INTRODUCTION TO SECURITY

FIFTH EDITION

INTRODUCTION TO SECURITY

OPERATIONS AND MANAGEMENT

Brian R. Johnson, Ph.D.
Michigan State University

P.J. Ortmeier (deceased)
Grossmont College

330 Hudson Street, NY NY 10013

Vice President, Portfolio Management: Andrew Gilfillan

Portfolio Manager: Gary Bauer

Editorial Assistant: Lynda Cramer

Senior Vice President, Marketing: David Gesell

Field Marketing Manager: Thomas Hayward

Product Marketing Manager: Kaylee Carlson

Senior Marketing Coordinator: Les Roberts

Director, Digital Studio and Content Production: Brian Hyland

Managing Producer: Cynthia Zonneveld

Managing Producer: Jennifer Sargunar

Content Producer: Nikhil Rakshit

Manager, Rights Management: Johanna Burke

Operations Specialist: Deidra Smith

Creative Digital Lead: Mary Siener

Managing Producer, Digital Studio: Autumn Benson

Content Producer, Digital Studio: Maura Barclay

Full-Service Management and Composition: iEnergizer Aptara®

Full-Service Project Manager: Rakhshinda Chishty

Cover Designer: StudioMontage

Cover Art: nirutft/Fotolia

Printer/Binder: LSC Communications

Cover Printer: LSC Communications

Text Font: Times LT Pro

Library of Congress Cataloging-in-Publication Data

Names: Johnson, Brian R., author. | Ortmeier, P. J. Introduction to security.

Title: Introduction to security : operations and management/P. J. Ortmeier, Ph.D., Grossmont College.

Description: Fifth Edition. | Hoboken : Pearson, 2016. | Revised edition of the author's Introduction to security, 2012. | Includes bibliographical references and index.

Identifiers: LCCN 2016041385 | ISBN 9780134558929 | ISBN 0134558928

Subjects: LCSH: Private security services—Management. | Buildings—Security measures. | Industries—Security measures. | Corporations—Security measures. | Security systems. | Computer security.

Classification: LCC HV8290 .J6196 2016 | DDC 363.28/9068—dc23 LC record available at https://lccn.loc.gov/2016041385

ISBN-10:   0-13-45589-28
ISBN-13: 978-0-13-45589-29

6 2019

To my wife Shari and my son Brian

Brief Contents

Contents

PART 4

Security Management 215

PART 5
Trends and Challenges 275

World events including the attacks of September 11, 2001, warfare, man-made and natural disasters, concern over crime, and security-related legislation have led to individuals, institutions, and governmental units to discover, re-examine, and explore the practices, roles, and functions of private security in society and organizations. The fifth edition of *INTRODUCTION TO SECURITY: Operations and Management* is the culmination of years of classroom teaching and practical experiences by the authors that provides readers with an understanding of the diverse and complex field of private security. It is particularly designed for two audiences: individuals exploring or seeking careers in private security, and those who want to gain a better understanding of the practice and field of security and how it differs from and complements the public sector criminal justice system.

The primary goal of this edition is to provide students and practitioners a detailed description and understanding of the private security industry and its diverse roles and functions in the twenty-first century. The book is balanced between security and management and leadership principles and practices. As such, it is relatively unique among other security texts, integrating security and managerial practices into one comprehensive text. Because of its design and content, it can readily be used in traditional and online undergraduate and graduate courses related to private security and security management. This text will also serve as a useful desk reference for security personnel and serve as study guide and aid for professional certifications, including the ASIS Certified Protection Professional (CPP) examination.

New to this Edition

This new edition has been updated to include the following:

- Most recent information related to the security industry and contemporary leadership and managerial practices.
- Many of the previous edition's topics have been reorganized and condensed into a more cohesive format, concentrating on major themes.
- Application of the course content has also been enhanced through more applied learning opportunities found throughout the text, and there are updated exercises at the end of each chapter.
- Many of the topics and issues reviewed in this edition are also approached in an interdisciplinary style, reflecting the diverse character of the security industry itself.
- A new chapter on security in an international perspective.

▶ Organization of the Book

The book is divided into five major parts that are additive and complementary in nature. Part 1 introduces the reader to foundational information related to the history and evolution of security, and security's function and role in society. Chapter 1 presents a brief history and overview of private security. Chapter 2 provides the reader with an understanding of the role of security in society and organizations. Chapter 3, meanwhile, focuses on the legal aspects that private security operations are exposed to and follow. Part 2 examines the fundamental elements of private security programs and practices, concentrating on the three pillars on which security programs are built. Chapter 4 focuses on *physical security*.

Chapter 5 presents topics related to *personnel security*. *Information* security is the primary subject of Chapter 6. Following an understanding of security's role and its fundamental activities within organizations, Part 3 reviews specific security sectors. Chapter 7 explores security issues unique to specific institutions. Chapter 8 introduces the reader to security practices and applications in the context of commercial, office, and residential security, while Chapter 9 reviews key concepts and issues related to the concept and philosophy of homeland security. Section 4 explores concepts related to how to lead and manage security operations in the various security sectors that exist. For example, Chapter 10 reviews basic concepts related to the effective management and leadership of security organizations. Chapter 11, meanwhile, examines core human resource activities performed by security managers and financial management activities related to budgeting. This section concludes with Chapter 12, which includes information related to risk management: particularly risk assessment and continuity planning. The last section of this text explores trends and challenges. Chapter 13 provides the reader with a review of the private security industry in an international perspective while Chapter 14 explores future trends and issues.

This fifth edition also contains a variety of learning and study aids to assist in enhancing the reader's foundational knowledge to ensure that key information, ideas, and perspectives important to the field of private security, management, and leadership are mastered. Some of these study aids will also enhance critical, practical, and creative thinking skills, which are essential attributes needed to manage the twenty-first-century security organization. For example, each chapter begins with a set of learning objectives that serve to explain what knowledge a person should be able to exhibit upon completion of the chapter. Included within the chapters are "Quick Surveys" that serve to apply key concepts found in the chapter to practical issues and situations, while "Security Spotlights" are also found throughout the text where readers can further apply and synthesize information from the chapter to actual, real-life issues related to security operations and management. Each chapter also concludes with a list of key terms and exercises and discussion questions to further ensure mastery of the information found in the chapter. The text also has a comprehensive glossary that can serve as a ready reference guide for key security terms and concepts.

▶ Instructor Supplements

Instructor's Manual with Test Bank. Includes content outlines for classroom discussion, teaching suggestions, and answers to selected end-of-chapter questions from the text. This also contains a Word document version of the test bank.

TestGen. This computerized test generation system gives you maximum flexibility in creating and administering tests on paper, electronically, or online. It provides state-of-the-art features for viewing and editing test bank questions, dragging a selected question into a test you are creating, and printing sleek, formatted tests in a variety of layouts. Select test items from test banks included with TestGen for quick test creation, or write your own questions from scratch. TestGen's random generator provides the option to display different text or calculated number values each time questions are used.

PowerPoint Presentations. Our presentations are clear and straightforward. Photos, illustrations, charts, and tables from the book are included in the presentations when applicable.

To access supplementary materials online, instructors need to request an instructor access code. Go to **www.pearsonhighered.com/irc,** where you can register for an instructor access code. Within 48 hours after registering, you will receive a confirming email, including an instructor access code. Once you have received your code, go to the site and log on for full instructions on downloading the materials you wish to use.

▶ Alternate Versions

eBooks This text is also available in multiple eBook formats. These are an exciting new choice for students looking to save money. As an alternative to purchasing the printed textbook, students can purchase an electronic version of the same content. With an eTextbook, students can search the text, make notes online, print out reading assignments that incorporate lecture notes, and bookmark important passages for later review. For more information, visit your favorite online eBook reseller or visit www.mypearsonstore.com.

Acknowledgments

I wish to express my deepest appreciation to the many people who provided support and assistance during the development of the fifth edition of this textbook. Gratitude is extended to my colleagues at Pearson including Gary Bauer, Jennifer Sargunar and Nikhil Rakshit, and to the excellent Aptara team led by Production Project Manager Rakhshinda Chishty and copy editor Tripti Khurana. Thank you so much for your professionalism, attention to detail, and dedication. Many thanks are also extended to the following individuals who shared their expertise in security for this edition: Thomas Ackerman, Director, Institute of Public Safety (Santa Fe College, Gainesville, Florida), Dan Bohle, Investigator, GVSU Security, Daniel Carncross, Director of Security (Columbia-Sussex Corporation, East Lansing Division), MACS (EXW/IDW) Steven J. Dyke, USN, Richard Grossenbacher (U.S. Secret Service (Ret), and Brian F. Kingshott, Ph.D., FRSA (London). I would also like to thank Andria Zwerk and Derek Manke for their assistance in the preparation of the manuscript.

I also appreciate the valuable contributions made by the reviewers of the previous editions: Jamie A. Latch, Remington College; Patrick Patterson, Remington College; Charles Green, Remington College; Jerome Randall, University of Central Florida; Richard Hill, University of Houston-Downtown; Dimitrius A. Oliver, Ph.D., Holly Dershem-Bruce, Dawson Community College, Glendive, MT; Stephen Jones, University of Maryland, College Park, MD; Sean Gabbidon, Penn State University, Middletown, PA; Neal Strehlow, Fox Valley Technical College, Appleton, WI; Donald Jenkins, Central Community College, Grand Island, NE; Michael Moberly, Southern Illinois University, Carbondale, IL; Charles Biggs, Oakland City University, Oakland City, IN; Terrance Hoffman, Nassau Community College, Garden City, NY; and Kevin Peterson, Innovative Protection Solutions LLC, Herndon, VA; John Bolinger, MacMurray College; Sonya Brown, Tarrant County College; Janice Duncan, Bauder College; and Bobby Polk, Metropolitan Community College—Omaha, NE.

Finally, I wish to express my heartfelt gratitude to my family, friends, and colleagues for their encouragement and patience.

Brian R. Johnson holds a Bachelor of Arts Degree in Criminal Justice from the University of Wisconsin-Eau, masters' degrees in Criminal Justice and Labor and Industrial Relations (emphasis in human resource management), and a Ph.D. in the Social Sciences (Criminal Justice) from Michigan State University. He served as a police officer and has years of experience in contract, proprietary security services, and security consulting in addition to police and security training-related activities. Johnson has also developed and implemented numerous courses in the field of criminal justice and has taught security-related courses at the undergraduate and graduate levels. Johnson is the author of *Principles of Security Management, Safe Overseas Travel and Crucial Elements of Police Firearms Training*. He has written several academic and practitioner-based articles in the fields of private security, policing, management, and criminology. He has worked with many local-, state-, and national-level organizations on security and poling-related issues. He is currently a Professor of Criminal Justice at Grand Valley State University, Grand Rapids, Michigan.

Comments regarding the book and suggestions for future editions are welcomed. The author is also available to provide assistance to any faculty who adopts this text for a course.

P.J. Ortmeier held bachelor's and master's degrees in criminal justice and a Ph.D. in educational leadership with an emphasis in public safety training and development. He is a U.S. Army veteran, a former police officer, and a former vice-president of United Security Systems, Incorporated. Ortmeier developed and implemented numerous courses and degree programs in law enforcement, corrections, security management, and public safety. He served as the chair of the 1,400-student Administration of Justice Department at Grossmont College in the San Diego suburb of El Cajon, California. P.J. died on September 15, 2012.

Ortmeier is the author of *Public Safety and Security Administration*, *Policing the Community: A Guide for Patrol Operations*, and *Introduction to Law Enforcement and Criminal Justice* as well as several articles appearing in journals such as *Police Chief*, *The Law Enforcement Executive Forum*, *California Security*, *Police and Security News*, and *Security Management*. With Edwin Meese III, former attorney general of the United States, Ortmeier coauthored *Leadership, Ethics, and Policing: Challenges for the 21st Century*. He also coauthored *Crime Scene Investigation: A Forensic Technician's Field Manual* with Tina Young as well as *Police Administration: A Leadership Approach* with Joseph J. Davis, a retired New York police captain. Ortmeier's publications focus on police field services, security operations, forensic science, professional career education, management, leadership, and competency development for public safety personnel.

Introduction
Security's Role in Society

The three chapters constituting Part 1 introduce readers to security's role in society. Chapter 1 presents a brief history and overview of functions of security. Chapter 2 reviews and addresses the wide range of threats to safety and security, from accidents, human error, and fire to natural disasters, civil liability, and numerous manifestations of crime. Chapter 3 focuses on the legal and regulatory environment of the private security sector, including the judicial process, a variety of types of laws and regulations, the regulation of the security industry, and professional certification and education programs.

1 History and Overview

LEARNING OBJECTIVES

After completing this chapter, the reader should be able to:

1. define what security is
2. explain some of the theoretical explanations related to the need for security
3. outline and describe the function of security in pre-modern England
4. know the three eras of security in the United States
5. understand and explain the contemporary security industry in the United States
6. explain contract, proprietary, and hybrid security
7. know the three essential elements of security
8. describe the different types of security organizations
9. describe the goals of security management
10. evaluate the roles of the security manager

▶ The Context for Security

"Security" encompasses a wide variety of definitions, concepts, and practices. The philosopher Thomas Hobbes (1588–1679) proposed that a natural right or value that is inherently recognizable through human reason or nature is the quest to seek out and live in peace—security (Bobbio, 1993). When examined in this broad philosophical manner, security can be considered a core need and social process whose end goal is to ensure individual, social, economic, and political security. In fact, perhaps it is better to understand that security exists to change a state of insecurity. To address these insecurities, security operates in the individual, organizational, and governmental domains. The need for security also creates and oftentimes relies upon social cohesion and relationships in order to ensure that individuals will effectively live with one another, while also strengthening organizations, governments, and nation states.

Security can be a subjective or psychological state of mind where at the individual level, the feeling or perceptions of security/insecurity or danger/safety coexist and intertwine. As a subjective state, individuals may feel insecure because of their surroundings, location, activities, life experiences, upbringing, or demographic characteristics, including age and gender. These subjective states can be shaped by real and intangible events that could decrease or increase perceptions of insecurity. These subjective states or perceptions can also exist at various social levels where the group, community, organization, and even a nation feel "unsafe" leading to a culture of "insecurity" (Weldes, 1999). For example, following a criminal activity, employees in a company may feel "unsafe," prompting employers to ensure that a state of security exists by increasing the amount of security personnel. This example also shows that insecurity has a mobilizing component where people, companies, and even nations have banded together to address insecurity. Security is also a measurable and objective state. And, effective security is an end goal. For example, a company may have an actual security event or not meet certain security standards for the protection of an asset—both of which are objective measures prompting the company to meet a measurable goal. In other cases, such as the 9-11 terrorist attacks, individuals, organizations, and governmental organizations soon realized that their security practices and operations were not adequate, prompting them to use private and public resources to reduce or eliminate the state of insecurity and reach the end goal of security.

security Freedom from risk or harm; ensuring safety.

Security is also a practice and industry. As a practice, security is needed by nations, organizations, institutions, and individuals. These security-related activities are carried out by a variety of individuals and organizations operating in the public and private domains. Security also exists on a practical level where individuals are concerned about their personal security in the context of being safe from predatory criminal and financial activities. As this text will show, security is also an industry composed of private and public sector organizations whose primary purpose is the provision of security-related products and services valued at $350 billion annually (ASIS, 2013). As a profession, security is a career choice that includes executives, managers, and staff whose positions and activities require specific knowledge, skills, and abilities in security-related principles and operations.

Finally, the field of security is multidisciplinary. Effective security operations and management rely on information that is drawn from several academic disciplines including the humanities, the social sciences (criminal justice, psychology, sociology, political science), the sciences (biology, chemistry, mathematics), and professions including business and law. For example, the risk management process requires an understanding of human nature and cultures (the humanities). Security operations include or collaborate with elements of the criminal justice system (police and the courts) to design crime prevention programs and assist in the prosecution of offenders. In some fields, security's mission includes protection from hazardous materials, and fire safety that requires an understanding of the chemistry of fire and physics. Security operations may also be used to generate revenue through the sale of products and services (Harowitz, 2003; Ortmeier & Meese, 2010; Peak & Glensor, 2008; Simonsen, 1998).

Because of the diverse ways in which security can be understood and examined, there is no single definition of security. Some broad definitions include the absence of risk or threat or freedom from fear or want, or eliminating threats that create a circumstance, condition, or event for loss, or the protection of assets from loss. Private security is defined as "individual and organizational measures and efforts (as distinguished from public law enforcement agency efforts) to provide protection for persons and property" (National Advisory Committee on Criminal Justice Standards and Goals, 1977, p. 3). Private security can also be defined as organizations or individuals other than the public police that require direct payment for security-related services (George & Watson, 1992). Meanwhile, corporate security is defined as a "security provision that seeks to achieve corporate organizational goals" (Walby & Lippert, 2014, p. 2).

Theoretical Foundations

There are several theoretical explanations that can be used to explain the need for security. It can be explained economically where because of governmental financial constraints, the private sector now provides a myriad of activities that were once the domain of the state. Combined with economic explanations, the growth of security can be examined in the context of governmental policy and politics, where at the local, county, state, and federal levels, policymakers have made the decision to increase security operations, or in some cases decide to use private security services that were

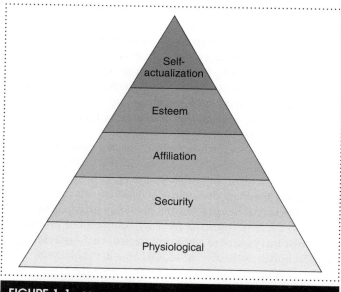

FIGURE 1-1 Maslow's Hierarchy of Needs
Source: Motivation and Personality, 3rd edition by Abraham H. Maslow, edited by Robert D. Frager & James Fadiman. Copyright (c) 1987. Pearson Education, Inc., Upper Saddle River, NJ 07458..

traditionally the responsibility of government. Private security can also be explained sociologically, examining the social process of security based on individual, class, and organizational behaviors.

One theory that has been used to explain the need for security is Maslow's hierarchy of needs (Figure 1-1 ■) that explains human motivation and development. Created in 1958, Abraham Maslow hypothesized that in order for humans to excel, they have prepotent or *a priori* needs that must be met before progressing on to more advanced, complex needs. The first needs according to Maslow are physiological, which comprise the physical requirements of human survival that include clothing, shelter, food, and water. Once these needs are adequately met, Maslow proposed that individual safety and security needs take precedence in one's life that include protection from personal and economic harm and having family and friends to ensure one's safety. Once these safety-related needs are adequately met, humans can progress to meeting their interpersonal needs that include developing effective interpersonal relationships and a sense of belongingness, subsequently improving one's level of self-esteem—another need on the hierarchy. Following these four needs, then humans can reach or achieve their full potential or self-actualization.

Using this theory to understand security, it becomes clear that safety and security needs and issues are priority needs that must be met. Failing to meet safety and security needs can have profound effects on individuals' abilities in establishing positive interpersonal relationships and a sense of belonging, impacting their levels of self-esteem. Applying this theory to an industrial security example, consider a company that has a security program to protect its assets and to ensure that employees feel safe and secure in the course of their daily work activities. Because of effective security, employees will have positive social interactions, high levels of self-esteem, and increased productivity. If, however, security is lacking, individuals may not feel safe or secure; hence, the organization could experience low productivity, morale, and employee resignations.

Next, the theory of collective security suggests that individuals will engage in self-protection activities when they perceive instability or insecurity with existing forms of protection provided by the government. In societies where there are strong forms of social

Maslow's hierarchy of needs A theory that explains human motivation and development. Created in 1958, Maslow hypothesized that in order for humans to excel, they have prepotent or *a priori* needs that must be met before progressing on to more advanced, complex needs.

theory of collective security Posits that individuals will engage in self-protection activities when they perceive instability or insecurity with existing forms of protection provided by the government.

control where effective forms of security are provided by the government, the citizens accept it and collective security exists. However, in times of instability or insecurity this collective security is threatened and people will resort to relying upon themselves and others for protection instead of the state. In these cases, individuals may engage in security-related activities, arming themselves, and making their homes more difficult to break into through better lighting and locks. They will use private security services to meet their needs (McDowall & Loftin, 1983). Similarly, when organizations perceive that the state cannot provide or meet their necessary security-related needs, they may create their own security forces to meet their specific needs.

Finally, there is the **mass private property hypothesis**. The mass private property hypothesis posits that areas of public life that were once the domain or control of the public police are now under the control of private companies. Because of the growth of office complexes, theme parks, gated residential communities, shopping malls, health care campuses, educational institutions, and other large private properties, the domain of the public police has shrunk. Therefore, the need and demand for increased numbers of private security personnel and technologies has increased in order to protect the users of these mass private properties (Kempa, Stenning, & Wood, 2004; Shearing & Stenning, 1981).

> **mass private property hypothesis**
> A hypothesis posits that areas of public life that were once the domain or control of the public police are now under the control of private companies.

SECURITY SPOTLIGHT

Think about your typical day. In what respects is security being provided to you during each part of your day? For example, as you leave your home, drive to school or work, shop at a store or online, or go out for the evening with family or friends, what forms of security are in place in each of those settings and during each of those activities?

▶ Security: A Brief History

Ancient Traditions

The need for and the practice of security is as old as mankind and civilization. In early prehistoric societies, the protection of persons and property was the responsibility of individuals, clans, and tribes that often "target hardened" or protected themselves and their properties in some manner. Some examples of physical security measures include the Great Wall of China that was built by Emperor Chen to protect his citizens and country from invasion from the Mongols (Fisher, 1995). Roman fortresses and other walled cities and castles whose remnants can still be seen throughout the world today also demonstrate the collective need for security. If not the protection of civilizations, assets needed to be protected. Deceased Egyptian Pharaohs were buried in secrecy in deep massive vault-like tombs that were sealed with heavy stones and mud to deter grave robbers (Dębowska-Ludwin, 2011). The Egyptians are also credited with inventing the mechanical lock over 4000 years ago while the Romans used heavy wood chests with locks and steel hardware to secure their valuables (Çelik, 2015; Wardle & Wardle, 2004). In other cases, the ancient historical record is also replete with stories of assassination where leaders used personal bodyguards for their protection. As the concepts of territoriality and personal property increased and societies became more complex, ultimately written laws were developed and formalized to proscribe (forbid) and prescribe (encourage) specific types of human behavior. Eventually, private and public security systems were created to deter potential offenders, enforce societal rules and laws, and provide protection for persons and property (Purpura, 2003; Simonsen, 1998).

English Origins

Under the Anglo-Saxon period in England (400–1066 A.D.), no formal police system existed. Policing was at the community and kinship level where family groups of 10 belonged to a territorial-based tithing unit and able-bodied males were responsible for social order and preventing crime in the tithing. These *tything* (or tithing) *units* were supervised by a tythingman (a forerunner of the constable) who was responsible for dealing with crime and disorder in the tythings and sometimes beyond. In turn, 10 tythings were organized into hundreds that were supervised by hundredmen. These hundreds were then organized into geographic areas known as shires. These shires were then supervised by a shire reeve who was elected by the hundredmen in the shire. The reeve was responsible to the Crown and had full administrative powers (including taxing) over the shire while the hundredmen answered to and followed the reeve's directives (Mawby, 2013; Morris, 1968).

After the Norman invasion and conquest of England in 1066 A.D., a more centrally controlled county (shire) government system was created through which the king appointed a law officer (the reeve) to act as the magistrate for each county. While keeping the tithing structure and the watch, the Normans also instituted the Frankpledge, a compulsory system of mutual responsibility, where every able-bodied male had to belong to a tything and was responsible for the collective security of the community and crown. As part of the Frankpledge system, all able-bodied men were required to serve the crown by participating in security-related activities (called the watch), patrolling the tything unit and responding to criminal activities when citizens raised the hue and cry, alarming others that a crime or an emergency occurred. Under this system, the shire reeve could also deputize a posse to seek out criminals and enforce the common law of England (Joyce, 2011). This structure of policing became more formalized under the Statute of Westminster of 1285 that further established local responsibility for police and security-related activities in walled cities and towns. Under the Statute of Westminster, it was the responsibility of all able-bodied males between the ages of 15 and 60 to engage in security-related activities by keeping a weapon at home and participating in the watch system, taking turns as nonpaid night watchmen in the community and guarding the entrances into towns. It was also the responsibility of these individuals to participate in the hue and cry. The hue and cry required citizens to come to the aid of others, assisting in the pursuit and arrest of criminals when called upon (Rawlings, 2002).

In the late 1600s and early 1700s, the industrial revolution dramatically transformed the economic and social conditions in England. Villages became cities and crime increased. The watch, with some modifications, still remained as the primary form of policing. In London in 1735, for example, individuals could hire watchmen as a substitute for themselves. However, in many of these urban settings, the volunteer watch system and the hue and cry simply could not keep up with the nature and extent of social disorder and crime (Rawlings, 2002). In response, the central government in England passed additional laws. For example, The Highwayman Act of 1692 made provisions for the use of thief takers, persons who captured thieves and recovered stolen property for a fee paid by the victim and, in some cases, by the government. While this system led to some serious abuses because the thief takers sometimes stole the property themselves or were in collusion with the criminals, it was nevertheless the impetus for the creation of private detectives and the public police. In 1742, Henry Fielding, a magistrate of the court on Bow Street in London, established a small group of legitimate and salaried thief takers who were paid through governmental funds. Known as the Bow Street Runners because they operated out of the Bow Street Court, these individuals were effective in patrolling, responding to incidents, investigating crimes, and capturing criminals. Later taken over by his brother John in 1754, the Fieldings' model of policing became the foundation for the first public police

---

shire reeve Individuals who were elected by the hundredmen who supervised the tything systems within shires.

Frankpledge system Ancient policing/watch practice in England where all able bodied men were required to serve the crown by participating in security-related activities (called the Watch).

watch Pre-modern/ancient form of policing in England and America where citizens were responsible for security-related activities.

Statute of Westminster of 1285 Established local responsibility for police and security-related activities in walled cities and towns.

thief takers Forerunners of modern day detectives that recovered stolen goods for a fee; provided for in British Highwayman Act of 1692

Bow Street Runners Created in 1742. Were legitimate and salaried thief takers that were paid through governmental funds and operated out of the Bow Street Court.

force where eventually in 1829, Home Secretary Sir Robert Peel introduced the Metropolitan Police Act to the English Parliament. This Act replaced the existing watch system in metropolitan London (not the city of London) with paid, full-time police officers. It was the first public police force in England and eventually a model of policing for other nations, including the United States (Durston, 2012; McLynn, 2013).

Sir Robert Peel The British Home Secretary credited with creating the first full-time police department in 1829 in metropolitan London.

Metropolitan Police Act 1829 British law, promoted by Sir Robert Peel, that established first public, full-time police department in the world.

The American Experience

The review of the American Experience reveals that the growth of security paralleled the growth of industries, society, technologies, and various social movements. One of the underlying themes of the American experience is that the private security industry was (and still is) entrepreneurial, finding new opportunities based on market and societal needs, "filling the voids" that the public sector could not provide.

Another theme to consider is that as society and institutions have become more complex, the problems of security enlarge and oftentimes magnify in importance. In a broad sense, the American Security Experience can be placed into three eras: colonial to WWI, post-WWI–2001, and the post-9-11 era.

Security in America: Colonial Origins to WWI

The criminal justice and private security systems in the United States developed primarily from the English common law structure and practices and the philosophical underpinnings of collective security. Most of the original American colonies were settled by the English. Thus, the colonists simply transplanted the laws of England and existing policing practices onto American soil. For example, as in England, the sheriff was the primary legal official in many jurisdictions. Likewise, in colonial America and even into the early 1800s, many cities still relied upon the watch system to perform security functions. The first watch in the city of Boston was created in 1636 where the main responsibilities of the citizen force that was supervised by the city marshal were to control public order crimes and to raise the alarm in the instance of fire (Lane, 1971).

In pre-WWI society, the infrastructure of the United States was in its infancy. Local, state, and federal governments were generally small and undeveloped, providing limited social service functions related to the provision of police and security-related services. Historians trace the beginnings of formal governmental police departments to Detroit in 1801 and Cincinnati in 1803, and the first national investigative agency to the U.S. Post Office in 1828. Boston created the first formal police department in the United States in 1838. New York City followed suit in 1844, San Francisco in 1847, and Dallas in 1856. At the federal level, an investigative arm was formed in the U.S. Treasury Department in 1864, and the Border Patrol was created in the U.S. Justice Department in 1882. In most cases, these agencies were rudimentary in nature. In the case of local police, they were oftentimes corrupt and controlled by the local political machines, lacking specialized detective units and the personnel needed to address many of the social issues and property crimes that existed. On the American frontier, meanwhile, police services (if they existed) were provided primarily by county or city sheriffs, constables, and marshals. Lacking assistants, sheriffs, and marshals were authorized to deputize citizens and form posses when a threat to security existed—an artifact of the English hue and cry. When police officials were not available, citizens often formed vigilante groups, which were organized attempts by citizens to maintain law and order (Abrahams, 2003).

With the birth of the coal, steel, railroad, and chemical industries, the need to protect private property led companies to create their own specialized security forces. One specific issue that needed to be addressed was labor unrest. As early as 1829, workers constructing the Baltimore and Ohio railroad were engaged in various forms of labor protest (including strikes, riots, and other forms of violence, including murder) over issues related to pay, job security, and working conditions. In other cases, gangs of workers attacked slaves and clashed with other ethnic groups, such as the Irish and Germans, working for the B&O Railroad over perceived inequities and bias. In some of these incidents, the B&O Railroad relied upon local sheriffs, volunteers, and state militia to arrest and quell the violence. However, in other cases, these public sources were limited, resulting in the company creating its own police force in 1849, hiring 25 armed guards to keep peace on the railroad lines. This was the first railroad police agency in the United States (Mason, 1998).

Unrest existed in other parts of the country. In 1865, the state of Pennsylvania passed the Railway Police Act, the first of its kind in the United States, which granted police powers to railway security personnel, leading to the creation of the Reading Railroad Rail and Coal Police. Working alone or sometimes with Pinkertons, these police forces protected railroad and coal companies from labor agitators, including the Molly Maguires. In 1866, this Act was extended to the steel companies who, like the railroads, could have their own security police by simply petitioning the governor that the company needed police powers to protect its properties (Kenny, 1998; Shalloo, 1929). This labor unrest was not restricted to the eastern United States. In a series of strikes in the Mesabi Iron Range in 1916, the Governor of Minnesota deputized private mine guards employed by the iron and steel corporations, giving them the same powers as sheriffs to combat the 20,000 strikers throughout the iron range (Marcy, 1916). In other cases, public law enforcement relied upon private company police to supplement its meager forces. In the Lattimer Massacre that occurred in the state of Pennsylvania in 1897, for example, the local sheriff used company police to build up his force to 150 men who subsequently opened fire on the 400 protesting miners, killing 19 and wounding 38 more (Wolensky, 2008). Besides their role in labor unrests, many corporations had established company towns where private security forces employed by the corporation were responsible for maintaining order throughout the town (Wagner & Obermiller, 2011). This role of private security in "union busting" activities continued into the 1930s.

The origins of contract security can also be traced to this era. As early as the 1840s, the need to protect money and financial instruments was recognized as a new security concern for companies where some entrepreneurial individuals formed courier companies. Later, to meet the needs of the growing financial sector, Henry Wells and William Fargo created the American Express Company in 1850 to transport gold, money, and financial instruments in New York and the eastern United States. Seeing the need and opportunity in the emerging west, in 1852, he and William Fargo created the Wells Fargo & Company to operate west of the Missouri River to transport goods and money from the gold-based economy of California (Fradkin, 2002). Other companies were also involved in the secure transportation of goods. In 1859, Washington Perry Brinks from Chicago formed a company to transport valuables. Later, the Brinks Company became known throughout the United States for its transportation of money, deposits, and company payrolls (McCrie, 1988).

This era also saw the growth of contract security guards and detectives. In 1847 Allan Pinkerton, a barrel maker, agent in the Underground Railroad, and amateur detective from Dundee, Illinois, gained fame as a detective after discovering a local counterfeiting operation and assisting the local police in other counterfeiting and kidnapping cases. Later serving as the city of Chicago's first detective in 1850, Pinkerton also created the North-Western Police Agency (later to become the Pinkerton National Detective Agency), the nation's first private detective agency. During this time period, Pinkerton and his agents provided private police, security, and investigative services for clients, and he and his staff functioned as the intelligence arm of the Union Army during the Civil War. In his role as the first Chief of the U.S. Secret Service, he is credited in thwarting an assassination attempt against President Lincoln in Baltimore in 1862. Pinkerton's fame, company, and services expanded after the Civil War where, oftentimes, Pinkertons were involved in preventing labor unrest by providing security officers in disputes and using undercover agents to detect labor agitators in companies (Dempsey, 2010; Lewis, 1948; Lipson, 1988; Weiss, 1986, 2007). Pinkerton was not the only contract security company that existed. Other companies included the Baldwin–Felts Detective Agency that was used by companies to address union-related issues in the coalfields of West Virginia and Colorado

Railway Police Act
Granted police powers to railway security personnel in 1865 in Pennsylvania, leading to the creation of the Reading Railroad Rail and Coal Police.

Allan Pinkerton
Founded the nation's first private detective agency in 1850 called the Pinkerton National Detective Agency.

(Lewis, 1993). There was also the William Burns International Detective Agency that was founded in 1909. Burns worked for the Secret Service before forming his agency, later becoming the Director of the FBI in 1921 (Weiss, 1986). These contract security companies performed a variety of services for the federal government and were arguably the only national police forces that existed until the FBI was created in 1909 (Hunt, 1990; Seigel, 2015).

Other types of security also emerged during this period. With the invention of the telegraph and electricity, the alarm market emerged. In 1844, Samuel Morse, the inventor of the telegraph, created a fire alarm telegraph system in Washington, DC and Baltimore. The first electric burglar alarm patent was also issued to Augustus Pope in 1853 (Greer, 1979). Later in 1857, Edwin Holmes created an electric burglar alarm that used existing telegraph wires to transmit signals to monitoring stations located throughout Boston. Later Holmes expanded his alarm business by partnering with the emerging telephone industry. After the Great Chicago fire in 1871, for example, it was estimated that the city had over 430 miles of telegraph and telephone wires linked to the city's fire stations in the 1880s (McCrie, 1988; Nye, 1997). By the 1880s, fire and burglar alarms were common security devices for homes, banks, and other businesses, and alarm companies including the American District Telegraph Company (ADT) (that still exists today) were created. Many of these alarm systems were quite specialized for their time, as was the case of Holmes' "Electrical Envelope for Safes" 1879 patent application that was basically a series of electrified tin foil strips wrapped around a safe that sensed changes in the electrical current. With the creation of "modern" retail model in 1879 by F.W. Woolworth where customers now had direct contact with merchandise, the problem of retail theft or shoplifting by customers also became an issue for merchants (Hayes, 2014). This issue led to some retailers creating private security or store detective forces, which was

Allan Pinkerton, 1819–1884. Pinkerton founded the first private detective agency in the United States. During the Civil War, he and his staff functioned as the intelligence arm of the Union Army. Civil War: Antietam, Maryland. Seated: R. William Moore and Allan Pinkerton (Right). Standing: George H. Bangs, John C. Babcock, and Augustus K. Littlefield.
(Photo courtesy of Library of Congress.)

William Burns, 1861–1932. Burns founded the Burns International Detective Agency in 1909. He worked for the Secret Service before forming his detective agency. In 1921, he became the director of the FBI.
(Photo courtesy of Library of Congress.)

the case with then "mega" discount stores such Klein's and Ohrbach's in New York City where private security had to contend with shoplifters, mobs of people during sales, and labor unrest where the strikers used a variety of tactics to disrupt store operations (Opler, 2002).

▶ Security in the Twentieth Century

The era of the twentieth century saw the continued growth of security based on the need to protect private property and the absence of security and law enforcement-related services in the public sector. However, a new issue and theme emerged in the twentieth century: national security. With the entry of the United States onto the Allied side in 1917 in World War I, concerns over the sabotage of some of the nation's critical infrastructure by German spies, particularly the railroads, munitions, and express companies, became a national security concern. These concerns led to the takeover of these industries by the military where company security employees became government employees (Lipson, 1988). The concern over sabotage also led to partnerships between governmental agencies such as the Office of Naval Intelligence (ONI) that was tasked with detecting enemy espionage activities. Because of the lack of personnel in the ONI, it was necessary to partner with Pinkerton for its counterespionage activities (Dowart, 1979). As was the case prior to WWI, oftentimes the military was also called to ensure security in key industries. The U.S. Army was called out at least 29 times throughout the United States during WWI to address domestic disorders that included labor strikes (Adams, 1995).

The twentieth century also saw continued growth of security based on labor issues. Regardless of the fact that the Great Depression led to high unemployment rates, there were

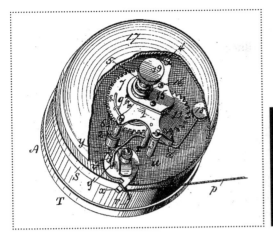

Burglar Alarm Patent. In post-civil war society, burglar alarms were common security devices for homes. This spring wound burglar alarm was activated by a sash cord that the user could install around windows and doors. (Image: U.S. Patent Office.)

still large numbers of strikes and labor unrest throughout the United States where private security was used to control and spy on union-related activities. If not contract security, other large companies created their own forces. For example, the Ford Motor Company's Security Services, which has been identified as the first modern proprietary security entity in the United States (Walby & Lippert, 2015), was created in 1917 to thwart union activities through the use of undercover spies and using security guards to "break" union strikes—oftentimes through violent encounters with the strikers. With the passage of the National Labor Relations Act (NLRA) in 1935, union-related activities (pickets, organizing, and elections) and belonging to a union became legal. While the role of security guards was no longer related to "union busting," some companies now had to use their security to address the now legal labor disputes, such as the General Motors sit-in strike of 1937 in Flint, Michigan (Lichtenstein, 1980). Other companies including the Ford Motor Company now had to deal with the legacy of the security guard as a strike breaker and union buster that created animosity between employees and security personnel, sometimes leading overt aggression toward security staff (Meyer, 2002).

World War II

With the entrance of America into WWII (1941–1945), the need to protect the United States' infrastructure and military, and industrial facilities from sabotage led to the expansion of private security. Plant protection employees in companies that held defense contracts were militarized and inducted into the military as civilian auxiliaries to the military police where they had to follow the Articles of War (Witey, 1947). The companies themselves also fell under continuing protection of the War and Navy Departments where the company's Defense Coordinator, who was supervised by military personnel, was responsible for preventing sabotage and espionage. To assist companies, the War Department established minimum security standards and provided specific guidelines on how to improve physical and personnel security measures in these defense-related industries (War Department, 1943). For example, the Westinghouse Corporation (that produced a variety of weapons including torpedoes) East Pittsburgh Plant had a 105-page Plant Protection Manual that outlined the responsibilities of the 14 different security-related positions that included plant protection squads, air raid wardens, and plant guards. The manual also included information on chemical weapons, air raid signals, and defense-related drills, while also identifying specific threats the company and employees could be exposed to (Vitale, 2011). Undoubtedly, these standards left a lasting impression on companies, increasing security's role, operation, and legitimacy. It also led to industrial security becoming a profession.

The Cold War and the National Industrial Security Program

Concerns related to national security did not diminish with the end of WWII. With the advent of the Cold War and the existence of a new enemy—the USSR and its Warsaw Pact allies, along with the Korean War (1950–1953), new security concerns related to espionage and industrial sabotage by subversives and Soviet spies in the nation's key defense industries became an issue. To address these concerns, the Industrial Defense Program was created in 1952 by the U.S. government. This program identified government-owned, contractor-operated industrial facilities that were on the Department of Defense's Key Facilities List. Those military branches affiliated with the Key Facility were responsible for working with that particular company that had primary responsibility for physical security and emergency management (Dempsey, 2010; Department of the Army, 1966). This program later led to the creation of the National Industrial Security Program (NISP) in 1993 by President Clinton. NISP consolidated the oversight of defense contractors into one agency, which is administered through the Defense Security Services (DSS), an agency of the Department of Defense. The NISP program and operating manual establishes minimum security standards for defense contractors working with classified information. Companies must possess a facility clearance prior to receiving and working with classified information, while employees working for the company must also have personnel clearances and be investigated by DSS personnel before having access to classified information (Clark & Jayaram, 2005; Herbig, 2011). Currently, 13,500 facilities are cleared under the DSS (Defense Security Services, 2015).

For more information on NISP and the DSS go to www.dss.mil/

During WWII industries producing defense-related items fell under the jurisdiction of War and Navy Departments. Here, two men of the plant protection force guard the stacks of vital magnesium produced at Basic Magnesium's giant plant in the southern Nevada desert. (Photo courtesy of Library of Congress.)

This era also saw the creation of professional security organizations. In 1955, a group of security professionals formed the American Society for Industrial Security (ASIS), which was later renamed ASIS International. Today, ASIS International's membership exceeds 35,000 members, making it the world's largest organization of security professionals. Dedicated to protecting the people, property, and information assets of a diverse group of private and public organizations, its members include management professionals who formulate security policy and direct security programs in a wide range of businesses, industries, and government operations. Besides ASIS, other organizations such as the International Association of Healthcare Security and Safety have certification programs for line level and managerial positions, while the Loss Prevention Foundation provides training and certifications for security personnel operating in the retail sector.

American Society for Industrial Security (ASIS) ASIS International; international organization of security professionals founded in 1955.

Federal Initiatives

In 1965, a national commission was established to investigate the nature and extent of crime in the United States and develop recommendations for the improvement of the criminal justice system. The President's Commission on Law Enforcement and Administration of Justice, commonly referred to as the President's Crime Commission, issued its report in 1967 and recommended improvements in law enforcement, courts, and corrections. In response to the President's Crime Commission report, in 1968, Congress enacted the Omnibus Crime Control and Safe Streets Act, budgeting billions of dollars to fight crime and make improvements in the administration of justice. Among its provisions, the Act established the Law Enforcement Assistance Administration (LEAA) in the U.S. Department of Justice. The LEAA was responsible for administering federal grant programs to local, county, and state governments to establish and improve police training programs and upgrade equipment and facilities. Colleges and universities throughout the country were also eligible for federal funding that enabled them to establish education programs in law enforcement and criminal justice. Although LEAA was eliminated during the Carter Administration, the LEAA and the Law Enforcement Education Program (LEEP) helped to launch an era of professionalism throughout the criminal justice system (Gest, 2001). While these monies were directed toward the public sector, the improvements in education, crime prevention, and policing undoubtedly "trickled down" to the private security industry that adopted many of these practices and new technologies generated through LEAA funding.

Law Enforcement Assistance Administration (LEAA) Now defunct federal program, established through the Omnibus Crime Control and Safe Streets Act of 1968 that provided federal monies to fight crime and improve the criminal justice system.

In 1969, the LEAA sponsored the Research and Development (RAND) Corporation to examine the private security industry. Its subsequent report "*The Private Police Industry: Its Nature and Extent*" is basically the first in-depth analysis of the private security industry in America. The study determined a sharp upward trend in the use of contract security for the 1970s and an increase in total guard and private police employment. The report also identified that the relationship between security and police was generally good, but some issues including abuse of authority, poor business practices, the lack of training, high false-alarm rates, and the use of low-quality, undertrained, and ill-supervised staff needed to be addressed through licensing and regulatory control (Kakalik & Wildhorn, 1971). The RAND report's solutions to private security's personnel problems focused on licensing security businesses and the registration of security officers (Kakalik & Wildhorn, 1971, 1972; Purpura, 2003).

The LEAA also established the Private Security Advisory Council (PSAC) in 1972 that was tasked to advise the LEAA on security-related issues and how the private sector could assist in preventing crime. From 1972 to 1977, the PSAC produced advisory reports for the LEAA. One of PSAC's publications, for example, reviewed the relationship between the police and private security industry. While determining that law enforcement and private security generally have a good working relationship, they also identified areas of conflict including the lack of mutual respect, communication, law enforcement's

Private Security Advisory Council (PSAC) Was tasked to advise the LEAA on security-related issues and how the private sector could assist in preventing crime.

knowledge about the industry, low employment standards, and perceived competition and corruption that needed to be addressed to ensure strong working relationships between the two (PSAC, 1976). The PSAC also published model state statutes for licensing burglar alarm companies and security officers. It also published a code of ethics for security operations and personnel, standards for armored car and armed courier services, and guidelines outlining the scope of authority for security personnel. (U.S. Department of Justice, Private Security Advisory Council to the Law Enforcement Assistance Administration, 1977).

In 1976, the National Advisory Commission on Criminal Justice Standards and Goals published the report of the Task Force on Private Security. For the first time, a national commission composed of leading law enforcement and private security academics and practitioners recognized the field of private security as an essential ingredient for public safety. The Task Force determined that the security industry was significantly under-regulated. It recommended minimum training and regulation standards in order to improve the nature and quality of security services to complement the law enforcement community in its efforts to fight crime. Specifically, the Task Force placed emphasis on licensing security businesses; minimum security personnel selection standards, training, and registration standards; codes of ethics and conduct; increased cooperation with the public police; improvement of security alarms and other crime prevention systems; state regulation; and continuing professional education and training (National Advisory Commission on Criminal Justice Standards and Goals, 1976). While no comprehensive degree programs existed at the time of the report's publication, the Commission also recommended specific private security degree programs in order to enhance professionalism in the field while promoting technological advances and research.

Following the publication of the Task Force Report, in the 1980s and 1990s the National Institute of Justice, U.S. Department of Justice funded two additional studies of the private security industry. The results of these studies, the Hallcrest Report I (1985) and the Hallcrest Report II (1990), reaffirmed the need for training and regulation of the security industry. The Hallcrest Report II contained numerous findings, recommendations, and forecasts. The Report addressed general and economic crime; selected crime concerns, including unethical business practices and terrorism; the dimensions of protection; security personnel issues; security services and products; comparisons of public police and private security; and, future research needs (Cunningham, Strauchs, & Van Meter, 1990; Cunningham & Taylor, 1985).

During the last quarter of the twentieth century, the security industry continued to grow rapidly due to increasing concern over crime and the limited availability of law enforcement resources. In the 1960s, it was estimated that there were 222,000 private security personnel. By 1975, this had increased to 435,000 (Shearing & Stenning, 1981). Other research found that in 1980, an estimated $22 billion was spent on private security activities in the United States, compared to $14 billion in local, state, and federal law enforcement (Stewart, 1985). The 1990s also saw continued growth, which was attributed to the increased fear of crime in society, globalization issues, and recognition that security was an essential component of the modern organization. The Violent Crime Control and Law Enforcement Act of 1994 (HR 3355) provided municipalities funding for improvements in lighting, emergency phones, and other security-related activities and functions. Another $10 million in funding was allocated to increasing public transportation security, including the use of private security personnel. Millions of dollars more were awarded to collaborative crime prevention efforts between the public and private sector. The 1990s also exposed Americans to international and domestic terrorism, prompting the increased recognition and use of private security. In 1993, Ramzi Yousef organized the car bomb attack that successfully detonated in one of the parking structures under the World Trade Center in New York City, killing six and injuring others (Hamm, 2007). In 1995,

Task Force Report on Private Security
Published by the National Commission on Criminal Justice Standards and Goals in 1976; recommended minimum training and licensing requirements for private security.

Hallcrest Report I
A study of the private security in America that was published in 1985.

Hallcrest Report II
A study of the private security in America that was published in 1990; reaffirmed the need for training and regulation of the security industry.

Violent Crime Control and Law Enforcement Act of 1994
HR 3355 provided municipalities funding for improvements in lighting, emergency phones, and other security-related activities and functions.

U.S. citizen and anti-government militant Tim McVeigh detonated a car bomb outside the Murrah Federal Building in Oklahoma City, killing 168 and injuring hundreds more. This incident led to increased security measures and architectural changes that incorporated security into building designs for federal buildings throughout the United States (Prendergast, 1995).

▶ Post-9-11 Security

Since the terrorist attacks of September 11, 2001, security has moved from the periphery to the center. The terrorist attacks on the Unites States on September 11, 2001 that targeted the World Trade Center and Pentagon led to a profound change in security in the United States and throughout the world. In the aftermath of 9-11, the U.S. Department of Homeland Security (DHS) was created by the Homeland Security Act of 2002 (U.S. Congress, 2002). The DHS represents the largest transformation of the national government since President Harry S. Truman merged the branches of the armed forces in 1947 to create the U.S. Department of Defense. The DHS currently employs about 240,000 individuals in 22 separate federal agencies. The primary mission of the DHS is to consolidate and better coordinate national (federal) efforts to combat terrorism and protect the United States against other threats to the homeland. Besides providing a better coordinated defense for the United States, the DHS maintains liaison with state and local governments and the private sector (U.S. Department of Homeland Security, 2015; White, 2012). Additional information regarding the DHS, its organizational functions, and the federal agencies it consumed is reviewed in Chapter 12.

The growth of security post 9-11 also occurred at the state and local levels and in the private security industry to meet the new challenges and threats of the twenty-first century. The increased threat of terrorism, natural disasters, concern over crime, and new mandates at the local, state, and federal levels have made organizations more aware of the need for security. In fact, in the early 2000s, it was estimated that private security personnel outnumbered law enforcement by a ratio of at least 3 to 1 (Abrahamsen & Williams, 2007). Throughout the rest of the text, the contemporary security sector will be examined in detail.

> **U.S. Department of Homeland Security (DHS)** A department of the federal government responsible for protecting the United States from and responding to terrorism, disasters, and other major national incidents.

> **Homeland Security Act of 2002** Federal law that created the U.S. Department of Homeland Security and consolidated 22 separate federal agencies from several departments into one; effective March 1, 2003.

▶ The Contemporary Security Industry

While this textbook primarily explores the private security industry, it needs to be understood that the practice of security exists in different domains. One way to classify security functions is by examining it in the context of sponsorship or who pays for the services performed—for the public good or for a specific client (Becker, 1974). In a simplistic sense, security can be divided into the binary categories of the public and private sectors. However, it can be further subdivided into defense-related, public security, homeland security, corporate security, private security, and individual or personal security sectors (Smith & Brooks, 2013). While different in their primary missions, all of these sectors and domains require knowledge of security principles, management, and operations. As shown in Table 1-1 ■, each of these domains also has primary and secondary objectives. They also provide many different career opportunities for individuals interested in security as a career.

The domain of the public sector security is defense/military, homeland security, and public security/policing. The defense domain's primary goal is protecting the United States. This domain is readily seen with the U.S. Military that is involved in many conflicts and peacekeeping missions throughout the world to ensure national security. Secondarily, the defense/military sector protects communities in the United States from

TABLE 1-1 Security Domains

Security Level	Public Sector			Private Sector		
	Defense/Military	Homeland Security	Public Security/ Policing	Corporate	Private	Personal
International	—					
National	●	●	—			
Communities	—	—	●	—	—	
Organizations			—	●	●	
Groups			—	—	—	
Peer/associates					—	
Families						—
Individuals						●

Source: Patrick J. Ortmeier, Johnson, Introduction to Security: Operations and Management, 5e. © 2018, Pearson Education, Inc., New York, NY.

various threats, including international terrorism. Next, the homeland security domain's primary goal is securing the nation followed by protecting communities against man-made and natural threats. Existing primarily in the federal public sector, the principal mission of security organizations in the DHS is based on national and domestic security. Other agencies at the state and local level and even the private sector are also involved in homeland security through resource and intelligence sharing activities. The last domain of the public sector is public security/policing. Seen primarily in the context of policing, these activities are directed toward crime fighting activities at the community level. This domain also has secondary benefits of ensuring national security and the protection of groups and individuals.

The final three classifications can be considered the "private" security sector. The primary mission of corporate security is the protection of company assets at the organizational level. However, this corporate domain also secures employees (groups), communities, and individuals through its provision of security-related services. Another domain is that of private security, which provides client-specific services primarily to organizations, while groups (including neighborhoods) and communities can also use their services and enjoy the resulting benefits of the private security services. Finally, there is the personal security domain. Here, individuals engage in a variety of security-related activities on their own, installing home alarm and lighting systems to protect themselves from various human and man-made threats. These personal level activities also serve to improve security among families.

▶ Security Personnel

An important consideration for any organization is determining who will perform security-related tasks. Generally, security personnel can be grouped into proprietary (in-house), contract (vendor-based), or hybrid, a combination of proprietary and contract personnel.

Proprietary Security

Security personnel who are direct employees of the parent agency, business, or institution are referred to as proprietary security or in-house security. In-house security personnel are

proprietary security
Security program controlled and financed directly by the protected organization.

not under contract through a third-party agency or business. Some of the advantages of proprietary security include the following:

- **Higher Quality.** personnel are generally paid more. This may result in higher quality personnel based on their experience, education, and commitment levels.
- **Training.** personnel can receive specialized training that meets the specific security needs of the organization. This may not be the case for some contract personnel.
- **Loyalty.** proprietary personnel only work for the organization and site where employed.
- **Lower Attrition Rates.** higher pay and benefits promote retention. In some contract organizations, the turnover rate may approach 300 percent.
- **Stability.** a stable workforce, with knowledge of the facility and its personnel, is an important consideration; an important consideration for an effective security program.
- **Respect.** because security personnel are actual employees, there may be greater levels of respect and cooperation with fellow nonsecurity employees in the organization.
- Increased direct control and supervision over the security force.
- High morale and motivation levels.

Sources: Canton, 2003; Fischer & Green, 2008; Maurer, 2000b.

The disadvantages associated with the employment of proprietary security personnel include generally higher costs because the employer must pay for certain benefits, lengthy disciplinary and termination procedures, and the administrative burden associated with human resource management activities.

Contract Security Services

In contrast to proprietary security are companies that are in the business of providing security services to other individuals or organizations for a fee. These are referred to as contract security services. Security services provided under contract include personnel, patrol, alarm

> **contract security service** Security organization that provides security services to individuals or other organizations for a fee.

Proprietary Security are often well trained and equipped: Security Police Officers (SPO) at Sandia/California.
(Photo courtesy of Sandia National Laboratories.)

systems, armored delivery, consultants, executive protection, information security, pre-employment screening, drug testing, and investigative services. With respect to investigations alone, contractors may provide services including criminal defense, personal injury, surveillance, expert testimony, workers' compensation and insurance fraud, undercover operations, trademark infringement, and personal protection.

The component of the contract service industry that experienced the most growth in the past 25 years is uniformed security. Downsizing and financial issues by many U.S. corporations during the 1980s and early 1990s resulted in layoffs for many proprietary security personnel. Many of these security officers were replaced with less expensive contract officers—sometimes referred to as the "McDonaldization of Security" (van Steden & de Waard, 2013). Additionally, as fear of crime and terrorism increased, many organizations began to employ contract security firms to protect personnel and other assets and reduce liability by creating a safer workplace (Fischer, Halibozek, & Walters, 2012).

The trend toward personnel outsourcing and the use of temporary employment services in the United States has created tremendous demand for contract security services. From a consumer standpoint, there are advantages and disadvantages to the use of a contract service. Some of the advantages include the following:

- *Lower Cost.* Expenses can be as much as 20 percent lower than proprietary services, not counting the costs associated with benefit packages (health insurance, retirement, vacation, etc.).
- *Administrative Unburdening.* The contractor is responsible for hiring, training, equipping, scheduling, supervising, evaluating, and terminating employees.
- *Flexibility.* As security needs change, the number of contract personnel required can be increased or decreased easily.
- *Fewer Direct Personnel Issues.* Problem contract employees may be replaced through a phone call to the contractor, while issues related to discipline and discharge are not the responsibility of the company.
- *Objectivity.* Contract employees are likely to be more objective and less susceptible to collusion with nonsecurity employees of the host company or agency.
- *Expertise.* In some cases, organizations have specific and specialized security needs that they cannot meet. A specialized contract agency can provide these services.

The disadvantages associated with the use of contract security personnel include higher attrition, inadequate training, and the contractor's failure to conduct thorough background investigations on employees. Ultimately, outsourcing security personnel and services is a management decision that should not be taken lightly. Careful consideration should be given to the needs of the organization. Cheaper is not necessarily better. In fact, if a contract service is used, the host organization should specify the qualifications, training, wage, supervision, and evaluation requirements in the contract.

Hybrid Security Organizations

hybrid security organization A security operation that employs proprietary security staff and uses contract security personnel to supplement existing proprietary security staff.

Some organizations use both contract and proprietary personnel allowing them to benefit from the advantages of both. A hybrid security organization employs contract security personnel to supplement existing in-house proprietary operations. Many large businesses, for example, employ a behind-the-scenes in-house security staff who may have a great deal of expertise in a particular security issue, such as information security. They also employ contract personnel to monitor surveillance equipment, screen visitors, and patrol parking structures.

▶ Determining Security Needs

The type of security required and the degree of complexity and mission of the security function depends on several factors. Every enterprise differs in its mission, in its culture, and in the way it conducts its internal and external affairs. This difference is a result of a culture emanating from the organization's history, personnel, and interrelationships. Organizational ethics also play an important role in the development of the security environment. Some organizations have very strict policies regarding personnel behavior, while others do not. In addition, private enterprises generate rules, regulations, and standards of conduct that form the foundation for a private justice system. These specific rules and procedures are found in employee handbooks and policy and procedure manuals that are basically the "Constitution of the Workforce." These private justice systems codify and implement certain types of sanctions for misconduct, much like criminal codes define and punish individuals for violations of societal rules. The security environment also depends on the relationship between security and public safety personnel. In the past, the relationship between public law enforcement and corporate security was often strained due to the low quality of some security personnel and the fact that many private police forces engaged in a protective function that many in public law enforcement believed fell under the purview of public policing.

> **private justice system** Rules, regulations, standards of conduct, and punishments established by private enterprises.

Another compounding factor involves the relationship between security personnel and the organization being protected. Many security employees are contract workers provided by third parties. Following a trend in American business, numerous organizations are replacing some of their proprietary employees with contract workers. Loyalty to the organization, therefore, often remains with the contractor rather than with the site being protected. Finally, a major challenge for security management in the electronic age is the protection of proprietary information. Competitive pressures, foreign and domestic, combined with the ability to invade an institution or country electronically, pose enormous threats to national security and business enterprises.

> **private police** Private security; protective services typically financed through private funding sources.

In spite of any shortcomings within the security environment, the future seems relatively unlimited for the security profession and for individuals who choose security as an occupation. Among other factors, constraints on public law enforcement budgets are likely to continue and necessitate increased use of private police (security) services. Security's positive impact in the modern world is without question. As security concepts are integrated into organizations, leaders are becoming more aware of the importance of security's value and contribution to the enterprise (American Society for Industrial Security, 2013; Dalton, 2003; Schmalleger, 2010).

Exciting career opportunities also exist in the security field (Harr & Hess, 2006). Salaries for security managers are generally competitive with those received in other professions. The results of a salary survey conducted in 1999 by the publisher of a security trade journal indicated that the average salary for security management personnel ranged from $30,000 to over $150,000 annually (Access Control & Security Systems Integration, 1999). A salary survey conducted in 2002 indicated that the highest average business-sector security manager salaries are earned in information technology ($109,105), followed by security professionals employed in the utilities and energy industry ($103,636) (Anderson, 2002). By 2007, the average annual salary for security professionals reached $117,000 (Moran, 2007). The salary for chief security officer (CSO) positions in large multinational organizations was expected to reach $400,000 annually (Lohr, 2002). By 2006, the salary range for CSOs reached $199,000–$294,000 (Scalet, 2006). In 2010, the median compensation for security professionals in the United States was $93,000, a 6 percent increase from 2009; those who held a Certified Protection Professional (CPP) certification earned a median salary of $111,000 and an average salary of $130,000 (American Society for Industrial Security, 2012). Based on the growth in the number of people employed as well as the increase in compensation levels, it is apparent that career opportunities and salaries are excellent for those interested in security services. While the actual number of security personnel is difficult to estimate

> **Certified Protection Professional (CPP)** Security professional designation awarded by ASIS International.

because job titles and classifications often vary among organizations, estimates from the U.S. Bureau of Labor Statistics (2015) show that there were over 1 million security guards, 80,000 information security specialists, over 60,000 alarm system installers, and approximately 30,000 private investigators. Other estimates show that there are approximately 2 million security personnel in the United States (ASIS, 2013).

Security's Impact

The singularly most important and conspicuous purpose of security is that of protector or guardian. As the guardian against harm to people, property, and information, security is a service function with a tremendous impact. However, security's value may be difficult to measure or quantify. Therefore, security's impact may be determined more appropriately by what does not happen, rather than by what does.

Security may add value to an organization by aggressively seeking cost reduction initiatives. Security managers may cut costs through entrepreneurial ventures and articulation arrangements with other security service providers. Collaborative business arrangements and consortiums are formed to increase efficiency and reduce expenses. In Washington, DC, five independent high-rise building management groups entered into an agreement to share services provided by a third-party vendor. Hospitals share services, including security services, with other hospitals. Multiple facilities with proprietary (in-house) alarm and video surveillance systems can collaborate to create a single central station to share in the cost or can charge member organizations for the service. Large facilities can utilize security personnel, instead of mailroom staff, to provide internal mail and delivery services, thus adding value to the organization by cutting delivery costs while increasing patrol activity (Colling, 2001; Dalton, 1995; Ortmeier & Davis, 2012).

Security involves government, nonprofit, and for-profit institutions. In an organizational sense, security is a function and responsibility that is woven increasingly throughout the operation of all public agencies and private institutions. As a function within an organization, security may be defined as a public or private service-related activity that provides personnel and equipment to prevent or reduce losses caused by criminal actions as well as by non-criminal events resulting from human error, emergencies, and natural and man-made threats.

▶ Security: Essential Functions

The management of security operations may be categorized according to the security functions performed. These functions include the essential elements of physical, personnel, and information security (INFOSEC) (see Figure 1-2 ■).

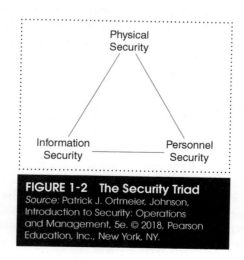

FIGURE 1-2 The Security Triad
Source: Patrick J. Ortmeier, Johnson, Introduction to Security: Operations and Management, 5e. © 2018, Pearson Education, Inc., New York, NY.

Physical security refers to tangible objects, such as walls, fences, locks, and building designs, that promote the protection of persons and property. It also includes lighting, surveillance and alarm systems, and security personnel devoted to access control activities. The physical safety and security requirements for persons and property are balanced with operational needs and the aesthetic qualities required in the environment. Good physical security protects a facility and its people. It can affect a potential criminal offender's perception of a possible crime target. The protection of electronic systems from loss due to accidents, natural disasters, or unauthorized access is another function of physical security. Computer systems, data, software, transmission lines, airwave frequencies, voice communications, electronic mail, and Internet servers must be protected. Revolutionary changes in technology have radically changed the nature of business and the environment in which organizations and governments operate. As a result, special attention must focus on the protection of these systems. Security measures must also be designed and implemented to protect the operation itself. In other words, an organization's processes must be protected. Without redundant systems, such as backup power supplies, temporary inactivity may occur in a critical stage of the operation, resulting in expensive downtime. This will be reviewed in detail in Chapter 4.

Personnel security involves the protection of persons associated with the organization and the protection from individuals who might harm the organization. Protection of employees, customers, and guests is inherent in the security function. Unique strategies may be required to protect dignitaries, corporate officers, and celebrities. Personnel security also involves hiring the right people and maintaining their integrity. It includes the utilization of an effective pre-employment screening process as well as policies and procedures to reduce the opportunity and motive for employee theft and poor productivity. This will be reviewed in detail in Chapter 5.

Information security is the third leg of the security management triad. Other than death or injury to a person, the greatest single threat to any individual, agency, institution, or nation is the loss of intellectual property or proprietary and confidential information. All stages of the information cycle must be protected. The methods used in the creation, processing, storage, retrieval, transmission, dissemination, and disposition of information in any form must be secured. The level of protection required at each stage depends on the information's value to the organization, the ability of an outsider to duplicate the information, and the potential harm that could result if the information is acquired by the wrong individuals, organizations, or nations. This will be reviewed in detail in Chapter 6.

physical security One of the pillars of an effective security program. Devices, lighting, surveillance and alarm systems, and security personnel devoted to access control.

personnel security One of the three pillars of any security program. Protection of persons associated with an organization as well as protection from individuals who seek to harm the organization.

information security (INFOSEC) One of the three pillars of an effective security program. Security of information creation, processing, storage, retrieval, transmission, dissemination, and disposition. The protection of information assets and systems against any threat.

SECURITY SPOTLIGHT

Identify an individual who works in security services, perhaps at your school, at your place of employment, or in your community. Determine whether this person would be willing to talk with you for a few minutes about security work. If so, consider asking the individual questions such as: What attracted you to security as a profession? What do you enjoy most about the work? What do you enjoy least?

► Roles of the Security Manager

Already, the reader of this chapter has most likely gained an appreciation for the complexity of security, recognizing that it is a profession requiring many skills. As pointed out by Rogers (2008):

Security risks confronting organizations must be managed in a security-discipline specific, integrated and systematic manner that is based on acceptable management, legal, financial, security, technological, engineering, safety and business principles. Gone are the days when a retired policeman or even a former military person could merely step into the position of a senior security manager, and successfully manage crime (security) risks. The modern corporate demands for effective security in the private sector no longer make it acceptable or allow for an ad hoc approach to security risk management. (Rogers, 2008, p. 150)

Since security management is a multifaceted occupation, the roles of the security manager are varied. The security manager simultaneously assumes managerial, administrative, preventive, and investigative roles and responsibilities.

As a *manager*, the security professional is responsible for selecting, training, scheduling, supervising, motivating, and evaluating security personnel. The manager is responsible for issues related to productivity, morale, compensation, well-being, and professional growth of security personnel as well as safety and security indoctrination and training of all employees. Employee attitudes and expectations toward authority are changing. Workforce diversity is commonplace and workplace violence has become a major issue. Organizations are also requiring higher productivity and improvements in the quality of output.

In the role of an *administrator*, the security professional is responsible for the establishment of security's organizational vision, mission, goals, and objectives. The security administrator must create a vision for the security operation as well as administer the day-to-day operations of the department. This involves planning, financial control, public relations, and community liaison activities. Security managers have become risk managers. They must anticipate, analyze, and protect an organization from virtually every conceivable threat, from liability to terrorism.

As a primary *prevention officer* of an organization, the security manager is ultimately responsible and accountable for prevention of loss from any source. It is the manager's responsibility to recognize and appraise hazards, and initiate action to reduce or remove the risk of loss. A high number of arrests for crimes committed on the premises are not a good measure for security program effectiveness, since it suggests that there is a problem with existing security measures and practices. The measure of the best security program is how many crimes and incidents are prevented.

When a loss or incident does occur, the security manager must become an *investigator* and determine the cause. Conducting background investigations on prospective employees and auditing the site to ensure that security measures are working are also part of the investigative function. However, the security manager is not a police officer. Security management and public policing are not synonymous. The language of the security manager is the language of business, loss prevention, and asset protection, not law enforcement. Similarities between public policing and security in the actual functions performed often end with appearance and structure. Although security personnel are involved in the detection and investigation of crime and the arrest of suspected criminal offenders, most of their time is spent on preventive efforts to reduce losses from noncriminal sources. Conversely a great deal of law enforcement activities are spent responding to incidents and crimes that have already occurred. In fact, former law enforcement officers do not always make the best security managers. Individuals and organizations that employ security personnel prefer individuals with specialized training, education, and experience in security services rather than in law enforcement. Security management and business skills, such as planning, accounting, budgeting, public relations, and value-added contribution techniques, are not taught in police academies. In a study conducted by one of the authors of this text, consumers of security services as well as security professionals preferred management candidates who possessed knowledge of security and skills in general business practices, personnel management, labor relations, planning, threat assessment, and policy formulation. Much less emphasis was placed on criminal law enforcement skills. In the post-9-11 environment, security knowledge and business skills remain important, with increased emphasis placed on intelligence (information gathering) capabilities and investigative skills (Burstein, 1996; Fischer & Green, 2008; Harowitz, 2003; Johnson, 2005; Maurer, 2000a; Ortmeier, 1996b).

security management
Multifaceted and interdisciplinary management tactics and strategies designed to secure persons, property, and information and prevent losses from any source.

Summary

In the past, security's image usually reflected a poorly trained individual who earned near minimum wage and guarded a gate or patrolled a business at night. Unfortunately, the popular media often portrays the private security industry in a negative and oftentimes contemptuous manner. Most contemporary security personnel, however, are much more sophisticated. Security personnel are used for emergency response, access control, deterrence, investigations, and personal and property protection. They monitor and operate security equipment utilized for access control, surveillance, fire protection, and patrol activities. As shown in this chapter, these security personnel can be proprietary, contract, or hybrid in nature.

The historical review of security shows that is has always been entrepreneurial, meeting the specific needs of private industries and governments. In pre-modern England, the practice of security was carried out by the citizenry to meet their collective security needs. This was also the case in pre-modern America where citizens carried out security-related functions prior to the introduction of formalized police structures. Later, with the birth of large corporations in the United States, companies created their own security/police forces to deal with loss and to address labor-related issues. This era also saw the growth of contract security agencies that provided a variety of services to industries and even the public sector. With the World Wars, meanwhile, the security function became more advanced, addressing new threats related to homeland security where the U.S. government became more involved in ensuring that key industries were protected. With the 9-11 terrorist attacks combined with other emerging security needs, the private sector has advanced, serving the needs of organizations and the public.

An effective security program relies upon physical, personnel, and information security. It requires effective management where security managers are called upon to establish policies and procedures for disaster recovery, emergency management, fire prevention, security education, loss prevention, and asset protection. To accomplish all of these goals and objectives, the role of a security manager is to serve as an administrator, a prevention officer, and an investigator. Ultimately, the goals of security promote a safe and secure environment and prevent loss. The result is maximum return on the investment of public or private capital. Security involves all those activities and objectives designed to meet asset protection goals to ensure that security problems do not materialize (Bratton, 2011; Dempsey, 2010; Kakalik & Wildhorn, 1971; Sennewald, 2003; Simonsen, 1998).

Key Terms and Concepts

Allan Pinkerton *8*
American Society for Industrial Security (ASIS) *13*
Bow Street Runners *6*
Certified Protection Professional (CPP) *19*
Contract security services *17*
Defense Security Services (DSS) *12*
Frankpledge system *6*
Hallcrest Reports I *14*
Hallcrest Reports II *14*
Homeland Security Act of 2002 *15*
Hybrid security organization *18*
Industrial Defense Program *12*

Information security (INFOSEC) *21*
Law Enforcement Assistance Administration (LEAA) *13*
Maslow's hierarchy of needs *4*
Mass private property hypothesis *5*
Metropolitan Police Act of 1829 *7*
National Industrial Security Program (NISP) *12*
Personnel security *21*
Physical security *21*
Private justice systems *19*
Private police *19*
Private Security Advisory Council (PSAC) *13*

Proprietary security *16*
Railway Police Act *8*
Security *3*
Security management *22*
Shire reeve (sheriff) *6*
Sir Robert Peel *7*
Statute of Westminster of 1285 *6*
Task Force Report on Private Security *14*
Theory of collective security *4*
Thief takers *6*
U.S. Department of Homeland Security *15*
Violent Crime Control and Law Enforcement Act of 1994 *14*
Watch *6*

Discussion Questions and Exercises

1. Discuss the theoretical foundation for security and the reasons for the growth in security services.
2. What are the three eras of security in the United States?
3. List and describe the functions and roles of security.
4. Describe the responsibilities of the security manager.
5. What are the three essential elements of security?
6. List and describe the different types of security personnel.
7. What are some federal initiatives that led to the growth and modernization of private security in the United States?
8. Why the growth of security in contemporary society?
9. Explain the main components of the contemporary security industry.
10. Explain security in pre-modern England. What did the United States adopt from England?

Your Turn

This chapter has shown that oftentimes the number of private security personnel outnumber public sector law enforcement personnel in a given area. To investigate if this point is true in your area, compare the number of sworn police officers to the number of contract, proprietary, or hybrid security officers in your hometown (or another area you are familiar with). Answer the following questions:

a. In what industries are they located?
b. Are they concentrated in a specific area in your chosen city?
c. What activities do they perform?
d. What is the ratio of security to sworn police?

2 Threats to Safety and Security

LEARNING OBJECTIVES

After completing this chapter, the reader should be able to:

1. identify and describe threats to safety and security
2. discuss the nature and importance of unintentional threats against an organization
3. discuss the importance of accident prevention
4. describe the fire triangle and classifications of fire
5. distinguish between natural and environmental disasters and civil disorder
6. analyze factors that create civil liability
7. demonstrate knowledge of substance abuse prevention, intervention, and treatment strategies
8. discuss the nature and extent of crime
9. list and describe types of crime
10. evaluate crime prevention strategies

▶ Introduction

One key consideration for security personnel to understand is that organizations are microcosms of society where the activities, actions, and social problems that exist in society often "spill over" into the organization to some degree. As such, companies, organizations, and institutions can be exposed to particular vulnerabilities that are weaknesses or gaps in the protection of an organization's assets (Field Manual, 2001). These vulnerabilities increase the level or degree of risk, which is the uncertainty or potential for injury, loss, or harm in defined circumstances. This risk is based on a variety of natural and man-made perils. Perils are the presence of factors or elements that expose assets to a given risk that can subsequently cause some type of loss. Perils are events that cause loss (McLeman & Smit, 2006). These perils can be natural where wind, extreme temperatures, earthquakes, epidemics, and floods can lead to and cause loss. In other cases, perils can be human-based that include crime, civil unrest, warfare, terrorism, and accidents.

There are also hazards. Hazards are underlying conditions or situations that increase the potential that harm will occur from a peril. Hazards make the occurrence or emergence of a peril more likely. For example, a chemical company that builds a factory in a floodplain (the hazard) is vulnerable to the risk of flooding (the peril), whereas a convenience store that is located in a high-crime neighborhood (the hazard) may be more vulnerable to a higher number of crimes (the specific peril) than another store located in a low-crime area of the city. Finally, there are threats. A threat is where the hazard has materialized into a tangible or definite human or non-human entity. These threats, which are oftentimes difficult to control, can cause some type of damage, injury, or loss, increasing risk. For example, if a hurricane develops (a peril), and people live in a coastal area (a hazard) where the hurricane strikes land, the resulting high

vulnerability Gaps or weaknesses in the protection of an organization's assets.

risk Possibility of suffering harm or loss; exposure to probability of loss or damage.

perils Situations or events that can cause loss, injury, or damage. Threats are a synonym of perils.

hazards Underlying conditions or situations that increase the potential that harm will occur.

threats Where a hazard has materialized into a tangible or definite threat that can cause some type of damage, injury, or loss.

risk management Process involved in the anticipation, recognition, and appraisal of a risk and the initiation of action to eliminate the risk entirely or reduce the threat of harm to an acceptable level.

all-hazards approach Being prepared to take appropriate actions for managing all types of risk.

accident An unfortunate event caused unintentionally by a human agent.

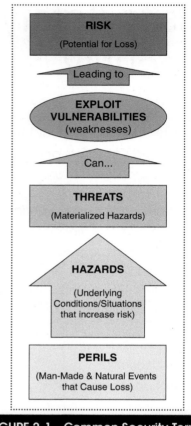

FIGURE 2-1   Common Security Terms

winds and flooding is a threat to humans and assets, including homes. Consider the following example that ties together all of these terms: Individuals are at a higher risk of loss due to a personal crime such as robbery in some cases because they do not have the means to fully protect themselves (a vulnerability). It is oftentimes hazardous to go into a known high crime neighborhood because the human peril of crime exists. A criminal emerges from a concealed area (a threat which is a materialized hazard), robbing the person, subsequently causing financial loss and psychological harm. A graphic representation of these terms can be found in Figure 2-1 ■.

It is the responsibility of the security function to identify the wide variety of potential perils and underlying hazards and address them through the risk management process (which will be explored in detail in Chapter 12), in order to prevent or mitigate the impact of these man-made threats on the organization. This requires companies to take an "all-hazards" approach, where organizations should be prepared for specific types of hazards while also being prepared to take appropriate actions for managing all types of risks. This approach does not mean that all safety and security issues need to be identified. Instead, this framework assumes that there are often common elements to many hazards that organizations need to be prepared for, in the event that they should occur (Calder & Bland, 2015).

▶ Accidents

Unfortunately, accidents occur in the workplace. An accident is "an acute and unintended event that leads to an injury" (Jeong, 1999, p. 566), "occurring when a plant [company] proceeds to an abnormal state or a transient situation from a normal state" (Kwon & Kim, 1999,

p. 491). It can also be understood as "an event involving an unplanned and an unacceptable loss" (Leveson, 2011). Accidents are different from disasters in the context of scale. In more extreme events, organizations may also encounter disasters, which are extremely large-scale, man-made, or natural events that result in casualties, destruction, damage, and disruptions. Disasters also affect large groups of people while the degree of damage often overwhelms the response capabilities of local emergency response systems, communities, and individuals (Alexander, 2005; Collins, 2000). The majority of workplace accidents result from the carelessness or failure to enhance safety-related work rules—oftentimes human error. These accidents can involve humans and property. In the context of humans, workplace accident data shows that accidents have been decreasing over the last decade. Nevertheless, in 2013, employers reported approximately three million cases of nonfatal workplace injuries (U.S. Department of Labor, 2015). Finally, the goal of any organization is to increase the safety of its workers. Safety is defined as the absence of accidents (Leveson, 2011).

One useful tool or model for understanding human-based accidents that has been applied to a variety of industry groups is the Human Factors Analysis and Classification System. This model examines the causal factors of accidents in a systems perspective. It takes the position that human error accidents are a symptom of a larger problem in the organization. It also assumes that there are "holes" in the safety barriers of organizations that exist at four different levels: (1) unsafe acts by operators; (2) preconditions for unsafe acts that include factors in the work environment and the physiological and mental states of employees; (3) unsafe supervision; and (4) organizational influences that include top-level decisions that have an impact on resources, and the organizational climate related to safety and policies and procedures (Wiegman & Shappell, 2003).

The research shows the nature and extent of human error that leads to accidents. In one study of process/storage plants and the transportation of hazardous materials in the chemical industry, approximately 20 percent of the accidents were directly attributed to human errors, which contributed to the "domino effect," where relatively minor accidents such as overfilling a chemical tank caused severe consequences over a much larger area (Darbra, Palacios, & Casal, 2010). Another study of more than 400 businesses in the United Kingdom and the United States found that as much as 23 percent of employees did not understand one critical aspect of their job, which led to an accident. The estimated loss to the U.S. and U.K. businesses due to accidents is roughly $28 billion per year (Cordin, Rowan, Odgers, Barnes, & Redgate, 2008).

Although safety legislation exists and companies have effective risk management, safety, and response activities, the potential for accidents is nevertheless high. This can be attributed to that fact that understanding production processes and responses to accidents in some complex systems (such as nuclear power plants) is simply beyond the comprehension levels of human beings (Perrow, 1984). In fact, regardless of governmental regulations and better practices and risk-management-related policies among corporations, there has been an increase in the actual number of workplace disasters per decade since the 1970s. However, the number of fatalities per incident has declined over the last 40 years (Coleman, 2006), decreasing by 26 percent since 2006 (U.S. Department of Labor, Bureau of Labor Statistics, 2010b).

To assist in the creation of a safe work environment, Congress passed the Occupational Safety and Health Act in 1970. The Act established the Occupational Safety and Health Administration (OSHA). The Act requires employers to provide a work environment that is free from recognized hazards that are causing, or are likely to cause, serious bodily injury or death to employees. An employer must also comply with specific OSHA-promulgated safety rules. The Act also prohibits any employer from discriminating against or discharging an employee who exercises rights under the Act. Employers must also know and comply with OSHA regulations and standards, eliminate hazards and provide a safe and healthy work environment; establish a record-keeping and reporting system covering all work-related injuries, deaths, and illnesses; conduct periodic safety and health inspections and correct any hazards found,

disaster Extreme large-scale man-made natural or natural events that result in casualties, destruction, damage and disruptions that affect large groups of people.

safety The absence of accidents.

Human Factors Analysis and Classification System Model that examines the causal factors of accidents in a systems perspective.

OSHA Occupational Safety and Health Act. Passed in 1970, the Act established the Occupational Safety and Health Administration (OSHA) and established specific safety requirements for employers.

and allow OSHA officials to inspect company facilities. Employers are also responsible for providing protective equipment, developing and enforcing safety and health standards, keeping workers informed of their OSHA rights, maintaining safety records, and training employees in workplace safety. All states also have their own state-level OSHA requirements and departments that provide additional safety-related guidelines and requirements.

Enforcement of the Act may involve OSHA inspections and citations of employers for breach of the general duty of care, breach of a specific safety and health standard, or failure to document incidents, maintain appropriate records, or conspicuously post notices required under the Act. Penalties for violating the Act can be both civil and criminal (Mann & Roberts, 2009). Initially, the cost of OSHA compliance can be considerable. Strategically, however, the costs related to occupational safety and health save money for companies, since accidents, long-term illnesses, and deaths resulting in loss and liability are decreased.

The security element of the organization is often responsible for OSHA enforcement and compliance activities through a variety of safety engineering-related activities that include risk management, and responding to and investigating workplace safety issues. To address safety-related incidents in organizations, it is recommended that they be examined in a systems perspective. For example, oftentimes, workplace accidents are attributed to "operator error" where the organization may take a behavioral approach to correct the actions of workers in order to avoid safety issues. While correcting the behaviors of employees is significant in preventing accidents, it is also important for security managers and staff to identify those underlying and often complex issues, factors, and root causes that lead to accidents. This can be done by looking at accidents systematically, analyzing the environment in which the accident occurred (Leveson, 2011).

Human Error and Accidents

human error Unintentional, human mistake.

One of the common causes of accidents is human error. Human error can be defined as "unintentional random events that are inherent in all human activities and professions" (McCrory, LaGrange, & Hallbeck, 2014, p. 2). They include: (1) mistakes or errors in planning; (2) slips or lapses—errors in carrying out job duties; (3) violations—deliberate deviations from safe practices; and (4) technical failures that occur when the actions or techniques are appropriate, but an accident nevertheless occurred (Reason, 1990). These human errors can result in financial loss. In the case of an industrial accident, the facility itself or some equipment could be temporarily or permanently damaged. In the case of nonproduction issues, inaccurate record keeping and inadvertently discarding valuables are commonplace in organizations. *Shrinkage* (loss of assets) within a retail organization, for example, is not always the result of an internal or external criminal act. Merchandise may be inadvertently under-rung at a cash register. Damaged merchandise may be discarded without proper documentation, and defective merchandise may be destroyed when it could be returned to the manufacturer for credit (Davies, 2007; Fay, 2000). Although a very broad topic, one of the primary roles of security includes anticipating, detecting, and preventing these errors.

▶ Fire

Fire is a serious concern for all organizations. In 2012, there were 92,800 nonresidential building fires in the United States, causing over $2 billion in losses (U.S. Fire Administration, 2013). At a minimum, fires can lead to business interruptions whose costs can far exceed the actual losses caused by the fire. Fires can also lead to injuries and death for employees. For example, one of the worst fire disasters in U.S. history (besides the 9-11 World Trade Center fire) was the 1911 Triangle Shirtwaist Fire disaster that resulted in the death of 146 workers. The resulting investigation found that fire suppression

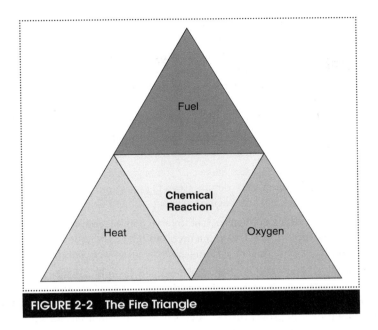

FIGURE 2-2   The Fire Triangle

equipment was inadequate and nonfunctioning, the doors opened inward, blocking the rush of employees trying to escape, and the stairways in the building were too narrow to accommodate the evacuation of employees. The fire was caused by human error—someone threw a match or cigarette into a pile of scrap fabric (McEvoy, 1995). Today, organizations must comply with a variety of fire-related laws and codes. Moreover, they must have effective fire prevention policies and practices that focus on preventing a fire from occurring. Fire protection and suppression tools to minimize personal injury and damage to property are also part of a comprehensive fire program.

A *fire* is actually a complex event. It can be understood as a state, process, or instance of combustion in which fuel or other material is ignited and combined with oxygen, giving off heat, light, and flame (Merriam-Webster, 2015). Although "fire" may appear to be simplistic in nature, it is actually a complex chemical process that involves a thermochemical process known as pyrolysis. Pyrolysis is a chemical or thermal decomposition of combustible organic materials that are broken down by heat, and oxidation, which is an exothermic reaction or process where oxygen combined with other substances releases heat energy (Drysdale, 2011). One way to understand the combustion process is through the fire tetrahedron model. The fire tetrahedron model incorporates the traditional elements of the fire triangle that explains that combustion is dependent upon the presence of three elements in specific levels or quantities: heat, fuel, and oxygen. The tetrahedron model adds a fourth element—a chemical chain reaction (Figure 2-2 ■). Under this model, if any of the elements are eliminated, then combustion cannot occur.

Fires are classified according to the types of combustibles present:

- *Class A:* Ordinary combustible materials including cloth, wood, rubber, and many plastics. Class A fires can be extinguished with water or dry chemical agents to cool the fire below ignition temperatures.

- *Class B:* This class contains liquids that are based on their flash points, which is the minimum temperature at which sufficient vapor is given off the liquid to form an ignitable mixture with air. These fuels burn only at the surface because oxygen cannot penetrate the depth of the fluid. Only the vapor burns when ignited. They include

pyrolysis A chemical or thermal decomposition of combustible organic materials that are broken down by heat, and oxidation.

oxidation An exothermic reaction or process where oxygen combined with other substances, releases heat energy.

fire tetrahedron model A fourth element of the fire triangle that consists of a chemical chain reaction.

fire triangle Heat, fuel, and oxygen necessary for a fire to occur.

Class I flammable liquids (e.g., alcohol, gasoline) that ignite and burn at normal working temperatures and have flash points below 100° F, and Class II combustible liquids (e.g., kerosene and many solvents) that require increased temperatures to burn, having flash points above 100° F. These types of fire require a dry chemical or CO_2 extinguisher that creates a barrier between the fuel and oxygen (i.e., a non-combustible chemical or foam) to "smother" the fire.

- *Class C:* Energized electrical equipment (computers, appliances, electrical panels, wiring, motors). When the electricity is turned off, the fire becomes a Class A fire. Class C fires require non-conductive extinguishing agents (no water).

- *Class D:* Fires involving powders, flakes, or shavings of combustible metals such as magnesium, titanium, potassium, and sodium. Class D fires require the use of specialized chemical agents and powders that are specific to the type of metals that need to be extinguished.

- *Class K:* Fires in cooking appliances that involve combustible cooking media (vegetable or animal oils and fats). These fires often involve high temperatures, requiring specialized hand-held and fixed extinguisher systems that rely upon wet chemical agents.

Different types of fire extinguishers are designed to fight different types of fire. The three most common types of portable fire extinguishers are: air pressurized water, CO_2 (carbon dioxide), and dry chemical (Federal Emergency Management Agency, 2011; National Fire Protection Agency, 2015a; OSHA, 2016). (*Note:* Some of the information from the National Fire Protection Agency has been used too—no direct quotes are used from the NFPA.)

There are three stages of combustion. In the *incipient stage,* the fire is in its beginning stage. It is small, where some heat and small amounts of fire gases are being produced. Generally, in this stage, hand-held fire extinguishers can be used to put the fire out. Next is the *free-burning phase,* where the fire has become more intense and there is an ample supply of oxygen where open or visible flaming is present. This oxygen is drawn into the fire and super-heated gases from the fuels increase the temperature of the area, oftentimes above 1,000 degrees, igniting other combustible materials in the area and creating a lot of smoke that serves as a fuel source. In some cases, this rapid increase in heat, combined with the presence of fuels, results in a *flashover,* which is the sudden increase in flame in the fire setting. The *smoldering* stage can be considered the last stage of the fire. Here, oxygen levels are not high enough to sustain the fire, even though there is the presence of heat and fire gases. In these situations, as soon as oxygen is reintroduced, the fire will resume again. Because of the presence of a large amount of flammable fire gases and heat in the smoldering stage, there is potential for a backdraft explosion. A backdraft explosion occurs when the reintroduction of oxygen leads to the fire gases igniting rapidly, causing an explosion (Norman, 2012).

Individuals are vulnerable to injury and the loss of life in fires. Generally, these combustible hazards can be grouped into toxic gases, heat, and smoke (Stec & Hull, 2010). Depending upon combustible products present, the type of combustion, and the temperature of the fire, a variety of toxic chemicals are present in fire gases and smoke that can adversely affect individuals exposed to them. The most dangerous category is *asphyxiant gases,* which may choke and suffocate individuals who are exposed to the fire. These include carbon monoxide (which is the most common gas produced), hydrogen cyanide (which is the byproduct of many polymers), carbon dioxide, and depleted levels of oxygen as a consequence of combustion. There are also a variety of *irritant gases* that are generated. These irritant gases can also be lethal, but at a minimum they impair one's vision and ability to breathe. Some of the common irritant gases include ammonia, hydrogen chloride, chlorine, sulfur dioxide, phosphoric acid, formaldehyde, and particulate matter or ash (Wakefield, 2010).

Thermal or heat-related injuries can also occur. Heat energy from fire can cause thermal injury through conduction. *Conduction* is the transfer of heat within or between solids, which requires direct contact with the heat. Injury can also occur through *convection*, which is the transfer of heat energy through the means of gases or liquids. It is often the movement of hot masses of air. Injuries and burns are also caused by radiant (or reflected) heat transfer. *Radiation* heat transfer occurs through electromagnetic waves. This type of heat transfer does not require direct contact with the heat source. An example of radiant heat is the sun which transfers heat energy to the earth and can cause sunburns (Prahlow, 2010).

Even though the research shows that most individuals die from fire toxicity as a result of the presence of fire gases—not flame or direct heat—it also needs to be understood that humans have relatively low tenability limits to the effects of heat. For example, burns to the respiratory tract begin at 140 degrees while skin tolerance to heat is about 248 degrees. This heat also causes mental deterioration, impeding decision-making and speed of evacuations. The presence of smoke also causes mental deterioration, panic, increasing the time period for evacuation and evacuation-related injuries, such as slip and fall-related accidents (Stec & Hull, 2010). Smoke-filled areas can also lead to a slow response time in fighting fires by fire personnel.

The causes of fire can be categorized as incendiary (arson-based), accidental, and natural (Almirall & Furton, 2004). Recent data from Federal Emergency Management Agency (FEMA) shows that arson is the cause of nonresidential building fires in 10 percent of all known fires. Other causes include electrical malfunctions (9.8 percent), followed by carelessness (6.8 percent), exposure (5.9 percent), which is when a fire from an outside source spreads to the building, open flames (5.4 percent), and open heat (5.4 percent). The frequency of fire also varies by industry group. Stores and offices (19 percent), outside and special properties (18 percent), and fires in storage areas (15 percent) were the top three sites for fires in 2006 (U.S. Fire Administration, 2010). This suggests that human activities in combination with the mass of combustibles, including furnishings and building components in a given area, known as the **fuel load**, as well as knowing the **fire load**, which is the total energy content of these combustible materials in a given area (including the structure itself and contents), are very important factors for consideration (Zalok & Eduful, 2013). Finally, natural events need to be considered a fire hazard. Lightning, for example, causes over 31,000 fires per year (Ahrens, 2008). Other "Acts of God" such as lava can also result in fires that can threaten the safety of employees and organizations in those areas where volcanism is present and active, such as the Hawaiian Islands (Smith, 2013).

Examples of severe accidental fires abound. Consider the fire that broke out in February 2003, during the Great White concert at the Station nightclub in West Warwick, Rhode Island. Pyrotechnics (fireworks) used during the band's performance inside the club ignited combustible building materials near the stage. The resulting fire spread quickly. Most concertgoers were unaware that the flames were not part of the show. Within minutes, flames and heavy smoke engulfed the club where 99 people died and nearly 200 more were injured in the frantic struggle to escape the aging wood structure. The West Warwick fire was the deadliest nightclub fire in the United States since the Beverly Hills Supper Club in Southgate, Kentucky in 1977 that killed 165 people (Zuckerman, 2003).

Another example of a fire and subsequent explosion occurred in February 2008 at the Imperial Sugar Refinery located in Port Wentworth, Georgia. Because of the presence of oxygen in the air, high concentrations of combustible dust in the air, and a confined environment that created overpressures in the fire (that leads to explosions), a dust explosion occurred, killing 14, injuring another 38, and extensively damaging the facility. The cause of this fire was sugar dust that was ignited by a hot bearing on a conveyor line. This initial fire then led to successive secondary dust explosions throughout the factory. The cause of the fire was attributed to poor maintenance. Management allowed sugar dust to pile up on the floors and equipment throughout the facility, not recognizing that sugar was a combustible hazard. Management was also not aware of the dangers of dust explosions (Taveau, 2012).

fuel load Human activities in combination with the mass of combustibles, including furnishings and building components in a given area.

fire load The total energy content of combustible materials in a given area.

Companies also need to be aware that they can be directly impacted by fires that do not occur within their own organizations. One of the largest fire-related disasters in the context of dollar losses occurred in 2000 when lightning struck a power line in New Mexico. Because of the power fluctuations, a small fire broke out in the Royal Philips Electronics silicon chip manufacturing plant in Albuquerque, New Mexico. Although the company effectively controlled and extinguished the fire in approximately 10 minutes, the smoke and water damage contaminated millions of chips that were awaiting shipment to cell phone manufacturers. The fire also contaminated the clean rooms of the company where chips were manufactured. Because of this "small" fire, Philips could not produce and ship enough chips to Ericsson, a major cell phone manufacturer at the time. As a consequence of not having chips for its phones, in 2000 alone, Ericsson lost $1.68 billion and had to lay off thousands of employees. As a result of its losses, Ericsson had to merge with Sony Corporation in 2001 (Mukherjee, 2008).

These examples show the dangers of fire. Organizations need to follow fire codes and fire-related legislation. They must also have proper fire prevention programs to prevent and mitigate fire loss. Additionally, proper and effective suppression strategies must be used after a fire starts. These strategies include the use of personnel and fire protection and suppression equipment and devices such as alarms, extinguishers, sprinkler systems, and firefighting equipment. Strategies also include the use of fire escapes, exit routes, evacuation procedures, and fire doors to help contain the fire (National Fire Protection Association, 2008). Specific fire prevention, protection, and response strategies will be examined in detail in Chapter 4.

► Counterproductive Workplace Behaviors

In many instances, the primary responsibility of security managers and staff is to work with other members of the organization in enforcing workplace rules. These workplace rules are often prescribed in the organization's policy and procedure manual, which can be considered the "Constitution of the Workplace," defining and explaining acceptable conduct. The activities deemed unacceptable can be considered forms of workplace deviance. Workplace deviance is defined as "voluntary behavior that violates significant organizational norms and, in doing so, threatens the well-being of the organization or its members, or both" (Robinson & Bennett, 1995, p. 556). These counterproductive activities exist across the dimensions of minor and serious and interpersonal and organizational behaviors that can be categorized into political deviance, property deviance, production deviance, and personal aggression (Robinson & Bennett, 1995). These types of deviance have different targets and degrees of severity. For example, political deviance-related activities are often minor and interpersonally directed, including activities related to "backstabbing" and spreading rumors. Likewise, personal aggression is more severe and is also interpersonal in nature. Conversely, production and property deviance activities are directed at the company and respectively include absenteeism, "slacking" or not working to full potential, theft, vandalism, and sabotage (Lawrence & Robinson, 2007). In some cases, these deviant activities are also crimes that may include illegal drug use and assaultive behaviors.

> **workplace deviance**
> Voluntary behavior that violates significant organizational norms and, in doing so, threatens the well-being of the organization or its members, or both.

Workplace Violence

One type of workplace deviance and specific crime category is workplace violence. According to the U.S. Department of Labor (2015), "workplace violence is any act or threat of physical violence, harassment, intimidation, or other threatening disruptive behavior that occurs at the work site" (np). This broad category of activities can include harassment, bullying, assaultive behaviors, and even homicides. Although workplace violence has been on the decrease for the last 15 years, it still accounts for approximately 15 percent of all nonfatal violent crime in the United States. It also affects over half a million workers

> **workplace violence**
> Violent acts including both physical assaults and threats of assaults directed toward workers and those in the workplace.

annually (Harrell, 2011). These acts can have a profound impact on organizations in the context of employee stress and turnover, fear of being victimized, and decreased productivity. Therefore, violence prevention is a key concern for organizations (Taneja, 2014).

These activities can be categorized into four groups: (1) criminal intent, where the perpetrator has no legitimate relationship with the business and employee; (2) customer/client, where the perpetrator has a legitimate business purpose but becomes violent; (3) worker-on-worker that can include physical fights; and (4) personal relationships, where the offender has some type of personal relationship with an employee in the company and accesses the company to commit an act of domestic violence (Islam, Edla, Mujuru, Doyle, & Ducatman, 2003). Of these categories, strangers commit the greatest proportion of workplace violence, accounting for 70 percent of all fatal violence (Harrell, 2011). While approximately half a million workers reported being a victim of workplace violence in 2009, these events are not distributed evenly across all occupations. Between 2005 and 2009, police officers, security guards, and bartenders had the highest rates of nonfatal violence. Other service-related occupations (such as retail and convenience stores) that have direct contact with clients also had high rates of violence (Harrell, 2011). The causes of workplace violence will be reviewed in detail in Chapter 5.

▶ Crime

A crime is "an act or the commission of an act that is forbidden, or the omission of a duty that is commanded by a public law and that makes the offender liable to punishment by that law" (*Merriam-Webster Dictionary*, 2015). Although a majority of the time is spent by security personnel in addressing noncrime-related matters, crime prevention and the detection of criminal activities are major security concerns. While all types of crimes can cause loss for organizations, security personnel often deal with property crimes such as theft, burglary, and vandalism.

Nature and Extent of Crime

There are two primary data sources for crime and victimization in the United States: the Uniform Crime Reports (UCR) and the National Crime Victimization Survey (NCVS). One of the primary data sources for crimes known or reported to the police in the United States is the UCR. Currently, there are approximately 18,000 local, county, state, federal, campus, and tribal law enforcement agencies that voluntarily submit their crime-related data to the FBI for analysis. This crime data is used to generate the crime rate, which is the number of known or reported crimes to the police per 1,000,000 persons. This data is also published in the report: *Crime in the United States*. Published annually since 1930, this comprehensive report provides meaningful information on crime and crime trends in the United States. The FBI classifies crime into two parts or categories. Part I offenses include the violent crimes of murder and nonnegligent manslaughter, forcible rape, robbery, and aggravated assault. Part I offenses also include serious property-related crimes that include burglary, larceny-theft, motor vehicle theft, and arson. Some of the Part II crimes include simple assaults, drug crimes, fraud and embezzlement, vice-related crimes, sex crimes including prostitution, gambling, and weapons-related offenses.

Figure 2-3 ■ shows that crime rates have actually decreased in the United States since the 1970s. Although the overall crime rate has dropped, security practitioners must keep in mind that these are national crime rates. As such, crime in certain cities or regions of the United States may not have dropped as much, or crime may have actually increased. Therefore, it is important to also review specific crime rates that the FBI generates in its annual UCR publications.

Uniform Crime Report (UCR) Annual report published by the FBI; includes crime statistics reported voluntarily to the FBI by law enforcement agencies throughout the United States. Generates the crime rate.

National Crime Victimization Survey (NCVS) Random-sample survey conducted by the U.S. Census that determines the victimization crime rate per 1,000 persons.

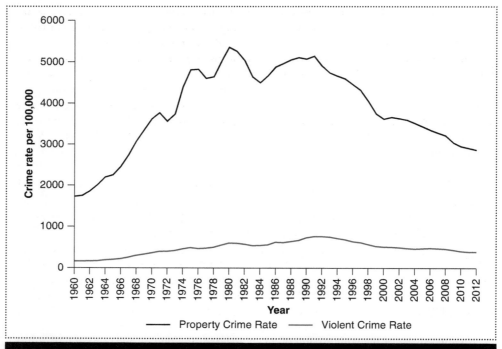

FIGURE 2-3 Crime Trends in the United States
Sources: FBI, Uniform Crime Reports, prepared by the National Archive of Criminal Justice Data.

Another data source for crime in the United States is the National Crime Victimization Survey (NCVS). Published annually since 1972, it uses a sample of approximately 50,000 households, surveying more than 100,000 individuals of age 12 or older. The NCVS data generates a victimization rate per 1,000 individuals. In 1995, the NCVS redesigned its questionnaires to include more detailed information of the interaction between the victim and the offender, victim crime deterrence efforts, perceived effectiveness of crime deterrence efforts, bystander behavior, perceived alcohol and drug use by offenders, and suspected gang involvement (Ortmeier, 2002; Schmalleger, 2010).

In response to some of these criticisms related to the UCR and NCVS and to collect more detailed information about crime events, the FBI introduced the **National Incident-Based Reporting System (NIBRS)** in 1989. As an alternative to the summary reporting or crime counts as found in the UCR, NIBRS was developed to collect more detailed information on known, reported crimes to the police. Among the major changes is the substitution of Part I and II offenses with Group A and B offenses. The traditional Part I offenses include eight street crimes, the Group A NIBRS category has 22 offenses, including economic crimes. Moreover, more detailed information is provided for each criminal event. For instance, the NIBRS includes 52 data elements that include the circumstances of the crime, offender characteristics, arrestee data, victim information, and offense and property-related information. While fewer agencies currently participate in the NIBRS (about 6,000) than the UCR program (U.S. Department of Justice, 2011), this data nevertheless provides rich, detailed information to security personnel that could prove to be useful in designing crime prevention programs and gaining a better understanding of the nature and extent of crime in their area of operations (U.S. Department of Justice, 2013).

By comparing crime and victimization rates, security managers may be able to develop a better understanding of the nature and extent of crime and victimization in their particular area. For example, UCR data can assist security personnel in gaining a better understanding of what types of crime the organization, employees, and visitors may be exposed to.

National Incident-Based Reporting System (NIBRS) Enhanced UCR; requires and provides more detailed information than UCR.

Because the UCR data has been collected over 85 years, trend analysis can be conducted, assisting security managers in making strategic decisions on where to relocate or build new factories. NIBRS and NCVS data also provides rich information on crime events and the dynamics between the victim and offender, resulting in better designed crime prevention efforts and patrol practices for security personnel.

Additional information regarding crime statistics and trends can be obtained from the FBI (www.fbi.gov) and the Bureau of Justice Statistics (www.bjs.gov).

White-Collar Crimes

Besides "traditional" street-related crimes, organizations, governments, businesses, and other enterprises are often easy targets for economic crimes, which are crimes that are committed for financial reward (Siegel, 2010). These crimes can affect the economic health of companies. The noted criminologist Edwin Sutherland created the term "white-collar crime" in 1939, defining it as an offense committed by a person of respectability and high social status in the course of an occupation (Sutherland, 1949). Later, Coleman (1994) expanded the definition, referring to it as a violation of the law committed by a person or group of persons in the course of an otherwise respected and legitimate occupation or financial activity. Unlike street crimes that are committed in public, these crimes are committed oftentimes in the privacy and comfort of company offices or an executive's home. They can also be committed by internal threats—employees—and include a wide range of financial crimes. The motives behind these types of crime are based primarily on personal financial gain.

> **white-collar crime**
> Offense committed by a person or group in the course of an otherwise respected and legitimate occupation or financial activity.

Organized Crime

Organized crime is defined as any relatively permanent group of individuals who systemically engage in illegal activities and provide illegal services. Organized crime is committed by entrepreneurial criminal enterprises or groups of individuals. These activities are continuous and conspiratorial in nature where economic gain is the primary goal. It involves the coordination of numerous persons in the planning and execution of illegal acts or the pursuit of legitimate goals through unlawful means. Organized crime's existence is maintained through the use of threats, intimidation, force, monopoly control, and corruption. Oftentimes, the revenues from illegal activities are used to develop legitimate businesses that are then used as a "front" to commit future criminal activities. Organized crime is old and constantly evolving. Once associated with the Italian Mob and the Prohibition era (1919–1933), organized crime groups still operate in the traditional vice-related crimes including drug sales and distribution, gambling, and prostitution. Because participants in these crimes often seek out these activities, they are often referred to as victimless crimes (Abadinsky, 2013). In other cases, modern organized crime groups are also involved in more specific ventures including organized retail crime (ORC), which involves large scale theft of retail goods from stores and the theft of cargo, costing retailers about $30 billion per year (*Organized retail crime*, 2015).

> **organized crime**
> Refers to a relatively permanent group of individuals that systematically engage in illegal activities and provide illegal services.

Another contemporary issue facing organizations is transnational organized crime (TOC). TOC is defined as "a structured group of three or more persons existing for a period of time and acting in concert with the aim of committing one or more serious crimes or offenses in order to obtain, directly or indirectly, a financial or other material benefit." (Finckenauer & Chin, 2007, p. 1). Characteristics of these crimes include the following: it is committed in more than one state, preparation for the crime occurs in another state, the criminal activities occur in more than one state, and the activities have substantial effects in another state. Some of the common TOC-related crimes include human trafficking, smuggling, weapons trafficking, prostitution, piracy, and illegal immigration (Finckenauer & Chin, 2007; United Nations, 2010).

> **transnational organized crimes**
> (TOCs) Criminal acts that are committed in more than one state, where the planning, preparation, control, and direction take place in a different country from where the crime is actually being committed.

▶ Theories of Crime

Understanding what causes criminal events and activities is paramount to effective security operations. This understanding must be based on factual and objective information, not subjective or speculative ideas. To assist security managers and personnel in developing a sound understanding of any issue, it is important to ground explanations and subsequent policies and actions on theory. Essentially, a *theory* is a thought or an idea that is supported by a hypothesis (a proposed explanation) and scientific evidence. While theories exist in any discipline, since security often has to address crime and disorder, many theories related to security originate from *criminology,* which is the scholarly and scientific examination of the causes of crime and deviance. These criminological theories are useful in gaining a better understanding of the role of security in organizations and predicting how human motivations and actions are related to deviance, crime, and security. Some of the major criminological theories are examined in this section.

One of the oldest explanations for crime is based on the Classical School of thought. This philosophical perspective posits that all human beings have *free will* where they rationally and freely choose their actions, always choosing to engage in pleasurable activities while avoiding or minimizing any pain related to their action(s). Based on these classical assumptions, individuals must be deterred from committing deviant or criminal acts through the fear of punishment. Punishment, meanwhile, must have some utility or purpose. This punishment must also be certain, swift, and severe and proportional to the offense committed to be effective. At the core of the classical perspective is the concept of deterring individuals from engaging in deviance acts through general and specific deterrence strategies. Under the concept of *general deterrence*, individuals will be deterred from engaging in a criminal or deviant act out of the fear of getting caught and punished. Under *specific deterrence*, meanwhile, the actual infliction of a punishment on a person caught committing an offense would serve to prevent that person from committing future offenses (Bernard, Snipes, & Gerould, 2010).

While the classical perspective can be readily seen in the U.S. legal system and the punishment of offenders, these classical assumptions tie directly into the role of security. Because security oftentimes has an authoritarian role in companies, its simple presence could increase the certainty of detection, serving as a general deterrent to deviant and criminal activities by internal and external threats. In the context of specific deterrence, meanwhile, if an individual is detected and caught, he or she could also be punished in some manner by the organization, which could serve to prevent future offending. Besides security personnel, technologies such as CCTV surveillance can also serve as a form of general deterrence: such technologies increase the potential for detection, deterring people from committing offenses.

One specific criminological theory that is based on the classical perspective is Cohen and Felson's (1979) *routine activities theory* (Cohen & Felson, 1979; Felson, 2002). Felson proposes that the opportunity to commit a deviant or criminal act consists of three elements: (1) a suitable target; (2) a motivated and likely offender; and (3) lack of capable guardianship. All three of these elements must be present to some degree for a deviant or criminal act to occur (Figure 2-4 ■). Meanwhile, the removal of one of these variables can serve to reduce or eliminate crime. Consider, for example, shoplifting. The crime of shoplifting involves a motivated and likely offender who rationally considers the criminal act, based on the availability of a suitable target (merchandise) and the lack of effective guardianship of the merchandise. If the suitable target is readily available and the offender believes that the item is not protected well, then a shoplifting incident may occur. However, shoplifting can be prevented (or at least reduced) by increasing guardianship and making the target more difficult to obtain. For example, retail establishments use visible guards at entrances and undercover loss prevention associates throughout their stores to deter such activities, while CCTV technologies may give the impression that the person will be caught for trying to steal the item. Stores, along with increasing guardianship may also use *target hardening* strategies, making items more difficult to steal.

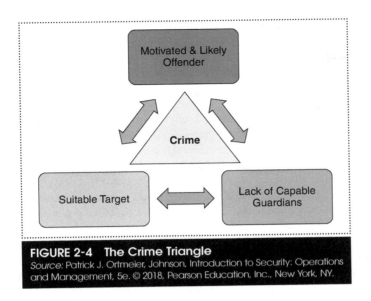

FIGURE 2-4 The Crime Triangle
Source: Patrick J. Ortmeier, Johnson, Introduction to Security: Operations and Management, 5e. © 2018, Pearson Education, Inc., New York, NY.

Some examples of target hardening include placing items in locked display cabinets or attaching various sensors to the item that will sound an alarm if taken. Some other specific studies that have used *routine activities* as a theoretical foundation to understand a social phenomenon include the drop in crime at the O'Hare International Airport post 9-11. Here, the researchers determined that the increased number of police and TSA (Transportation Security Administration) employees and more restrictive policies and procedures (all of which increased guardianship), made airport travelers less of a suitable target to would-be offenders, leading to a pronounced and consistent decrease in property crime since 9-11 (Johnson, Yalda & Kierkus, 2010).

There are also some *psychological perspectives* that explain crime. The main emphasis of these theories is that the offender has some underlying psychological abnormality that was a causal factor in his or her commission of the crime. Consider, for instance, Sigmund Freud's psychoanalytical approach that proposes that crime is caused by unconscious motivations. Here, Freud proposed that the human personality is composed of three elements: (1) the id, which is the chaotic, unreasonable, and impulsive part of human personality that contains unconscious pleasure seeking primitive drives, such as anger and aggression; (2) the Ego, which is the regulator of the id, balancing the id by finding realistic ways for the id to be satisfied and to express itself; and (3) the Superego (or conscience), which plays a moralizing role, striving for perfection by internalizing social values and morals that are taught by parents and other pro-social sources. These sources regulate the id's impulses while also persuading the ego to turn to moralistic goals, and if not, it punishes the ego through guilt. Freud proposed that all three of these elements develop in different stages in humans. However, in some cases, there is an imbalance between the three that can lead to violence (Coon & Mitterer, 2012; Weiten, 2004). Consider, for example, a worker who commits a violent act against another worker. The psychoanalytical approach would propose that the offender had an underdeveloped Superego. Because this person basically did not have a conscience or capacity to feel guilt, nothing in his personality prevented him from acting out the violent actions of the id.

Other psychological explanations use psychological abnormalities as a basis. In some instances, offenders may have psychopathologies or mental illnesses that make them commit deviant acts. Consider, for example, *psychopaths*, who have underdeveloped regions of the brain that regulate and control impulse and emotion. Because of this defect, psychopaths may be highly aggressive or impulsive, show little remorse for their actions, and lack empathy (Dolan, 2004). By contrast, there are many other psychopathologies, including schizophrenia and bi-polar disorders, that can be caused by genetic or environmental factors. Some of these disorders can also lead to *psychosis*, which is a break from reality, where a person suffers from hallucinations and delusions and is not aware of his or her break with reality (Alekseeva et al., 2012).

There are also sociological theories that explain crime by examining the social environment in which crime occurs or exists. One group of sociological explanations for crime are *social learning theories*. These theories propose that people learn how to be deviant. Because these theories posit that crime can be learned, obviously such actions can be "unlearned." As such, organizations that have effective policies and a proactive security staff that "model the way" can serve to educate employees in acceptable conduct in the workplace.

One well-known social learning theory is the principle of *differential association*, which was created by Edwin Sutherland in 1947. Sutherland proposed that deviance is a normal and learned behavior. The nine key points of his theory is that: (1) crime is learned; (2) it is learned through the process of communication; (3) it is learned in intimate groups; (4) the learning includes techniques and attitudes; (5) the specific direction of motives and drives is learned from definitions of the legal codes as favorable or unfavorable; (6) a person becomes delinquent because of an excess of definitions favorable to violation of law over definitions unfavorable to violation of the law; (7) differential associations may vary in frequency, duration, priority, and intensity; (8) the process of learning criminal behavior by association with criminal and anticriminal patterns involves all of the mechanisms that are involved in any other learning; and (9) while criminal behavior is an expression of general needs and values, it is not explained by those needs and values, since noncriminal behavior is an expression of the same needs and values (Bernard et al., 2010).

This theory may be applicable to explaining many workplace safety violations and deviance. Consider, for example, human error and workplace safety issues. In many cases "shortcuts" are learned from social interactions with other coworkers. Moreover, they are deemed acceptable among the intimate group of coworkers. In other cases, the theory can be used to explain workplace deviance. Consider, for example, the book *Rivethead: Tales from the Assembly Line*, where Ben Hamper (1991) provides the reader, rich first-hand information on his personal experiences regarding workplace deviance at the General Motors truck and bus factory in Flint, Michigan in the 1970s and 1980s. Some deviant activities that occurred on the job included drug and alcohol use, time card fraud, sleeping on the job, and shoddy work. Applying the principles of differential association, these and other activities were learned from other coworkers (intimate groups) and they were seen as acceptable among the workers. And, even though they were violations of work rules, they were nevertheless seen as favorable. These behaviors and activities were part of the assembly line culture, reflecting the needs and values of the workers.

There are also *social structure theories* that use social and environmental characteristics of the place or location to explain crime. One particular theory is *social disorganization*. Social disorganization theory posits that the ecological characteristics of neighborhoods can lead to increased levels of crime and deviance. For example, communities that are characterized by poverty, unstable and changing populations, and have weakened institutions of social control (including schools, churches, families, and governmental services), are impacted more by social problems, including crime. This social disorganization can then lead to a lack of common norms and values. When faced with this lack of a common culture, individuals may create their own, leading to a subculture of beliefs, rules, and values. This leads to "culture conflict" where there is disagreement on what the societal rules should be, resulting in crime as an acceptable form of conduct. These subcultural values can be culturally transmitted from one generation to the next. Consider, for example, gangs. These gangs often have subcultural values based on violence and they thrive in socially disorganized areas. In many cases, these gangs are persistent over time, suggesting that the culture of the gang is intergenerationally transmitted (Siegel, 2010).

This group of theories has been heavily used in criminal justice policy. For example, the philosophy of community policing seeks to build prosocial relationships where the police and community address crime and quality-of-life issues. It has also been used in urban planning initiatives, such as the Chicago Area Project, whose ultimate goal was to rebuild deteriorated communities and provide affordable quality housing (Warner, Beck, & Ohmer, 2010) Social disorganization theories can also be applied to security operations. Consider, for example, companies that operate in high-crime socially disorganized areas. Based on the tenants of this theory, the presence of a company in a socially disorganized area could make it and its employees more vulnerable to a variety of property and personal crimes, due to the subcultural crime-related values that exist. One example is in the healthcare industry that has experienced gang violence. This violence can be attributed to the presence of rival gang members in the facility or gangs seeking retaliation against rival members admitted to the hospital (Henson, 2010). Employees from socially disorganized areas may also possess some subcultural values that could lead to security-related issues. For example, street gangs could infiltrate a workplace to steal products. In addition, if a company hired rival gang members to work together, the strong subcultural values associated with the gang affiliations could result in animosity and even open aggression in the workplace.

Another group of social structure theories are the *strain/anomie theories.* These theories do not use the "place" or location to explain crime. Instead, they posit that the entire value system and socio-economic structure of the modern U.S. economy promotes deviance and crime. In essence, it looks at the cause of crime in macro-micro approach, arguing that society values lead to individuals experiencing "strains" that lead to crime. One heavily used strain-based theory is Robert Merton's Five Modes of Adaptation. Originally created in 1938, Merton proposed that crime and deviance was the result of "an acute disjunction between the cultural norms and goals and the socially structured capacities of members of the group to act in accord with them" (Merton, 1968, p. 216). This disjunction or unintended latent consequence of the U.S. culture has created a sense of normlessness on how to reach these goals, where, in some cases, individuals become innovators and engage in criminal activities to reach these goals. Although Merton's theory has undergone several modifications, the resulting strain or anomie theories are based on the premise that crime and deviance is the product of two elements: (1) the goal orientation of modern day society, which is based on economic success; and (2) the available means to achieve those goals (Bernard et al., 2010). A more refined definition of strain is Messner and Rosenfeld's (1997) *institutional anomie theory.* Messner and Rosenfeld define the "American Dream" as the "commitment to the goal of material success, to be pursued by everyone in society, under conditions of open, individual competition" (p. 69). They also propose that crime exists in higher rates in the United States because the economy dominates over other social institutions that create norms and controls, such as the family, education, and polity (the government or political restraint of the market economy).

These strain theories also posit that not all individuals have the same opportunities to achieve economic success. Consider, for example, drug dealers or armed robbers. Under the strain/anomie perspectives, they engage in these criminal activities to obtain money because they have no other legitimate means to achieve material and financial success. The strain/anomie perspective has also been used to explain white-collar crime. In this context, employees may embezzle or steal from a company for the same reasons a street criminal does—economic strains or frustrations based on cultural expectations related to the "American Dream" (Schoepfer & Piquero, 2006).

SECURITY SPOTLIGHT

Reflect on a crime that has recently occurred where you live. What criminological theory would explain the actions of the offender?

Crime Prevention

Crime prevention strategies are proactive efforts and policies that reduce the occurrence of criminal activities (Schneider, 2014). They include education, treatment, diversion, rehabilitation, and deterrence activities. Prevention of crime in organizations involves comprehensive loss prevention and asset protection tools, policies, and procedures. In addition, the prevention of serious street crime, which always impacts individuals and organizations in a negative way, requires early intervention. When one realizes that crime is caused by a complex array of risk factors, it is not difficult to understand why single-focus intervention strategies are unlikely to succeed. Crime prevention must involve comprehensive intervention approaches that address multiple risk factors. To be effective, these strategies require collaboration between and among individuals, groups, and institutions. Therefore, it is important that individuals, families, social services agencies, schools, public safety organizations, security professionals, and businesses work together to prevent or reduce the likelihood of criminal behaviors. Intervention as well as deterrence through security before a crime is committed may be the best strategy for solutions to crime prevention (Bratton, 2011; Wasserman, Miller, & Cothern, 2000).

One crime prevention technique that is grounded in academic theory is *crime prevention through environmental design* (CPTED). Based on the principles of behavioral psychology, Jeffery (1971) proposed that human behavior is influenced by an environment that positively reinforces criminal behavior. In order to reduce and control crime, crime prevention efforts should be directed at modifying the environment in order to change the offender's decision to commit a crime. For example, increased lighting, the planting of trees and flowers, and the placement of buildings are all CPTED strategies to get criminals to "think" not to commit crimes. CPTED strategies also improve the quality of life and reduce the fear of crime (Crowe, 2000). Similar CPTED strategies can exist within companies where retailers use CCTV surveillance cameras, staff, and even a clean and well-kept shopping environment to deter would-be shoplifters (Kajalo & Lindblom, 2011).

▶ Terrorism

terrorism Use of violence or threats to intimidate or coerce.

The United States, along with many other countries, finds itself immersed and preoccupied with terrorism. Although there is no universal definition of terrorism, the University of Maryland's Global Terrorism Database (START, 2015) defines these acts as "the threatened or actual use of illegal force and violence by a nonstate actor to attain a political, economic, religious, or social goal through fear, coercion, or intimidation." (np). According to the Institute for Economics and Peace (2014), in 2013, there were over 10,000 attacks in 83 countries where private property and citizens were the primary targets.

Unfortunately, U.S. companies and citizens in these high-risk regions or nations may be vulnerable. Consider, for example, the numerous terrorist attacks on U.S. affiliated hotels, including Marriott, Hilton, and Sheraton, throughout the world where U.S. business personnel (and other Western citizens) have often been targeted (Wernick & Von Glinow, 2012). To address this growing concern, many hotel security programs are now based on proactive, intelligence-led initiatives where the security function works directly with the police and the intelligence sector, while also increasing its physical security measures to protect hotel guests (Paraskevas, 2013). For example, in September 2008, an Al-Qaeda terrorist detonated a car bomb in front of Marriott Hotel in Islamabad, Pakistan. While the blast caused severe damage to the facility, killing 56 people and injuring another 270, it was estimated that if the hotel did not have a vehicle checkpoint manned by armed security and blast barriers, the terrorist would have been able to get closer to the hotel, resulting in the death of thousands (Wernick & Von Glinow, 2012). Additional information on terrorism and the roles and responsibilities of the private sector in antiterrorism initiatives is presented in Chapter 12.

▶ Civil Unrest

The term civil unrest is a broad concept and term used to describe an event where a group of individuals somehow disrupt the peace and tranquility of a community or business. Some of the other words often used interchangeably for civil unrest include civil disorders, disturbances, disobedience, and protests. According to FEMA (2015), a civil disturbance is "a civil unrest activity such as a demonstration, riot, or strike that disrupts a community and requires intervention to maintain public safety" (np). In a legal sense, civil disorder is defined by federal law (see 18 U.S.C. § 232) as "any public disturbance involving acts of violence by assemblages of three or more persons, which causes an immediate danger of or results in damage or injury to the property or person of any other individual" (np).

Civil unrest has general and specific elements. The number of people initially involved can fluctuate; they can also be spontaneous or planned. Size-wise they can start small and grow exponentially. They can be short term or long term in duration and can be based on positive and negative issues or events. Civil unrest can also be directed against governments or organizations. They may vary geographically, while the demographics of participants may also vary. They may also be the result of man-made and natural events, and they can be peaceful celebrations or be violent (Ballantyne, 2006). Although different, perhaps the common denominator is that these events have the potential to lead to injuries and damage to property, and they may pose a significant challenge to governments and private sector organizations.

Civil unrest can lead to riots. A riot is defined as "relatively spontaneous group violence" (Marx, 1972, p. 50). In many cases, state laws actually provide a numerical number of people who need to be involved in an event before it is officially a riot. However, the common denominator is that riots are violent. The causes of these riots are broad. They can be: (1) issueless, having no purpose—such as looting after an earthquake; (2) purposeful, such as riots that occur as a result of some specific reason—such as labor unrest or police brutality; (3) revelous, which are celebratory in nature—such as college students celebrating a sports title or victory; and (4) symbolic that show discontent but have no specific goals (Goode, 1992).

Oftentimes, these events are small and local, but they can rapidly spread. Consider the 2011 riots in England that were spurred by the police shooting of Mark Duggan in the neighborhood of Tottenham in north London. Initially, about 100 people gathered outside the local police station requesting that a senior police officer answer questions about the shooting. Soon, however, bottles were thrown, fires were set, and shops were looted. Over a period of 5 days, the rioting and looting spread to other parts of England, involving thousands of rioters. While the initial police shooting was the "spark," it was later determined that the true roots or cause of the widespread damage was related to underlying frustrations the rioters had with existing police practices and economic injustices in the context of opportunity, money, and jobs (Lewis et al., 2011). The total losses of these riots were estimated at £300 million in London alone (Dodd, 2011). Likewise, the police shooting of Michael Brown in Ferguson, Missouri in 2014 resulted in both peaceful demonstrations and riots. Over a 2-week period, at least 10 businesses were completely destroyed by arson while many others were looted and vandalized (Stewart, 2014).

civil unrest A broad concept and term used to describe an event where a group of individuals somehow disrupt the peace and tranquility of a community or business.

civil disturbance A civil unrest activity such as a demonstration, riot, or strike that disrupts a community and requires intervention to maintain public safety.

riot Relatively spontaneous group violence.

Labor Unrest

Currently, approximately 15 percent of the labor force in the United States is unionized (Bureau of Labor Statistics, 2015). The legal right to belong to unions can be traced to the National Labor Relations Act of 1935 that provided the right for workers to unionize and engage in other concerted and protected labor-related activities including picketing, passing out union-related information, and holding meetings. In some cases unions strike, which is basically a work stoppage where employees subsequently picket to force employers to bargain. In some cases, labor unrest can lead to violence. This violence could be associated with strike-related activities where strikers could damage company property. In other cases, workers could engage in the sabotage of equipment or products as retaliation against the employer, based on a "burning" or very important labor-related issue. This labor unrest can also occur in nonunion settings where employees are attempting to organize or are angry over issues related to pay, benefits, and working conditions.

▶ Man-made Disasters

man-made disasters
Disasters that are result of hazards that are created by humans, not the natural environment.

Man-made disasters, as the term implies, are the result of events that are created by humans—not the natural environment—that expose humans to some type of threat. These events can also be considered to be events that are the result of human decisions and actions that lead to widespread damage, injury, loss of life, and economic loss and disruption, overwhelming the human capacity to respond to and control the event. These disasters can be categorized into technological, transportation-related, structural collapses, and production failures (Mohamed Shaluf, 2007). In some cases, their impact could be short-term and restricted to a certain group of individuals, such as the 2005 British Petroleum Texas City refinery explosion that killed 15 and injured 180 people. The ensuring investigation found a poor safety culture in the company and other "human errors" that included poor maintenance, worker fatigue, and poor site leadership that led to the disaster (U.S. Chemical Safety, 2007). In other cases, man-made disasters can be immense, long term, and are not geographically restricted. An example of this type of man-made disaster is the 1986 explosion of the Chernobyl nuclear power plant in the former Soviet Union that resulted in radioactive gases being released into the atmosphere, spreading throughout the world. Besides the immediate deaths of over 30 individuals, 50,000 citizens were evacuated and banned from returning to the area (Jaworowski, 2010). Approximately 30 years later, the legacy of this disaster still exists in the form of socio-economic impacts and medical issues among those initially exposed (and even those born after the event) (Bromet, Havenaar, & Guey, 2011). To mitigate (or lessen) the impact of these disasters, security organizations need to properly plan and prepare for such events. A detailed discussion of this process will be conducted in Chapter 12 of this text.

Environmental Accidents/Disasters

Environmental accidents and disasters include events associated with exposures to hazardous materials, diseases, conventional and nuclear power failures, mine explosions, and gas or oil line or water main breaks. The key element of these accidents or disasters is that they somehow impact the natural environment. These accidents and disasters can be the result of man-made or natural disasters or a combination of the two. Consider, for example, the Gulf of Mexico Deepwater Horizon drilling rig explosion on April 20, 2010 and subsequent oil spill that contaminated the Gulf of Mexico, wetlands, and beaches throughout the Gulf States. The explosion aboard the British Petroleum financed oil rig left 11 workers dead and precipitated the largest offshore oil spill in U.S. history. The disaster increased focus on the safety of offshore drilling and oil exploration and production (Banerjee, 2011).

NEW ORLEANS—Fire boat response crews battle the blazing remnants of the offshore oil rig Deepwater Horizon on April 21, 2010. Multiple Coast Guard helicopters, planes, and cutters responded to rescue the Deepwater Horizon's 126 person crew.
(Photo courtesy of U.S. Coast Guard.)

Warfare

Today, most companies have offices and assembly facilities throughout the world. Even if not directly operating in another country, an organization's assets and supply chain network could be linked to a foreign country or region in the world experiencing warfare. As such, companies can face a variety of threats to their physical and financial security because of direct and indirect consequences of war.

Warfare is a man-made event. It can include conventional, civil, and insurgency-related events. Regardless of the type of war, these activities can result in the destabilization of countries and regions of the world. Warfare can lead to humanitarian issues including decreased agricultural production and famine, the displacement or migration of populations, and disease (Homer-Dixon, 1999). Warfare can also create animosity toward foreign owned corporations operating in those countries (or regions), especially if these companies had some role in supporting the war. For example, in some cases multinational companies indirectly finance or support wars through their state-level contracts with the host nation to extract natural resources including oil, diamonds, timber, and precious metals. Or, to ensure effective operations, oftentimes these companies also develop relationships with the local communities and politicians supporting the conflict. In fact, in the Sudan conflict, it has been argued that the presence of multinational oil companies has actually prolonged the civil war, providing the Sudanese government about $1 million per day (Fishman, 2002; Patey, 2006). Conversely, multinational companies have also positively shaped global security and reduced warfare where governments and policy-makers throughout the world have considered their economic objectives and stability over aggression (Brooks, 2005).

► Natural Disasters

natural disaster
Sudden, extraordinary misfortune caused by a force of nature.

A natural disaster is defined as "a situation or event caused by nature, which overwhelms local capacity, necessitating a request to a national or international level for external assistance; an unforeseen and often sudden event that causes great damage, destruction and human suffering" (Khan, Amatya, Gosney, Rathore, & Burkle, 2015, p. 1711). These hazards exist in the natural environment and they pose a threat toward humans in some manner (Mohamed Shaluf, 2007). In 2013, there were 330 natural disasters reported worldwide in 108 countries, impacting over 96 million individuals. The country most often impacted by a disaster is the United States (Guha-Sapir, Hoyois, & Below, 2014), which had 84 major disaster declarations in 2014 alone (FEMA, 2015). The Centre for Research on the Epidemiology of Disasters (CRED) classifies natural disasters into five main categories: (1) geophysical events that include earthquakes and volcanoes; (2) meteorological storms; (3) hydrologic or water disasters including floods; (4) climatological events cases by extreme changes in the weather that result in drought, extreme temperatures, and wildfires; and (5) biological events that can include epidemics and insect and animal infestations (Guha-Sapir et al., 2014).

One example of a natural disaster was Hurricane Sandy that struck the Eastern Seaboard of the United States in 2012. The hurricane created a 14-foot storm surge, flooding parts of lower Manhattan, causing more than $19 billion damage to New York City (Aerts & Botzen, 2014). Another common disaster scenario that is encountered by organizations operating in the Great Plains states is tornadoes. Take, for example, a tornado that struck Joplin, Missouri, in 2011 that killed 116 individuals and destroyed or damaged multiple businesses, churches, and the local hospital. In this particular incident, FEMA, local law enforcement, and merchants including Home Depot and Wal-Mart engaged in joint recovery activities (Givens & Busch, 2013).

hybrid disasters
A type of man-made disaster. Are the result of human activities and decisions compounded with natural forces.

Hybrid disasters are another type of man-made disaster. Hybrid disasters are the result of human activities and decisions compounded with natural forces such as wind, tornadoes, earthquakes, and lightning (Shaluf, 2007). Another term that is used for these types of

Flooding near St. Louis Missouri, 2016: Valley Park, MO, January 1, 2016. High flood waters cause the busy intersection of I-44 and Route 141 to close. (Photo courtesy of Steve Zumwalt/FEMA.)

events is "*natech*" ("natural-technological") disasters where natural forces "trigger" technological disasters (Krausmann, Renni, Campedel, & Cozzani, 2011). These natech disasters
can be large, such as an oil pipeline breaking after an earthquake. Or, they can be small,
such as paints and solvents from thousands of homes washing into floodwaters (Young,
Balluz, & Malilay, 2004). Take, for instance, Hurricane Katrina that ravaged the U.S. Gulf
States in 2005. A cursory review of the Hurricane suggests that the flooding of the City of
New Orleans was the result of storm surge—a meteorological event that caused a natural
disaster. However, a closer inspection of the disaster shows that the flooding was precipitated by the storm surge, compounded by a technological disaster due to the man-made
levees in New Orleans being breached by the flood waters (Miller, 2007). Another example
of a large natech disaster is the Fukushima Daiichi Nuclear Power Plant disaster in Japan in
2011. As a result of the great Japan earthquake, a tsunami (tidal wave) struck the plant,
disabling the reactors' cooling capabilities, leading to reactor core meltdowns, fires, and the
release of radioactive gases into the atmosphere (Leon et al., 2011). Disasters will be
explored in greater detail in Chapter 12.

► Civil Liability

Civil liability has become a major concern for public and probate organizations and institutions. Civil liability is a legal risk that can impact a company financially and reputation-
ally. Civil liability is when a party or parties are harmed or injured through the actions or
inactions of another. Large punitive damage awards by juries and out-of-court settlements
have been awarded to plaintiffs who have prevailed in sexual harassment, unsafe environments, negligence, wrongful death, defects in products, invasion of privacy, excessive
force, personal injury, violation of civil rights, and conspiracy to defraud cases. This issue
will be explored in detail in Chapter 3.

> **civil liability**
> May occur when a
> person is harmed or
> injured through the
> action or inaction of
> another. The harm may
> or may not be the result
> of criminal activity.

Summary

Through their activities organizations are vulnerable to
man-made and natural threats. Many of these threats can
cause some type of damage, injury, or harm to employees,
patrons, and the organization itself. Accidents occur in
organizations. These accidents can lead to human and
property-related losses. Oftentimes accidents are the
result of human error. In order to control and prevent accidents, organizations need to have well-designed and
administered safety programs. To assist organizations in
creating a safe working environment, in 1970 the U.S.
government created OSHA, which has established
specific safety requirements that employers must follow.
In combination with an effective safety and security
program, the many risks against companies can be
properly controlled or managed.

This chapter also reviewed some of the common
threats against organizations. Fire is a serious concern for
all organizations. Oftentimes, the term "fire" is used gener-
ically. However, a fire is actually a complex chemical process that involves different stages. Depending upon the
stage and the combustibles present, fires can be quite dangerous for employees. Fires can also impact a company
financially through the loss of production capabilities.
Other threats to organizations and employees include
workplace violence and other personal and property
crimes. Companies are also vulnerable to organized crime,
terrorist activities, and civil unrest that can take the form of
protests, riots, and labor unrest. To help understand the
causes of these activities, several criminological theories
exist. These theories are oftentimes based on classical
assumptions of human behavior, psychological explanations, and social learning. From these theories effective
crime prevention programs can be designed and administered. Finally, companies are at risk and vulnerable to
other man-made disasters that can be caused by environmental accidents/disasters and warfare. Companies also
face risk from natural and natech disasters. All of these
issues and others will also expose companies to legal risk,
which can be mitigated through a well-planned comprehensive safety and security program.

Key Terms and Concepts

Accident 26
All-hazards approach 26
Backdraft explosion 30
Civil disturbance 41
Civil unrest 41
Civil liability 45
Combustible hazards 30
Disasters 27
Fire load 31
Fire tetrahedron model 29
Fire triangle 29
Fuel load 31
Hazards 25
Human error 28
Human Factors Analysis and
    Classification System 27

Hybrid disasters 44
Man-made disasters 42
National Crime Victimization
    Survey (NCVS) 33
National Incident-Based Reporting
    System (NIBRS) 34
Natural disaster 44
Occupational Safety and
    Health Administration
    (OSHA) 27
Organized crime 35
Oxidation 29
Perils 25
Pyrolysis 29
Riot 41
Risk 25

Risk management 26
Safety 27
Stages of combustion 30
Terrorism 40
Threats 25
Transnational organized crimes
    (TOCs) 35
Uniform Crime Report
    (UCR) 33
Vulnerabilities 25
White-collar crime 35
Workplace deviance 32
Workplace violence 32

Discussion Questions and Exercises

1. Individuals, businesses, public agencies, and nations are threatened by numerous criminal and non-criminal hazards. List these hazards and describe the ramifications of each.
2. What are some of the components of civil unrest?
3. What are some of the crimes that security personnel will encounter?
4. What are some of the categories of workplace violence?
5. Explain the Human Factors Analysis and Classification System.

6. What is OSHA? What is its role in safety and security?
7. What is a hazard? What is a peril? What is vulnerability? Provide an example of each.
8. Explain the Fire Tetrahedron Theory. What are the stages of combustion?
9. What is the difference between a natural and man-made disaster?
10. What are some of the common causes of fire in organizations? How can these be prevented?

Your Turn

Assessing Threats to Safety and Security in Your Area

Threats to safety and security take numerous forms—accidents, human error, fire, natural and environmental disasters, civil liability, substance abuse, civil disorder, and crime in all its many types. Assess and address your vulnerability to these threats by taking the following steps:

1. For your town, city, or state, research the statistics available on each of these threats. For example,

consult FBI reports on various types of crimes in your area, and look for studies on the other types of threats and how the findings relate to your area.
2. Select a human and natural hazard in your community that may materialize into a threat. Explain in detail why this is a concern or issue.
3. Formulate a strategy for addressing the threats you identified in Question 2. For instance, what kind of contingency plan or disaster-recovery strategy would you recommend to address this threat?
4. Use a criminological theory to explain a security-related issue.

3 The Legal and Regulatory Environment of the Private Security Industry

LEARNING OBJECTIVES

After completing this chapter, the reader should be able to:

1. describe the judicial system of the United States
2. explain the judicial process for criminal cases
3. distinguish a tort from a crime
4. discuss types of situations conducive to tort liability
5. explain and compare the two types of torts
6. explain some remedies and defenses under tort law
7. explain how the legal and regulatory environment influences security operations
8. explain how administrative law differs from criminal law
9. explain the main elements of a crime
10. compare arrest authority of public police with private security
11. explain and define industrial self regulation

▶ Introduction

This chapter is devoted to legal concepts and processes that apply to the security profession. The legal and regulatory environment in which security operates involves a mixture of criminal, civil, and administrative laws. Security personnel encounter relatively unique legal obligations and face a multitude of legal issues. People, physical property, and information must be protected without incurring civil liability or violating anyone's rights. Personnel matters must be dealt with in a manner consistent with existing criminal and employment laws. Security managers must enter into and audit contractual agreements. They must also prevent and investigate crime and collect and preserve evidence that may be used in criminal and civil cases. Organizational activities must be monitored to ensure compliance with a wide array of local, state, and federal laws. Consequently, the contemporary security professional must be well versed in the law and anticipate situations where expert legal representation is necessary. As shown in Figure 3-1 ■, this legal environment is complex, where security managers and the security function are influenced by and must be aware of the various legal issues that they may be exposed to.

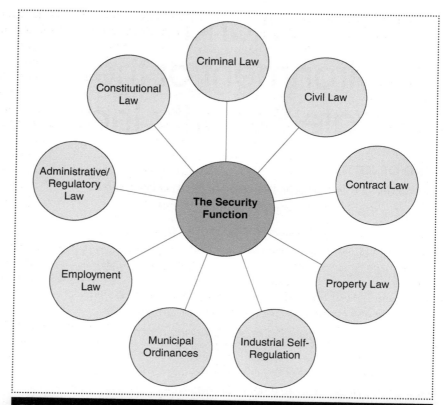

FIGURE 3-1 The Legal and Regulatory Environment of Security
Source: Patrick J. Ortmeier, Johnson, Introduction to Security: Operations and Management, 5e. © 2018, Pearson Education, Inc., New York, NY.

▶ Constitutional Law

constitutional law
That branch of law that is concerned with the examination, interpretation, and application of the U.S. Constitution.

Bill of Rights The first 10 Amendments to the U.S. Constitution.

Constitutional law is that branch of law that is concerned with the examination, interpretation, and application of the nation's constitution. In a broad sense, the U.S. Constitution creates the structure and branches of the federal government while regulating the role of governments and their actors for national self-governance. It is the "Supreme Law of the Land" for the United States, and it sets the rules that state actors must follow when governing the daily activities of individuals. It also provides guiding principles and specifies the rights guaranteed to all people in the United States. The Bill of Rights, which is the first 10 Amendments to the U.S. Constitution, protects individual rights from the actions of federal and state governments (and its actors), in what they can and cannot do. Freedom of speech, the right to bear arms, search and seizure, due process, self-incrimination, the right to counsel, trial by jury, and cruel and unusual punishment are some of the key issues that the Bill of Rights addresses. The U.S. Constitution is also a living document that is constantly being re-evaluated and interpreted by the federal courts to guide and assist governments in the execution of their activities. All states also have their respective state constitutions. These constitutions also structure and define the role of state governments and provide people in that state additional protections that may not be afforded to them through the U.S. Constitution.

The U.S. Constitution governs and regulates governments and their agents or actors. It does not govern the actions of private parties (citizens and companies). For example, companies often have restrictive policies and practices regarding free speech in the

▼

workplaces. Likewise, companies that have search policies to prevent workplace theft and violence may have some individuals perceive that these actions are a violation of a constitutionally protected right, even though they are not. In order to be a violation of the U.S. Constitution, state action must exist. State action is defined as "an intrusion into a person's rights either by a governmental entity or by a private requirement that can only be enforced by governmental action" (Black, 1990). In some cases, this state action may be remote. For example, in Romanski v. Detroit Entertainment LLC (2003), the Sixth Circuit Court of Appeals determined that security guards employed by the MotorCity Casino were state actors and performing a public function when Stella Romanski was detained and then ejected from the casino for picking up an abandoned 5 cent token from the tray of a slot machine. Because casino security police were performing a public function (arresting a person that was exclusively once reserved for the public police), they subsequently violated the Constitutional rights of the defendant under the Fourth Amendment. The decision was based on the fact that the security guards received their arrest powers through state licensure, giving them exclusive powers of arrest that were traditionally reserved for the police (state actors) and beyond those of other types of security guards licensed through the state. Because they were now state actors, the Court determined that the plaintiff had recourse under federal civil rights legislation to sue the casino for violating her constitutionally protected rights under the Fourth and Fourteenth Amendments (Pastor, 2007).

The previous example shows that private security personnel are not fully exempt from the provisions of the U.S. Constitution in the course of their actions. For example, a company that violates the civil rights of individuals through discriminatory employment practices and actions in the workplace can be prosecuted under a variety of federal laws. In addition, these actions can lead to a civil suit against the parties for injuries they caused. Provisions in state constitutions may also provide additional protections for individuals, and this chapter will show that individuals have other legal options to pursue if security personnel should engage in unethical or illegal activities. As such, security personnel and managers must ensure that their daily activities, practices, and policies do not infringe upon the rights given to people through the U.S. and state constitutions. Symbolically, adherence to the inherent rights of individuals should be an underlying philosophy for any progressive security function.

> **state action** An intrusion into a person's rights either by a governmental entity or by a private requirement that can only be enforced by governmental action.

> **criminal law** The body of law that relates to crime. It regulates social conduct and/or prescribes whatever is threatening, harmful, or otherwise endangering to the property, health, safety, and moral welfare of people.

▶ Criminal Law

Criminal law is the body of law that relates to crime. "It regulates social conduct and prescribes whatever is threatening, harmful, or otherwise endangering to the property, health, safety, and moral welfare of people. It also includes the punishment of people who violate these laws" (Farmer, 2005; p. 11). When a crime is committed, the offender commits an offense against society. Therefore, if a person violates a state criminal law, the offender has harmed all the citizens of that state, regardless of who the specific victim is. When one commits a violation of the federal criminal law, the offense is committed against all the citizens of the United States. In a criminal case, the government, through state and federal prosecutors, must establish proof of guilt beyond a reasonable doubt that the accused committed the crime. Reasonable doubt means that the evidence presented by the prosecution leaves "no reasonable doubt" in the belief of a juror or judge that the defendant is guilty of the crime in question (Samaha, 2013). The defense, meanwhile, works to refute the government's case.

Sources of criminal law include the U.S. Constitution, federal statutes, state constitutions and statutes, county and municipal ordinances, judicial decisions (case law), and common law (law based on custom or tradition). Statutes and ordinances are written laws that are the product of a legislative activity. At the state level, the actual elements and

> **reasonable doubt** The evidence presented by the prosecution leaves "no reasonable doubt" in the belief of a juror or judge that the defendant is guilty of the crime in question.

> **common law** Unwritten law based on custom or tradition.

> **statute** Written law that is the product of legislative activity.

definitions of crime may vary. However, most legal jurisdictions model and write their criminal codes from the Model Penal Code. The Model Penal Code, as the name suggests, are "models" or sample sets of criminal laws that were written by judges, legal scholars, and attorneys from the American Law Institute. These statutes have been adopted by legislatures and written into state statutes (Dubber, 2015).

There are two main elements or parts of a crime. *Mens rea* is the element of a crime that focuses on the offender's guilty mind or criminal intent (a design, resolve, or purpose of the mind) to commit a criminal act. Types of intent fall into four basic categories: general, specific, transferred, and criminal negligence. General criminal intent may be inferred from merely doing the act. Specific criminal intent requires a specifically intended and desired result. Some specific intent crimes include assault, crimes that involve attempts, burglary, conspiracy, embezzlement, false pretenses, first degree murder, forgery, larceny, and solicitation. Although each of the criminal acts is different, the common denominator of each of these is that a prosecutor must prove that the person specifically intended to engage in these activities in order to secure a conviction. With transferred (constructive) intent, a person may be liable for unintended consequences, such as when A shoots at B, misses, and kills C, an unintended victim. Criminal negligence is the failure to exercise the degree of care that a reasonable and prudent person would exercise in similar circumstances. A person who operates a motor vehicle while under the influence of alcohol or drugs does so in a criminally negligent manner (Samaha, 2013).

Actus reus, meanwhile, is the criminal act itself. It is an act or a failure to act. These acts can be divided into conduct-related and results crimes. Conduct-related crimes are criminal simply because of the act's dangerousness. Often referred to as *strict*, or *absolute liability* offenses, these crimes require no culpable mental state and present a significant exception to the principle that all crimes require a proximate causal connection between the act and intent. Strict liability offenses make it a crime simply to do something, regardless of the actor's intent. Such offenses are based upon the presumption that causing harm is in itself blameworthy. An example of a strict liability offense would be speeding. Here, the state does not have to prove the mental state of the driver. Because the act itself is inherently dangerous, the operator can be cited and sometimes arrested for committing the act. There is also a category of crimes called inchoate offenses. Inchoate offenses are incomplete crimes. Here, the offender did not commit the crime. Even though the crime was not committed, society has nevertheless determined that planning or preparing to commit the crime in itself threatens society. Examples of these types of crimes are attempt, solicitation, and conspiracy-based crimes. With results crimes, meanwhile, the results of the person's actions are criminal in nature. Examples include assault, battery, murder, and manslaughter. In these results crimes, causation needs to be proved to secure a guilty verdict (Samaha, 2013).

There are also types of crimes. Offenses are classified as felonies, misdemeanors, and violations or even infractions. Felonies usually carry a potential penalty of a fine, over 1 year in prison, or even death. Misdemeanors carry a potential penalty of a fine or up to 1 year in a municipal or county jail. Violations or infractions carry a potential penalty of a fine and are not usually punishable by imprisonment (Brody, Acker, & Logan, 2010; Cheeseman, 2010; Nemeth, 2004; Ortmeier, 2006; Siegel & Senna, 2008).

Crimes can also be classified according to who is affected. Crimes against persons include the crimes of murder, rape, robbery, and assault. Property-related crimes include automobile theft, theft of property (real and tangible), and others. Another category is victimless crimes where the parties (to some degree) consensually engage in the criminal act and there is no apparent or evident injury. These crimes may include prostitution, gambling, and drug use.

mens rea The element of a crime that focuses on the offender's guilty mind or criminal intent (a design, resolve, or purpose of the mind) to commit a criminal act.

criminal negligence A form of criminal intent; the actor can foresee the result and fails to exercise the degree of care that a reasonable and prudent person would exercise in similar circumstances.

actus reus The criminal act.

felony A crime for which the potential penalty may be a fine and/or imprisonment of more than 1 year in jail.

misdemeanor Crime for which the potential penalty may be a fine and/or confinement for up to 1 year.

In some cases, criminal activities can also result in a civil claim against the offender. In these situations, the offender could be found guilty of the offense in the criminal courts, which uses the beyond a reasonable doubt standard to secure a conviction. Following this conviction, the injured party can then seek civil recovery for any damages caused by the offender as result of his or her criminal activity in the civil court system. In the civil court, the less standard degree of proof based on the preponderance of evidence is used.

Many crimes are arrestable offenses. An arrest involves the taking of a person into custody for the purpose of answering to a criminal charge. Laws of arrest differ between public peace officers and private citizens. In the vast majority of situations, security personnel operate as private citizens unless statutory authority as peace officers is granted to them. Under most state laws, a private citizen may arrest if the private person observes a felony being committed. For a felony not observed by the private person, an arrest can be made, if in fact the felony was committed and the arresting person has probable cause to believe that the person committed the crime. In other cases, private persons can arrest for misdemeanor offenses. The best example is the merchant's privilege statute, which allows retail merchants and their agents to arrest for misdemeanor retail crimes. This will be examined in detail in Chapter 8.

Effecting an arrest is a risky proposition. The arresting person and others in proximity to the arrest can be physically injured. The person being arrested can also be injured, and in some cases even die. Furthermore, in probably no other situation is the risk of a civil lawsuit greater, especially when the arresting person is not a public law enforcement officer where an individual can be challenged under a false arrest and false imprisonment claim. To avoid liability, some organizations do not allow personnel, such as security officers, to effect an arrest under any circumstances.

> **arrest** The taking of a person into custody for the purpose of answering to a criminal charge.

SECURITY SPOTLIGHT

Select two types of crime, such as crimes against property and crimes against persons. Using the resources suggested in this chapter, research the laws regarding the two types of crime you selected in the state where you live. Select another state, and research that state's laws regarding the two types of crime you selected. In what ways are the two states' laws regarding these crimes similar? In what ways are they different? To what extent (if any) have they changed over the years?

▶ Civil Law

Civil law governs relationships between individuals, organizations, corporations, and governmental bodies. In these cases, a civil wrong or injury, known as a tort, has occurred for which the law provides a remedy. Unlike a crime, which is a public wrong against society, a tort is a private wrong committed against a person or property. In civil cases, a complaint (lawsuit) is initiated by a plaintiff (the injured party), claiming a civil wrong committed by the respondent (or tortfeasor). Since a civil lawsuit is not a criminal prosecution, neither a state's prosecuting attorney nor the U.S. attorney represents either party. Civil liability, rather than criminal culpability, is the issue in civil cases where the party at fault does not serve a criminal sentence, but instead is responsible for correcting a wrong in some manner. The wrong can be based on malfeasance, which is conduct that is illegal and inherently wrong. Or, it can be based on misfeasance, which is a lawful act that is carried out in an unlawful manner (Reamer, 1995).

> **civil law** Governs relationships between individuals, organizations, corporations, and governmental bodies.

> **tort** Private wrong committed against a person or property.

The standard or degree of proof needed to prevail in a civil case is the *preponderance of the evidence*. This degree of proof is met if the evidence demonstrates a probability—at least a 51 percent likelihood—that the facts in the issue are true (Samaha, 2013).

Procedurally, a civil suit parallels the steps in a criminal proceeding. The respondent files an answer to the plaintiff's claim and states a defense against the complaint. Pretrial motions requesting discovery of the opponent's information are filed by both parties. Jury selection (if applicable) follows a procedure similar to that which occurs in criminal cases. At trial, opening statements are made by the plaintiff (or plaintiff's counsel) and the respondent (or respondent's counsel). The plaintiff's case is presented first, followed by the respondent's case. Direct and cross-examination of witnesses is similar to criminal proceedings, although evidentiary rules, testimonial privileges, and prohibitions against admission of hearsay evidence are more relaxed. Both sides make closing statements, the judge provides instructions to the jury, and the jury (if a bench trial is not used) deliberates to reach a verdict. Unlike criminal cases, in which unanimous verdicts are required, substantial majority verdicts are permissible in states.

Oftentimes acts of omissions and accidents are the result of employees acting in the course of their employment where the person's intent is irrelevant—only the end result is considered in the case. Under the common law doctrine of respondeat superior (or "let the master answer"), employers are responsible (or vicariously liable) for the negligent actions of their employees when their actions are within the scope of their employment. For example, if a driver of an armored car crashes into a vehicle, causing personal and property damage to the vehicle and driver (e.g., financial and personal losses), the armored car company will be held vicariously liable under the doctrine of respondeat superior for the damages in civil court. Because driving the vehicle was job-related and within the scope of the person's employment, the employer can be held liable for the employee's failure to operate the vehicle in a safe and prudent manner. Accordingly, a judge or jury may award financial compensation to the injured party.

Managers and organizations can be civilly liable for numerous personnel and management-related practices. Management may be liable for negligent hiring, training, supervision, and retention, as well as for wrongful termination of personnel. Organizations and individuals may be held liable for invasion of privacy, malicious prosecution, defamation of character, foreseeable acts of violence, false arrest and false imprisonment, use of excessive force, and failure to protect confidential information. The increasing number of liability-related lawsuits should be a concern for professionals in all fields, not just security. To protect against civil charges, people should practice good human relations, become familiar with relevant federal and state laws, make every reasonable effort to comply with those laws, and adhere to a professional code of ethics and standards of conduct. Managers and staff should also be aware of the types of civil liability that exist in their industry sector and engage in proactive efforts to identify and prevent such activities from occurring. The two primary types of torts that security companies, managers, and personnel may be liable for include negligence and intentional torts.

> Additional information about the judicial process as well as legal concepts and laws may be obtained from the American Bar Association at www.abanet.org.

Negligence Torts

Negligence torts emerge from those situations in which a tortfeasor fails to exercise ordinary and prudent care when carrying out specific tasks and activities, causing some type of loss to another. The accused may have failed to perform an act that a reasonable person, in similar circumstances, would do, or may have done something that a reasonable person would not do. In these situations, the actor is said to be negligent (Samaha, 2013).

respondeat superior
A legal doctrine where employers are responsible (or vicariously liable) for the negligent actions of their employees.

negligence torts
Emerge from those situations in which a tortfeasor fails to exercise ordinary and prudent care when carrying out specific tasks and activities, causing some type of damage, injury, or harm to another.

There are four elements that need to exist to win (or prevail) in a negligence-based tort: (1) duty; (2) breach of duty; (3) proximate cause; and (4) damage, injury, or harm. Under the concept of duty, persons and organizations have a duty or responsibility to act (or not act) in some manner. For example, hotels, restaurants, retail establishments, and other organizations and institutions have a duty of care to people using their properties and services. Users have a reasonable expectation that the company or institution will provide that level of care. Duty is also based on the concept of foreseeability. Foreseeability is the concept that the person or organization knew or should have reasonably known what dangers exist or could exist, and then provided an appropriate level of care to address them. Using the earlier accident example, a reasonable expectation of an armored car company is to ensure that drivers have a good driving record and are trained in operating an armored car. Under breach of duty, meanwhile, the plaintiff needs to prove that the respondent failed to act in a reasonable and prudent manner toward the duty of care that was needed. This is based on what a reasonable person would have done, in the same situation. It is also based on existing industry standards and practices. The plaintiff also needs to establish that the actions (or inactions) were the proximate cause of the injury or harm that occurred. This injury or harm can be the result of mental anguish, emotional distress, pain and suffering, actual medical expenses, loss of property, and future costs related to medical expenses and lost income (Samaha, 2013).

Security operations and the organizations in which they operate face a myriad of activities that could lead to a negligence-based lawsuit. In fact, in any situation where the company or a person was expected to act and did not, or acted in an inappropriate manner, the potential for a negligence-based tort claim could arise. Some common negligence claims in the field of security include negligent: entrustment (entrusting another with equipment or a task that then leads injury); supervision (the failure to reasonably control and/or supervise employees); training (a.k.a. "failure to train" where training of the employee or lack thereof fails to prevent the employee from engaging in the acts that injured the complainant); retention (the employee was unfit for the position which created the harm); and, investigations (not conducting an effective "good faith" investigation of a person or issue) (Kleiman & Kass, 2014).

Intentional Torts

Another category is intentional torts. This category of tort includes civil wrongs that are the result of an intentional act—not an accident—by the tortfeasor. Under these types of torts, the plaintiff must prove that the tortfeasor intended to perform the underlying act that led to the injury, harm, or damage. Another way to understand an intentional tort is that the tortfeasor was indifferent to the rights and protection of persons and/or the properties of others through his or her actions. Some of the common types of security-related intentional torts include: false arrest, false imprisonment (the unlawful violation of the personal liberty of another), assault (the threat of bodily harm against another) and battery (any harmful or offensive bodily contact), wrongful death (causing another's death through negligent conduct), malicious prosecution (wrongful prosecution of a person, not based on probable cause), and trespass. These intentional torts can also lead to punitive damage awards, which are awards above and beyond the actual loss incurred by the injured party (Pastor, 2007).

intentional torts Willful tort activity. Examples include assault, false imprisonment, and defamation of character.

Defamation

One particular concern for security administrators is defamation. Defamation involves damaging a person's reputation by making public statements that are both false and malicious. Defamation can take the form of libel or slander. Libel includes statements in print, writing, pictures, signs, or publications that injure another person's reputation. The words can also be

defamation Damaging a person's reputation by making public statements that are both false and malicious. Defamation can take the form of libel or slander.

read aloud by a speaker or broadcast for the public to hear. Slander is speaking defamatory words intended to prejudice others against an individual, jeopardizing the person's reputation or means of livelihood. Employers may be sued for defamation when they provide derogatory information to a prospective employer regarding a current or former employee. Usually, the truth of the information provided is a complete defense to the lawsuit. However, even when the disclosure is truthful, statements made in a malicious or reckless manner may establish the foundation for a damage award to the plaintiff. Generally, the respondent in a defamation lawsuit will be liable if any of the following conditions exist:

- Actual malice on the part of the information provider is established.
- False defamatory information was published intentionally.
- False defamatory information was provided to someone who has no legitimate reason to receive it.
- False defamatory information was published recklessly, without regard to its truthfulness.
- False defamatory information was published for other than legitimate reasons (Samaha, 2013).

There are situations other than employment reference inquiries that may give rise to liability for defamation. These situations include statements made in the course of an employee misconduct investigation and accusations of misconduct directed toward a customer or client. To avoid defamation claims, employers and security personnel are cautioned to refrain from making specific accusations, either verbally or in writing. Even when an adequate defense is available, the costs associated with litigating a claim can be considerable.

Remedies under Tort Law

> **compensatory damages** Compensate compensate a plaintiff in a lawsuit for actual losses incurred.

There are several remedies under tort law. The main goal of compensatory damages is to make the person whole again for damages. Here, the court awards financial compensation for the actual damages received. For example, if medical costs, lost wages, legal fees, and property damage amount to $45,000 in an accident-related injury, the plaintiff is compensated that amount (Lens, 2011). Punitive damages can be awarded in some tort cases. These awards are above and beyond the actual losses experienced by the action. The primary goal of these damages is to punish the respondent for outrageous conduct and to deter defendants and others from committing similar actions in the future, protecting others including the public in the process. As such, these large awards can serve as a regulatory effect upon industries and individuals (Popper, 2011). Using the previous example, if the accident was the result of a security officer driving recklessly and purposely exposing the public to harm, instead of a simple accident, the tort is intentional in nature. Because of the intent to engage in the act, the court can determine an appropriate level of financial punishment in addition to actual losses. However, not all remedies may be financial. In some situations injured parties can seek an injunction. An injunction is a judicial decree by the court that the tortfeasor engages in or ceases a particular activity or course of conduct. In doing so, the tortfeasor now has a duty to do something, limiting their options regarding the particular activity (Mendlow, 2011).

> **punitive damages** Civil awards above and beyond the actual losses experienced by the action. Designed to punish a respondent in a lawsuit.

> **injunction** A judicial decree by the court that the tortfeasor engages in or ceases a particular activity or course of conduct.

> **assumption of risk** A legal doctrine that is based on the premise that the plaintiff knowingly and voluntarily assumed the risk of the activity or action that led to damage, injury, or harm.

Defenses under Tort Law

Respondents do have some defenses under civil law that can reduce or even bar (prevent) a plaintiff from recovering damages. The doctrine of assumption of risk (that is used in personal injury and negligence-based claims) is based on the premise that the plaintiff knowingly and voluntarily assumed the risk of the activity or action that led to damage, injury, or harm. Here, the tortfeasor would have to prove that the plaintiff knew of the dangerous activity and voluntarily exposed him or herself to it. The doctrine of comparative negligence takes the position that the plaintiff did something that contributed to the damage, injury, or harm. Under this defense, the respondent will "compare" the negligent actions of the plaintiff to his own negligent actions in order to convince the court that any damage award should be reduced because of those actions. This defense generally does not eliminate fault. Instead, it is designed to reduce the amount of the award because of the plaintiff's actions. In some states, under the legal principle of modified comparative negligence, the plaintiff can only recover if their fault is less than the tortfeasor's (Nemeth, 2011; Pastor, 2007).

> **comparative negligence** Legal doctrine that takes the position that the plaintiff did something that contributed to the damage, injury, or harm.

▶ Administrative Law

Administrative laws create and establish agencies that are given powers to enact rules and regulations that govern specific individuals and organizations. Administrative agencies derive their authority from state and federal statutes that authorize the agency, often referred to as a department, commission, bureau, or office, to regulate conduct involving safety, education, welfare, national security, taxation, environmental and consumer protection, transportation, communications, commerce, and trade. Because societies are complex, countless administrative agencies have been created to regulate and control human and organizational behaviors. Legislatures have also passed enabling statutes that empower these agencies with broad discretionary authority to formulate, implement, and enforce public policy that has the impact of law. Some examples include the Internal Revenue Service that enacts and enforces tax law, the U.S. Department of Labor, Occupational Safety and Health Administration that sets workplace safety rules, and the Food and Drug Administration that establishes rules for drug development, testing, and purity as well as food safety requirements (Samaha, 2013).

> **administrative law** The branch of public law created by administrative agencies and presented in the form of rules and regulations that dictate duties and responsibilities of individuals and organizations.

Administrative agencies are usually granted executive powers, such as the power to investigate and prosecute violations of statutes and administrative regulations and orders. At the federal level, agencies may also issue an administrative subpoena to collect documents and testimony related to the issue of the investigation (Doyle, 2006). As an example, the Equal Employment Opportunity Commission (EEOC) uses administrative subpoenas in its investigations of employment discrimination. It can have these subpoenas enforced in the courts if the parties do not comply with the subpoena (Morrison, 2014). Administrative agencies may also conduct physical inspections of business and governmental premises and facilities. However, the executive powers granted to administrative agencies are subject to certain constitutional constraints. For example, administrative inspections or searches are subject to the same restrictions placed on other government agents by the Fourth Amendment to the U.S. Constitution (Cheeseman, 2010). Parties found to be in violation of administrative law can be fined, civilly sued, or in some cases criminally prosecuted for their actions.

Security personnel operate directly under many regulatory laws. In most states, contract security personnel must follow minimum training and selection and pre-employment standards. These can include minimum age and educational levels and the mandatory fingerprinting of job applicants (Nalla & Crichlow, 2014). At the federal level, regulations vary depending upon what industry sector the security function operates in. The 3,000+ contract protective security forces used at various Department of Energy sites throughout the United States must meet pre-employment, physical fitness, and training standards. Oversight of these standards is carried out by the Department of Energy's Health, Safety and Security division. If not directly impacted by regulations, the daily activities of security personnel and managers must also

▼

comply with other regulatory laws. OSHA-related laws governing workplace safety and violence prevention activities must be administered and followed. Likewise, security operations and practices must comply with the U.S. Department of Health and Human Services privacy-related regulations on individuals' health records and information under the Health Insurance Portability and Accountability Act (HIPAA). Meanwhile, the Nuclear Regulatory Commission and the Defense Security Services have minimum security standards for facilities under their control, while countless other agencies have established minimum standards related to information security. As such, the actions of administrative agencies can disrupt daily activity and business operations if, in the judgment of agency representatives, conduct does not conform to the requirements of the regulations. Security professionals must acknowledge the power and control administrative agencies retain and ensure that human and organizational behaviors conform to regulatory requirements.

► Contract Law

A contract is a legally binding and voluntary agreement between two or more parties that creates specific obligations on another party to do or not do something. If a contract is violated, the injured party has legal recourse in the civil courts to seek a remedy for the breach of the other party's duty (Black, 1990). There are two types of contracts. An expressed contract is a written agreement between the parties where the terms are explicitly stated and agreed upon. An implied contract is unspoken and results from the actions of the parties where the parties believe that an agreement exists (Feinman, 2000). Although the vast majority of contracts in professional settings are expressed or written, in some situations one of parties may still nevertheless violate the conditions of the contract, leading to subsequent legal issues.

A legally binding contract contains four elements: (1) an offer; (2) consideration; (3) acceptance; and (4) mutuality of obligation. An offer is basically a promise made by one of the parties to do or not to do something, provided that the terms of the offer are accepted. A contract security company that states it will provide 10 security personnel at a particular location to perform specific services for a certain set price per month to a client is an offer. In many instances, the negotiation of a contract also involves exchanging counter offers. These counter offers are not contracts, but are simply new offers to the other party. *Consideration* (e.g., "consideration for the promise" or benefit given to the other party) is the point that the contract must have some type of value. This value induces the parties to enter in the contract. It is an exchange of promises and it is based on something of value that is bargained for as part of the agreement. This value could be based on financial expenditures, the promise to do (or not do) something, or the promise to perform a service. In the case of the earlier example, the provision of security personnel for a set fee is the consideration. Next, acceptance means that the offer was accepted by the parties. There is no contract without acceptance. Usually contracts are signed agreements between the parties. The last element, which is the doctrine of mutuality of obligation means that the parties "have a meeting of the minds" and have agreed to the basic terms and conditions of the contract and agree to be bound by the contract (Bix, 2012). Under this doctrine, if one of the parties does not meet their mutual obligation, then the law will determine that neither one is bound to perform. Using the above example again, an enforceable contract exists when both parties follow the contract—the contract security company provides personnel while the other party pays the agreed upon monthly fee—mutuality of obligation. If, however, the site fails to pay its monthly fees to the contract security agency, then the agency does not have the legal responsibility to continue providing personnel since mutuality of obligation no longer exists.

contract Legally binding voluntary agreement between or among parties.

expressed contract Contract in which all terms are explicitly stated and agreed upon.

implied contract A contract that is "unspoken" and results from the actions of the parties where they believe that an agreement exists.

offer Part of a contract. A promise made by one of the parties to do or not do something, provided that the terms of the offer are accepted.

acceptance Part of a contract. Means that the offer was accepted by the parties. There is no contract without acceptance.

mutuality of obligation An element of a contract. The parties "have a meeting of the minds" and have agreed to the basic terms and conditions of the contract and agree to be bound by the contract.

Many contracts also contain provisions that shift or limit the liabilities of the parties in the contract. Limitations of liability clauses are sections in the contract that limit, define, and articulate the maximum liabilities of the party if there is some type of legal challenge or action. There are also "hold harmless" clauses. Hold harmless clauses prevent the parties from holding one another responsible for certain types of loss, damage, or injury under the contract. For example, many software companies in their agreements "hold harmless" the manufacturer for any losses that may occur by the user for glitches or defects in the software that the user agrees to before the program is opened and installed. In the case of a contract security provider, an example of a hold harmless clause is "the XYZ corporation will hold harmless the ABC contract security firm and its agents and employees from and against any claims, damages, cause of action, losses, and expenses that arise from the work performed at the . . . that is caused whole or in part by the ABC company and/or any of its agents or employees, subcontractors or independent contractors . . . ." There are also indemnification clauses. An indemnification clause requires or obligates a party in the contract to compensate the other for damages. An example would be a person who has vehicle insurance. Here, the insurance company is the indemnifier who will pay for losses as explained in the insurance policy. A security-related indemnification clause could hold a contract security company responsible for all legal fees associated with any false arrest related lawsuit (Young, 2002). These clauses "indemnify" or absorb the losses associated with an act where one party basically assumes the responsibility and liability for an action that would be the responsibility of someone else.

Although security professionals are likely to engage in numerous contractual relationships, the most common situation will involve contracts for some type of security service. Outsourcing (utilizing contracted vendors) for security services and personnel is common. Potential outsourcing situations include facility reviews, program planning, security system design and installation management, system monitoring, training, and investigations of security personnel (Maurer, 2000b). In many cases, these contracts can be quite complex, including special clauses that stipulate liquidated damage arrangements and limitations on damages.

The periodic review of contractual arrangements is necessary to ensure that the contracts are legal and do not expose the company to the potential for liability. In some cases, restructuring contracts can result in considerable cost savings. One major financial institution, headquartered in Pittsburgh, Pennsylvania, decreased the number of contractors, obtained volume discounts, and reduced the organization's annual contracted security expenses by 9 percent through its review of existing contracts (Mann, 1999). This example also shows that managers need to be financially literate when reviewing financial contracts.

> **limitations of liability clauses** Are sections in the contract that limit, define, and articulate the maximum liabilities of the party if there is some type of legal challenge or action.

E-contracts

The Internet is a heavily used tool in carrying out different types of businesses where contracts can now be negotiated and executed in electronic format. Perhaps one of the most common types is a clickwrap contract where a website-based company sets the terms and agreements for downloading software and music (Dickens, 2007). Assuming all the elements to create a contract are present, an electronic contract or E-contract is valid and enforceable. The Electronic Signature in Global and National Commerce Act (E-Sign Act), enacted by Congress (2000), provides that a signature, contract, or any other record that exists in electronic form is enforceable and basically the same as a traditional "paper and pen" contract (Cheeseman, 2010). The Uniform Electronic Transaction Act (1999) also reiterates that electronics contracts are also legal and binding. However, to overcome evidentiary problems in the event of a lawsuit, the parties should always print and retain paper versions of any electronic contract negotiations.

> **E-contract** An electronic contract.

Noncompete Agreements

Another type of contract that employers often require employees to sign, particularly in the private industry, is a noncompete agreement. Also known as "covenants not to compete (CNCs)," these contracts (also known as restrictive covenants because they restrict behaviors) are designed to prohibit direct competition and knowledge transfer by former employees to other organizations competing with the company. In order to prevent this transfer of information, the "noncompete" contract specifies the time period and other conditions (including geographical distances) that prohibit the former employee from obtaining similar jobs and competing with his old employer.

CNCs are heavily used in many sectors. Approximately 80 percent of managers employed in S&P 500 companies have CNCs in their employment contracts (Conti, 2014; Thomas, Bishara, & Martin, 2014). Consider, for example, a security manager in the alarm sector. If this person would accept a position with "the competition," the manager could use existing marketing information, his list of contacts and current contract holders, and even take technological secrets with him to the new rival company, subsequently harming the old company in the process. In order to prevent this, the noncompete agreement would specify that the manager could not work in this industry for a set period of time (e.g., 2 years) post-resignation. By having a 2-year restriction, the existing client list, marketing plans, and technologies would be outdated after the 2-year restriction, preserving the needs of the old company while nevertheless allowing the employee to seek a new career in the same field. These CNCs can also include other provisions and stipulations established by the employer and employee.

The enforcement of noncompete agreements involves litigation through the courts. They are upheld in most states if the contract is confined to legitimate business interests, states the irreparable harm to be suffered by disclosure, narrowly defines the scope of the restrictions to a reasonable time and place, and describes the prohibited conduct. Protectable business interests include trade secrets, intellectual property, and business goodwill (intangible assets) arising from the name, location, or reputation of the company. Some courts also hold that an employee's unique skills acquired on the job are a protectable business interest (McDonald, 2003). Generally, the courts uphold these covenants when there is a legitimate business and employer interest, there is no harm to the public interest, and there is no real hardship for the former employee. When noncompete agreements are enforceable, the enforcement is not unlimited. The noncompete restriction is limited to a reasonable period of time; the courts have upheld such agreements for periods up to even 3 years in length (Estlund, 2006; Pivateau, 2014).

In lieu of CNCs, some companies use nonsolicitation agreements. Like CNCs, these are contracts between the employer and employee. Instead of completely prohibiting competition, nonsolicitation agreements are narrower in their restrictions, preventing a former employee from soliciting the previous employer's clients or employees. As is the case with CNCs, these agreements are enforceable in the courts where former employees can be held liable for their actions if in violation of the agreement (Anderson, 2011).

▶ Property Law

Although property rights hold a unique position in the American society, the term *property* is not easily defined. Property rights protect lawful possession, use, and ownership. In the United States, property is a legally protected interest or group of interests, including the exclusive right of a private person to control private property, as well as the right of a political unit (city, county, state, and nation) to control public property for an economic good.

The concept of property is extremely important in a democratic and free society. In a sense, property rights are almost sacred to many people. Security managers, therefore, should familiarize themselves with the nature, scope, rights, and legal consequences associated with personal and real property laws.

Property can be tangible, such as an automobile or building to which an interest holds a possessory right or title. In contrast, intangible property does not take a physical form. Stock certificates, proprietary information, intellectual property, copyrights, and patents represent property interests that, although not physical, are legally protected by law. As technological knowledge expands more rapidly and data processing and communication systems become more sophisticated, the classifications of personal property broaden. The rise in patent applications, for example, can be explained partly by new classes of discoveries and innovations that have been granted property protection by the courts. For example, although the U.S. patent system has existed for over 200 years, biotech companies could not patent genetic discoveries until 1980 because DNA was not considered a property. Likewise, patents on software were not allowed until 1981. And, in 1998, patent rights were expanded to include business methods. Even techniques owned by a company can be considered property. In some high-profile lawsuits in 2000, Amazon.com claimed its one-click ordering system patent must force Barnesandnoble.com to use two clicks. Priceline.com sued Microsoft and its Expedia subsidiary for infringement on Priceline.com's name-your-own price auction model, a business methods patent (Jones, 2000). Although these disputes may appear to be trivial, when examined in the context of marketing and consumer practices, millions of dollars could be at stake for companies.

The most significant distinction in property law emanates from the difference between personal property and real property. Personal property includes virtually anything, tangible or intangible, other than land and anything in it or permanently attached to it (real property, real estate). When real property, such as minerals or buildings, are extracted or removed from land, they are theoretically transformed into personal property. Important legal considerations emanate from the distinction between personal and real property. Transfer of title to personal property is relatively simple and is typically controlled by a uniform commercial code. Transfer of real property (real estate) is much more formal and includes the delivery of an instrument referred to as a deed. In some cases, an individual, political entity, or corporation (considered a "paper" person in the perspective of the law) may have a legal right to possess, rather than own, property. Renting a vehicle (personal property) or leasing a building (real property) represents contracted possessory rights rather than ownership. Under the terms of the contract, the lessee is subject to agreed-upon conditions of use, and the lessor retains ownership rights.

► Employment and Labor Law

Employees have a right to a safe and secure workplace, equal pay, compensation for work-related injuries, financial security upon retirement or loss of employment, and protection against unfair dismissal from employment. Employment law covers a vast array of common law and statutory provisions that regulate the employment relationship. Employment laws include labor laws, employment discrimination laws, and laws that are created to protect employees. Some of the more prominent pieces of legislation include the Fair Labor Standards Act and Title VII of the Civil Rights Act of 1964.

The Fair Labor Standards Act (FLSA) was passed by Congress in 1938. The Act forbids the use of oppressive child labor, and it established minimum wage and overtime pay for workers. Under the FLSA, an employer cannot require a nonexempt employee (nonmanagerial worker) to work more than 40 hours per week unless the employee is paid one-and-a-half times the regular pay for each hour worked over 40. In some cases, however,

property law
The body of law that deals with the lawful possession and ownership of tangible and intangible property.

personal property
Anything, tangible or intangible, other than land and anything in it or permanently attached to it (real property, real estate).

real property Land and anything permanently (or semipermanently) attached to land; real estate.

employment law
Common law and statutory provisions that regulate the employment relationship.

Fair Labor Standards Act (FLSA) Passed by Congress in 1938. The Act forbids the use of oppressive child labor; established minimum wage and overtime pay for workers.

companies may violate the FLSA, which was the case with Wal-Mart Stores. In 2002, a federal trial jury in Portland, Oregon, found Wal-Mart Stores, the world's largest retailer and private employer, guilty of pressuring employees to work unpaid overtime. More than 400 current and former employees from almost two dozen Oregon Wal-Mart Stores sued the retailer for violating state and federal wage laws. More than 35 similar lawsuits were filed against Wal-Mart in 30 other states. Those suits, from New York to California, involved thousands of workers seeking millions in back pay. Other suits and complaints against Wal-Mart alleged that the company discriminated against female workers and that Wal-Mart thwarted employee efforts to unionize (Armour, 2003; "Wal-Mart loses overtime pay lawsuit," 2002).

In the area of employment discrimination law, a number of federal and state statutes govern the employment relationship. Paramount among these laws is Title VII of the Civil Rights Act of 1964, as amended. Title VII legislation prohibits discrimination in employment on the basis of gender, race, religious preference, national origin, and age throughout the employment relationship that includes hiring, promotions, pay, and retirement. The Civil Rights Act also led to the creation of the EEOC that is tasked with investigating and enforcing federal antidiscrimination legislation. Later in 1990, the Americans with Disabilities Act was enacted. This Act prohibits actions by employers against prospective and actual employees who have actual or regarded disabilities. Like Title VII violations, claims related to discrimination because of a disability are investigated by the EEOC and enforced in the courts if necessary, where employers may be fined and required to change their discriminatory practices (DeLeire, 2000). Affected individuals can also sue employers to seek recovery for damages under civil law.

There are other laws that security staff and managers need to understand. The Employee Polygraph Protection Act of 1988 (EPPA) prohibits private sector employers from using polygraphs as a pre-employment selection tool while also preventing their use among existing employees in some workplace-related issues. However, a polygraph (with restrictions) can be used in investigations involving financial loss. The Act exempts pharmaceutical-related, private security companies, and companies involved in national security-related activities (Cohen & Cohen, 2007). Some states also have even greater restrictions to polygraph use in the public and private sectors (Barnhorn & Pegram, 2011).

Collective Bargaining Laws

In 1935, Congress enacted the National Labor Relations Act (NLRA), also known as the Wagner Act. This Act gave employees the right to belong to labor unions (and strike) in the private sector. It also legalized unions and required employers to recognize and bargain with labor unions. The Act outlined the federal government's support for collective bargaining and unionization. It also established the National Labor Relations Board (NLRB), an independent federal agency that monitors union-related activities and investigates unfair labor practices by employers and unions. The NLRB also issues precedent setting decisions that employers must follow. In this context, many NLRB decisions impact security operations and practices. For example, some security-related surveillance practices, such as photographing union activities, may be determined by the NLRB as an unfair labor practice since they could interfere with or "chill" an employee's legal right to join and engage in concerted labor activities (Johnson, 2015). While the NLRA and its subsequent amendments including Taft-Hartley in 1947 and the Labor Management and Reporting and Disclosure Act of 1959 (also known as Landrum-Griffin Act) have further refined private sector labor relations, beginning in the late 1950s, many states have also passed public sector laws granting public employees the right to collectively bargain and unionize. These laws are very

Title VII of the Civil Rights Act of 1964 Prohibits discrimination in employment on the basis of gender, race, religious preference, national origin, and age throughout the employment relationship including hiring, promotions, pay, and retirement.

Employee Polygraph Protection Act of 1988 1988 federal law that severely restricts the use of the polygraph or similar instruments by private-sector organizations.

National Labor Relations Act (NLRA) Also known as the Wagner Act. Federal law that grants employees the right to belong to labor unions in the private sector.

similar to the NLRA and often have specific agencies that are responsible for investigating labor issues and rendering precedent-setting decisions related to labor disputes in the public sector (Kearney & Mareschal, 2014).

Collective bargaining contracts can also define and regulate the security function in the workplace. Collective bargaining contracts can be considered the "constitution of the workforce." These agreements define the roles and responsibilities of employees and employers. They also set forth what actions are appropriate for management. For example, collective bargaining agreements can set restrictions on surveillance actions of management, defining where and when security surveillance is acceptable. Collective bargaining agreements also define specific procedures that need to be followed in investigations that could have an adverse impact on those individuals being investigated, where the union member may be entitled under Weingarten Rights to have a union representative present during any investigation of the employee, when requested by that employee (Johnson, 2005; True, 2005). As these two examples suggest, because many constitutional rights "stop at the workplace door" the provisions found in the collective bargaining agreement may re-establish and even enhance personal and workplace rights. If violated, there are provisions in the contract for investigating and correcting any wrongs, including judicial enforcement of the contract provisions, if necessary. Security personnel must be well informed of the content (following the "four corners of the contract") of collective bargaining agreements in order to ensure labor peace in the organization.

▶ Municipal Ordinances

Security professionals must also be informed of municipal ordinances that can impact security administration and operations. Municipal ordinances are laws and regulations passed by municipalities and counties. For example, many cities including Louisville, Kentucky have false alarm ordinances that are designed to ensure that businesses have functional alarm systems in their organizations. As part of these ordinances, alarm technicians/installers are required to install commercial security systems and alarm holders and companies can be fined for false alarms that occur (CryWolf, 2015). In an effort to reduce crime in some business settings, other cities require businesses to have CCTV systems. Ordinances related to fire detection and suppression systems are also commonplace. In other cases, municipalities have the ability to pass laws to create Business Improvement Districts (BIDS) and levy taxes to fund private security patrols in those areas to control crime and disorder (Vindevogel, 2005). The failure to follow municipal ordinances can result in security companies being cited and in some cases being prevented from operating in that jurisdiction.

> **municipal ordinances** laws created by cities, towns, or villages.

▶ Industrial Self-Regulation

In spite of the lack of uniform governmental standards for the regulation of the security industry, organizations within the industry, as well as private and public instructional providers, have voluntarily developed certification, training, and education programs. Voluntarily adhering to industry standards and self-created codes or principles of conduct, is called industrial self-regulation. This self-regulation of activities governs industry practices, establishes social norms among individuals and organizations, and can be a complement to traditional laws and regulations (Nysten-Haarala, Klyuchnikova, & Helenius, 2015).

There are some examples of industrial self-regulation in the security industry. Diligent efforts on the part of ASIS International led to the development of a professional code of ethics and the Certified Protection Professional (CPP) program. To acquire the CPP designation,

> **industrial self-regulation** Organizations voluntarily adhering to industry standards and self-created codes or principles of conduct.

the candidate must meet minimum experience and education criteria and pass a professional certification examination. The program focuses on security management and is administered by a professional certification board under the auspices of ASIS International. Additional certification programs offered by ASIS International include the Physical Security Professional (PSP) and the Professional Certified Investigator (PCI) designations. The Loss Prevention Foundation also offers two training and certification programs: Loss Prevention Qualified (LPQ) and Loss Prevention Certified (LPC). The LPQ certification is designed for entry-level retail loss prevention personnel. The LPQ program focuses on the retail environment, business practices, and basic loss prevention techniques. The LPC program offers advanced education and certification of retail loss prevention for managers and executives. The LPC program focuses on leadership, advanced business practices, operations, crisis management, and supply chain management (The Loss Prevention Foundation, 2007). Similar efforts to improve the quality of security personnel have been articulated through programs developed by the International Foundation for Protection Officers (focusing primarily on security officers), International Association for Healthcare Security and Safety, Academy of Security Educators and Trainers, International Association of Professional Security Consultants, and the International Association for Computer Systems Security.

Education and certification programs are important ingredients to professionalism. Education programs assist individuals with acquisition of the philosophy and knowledge specific to a discipline. A legitimate certification program ensures that members of a profession are competent to practice in the field. The contemporary security manager can no longer survive simply with a high school diploma and 20 years' experience in military or public law enforcement (Johnson, 2005; Simonsen, 1998).

▶ Regulation of the Security Industry

Generally, it can be concluded that the local, state, and federal governments have traditionally taken a "hands-off" approach to the regulation of private security operations. One of the earliest examples of the government restricting the private security industry was the **Anti-Pinkerton Act of 1893** that prevented the federal government from hiring Pinkerton Detectives (and other private detective companies) due to the union busting, corrupt and unethical activities they were involved in at that time. Later, the La Follette Civil Liberties Committee (1936–1941) investigated unions' right to free speech and the right to assemble. In its ensuing investigation of many security-related practices of companies in the steel, coal, and automobile industries, the Committee cited the actions of company police in thwarting the constitutional rights of workers. In particular, there were four antiunion actions by companies: espionage, munitions, strikebreaking, and the use of private police. The Commission determined that espionage or spying on union activities was a universal practice among companies, citing the vast amount of money that General Motors had allocated to espionage, oftentimes using undercover Pinkerton employees to infiltrate union ranks. The investigation also found that some of the steel companies had more chemical munitions than the Chicago Police Department, and used contract security officers as strikebreakers that resulted in violence and resentment; company guards used in company towns and factories were also found to violate the civil rights of workers and their families. The actions of the Commission served to expose some of the abuses of the private security industry and operations leading to some criminal investigations and prosecutions. It did not lead directly to any legislative controls on the private security industry (Auerbach, 1964; Calder, 2010). However, changes in labor laws did result in approximately 200 contract security firms involved in strikebreaking and espionage to go out of business, while plant police forces deceased in size (Schweitzer, 1980).

Anti-Pinkerton Act of 1893 Prohibited the federal government from hiring Pinkerton Detectives and other private detective companies.

The first federal government effort to regulate the security industry commenced with the introduction of a bill by former vice president Al Gore when he was a senator from Tennessee. If passed, the bill would have required minimum standards for proprietary and contract security personnel working in U.S. government operations. Subsequent initiatives by Congressmen Matthew Martinez (D, OK) in 1992, and Don Sundquist (R, TN) in 1993, and Senator John Edwards (D, NC) in 2003 did not result in the passage of any federal law regulating the industry. On April 2, 2003, U.S. Senator Carl Levin (D, MI) introduced a bill, the Private Security Officer Employment Act of 2003, to permit authorized employers of security personnel access to FBI criminal history data (and state databases) to review the criminal histories of employees and applicants. Cosponsored by Senators Lamar Alexander (R, TN), Joseph Lieberman (D, CT), Mitch McConnell (R, KY), and Charles Schumer (D, NY), the bill was read twice and referred to the Senate Committee on the Judiciary. This Bill became law in 2004 as part of the Intelligence Reform Bill, President George W. Bush signed this Bill the **Private Security Officer Employment Authorization Act of 2004** into law on December 17, 2004. Under the Act, employers may conduct criminal history checks of applicants for, and holders of, positions in which the primary duty is to perform security services, including positions held by contract and proprietary security personnel. The Private Security Officer Employment Authorization Act program is completely voluntary. Employers may, if they choose and if the applicant or employee consents, send fingerprints or other types of positive identification to a state identification bureau as well as the FBI. Employers do not have direct access to the results of the criminal history search. However, employers are provided with enough information to make an informed employment decision. The program is supported financially through user fees.

> **Private Security Officer Employment Authorization Act of 2004** Allows employers to conduct criminal history checks of applicants for, and holders of, positions in which the primary duty is to perform security services, including positions held by contract and proprietary security personnel.

Information regarding specific training, education, and certification programs may be obtained by contacting ASIS International at www.asisonline.org.

▶ Judicial Systems and Processes

Each of the above types of laws and regulations can be enforced in the courts if necessary. As such, it is important to possess knowledge of the judicial systems and their processes that exist in the United States.

The judiciary in the United States operates as a dual system consisting of state and federal courts. State courts address violations of law and other legal matters pertaining to the laws of a particular state. Federal courts address violations of law as defined by the U.S. Congress. State and federal court systems operate autonomously. In some cases, both systems have concurrent jurisdiction over the same criminal activity. Robbery, for example, is a criminal law violation in every state. If a robbery is committed against a federally insured financial institution, such as a bank, the criminal activity (the robbery) is also a violation of federal law. Thus, the state government and the federal government have concurrent jurisdiction over the same case. Under such circumstances, a defendant can be tried, convicted, and sentenced in both systems without violating the Fifth Amendment's double jeopardy provision because the perpetrator committed two separate offenses. The bank robbery represents an offense against the citizens of the United States as well as an offense against the citizens of the state in which the robbery was committed.

The U.S. Constitution specifically provides for only one court, the Supreme Court of the United States. Article III, Section 1, of the Constitution reads that the judicial power of the United States shall be vested in one Supreme Court, and in such inferior courts as the Congress may from time to time ordain and establish. It was the Judiciary Act of 1789 that established other federal courts, namely the U.S. district courts and the U.S. circuit courts of appeals. There are at least 56 separate and distinct court systems in the United States and its territories. They include the federal system, 50 state systems, and one system each in the District of Columbia, Guam, Puerto Rico, the U.S. Virgin Islands, and the Northern Mariana Islands.

The federal court system consists of 94 U.S. district courts (trial courts) situated in 13 U.S. courts of appeals circuits. The U.S. Supreme Court functions as an appellate court. It reviews constitutional challenges to federal and state statutes, as well as appeals from criminal and civil trial court cases brought before it through state appellate courts or one of the 13 U.S. courts of appeals. In the case of state court judgments, an appeal from a state's court of last resort is a matter of right when the validity of a federal statute is questioned in a state court or when a state statute is challenged because it is alleged to violate the U.S. Constitution (Cole & Smith, 2011; Fagin, 2007; President's Commission on Law Enforcement and Administration of Justice, 1967; Rutledge, 2000).

The U.S. district courts are the trial courts of general jurisdiction in the federal system. They have trial jurisdiction over civil actions involving copyrights, patents, postal matters, civil rights, and almost all other civil and criminal cases arising under the laws and treaties of the United States and the U.S. Constitution. They have concurrent jurisdiction with the states in criminal cases when a criminal act violates federal as well as state law. U.S. district courts have jurisdiction in civil cases in which the dollar amount in dispute is over $10,000 and the parties to the action are residents of different states.

The U.S. magistrate courts have authority to issue federal warrants, set bail, hold preliminary hearings in federal cases, and conduct summary trials for minor federal crimes in which the defendant waives the right to a trial in U.S. district court. Other specialized federal courts include the U.S. Court of Claims, which hears financial lawsuits against the United States, the U.S. Court of Customs and Patent Appeals, the U.S. Tax Court, and military and territorial courts.

The intermediate appellate courts in the federal system are the U.S. courts of appeals (see Figure 3-2 ■). They have appellate jurisdiction over all U.S. district court decisions except under three conditions: (1) when a three-judge district court has enjoined (stopped) enforcement of a federal or state statute on grounds of unconstitutionality, and the case proceeds directly to the U.S. Supreme Court; (2) when a U.S. district court declares a federal statute unconstitutional, and the United States is a party to the action; and (3) when a case requires immediate settlement because of imperative public importance.

Learn more about the federal courts through the Federal Judiciary home page located at www.uscourts.gov/about.

The U.S. Supreme Court has no authority to make a final determination in a state case. The Court may affirm (let stand) the decision of the lower court or reverse the decision and remand (return) the case to the lower court for a decision that is consistent with Constitutional law. If the constitutionality of the entire state court case is at issue, the charge against a defendant in a criminal case must be dismissed. If only a portion of the evidence is declared inadmissible, the state court may order a new trial based on admissible evidence only. A new trial does not violate the Fifth Amendment double jeopardy clause, since there has not been a final judgment in the case and the new trial is considered *de novo* (new), as if the original trial had not taken place.

U.S. district court Trial court in the federal court system.

U.S. court of appeals Intermediate appellate court in the federal court system.

intermediate appellate courts Appellate courts between trial courts and courts of last resort.

The United States
Federal Courts

SUPREME COURT	**UNITED STATES SUPREME COURT**
APPELLATE COURTS	**U.S. Courts of Appeals** 12 Regional Circuit Courts of Appeals 1 U.S. Court of Appeals for the Federal Circuit
TRIAL COURTS	**U.S. District Courts** 94 judicial districts U.S. Bankruptcy Courts **U.S. Court of International Trade** **U.S. Court of Federal Claims**
FEDERAL COURTS AND OTHER ENTITIES OUTSIDE THE JUDICIAL BRANCH	**Military Courts (Trial and Appellate)** **Court of Veterans Appeals** **U.S. Tax Court** **Federal administrative agencies and boards**

Federal courts.
(Photo courtesy of United States Courts.)

State Courts

State and local courts try criminal and civil cases arising out of incidents occurring within the state and cases involving violations of state and local laws. Each state has a court of last resort, usually called the state supreme court. Appeals from these courts are taken directly to the U.S. Supreme Court, the highest court in the United States. All states also have some form of intermediate appellate court. They review decisions on appeal from state trial courts. Appeals from state intermediate appellate courts are taken to the state court of last resort.

State trial courts generally fall into two categories: limited and general jurisdiction. Courts of limited jurisdiction are restricted in their authority. These courts adjudicate small civil claims, typically try misdemeanor cases, and conduct preliminary hearings in felony cases. If, as the result of a preliminary hearing, the court of limited jurisdiction determines that probable cause exists to hold the defendant on the felony charge, the defendant's case is transferred to the state court of general jurisdiction for arraignment and trial. Courts of general jurisdiction may try any state criminal or civil case brought before it. Criminal and civil trials take place in trial courts. They have original jurisdiction in these cases. *Appellate courts*, on the other hand, with rare exception, do not originate or try cases. They only review cases and decisions appealed

courts of limited jurisdiction Courts that are limited in the types of cases they are authorized to try.

court of general jurisdiction A level in state courts that can try any case brought before it.

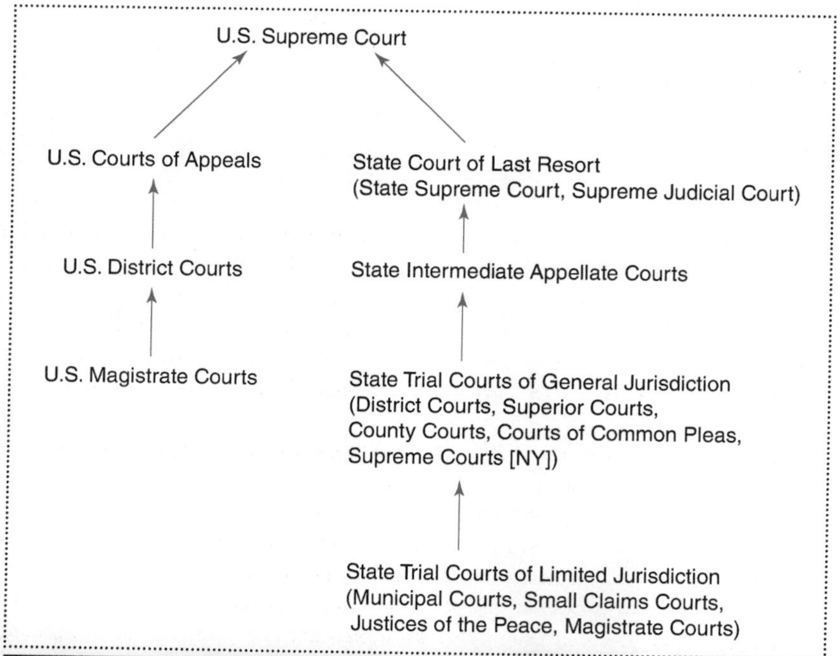
U.S. Supreme Court
U.S. Courts of Appeals
U.S. District Courts
U.S. Magistrate Courts
State Court of Last Resort
(State Supreme Court, Supreme Judicial Court)
State Intermediate Appellate Courts
State Trial Courts of General Jurisdiction
(District Courts, Superior Courts,
County Courts, Courts of Common Pleas,
Supreme Courts [NY])
State Trial Courts of Limited Jurisdiction
(Municipal Courts, Small Claims Courts,
Justices of the Peace, Magistrate Courts)

FIGURE 3-2 Court Systems

to them from trial courts or lower appellate courts. Appellate courts review *the transcript* (written record) of the trial court proceeding as well as written briefs submitted by the parties in the action. The appellate court may also hear short oral arguments from the petitioner and the respondent or their representatives. Appeals from trial courts proceed through either a state or a federal appellate review process and may culminate at the U.S. Supreme Court.

SECURITY SPOTLIGHT

Review and explain the court structure that exists in your particular state. How many levels exist? What are the roles of the court at each level?

▶ The Judicial Process

Criminal Cases

initial appearance The defendant's first appearance before a court. A nonadversarial proceeding before a magistrate (or judge) to set bail.

In a criminal case, initiation of the pretrial process is made through a physical arrest or issuance of an arrest warrant. A criminal citation is issued in lieu of an arrest for minor offenses. If arrested, the arrestee is "booked." A booking is the official recording of the arrest in the records of the arresting law enforcement agency. If the arrestee cannot be released on recognizance (ROR) without a bail hearing, and a judge is not immediately available, the arrestee may be detained in a jail for a reasonable time (about two court working days) until a first appearance before a judge. At the **initial appearance**, the arrestee is informed of the charge(s), advised of rights under the Constitution, and, if possible, bail is set. In some jurisdictions, the first (or initial) appearance is referred to as the arraignment on the complaint, which should not be confused with a post-indictment or post-information proceeding, called an arraignment. The first appearance is a nonadversarial proceeding.

In federal felony cases, a formal charge against the accused must be issued by a federal grand jury in the form of an indictment. In state cases, the prosecuting attorney may present the case to a grand jury for possible indictment, or may file an information, which is a formal charge for a felony issued from the prosecuting attorney's office subsequent to a preliminary hearing. The formal charge for a misdemeanor case is usually called a criminal complaint.

Many states do not utilize a grand jury. In lieu of a grand jury proceeding, a preliminary hearing is conducted to determine if probable cause exists to hold the accused to answer to the charge. The preliminary hearing is an adversarial proceeding. It is an evidentiary hearing. During this hearing, the prosecution must establish a *prima facie* case, which means that on the face of the evidence presented, probable cause exists that a crime occurred and the defendant committed the offense.

If probable cause is established at the preliminary hearing, the case proceeds to the arraignment. At the arraignment, the accused is asked to enter a plea. The pleas available include guilty, not guilty, not guilty by reason of insanity, or no contest (*nolo contendere*). If the defendant pleads not guilty or no contest and proceeds to trial, the defense attorney usually files pretrial motions to have the charges dismissed, suppress prosecution evidence as inadmissible, discover evidence the prosecution has, or delay the trial. Motions may also be filed to change the venue (location) of the trial, consolidate multiple charges arising from a single criminal transaction, sever multiple counts or defendants, and disclose the identity and location of an informant. In many states, the arraignment occurs prior to the preliminary hearing.

If the case qualifies for, and the accused selects, a jury trial, the next step is jury selection. An initial list of potential jurors is selected from property tax records or from a list of registered voters or vehicle owners, or from the department of motor vehicle's list of those who hold driver licenses. From the initial list, a jury pool (venire) is randomly selected. Members of the jury pool receive jury duty notices and are asked to report to a court facility. From the jury pool, a jury panel of approximately 30 people is randomly selected and referred to a courtroom for trial jury selection. Members of the jury panel are interviewed by the judge, prosecution, and defense during a *voir dire* examination (*voir dire* means to speak the truth) to determine their suitability for service on the trial jury. Potential jurors may be excused from the jury panel for cause or due to a *peremptory challenge*. Challenges for cause are not limited. However, peremptory (no cause or reason need be given) challenges are limited in number, usually from six to 10 challenges, depending on the seriousness of the criminal charges.

After the trial jury is selected, the jury is sworn in (impaneled) and the government presents its case. During the opening statement, the prosecutor explains to the court what evidence will be presented as proof of the allegations in the complaint, indictment, or information. Subsequently, the defendant or the defendant's attorney outlines how the allegations made by the prosecutor will not be proven. Following the opening statements, the prosecution and the defense present their cases. A witness is examined directly by the side calling the witness, followed by cross-examination from the opposing party. Impeachment (reducing a witness' credibility) is the intended outcome of cross-examination.

When the defense rests its case, the prosecutor may offer rebuttal evidence to respond to the defendant's proof. If the prosecutor offers rebuttal evidence, the defendant may present a surrebuttal to refute the prosecutor's rebuttal evidence. States vary regarding the number and order of closing arguments. Nearly all states allow the defense to make a final argument (summation) first, followed by the prosecution. A few states permit three arguments (summaries) at the end of the trial. Where three arguments are permitted, an opening argument is made by the prosecution. The prosecutor summarizes the evidence presented, states how the evidence has satisfied the elements of the charge, and asks for a finding of

indictment Formal criminal charge issued by a grand jury.

information In a criminal proceeding, the formal criminal charge issued by a prosecutor in a state felony case.

preliminary hearing In the pretrial stages of a criminal proceeding, hearing at which the judge determines if probable cause exists that a crime was committed and that the person charged committed the offense.

arraignment The pretrial judicial hearing at which a defendant enters a plea to a criminal charge.

***voir dire* examination** "Speak the truth" examination of a prospective trial juror to determine juror's suitability for jury service. The prospective juror's qualifications may be challenged for cause or a party may exercise a peremptory challenge.

challenge for cause A challenge to a potential trial juror's qualifications that must be accompanied by a reason; there is no limit to the number of challenges for cause.

impeachment In a judicial proceeding, refers to an attack on the credibility of a witness; possible result of cross-examination of a witness.

guilt. This is followed by an argument from the defense. This is similar to opening argument by the prosecution, except the defense asks the court for a finding of not guilty. Finally, during a closing argument by the prosecution, the prosecutor may reply to statements in the argument made by the defense.

After all closing arguments are presented, the judge instructs the jury (if a jury is used) regarding the points of law that apply in the case. These instructions are critical to the final determination in a jury trial. As exemplified by the Charles Keating, Jr. fraud case, an appellate court may reverse a conviction if the judge's instructions are improper. Keating was convicted in 1992 in Los Angeles Superior Court of fraud involving the sale of $200 million in worthless bonds that ultimately led to the collapse of the Lincoln Savings and Loan Company. Public funds in the amount of $3.4 billion were used to keep the entire savings and loan industry from collapsing. According to the appellate court, the judge in the Keating state trial, Lance Ito (the judge in the O.J. Simpson trial), presented faulty instructions to the trial jury. Ito did not instruct the jury to consider whether Keating intended to swindle the investors (Krasnowski, 2000).

Subsequent to the judge's instructions to the jury, the jury retires to deliberate. These deliberations are not public, and the jury may be sequestered. Sequestration (or jury isolation) is used to ensure that jury members' objectivity in the trial is not deliberately or accidentally tainted. A unanimous verdict by the jury is required in criminal cases. If the jury's verdict is not guilty, the defendant is released. Not guilty verdicts are final. If the defendant is found guilty, the judge may order the probation department to conduct a presentence investigation. A presentence investigation is a comprehensive investigation of the accused's background, including his or hers criminal, social, and employment history. The results of the investigation assist the judge in determining the most appropriate sentence. At sentencing, the judge may impose a fine, jail or prison sentence, probation, or a suspended sentence (Acker & Brody, 2004; Hails, 2012).

Summary

This chapter has shown that the legal and regulatory environment in which security operates involves a mixture of constitutional, criminal, civil, administrative, contract, property, and labor law. The U.S. Constitution governs and regulates state agents and actors. It does not govern the actions of private parties unless these parties violate constitutionally protected rights of individuals granted to them under federal law. Criminal law, meanwhile, is that body of law that relates to crime while civil law governs relationships between individuals and organizations. Security personnel and managers must also be informed of the various administrative laws that regulate human and organizational behaviors that include EEOC and OSHA legislation. Furthermore, since the security industry and personnel are often involved with creating and following contractual agreements, staff and managers must also have a working knowledge of contract law. Finally, since security is concerned with the protection of property and persons, a working understanding of property and employment and labor law is critical. Besides official legal controls, this chapter has also shown that in many cases, the security industry has created its own regulations to complement existing laws and regulations.

This chapter has also reviewed the U.S. legal system and the judicial process. The judiciary in the United States operates in a dual system consisting of federal and state courts. The federal system is relatively straightforward: the lowest court level is district courts followed by the appellate courts—the U.S. court of appeals and the U.S. Supreme Court. State courts differ in name and structure from state to state. State trial courts generally fall into two categories: courts of limited and general jurisdiction. Like the federal courts, states also have appellate courts, including a Supreme Court. This chapter has also reviewed the basic components of the court process that includes the initial appearance, preliminary hearing, arraignment, and trial. Since security personnel can be involved in both criminal and civil cases, a full understanding of their respective state's court structure and processes is important.

Key Terms and Concepts

Discussion Questions and Exercises

1. Describe the U.S. federal court system. Include types, levels, and jurisdiction of courts in the description.
2. What are the elements of a tort?
3. Distinguish a tort from a crime and describe types of situations that give rise to tort liability.
4. Why should a security manager, or any person nominally in charge of a loss prevention function, be familiar with contract, property, administrative, and employment law?
5. What constitutes criminal activity? In other words, what are the essential elements of a crime?
6. Explain and provide an example of industrial self-regulation.
7. What is defamation? How can the claim of defamation be avoided?
8. To what extent is the security industry regulated? How is it regulated?
9. Review your states' court system. Explain each level in detail.
10. What are some defenses under civil law? Explain and provide an example of each.

Your Turn

Researching and Writing a Case Brief

In addition to statutory law, much of the law applicable to the rules of evidence and criminal procedure is the product of judicial decisions (case law) in actual criminal cases. The ability to conduct research on case law, understand a court's reasoning for its decision, and write a synopsis (brief) of the case and the court's opinion can be very helpful to students and practitioners.

Using the following basic legal research and case brief writing guidelines, research and write a brief on a recent appellate court case of your choice.

Guidelines for Legal Research

Official and unofficial appellate court case reports contain the court majority's opinion and the dissenting opinion (if any) in individual cases. Official reports are published by the government and contain the entire text of the court case opinions. Unofficial reports are published by private companies. The following are examples of each, along with their abbreviations.

United States Reports (U.S.)—Official report containing U.S. Supreme Court decisions.

United States Supreme Court Reports—Lawyers Edition (L. Ed.). Unofficial report containing U.S. Supreme Court decisions.

Federal Reporter (F. or F. Rep.)—Official report containing decisions of the 13 U.S. courts of appeals.

American Law Reports (ALR)—Unofficial report containing selected appellate decisions across the United States.

A citation is used to locate a case in a law library.

Example:	Miranda v. Arizona, 384 U.S. 436 (1996).
Case name:	Miranda (appellant) v. Arizona (respondent)
Report volume number:	384
Report symbol:	U.S. (United States Reports)
Report page number:	436
Year of decision:	1966

To locate the case in a law library, proceed to the section containing the relevant reports, select the appropriate volume (numbered on the outside binder of the text), and turn to the designated page number. Learn how to access a law library online through the Law Library of Congress at www.loc.gov/law/public/lawguide. Or, go to your University's library online databases to locate a legal database that contains cases.

Guidelines for Writing the Case Brief

Case briefs contain 400 words or less and usually follow a format similar to the following.

Case name and citation.

Type of case—A statement describing the type of case (criminal or civil) and how the case was brought on appeal to the present appellate court.

Facts—This section contains a brief summary of the key facts of the case.

Issue(s)—This section describes the issues or questions of law the court is asked to decide. Example: Was the evidence seized illegally or unconstitutionally?

Findings—This section contains the ruling (decision, holding) of the present appellate court. The present court may affirm (agree with and let stand) the decision of the lower court or it may reverse (overturn) the lower court's decision and/or remand (send the case back) to the lower court.

Discussion—This section contains the reasons for the present court's findings based on the facts and issues presented.

PART 2

Security Operations
Essential Functions

The chapters in this section of the textbook focus on security's essential functions. These core or essential functions are divided into three main elements: physical, personnel, and information security. These three key components of an effective security program are complementary and overlapping in nature as shown in Figure 4-1 ■.

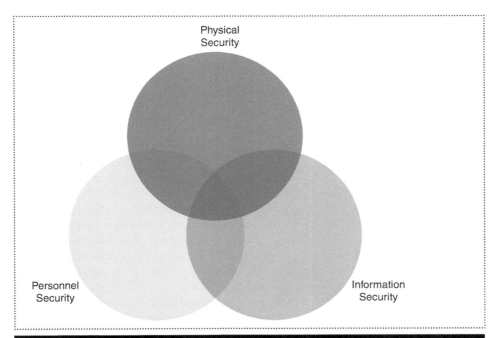

FIGURE 4-1   Core Elements of the Security Function
Source: Patrick J. Ortmeier, Johnson, Introduction to Security: Operations and Management, 5e. © 2018, Pearson Education, Inc., New York, NY.

Chapter 4 focuses on *physical security*, including building security, sensors and systems, fire prevention and protection, and human protection systems. Chapter 5 reviews issues related to *personnel security*, emphasizing the need to protect human assets. *Information security* is the subject of Chapter 6.

4 Physical Security

LEARNING OBJECTIVES

After completing this chapter, the reader should be able to:

1 *describe the basics of defense in depth*

2 *understand and apply the core elements of a physical protection system*

3 *demonstrate knowledge of sensors*

4 *analyze the protective value of building exteriors and interiors*

5 *discuss the importance of lighting*

6 *demonstrate knowledge of different types of access control*

7 *list and describe types of alarm systems*

8 *describe the access control function of security personnel*

9 *explain the importance of having effective fire protection systems*

10 *understand the function of guard forces in a comprehensive physical protection system*

▶ Introduction

Physical security is the first line of defense against human threats. The U.S. Army defines physical security as "that part of security concerned with physical measures designed to safeguard personnel; to prevent unauthorized access to equipment, installations, material, and documents; and to safeguard against espionage, sabotage, damage, and theft….Challenges relative to physical security include the control of populations, information dominance, multinational and interagency connectivity, antiterrorism, and the use of physical security assets as a versatile force multiplier." (Field Manual, 2001; p1-1) Facility perimeters, tangible property, personnel, and information are protected using an appropriate combination of physical security measures that use the elements of lighting, hardware, equipment, human agents, and policies and procedures. These elements form protective systems that target harden assets against both internal and external human adversaries.

▶ Physical Security Systems

To protect against human-based threats, organizations need to have well-designed and comprehensive physical security programs. Any effective physical security program encompasses two mutually supporting elements. It includes physical protective measures, which are basically the physical elements of security (lighting, locks, fences, sensors, etc.)

that are designed to protect specific assets. In addition, there are procedural security measures. These are policies and procedures that are in place to address a security concern (FM 3-19, 2001). These policies and procedures are the pillar or foundation for any security program. For example, a company could have sophisticated security technologies. However, if the company does not have effective policies and procedures that regulate the use and response to these systems, security forces may not know what to do, making these technologies worthless.

procedural security measures Policies and procedures that are in place to address a security issue/concern.

An effective physical security program integrates equipment, people, and procedures to protect an organization from threats (Garcia, 2001). These programs should be based on the concept of defense in depth. Defense in depth strategies use a layered approach to security where mutually supporting security countermeasures are used to protect assets (Field Manual, 2001).

defense in depth Strategies that use a layered approach to security where mutually supporting security countermeasures are used to protect assets.

Perhaps the best way to understand defense in depth strategies is to think of them as the layers of an onion. Like an onion, a security program should have multiple layers of interconnected security functions that an adversary would need to defeat or "peel away" in order to succeed in his efforts. The strategy for defense of any asset focuses on the outer perimeter and progresses through the inner perimeter, areas within a building, rooms, and specific assets in those rooms. In this sense, countermeasures form concentric circles of protection around an asset (see Chapter 12 for a diagram of defense in depth). This layered effect provides a greater degree of protection than a single layer. Since several different types of countermeasures may be necessary to combat each threat, these countermeasures should complement rather than compete with each other.

Comprehensive defense in depth programs are far more effective than other security measures that exist. In some cases, organizations use a "plugging the hole" approach to physical security, which is a piecemeal approach to security where an organization adds a new technology in response to a security issue or event to "fix" an issue that arises. Other approaches can include "more is better," which is based on the idea that adding more layers of security is better, which may not be the case. Finally, the "silver bullet" analogy is based on the belief that high tech solutions will fix the security issue (Nunes-Vaz & Lord, 2014). While they may work, what all of these approaches fail to consider is how these measures complement or contribute to the comprehensive goals of a security program.

The goal of defense in depth is to deter and defeat an adversary's actions. Deterrence-based strategies are designed to deter an adversary from committing the act. These strategies make the facility or the particular target unattractive or too difficult to defeat in the mind of the adversary (Garcia, 2001, 2006). For example, in some instances, a "No Trespassing" sign or a fence may deter a person from accessing private property. In other cases, where the adversary is highly motivated and is seeking a high value asset, other forms of physical security will be needed to deter the individual from committing the act while also stopping, denying, or defeating the adversary's actions through a variety of security measures. With defeat, meanwhile, an effective security program will ensure that the adversary fails in his or her efforts.

deterrence-based strategies Security strategies to deter an adversary from committing the act.

▶ Levels of Protection

The level of protection that an organization needs depends on the asset(s) that needs to be protected. While no physical protection system (PPS) is 100 percent defeat-proof, an appropriately designed program can nevertheless strive for the 100 percent goal through an effective PPS. There are some examples of protection levels. Following the 1995 bombing of the Murrah Federal Building in Oklahoma City, President William Jefferson Clinton

FEDERAL SECURITY LEVELS

- **Level I**—buildings with no more than 2,500 square feet, 10 or fewer federal employees, and limited or no public access;
- **Level II**—buildings with 2,500 to 80,000 square feet, 11 to 150 federal employees, and moderate public access;
- **Level III**—buildings with 80,000 to 150,000 square feet, 151 to 450 federal employees, and moderate to high public access;
- **Level IV**—buildings with 150,000 square feet or more, more than 450 federal employees, and a high level of public access; and
- **Level V**—buildings that are similar to Level IV but are considered critical to national security (e.g., the Pentagon).

Source: Reese (2014).

established the *Interagency Security Committee* (ISC). Chaired by the Department of Homeland Security, the ISC is composed of representatives from approximately 53 federal agencies; the goal of this committee is to develop model physical security standards for federal buildings, based on the threats and vulnerabilities present and industry best practices (Interagency Security Committee, 2013). The U.S. government also classifies facilities by security levels where the higher the level, the greater is the threat level, and the need for more security (Reese, 2014). These levels can be found in Box 4-1.

Another example of security levels is presented by Vellani (2007):

Level 1—Minimum Protection. Designed to *impede some unauthorized external threat activity*. Examples include using locks and simple barriers to restrict access to restrooms and stockrooms in retail stores.

Level 2—Low-Level Protection. Designed to *impede and detect some unauthorized external threat activity*. Includes the use of basic local alarms, physical barriers, security lighting, and high-security locks. Examples of settings where this level of protection would be provided include low-risk parking facilities, office buildings open to public access, and shopping centers.

Level 3—Medium Protection. Designed to *impede, detect, and assess most unauthorized external threat activity*. Includes the use of high-security physical barriers, monitored alarm systems, security personnel, and a basic communications system. Examples include perimeter protection, including chain-link fences for elementary schools in high-crime neighborhoods, and data centers.

Level 4—High-Level Protection. Designed to *impede, detect, and assess most unauthorized external and internal threat activity*. Includes the use of perimeter alarms, surveillance systems, security personnel, advanced communications systems, access controls, high-security lighting, coordination with local public law enforcement, and formal contingency plans. Examples of settings requiring such protection include major hospitals and most government buildings.

Level 5—Maximum Protection. Designed to *impede, detect, assess, and neutralize all unauthorized external and internal threat activity*. Includes the use of on-site armed security response personnel and sophisticated alarm systems (Gigliotti & Jason, 1999). Examples of settings requiring such protection include nuclear power facilities and courthouses.

► Core Elements of Physical Protection Systems

Any effective security program must rely upon countermeasures. Countermeasures are actions directed against threats or the actions of adversaries. Generally, countermeasures used in any physical security program include site work, building, detection, and procedural elements. Common site work elements, which is anything beyond 5 feet from the facility or asset, include landforms (such as hills or depressions), standoff distances, and perimeter barriers such as fences that could assist or impede security efforts (Field Manual, 2001; Steffey, 2008). Another site work practice is to ensure that there are clear zones around assets, so detection elements can readily detect threats in the protection zone. Building elements are protective elements associated directly with making structures more resilient to the actions of an adversary. These include what the building is constructed of (brick, concrete, wood, metal), as well as windows, roofs, and doors (Field Manual, 2001). For example, in Israel, many existing structures are hardened against terrorist attacks by retrofitting walls, doors, and windows to be more resistant against blasts and projectiles (Eytan, 2005). Next, there are detection elements. Detection elements detect adversaries, weapons, contraband, and other threats. These elements include various technologies and security personnel. Last, there are *procedural elements*. These are the policies and standard operating procedures for security operations and personnel. These elements are the foundation for the other three elements of an effective security program (Field Manual, 2001).

Any well-designed PPS also uses: (1) Detection; (2) Delay; and (3) Response functions that are used in a defense in depth approach.

Detection-based elements discover an adversary's actions. These detection-based strategies rely upon various sensors and human beings to detect the actions of adversaries. Their primary purpose is to alert security staff (and others) that a security issue may exist. Sensors, for example, detect an action and then generate an alarm which is assessed by guard forces. In some cases, visible sensors can deter a human adversary. Visible sensors, for example, may make an adversary change his or her mind to enter a facility. Generally, technology-based sensors are more effective in detecting an adversary's actions than human beings. Human beings, however, are nevertheless very important in assessing if a security issue exists (Garcia, 2006). Humans are also very important detection elements in screening and access control activities where they can examine individuals and materials moving in and out of the facility.

Delay functions are designed to slow an adversary's progress. Some delay-based measures include fences, locks, physical barriers, concrete walls, and security forces. The goal behind delay functions is to slow an adversary from reaching the asset. Delay effectiveness is measured in the time required by an adversary (after being detected) to circumvent or defeat each delay element that is present. Delay functions also increase the time period for guard forces to respond to the adversary (Garcia, 2001; 2006).

Response strategies interrupt the actions of an adversary. An effective response strategy requires the detection of an adversary who is also delayed, so a guard force can have enough time to verify and respond to the threat. The goal of a response is to interrupt and neutralize the adversary's actions. Without an immediate response to a threat, the risk of loss increases (Garcia, 2006).

A well-designed security program should examine the potential threats in a 360 degree perspective, identifying potential vulnerabilities above, under, and around the asset to be protected. For example, one large grocery chain built a new distribution warehouse that included a secure storage area for pharmaceuticals. When building the large vault-like structure in the warehouse, the concrete floor of the pharmacy vault was approximately 10 feet thick and included vibration-related sensors to detect any signs of tunneling. Well-designed programs also use the defense in depth approach, beginning with the

countermeasures
Actions directed against man-made and natural threats.

site work elements
Anything beyond 5 feet from the facility/asset that could assist or impede security efforts.

building elements
Protective elements associated directly with making structures more resilient to the actions of an adversary.

detection elements
Detect adversaries, weapons, contraband, and other threats.

sensor Device that senses a specific condition, including motion, sound, temperature, or vibration.

guard forces Proprietary, contract or hybrid security personnel.

exterior of the facility and subsequently working inward. Well-designed programs also allow for the continuous and uninterrupted surveillance of threats (Tyska & Fennelly, 2000). For example, if a threat should enter the facility and then advance deeper into the complex, sensors and cameras should be able to continually monitor the adversaries' actions and progress.

▶ Perimeter Security

The security of any facility begins with a continuous line of security along its perimeter in order to prevent adversaries from entering the facility or attacking an asset. When evaluating what type of physical security is necessary, it is important to identify security vulnerabilities and the surrounding environment. If a new facility is planned, management is well advised to conduct a site survey to determine the availability of public services, analyze crime rates, and evaluate human threats. Natural barriers should not be discounted. In some instances, natural barriers, such as streams, lakes, and rugged terrain, are excellent perimeter controls.

One of the key considerations for perimeter security is standoff zones. A standoff zone is the distance of the asset from the threat. In the context of perimeter security, it is the distance from the external perimeter of the property to the asset being protected. The goal of any standoff zone is to keep threats as far away from the assets being protected. For example, if a building is 200 yards from a public roadway, this standoff distance would allow for the effective use of surveillance cameras and sensors to detect and then assess any potential threats entering the property. However, if this distance was only 20 feet, the small standoff distance would impede the assessment and response to threats, since staff would most likely not have the time to respond to the threat. Areas within standoff zones can be further divided to increase security. Nonexclusive zones are the distance from the perimeter to the asset being protected. These zones limit access to some degree. For example, only employees could enter the nonexclusive zone and park in company parking lots. Next, there are exclusive zones located within the nonexclusive zone. Here, certain individuals are allowed to progress to the asset being protected by foot, followed by using their card access to enter the building, followed by a search of the person at a controlled entry point (Remennikov & Carolan, 2005). A diagram of these zones can be found in Figure 4-2 ■.

> **standoff zone** The distance of the asset from the threat.

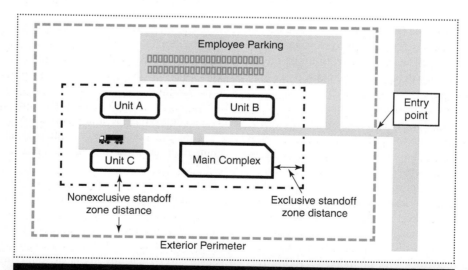

FIGURE 4-2 Standoff zones.
Source: Adapted from FM 3-19 Army Publication.

The standoff distance should be based on the different types of threats that an organization may be vulnerable to. For example, standards by the U.S. Department of State (2014) for the construction of new foreign U.S. embassy office buildings call for a minimum 100 foot standoff distance from the perimeter of the U.S. property and the building exterior in order to protect the structure from car bomb attacks. The U.S. Army has a design strategy that calls for the greatest distance possible for a standoff distance, followed by hardened exterior walls on buildings to protect against armed adversaries (Field Manual, 2001).

► Lighting

One of the best and least expensive security measures is artificial lighting. Lighting should be considered an inner as well as an outer defense. Many crimes are committed because the opportunity for detection is limited. Light increases the likelihood of detection and it also serves as a deterrent. To ensure detection, continuous and even lighting is necessary to protect assets. Portable lighting should also be available for special needs. Emergency or standby lighting is also used during power failures to ensure adequate levels of illumination (Ricks, Tillet, & Van Meter, 1988).

Perimeter lighting illuminates the perimeter of the protection zone. It can involve the use of streetlights, floodlights, searchlights, and Fresnel lights (which provide a long, narrow, horizontal beam without glare). Floodlights, for example, are typically used at facility boundaries to deter intruders. Artificial perimeter lighting can also be mounted on freestanding masts and towers, walls, or other structures.

> **perimeter lighting**
> Use of street lights, floodlights, search lights, and Fresnel lights to illuminate facility perimeter and/or protection zone.

Light fixtures should be tamper-resistant while the wiring must not be exposed to damage or a possible intruder. A backup power supply or generator should be available to support lights in the event of a power failure for both interior and exterior lighting. Building exterior openings, doors, and windows should also be illuminated to deter and increase the ability to detect adversaries.

The proper design of security lighting can be complex. The amount of illumination, which is the quantity of light shining directly on an object, depends on the purpose of the lighting and what is being illuminated (Doboli et al., 2008). As a general rule, artificial lighting should provide even coverage of the assessment zone (the area under observation), allowing for no dark areas which could serve as an area for concealment. Lighting should also be used continuously, and in some cases it should not just be used at night. Artificial lighting should be used in any situation where natural light is not sufficient to effectively monitor an area, or where the contrast between lighting/darkness creates a safety issue for employees. Generally, complex tasks and smaller and darker objects that need to be observed require more light to properly surveil than larger ones (Garcia, 2006). In operations areas, such as workspaces, the amount of lighting and brightness required is usually much higher than for security purposes. Protective lighting must be of sufficient brightness to permit adequate human or technological surveillance, illuminate exit routes, identify hazards to prevent personal injury, and create a psychological barrier to unauthorized intrusion. Protective lighting must also be positioned to avoid glare that might reduce visibility for security personnel and others with authorized access to a facility. Lighting standards must also comply with industry standards, which are established by the American National Standards Institute (ANSI) and security organizations.

Security managers also need to consider what types of lamps to use, based in part of their application, the environment they will be operating in, and the initial and maintenance costs associated with lamps and fixtures themselves. Commonly referred to as bulbs or tubes, lamps generally fall into six categories. The oldest and most common type is the incandescent lamp, which produces light by heating a filament. Although inexpensive to purchase initially, the incandescent lamp is the least efficient and most expensive in the long term because most of the energy consumed by the lamp creates more heat rather than light. Mercury vapor lamps produce a strong light with a bluish cast, have a long lamp life, and can tolerate low temperatures. However, they have a long start-up time. Florescent lamps are typical of a mercury vapor type and are highly efficient. They are temperature sensitive and may have limited value in cold climates. Metal halide lamps are expensive, but they depict true colors and can tolerate low temperatures. They are often used in stadium lighting. However, like mercury vapor lamps, metal halide lamps require considerable start-up and restart time. Therefore, they are not practical where continuous lighting is necessary. Frequently used in transportation environments or areas where fog is common, sodium vapor lamps emit a soft yellowish light that penetrates moisture. Produced as low-pressure or high-pressure lamps, sodium vapor lamps are more efficient than mercury vapor lamps. Quartz lamps are excellent sources of illumination for perimeter control systems. They emit a very bright white light, and the start-up time is short (Ricks et al., 1988). New lighting technologies, including LED lamps, may also be an effective illumination option because the lamps have a long life that reduces replacement and maintenance costs. They also save energy and even attract fewer insects because they do not emit ultraviolet light that insects are attracted to (Bessho & Shimizu, 2012).

▶ Fencing and Barriers

Security-related fencing is a common perimeter control used as part of a comprehensive security program. Although fences typically provide minimum security, they mark and define the perimeter, delay an intruder, channel employees and visitors to appropriate areas, and act as a platform for alarm sensors. Fences should be considered to be a deterrent only, even though they can delay and defeat the actions of some adversaries (Garcia, 2006). Depending on the aesthetic qualities desired and balanced with the security need, fences may be constructed of wood, masonry, or wire. Wood, stone, brick, and masonry fences possess aesthetic qualities not typical of wire fences. However, unlike wire fences, solid barriers obstruct visibility of the area outside the fence. If concealment of inside

Nuclear plant security—protective layers. A barbed wire fence that provides a physical layer of protection at a nuclear facility.
(Photo courtesy of U.S. Nuclear Regulatory Commission.)

activities to passersby is a consideration, solid walls are very effective. In some cases, organizations may also use barbed wire or concertina wire as a form of temporary fencing, or use it to enhance existing security measures in a facility.

Chain-link fencing is the most commonly used type of perimeter fence. It requires little maintenance, is simple to erect, and provides for greater visibility in comparison to wood or masonry forms of perimeter control. To be fully effective, chain-link fences should be constructed of 11 gauge or heavier wire, and be at least 8 feet high, with mesh of 2 square inches or less (Reid, 2005). For maximum security effectiveness where appearance may not be a concern, barbed, razor ribbon, or concertina wire as fence treatment or a top guard may be added to the top of the 8-foot chain-link fence. The addition of top guard increases a fence's deterrent value while also serving to delay or slow the actions of the adversary (American Public Transportation Association, 2010).

Basic requirements for security fencing are that it should be straight and free from any obstructions (such as weed and brush). Straight fences allow for effective surveillance and limit areas of concealment of adversaries. Fences should also have clear zones on each side in order to enhance surveillance so a threat does not bypass or easily defeat the fencing (Garcia, 2006). For example, if a tree is located in close proximity to a fence, an adversary could use the tree as a bypass, using the tree as means to scale the fence. The bottom of the fence should also be secured to prevent lifting or crawling under by tying the lower edge of the fence to rigid metal straps or weaving steel cables through the mesh to prevent it from being lifted. If the earth below the fence is loose or subject to erosion, the fence should be buried and secured below ground level. To maintain the protective integrity of a fence, sensors may also be added. Electromagnetic and fiber optic cables, taut wire, vibration, and CCTV cameras can also be used for this purpose. Periodic and random security patrols should also be used to ensure fence integrity and to check for any signs of tampering or intrusion (Fitzhenry, 2007; U.S. General Services Administration, 2011).

Every opening in a fence presents a potential security risk. These openings (called portals) should be kept to a minimum, and access through gates should be controlled by security personnel, sensors, or other access control devices, such as card access. Some of the common fence portals include hinged mesh gates, turnstiles, decorative wrought iron gate and gate-arms that can be operated manually or electronically (Hicks, Snell, Sandoval, & Potter, 1999). Obviously, there should be sufficient openings to accommodate the safe and efficient movement of pedestrian and vehicular traffic. A careful analysis of needs and traffic patterns will determine how many openings are necessary.

There are other types of physical barriers that security personnel can use to define public from private spaces while target hardening certain locations. *Vehicle barrier systems* may be a need for some organizations. Depending upon the security threat, these can be quite strong and technologically advanced, having the ability to stop large vehicles from entering the facility while also deflecting blast waves or pressures away from the assets being protected (Ellison & Brokaw, 2014). Vehicle barriers are classified as flexible or rigid. Flexible barriers move to some degree when struck by a vehicle. They include mesh fences, cables, and even large decorative concrete planters that will slow a vehicle's movement (Terry & Tholen, 2006). One type of flexible barrier is the *Jersey Barrier*. These are modular concrete barriers that can be used to prevent and control traffic flow and speed, or deter vehicular traffic. They can be set up in a wall fashion to prevent vehicles from entering an area or be used to separate vehicles into lanes. In other cases, they can be set up in a serpentine manner, forcing a vehicle to slowly weave its way through the barriers, allowing detection elements (including guards) to assess the threat level of the vehicle and its occupants (Stanford, 2007). Another type of flexible barriers are the *traffic treadles* that shred and deflate vehicle tires. These retractable spike-like barriers can be permanently mounted into the driving surface or used in a temporary application where they can be manually or automatically deployed. Rigid barriers withstand large kinetic energy forces and prevent a

The active vehicle barrier system, or pop-up barrier, is designed to physically prevent unauthorized vehicles from entering Joint Base Andrews. The pop-up barriers are hydraulic, manually operated, systems that deploy in just over one second. As a safety feature, there are light systems immediately next to each barrier.
(Photo courtesy of Joint Base Andrews.)

vehicle from running over or pushing the barrier out of the way (Terry & Tholen, 2006). These include cylindrical bollards that vary in size and strength (Liu, Li, Phang, & Sun, 2008). These bollards are designed to deter and stop vehicles from accessing a certain area. They can be fixed or stationary, and they can be retractable, allowing security personnel to manually or electronically rise or lower them into a secure concrete foundation to allow vehicular access. There are also *wedge barriers* that are electronic or hydraulically operated retractable barriers that are securely mounted in a solid foundation. By their construction, they are designed to stop large vehicles from entering a protected area (Murray-Tuite, 2007).

▶ Sensors

Sensors measure changes in something. Based on these changes, they can sound an alarm, alerting security personnel to assess the situation that led to the alarm activation. There are various sensor classifications. They can be classified as active or passive, covert or visible, line of sight or terrain following, and volumetric or line. They are also classified by their mode of application (Garcia, 2001; 2006).

Active sensors emit energy. By emitting energy these sensors basically function by detecting changes in the signal from the amount of energy being sent out and then received (Rajendran & Rathinasabapathy, 2007). An ultrasonic motion sensor transmits an extremely high (beyond a human being's audible range) sound energy that fills the volume of a protected area (e.g., a room). When an object or a person moves through the protected area, the motion creates a shift in the frequency of the transmitted sound energy, known as a Doppler shift. The shifted frequency is detected (sensed) by one or more receivers, and an alarm is activated. Microwave motion sensors are similar in operation to ultrasonic motion sensors except that microwave systems utilize high-end radio frequencies rather than sound. Microwave sensor units transmit microwave energy and detect the energy as it is reflected from objects and returned to the transmitter/receiver unit (Guo, Tiller, Henze, & Waters, 2010).

ultrasonic motion sensor Transmits extremely high frequency (beyond a human being's audible range) sound energy.

microwave motion sensor Sensor that utilizes high-end radio frequencies rather than sound. Similar in operation to ultrasonic motion sensor.

Passive sensors absorb and measure changes in energy. They do not emit energy or a signal *per se*. Instead, they monitor an area for changes. A common passive sensor would be temperature-related, where a certain rate in rise over a set period of time would activate an alarm. For example, passive infrared sensors are designed to detect changes in heat or thermal energy (Keller, 1993). If a person with a body temperature of 98.6 degrees Fahrenheit passes through a protected area with a temperature of 70 degrees Fahrenheit, the infrared sensor will detect the person's presence through his infrared radiation and activate an alarm.

There are also vibration and acoustic sensors that can be mounted on objects or even buried. In addition, there are capacitance-based sensors that measure changes in an electrical field. Also known also as a proximity sensor, these sensors measure changes in capacitance (electrical charges) as a human body enters (or something else that can hold an electrical charge) an electronic field (Sullivant, 2007). For example, a safe or a file cabinet may have a capacitance sensor attached to it. When a human being touches the safe, the electronic field is changed, which is subsequently detected by the sensor.

There are two other ways to classify sensors. Sensors can be line of sight (LOS) or terrain following. LOS sensors require a clear "line of sight" between the sensor's sending and receiving unit. Terrain-following sensors follow the contours of the terrain, allowing for full coverage of the area with no "blind spots" that could exist with the LOS sensor if the terrain is uneven. Sensors can also be classified according to their detection zones. Volumetric sensors are designed to fill a certain area, such as a room. Line detection sensors have a detection zone along a specific line. An example of a line sensor would be a fence that has sensors placed on it. Here, the detection zone is the fence itself. Finally, how the sensor is used needs to be considered. Some different applications include buried line, fence-associated sensors, and freestanding sensors that are not buried or mounted on a fence (Garcia, 2001; Harman & Messner, 2012). An example of a buried active sensor would be an invisible pet fence. Here, a transmitter emits a radio signal from a wire that is buried around the perimeter of a yard. As a dog approaches the perimeter where the wire is buried, the receiver unit (which is a part of the dog's collar) receives the signal from the buried wire, sounding an audible alarm and then delivering a shock, hopefully preventing the dog from moving closer to or outside the perimeter.

> **passive infrared sensor** Detects changes in heat or thermal energy (infrared light radiation) in protected area.

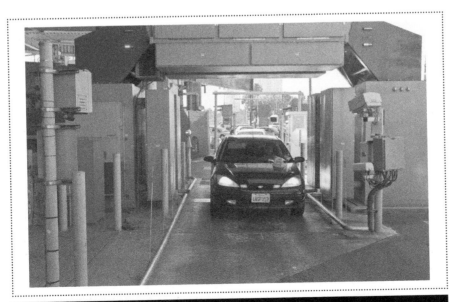

Sensor photo. Border crossing X-ray at San Ysidro.
(Photo courtesy of Josh Denmark/U.S. Customs and Border Protection.)

The type of sensors used depends upon cost, the asset that needs to be protected, and environmental conditions. For example, if the cost of a sensor (including the cost of using it) is more expensive than the asset that needs to be protected, management may want to re-evaluate the need for that type of sensor. Also, all sensors have their limitations. In order to compensate for these limitations, an effective security program will use multiple types of sensors simultaneously that are mounted covertly or visibly, and oftentimes buried or tied into other physical security applications, such as fences. Many manufacturers also market dual technology sensors that, for example, incorporate passive infrared and microwave technologies to ensure a higher probability of detection (Guo et al., 2010).

When using sensors, security personnel need to be aware of false and nuisance alarms. The goal of any sensor is to have as close to a 100 percent probability of detection along with a 0 percent nuisance alarm rate. Nuisance alarms are caused by an event that is not a true intrusion or a security issue. Nuisance alarms occur when the sensor is working properly, but it does not detect a threat. For example, motion-related sensors could detect wildlife, vibration-related sensors mounted on fencing could activate in high winds while similar buried vibration sensors placed near roadways could lead to nuisance alarms because of the vibration associated with heavy vehicles driving on the adjacent road. A false alarm, meanwhile, is the result of a defect in the sensor or its application. Here, the sensor did not detect anything—it was a false alarm because of a defect in the equipment (or installation). In these cases, the source of the alarm cannot be determined or verified since it is a defect in the sensor itself (Dabling, McLaughlin, & Andersen, 2012; Garcia, 2006).

nuisance alarm An alarm caused by an event that is not a true intrusion or security issue.

false alarm An alarm that is activated as a result of a defect in the sensor itself or its application.

▶ Alarm Systems

Sensors are one element of an alarm system. An alarm system includes an array of interconnected parts designed to function as a unit. An alarm is a communicator designed to notify a receiver of an issue. Today, alarm systems range from simple to complex and are used to detect fire, intrusion, medical emergencies, and other safety and security concerns. They can be used to secure perimeters and buildings as well as sensitive areas within a facility. They may also be used to control energy consumption, and alert the staff of any mechanical failures that could compromise the organization in some way.

Every alarm system consists of three basic components: (1) a triggering, initiating, or activation device, or a sensor (detector) that detects a condition; (2) an alarm system circuit that transmits information; and (3) an annunciator (signal) that notifies the recipient of the detected condition. The alarm system circuit is the communication link between the sensor and the annunciator. In some cases, the circuit also connects with an audio–video recorder or communications device. A circuit communicates via wire, radio wave, electric circuit, telephone line, fiber-optic cable, microwave, satellite, or a combination of these. Advances in fiber-optic technology greatly improved materials available for alarm circuitry. Optical fiber transfers a pulsating light through a fine glass, or fiber. Optical fiber transmission has many advantages over other types of circuits. Fiber optics cables are low cost, safe to operate, and immune to interference from other power sources. At the end of a circuit, the annunciator notifies, or signals, a recipient that an event (intrusion, fire, medical emergency) is taking place. Annunciators include audible or silent signals, such as a light, bell, buzzer, horn, or siren, or a visual text display on a computer screen (Bowers, 2013).

alarm Communicator designed to notify a receiver of an issue.

annunciator Signaling device that notifies recipient of detected alarm condition.

alarm system circuit Communication link between alarm sensor and annunciator.

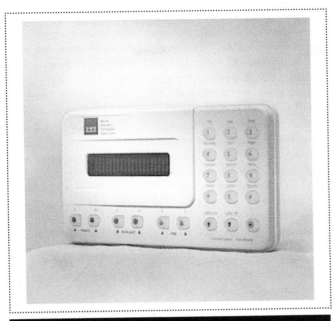

Alarm control system touchpad.
(Photo courtesy of Interlogix, Inc.)

Alarm systems can be grouped into four basic categories. A local alarm system, such as a car alarm, notifies anyone who is within hearing distance. A proprietary alarm system is owned and operated on site by the user and requires continuous control-panel monitoring. A *public alarm system* is connected directly to a public 911 emergency dispatch center or a local police department. A central station alarm system, although similar to the proprietary system, may be monitored at a remote location. Utilizing modern communications technology, a central station alarm system can have a sensor in New York City with an annunciator in San Diego, California. Central station alarm systems also allow for monitoring of numerous locations simultaneously. Typically, a telephone dialer in a central processing unit (CPU) located at the facility where the event is occurring sends a signal through the circuit to the central station. The CPU is the brain for the system. It receives, processes, stores, and transmits information detected by the sensors. Most CPUs also have fail-safe mechanisms that notify the central station when electric power to the alarmed facility has been interrupted (National Fire Protection Association, 2007; Sweet, 2006; Trimmer, 1999; U.S. General Services Administration, 2011).

Alarm System Management

An improvement in protection usually results when alarm systems are properly installed and monitored continuously. Otherwise, continuous protection can only be achieved by assigning personnel to observe the protected area. However, over time, using personnel in lieu of alarm systems is costly. Alarm systems, although expensive to purchase and install, are usually economical in the long run and provide a substantial return on the initial investment. Security professionals must recognize that alarm systems are becoming very sophisticated. The increased use of automated, personal computer (PC)-based technologies to perform critical security monitoring functions presents new challenges for the security manager.

local alarm system When activated, produces an alarm signal in the immediate vicinity of the protected premises.

proprietary alarm system Alarm system owned and operated onsite by the protected user.

central station alarm system Alarm system that is monitored from a facility at a remote location. The central station may monitor several alarm systems simultaneously.

The manager must be able to effectively integrate electronic technologies into the total security management system in a way that does not conflict with an organization's operational environment. Therefore, the security manager's ability to control risk with minimal operational interference is determined by certain critical alarm systems design and integrated decision-making functions: the relevance and completeness of the risk assessment, the degree of the security alarm system's applicability to the facility, the quality of the equipment selected and its installation, and how the system facilitates organizational operations. Careful planning and management of alarm systems will help avoid the costs associated with events such as false alarms while reducing costs through integrated systems design (Gallagher & Grassie, 2000; "Sun Microsystems integrates access control worldwide," 2000; Wilberg Fitzsimons, 2000).

The first step to effective alarm system management involves identifying alarm points. These are specific locations where sensors and alarms will be placed. They are basically substitutes for human security guards, and they must correspond to and tie into the organization's comprehensive PPS (Fay, 2007). Some issues security managers must consider include:

- determining how and when the facility operates and who uses the facility.
- identifying assets, threats, vulnerabilities, and security countermeasure requirements.
- integrating the concept of security operations with organizational (facility) operations.
- defining alarm point active and inactive times.

After alarm points are identified and integrated with facility operations, the security manager can develop effective alarm response procedures. These procedures should be concise, unambiguous, consistent, and tailored to each specific alarm point, with consideration given to the time necessary for the response. Finally, alarm monitoring and response personnel must receive training consistent with the operational demands of the system. Without appropriate alarm systems management, even the best-intentioned capital investment in systems can become difficult for the security manager to administer.

Security systems integration is the unification of all computer-based systems (including security systems) into one system in order to control any issue or situation an organization may experience (Davies & Hertig, 2007). This practice is advancing rapidly as the availability of new technologies provides unprecedented levels of performance and effectiveness for security systems. Experts outline at least seven trends in security systems integration:

- Standardization of operating systems is often insisted upon by information technology departments to simplify support requirements.
- Computer networks, such as local area networks (LAN), are replacing dedicated security hardware as the standard infrastructure for connecting security system components.
- Regarding card-key access and card-reader technologies, magstripe cards continue in use where cost is a consideration. However, the overwhelming choice for new card-key access systems involves the use of proximity card technology since patents for proximity cards and card readers are about to expire and the cost should decrease considerably.
- There is greater integration of systems so that useful information can be shared, enabling more intelligent operational decisions and often reducing costs of operation.
- Video recording and transmission standards are shifting from analog to digital technology. Higher processor power as well as increased speed and memory capacity are cited as the major reasons for the shift toward digital technology.

> **alarm system management** Alarm point definition (identification) and integration with facility operations, the development of effective alarm response procedures, and training of alarm monitoring and response personnel.

> **alarm points** Identified points where sensors and alarms are placed.

- The demand for asset tracking capability has been heightened by an increase in thefts of small high-value items, such as computer laptops. The challenge for the security manager involves the task of designing, managing, and maintaining sophisticated, large-scale security systems. Facing the challenge requires the development of new skills by security personnel.

- Real-time online access to security video recordings and associated alarm event information is increasing. Online access to video recordings of events such as alarm verifications, facility openings and closings, and officer patrols allows personnel to view activities anytime from anywhere (Coleman, 2000; Fitzhenry, 2007; Gallagher & Grassie, 2000; Sweet, 2006).

Additional information regarding alarm systems may be obtained by contacting the Central Station Alarm Association at communications@csaaul.org or the National Burglar and Fire Alarm Association at www.alarm.org.

▶ Building Exteriors and Interiors

In addition to physical security mechanisms, including barriers, lighting, alarms, locks, and personnel, organizations also control and restrict access into general and specific locations within their organizations. The underlying goal behind these physical security systems is that they should control and limit access to certain areas and assets. Access control also applies to information and technologies in organizations.

Access Control

Like other forms of physical security, access control can be examined using the principles of defense in depth or a layered approach to security. The building exterior, often referred to by architects as the *envelope*, includes the walls, doors, windows, and locking devices. The roof and main floors should be hardened and alarmed, if possible. The roof of a building is often overlooked when protection features are incorporated into building design. Usually constructed with lightweight and easily penetrated materials, a roof is rarely alarmed, and visibility of the roof is often restricted. Therefore, intruders may gain access to a building through the roof without detection. Likewise, floors, especially those in multistory buildings, provide access if adequate security does not prevent access from an occupancy located below the protected enterprise. Exterior walls should be constructed of intrusion-resistant and impact-resistant materials. This also applies to walls in common with adjoining occupancies. Access to a business can be gained easily if the common wall with an adjacent business is constructed merely of wood or metal studs and drywall, plaster, or paneling (Reid, 2005; San Luis, Tyska, & Fennelly, 1994).

Doors and other exterior openings are another security issue. Exterior doors should be solidly constructed. Hinges with nonremovable pins should be located on the inside. Door frames, locks, and panels are also extremely vulnerable to attack. The frame of the door should resist prying or spreading with a crowbar. Exterior door locks should be high-quality and intrusion-resistant. Although high-quality modern door locks are pick-resistant, many can be slipped or pulled if the tools required are available. Door panels should be solid and 2 inches thick. Steel plates may be used to reinforce door interiors. Windows in door panels can be reinforced with bars or steel mesh or constructed of impact-resistant materials. Other

access control
Activities that limit access to a facility or certain locations.

exterior openings larger than 96 square inches should receive special attention. Air ducts, elevator shafts, skylights, and windows should be covered with security glass (known as glazing in the field of security) or protective screening and, if possible, be alarmed. Unauthorized human intrusion into a building is often accomplished by entering through a window (Perdikaris 2014; Roper, 1997; San Luis et al., 1994).

Next, physical access controls should deter individuals from entering a location. Deterrence-based access control strategies could include signage and even greeters that through their actions establish a sense of territoriality. The next layer includes gates, doors, and locks and procedural controls that limit the movement of individuals. The goal behind all of these strategies is to control and limit the flow of traffic, allowing individuals access to some areas while restricting the movement of individuals in other cases. If the interior of a building has been designed properly, activities may be assigned to functional areas based on their level of risk and vulnerability to loss. Sensitive and high-risk areas should be located deep within the building and away from the building's exterior. These areas can be target hardened with intruder-, fire-, and disaster-resistant materials as well as alarm and access control devices and personnel (Fischer & Green, 2008; Hess & Wrobleski, 2009).

Locks

Locking devices are used to deter the undetermined and delay the determined. Locks tend to increase the amount of time required for an intruder to gain access to a protected area. They are delay devices only. They increase the probability of detection and apprehension if used in conjunction with sensors and alarm systems and if security personnel are available to respond to the affected area.

Key-operated locks are the most common. Examples include most padlocks and door locks. A notched key is inserted into a keyway containing obstacles or tumblers that can be bypassed by using the correct key. When the appropriate key is turned, a bolt, arm, or shank in the locking device is moved. In the case of a doorknob, rotating the key inside the keyway inserts or withdraws a bolt to or from a strike plate hole embedded in the door frame, thus opening or closing the lock. The lock's bolt can be a spring-loaded bolt or a deadbolt. Spring-loaded bolts (latches) automatically enter the strike plate when the door is closed. Deadbolts require insertion and rotation of a key or operation of a thumb latch to secure the bolt in the strike plate. Spring-loaded bolt locks, unless otherwise protected by a latch guard or metal plate, are easily compromised by slipping a knife or a screwdriver between the door and the jamb, moving the bolt, thus releasing the spring. Deadbolt locks are not spring-loaded and require manual operation with a key. Deadbolt locks with an antiwrenching exterior collar and a minimum 1-inch throw into the strike plate hole provide the best security where key-operated locks are used (Fennelly, 2012; Ricks et al., 1988).

Obviously, key control is a very important consideration with any key-based lock system. An inventory of the keys, as well as a key assignment record is vital to system integrity. One major disadvantage to key-based systems surfaces when locks must be rekeyed frequently. Organizations with numerous locations or high personnel attrition may find it necessary to rekey often. The cost can be considerable. However, the expense associated with rekeying can be reduced by utilizing multiuse, instant rekeying lock systems. These systems allow up to 12 easy-to-complete key sequence changes during the life of the lock cylinder, thus reducing labor expenses associated with locksmith-assisted hardware changes. A special lock-change key is inserted into the keyway and rotated, and the cylinder is reprogrammed for a new key set (Fennelly, 2012; Ricks et al., 1988).

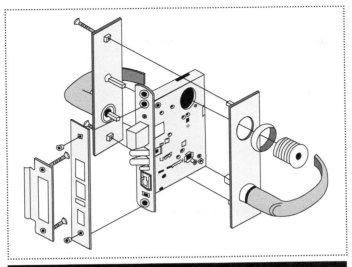

Components of a durable door locking device.
(Photo courtesy of Yale® Security Inc.)

Combination locks (dial or push-button) are often used on safes, vaults, padlocks, and vehicle doors. They cannot be picked, but can be compromised if the combination to the lock is readily available to unauthorized users. Keypad locks generally rely on microcomputer technology and can be applied in a wide range of settings. Telephones, radios, automatic teller machines (ATMs), calculators, and microwave ovens all utilize keypads to enter data and operate the device. Electronic locks are commonly used when control of the locking device is maintained at a location some distance from the lock. These locks are used to control gates and visitor access to businesses and apartment buildings.

A card-operated lock is often used to control access to restricted areas or an organization's physical assets and computer networks. A typical card-operated lock system requires the user to swipe, slide, or place a card near or into a reader that uses magnetic or radio frequency identification (RFID) to validate the card, and releases the lock if the card is valid. Some card-key access systems also record the card number, and the date and time entry is granted. These systems make the controlled access decision based on preauthorization. They record and store access information and can summon assistance if necessary (Southerland, 2000; Tyska & Fennelly, 2000). For example, employees use these cards when moving around an office building and using computers at various workstations. When an employee leaves a workstation and removes the card, this action causes the machine to lock down, preventing the risk of anyone else sitting at the person's desk and stealing sensitive information (Wagley, 2010). Some organizations are exploring the use of smart cards in their personnel identification systems. About the size of a credit card, these cards contain an embedded microchip circuit that contains information about the cardholder regarding access rights in the organization. These cards can also be programmed to contain other information including medical and personal contact information. They can even serve as a debit payment card for use in company cafeterias and stores. These smart cards can also be used to further authenticate the identity of a person at secure workstations where the person may be required to pass the card in front of a RFID reader or "swipe" the card while typing in a password, or even use a biometric-based feature such as a retina or a fingerprint scan to gain access (Rankl & Effing, 2010).

combination lock Dial or push-button lock commonly used with safes, vaults, padlocks, and vehicle doors.

keypad lock Generally, an electronic lock that utilizes microcomputer technologies and touch pads.

electronic locks Access control devices that do not rely upon traditional keys and instead use some type of proximity or card access device.

card-operated lock Cards with magnetic strips that are slid or inserted into a card reader connected to a microcomputer that activates the locking device.

Access control security gates combined with biometric hand readers provide layers of protection at a nuclear facility.
(Photo courtesy of U.S. Nuclear Regulatory Commission.)

biometric system An access control system that must recognize a human biological feature before access to a protected area is granted.

Other sophisticated locking devices integrate biometrics. A biometric system is designed to recognize certain biological features of an individual before access to a protected area is granted. Biometric locking systems may be programmed to recognize facial features, voice patterns, an eye's retina, fingerprints, hand geometry, or the physical pressure one applies when writing a signature. It appears that biometrics may also be useful for controlling access to the Internet. For example, one researcher has developed a system that allows the identities of owners of web accounts to be verified with fingerprints rather than usernames and passwords. Here, users provide their fingerprints during a one-time registration process. After they register, they can use their fingerprints to gain access to various online accounts. The system may also be expanded to include palm prints and facial expressions as ways of identifying users (Online access with a fingerprint, 2010).

Security personnel should not be lulled into a false sense of security simply because a door lock is durable. Even the strongest of locks is useless if facility personnel do not restrict access to keys (key control), or if the door or its frame is weak. Further, strong locks, doors, and framing are useless if the building construction materials that surround the protected area are weak. Building interiors with suspended (drop) ceilings and crawl spaces, for example, typically allow an intruder to bypass the door altogether. The intruder simply removes a ceiling tile in the hallway or the room adjacent to the protected area and gains access to the crawl space and the protected area without entering through the secured door.

In large facilities frequented by numerous visitors, consideration should be given to a pass system. Typically, personnel identification systems include the use of color-coded, tamper-resistant identification cards, passes, or badges that indicate the level of access authorized. In some cases, a person will need to exchange passes while in the institution. For example, a person will need to have a green pass to enter. Then, to seek access to another part of the building, the person will need to trade the green pass with security personnel (who again verify the identity of the person), who then issue a yellow pass. These multiple pass systems ensure multiple checks or verifications of guests while also ensuring that the passes are not exchanged or given to adversaries (Fisher, 2010). In some cases, these passes are also time sensitive, where for example, the pass will change color after a set period of time, such as 24 hours. For example, in a local health care facility, individuals have limited access to the children's hospital. To gain access, a person must have a valid reason to be there (visitor or parent for example), and provide security staff with photo identification which is scanned and recorded. Security staff then issue a time-sensitive color-change pass that is worn by the visitor that clearly specifies the floor that the visitor can use and the date of visit. The person is then required to check out at the end of the visit. Although this procedure is not practical in some facilities, such as retail shopping centers or entertainment venues, passes can be effective access control mechanisms in many facilities if the system is properly implemented and enforced.

▶ Fire Sensors and Alarms

Already Chapter 2 has provided a review of the principles and causes of fire. Fire safety is probably more regulated than any other component of a safety and security program. Numerous federal, state, and local laws prescribe fire safety practices. Since fire prevention and protection principles are well established, one could assume that the application of fire safety fundamentals is very similar between and among facilities. Although similarities may exist in small facilities with common fire hazards, fire prevention and protection strategies depends primarily on the types of fire hazards present. Through a comprehensive planning approach to fire safety, the security manager can design a fire prevention and protection program that meets the need of the facility.

Fire prevention is defined as fire service activities that decrease incidents of uncontrolled fire. Fire prevention activities include inspections, investigations, fire hazard abatement activities, enforcement, plan reviews, inspection activities, and educational activities. The main objective of a fire prevention inspection is to determine if reasonable life safety conditions exist within a given facility. Inspections are intended to identify hazards that could cause a fire or allow a fire to develop or spread. Accurate inspection documentation is an essential factor in fire prevention because inspection reports are used to enforce fire safety regulations, including those related to violation notices, plan reviews, and issuance of permits. Fire investigation involves fire cause determination and the investigation of criminal actions that may have contributed to a fire. Fire cause determination is important because the analysis of causes and gathered data will, over time, indicate trends in certain fire-prone areas. Moreover, the information will provide data for the development of a fire prevention program. Fire hazard abatement activities are carried out and planned accordingly to comply with various fire codes. Abatement codes focus on building, zoning, planning, electrical, plumbing, heating, air conditioning, landscaping, air pollution, and environmental protection. The codes are usually updated at 5-year intervals and are designed to correlate with the fire prevention standards of the American Insurance Association (Robertson, 2010). Fire prevention enforcement encompasses the adoption and administration of fire prevention codes, enforcement procedures, and notices. Enforcement procedures involve compliance with fire permits, certificates, and licenses. Enforcement notices involve fire prevention personnel who inspect occupancies that have been issued warnings or notices of violation, red tag or condemnation notices, citations or summons, or warrants in violation of fire codes. It is the public fire inspector's duty to ensure that corrective action is taken so occupants are in compliance with all fire safety codes.

Fire prevention also requires plan reviews and inspection programs. An effective (and legal) fire prevention plan also requires a facility plan review, which is conducted by the local fire department. Generally, this review focuses on four areas: site plans, preliminary building plans, final building plans and specifications, and certificates for occupancy.

fire prevention Policies and practices designed to prevent a fire from occurring.

fire investigation Involves fire cause determination and investigation of criminal actions.

fire hazard abatement Involves the use of fire abatement codes typically established at the municipal government level.

fire prevention enforcement Adoption and administration of fire prevention codes; enforcement procedures, and notices.

plan review A process or requirements used by local governments to ensure that businesses are in compliance with building codes and other laws and ordinances.

Most sites are reviewed in conjunction with the local building, zoning, and public works departments or with state regulatory agencies. Fire officials also participate in preconstruction conferences to answer questions relating to building fire protection features, building codes, fire prevention code requirements, and other plan review processes. If an existing facility requires an upgrade or a remodel, retrofitting the fire safety apparatus also requires special consideration and planning.

The fire safety retrofit design plan should include specific elements. The plan should address applicable fire codes and standards, an identification of new fire systems arrangements, existing building characteristics and fire protection systems, a timetable for phasing in new fire safety equipment, and provisions for future needs (Greene & Tappen, 2000; National Fire Protection Association, 2007; Schumacher, 2000). Company fire inspection programs include building surveys and the correction of common problems concerning life safety conditions. They also involve locating and correcting fire hazards, and testing fire protection systems. These inspections may be conducted by company personnel. If situations are detected that need to be corrected, it is the inspector's duty to conduct all follow-up or re-inspections.

Fire safety education is also an important element of a fire prevention program. The two main purposes of education are fire prevention and fire reaction training. Life safety and asset protection in the event of a fire depend on good planning and proper training of employees. When a fire occurs or when a fire alarm is sounded, all occupants should react instinctively. All fire alarms should be treated as real. Plans for notification of occupants, as well as firefighting and other emergency personnel are essential. Evacuation plans and routes must be developed and practiced. Educating occupants about fire prevention and protection systems as well as evacuation procedures is critical to safety and injury prevention. Indoctrination of all new employees and periodic refresher training should be a part of every employee's continuing education program. Fire prevention, reporting and evacuation procedures, use of extinguishers, basic first aid, and fire drills should be part of every fire safety training session.

When designing an educational plan or a program, it is very important to engineer in human behavior in any fire evacuation plan. Human behaviors in a fire can be divided into three stages: detection, response, and travel. The detection time is that period of time from the ignition of a fire until it is detected. These detection times vary: those directly involved with the fire will know first, while those not involved will require a fire alarm to be activated before they begin their evacuation. Next is response, which involves the time period from detection until a person begins to evacuate or escape the fire. According to a research, it takes about 45–75 seconds for an average person to respond to a fire alarm. The final phase is travel time. Travel time is that period of time from escape to reaching a safe area outside the building (Nystedt, 2003). Knowing the psychological dynamics of fire also needs to be a part of the educational process. Under the affiliation model, for example, under stressful situations there is a tendency by human beings to act in irrational ways, limiting their decision-making process and slowing the evacuation time because they may move toward familiar places and persons and not toward exits (Sime, 1985).

Some situations require the development and training of a private company fire unit or fire brigade. Facilities located in remote areas, away from public fire departments, or are serviced by fire departments that lack the expertise and equipment to effectively meet the organization's fire-related needs may require an in-house firefighting team. Manufacturing facilities located in some foreign countries may not be located near adequate firefighting services. It may be necessary to create a company fire brigade made up of selected, well-trained employees who are competent to handle firefighting assignments. The size of the fire brigade will depend upon the location and size of the facility as well as on the nature of the fire risk.

fire inspection program Fire safety surveys, testing of fire systems.

fire safety education Fire prevention and fire reaction training.

fire brigade Private firefighting units and personnel.

► Fire Protection Systems

Fire protection systems focus on fire detection, containment, and suppression of fires. It is a primary consideration during construction of new facilities, as well as when upgrading existing facilities. Model building codes, statutes, and regulations for new construction have existed for many years. The codes and regulations provide for alternative methods, materials, and equipment that may be used to provide equivalent levels of safety. Performance-based fire safety design principles are used to analyze, document, and evaluate fire safety alternatives. Consultation with qualified experts and fire safety engineers is often necessary to ensure compliance with regulatory fire safety goals.

Four types of fire sensors (detectors) are commonly used in fire protection systems. Thermal sensors provide the least amount of advanced warning time. It senses the heat in a protected area. Some thermal sensors are preset and respond at a specific temperature. Others, known as rate-of-rise sensors, respond to rapid increases in temperature. Infrared sensors respond to infrared light emissions in flame. Photoelectric sensors, detect smoke and particulates in the environment. Here, air enters a sensing chamber that measures changes in the amount of light emitted by the sensor. When the amount of light is restricted by smoke particulates, an alarm is activated. Ionization sensors, respond to invisible products of combustion, such as toxic gases. These "smoke detectors" are commonly used in residential settings. Here, particulates entering the sensor pass through two electrically charged plates that ionize the air. Smoke and other particulates entering the chamber change the electrical field, breaking the path of electricity between two metal plates (basically interrupting a circuit), which results in the sensor sounding an alarm (Bukowski et al., 2007; National Fire Protection Agency, 2015). There are also flame detectors. As the name suggests, these types of sensors use infrared light wavelengths or ultraviolet radiation to detect the presence of light, which is created by the presence of flame (Middleton, 1983).

All organizations also have fire annunciators, which are devices that control and monitor the various parts or components of a fire alarm system. Oftentimes, these are simply called fire panels and they are located near the main entrances of facilities so they can be easily accessed by firefighting personnel in order to determine the location of the alarm and fire in the facility. In many cases, these annunciators incorporate a series of smart technologies that provide extremely detailed information on the location and type of fire, as well as the movement of first responders in the building (Reneke, 2013). In some cases, annunciator systems transmit the fire alarm signal to another location, such as a central station security console, 911 emergency communications center, or fire department. Remote annunciators may be monitored at some distance from the sensor location while other technologies now offer the ability to use smart phones as an annunciator.

Fire Extinguishers and Sprinkler Systems

There are several types of portable fire extinguishers. Water, fog, and foam extinguishers are effective for Class A (ordinary combustibles) and Class B (flammable liquid) fires. Carbon dioxide (CO_2) extinguishers are generally used on Class B and Class C (electrical) fires. Dry chemical extinguishers are designed to deal effectively with Class A, B, and C fires. Dry powder extinguishers are effective against Class D (combustible metals) fires (Cote, Grant, Hall, Powell, & Solomon, 2008). In most cases, these portable fire extinguishers are delivered by hand and are intended to extinguish small fires only (about the size of a trash can). Extinguishers can also be considered to be escape tools because they "beat back" fires and allow extra time for the evacuation of individuals from the fire zone (Subramaniam, 2004).

---

fire protection systems Procedures and fire suppression systems and activities designed to minimize harm to persons and property after a fire has started.

thermal sensors Detect heat in a protected area.

infrared sensors Detect changes in heat or thermal energy.

photoelectric sensors A fire-related sensor; detect airborne particles, including smoke, in an environment.

ionization sensors Detect products of combustion, including heat, flame, smoke, and invisible toxic gases.

fire annunciator Devices that control and monitor the various parts and components of a fire alarm system.

inergen systems Fire suppression systems that provide a gaseous alternative to other types of fire extinguishing agents.

Another common extinguishing agent relies upon inergen systems. Inergen fire suppression systems provide a gaseous alternative to other types of fire-extinguishing agents. Inergen fire suppression systems use a combination of inert gasses that basically interrupt the combustion reaction process. They are ideal for environments that should not be exposed to water, fog, foam, dry chemical, or powder. Inergen-based gases can be applied in vaults, computer or telecommunications facilities, or any area containing sensitive electronic equipment (Schroll, 2002; Su, Kim, Crampton, & Liu 2001).

sprinkler systems Fire suppression systems that use pipes containing suppression fluids that are distributed through sprinkler heads.

Sprinkler systems provide one of the best-known protections against personal injury and property loss due to fire. These systems provide concentrated fire suppression in a specific area. Sprinkler systems use underground or overhead water pipes with sprinkler heads plugged with a heat-sensitive metal strip or plastic sensor or plug that melts at a specified temperature, and automatically disperses water or fire-suppression chemicals through sprinkler heads. Depending upon the application, these systems can be dry or wet pipe. Dry pipe systems are used in environment settings that are subject to cold temperatures and freezing. These systems contain compressed air in their piping systems that hold back water or some other extinguishing agent. However, when the heat sensor is opened, the air escapes from the pipe allowing the extinguishing agent to travel down the system and out of the sprinkler heads. Wet pipe, meanwhile, does not contain compressed air. The lines are prefilled with the extinguishing agent (usually water). Here, once the sensor head is activated, the system reads a pressure drop which activates the entire system, pumping extinguishing agents through the pipes. Properly installed and maintained sprinkler systems rarely fail to operate if there is an adequate water supply to support the system (Hall, 2006; National Fire Protection Association, 2007).

To learn more about alarm systems and management through the U.S. General Services Administration, visit www.gsa.gov/portal/content/104644.

SECURITY SPOTLIGHT

Do you currently use an identification card to gain access to your residence, to the educational institution you attend, or to a workplace facility where you are employed, or to use information technology systems in a facility? If so, what data is stored in the card's technology—your photo? fingerprint? a unique identification number? level of access authorized to you? If possible, speak with someone in the organization's security department to find out how this physical security system has evolved over the years. For example, has the organization adopted more sophisticated technology in its personnel identification system over time? If so, why? And how effective has the new technology proved?

▶ Cameras and Surveillance Systems

closed-circuit television (CCTV) Video surveillance system closed to external transmission.

Organizations also use camera surveillance systems to monitor the flow of individuals and to detect and perhaps deter or prevent criminal activities. Where security personnel are limited, camera surveillance systems provide extra "eyes and ears" to the human observer. CCTV or closed-circuit television capability enhances safety and security effectiveness and efficiency. These CCTV systems are not publicly broadcasted. They are internal or "closed" by design where their main purpose is to monitor and record activities within an organization. CCTV can be used in a wide variety of security settings. Moreover, CCTV operates as an extension of the human operator's "eyes and ears." Although expensive to install and maintain, CCTV can generate considerable personnel cost savings because one person can monitor numerous locations simultaneously. Often coupled with time lapse recording, pinhole lenses, opaque domes, and pan–tilt–zoom (PTZ) options, CCTV increases personnel productivity and efficiency. CCTV systems can also provide a permanent record of an incident or event through the use of video and digital recording.

CCTV systems consist of three components. First are the cameras themselves. Because of technological advances, cameras have many features including the ability to pan, tilt, and zoom. Modern cameras also capture color images (instead of monochromatic black and white) and they also use infrared and ultraviolet technologies that enhance night vision surveillance capabilities. Next, the cameras can send their signals to monitors located at a central location or off-site. Operators at these locations have the ability to control cameras while watching single camera images or multiple cameras that may have their own independent monitors. In most cases, however, there is one main monitor called a multiplexor. Multiplexers have the ability to display one camera image, periodically switch from one camera to another or display multiple images at a time through split screen technologies on a monitor. Personnel also have the ability to determine which cameras to watch at any given time while also controlling the functions of each camera (e.g., pan, tilt, and zoom) from this location. These systems can also attach peripheral devices (devices that have one single task) such as sensors and alarms that may have the capacity to directly activate the camera on the multiplexor where the threat is detected. Last, most CCTV systems also have a recording device that has the ability to record all of the cameras for future playback, and to preserve footage for use in investigations and criminal and civil complaints (Matchett, 2003). Historically, CCTV systems were analog and relied upon magnetic tape storage using (video tapes) to preserve and store video footage. In many cases, these video libraries were quite large, oftentimes taking up small rooms to store the video footage for periods of time up to a year. Now, modern surveillance systems use digital technologies. These digital images are stored electronically, increasing the storage capacity and portability of data compared to the earlier analog technologies. These new systems also allow for the easy retrieval of high quality still and motion images.

A CCTV camera.
(Photo courtesy of U.S. Custom and Border Protection.)

CCTV systems can be very sophisticated. Many modern video security systems are linked to computer software that is programmed to identify suspicious behavior and abnormal events, and notify security personnel. Video analytics software is designed to detect a wide range of abnormalities (e.g., someone falling, a package left unattended, and a vehicle proceeding in the wrong direction) and notify human agents through audio or visual alarms and even through smart phones. Using the software system greatly reduces the amount of personnel time required to monitor videos in search of abnormalities (Fitzhenry, 2007; U.S. General Services Administration, 2011; Wimmer, 2000). Three-dimensional (3D) graphics technology is also promising to improve surveillance systems' effectiveness by helping physical security personnel organize the ever-increasing volumes of data generated by cameras, access logs, alerts from analytics systems, and so forth. A 3D map of a facility provides a more intuitive visual framework for security personnel. Personnel can "fly" through the virtualized facility and watch a fusion of all videos in their real locations, instead of memorizing the locations of hundreds of cameras. When locations of emergency exits and access points are included in the 3D image, security personnel have an even bigger, more useful picture. 3D also makes surveillance planning easier. Such planning typically involves diagrams of floor plans, photos, and extensive site visits. Armed with realistic 3D maps of a facility, planners can make fewer site visits—saving time and money. They can also make a more convincing business case to finance managers by using a 3D map to show how a planned upgrade of surveillance equipment would remedy gaps in coverage (Laforte, 2010).

SECURITY SPOTLIGHT

Research statistics and viewpoints on the use and effectiveness of public CCTV camera systems. Where are these systems used most often? What does the prevailing viewpoint seem to be regarding how effective they are in providing physical security? What concerns, if any, have their use raised?

▶ Guard Forces

People constitute the most significant protection resource. Although technology can be used to reduce or augment existing security personnel requirements, hardware and high-tech devices cannot totally displace the need for security personnel. Security personnel are still needed to respond to, assess, and oftentimes defeat the actions of an adversary. Monitoring, critical analyses of situations, and effective intelligent response can be accomplished only through the appropriate use of security personnel. Even when alarm and surveillance systems are monitored at some remote site, such as a central station, someone (a human agent) must be in place to receive an alarm signal and respond or notify appropriate response personnel.

Security personnel take many forms. Receptionists, secretaries, janitorial and maintenance workers, supervisors, executives, retail clerks, cashiers, and operations personnel can fulfill a security function. Every person can function as a deterrent to crime, and all are in a position to control access and observe and report unsafe conditions and suspicious behavior. Proper security training and awareness for all personnel expands the number of people available for loss prevention.

In all but the smallest organizations, the primary responsibility for the protective function usually rests with the facility or security manager and asset protection personnel. The security force may consist of any combination of uniformed or plainclothes protection officers, investigators, CCTV and alarm console monitoring personnel, health and safety compliance inspectors, firefighters, or emergency response specialists. The security force

Well-armed and -trained security officers are one component of the robust security at U.S. commercial nuclear power plants.
(Photo courtesy of U.S. Nuclear Regulatory Commission.)

may be proprietary, contract, or a combination of the two. Even in organizations that have no one assigned full time to asset protection duties, someone is nominally responsible for the security function (Canton, 2003; Fischer & Green, 2008; Walsh & Healy, 1987).

Because human beings constitute the most significant protection resource, caution must be exercised to hire the right people, train and treat them well, and maintain their integrity. Pre-employment selection procedures, leadership and supervision, workforce planning, training, and education of employees will be reviewed in future chapters of the textbook.

A QUICK SURVEY

Which of the following physical security systems is in place at the educational institution you attend or the organization that employs you? Check all that apply.

- Perimeter controls
- Walls, doors, and other elements of building exteriors and interiors
- Lighting systems
- Locks
- Visual assessment and surveillance systems
- Alarm systems
- Fire prevention and protection systems
- Human protection systems
- Other

In your view, does the facility where you attend school or where you work have adequate physical security? Why or why not? If not, what changes would you recommend?

Summary

Physical security is the first line of defense against human threats. It is a core element of any security program. Physical security may be defined as the use of structural, electronic, and human protection systems. The core elements of a PPS rely upon site work, building, detection, and procedural elements. A good PPS also needs to consider perimeter security issues, lighting, fences and barriers, sensors, and alarm systems. Some of the primary issues organizations need to consider include access control, fire sensors and protection systems, camera surveillance systems, and guard forces.

Career opportunities

United States Secret Service: Physical Security Specialists provide technical expertise and operational support to identify hazards and implement countermeasures while conducting security surveys, vulnerability assessments, and protection assignments. They also perform technical security functions such as: intrusion detection and surveillance systems; technical surveillance countermeasures; chemical, biological, and radiological hazard countermeasures; and fire protection at the White House and other protected sites located throughout the United States.

To learn more about this position or other position categories, go directly to www.usajobs.gov and navigate down the listing of available vacancies at the Secret Service.

Key Terms and Concepts

Access control 85
Alarm 82
Alarm points 84
Alarm system circuit 82
Alarm system management 84
Annunciator 82
Biometric system 88
Building elements 75
Card-operated lock 87
Central station alarm system 83
Closed-circuit television (CCTV) 92
Combination locks 87
Countermeasures 75
Defense in depth 73
Detection elements 75

Deterrence-based strategies 73
Electronic locks 87
False alarm 82
Fire annunciator 91
Fire brigade 90
Fire hazard abatement 89
Fire inspection programs 90
Fire investigation 89
Fire prevention 89
Fire prevention enforcement 89
Fire protection systems 91
Fire safety education 90
Guard forces 75
Inergen systems 92
Infrared sensors 81
Ionization sensors 91

Keypad locks 87
Local alarm system 83
Microwave motion sensor 80
Nuisance alarms 82
Passive infrared sensor 81
Perimeter lighting 77
Photoelectric sensors 91
Plan review 89
Procedural security measures 73
Proprietary alarm system 83
Sensors 75
Site work elements 75
Sprinkler systems 92
Standoff zones 76
Thermal sensors 91
Ultrasonic motion sensor 80

Discussion Questions and Exercises

1. Outline and describe the basics of a physical security program. Include outer and inner perimeter controls and the roles of protective lighting and access control devices in the description.
2. Compare and contrast visual assessment, surveillance, and alarm systems. What role does each fulfill?

3. Physical security and access control systems are not complete without a human resource component. Explain. Are dedicated security personnel necessary in all organizations?
4. Explain the concept of defense in depth? Why is this important in a physical protection system?

5. What are the core elements of physical protection systems?
6. Explain the various types of sensors. What are some key issues or factors to consider when using these various sensors in physical security?
7. What are the roles of lighting and fences in physical security? What are some similar roles or functions each has? What are some differences?

8. What is access control? E its importance by using t depth."
9. Explain the role of guard f program.
10. Explain the importance of and control as part of an eff gram. What are some comr

---

Your Turn

Strengthening Physical Security for a Small Business Owner

Nishant Patil operates a small electronic component manufacturing business in a leased building located in an industrial park of a medium-sized city. The facility has no perimeter fencing because Patil's landlord will not permit exterior fences. Patil employs 10 full-time people who work normal daytime hours, Monday through Friday. His facility has been burglarized on three separate weekends over the past 6 months. On each occasion, small hand tools were the burglars' target. During the last burglary, the perpetrator(s) started a fire in Patil's office. The building does not have a sprinkler system. It does, however, have a local fire detection and alarm system. Fortunately, a passer-by heard the alarm on the night of the fire and

contacted the fire department minimal. The building has no alarm) system, and Patil has security-related improvement

1. Based on the informati security measures w Nishant Patil? Explain y

2. What additional inform ful in developing recor example, would you v day each burglary occu place of business? Infor backgrounds and finan these and other kinds recommendations?

5   Personnel Security

LEARNING OBJECTIVES

After completing this chapter, the reader should be able to:

1. describe the key elements of a comprehensive personnel security program
2. articulate the purpose and goals of personnel security programs
3. understand some of the common screening tools used in background investigations
4. know some of the common personnel security threats
5. understand the function, role, and activities of executive protection programs
6. know the nature and extent of workplace violence
7. know the main elements of a workplace prevention program and prevention strategies
8. identify international travel issues related to personnel security
9. understand and identify threats to employees when traveling abroad

▶ Introduction

Personnel security involves the protection of individuals and the organization's physical and information assets. It involves measures and activities to protect employees and those coming to the organization for business purposes, including customers, visitors, contractors, or consultants and even unauthorized persons. It is also important in protecting company property. Personnel security is considered the foundation on which all other security-related safeguards exist (*"Final report,"* 1999). It is integral to organizational success.

▶ Personnel Security: Key Elements

The foundation of any effective personnel security program begins with policies and procedures that promote safety and security, protecting employees from strangers, business associates, coworkers, and invitees (such as subcontractors). The security function should also ensure that employees are aware of the security program and are persuaded to comply with all policies, procedures, and practices. While employees need to be trained and educated in security-related policies, an effective personnel security program also requires security awareness. Security awareness is basically the depth and degree of security-related knowledge that organizational members possess, apply, and use in the workplace. It can also be understood as the level of awareness that employees have of the security mission and the degree of commitment they have toward that mission. It is also a mindset that everyone in the organization is responsible for security to some degree (Bauer, Bernroider, & Chudzikowski, 2013). This concept also emphasizes that security should become a cultural norm that is led and reinforced by the security personnel and carried out by all members of the organization, who are considered key elements of the organization's security plan. Consider, for example, a common security issue in many organizations: the propping open of external doors for various purposes. While considered "no big deal" by the uninformed employee, an open door can lead to threats entering an organization undetected. By educating and training employees on the dangers of propping doors, their awareness of the various risks they create through this practice is enhanced. The training would also increase their level of security awareness.

Personnel Security and Hiring Practices

One primary goal of a personnel security program is to ensure that human threats are kept out of the organization. To prevent threats from legitimately entering the workplace, organizations must have a properly designed applicant selection and screening process to determine the suitability of personnel in the context of their knowledge, skills, and abilities and their security threat to the organization. Depending upon these needs, the nature and extent of the applicant selection process varies among organizations. In some cases it can be quite extensive. When an employee is needed for a highly trusted position or is required to hold a top secret clearance issued by a federal agency, many screening tools and in-depth background investigations will be conducted.

In most cases, the human resource function is responsible in determining employment criteria through a comprehensive job task analysis, which is the process of breaking a job down to its essential tasks and activities in order to determine what knowledge, skills, and abilities are needed to perform the job (Hartley, 2004). Since personnel can be a security threat, the security function should also be involved in the development of selection and screening tools. These are needed in order to ensure that candidates meet the security pre-access suitability criteria or standards, which are the minimum requirements to get hired while also ensuring personnel reliability throughout the employment relationship. This is known as suitability determination (Cane, 2015). In many cases, these pre-access suitability criteria are already determined for the organization by regulatory agencies and law. Following the creation of these criteria, various job-related and nondiscriminatory selection techniques that conform to state and federal employment laws are used to "screen in" qualified individuals.

The selection process normally begins with a request for, or submission of, an *application*. Employment application instruments should be objective, uniform, consistent, and job-task related. Care should be exercised in the development of application forms to ensure that information is not requested in violation of any state or federal laws. Age, birthplace, race, citizenship, religious affiliation, and arrest information is often protected by antidiscrimination and privacy laws. An application form should not contain questions other than those pertaining to the applicant's ability to perform the job for which the application is made. An appropriately constructed application form, once completed by the applicant, provides insight into the candidate's past and assists in the candidate's background verification process. Signed and dated below a statement affirming to state the truth, the application becomes a legal document. It can be used by the employer as a defense in a subsequent legal proceeding if the employee is terminated due to false or misleading information presented in the application (Bland & Stalcup, 1999; Cheeseman, 2010; Greer & Plunkett, 2007; Lewis, Goodman, & Fandt, 2008).

The interview is a face-to-face encounter between the candidate and the employer's representative or a screening committee. The interview provides an opportunity to observe the candidate's appearance, demeanor, and response to questions designed to probe the candidate's abilities, honesty, dependability, judgment, and initiative. During an interview,

personnel security One of the three pillars of any security program. Protection of persons associated with an organization as well as protection from individuals who seek to harm the organization.

security awareness The depth and degree of security-related knowledge that organizational members possess, apply, and use in the workplace.

job task (occupational) analysis Identifies the job functions (duties) a worker is expected to perform. Breaking the job down to its essential tasks.

interview Face-to-face encounter between the candidate and the employer's representative.

questions that may be in violation of local, state, and federal statutes relative to marital status, lifestyle, and equal employment opportunity must be avoided (Lewis et al., 2008; Nixon, 2007). Ethical dilemmas as well as various types of situations may be presented to the candidate to evaluate the candidate's problem-solving skills under pressure and predict decision-making behaviors. The interview also provides the opportunity for the employer to provide the potential employee with a *realistic job preview*. Employee retention begins with policies and open lines of communication designed to ensure realistic expectations on the part of new and existing employees. The job description and specifications, compensation and benefits plan, and minimum activity requirements should be discussed. Employers need to be honest with job applicants.

Various job-related tests can also be administered. Aptitude, knowledge, and skill tests determine suitability for the position and provide objective verification of the knowledge and skills claimed in the resume (if submitted) and application. The tests can assist in determining the level and amount of training necessary to prepare the candidate for the position. A wide range of valid pencil and paper (and online) *psychological tests* are available that can be used to determine a candidate's emotional stability and mental health. The test procedures often include the use of staff psychologists to interpret the results. However, employers are cautioned that the use of any test designed to diagnose psychological disorders of a candidate may lead to an unintended violation of the Americans with Disabilities Act (ADA).

integrity tests Tests used to detect a person's propensity toward dishonesty and unethical acts.

Integrity tests can be used to detect a propensity toward dishonesty, substance abuse, violence, or a high level of tolerance for such behavior in others. Similar in format and application to psychological tests, several integrity testing instruments are commercially available. Test producers should provide validity data for psychological and integrity tests (Jones & Arnold, 2003). Using tests to identify attitudes toward substance abuse and theft, and to predict behavior based on these attitudes, is not always foolproof. Employers should not rely solely on the results of such tests when making hiring decisions. The tests should be viewed as complementary tools in a comprehensive pre-employment screening arsenal. Additionally, organizations risk the violation of federal and many state laws if these tests discriminate against anyone on the basis of race, and gender.

background investigation A comprehensive investigation of a candidate's personal, financial, and criminal background.

Another component of any selection process is a comprehensive background investigation, which is the process of investigating the candidate's suitability for employment. These background investigations rely on application information provided by the candidate, the interview, and other selection tools. Usually, an applicant is asked to authorize the disclosure of relevant background information by third parties. To release the prospective employer and the third parties from liability associated with disclosure of the information requested, the candidate should be required to sign an *authorization to release information document* as a condition for employment. Prospective employers should consult in-house or contracted legal counsel regarding the appropriate language to be included in the authorization to release information document.

criminal history checks Criminal background investigations conducted by human resource or security personnel on new and current employees.

As part of the background investigation, criminal history checks are imperative. In some industry sectors, for example, federal laws require banks, brokerage houses, and insurers to conduct criminal history checks on all prospective employees who are required to handle cash or other financial assets. As a general rule, conviction data is a matter of public record, accessible to anyone. For example, many public sector websites have registries and information through which employers can obtain conviction data as well as the identity of those in jail or prison or have outstanding arrest warrants. Another common practice is the submission of an applicant's fingerprints, as part of the criminal history. In the past, the submission and review of fingerprints was a timely process, sometimes taking months. However, with the advent of digitized and automated fingerprint identification systems (AFIS), many institutions now scan fingerprint images directly into a computer database that automatically classifies the prints, completing a criminal history check in minutes (Lushbaugh & Weston, 2012; Millwee, 2000).

If you are employed by an organization, how does the organization conduct background investigations during the selection process? Consider the investigative techniques the organization used with you when you applied for an open position there. If you can, meet with someone in the human resources department to learn whether the organization's approach to background investigations has changed over the years and, if so, what prompted those changes?

A credit history check of the applicant should also be conducted. Late payments, nonpayments, bankruptcies, liens, and judgments against a candidate can be uncovered through a comprehensive credit investigation. Most employees are placed in positions of trust and are charged with the responsibility of protecting assets. Although a poor credit history does not mean that the employee would steal to pay off debt, it may show inadequate financial literacy and management skills, poor judgment, and lack of responsibility, especially with respect to the management of financial assets. Most financial institutions will not employ individuals with poor credit histories. If employees cannot manage their own money, they cannot be expected to manage another person's assets. Although some bad credit may be unavoidable, such as a catastrophic illness that leads to personal financial disaster, poor financial management is often linked to irresponsible behavior. A wise employer does not hire irresponsible people.

> **credit history**
> An applicant or employee's financial history.

A thorough background investigation on a prospective employee is not complete until personal references are checked, and academic credentials and employment histories are verified. A high percentage of resumes, job applications, and interviews produce information that may be less than the whole truth. Likewise, candidate-provided references rarely result in any negative information about the applicant. Since applicants provide references who will provide favorable comments, interviewing coworkers and applicants' neighbors may be a good practice to gain additional information (Johnson, 2005).

Continued Reliability

Background investigations may also be conducted periodically or continuously post-hire to ensure that employees have ongoing suitability and trust to hold their positions. In some cases, governmental agencies have requirements that certain employees in trusted positions who deal with sensitive or classified information have periodic reviews in order to renew their security clearances (Fischer & Morgan, 2002). For example, Defense Security Service personnel are responsible for performing a *continuous evaluation process* (CEP) for individuals in the private and public sectors who have access to top secret, secret, and confidential defense-related information. Depending upon the sensitivity designation of the position the person holds, the CEP may be conducted every 5, 10, or 15 years where investigators examine the various conditions that raise concerns. Some factors that could cause a revocation of a person's clearance include: financial issues, sexual behaviors, gambling debts, questionable allegiance to the United States, foreign influences, criminal conduct, alcohol consumption, and drug use. Another example of the background investigation processes conducted by federal government agencies can be found in Figure 5-1 ■.

Companies may also engage in continued verification activities to ensure that employees (aka: trusted insiders) are still suitable to perform their functions. Without an invasion of an individual employee's right to privacy, continuous screening permits an organization to extend its due diligence of employees, from the initial contact with employee candidates through the complete lifecycle of the employee–employer relationship. Without continued reliability checks some organizations could be exposed to civil liability. Consider, for example, the Germanwings Flight 9525 plane crash in 2015 that was the

> **continued reliability**
> Employee background investigations conducted continuously or periodically to ensure that employees have ongoing suitability to hold their positions.

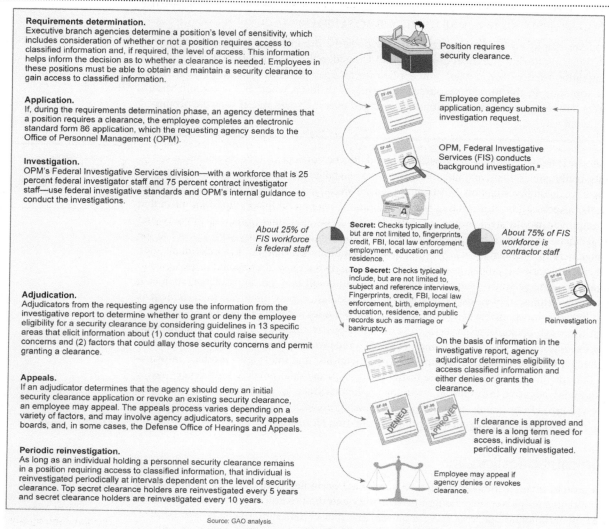

Requirements determination.
Executive branch agencies determine a position's level of sensitivity, which includes consideration of whether or not a position requires access to classified information and, if required, the level of access. This information helps inform the decision as to whether a clearance is needed. Employees in these positions must be able to obtain and maintain a security clearance to gain access to classified information.

Application.
If, during the requirements determination phase, an agency determines that a position requires a clearance, the employee completes an electronic standard form 86 application, which the requesting agency sends to the Office of Personnel Management (OPM).

Investigation.
OPM's Federal Investigative Services division—with a workforce that is 25 percent federal investigator staff and 75 percent contract investigator staff—use federal investigative standards and OPM's internal guidance to conduct the investigations.

Adjudication.
Adjudicators from the requesting agency use the information from the investigative report to determine whether to grant or deny the employee eligibility for a security clearance by considering guidelines in 13 specific areas that elicit information about (1) conduct that could raise security concerns and (2) factors that could allay those security concerns and permit granting a clearance.

Appeals.
If an adjudicator determines that the agency should deny an initial security clearance application or revoke an existing security clearance, an employee may appeal. The appeals process varies depending on a variety of factors, and may involve agency adjudicators, security appeals boards, and, in some cases, the Defense Office of Hearings and Appeals.

Periodic reinvestigation.
As long as an individual holding a personnel security clearance remains in a position requiring access to classified information, that individual is reinvestigated periodically at intervals dependent on the level of security clearance. Top secret clearance holders are reinvestigated every 5 years and secret clearance holders are reinvestigated every 10 years.

Position requires security clearance.

Employee completes application, agency submits investigation request.

OPM, Federal Investigative Services (FIS) conducts background investigation.[a]

About 25% of FIS workforce is federal staff

About 75% of FIS workforce is contractor staff

Secret: Checks typically include, but are not limited to, fingerprints, credit, FBI, local law enforcement, employment, education and residence.

Top Secret: Checks typically include, but are not limited to, subject and reference interviews, Fingerprints, credit, FBI, local law enforcement, birth, employment, education, residence, and public records such as marriage or bankruptcy.

Reinvestigation

On the basis of information in the investigative report, agency adjudicator determines eligibility to access classified information and either denies or grants the clearance.

If clearance is approved and there is a long term need for access, individual is periodically reinvestigated.

Employee may appeal if agency denies or revokes clearance.

Source: GAO analysis.

[a]OPM provides background investigation services to over 100 executive branch agencies; however, others, including some agencies in the Intelligence Community, have been delegated authority from the Office of the Director of National Intelligence, OPM, or both, to conduct their own background investigations.

FIGURE 5-1   The Federal Personnel Security Background Investigation Process
Source: From Personnel Security Clearances. © 2013. Published by Government Accountability Office.

result of the co-pilot locking the pilot out of the cockpit and then setting the autopilot to 100 feet, crashing the aircraft into a mountain in the French Alps, killing all 150 aboard. It was reported that the co-pilot had a history of mental health issues, which may have been the cause of his actions. While Lufthansa, the parent company of Germanwings, required periodic medical examinations that included asking rudimentary mental health questions, these examinations did not include any psychological testing by a psychiatrist (Alexander & Green, 2015; Hussain, Malik, & Menezes, 2015).

Reliability/trust-related indicators used in these investigations include criminal and financial issues the employee may have been involved in, after the last investigation was conducted by the organization. Other reliability measures can include changes in employee performance, incidents in the workplace, and other work-life events such as divorce, death, and illnesses (Nixon & Kerr, 2011). In some cases, an organization may have continued verification policies and procedures that require employees to submit to some types of testing. They commonly include drug screening and medical and psychological testing. In other situations, policies and procedures require employees to report to management any criminal, medical, or financial issues that may compromise their ability to perform their job.

Other Personnel Security Issues

While an effective selection process will help in screening out potential threats, organizations nevertheless need to accept the fact that there will still be internal and external threats that will affect the welfare and safety of employees. Some of these actions include crimes against property and persons in the workplace. Property-related offenses against the company, including theft, embezzlement, fraud, and the theft of intellectual property, may also occur (which will be covered in Chapter 6). These personnel security issues can be mitigated through the use of physical security measures, effective policies and procedures, increased security awareness among all employees, and effective leadership that maintains a culture of integrity and honesty.

To address these issues, security and other managerial functions in the organization, such as human resources and risk management, must develop a comprehensive security audit of all of the risks that employees may be vulnerable to, based on the various threats identified through the risk analysis process. In some cases, the threats to employees can be remote but nevertheless devastating for companies and personnel. For example, on 9-11, seven executives from TJ Maxx (a clothing retailer) were killed when the aircraft they were passengers in was crashed into the World Trade Center. Besides losing key executives, which could have been mitigated to some degree if the company had a travel security policy that prohibited the travel of executives together, the organization also had to address the needs and concerns of other executives who were now perhaps afraid of flying. The company hired counselors to work with the 600+ employees who also traveled by air to address their concerns (Hays, 2001).

Personnel Safety

The practice of personnel security also includes occupational safety. Occupational safety is the protection of a company and its human assets against accidents, injuries, and harm as the result of noncriminal actions by humans and mechanical/industrial failures. The security function is often responsible for health, and safety-related issues. In other cases, organizations may have dedicated staff that is responsible for occupational health and safety, enforcement, and compliance activities. Even in these settings, however, the security function is integral in ensuring a culture of safety in organizations. This is achieved through detecting safety-related hazards and responding to various safety-related events, including fires and accidents, while mitigating the effects of such incidents on employees and the organization.

In other cases, personnel safety extends to natural disasters. In these incidents, management will need to have well-designed disaster response plans that include mitigation, response, and recovery activities (Disaster response will be reviewed in detail in Chapter 9). Consider the case of Shell Oil that has extensive operations in the Gulf region of the United States. In 2005, Hurricane Katrina struck the Gulf Coast region, devastating large areas of Mississippi, Louisiana, and the city of New Orleans. To address the safety and security needs of the critical staff that stayed behind to assist the company during the hurricane, these employees and their family members (including grandparents and pets) were all evacuated to the Shell Training Center that was equipped with backup generators and located on higher ground out of the main path of the hurricane. By including family members in the evacuation, the staffs' families were close and safe, easing any psychological trauma and associated stress related to the safety and security of their loved ones ("Bouncing back," 2005).

> occupational safety
> The protection of a company and human assets against accidents, injuries, and harm as the result of noncriminal actions by humans and mechanical/industrial failures.

Executive Protection Details

The practice of using security personnel to protect a specific person or principal is commonly referred to as *executive protection*. Executive protection (EP) is a comprehensive term and practice, encompassing all activities designed to maintain the safety, security, and health of a human asset, including executives, citizens, and political leaders. In some cases, EP is considered in a narrow viewpoint where protection activities are thought to be provided only to individuals who have senior managerial responsibilities in organizations. While high-profile executives such as chief operating officers and presidents often need protection, modern EP activities extend to all individuals whose knowledge, skills, and abilities are critical to the operation and success of the organization.

The practice of EP is simply not providing a single "bodyguard" to protect a principal. EP is a complex and oftentimes continuous security activity and program involving multiple individuals who have diverse skill sets that include the ability to conduct comprehensive threat-based risk analyses, engage in surveillance and counter-surveillance activities, perform logistical movements of persons down to the second, be medically trained, and possess personal defense skills and tactics related to protecting the principal. Because of these skill demands, oftentimes companies will contract with EP companies that specialize in EP. In other cases, an organization will have an in-house staff whose main responsibilities are the protection of key personnel.

Any EP activity begins with the creation of an EP plan. The three essential components of an effective EP plan are shown in Box 5-1.

The EP activity begins with a risk assessment. This is used to develop a specific EP plan for a particular event and person(s). Here, EP personnel must conduct a comprehensive risk analysis, identifying known and potential human and natural threats and the means by which these threats could harm the *principal*. It also includes an analysis of prior issues and incidents that a principal may have encountered. This risk assessment occurs before, during, and even after the particular event, where the risk assessment staff are continually monitoring the threat environment to protect the principal. One of the key points to consider in any executive detail program is that the threat environment is constantly changing as the principal moves from location to location. The threat environment could be "fixed" or stable if the principal is at a particular location on one day. The following day, meanwhile, the threat environment may be dynamic, changing as the principal travels to another region of the world, stays at various locations, and frequents public and private events. In addition, protection details in a remote area with few structures and people present have a different threat environment to manage than an urban area with a high number of individuals present, heavy traffic, and structures that can provide cover and concealment for threats (Johnson & Kingshott, 2009).

BOX 5-1

COMPONENTS OF AN EXECUTIVE PROTECTION PLAN

- A *risk assessment* is used to examine an environment and attendant circumstances to identify threats that could harm a principal, predict the likelihood of a negative event, and assess the damage if a negative event materializes.
- *Advanced procedures* involve touring the principal's intended route and coordinating security arrangements before, during, and after the principal's travel.
- Through *protective operations*, EP personnel accompany the principal, engaging in counter surveillance and defensive tactics (Gips, 2007).

This risk assessment extends far beyond human threats. An effective program will also include health-related issues that could compromise the principal. In all cases, a well-constructed EP plan will also consider the risk of adverse events, such as weather that could basically "trap" an executive in a country or region. A good plan will also monitor events related to warfare and politics. These events could cause a "ripple effect" where one small incident in one nation could rapidly spread in a region (or even the world), trapping, delaying, and exposing the principal to various risks and threats. These plans also require a great deal of outreach and collaboration with law enforcement and security organizations in those locations where the principal(s) will be traveling. Moreover, these plans need to be adaptable where different contingency plans based on unforeseen issues will need to be created, including emergency procedures and a sound evacuation plan (Johnson & Kingshott, 2009).

Once a plan is made, it must be tested, assessed, and evaluated for its effectiveness. This requires the use of individuals who often have a different set of EP skills than those who are responsible for performing risk analyses. These advanced procedures involve executing the EP plan without the presence of the principal(s) at the specific locations where the principal will be. These activities carried out by the advance team can be considered practice and continued preparation for the actual protective operation. These advanced procedures are also important in identifying any additional risks and threats that the initial risk assessment may have overlooked. Another responsibility that the advance team has is to work with law enforcement agencies and private security personnel in the area where the principal will be, practicing the plan, traveling the selected route, and preparing the locations where the principal will be (Holder & Hawley, 1988). Advance teams will also engage in counter-surveillance activities, taking measures to prevent the surveillance of the principals when they arrive, at times even sweeping for "bugs" or listening devices. At this stage (if not earlier), the EP team will also brief the principal on specific risks and threats and the principal's role and responsibilities during the operation.

Protective operations are the final stage in the EP process. These are complex and require coordinated efforts between mobile and fixed protection staff, and a command center to monitor and protect the movements of the principal(s). Consider, for example, when a principal is moving. Protecting a principal in a moving vehicle (a motorcade) will require a minimum of three vehicles where normally the principal will be in the center car (but not all times), while additional EP staff will be stationed along the motorcade route. In cases where the principal is on foot, a minimum of four EP staff will be needed, positioned around the principal, in addition to other EP staff that are monitoring the threat environment.

There is also a final stage that is not directly related to protecting the principal, but is nevertheless important in the administration of an EP program: post-analysis. In this stage, all of the EP team members (planners in the risk analysis stage, advance team, and operations team) debrief and review the success of the EP event. Through these activities, future EP events may be made more successful using the information gleaned from the post-analysis debriefing activities.

While the above information provides insight into traveling executives, EP programs are also used in the workplace and home. One major domestic automotive company, for example, has EP activities that are directed toward the homes and families of executives. Security staff are assigned to the executives' homes while residential alarm systems are monitored at the corporation's central control center. In another large corporation, medical staff that are assigned to the EP team are available nonstop to address health issues. Like mobile EP details, an effective EP program in the home and workplace will require risk analysis and the use of protective details. However, because of the fixed location, advanced procedure activities will be more limited in nature.

advanced procedures Executing the Executive Protection plan without the presence of the principal at specific locations where the principal will be.

advance team Part of the executive protection process. Individuals in the EP team that perform security-related activities in advance of the arrival of the principal.

protective operations The final stage in the executive protection process. Complex and coordinated efforts between mobile and fixed protection staff and a command center to monitor and protect the movements of the principal(s).

▶ Workplace Violence

Workplace violence is a major personnel security concern in the modern organization. Consider the following examples:

- 23-year-old Joshua Golson-Orelus is facing murder, robbery, and other charges in a 17-count indictment. The suspect allegedly targeted 11 gas stations and convenience stores over a 7-month period in the cities of Westbury, Hicksville, Jericho, and East Meadow in New York, netting about $11,000 from all of the robberies. Some of the businesses he robbed twice. The most serious robbery involved the fatal shooting of a gas station clerk in Levittown, New York in January, 2015. At a news conference in Mineola, Acting District Attorney Madeline Singas stated that his crimes were "very brazen" and that he was "terrorizing" employees ("Man accused of murder," 2015).

- On February 3, 2011, 38-year-old Alex Figueroa shot and killed his ex-wife, Guimmia Villia, at a small pharmacy in Queens, New York. Figueroa walked into the pharmacy carrying flowers and shot Villia, who had an order of protection against him. He later shot and killed himself. Domestic violence charges had previously been filed against him, but the charges were dismissed and the file sealed. One order of protection against Figueroa had expired on January 25; another was set to expire in April (O'Connor, 2011).

- On August 3, 2010, Omar Thornton, 34, went on a rampage after being fired from a beer depot, Hartford Distributors, in the town of Manchester, Connecticut. Thornton pursued his victims as they hid in offices, closets, and the parking lot. Armed with two 9-millimeter handguns, Thornton killed eight people before turning a gun on himself. Police believed that Thornton, a warehouse driver, had gone to the depot to confront his bosses and union officials over allegations that he had been stealing alcohol. Thornton had brought the two pistols into the facility hidden in a lunch box prior to his termination meeting. According to police, a shotgun was also found in his car, but was not used. The first two individuals killed by Thornton were the employees who had been assigned to escort him out of the building. After shooting them, Thornton sought out additional victims (Smith, 2010).

These and many other incidents reveal that employees can be exposed to a myriad of internal and external threats that can jeopardize their welfare, safety, and even their lives. All organizations are prone to violent episodes due in part to the point that they are a microcosm of society, employing individuals who may be crime-prone, inviting others onto their property who may commit crimes, and operating in high-crime cities and neighborhoods. In fact, no location is immune from violence. Even military bases and police agencies have been the sites for workplace violence episodes.

> **workplace violence (WPV)** Violent acts including both physical assaults and threats of assaults directed toward workers and those in the workplace.

Workplace violence (WPV) is defined as violent acts, including both physical assaults and threats of assaults, directed toward workers and those in the workplace (Centers for Disease Control and Prevention, 2002). The National Institute for Occupational Safety and Health (NIOSH) (2015) defines WPV as "violent acts (including physical assaults and threats of assaults) directed toward persons at work or on duty." The World Health Organization (WHO) defines WPV as "the intentional use of power, threatened or actual, against another person or against a group, in work-related circumstances, that either results in or has a high degree of likelihood of resulting in injury, death, psychological harm, mal-development, or deprivation" (Cooper & Swanson, 2002; p. v). The concept of WPV has been further refined into the concept of *workplace aggression*, which includes behaviors by a person or persons in or outside of an organization that are intended to psychologically or physically harm a worker in a work context. This definition takes the perspective that not all aggressive behaviors are violent, but they are nevertheless aggressive in nature (Barling, Dupré, & Kelloway, 2009; Schat & Kelloway, 2005). Under this broader definition, nonphysical

BOX 5-2

TYPOLOGY OF WORKPLACE VIOLENCE

Type	Description
Criminal intent	The perpetrator has no legitimate relationship to the business or its employee, and is usually committing a crime in conjunction with the violence.
Customer/client	The perpetrator has a legitimate relationship with the business and becomes violent while being served by the business. This category includes customers, clients, patients, students, inmates, and any other group for which the business provides services.
Worker on worker	The perpetrator is an employee or past employee of the business who attacks or threatens another employee(s) or past employee(s) in the workplace.
Personal relationship	The perpetrator usually does not have a relationship with the business but has a personal relationship with the intended victim.

Source: Patrick J. Ortmeier, Johnson, Introduction to Security: Operations and Management, 5e. © 2018, Pearson Education, Inc., New York, NY.

activities related to bullying and sexual harassment are also considered as WPV issues. Another term that is used in the field of security to describe WPV is occupational violence.

OSHA (Occupational Safety and Health Administration) classifies WPV into four types, based on the relationship between the offender and the target. These include: (1) criminal intent, (2) customer/client/patients, (3) worker on worker, and (4) personal relationships. These are found in Box 5-2.

The Nature and Extent of Workplace Violence

According to the NIOSH, even though workplace homicides have decreased annually over the last 15 years, there were still over 14,770 workplace homicides between 1992 and 2012, an average of 700 per year. The research also shows that about 70 percent of workplace homicides are the result of robberies, while another 21 percent were committed by workplace associates. Of these workplace homicides, 28 percent of the victims were in a retail sales-related position, 17 percent were employed in a protective services profession, and 13 percent were employed in material moving and transportation-related occupations. In the majority of these incidents (80 percent), firearms were used (Harrell, 2011; "Occupational violence," 2015).

Nonfatal incidents, which are far more common than fatalities, are also an issue. OSHA estimates that 2 million workers are victims of WPV annually ("What is workplace violence," 2002). In 2009, an estimated 572,000 nonfatal crimes (rape/sexual assault, robbery, and simple or aggravated assault) were committed against individuals in the workplace where 137,000 individuals had to be treated for injuries at hospital emergency rooms. Although simple assault is the most common WPV incident, domestic violence, stalking, threats, sexual harassment, and physical and emotional abuse are other issues that need to be addressed by organizations. These violence-related activities impact the productivity and profitability of organizations due to lost days, increased medical and worker's compensation costs, and increased security-related expenditures to address WPV-related issues (Rugala & Isaacs, 2003). These events can also lead to low morale, higher rates of employee stress and medical issues, quits, and a decreased or damaged reputation for those companies that have experienced WPV issues.

The research also provides some insight into the victim–offender relationship, the rate of WPV in the industry sector, and when they occur. First, most WPV actions in both the public and private sectors are committed by strangers: 53 percent of males and 41 percent of females were victimized by strangers, where approximately 25 percent of both males and females were victimized by someone whom they had a work relationship with. The most common age range for victims was the 20–34 age group (Harrell, 2013) while males (with the exception of rape and sexual assault) had higher rates of violent WPV than females. Most offenders, meanwhile, were male (82.3 percent), white (54.7 percent), 21 or older (69 percent), and acted alone (85.7 percent). The research also shows that most WPV crimes occur between the hours of 12 P.M. and 6 P.M. (Duhart, 2001).

Not all occupations have the same risk for occupational violence. As a generalization, the occupations that have contact with the public have higher incidents of WPV. Between 2005 and 2009, law enforcement officers, security guards, and bartenders had the highest rates of nonfatal WPV (Harrell, 2011; "Occupational violence," 2015). Violence rates against health care workers, especially those employed in the mental health sector or where workers are addressing a patient's medical and nonmedical needs are also high (Harrell, 2011; Hartley, Doman, Hendricks, & Jenkins, 2012). Another industry sector that has high WPV rate is the retail sector, especially those working at gas stations (Harrell, 2011).

Some specific workplace-related factors that increase the potential for WPV include:

- Contact with the public.
- Exchange of money.
- Delivery of passengers, goods, or services.
- Having a mobile workplace such as a taxicab or police cruiser.
- Working with unstable or volatile persons in health care, social services, or criminal justice settings.
- Working alone or in small numbers.
- Working late at night or during early morning hours.
- Working in high-crime areas.
- Guarding valuable property or possessions.
- Working in community-based settings (Sygnatur & Toscano, 2000).

Internal threats also need to be considered. When nonstrangers commit WPV, the perpetrator may be a coworker, supervisor, client, or domestic partner. Even though research shows that there is no definitive profile of persons who commit WPV, some warning signs of employee threats are shown in Table 5-1 ■. Perpetrators may also be depressed, paranoid,

TABLE 5-1 Workplace Violence Warning Signs—Internal Threats

- Blaming others whenever something goes wrong
- Acting impulsively
- Having difficulty controlling emotions
- Being fascinated with weapons
- Using drugs
- Being a loner
- Exhibiting a pattern of violent behavior or showing tendencies toward violence
- Being obsessed with death
- Experiencing feelings of worthlessness
- Having a deteriorating relationship with supervisors
- Having significant family, financial, and personal problems
- Perceiving or experiencing real discrimination
- Suffering psychiatric illnesses such as depression, paranoia, schizophrenia, or bipolar disorder

Source: Based on "Preventing Violence at Work, by Bonnie S. Michelman, 2011. https://sm.asisonline.org/Pages/Preventing-Violence-at-Work.aspx.

or psychologically imbalanced, have a fascination with weapons, hold antagonism toward others, and may be substance abusers. Often, the perpetrator is faced with a job termination or a layoff. In other cases, the offender may react violently to the leadership style of a supervisor. In some incidents, the perpetrator retaliates against a person who rejected romantic advances or reported the offender for sexual harassment ("*The USDA handbook,*" 2001).

Stress is also a factor in WPV. While worker productivity appears to be increasing, physical and psychological stress in the workplace is increasing as well. Pushed by longer workweeks, larger workloads, and pressure to produce more, job-related stress can lead to depression, anxiety, and illness. During economic recessions, stress can translate into increased WPV—in the form of suicides, shootings sparked by layoffs, violent conflicts with shoplifters, and racially charged rampages (IOMA/IOFM, 2011). The trauma associated with stress can result in harassment, verbal abuse, and physical violence events (Fest, 2001).

Organizations can also be civilly liable for failing to address WPV issues. In 2000, the Hawaii State Occupational Safety and Health Division cited Xerox Corporation for failure to have or enforce WPV policies that might have prevented Xerox employee Byran Uyesugi from shooting seven coworkers to death in 1999. Publicized as the worst mass killing in Hawaii's history, the state alleged that Xerox allowed Uyesugi to return to work after an on-the-job violent outburst that occurred in 1993. The state's citation also stated that Xerox did not have an effective WPV prevention program, and did not properly train managers to recognize and deal with potential employee violence ("Hawaii cites Xerox in worker shooting," 2000). Even verbal abuse in the workplace can cost an employer hundreds of thousands of lawsuit judgment dollars if the behavior is known, tolerated, and not addressed by the organization (Sofield & Salmond, 2003).

Preventing Workplace Violence

All organizations should have a comprehensive workplace violence prevention program to mitigate and address violent episodes in the workplace. Some key elements of these programs include: (1) managerial commitment and support, (2) a workplace safety analysis, (3) prevention and control, (4) administrative controls, (5) safe work practices, (6) training, and (7) post-incidence response (Cohen, 2004; "Occupational violence," 2015). The goal of any comprehensive WPV program is to keep threats out while also identifying and managing internal threats through proactive policies and interventions.

Managerial support begins with management's recognition that WPV is a serious health and safety issue for employees and the organization where management then commits to and supports a comprehensive WPV program that includes employee involvement in the development of the program. As part of this commitment, management is also responsible for creating a violence-free culture and providing financial, personnel, and information-based resources to make the program a success (OSHA, 2015).

The workplace safety analysis includes identifying and assessing hazards and threats (OSHA, 2015). Here, managers must review past incident reports and the frequency and severity of WPV-related incidents in their organizations. Managers must also analyze and understand the threat environment through a comprehensive review of criminal activities and trends or patterns in WPV in other organizations and industry groups. Part of an effective analysis will also include the use of employee surveys to detect areas of conflict and concern. These surveys will also build greater levels of trust and unity between employees and management (Lewin, 2002). The safety analysis will also require a comprehensive safety and security audit whose activities can be found in Chapter 12 of this text.

When designing a WPV plan against internal threats, the staff needs to consider the source of the problem by analyzing the aggressor and the target. In many cases, WPV is often considered to be a person on person issue. This may be a narrow approach to understanding and identifying sources of workplace aggression. Some research suggests that workplace

violence prevention program Specific security programs designed to mitigate and prevent workplace violence incidents.

safety analysis Identifying and assessing workplace hazards.

aggression should be examined based on the target and direction of the aggression. By looking at aggression and violence in this perspective, it can be examined at the individual, group, and organizational levels. For instance, violence may be attributed to individual on individual issues, which can be considered a lateral form of aggression where individual employees will engage in various actions against other individual workers for a variety of personal issues. There could be lateral group on group aggressive activities where one shift or department, for example, may not like another shift or department. In other cases, there could be upward forms of aggression where individuals could be aggressive toward other work groups or team members, based on work-related issues or personal bias. Individuals and groups could also target the organization, which in turn could create a toxic and unsettling work environment. Organizations themselves can create WPV issues in a downward direction toward groups and individuals. Organizations through their actions (or inactions) can inadvertently create hostile or toxic work environments. They may lack policies and procedures related to WPV and they may not enforce policies or recognize the need for policies and enforcement. In some cases, organizations may even have a culture that supports antagonizing groups and individuals for various purposes (Pinto, 2014).

prevention and control strategies The use of engineering and administrative controls to create a solid, comprehensive physical security program.

Prevention and control strategies begin with the creation of a solid, comprehensive physical security program. Here, various *engineering controls*, which are physical changes to the workplace, are used to separate workers from hazards and threats (OSHA, 2015). Physical changes to the workplace may include modifying the work environment by providing panic alarms and other forms of emergency communication that can be readily accessed by the staff, and adding secure doors and rooms. Many of these engineering controls are based on the principles of Crime Prevention through Environmental Design (CPTED) which uses modifications to the environment (building design and landscaping) to deter and prevent criminal behaviors (Crowe, 2000).

Coinciding with the creation of an effective physical security program, organizations also need to develop comprehensive administrative controls to reduce the risk of WPV. Administrative controls are policies and procedures that promote safe work practices. They rely upon human actions to be effective. These administrative controls can be quite extensive, including major changes to policies and procedures related to WPV, procedures for addressing complaints and incidents, stress, drug and alcohol abuse prevention, conflict management, harassment, and weapons policies. Changes to pre-employment screening tools and disciplinary measures associated with WPV may also be instituted (Pinheiro & Anderson, 2012; Sugahara & Sugahara, 2014). Another administrative control could include the use of early warning systems. Early warning systems (EWS) can be considered a form of preventative management where the organization uses a variety of baseline data to monitor employee actions with the goal of preventing a counterproductive action, such as WPV, before it occurs (Bell, Quick, & Cycyota, 2002). For instance, increased absenteeism, changes in work and productivity, and increased complaints from staff and customers may be an indicator of a personal problem that management could proactively address in order to prevent a WPV episode.

administrative controls Policies and procedures that promote safe work practices.

early warning systems (EWS) Preventative management where the organization uses a variety of baseline data to monitor employee actions with the goal of preventing a counterproductive action, such as workplace violence, before it occurs.

Next, organizations need to modify existing *work practices*. In many situations, organizations over time have inadvertently created work practices that do not support its anti-WPV program. Here, the organization needs to re-evaluate existing work practices by employees to identify any practices that could promote WPV. These work practice changes could include the mandatory reporting of all assaults and threats, establishing liaison with local police, enforcing sign-in procedures for visitors, pairing up employees (buddy systems) in high-risk areas, and requiring employee escorts to vehicle and bus stops ("Workplace violence," 2012). Next, employees should be trained in the new policies and procedures, and be trained to recognize the symptoms of WPV and the profile of potential perpetrators. Without proper training of all employees and managers, prevention and control strategies as well as administrative controls will be ineffective.

Any WPV program also has post-incident procedures. Post-incident procedures are organizational activities immediately after the event. Already, the organization should have established liaison with local law enforcement and other emergency management officials to address a violence-based incident. Post-incident response procedures include crisis response and victim support services to assist the staff in coping. Post-intervention procedures will also include business recovery and resumption plans, investigating the cause(s) of the incident, and media communication (Pinheiro & Anderson, 2012; OSHA, 2015).

<aside>
post-incident procedures
Procedures and activities by the organization immediately after an event.
</aside>

Violence in Health Care Settings

Already, this chapter has identified that health care workers have an increased risk of WPV. OSHA (2015) has created guidelines for health care workers that are based on managerial commitment, worksite analysis, and hazard prevention and control. Some engineering controls include:

- Panic buttons or paging systems at workstations and personal alarm devices worn by employees.
- Metal detectors in high-risk areas (such as emergency rooms).
- Closed circuit television inside and outside the facility.
- Curved mirrors.
- Glass panels/walls for better monitoring.
- Enclosed receptionist desk with bulletproof glass.
- Deep counters at nursing stations.
- Limiting access by locking doors.
- Provide lockable doors and secure bathrooms for staff members that are separated from clients and visitors.
- Secure furniture.
- Areas for patients/clients to de-escalate.
- Comfortable waiting areas to reduce stress among patients.
- Divide waiting areas to limit the spread of agitation among visitors/clients.
- Install bright effective lighting indoors and outdoors.

Some administrative (e.g., policies and procedures) and work practice controls, which change the way employees perform their work, include the following:

- Clearly state to patients, clients, and visitors that violence is not permitted.
- Traveling workers should have specific log in/out procedures and be required to contact the office after every visit.
- Supervise the movement of persons throughout the facility.
- Report all violent incidents to the employer.
- Treat/interview aggressive/agitated clients in open areas.
- Ensure that workers are not alone when performing services.
- Limit workers from working alone in high-risk areas.
- Establish liaison with local police.
- Establish a system (chart tags, log books, verbal reports) to identify patients and clients with a history of violence.
- Institute sign-in procedures and visitor passes.
- Have properly trained personnel to respond to incidents.

Violence in Retail Outlets and Convenience Stores

Statistics indicate that retail sales workers have one of the highest risks for injury on the job. In fact, one-half of all occupational homicides occur at night in small retail outlets (Northwood, 2011). OSHA has created guidelines for WPV prevention in nighttime retail establishments that incorporate physical and personnel security, and administrative and practice controls (*"Recommendations for,"* 2009). Some physical security measures include:

- Limiting signage on windows to increase natural surveillance by the public.
- Lowering shelving through the store so workers can see threats.
- Making sure the cash register area can be seen from outside the store.
- Using curved or convex mirrors at hallways and areas of concealment.
- Ensuring adequate lighting inside and outside the store.
- Placing height markers on door frames to better identify offenders.
- Installing sensors and alarms (including door detectors) that alert staff when a customer enters.
- Installing physical barriers including bullet-resistant glass, pass-through windows, and drop safes.
- Having signage notifying offenders that there is limited cash on hand.
- Using fencing to limit and control the flow of traffic on store property.
- Using CCTV systems to deter and identify perpetrators.
- Having staff panic alarms.

Some administrative and work practice controls include the following:

- Having more staff on duty during high-crime times (late evening/early morning hours).
- Enforcing policies and procedures related to locking doors, cash control, and inspections of CCTV, alarms, and other physical security devices.
- Implementing emergency procedures related to WPV.
- Preventing large currency transactions.
- Establishing liaison with local police.
- Providing security escorts for employees and creating policies and procedures for reducing the risk of assault when using outdoor storage areas and trash dumpsters.

Learn more about workplace violence prevention by accessing the Centers for Disease Control, National Institute for Occupational Safety and Health (NIOSH) website at www.cdc.gov.

▶ Personnel Security and International Issues

Business travel is expected to grow in some parts of the world such as the Asia Pacific region (Becken, 2012). With more world trade and subsequent travel, business professionals will be vulnerable to more human and natural threats. Consider the following examples of each:

- The attack and three-day siege by the Islamist group Al-Shabaab at the Westgate shopping mall in Nairobi, Kenya, in September 2013 led to the death of at least 67 individuals while 200 more were injured. Some of the victims included businessmen from Canada and Western Europe (Agbiboa, 2014).

- January 6, 2014 Venezuelan beauty queen and telenovela star Mónica Spear was in her native country of Venezuela where Spear and her ex-husband, Thomas Henry Berry, were gunned down on a desolate highway after the car they were driving struck a sharp object. Seven people have been arrested in the slayings (Cabera, 2014).
- A U.S. citizen who reportedly worked for a U.S.-based company in Mexico was kidnapped early on the morning of January 4, 2011, in Monterrey, Nuevo Leon state, in Mexico. The victim apparently was driving a company-issued armored luxury vehicle at the time of the kidnapping. The victim was severely beaten and was released later in the evening in the nearby city of Escobedo, Nuevo Leon state, just north of Monterrey. No ransom was demanded, indicating that the attackers' main objective was stealing the armored luxury vehicle ("Mexico security memo," 2011).

Some of the more common risks to international executives include kidnapping, health-related issues, and terrorism-related incidents.

Executive/Corporate Kidnapping

Corporate kidnapping is the abduction of employees for ransom, where the company is solicited for the ransom payment. Here, the company is considered to be the primary victim because it is the one that is being extorted for money, while the actual person(s) kidnapped are secondary victims (Johnson, McKenzie, & Warchol, 2003). Unlike political forms of kidnapping, which are common in some parts of the world, the primary motive of corporate-based forms of kidnapping is monetary gain. In one study of over 7,900 kidnapping incidents in Columbia, the majority of kidnappings were committed for financial purposes (Pires, Guerette, & Stubbert, 2014). In fact, the Al-Qaeda cell in the country of Mali made over $90 million over a 10-year period, and the kidnapping of crews and the vessels and their contents for ransom are commonplace off the African coast by Somali pirates. Such incidents are not rare: the number of persons kidnapped annually for ransom worldwide is estimated at 25,000 (Pires et al., 2014).

In some countries, executive kidnapping has become a cottage industry for local criminals looking for easy money, abducting naïve, unprotected, and unprepared businesspersons traveling for their companies. In other cases, corporate kidnapping is committed by highly organized criminal syndicates, rebel groups, narco groups, and even terrorist organizations that are seeking new funding sources for their activities (Johnson et al., 2003; Petersen & Petersen, 1993). Some of the top countries for kidnapping include Columbia, Mexico, Brazil, Ecuador, Peru, and Venezuela. Other high-risk countries include Nigeria and India (Briggs, 2001; Strizzi & Meis, 2001), while Mexico is currently the most dangerous country for business executives (Tuttle, 2015).

There are different types of kidnappings. Express kidnappings are short term in nature. In these types of kidnappings, abductors drive the hostage(s) to an ATM in order to withdraw as much cash as possible, and then release them. These are common in Mexico (Johnson et al., 2003). In other cases, there are long-term kidnappings where the hostage is kept for long periods of time and where ransoms can be quite large. For example, Thomas Hargroves, an employee of the International Rice Research Institute, was kidnapped in 1994 by FARC (*Fuerzas Armadas Revolucionarias de Colombia or the Revolutionary Armed Forces of Columbia*) rebels and held hostage for 11 months until his family paid a six-digit ransom (Hargroves, 2007). Another type is group-based, which often involves offenders setting up roadblocks between major cities and abducting individuals from their vehicles when they are forced to stop (Pires et al., 2014).

There are many proactive strategies used to address executive kidnappings. At the governmental level, countries can create or enhance criminal sanctions, while local governments can increase the number of police. However, companies relying only on these

corporate kidnapping The abduction of employees for ransom, where the company is solicited for the ransom payment. Also called executive kidnapping.

express kidnappings Short-term types of executive/corporate kidnapping.

strategies fail to consider that many of the areas where kidnappings occur have weak and corrupt governmental units where local police and other governmental officials are involved in the kidnapping business (Johnson et al., 2003). In other cases, corporations themselves need to be responsible for EP activities. Companies often educate employees on the dangers of foreign travel, regardless of the country, and provide training in safe travel tactics. This training includes a variety of topics including: dressing inconspicuously and "blending in," who to talk and socialize with, where to go, conduct outside of secure areas, and escape and evasion techniques (Johnson & Kingshott, 2009). Employees themselves can be target hardened by wearing and equipping their vehicles with GPS to track their movements (Pires et al., 2014), using security transport, armored vehicles, and lodging employees in target-hardened hotels or private facilities staffed by security personnel (Trotta, 1988). Additionally, organizations can use private security and EP personnel that may accompany business executives and oftentimes their families traveling to certain high-risk areas. Companies could also use contract personnel (and companies) who specialize in EP activities, or they can also employ reputable security forces in the host nations (James & Goldstaub, 1988). These programs often extend to the family members of executives who are often considered "soft targets" because they may be overlooked in the security needs assessments but are nevertheless targets for kidnappers (Johnson et al., 2003). An effective safe travel program should also include situational awareness training. In a broad sense, situational awareness is being aware of one's surroundings and having the ability to identify dangerous situations and threats. This mindset also requires that individuals take responsibility for their own safety and "trusting their gut" or having an intuition that a security threat exists (Stewart, 2012).

> **situational awareness**
> Being aware of one's surroundings and having the ability to identify dangerous situations and threats.

Corporations also use reactive measures to protect critical employees. One measure is to have kidnap and ransom (K&R) insurance. It is estimated that 75 percent of the Fortune 500 companies already have K&R policies to protect executives (Kravitz & O'Molloy, 2014). K&R insurance policies are taken out by companies and individuals to address the costs associated with a kidnapping incident. Like other forms of insurance, the cost of K&R insurance is based on individual characteristics and the region of world where the person is traveling. There are several different types of K&R insurance. Some policies only cover the cost of the ransom, while others cover the costs associated with ransom, the recovery of the person and post-incident issues including medical and psychological assistance (Johnson et al., 2003; Lobo-Guerrero, 2007).

There are governmental resources available for companies to combat corporate kidnapping. One major resource is the Overseas Security Advisory Council (OSAC). Created in 1985, OSAC is a partnership between 34 private and public sector organizations and the U.S. Department of State Diplomatic Security Service to address and identify security-related issues in foreign countries. As part of its mission, OSAC also provides best practices for security activities abroad. To date, approximately 3,500 organizations participate in the OSAC program (About OSAC, 2015). In addition to OSAC, the U.S. Department of State publishes travel advisories that provide up-to-date information on natural disasters, disease, and man-made threats country by country.

> **Overseas Security Advisory Council (OSAC)**
> Created in 1985, a partnership between 34 private and public sector organizations and the U.S. Department of State, Diplomatic Security Service to address and identify security-related issues in foreign countries.

Learn more about the Overseas Security Advisory Council and safe travel at www.osac .gov and the U.S, Department of state at www.state.gov.

Health Threats to Employees

Organizations that assign human assets to work in foreign lands must also ensure their health. Health care services in many foreign nations and regions of the world are substandard. A failure to receive adequate medical care immediately after the onset of a sudden illness can be fatal. Like other security-related issues, security personnel need to perform a health-related risk analysis of the specific region and countries that executives will be traveling to in order to determine what health threats are present along with the existing medical services that exist in the region of the world or particular country. Security personnel also need to participate in pre-travel consultation activities that include informing and training travelers in health-related issues while also determining specific pre-existing health issues that may exist. Some companies maintain or establish contractual arrangements with highly trained teams that specialize in medical evacuation of personnel from foreign countries. In other cases, companies will have paramedics (and appropriate medical supplies and equipment) accompany executives on their travels (Johnson & Kingshott, 2009). Based on the threat environment, companies may decide to avoid high-risk health areas. For example, the Ebola outbreak in West Africa in 2014 was declared a public health emergency by the WHO, leading to a large decrease in business travel where even the airlines temporarily discontinued flights to protect flight crews from exposure (Waheed, 2014). Another component of a comprehensive health program also includes post-travel debriefing activities in order to determine if travelers experienced any health issues, and to identify additional health issues that may have been overlooked in the initial risk analysis (Centers for Disease Control and Prevention, 2015; Lee & Spisto, 2004).

Terrorism

Like the risk of kidnapping, the threat of international and domestic terrorist attacks can lead to death or serious injury for employees. Such actions are also orchestrated to damage the reputation of the companies involved. Trends suggest that the United States and its citizens are preferred targets for terrorists. Luxury hotels in Jordan, Pakistan, Indonesia, India, and Afghanistan have been targeted by terrorist groups due in large part because they are frequented by citizens and business executives from Western nations and they are a symbol of Western culture (Paraskevas, 2013; Wernick & Von Glinow, 2012). To avoid these threats while nevertheless maintaining business relationships in some high-risk regions of the world, companies have also found options to physical travel. Some companies, for example, use videoconferencing or virtual meetings (Tarlow, 2011), while others may use private or chartered aircraft instead of commercial flights (Derudder, Faulconbridge, Witlox, & Beaverstock, 2012).

Summary

Personnel security involves the protection of human beings and security from individuals who pose threats to others as well as the organization's physical and information assets. Personnel security is a complex process. Any effective security program begins with a creation of effective policies and procedures. These policies and procedures are the foundation of any personnel security program, assisting in building a culture of security awareness in the organization. Organizations must also prevent employee-based threats from entering the workplace through the design and use of effective pre-employment tools, including background investigations, that serve to "screen in" qualified individuals in order to prevent personal and property-related crimes from occurring in the workplace while also protecting the assets of organizations. To further ensure personnel security, many organizations also have continued reliability practices to ensure the integrity and honesty of its employees throughout the employment relationship. In some cases, companies use executive protection personnel as a means to ensure the safety and security of their employees.

This chapter has also shown that unfortunately, crimes against personnel and companies can and do occur. One issue is workplace violence. Since WPV is a process involving offenders and victims, this "chain" needs to be interrupted, broken through prevention and control strategies using engineering and administrative controls, and modifying work practices that are effective means to mitigate the risk of WPV. Personnel security also needs to address other issues such as executive/corporate kidnapping, health issues, and terrorist-related attacks.

Careers in Personnel Security

Entry-level and advanced positions in personnel security include background and continued reliability investigations, training, and EP activities. These opportunities exist in both the contract and proprietary sectors. Salaries and qualifications vary depending upon the position desired. Some positions require experience, while others require advanced degrees (Associates and Bachelors). A review of career-related search engines using the key words "personnel security," "background investigator," and "executive protection" will provide additional details on requirements and salaries. There are also many public sector positions available. These positions can be found on usajobs.gov. For example, the Defense Security Services (DSS) employees are responsible for personnel security clearances. Some of the specific activities performed are shown below:

- Analyze investigative case files to determine whether a person is able and willing to safeguard classified national security information, based on his or her loyalty, character, trustworthiness, and reliability.
- Understand and apply national guidelines that determine eligibility for access to classified information.
- Educate industry on the personnel clearance process.
- Incorporate latest technology into the clearance process.
- Work both independently and in a collaborative environment with other security professionals.

Entry-level salaries range between $42,000 and $57,000 depending upon qualifications.

Key Terms and Concepts

Administrative controls *110*
Advance team *105*
Advanced procedures *105*
Background investigation *100*
Continued reliability *101*
Corporate kidnapping *113*
Credit history *101*
Criminal history checks *100*
Early warning systems *110*

Executive protection *104*
Express kidnappings *113*
Integrity tests *100*
Interview *99*
Job task (occupational) analysis *99*
Occupational safety *103*
Overseas Security Advisory
   Council (OSAC) *114*
Personnel security *98*

Post-incident procedures *111*
Prevention and control strategies *110*
Principal *104*
Protective operations *105*
Safety analysis *109*
Security awareness *98*
Situational awareness *114*
Violence prevention program *109*
Workplace violence (WPV) *106*

Discussion Questions and Exercises

1. Describe the role of personnel security in the protective function.
2. Outline and describe the process for the recruitment and selection of personnel.
3. What are some of the key elements of a background investigation?
4. What is continued reliability? How do you ensure continued reliability in the workplace?
5. What is occupational safety? What is the role of OSHA and security in occupational safety?

6. Explain executive protection. What are some of the major elements of any executive protection program?
7. What is workplace violence? What are some causes of WPV?
8. What are the four types of workplace violence?
9. What are some key elements of an effective WPV prevention program?
10. What is corporate kidnapping? How can it be mitigated or prevented?

Your Turn

Managing Workplace Violence

Apollo Communications provides technical support services to several major companies engaged in landline, digital, and satellite communications. Due to the nature of Apollo's business, it employs numerous technical experts who are difficult to retain because of their high-demand status. During a hiring surge initiated after Apollo took on several large new customers, the company hired a new employee, Bob Jones. Before being offered the position, Jones interviewed well. Moreover, his criminal, credit, employment, and academic histories were subjected to Apollo's pre-employment screening process. Although many of Jones' previous employment positions had lasted less than a year, Apollo hired Jones because managers believed that he had the technical expertise the company needed. However, within a few months, it became obvious to Apollo that Jones did not have the level and type of technical expertise his credentials had promised. Jones was terminated before the end of his probationary period.

Subsequent to his termination, Jones sent threatening emails to former coworkers. Futhermore, employees often encountered Jones in the company's parking lot as they ended their workday. On several occasions, Jones confronted and verbally threatened his former supervisor in the parking lot.

1. In your view, could a defective pre-employment screening process have led to Jones' hiring? If so, in what respects might the screening process have been defective?

2. If you had been involved in the process used to hire Jones, what warning signs would you have noticed and investigated?

3. Did Apollo exercise poor judgment when hiring Jones? If so, what may have led to the poor judgment? For example, could feelings of pressure to enhance staff quickly to serve new customers have caused hiring managers to overlook warning signs they normally would have noticed? If Apollo had successfully hired large numbers of new people in the past, could those involved in the hiring process become complacent?

4. In your opinion, how likely is it that Jones could become violent? Explain your reasoning.

5. How would you advise Apollo to respond to Jones' threats? Draw on what you learned in this chapter, including suggestions for securing office buildings, assessing the likelihood that someone in the workplace could become violent, and preventing workplace violence.

6. Who do you think should bear the primary responsibility for preventing workplace violence—employers? local law enforcement? mental health professionals? Explain your thinking. In what ways (if any) could these and other stakeholders work together to prevent workplace violence more effectively?

6 Information Security

LEARNING OBJECTIVES

After completing this chapter, the reader should be able to:

1. explain the importance of information security
2. explain and apply the CIA triad
3. know the major elements of an information security program
4. understand asset clarification and control processes
5. understand the importance of policies and procedures and physical security measures in an information security program
6. identify how human behaviors can compromise information security programs
7. explain the nature and extent of cybersecurity and some common types of cyberattacks
8. explain and understand the key elements of any network security program
9. understand the underlying principles of communications security
10. define intellectual property and ways to protect it

▶ Introduction

Information is a valuable asset and the lifeblood of organizations. As a basis for political power and defense, information is vital to national security. Information represents one of the most important components for survival within a competitive global economy. As a business resource, information is used for internal operations and strategic planning. Information provides the knowledge base necessary to identify risks and protect people and property. Information is extremely perishable and often costly to produce and protect. In addition, threats to information come in numerous and varied forms. They include environmental and natural disasters, fire, accidents, and intentional human actions. Information can be physically or electronically damaged, destroyed, or stolen. Authorized as well as unauthorized persons can manipulate data, deny access to authorized users, conduct economic and political espionage, and improperly destroy critical information. Bribery and extortion as well as physical and electronic eavesdropping undermine efforts to safeguard proprietary information and intellectual property. Employees, guests, vendors, foreign nationals, and computer hackers (computer intruders) can sabotage databases (American Society for Industrial Security, 1998; Boyce & Jennings, 2002; Jones, 2000; Maras, 2012; U.S. Department of Justice, Federal Bureau of Investigation, 2007).

Information exists in systems, which are interdependent and interacting components that are organized to accomplish a specific activity or objective. An *information system* is a discrete (and integrated) set of information resources organized for the collection, processing, maintenance, use, sharing, dissemination, or disposition of information. Some of the key elements of information systems include data, and people (employees and authorized users). Other key elements include information technologies (computer equipment/hardware, software and communications) used to store, retrieve and transmit data. While oftentimes information systems are examined in the context of computer systems and digitized information, in a broader perspective, information systems also include verbal and traditional "paper and pencil," or print-based information and media, which all organizations still heavily rely upon. Moreover, these information systems interact with other systems, including the environment in which they exist and operate. Oftentimes, this information is proprietary or the property of the organization that includes trade secrets and other information critical to the economic, commercial, and financial success of the company where its loss or theft could result in the loss of millions of dollars for the company or even its complete failure. Indirectly, the news that an organization has lost or mismanaged information will also damage its reputation (Syamsuddin & Hwang, 2010).

This information and the systems in which it exists must be protected through effective security measures. This chapter will provide a review of some of the main issues related to information security. Regardless of the type of organization, every organization needs to have a properly developed information security program.

> **hacker** A person who illegally accesses restricted computer systems and databases.

▶ Information Security

Information security (INFOSEC) in a broad perspective is the protection of information and information systems from threats. It is defined as "protecting information and information systems from unauthorized access, use, disclosure, disruption, modification, or destruction." (Hwang & Syamsuddin, 2009, p. 159). In a virtual cyberdomain, information security is related to the "protection of data and processing from unauthorized observation, modification, or interference" (Sehgal et al., 2011, p. 279). While a great deal of INFOSEC-related efforts are directed at computers and the information these devices store and transfer, the discipline of information security is much broader, encompassing the protection of all forms of information. To accomplish INFOSEC goals, management utilizes INFOSEC risk assessment and analysis processes to determine the criticality of the information, its vulnerability, and the probability that a threat will materialize. The cost of information replacement, waste, abuse, and liability associated with its unauthorized release must also be evaluated. In addition, the cost effectiveness of the information safeguards recommended and implemented must also be determined.

> **INFOSEC** The protection of information and information systems.

> **CIA triad** A security program that uses the goals of Confidentiality, Integrity, and Availability to ensure information systems security.

Information Security Objectives

An effective information security program relies upon the three elements, known as the CIA triad or *model* that uses the goals of confidentiality, integrity, and availability to ensure information systems security. A review of this triad can be found in Box 6-1. These are considered the three most important goals of information security, and they apply to both cyber and physical forms of information. First, confidentiality addresses keeping data private, allowing its access to authorized persons only. To keep data private, organizations will have rules and restrictions to ensure that information is accessible only to those authorized to have it and there is no loss of confidentiality. Integrity, meanwhile, is that an organization has processes to ensure that information is not modified, destroyed, or altered in some manner from storage and transfer (Mellado, Fernández-Medina, & Piattini, 2007; Stine, Kissel, Barker, Fahlsing, & Gulick, 2008). For example, one common issue that may arise is the unauthorized modification of software that can result in a malicious

> **confidentiality** Keeping data private, allowing its access to authorized persons only.

> **integrity** An organization has processes to ensure that information and/or data is not modified, destroyed, or altered in some manner from storage and transfer.

BOX 6-1

CIA TRIAD

Security objectives	Definition
Confidentiality: A loss of *confidentiality* is the unauthorized disclosure of information.	"Preserving authorized restrictions on information access and disclosure, including means for protecting personal privacy and proprietary information…"
Integrity: A loss of integrity is the unauthorized modification or destruction of information.	"Guarding against improper information modification or destruction, and includes ensuring information nonrepudiation and authenticity…"
Availability: A loss of availability is the disruption of access to or use of information or an information system.	"Ensuring timely and reliable access to and use of information…"

Source: Stine et al. (2008, August).

availability Ensuring that information is available to all authorized users.

software attack on the organization's information system. Next is availability. The objective of availability is to ensure that information is available to all authorized users (Stone & Merrion, 2004). Here, organizations must control access to data through administrative, technical, and physical controls. Administrative controls (as reviewed in Chapter 5) are policies and procedures and security awareness training for employees. Technical controls include firewalls, encryption, etc. Last, there is physical security. Like the other assets an organization needs to protect, there must be a layered approach to information security where threats must defeat multiple physical barriers to access protected information. These will be reviewed in detail in this chapter.

Designing an Information Security Program

The business community might save itself considerable time, effort, and money by adopting information protection strategies that replicate those employed in government operations. Paralleling government efforts, *operations security* (OPSEC) involves information risk assessment and business intelligence activities in a process through which business operations are analyzed to identify potential intelligence indicators that competitors might scrutinize to gain a competitive advantage. OPSEC views operations from an adversary's perspective in an effort to seek out an organization's vulnerabilities and protect its critical information, which is defined as information that is vital to a mission that if an adversary obtains it, correctly analyzes it, and acts upon it, the compromise of this information could prevent or seriously degrade mission success (OPSEC Professionals Society, 2007). This means that business-people must think like criminals, anticipating threats. Private businesses seeking government contracts for classified projects are often required to submit OPSEC plans along with their bids. Components of the development and implementation of an effective OPSEC plan include:

critical information Information vital to a mission. All forms and types of information as defined in the U.S. Economic Security Act of 1996.

- The identification and valuation of critical information.
- Identifying and analyzing potential threats, including the threat's motivation and capabilities.
- Evaluating the organization's information vulnerabilities.
- Assessing the impact of a materialized threat as well as a cost-benefit analysis of any protective measure implemented.
- Implementing the most cost-effective protective measure options (countermeasures) (Jelen, 1994; OPSEC Professionals Society, 2007).

► Key Components of an Information Security Program

Any organization needs to implement and maintain an information security program. Some of the key elements of these programs include: (1) asset classification and access control; (2) policies and procedures; (3) physical security controls; (4) controlling human activities; (5) technical/logical controls; (6) communications and operations management; (7) systems development and maintenance; (8) business continuity management; and (9) compliance.

Asset Classification and Access Control

Not all information has the same value. Asset classification is the process of assigning value to information. Classification criteria are developed through the risk analysis process and governmental regulations. In other cases, the value of information-based assets is determined by personal decisions. Once the value of information is properly assessed, then various access controls or security measures can be attached to the asset to protect it.

> **asset classification** The process of assigning value to information.

Three types of access control policies include: (1) role-based; (2) discretionary; and (3) mandatory. Role-based access control (RBAC) systems grant access based on the roles that individual users have in the organization. Oftentimes, under this type of system, access rights are based on the person's position, job assignments, or responsibilities in the organization. Generally, RBAC systems are easy to administer because they are not based on the personal characteristics of the user. Under this control policy system administrators (in the case of computer-based access control) can simply grant permissions in bulk, based on the position a person holds (Alhaqbani & Fidge, 2008). Discretionary access control (DAC) systems, which are common in many businesses, grant access to information by the owner of that information. Under these models, the owner of the information or the system administrator decides or delegates who is going to have access to it, adding or removing individuals from the access control list as needed (Biskup & Lochner, 2007). Mandatory access control (MAC) systems are nondiscretionary strategies that are considered more secure than discretionary models. Mandatory access systems have fixed rules or attributes that allow access to information or information systems. Oftentimes, these systems are based on hierarchical models of classification where users are given or assigned a security level based on their level of trustworthiness (Sandhu & Samarati, 1994). For example, the U.S. military uses four levels to classify its information (Boyce & Jennings, 2002; Maras, 2012):

> **role-based access control (RBAC)** An access control policy for computer-based information that grants access based on the job and tasks that individual users have in the organization.

> **discretionary access control (DAC)** Common in many businesses, grant access to information by the owner of that information. Under these models, the owner of the information or the system administrator decides or delegates who is going to have access to the information.

- **Top Secret.** Unauthorized disclosure of information in this category would cause *grave damage* to the United States.
- **Secret.** Unauthorized disclosure of information in this category could cause *damage* to the United States.
- **Confidential.** Unauthorized disclosure of information in this category would be *prejudicial to the interests* of the United States.
- **For Official Use Only.** Unclassified but sensitive. Unauthorized disclosure of this information would compromise trade secrets, give a contractor a competitive bidding advantage, or circumvent the Privacy Act of 1974.

> **mandatory access control (MAC)** Have fixed rules or attributes that allow access to information or information systems.

Mandatory models also use nonhierarchical categories of control that are assigned to users. This nonhierarchical categorization is based on the elements of compartments and caveats. Compartments refer to the subject matter of the information or object(s) that the user is given access to. An example of compartments used may include information security and communications security. Caveats (or markings on the information) are the actual markings on the document which are rules related to using and handling compartmental-ized information. These caveats can include "NOFORN" (no foreign access) and "U.S. EYES ONLY" (only U.S. citizens/viewers allowed) (Carroll, 2014).

Mandatory access control systems can also be used in organizations. After an organi-zation assigns a security level (the hierarchy), it can further compartmentalize and assign caveats to the information (the nonhierarchical elements). For example, an employee may have a secret clearance allowing him to access information related to "product develop-ment" and "testing and evaluation" (the compartments). The caveat, meanwhile, is that "proprietary information is involved." Another example includes: "ACME Confidential, Internal, No Copies." Here, the hierarchical level of security is confidential, while the nonhierarchical category of "Internal" restricts the information for internal use only (the compartment) and "no copies" is the caveat or marking that provides specific rules on how the information can be used.

The National Institute of Standards and Technology (NIST) has also created classifica-tion standards used by the federal government that are based on the security objective and impact. This can be found in Box 6-2.

Organizations need to be aware of the dangers of "over-classifying" information. Over-classifying occurs from doubt on classification criteria or rules, an attitude of "playing it safe," and personal uncertainty (Slaveski & Bakreski, 2014). Over-classifying

BOX 6-2

CATEGORIZATION OF FEDERAL INFORMATION AND INFORMATION SYSTEMS

Security objective	Potential impact		
	Low	Moderate	High
Confidentiality Preserving authorized restrictions on information access and disclosure, including means for protecting personal privacy and proprietary information. [44 U.S.C., SEC. 3542]	The unauthorized disclosure of information could be expected to have a **limited** adverse effect on organizational operations, organizational assets, or individuals.	The unauthorized disclosure of information could be expected to have a **serious** adverse effect on organizational operations, organizational assets, or individuals.	The unauthorized disclosure of information could be expected to have a **severe or catastrophic** adverse effect on organizational operations, organizational assets, or individuals.
Integrity Guarding against improper information modification or destruction, and includes ensuring information nonrepudiation and authenticity. [44 U.S.C., SEC. 3542]	The unauthorized modification or destruction of information could be expected to have a **limited** adverse effect on organizational operations, organizational assets, or individuals.	The unauthorized modification or destruction of information could be expected to have a **serious** adverse effect on organizational operations, organizational assets, or individuals.	The unauthorized modification or destruction of information could be expected to have a **severe or catastrophic** adverse effect on organizational operations, organizational assets, or individuals.
Availability Ensuring timely and reliable access to and use of information. [44 U.S.C., SEC. 3542]	The disruption of access to or use of information or an information system could be expected to have a **limited** adverse effect on organizational operations, organizational assets, or individuals.	The disruption of access to or use of information or an information system could be expected to have a **serious** adverse effect on organizational operations, organizational assets, or individuals.	The disruption of access to or use of information or an information system could be expected to have a **severe or catastrophic** adverse effect on organizational operations, organizational assets, or individuals.

Source: Stine et al. (2008, August).

▼

can restrict the access of information to those who need it to perform their work. Moreover, it leads to increased costs for organizations because of security protocols, operations, and even the cost of personnel investigations. Of greater concern is that the over-classification of information may erode existing policies and procedures for the handling of information. For example, if a person often receives emails that are classified "secret," but the information in them is basically public knowledge and obviously not secret, when actual "secret" classified information is received, the person may "de-value" that information and not follow established security protocols and practices.

Policies and Procedures (Operational Goals)

The goal of any INFOSEC program is to reduce the risk of fraud, error, and the misuse of information and computer resources by humans (Merkow & Breithaupt, 2014). To meet these broad goals, appropriate policies and procedures directed toward individuals and administrative/operational practices must be created.

Some of the specific categories of policies include operational controls that encompass administrative, managerial, and procedural activities that are designed to control human behavior (Van Niekerk & Von Solms, 2004). When considered in the perspective of information security, effective personnel screening tools and policies and procedures related to hiring staff need to be developed that are related to the protection of intellectual property, trade secrets, and sensitive information.

This element also includes the creation of policies and procedures and educating users about their security responsibilities, including the protection and creation of passwords, which is known as password stewardship. Personnel security-related policies should include restricting the use of recording devices, such as cameras, audio–video recording equipment, and cell phones on site to protect against the recording of information. Other policies are related to duplicating information. They can be as simple as having policies or guidelines on photocopying information, and limiting the use of photocopies and scanners to key personnel. Access to accounting, shipping, receiving, payroll, bank records, income, and financial information should be restricted to those who have an absolute need to view and use the information. Other policies include Internet and email use to reduce the threat of cyberattacks, secure storage, network usage, sharing information, and policies on the removal of information outside the workplace. Companies also have policies regulating the use of laptops and mobile devices, memory sticks and memory cards (which many organizations prohibit), and reporting procedures for security-related issues and violations (Carlson, 2001).

Policies should also address procedures for destroying or disposing of information that is no longer needed. Too often, critical information is discarded carelessly. In most jurisdictions, discarded materials placed in a trash can or dumpster are considered abandoned property, thus belonging to no one. An adversary may take the discarded materials and use the information against its former owner. For example, shredding or pulverizing documents and appropriate deletion of information stored in an electronic medium helps to prevent adversarial access to information. In other cases, companies may sell their scrap to recyclers. This scrap, however, could provide intelligence for the competition on what new projects a company is working on. And, in some cases, the scrap could provide the competition with actual new product designs (Winkler, 1997). In other situations, companies sell their entire computers for scrap. In some cases, scrap computers are sent to foreign countries to be recycled where critical proprietary information from the discarded computer hard drives are then recovered, sold, and used to compromise an organization (Doyon-Martin, 2015).

> **password stewardship** Protecting and maintaining effective computer passwords and effectively securing passwords.

Physical Security Controls

physical security measures Physical measures (i.e., locks, walls, gates) used to protect assets.

An effective information security program also requires physical security measures. Already reviewed in Chapter 4, the nature and the extent of the actual physical security measures will be dictated by the information or asset(s) that need to be protected and the threat environment. The protection of information first relies on "traditional" forms of physical protection systems. The physical facility is usually the building(s) housing the system and network components. Security personnel, employee and guest identification systems, sensors, surveillance and alarm systems, automatic door controls, fences, lighting, signage, and crime prevention through environmental design (CPTED) strategies all contribute to the physical protection of information. These physical security measures must take a "defense in depth" approach, providing multiple layers of defense against the human aggressor. In the case of a computer-based crime, for example, physical security measures must exist at the exterior perimeter, at entrances to buildings, and at specific locations within the buildings. If properly designed and administered, these measures can deter, delay, and deny access to information-based assets.

When designing the actual physical protection system, planners need to consider which elements of the information system are the target and the means by which a crime could occur. As a target, computers (and their internal components) are vulnerable to theft and vandalism. To protect against theft, for example, cable locks, vibration, and capacitance sensors are used to alert security personnel that the computer itself is being moved. In the case of theft of information found in an information system, physical security is still needed. Consider, for example, that an unauthorized access to a computer system oftentimes requires physical access to one of the components of the system. If an organization has computers secured in rooms that require some form of access control, the theft of cyber-related information can be deterred, detected, and perhaps denied, even if a person had stolen a password that would have granted access to the system, since the threat could not physically access the computer. In some cases, computers themselves are physically modified to prevent the theft of information. One common (and easy) way is to physically remove all ports (or access points to the computer system and data), preventing persons from inserting USB memory sticks or other types of portable storage devices into them.

Human Activities and Information Security Policy

absolute value The intrinsic value of a particular item without comparing it to other assets.

relative value The subjective value of a component piece of information, based on its contribution to the entire system.

While there are many methods of physically securing information, information security programs also need to consider that human actions and activities often compromise information, regardless of what types of policies and procedures and physical protection systems exist. Therefore, a primary element of any information security program is that human beings are trained in the safe handling of information. In this context, employees (and organizations) first need to recognize the absolute and relative value of information and that all information can have some type of value. Absolute value only looks at the intrinsic value of a particular item without comparing it to other assets. It is the actual monetary value of an item. For example, the theft of a computer itself has an absolute value, based on the cost of replacing it. Relative value, meanwhile, is the subjective value of a component piece of information, based on its contribution to the entire system (Herrmann, 2013; Winkler, 1997).

social engineering Nontechnical and nonphysical means to steal information. Psychologically manipulating people to divulge confidential information.

Consider the following example that shows the value of relative information. One nefarious way to steal information involves social engineering tactics. Social engineering involves nontechnical and nonphysical means to steal information. It involves psychologically manipulating people to divulge confidential information. For example, Ira Winkler (1997), a security consultant, in his book "*Corporate Espionage*" explains how he attacked a company by obtaining "small" seemingly innocent pieces of information. His attack first began when he called the corporation's mailroom where he obtained shipping codes from an employee. Once he got the shipping codes, he posed as an executive, calling human resources, instructing them to mail a corporate telephone directory (an internal document) to a fictitious subcontractor (himself), providing them with a valid shipping code (which served to gain credibility and trust with the human resources employee) that he obtained from the mailroom employee. Once he received the phone book in the mail, he then contacted various executives in the corporation using the ruse that he was from human resources, collecting sensitive corporate information that subsequently compromised the company. While some of this information seemingly had limited or no absolute value to the holder of the information, combining the "bits" of relative value information caused a serious security issue for the organization. This example also shows that part of any information security program involves educating employees about the need for information security and that common information has value.

There are several human activities in the workplace that can compromise information security. In some cases, common activities compromise existing physical security measures. For example, employees may leave file cabinets unlocked, fail to lock offices when not in them, leave information unsecured and available for others to view and take, hold secure doors open for other individuals (defeating physical security), allowing them to "tailgate" or follow a person through a secure portal without using their access control device, (Myyry, Siponen, Pahnila, Vartiainen, & Vance, 2009) write passwords on documents or calendars and Post-it notes in offices, and fail to shut down or log off on workstations. In fact, information security could even be compromised because of a messy desk or an unorganized office. By failing to have a "clean desk" where information is properly organized, the theft of information in a disorganized, cluttered, or "dirty" office may not be readily detected (De Maeyer, 2007).

Information can be compromised through social engineering activities outside the workplace. Information can be divulged in social settings, including bars and clubs, where a casual conversation about one's personal life and interests, occupation, and work is not innocent in nature, but is designed to obtain information to hack into a computer system, or to collect information about confidential projects. Social engineering can also occur online, through social network sites where the threat builds a level of trust with the victim(s) (Corritore, Kracher, & Wiedenbeck, 2003). Some of these social engineering incidents can involve long-term romantic relationships where the person's true motives are based on obtaining information from his or her unwitting partner. In one case, an employee of a biochip company shared trade secrets with her boyfriend (who was actually a corporate spy) whose "employer" was sending him back to Europe because he could not solve some research questions and his work was unsatisfactory. Out of fear that she would lose her boyfriend, she then gave him computer disks and over 2,000 pages of confidential DNA research information to assist him in his research, hoping he would not be transferred. He then fled back to Europe after stealing more documents from her apartment. The scam was detected by corporate security that contacted the FBI. However, the damage to the company was already done (Schweizer, 1993).

Technical/Logical Controls

Logical or technical controls are products and processes used to protect access to and the flow of data in an information system. They can be considered to be technical controls (not physical protection) that are software-based that prevent access to the system itself through some type of authentication. These nonphysical means of denying access include firewalls, antivirus software, encryption, and intrusion detection software (Baker & Wallace, 2007). They are not part of the physical architecture of a system, but they are very important as

> **technical controls**
> Products and processes used to protect access to and the flow of data in an information system.

"cyber-access" control measures. These technical controls also include activities related to identification and authentication, access control, confidentiality, integrity of data, nonrepudiation controls that guarantee the accurate transmission of messages (oftentimes through encryption), and denying a transaction or activity (Botha & Eloff, 2001). Like physical security measures, these are often used in a layered "defense in depth" approach to prevent a system compromise.

Some common technical controls include passwords, biometrics, and session locks. In many cases, passwords (or unique identifiers) are fixed, meaning they are valid for a certain period of time where the user will have to request a new password from a system administrator or update and change the existing password. In other cases, passwords are dynamic or one-time use. These passwords are often created by tokens (Personal Identification Numbers [PINs] that change with time) which generate a one-time password for the user. These types of passwords are preferred (Tseng, Jan, & Yang, 2007). Other types of technical access controls also include biometrics that include fingerprint and retinal scans that may be used in conjunction with passwords as an added layer of access control. There are also session locks that are designed to prevent unauthorized users from accessing information from "open" computers. Here the system "locks out" users who have not performed a computer function (such as a keystroke) for a set period of time, such as 2 minutes, requiring the legitimate user to log back onto the system (Choi & Lee, 2015).

Communications and Operations Management

The objective of this element of information security is to ensure that information processing facilities are secure. It concentrates on reducing the risk of failure "and its consequences by ensuring the proper and secure use of information processing facilities, and by developing incident response procedures" (Saint-Germain, 2005, p. 62). Communications and operations management activities focus on the organization's operational procedures, change control (which is concerned with the management of all changes and modifications to a computer system), incident management, the segregation of duties among staff to prevent internal security issues, the management of removable data, and capacity planning which deals with the ability of the system to meet new technological developments and demands while meeting the flow or volume of information (Franke, Johnson, & Konig, 2014; McAdams, 2004; Nsouli & Schaechter, 2002). Some of these elements include backup recovery processes, and processes to protect the integrity and security of software and information from intrusion and viruses (Ma & Pearson, 2005). Operations management also addresses "housekeeping" activities that include guidelines, procedures, and scheduling the backing up of data, the disposal of media, and controls related to the exchange of information within and outside of the organization (Carlson, 2001).

Systems Development and Maintenance

This element of a security policy defines and establishes the requirements for the planning and management of the organization's information security system. This element requires that security be part of any system from the initial development to the procurement of new components throughout its entire "lifecycle" (from initiation to discontinued use and disposal). It includes policies and standards related to cryptography, which is the science of secret writing, and cryptographic security which involves a transformation (secret writing) of the data being transmitted in order to make it unintelligible to an unauthorized interceptor. Converting plain text to crypto text is referred to as an encryption, while conversion of crypto text to plain text is referred to as a decryption. The primary goal of this element is to ensure system integrity of software and data, while being able to track and evaluate existing system security measures, and update and modify as needed (Carlson, 2001). In the context of

password Unique identifier necessary to gain access, as in a code inputted to access a computer file or program.

session locks Prevent unauthorized users from accessing information from "open" computers.

cryptographic security The transformation (secret writing) of the data being transmitted in order to make it unintelligible to an unauthorized interceptor.

encryption Conversion of plain text to crypto text.

decryption Conversion of crypto text to plain text.

computer security, organizations often have virtual private networks (VPNs) that encrypt information between two points. VPNs are used for internal and external communication to protect information flow through untrusted Internet connections when beyond the borders of a trusted internal network (Andress, 2011).

Business Continuity Management

Business continuity management (BCM) is designed to improve the resilience of a company. BCM requires three different activities: (1) planning for issues including interruptions; (2) testing to make sure the plan or program works; and (3) maintenance and reassessment of the BCM strategy (Carlson, 2001). Business continuity ensures that the organization plans and prepares for INFOSEC-related events due to both man-made and natural threats, including fire, earthquakes, and floods. (Goluch et al., 2008). For example, physical protection against damage from fire, flood, wind, earthquake, explosion, civil unrest, and other forms of natural and man-made risk should be designed and implemented. Critical IT equipment, cabling, and so on should be protected against physical damage, fire, flood, theft both on- and off-site. Power supplies and cabling should be secured. The facility's general *geographic location* determines the characteristics of natural threats, which include earthquakes and flooding; man-made threats, such as burglary, civil disorders, or interception of transmissions; and damaging nearby activities, including toxic chemical spills, explosions, and fires. More information regarding business continuity can be found in Chapter 12.

Compliance

Last, organizations need to follow all laws, regulations, and contractual agreements when developing an effective information security program. For example, in one instance, a company holding top secret defense-related information was cited by federal authorities for failing to properly control classified information. While the organization had strong physical security and computer-related measures to prevent access, the actual computer system design was at fault: every day, computer data was backed up to the organization's server that was located at its corporate headquarters in a foreign country. In effect, the company was transmitting top secret information to a foreign country, violating federal law and NISP requirements. This was fixed by changing company protocols and practices for the backup of information.

▶ Cybersecurity

Computer security is a major issue for organizations. It is also a major national security issue for the United States. Since the early 1970s, computer technology has dramatically changed the way information is acquired, transmitted, analyzed, stored, and retrieved. It has transformed the work world and is part of almost everyone's daily life. In most cases, computers rely upon the cyberspace and networks upon networks of interconnected devices (computers, smart phones, communication systems, computerized equipment) to communicate with one another through the Internet or World Wide Web.

Many (if not all) organizations now have the capacity to use off-site storage of information. This information can be stored in the cloud which is a metaphor for Internet-based computing where organizations (and individuals) use external computer services (storage, applications, and servers) from the Internet, instead of using internal computer resources (Babu, Kumar, & Tiwari, 2015). Cloud computing promises to help companies achieve flexibility and agility as well as reduce costs associated with their use of IT. For instance, instead

virtual private networks (VPNs) Computer networks that encrypt information between two points to protect information through untrusted internet connections.

business continuity management (BCM) Designed to improve the resilience of a company. BCM practices ensure that the organization plans and prepares for information-security related events due to both man-made and natural hazards and threats.

cloud A metaphor for Internet-based computing where organizations (and individuals) use external computer services.

of owning the hardware and software necessary to operate a customer call center, a company can pay a vendor to manage the computers, code, and store data involved in this business function. The company pays the vendor only for the number of "seats" (employees responding to customer calls) it needs at the time, scaling that number up or down to reflect business cycles. Despite these advantages, cloud computing has raised questions in some executives' minds about how secure and private their data (especially associated with customers) will be in the cloud. For example, cloud vendors may hire staff without doing sufficient background screening. And when data goes into the cloud, a software bug or malware could compromise it (Brenner, 2010). While off-site storage ensures that information can be recovered if there is a system failure in the organization while also ensuring business continuity, these sites can be compromised. For example, in August 2014, Apple's iCloud was hacked which led to some compromising photos of several celebrities being released to the public (Griffin, 2015).

> **cybercrimes** Criminal activities where computers and computer networks are the target, tool, instrument, or place of criminal activity.

Along with the increased use of computers has come a commensurate increase in cybercrimes, which are criminal activities where computers and computer networks are the target, tool, instrument, or place of criminal activity (Jidiga & Sammulal, 2013). The resulting cybercrimes are vast in type and number. And, unlike traditional crimes, a perpetrator does not have to physically enter the organization to successfully complete the crime. Cybercrimes are global in nature and oftentimes have an international component where the criminal(s) may be in one continent and the victim(s) in another.

The motives of cybercriminals vary and can include curious "cyberpunks (those who hack for notoriety)," "hacktivists (social disobedience related cybercrimes)," and those who engage in cybercrimes for financial and political purposes (Rogers, 2011). Regardless of the motives behind an attack, unauthorized users can steal data and use the victim's computer services for financial gain, or as a tool to attack the information systems owned by other organizations. To defend against cybercrimes an effective cybersecurity program must be developed. Cybersecurity is the "protection of information, infrastructure, and ingredients of information (data) from cyberthreats" (Jidiga & Sammulal, 2013, p. 6).

> **cybersecurity** Computer security efforts directed at the protection of information systems computers, networks, software, and computer-related information from theft or damage.

The Nature and Extent of Cybercrime

As organizations and governments increase their reliance on computer-based information networks, cyberattacks are a critical and growing threat. In a study conducted in 2014, it was estimated that over 80 percent of companies employing more than 2,500 employees were targets of cyberattacks. It was also determined that there are over 1 million new malware threats released into the Internet daily (ISTR, 2015). Verizon Corporation's 2015 Data Breach Investigations Report that investigated 70 companies throughout the world found that there were 79,700 incidents, and 2,122 confirmed data breaches that resulted in the compromise of 700 million records. The dollar losses related to cybercime are immense. Financial losses are estimated annually to be $105 billion, and it is estimated that cybercriminals make more money yearly than total profits from the illegal drug trade (Bose & Leung, 2014). At an individual level, the FBI's annual Internet crime report (that relies upon the voluntary submission of cybercrimes to its Internet Crime Complaint Center), shows that there were over 269,422 complaints received in 2014. Of these, 123,684 reported some type of financial loss, averaging $6,472 per incident. It is estimated that only 10 percent of all known incidents are reported to the ICCC (FBI, 2014).

Types of Cybercrimes

Numerous types of computer-related crimes are committed against organizations and individuals. One typology classifies cybercrimes based on whether the computer is the: (1) target or (2) instrument or tool used to commit the crime. These Type I and II classifications are shown in Box 6-3.

▼

CYBERCRIME CLASSIFICATIONS

	Type	Description
Type I: The computer as a target of crime	Unauthorized access	Hacking, copy, modify, delete or destruction of computer data or programs
	Malicious codes	Virus, worm, Trojan horse, logic bombs, etc.
	Denial of service (DoS)	Disruption of computer services
	Theft of service	Theft of service, misuse of service
Type II: The computer as an instrument of crime	Obnoxious content	Child pornography, hate crimes, harmful contents, forged or counterfeit documents
	Internet fraud	Identity theft, online fraud, sabotage, social engineering fraud, phishing, etc.
	Misconduct	Harassment, cyberstalking, conspiracy, spamming, drug trafficking, extortion, money laundering

Source: Modified from Banday & Mir (2012).

Of particular concern for organizations are Type 1 attacks. *Type I attacks* occur when the computer/computer system is the target. These systems are commonly targeted by *hackers* who are basically unauthorized persons (both internal and external to the company) who unlawfully or illegally access or break into a computer system (Ramdeyal & Eloff, 2004). A hacker's motives range on a continuum from curiosity on the details of an organization's programmable systems, the challenge of hacking into a system, or serious criminal intent where proprietary information or the computer system itself is the target (Rogers, 2011).

There are generally four steps involved in a hacker attack: (1) information gathering; (2) initial access; (3) privilege escalation; and (4) creating back doors and covering tracks. In order to break into a system, hackers first need to gather information. Information gathering involves "footprinting," where the hacker tries to gain as much information about the target and existing computer security, oftentimes scanning the computer system for ways to access it, and probing the system (called enumeration) to see if user accounts and network resources are not well protected. Following information gathering, the threat then usually performs an *initial access* which can involve the installation of malicious codes to gain entry into a system. Once in the system, unauthorized users can expand their privilege or access to other information (called root compromise), oftentimes using malicious codes again to achieve their criminal purposes. In the last stage, the hackers create back doors so they can readily gain access to the system again. One common back door technique includes creating a user account so hackers can readily reaccess the system. In order to ensure not being detected, hackers also need to "cover their tracks" from being detected by system administrators. This can be accomplished by deleting or modifying logs, and disguising the malicious software that was used to gain initial access to the system (Bento & Bento, 2004).

Cybercriminals also use malicious code attacks as a means of gaining entry, or as an end goal of the attack. Malicious code attacks occur when individuals (usually hackers) gain access to user and/or computer administrator accounts in order to shut down or raise havoc in a computer server or network (Bento & Bento, 2004). While numerous in type

> **information gathering** Part of a hacker attack. Where a hacker tries to gain as much information about the target and existing computer security.

> **back doors** A means for hackers to gain access to a computer system.

> **malicious code attack** Computer code designed to gain entry into a system in order to steal information and/or cause damage to data and systems.

and complexity, some of the malicious code attack methods (also known as vectors) use the following methods and *malware* (which is a generic term used to describe malicious software) to gain entry into a system:

spoofing Trickery to gain access to a computer/information system.

- Trojan horse—a program that appears to be a legitimate, useful program but it is actually malware. In Trojan incidents, a user opens a "legitimate" program which launches the nonreplicating malware program, installing a malicious software program that can compromise circuits, software, and hardware devices in the system. These are the most common types of malware (CISCO, 2014; Sharifi, Mohammadiasl, Havasi, & Yazdani, 2015).

phishing A form of computer-based identity theft where the perpetrator poses as a legitimate entity using email and malicious websites to obtain personal information.

- Viruses—are malicious pieces of code that are secretly installed or implanted into a computer system, "infecting" or contaminating the system and devices that use or are connected to the system (Ramdeyal & Eloff, 2004).

- Worms—carry viruses and allow Trojans to be replicated in the entire computer system (Saeed, Selamat, Abuagoub, & Abdulaziz, 2013). Worms basically copy themselves to a system (which Trojans do not do) which then automatically executes various operations. Unlike viruses, they are not a piece of code but are instead an entire program that can run on its own and spread to other machines and devices (Arce & Levy, 2003).

vishing Similar to the traditional phishing scam. Instead of being directed by an email to an Internet site, the victim is asked to provide personal information by means of a telephone, using Voice over Internet Protocol (VOIP).

- Logic bombs—are software programs that remain "silent" until a certain computer activity (keystrokes, opening a program) or date and time is met. Once the activation criteria is met, the software program is then "turned on," infecting the system with malicious code (Saeed et al., 2013).

There are other ways to gain access into a computer system. One way is through "brute force" where a person simply guesses passwords or steals unsecured passwords that individuals have not properly protected (Bento & Bento, 2004). Another kind of cyberattack is through spoofing which involves trickery to gain access to a system. Web spoofing (one type of spoofing) involves the creation of a hoax website that is very similar in appearance and function to a legitimate website. When a user opens the link, a virus or worm is launched. Another type of spoof is phishing. Phishing uses social engineering tactics that rely upon manipulating or tricking people to provide confidential information. Here, the user opens a spoofed website or email and then provides personal information, including passwords and account numbers (Dinev, 2006; Rajalingam, Alomari, & Sumari, 2012). A more recent type of phishing is vishing, which is similar to the traditional phishing scam. Instead of being directed by an email to an Internet site, the victim is asked to provide personal information by means of a telephone, using Voice over Internet Protocol (VOIP), which enables telephone calls to be made over the Internet. Victims are led through a series of voice-prompted menus that request account numbers, passwords, and other sensitive information. In another version of vishing, the caller is a live person or a recorded message that directs the victim to take action to protect a personal credit card or bank account (U.S. Department of Justice, Federal Bureau of Investigation, 2007).

denial of service (DoS) Attack occurs when a perpetrator uses a computer network to flood another computer server with large fictitious packets of data, overloading the system and causing the server to "crash" or to slow down considerably.

In some cases, the primary goal of a cybercriminal is to harm or destroy the computer system or network itself. A denial of service (DoS) attack occurs when a perpetrator uses a computer network to flood another computer server with large fictitious packets of data, overloading the system and causing the server to "crash" or to slow down considerably. There are also distributed denial of service (DDoS) attacks. Here, the perpetrator(s) use a large network of computers that have been compromised (often thousands that have been infected with malware) flooding the organization's server(s) with data to slow or crash it. Regardless of whether it is a DoS or DDoS attack, the underlying goal is to overload the victim's system to prevent it from performing normal Internet-based business activities (Bhandari, Sangal, & Kumar, 2015; Wang, Lin, & Wang, 2016). One analogy that has been used to describe these types of attacks is that they are not "picking the lock" to the system. Instead, they are blocking the

distributed denial of service (DDoS) attack Where a large network of computers have been compromised (often thousands that have been infected with malware), flooding the organization's server(s) with data to slow or crash it.

door from the outside with as much rubbish as they can pile up (Lizard Squad Member, 2015). In one DDoS attack, a hacker group known as the "Lizard Squad" performed DDoS attacks against Xbox Live and Sony's PlayStation on Christmas day, 2014 preventing online gamers the ability to log on to the systems. Besides actual dollar losses associated with the attack, the companies also had damage to their corporate brand (Cooter, n.d.).

Organizations also need to recognize the threat of Type II crimes. In some situations, employees (and nonemployees who have unauthorized access) can use computers as an instrument to commit various crimes, unknown to the owner(s) of the information system. In this context, individuals can use computer systems to store and transfer illegal and obnoxious content, and use systems to defraud customers and the general public. Employees can also use systems to send harassing and threatening emails to coworkers (a form of occupational violence).

SCADA-based Attacks

Specific components of a computer network can also be attacked and compromised. SCADA (Supervisory Control and Data Acquisition) is a category or specific type of application-based software that is used in various control systems to monitor processes and the physical function of equipment (Radvanovsky & Brodsky, 2013). These SCADA-based systems rely upon hardware components that send "real-time" data to a computer equipped with SCADA software that controls that particular piece of equipment. Based on the data received, the computer can then adjust functions on its own, or warn human beings that there is an issue. An example is a SCADA system that detects leaks in an oil pipeline. In this example, if the pressure or volume dropped in the pipeline, the SCADA system would alert personnel or immediately stop the flow of oil by shutting off a valve.

These SCADA systems exist in all organizations. Of particular concern is that some of these systems are tied to the vital production components, where an attack could compromise one small component of the system, leading to a complete system failure. As an example, a SCADA attack could simply target one key component of the production process, such as a motor or generator. By causing one piece of machine to fail, it could lead to a cascading series of events leading to widespread damage, shutting down the entire facility. One actual SCADA-based attack was detected and prevented by personnel in 2010, at Iran's Bushehr nuclear plant. Here, a Stuxnet malware cyberworm infected the plant's computer system, identifying critical functions running on the system's Programmable Logic Controller (PLC), injecting its own code into the system. The Stuxnet "cybermissile" may have entered the system through a USB stick used by a contractor employee building the facility (Clayton, 2010; McMillan, 2010).

Protecting Computer Networks

Some of the key elements of any network security program to prevent a cyberattack include: (1) network segmentation; (2) choke points; and (3) planned redundancy. Network segmentation involves securing, isolating, and separating vital network components into subnetworks to better protect the entire system by compartmentalizing an attack and any damage if it should occur (Genge, Graur, & Haller, 2015). In addition to network segmentation is the use of choke points to funnel network traffic through certain points where information can be filtered and inspected for malware and other threats. The next network design element is planned redundancy. For example, an effective network will have multiple firewalls (or filters) to prevent cyberattacks while also ensuring that if there are system failures or connectivity issues, the system will still be able to "switch" or route traffic through different devices or connect to the Internet (Andress, 2011).

Supervisory Control and Data Acquisition (SCADA) A category or specific type of application-based software that is used in various control systems to monitor processes and the physical function of equipment.

network segmentation Securing, isolating, and separating vital network components into subnetworks to better protect the entire system by compartmentalizing an attack and any damage if it should occur.

choke points Computer technology that funnels network traffic through certain points where information can be filtered and inspected for malware and other threats.

planned redundancy In the context of computer security, is the use of multiple firewalls to prevent cyberattacks while ensuring that there are no system failures or connectivity issues by being able to route traffic through different devices.

There are also specific mechanisms to protect networks and data. A firewall is basically a filter that is placed on a gateway between an organization's system and the Internet where traffic can be blocked based on protocols (or rules) that are created by system administrators (Andress, 2011; Mayer, Wool, & Ziskind, 2000). Other security practices involve the use of Network Intrusion Detection Systems (NIDS) that can monitor network traffic, inspecting or looking for potential attacks (Srivastava, Dwivedi, Pankaj, & Tewari, 2013). In some cases, organizations can also block certain social media websites, such as Facebook, in order to increase worker productivity and to prevent the introduction of malware to its system (Leitch & Warren, 2009).

► Communications Security

While organizations need to be concerned about information in computers, they also need to secure other communication-based technologies that often use and rely on their computer-based technologies. Communications security (COMSEC), which is considered a component of INFOSEC, includes all efforts to protect information transmitted by voice, electronic impulse, wire, microwave links, fiber optic lines, and satellite systems from unauthorized interception. An interception can be accomplished by wiretapping, through interception of electrical impulses radiated (emanated) from computer equipment, and by concealing audio or visual transmitters on the victim's premises (bugging).

Cryptography is one of the most secure methods of preventing unauthorized interception of data communications, requiring the hostile attacker to resort to acquiring the data before it is encrypted. Since traditional methods of communication theft, such as wiretapping, require some physical intrusion, threats can also intercept emanations (emissions) from electronic equipment. For example, electromagnetic emanations (or emissions) from equipment can be captured by electronic pickup devices. To address this issue, organizations have emanations security (often called TEMPEST) protocols and systems that are used to electromagnetically harden the inadvertent release of electromagnetic signals. Some of these security countermeasures include redesigning computer systems, constructing rooms and structures to shield against emissions, and using jamming countermeasures (Zhou, Yu, & Wang, 2012).

Technical security in communications involves prevention of adverse technical surveillance through the use of intrusion devices. Technical surveillance devices include microphones and wires as well as mechanical instruments used to listen through a heating duct or conduit. Carrier current devices, which capture voice communications by utilizing a facility's internal electric wiring system, visual-optical (CCTV) devices, and telephone bugging instruments, are also used. COMSEC defenses against technical surveillance include physical inspection (search) for devices, electrical wiring and equipment inspections, metal and harmonic detectors for electronic bugs, and instruments that detect electronic emanations from bugging devices (Maras, 2012).

SECURITY SPOTLIGHT

Assess the existing information security program where you work or at another location you are familiar with. What human activities currently compromise information security? How can INFOSEC be improved?

► Protecting Intellectual Property

Any information security program also includes protecting intellectual property. Intellectual property is defined as intellectual assets, including patents, trademarks, and trade secrets that the organization has a property right to (or owns) (Hayton, 2005). Traditionally, organizations have had three public methods to protect their intellectual property: copyrights, patents, and trademarks.

A copyright prevents unauthorized use of virtually any creative writing or expression that is physically observed. Materials that may be copyrighted include books, periodicals, lectures, videos, maps, musical compositions, drawings, and works of art. A copyright infringement occurs whenever a substantial and an important part of a copyrighted work is copied or reproduced without permission. However, under the fair use doctrine, copyrighted materials can be used in some situations, such as news reports, scholarly works, or by teachers or students. For individuals, a copyright expires 70 years after the death of the creator. For business copyright registrants, a copyright expires 120 years from the date of creation, or 95 years from the date of the first publication, whichever is shorter.

A patent protects a novel, useful, and nonobvious invention from unauthorized replication or use. The subject matter for patents includes processes, machines, compositions of matter, improvements to existing processes, designs of articles for manufacture, living material invented by a person, and asexually reproduced plants (e.g., plants produced by cuttings). Patent infringement occurs when the replication or use of a patent is unauthorized. Under the public use doctrine, a patent may not be granted if an invention is used by the public more than 1 year prior to the patent's application filing. Twenty-year terms are granted to patents on processes and manufactured articles. Design patents have a 14-year life term.

A trademark protects against unauthorized use of a distinctive mark, name, word, symbol, or device that identifies the product of a particular commercial enterprise. In addition, trade names (service marks) and quality certification marks can be protected by trademarks. The term for the original registration of a trademark is 10 years. Trademark registrations can be renewed for an unlimited number of 10-year terms. However, once a trademark becomes a common term (a generic name for something, such as Elevator which was once a trademark name) for a product or service, it loses its federal trademark law protection (Cheeseman, 2010; Greer & Plunkett, 2007; Moore, 2011).

All of these forms of intellectual property are public in nature, where the competition can easily access copyrighted information, patent applications, and trademarks. To prevent the competition from accessing some information, organizations use "trade secrets" protection. These are organizational assets or company property that is not published or made public that contributes to its commercial success (Bhattacharya & Guriev, 2006). Trade secrets can exist in the form of ideas, software code, organizational knowledge that has some type of commercial value, chemical formulas, sales lists, or even recipes (e.g., Coca Cola). It also includes marketing, financial and technical plans that the company has taken concerted efforts to protect and keep secret (Cheung, 1982; Goldstein, 2007). Unlike patents and copyrights, the organization (or person) has a right of nondisclosure of this information to the public (Paine, 1991), providing a broader scope of protection. The information is also protected in perpetuity, which is not the case for patents and copyrights (Hannah, 2005).

The theft of trade secrets is not a new crime. One of the first recorded incidents of industrial espionage was in the early 1700s where the French Jesuit priest Father d'Entrecolles was successful in stealing the ingredients for the production of porcelain from the Chinese. The theft of the secret ingredient of kaolin led to companies in France gaining a competitive edge from their rival Chinese manufacturers. Now, computer-related technologies and the Internet or global connectivity has also made trade secrets more vulnerable to theft. Meanwhile organizations may not fully recognize that they are vulnerable,

---

intellectual property Information created through research and development, such as chemical formulas and software designs.

copyright Protects against unauthorized use of virtually any creative writing or expression that can be physically observed.

patent A novel, useful, and nonobvious invention protected by federal law from unauthorized replication or use.

trademark Protects against unauthorized use of a distinctive mark, name, word, symbol, or device that identifies the goods of a particular commercial enterprise.

trade secrets Ideas, software code, organizational knowledge that has some type of commercial value.

and lack effective countermeasures and investigative tools to properly prevent and detect such activities ("*Annual report*," 2003 Carr, Morton, & Furniss, 2000). Combined with the global marketplace, the U.S. economy has also been characterized as an open economy that encourages foreign investment and open forms of research and development at universities throughout the United States ("*Annual report*," 2003). This "openness" has resulted in a lot of unsecured ideas and information made readily available to trade secret thieves. At the same time, organizational structures have changed where the location, structure, and flow of proprietary information has become more decentralized in nature, leading to more individuals and other institutions possessing "semi-finished" or complete blocks of knowledge related to the organization's success (Liebeskind, 1997). With information not held and secured by one entity, the threat of trade secret theft will naturally increase.

The theft of trade secrets can be divided into the specific acts of industrial or economic espionage. Industrial espionage is the theft of trade secrets by individuals and companies. With these crimes a person or a business sponsors or coordinates an intelligence activity for the purpose of enhancing the competition's advantage in the marketplace ("*Annual report*," 2003). Economic espionage is defined by the FBI (2015) as, "foreign power sponsored or coordinated intelligence activity directed at the U.S. government or U.S. corporations, establishments, or persons for the purpose of unlawfully obtaining proprietary economic information" (np). It is considered to be one of the most serious threats to the economic health of the United States ("Economic espionage," 2015). While oftentimes the terms are used interchangeably, the fundamental difference between the two is that industrial espionage is committed by persons and companies while economic espionage is coordinated or directed by a foreign power. Both of these activities are illegal in the United States and many other countries. However, they still occur and many progressive companies now have counterespionage units who are tasked with determining who is watching them and creating countermeasures to deter them (Benny, 2014). These illegal activities are not to be confused with

industrial espionage The theft of trade secrets by individuals and companies.

economic espionage Foreign power sponsored or coordinated intelligence activity directed at the U.S. government or U.S. corporations, establishments, or persons for the purpose of unlawfully obtaining proprietary economic information.

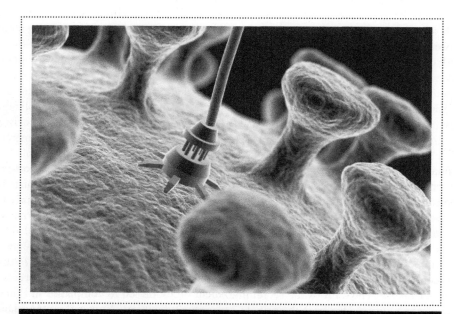

Nanotechnology and other cutting-edge technologies are vulnerable to economic espionage.
(Photo courtesy of U.S. Department of Energy.)

competitive intelligence which is "the art of defining, gathering, and analyzing intelligence about competitor's products, promotions, sales, etc. from external sources" (He, Zha, & Li, 2013, p. 465). Competitive intelligence is legal because it uses open or public sources of information where organizations can data mine annual reports, social media sites, press releases, trade journals, events, patent databases, and other financial reports to gain a better understanding of the competition (Wright, 2015). While legal, organizations nevertheless need to manage and protect these open sources of information as they would other proprietary information that is related to their success.

One particular law that exists to promote economic and national security in the U.S. is the Economic Espionage Act of 1996. The Economic Espionage Act (EEA) was created to deter and prosecute domestic and foreign efforts toward the theft of trade secrets and economic espionage activities (Horowitz, 1998). To be considered a trade secret theft under the EEA, the following criteria must exist: (1) intangible and/or tangible forms of information are protected; (2) the owner took objectively reasonable measures to protect and keep the information secret; and (3) the owner derives some type of independent economic value from the trade secret from not being publicly known (Krotoski, 2009). Section 1831 prosecutions address economic espionage where it must be proven that a foreign government or one of its instrumentalities (a foreign company the country assisted) committed the crime. Section 1832 violations deal with the theft of trade secrets where a person or company intended to convert the trade secret information for economic benefit for anyone other than the actual owner. Some of the specific elements needed for §1831 and §1832 prosecutions can be found in Box 6-4.

In 2016, the Economic Espionage Act was amended through the Defend Trade Secrets Act (DTSA). Some of the amendments to the original act include increased fines, where the courts can now impose a fine up to $ 5 million or three times the value of the stolen trade secret; "whistleblower" immunity from civil liability for employees, contractors and consultants for the disclosure of trade secrets to the government or a court filing; the forfeiture or seizure of property by those accused of trade secret theft to prevent the propagation or dissemination of the trade secret; and, civil actions including injunctions and damage awards for losses. The DTSA also added trade secret theft and economic espionage to the list of offenses under the Racketeer and Corrupt Influence Organizations (RICO) Acts (S.1890, 2016).

While 1831 violations are uncommon, the U.S. government has successfully prosecuted 102 cases of 1832 violations for the period 1996–2014. The review of 1832 prosecutions shows that most offenders are not foreign nationals or nonemployees that stole trade secrets

> **competitive intelligence** The legal act of defining, gathering, and analyzing intelligence about competitor's products, promotions, sales etc. from external sources.

> **Economic Espionage Act of 1996** Federal law created to deter and prosecute domestic and foreign efforts toward the theft of trade secrets and economic espionage activities.

> **Defend Trade Secrets Act** A 2016 legislation directed toward the enhancement of penalties for trade secret theft and economic espionage.

BOX 6-4

ELEMENTS OF SECTION 1831 AND 1832 VIOLATIONS

Elements of the Offense under 18 U.S.C. § 1831: In order to establish a violation of 18 U.S.C. § 1831, the government must prove: (1) the defendant stole or without authorization of the owner, obtained, destroyed, or conveyed information; (2) the defendant knew this information was proprietary; (3) the information was in fact a trade secret; and (4) the defendant knew the offense would benefit or was intended to benefit a foreign government, foreign instrumentality, or foreign agent.

Elements of the Offense under 18 U.S.C. § 1832: In order to establish a violation of 18 U.S.C. § 1832, the government must prove: (1) the defendant stole, or without authorization of the owner, obtained, destroyed, or conveyed information; (2) the defendant knew this information was proprietary; (3) the information was in fact a trade secret; (4) the defendant intended to convert the trade secret to the economic benefit of anyone other than the owner; (5) the defendant knew or intended that the owner of the trade secret would be injured; and (6) the trade secret was related to or was included in a product that was produced or placed in interstate or foreign commerce. Section 1832 shares the first three elements with § 1831.

Source: Criminal Resource Manual (2015).

using complex means. Instead, the majority of offenders were trusted personnel or insider threats that included current or former employees and invitees to the organization (such as subcontractors) that already had some level of legitimate access to the trade secrets that were stolen. In the context of demographic characteristics, most were males acting alone and were U.S. born or naturalized citizens. The research also shows that all organizations are vulnerable. Large companies as opposed to small companies, and manufacturing companies as opposed to other types of industries, were no more likely to be targeted by either current or past employees. The means of attack in many of these cases were not sophisticated. Because employees already had access to the information, they simply downloaded or transferred information to personal devices and accounts for reasons that were often based on personal financial gain. In other cases, they physically stole documents, carrying them out of the organization. These findings suggest that the traditional means to prevent the theft of information that include administrative and physical security measures were not effective in delaying, deterring, and denying the theft of information (Johnson, Kierkus, & Gerkin, 2016).

Summary

The protection of information is vital to nations, organizations, and individuals. The introduction of computers dramatically altered the manner through which information is collected, transmitted, analyzed, stored, and retrieved. Of particular importance is that organizations need to protect their information systems from natural and man-made threats. To protect against human threats, effective policies and procedures, personnel security, and physical protection systems must exist and be incorporated into a comprehensive information security program. Any comprehensive information security program will also include the proper classification and control of information, technical or nonphysical means of controlling access to computers, reducing the risk of systems failures through communications and operations management activities, and making sure that security is part of the design of the "lifecycle" of the information system from its design, implementation, and disposal of equipment and information. Other crucial elements also include business continuity management practices to ensure system resiliency against man-made and natural threats, and ensuring that the information security program complies with all laws, regulations, and contractual agreements related to the security and dissemination of information.

This chapter has also shown that organizations are vulnerable to cybercrimes and intellectual property theft. The nature and extent of cyber-related crimes are extensive in the content dollar losses and frequency. Some of the common means by which these attacks occur are through malware and malicious code attacks that include DoS and DDoS attacks to steal data or damage and destroy computer systems. In other cases, malware can target SCADA software leading to the disablement and destruction of key components of a production process. The theft of intellectual property from information systems is also a security issue for organizations. Intellectual property theft can include the theft of trade secrets by individuals and companies and economic espionage that is carried out by foreign countries. While individuals can be prosecuted under the Economic Espionage Act of 1996 (18 U.S.C. 1831–1839), preventing these crimes requires recognition that trade secrets are vulnerable to attack and that well-designed information security programs can serve to protect these vital assets.

Career Opportunities in Information Security

Information security (INFOSEC) is one of the fastest growing sectors in the security sector. Generally, information security specialists require a combination of computer-related and security skills. Virtually every organization must have an information security program and policies. Opportunities exist in both the public and private sectors where entry-level salaries are quite lucrative while managerial levels can easily top $100,000. Listed here is an example of a civilian information security specialist position for the Department of the Air Force:

Job Title: Information Technology Management (Information Security)

Salary Range: $31,994.00 to $150,830.00/Per Year

- Work involves ensuring the confidentiality, integrity, and availability of systems, networks, and data through the planning, analysis, development, implementation, maintenance, and enhancement of information systems security programs, policies, procedures, and tools.
- Utilizes knowledge of information technology principles, methods, and security regulations and policies to administer various information security programs.
- Promotes awareness of security issues among management and ensures sound security principles are implemented to ensure protection of information transmitted to the organization, among organizations, and from the organization to the local or wide area networks, the World Wide Web, or other communication nodes.
- Conducts risk assessments to identify possible security violations. Controls and protects all cryptographic material and administers applicable access programs.

Key Terms and Concepts

Absolute value *124*
Asset classification *121*
Availability *120*
Back doors *129*
Business continuity management (BCM) *127*
Choke points *131*
CIA triad *119*
Cloud *127*
Communications security (COMSEC) *132*
Competitive intelligence *135*
Confidentiality *119*
Copyright *133*
Critical information *120*
Cryptographic security *126*
Cryptography *132*
Cybercrimes *128*
Cybersecurity *128*
Decryption *126*

Defend Trade Secrets Act *135*
Denial of service (DoS) *130*
Discretionary access control (DAC) *121*
Distributed denial of service (DDoS) attack *130*
Economic espionage *134*
Economic Espionage Act of 1996 *135*
Emanations security *132*
Encryption *126*
Firewall *132*
Hackers *118*
Industrial espionage *134*
Information gathering *129*
INFOSEC *119*
Integrity *119*
Intellectual property *133*
Malicious code attack *129*
Mandatory access control (MAC) *121*
Network segmentation *131*

Password *126*
Password stewardship *123*
Patent *133*
Phishing *130*
Physical security measures *124*
Planned redundancy *131*
Relative value *124*
Role-based access control (RBAC) *121*
Supervisory Control and Data Acquisition (SCADA) *131*
Session locks *126*
Social engineering *124*
Spoofing *130*
Technical controls *125*
Technical security *132*
Trademark *133*
Trade secrets *133*
Virtual private networks (VPNs) *127*
Vishing *130*

Discussion Questions and Exercises

1. What is the purpose of INFOSEC?
2. Explain the elements of the CIA triad.
3. Identify three threats to critical information and describe strategies to protect the information. What role does risk assessment play in the information protection function?
4. What is social engineering? How do you protect against social engineering activities?
5. What is business continuity? Provide an example of a business continuity plan.
6. What are the three types of access control policies used in organizations?
7. Outline and describe the strategies for protecting computer systems and databases.
8. What are trade secrets? How do they differ from other types of information?
9. Traditional criminal identification and investigation methods are inappropriate for computer-related crime. Explain.
10. Reflect on your personal actions and activities that compromise information security. What are some ways to correct these actions?

Your Turn

Preventing Cyberstalking

Advances in GPS technology, the proliferation of smart phones with embedded GPS, and the increasing popularity of social networking media, such as Facebook, Twitter, and Flickr have all made cyberstalking easier than ever. To protect yourself and your loved ones from this particularly dangerous form of cybercrime, learn as much as you can about these technologies. Next, consider the following questions:

1. How do these technological advances enable cyber-stalkers to capture and use personal information about potential victims?
2. In what ways (if any) are you and your loved ones currently using such technologies that could make you vulnerable to cyberstalking?
3. What changes could you make in your own and your loved ones' use of these technologies to enhance your and your loved ones' safety from stalking?

PART 3

Security Sectors

The chapters in this section examine specific security sectors composed of institutional, commercial and industrial, and homeland security. Chapter 7 reviews security activities that are performed in various institutions that include: financial, courthouse and courtroom, K–12 schools and institutions of Higher Education, health care, entertainment, and religious organizations. Chapter 8, meanwhile, reviews commercial, office, and residential security issues. Last, Chapter 9 is devoted to homeland security, reviewing issues related to terrorism, natural disasters, airline and critical infrastructure security.

7 Institutional Security

LEARNING OBJECTIVES

After completing this chapter, the reader should be able to:

1 *identify security threats unique to specific institutions*

2 *describe asset protection priorities as well as loss prevention policies, procedures, and systems associated with the following:*

- *banking and financial institution security*
- *courthouse and courtroom security*
- *educational institution security*
- *health care security*
- *entertainment security*
- *religious institution security*

▶ Introduction

Although many general security management principles apply across a broad spectrum of public and private environments, some security practices in these institutions are relatively unique, requiring specific practices and techniques. This chapter will examine security activities in institutions, which are defined as a permanent governmental, social, or commercial organizations that cater to the interests of the public at large and to no one special class or group (Schettler, 1943). What is distinctive about these locations is that they can often be large. Oftentimes, these institutions are also private properties that the public can easily access.

▶ Financial Institution Security

A financial institution is defined by federal law as "any business or agency which engages in any activity which the Secretary of the Treasury determines, by regulation, to be an activity . . . or any other business designated by the Secretary whose cash transactions have a high degree of usefulness in criminal, tax, or regulatory matters" ("Money and finance," 2015). Examples include: insured banks, commercial banks and trust companies, credit unions, investment bankers and companies, operators of credit card systems, and insurance companies. Financial institutions can also be considered to be intermediaries or businesses that perform transactions on deposit accounts and process financial documents, such as loans (Sufian & Majid, 2014).

Financial institutions provide attractive targets for insider and outsider threats. Robbery, burglary, embezzlement, loan fraud, manipulation of funds, computer hacking, and credit card and check fraud are major threats. Losses to financial institutions are direct, since the object of the theft is money, not goods or services. Losses from fraud alone are estimated to exceed $30 billion annually. E-commerce banks and other institutions have increased their risk exposure because they are connected internally and externally through online banking services and electronic fund transfers. Unauthorized use of an electronic database by an employee may result in invasions to privacy. Data manipulation through computers is particularly dangerous. Account and loan balances as well as credit lines can be altered or completely deleted. Financial institution websites can be penetrated (hacked) and the content altered to display false or slanderous information. Through denial of service attacks, a hacker can electronically flood the institution's computer with email messages, collapsing the system. Computer malware is always a concern, where confidential customer information can be obtained and redirected to different accounts, sold to illegitimate users, held hostage, or sold back to the financial institution for a fee. All of these vulnerabilities require comprehensive personnel, physical and information protection strategies to prevent these types of incidents and crimes from occurring (Hess & Wrobleski, 2009; Spivey, 2001).

> **financial institution** Bank, credit union, brokerage house, insurance company, or any other institution where financial transactions are the primary function.

Banks are perhaps the most commonly recognized financial institution. Historically, the threats against banking institutions were burglaries and robberies where banks relied upon architectural design for their physical security, constructing large monolithic stone and concrete buildings that had large vaults to protect money and other financial assets against after-hours burglars and safe crackers. The physical construction of these banks, combined with the presence of other physical security measures, such as high counters and decorative bars separating staff from customers, served to prevent and deter some crimes while also serving a symbolic function of "telling" customers that their money was safe and the bank was trustworthy and dependable (Frandsen, Hiller, Traflet, & McGoun, 2013). The construction and physical security practices, including guards also served to protect (to some degree) against bank robberies that were made famous in the 1930s by some notorious criminals, including Bonnie and Clyde, John Dillinger, and Pretty Boy Floyd (Burrough, 2009). Beginning in the mid-twentieth century, banks changed philosophically, switching from a "money storage" facility to a "money store," marketing financial products to customers. They also changed architecturally, shifting to an open design or layout making them more inviting, resembling a retail store (Frandsen et al., 2013). Banks have also increased in number. Retail banks have now branched out into the suburbs and are located at convenient satellite locations to meet customer needs, such as strip malls where their sheer numbers alone may increase the bank's vulnerability for crimes including robbery.

Banks are still a relatively easy target for robberies. In 2014, there were 3,866 robberies of federally insured financial institutions reported to the FBI. Most of the robberies were committed at branch locations (not the main bank office) in metropolitan areas and were committed by males. Most robberies took place at a counter and were accomplished through the use of a note demanding money, an oral demand for money, or threatening the use of a weapon (FBI, 2014). While appearing high in number, they actually are not. Bank robberies account for about every two in 100 robberies in the United States (Weisel, 2007).

Three reasons explain why banks can be considered an easy target. First, and perhaps the most obvious, is that banks are lucrative targets because they have money; on average a bank robber nets $4,000. Second, there has been an increase in the number of banking branches and extended banking hours since the 1970s. This increase in banks along with extended hours provides more opportunities for offenders. Last, bank robberies may actually be considered to be low-risk forms of robberies. Generally banks have the same layout allowing for easy entry and exit, and staff is not armed and is trained to comply with the demand(s) of the robber(s) and not resist (Weisel, 2007).

> **Bank Protection Act of 1968** Federal legislation designed to reduce the vulnerability of financial institutions. Requires all banks to have written security plans and a designated security officer.

In an effort to reduce the vulnerability of financial institutions, in 1968, Congress passed the Bank Protection Act of 1968, as amended ("Banks and banking," 2015) in response to the increased number of bank robberies that were occurring throughout the

United States in the 1960s (Hannan, 1982). The main goal of the Act is to "discourage robberies, burglaries, and larcenies and to assist in the identification and apprehension of persons who commit such acts." This Act requires that all banks and Savings and Loans, which are a member of the federal reserve system, have written security plans and a designated security officer who is responsible for developing the security program and reporting to the board of directors on an annual basis on the implementation, effectiveness, and administration of the security program (12 CFR 208.61). Banks that fail to comply with the provisions of the Bank Protection Act can be fined up to $100 a day (Mullins, 2012). Some of the specific elements of a bank security program are found in Box 7-1.

BOX 7-1

THE BANK PROTECTION ACT OF 1968

§ 326.3 SECURITY PROGRAM

a. *Contents of security program.* The security program shall:

1. Establish procedures for opening and closing for business, and for the safekeeping of all currency, negotiable securities, and similar valuables at all times;

2. Establish procedures that will assist in identifying persons committing crimes against the bank, and that will preserve evidence that may aid in their identification and prosecution; such procedures may include, but are not limited to:

   (i) retaining a record of any robbery, burglary, or larceny committed against the bank;

   (ii) maintaining a camera that records activity in the banking office; and

   (iii) using identification devices, such as prerecorded serial-numbered bills, or chemical and electronic devices;

3. Provide for initial and periodic training of officers and employees in their responsibilities under the security program, and in proper employee conduct during and after a robbery, burglary, or larceny; and

4. Provide for selecting, testing, operating, and maintaining appropriate security devices, as specified in paragraph (b) of this section.

b. *Security devices.* Each insured nonmember bank shall have, at a minimum, the following security devices:
   1. A means of protecting cash or other liquid assets, such as a vault, safe, or other secure space;

   2. A lighting system for illuminating, during the hours of darkness, the area around the vault, if the vault is visible from outside the banking office;

3. An alarm system or other appropriate device for promptly notifying the nearest responsible law enforcement officer of an attempted or perpetrated robbery or burglary;

4. Tamper-resistant locks on exterior doors and exterior windows that may be opened; and

5. Such other devices as the security officer determines to be appropriate, taking into consideration:

   (i) the incidence of crimes against financial institutions in the area;

   (ii) the amount of currency or other valuables exposed to robbery, burglary, and larceny;

   (iii) the distance of the banking office from the nearest responsible law enforcement officers;

   (iv) the cost of the security devices;

   (v) other security measures in effect at the banking office; and

   (vi) the physical characteristics of the structure of the banking office and its surroundings.

[Codified to 12 C.F.R. § 326.3]

[Section 326.3 amended at 56 Fed. Reg. 13581, April 3, 1991, effective May 3, 1991]

§ 326.4 REPORTS

The security officer for each insured nonmember bank shall report at least annually to the bank's board of directors on the implementation, administration, and effectiveness of the security program.

[Codified to 12 C.F.R. § 326.4]

[Section 326.4 amended at 53 Fed. Reg. 17917, May 19, 1988; 56 Fed. Reg. 13582, April 3, 1991, effective May 3, 1991]

Source: From Compliance Laws and Section 1405 Regulations, published by U.S. Department of Treasury.

In order to deter and/or prevent bank robberies, there are some specific policies and work practices that banks use. These can be divided into: (1) reducing the rewards of the robbery; (2) increasing perceptions of risk; (3) increasing the risk of apprehension; and (4) increasing the difficulty of offending. Efforts at reducing the reward are accomplished by limiting the amount of money available by having cash management policies that require small amounts of cash in drawers, the use of automatic cash dispensing units that limit the amount of cash that can be withdrawn by tellers, and dye packs that detonate once a person leaves the bank, staining the money and making it useless. Banks also have strategies to increase perceptions of risk. These can include tactics by staff to slow handing over money to the robbers (which can be dangerous) and the installation and use of physical barriers, such as counters and revolving doors to slow an escape. Banks can also have policies that restrict the wearing of hats and glasses, and other forms of disguise by patrons, having greeters to discourage robbers, and use security guards. In order to increase the risk of apprehension, banks can also hide tracking devices, such as microchips with transponders in money to "follow" the money, use sequentially numbered money known as bait money to track the money once it re-enters circulation, offer rewards, and have effective physical protection systems, including high quality surveillance and alarm systems. To increase the difficulty of offending, banks can also use physical security measures. These can include limiting access to bank lobbies by requiring customers to use their ATM swipe cards to gain access. Banks (and other organizations) can also use man traps, which are small vestibules that have two interlocking doors on each side, where one door must be closed before the other can open. While just considered a small waiting area to some, these man traps or bandit barriers allow bank staff to electronically control who is entering the bank, allowing them to "buzz in" or lock out any potential threats. And, if a threat is present, bank staff could actually lock the person in the vestibule (Schoenberg, 2005; Sennewald & Christman, 2011).

> **man trap** Used in physical security and access control applications. Are small rooms or vestibules that have two interlocking doors, "trapping" a person in the room, if necessary.

ATM Security

Another banking security issue is related to automatic teller machines (ATMs). ATMs are basically portable computers and cash machines that allow users to perform a variety of out-of-home financial transactions around the clock, including the withdrawal of money without the assistance of bank personnel. ATMs provide convenience for customers and they are a cost-saving measure for banks, eliminating the need for human beings to conduct transactions. These are used extensively by financial institutions throughout the world. These ATMs are oftentimes connected to the bank's main server through a GSM (Global System for Mobile Communications) cellular connection that securely transits financial information (Lizie & Dhas, 2015).

> **ATM** Automated teller machine. Used in electronic banking.

ATMs are vulnerable to physical attacks. In some cases, thieves will perform a brute force attack to open the machines for money. These attacks could include "ram raiding," which involves ramming the ATMs with vehicles or heavy equipment to demolish and force them open for their cash (Saket, Sagar, & Singh, 2012), or using sledge hammers and cutting torches to access the ATM's contents. In other cases, individuals may take the entire machine and then later attempt to open it at another location. To combat these efforts, ATMs are often target hardened by installing them in walls, or mounting them on concrete pads and surrounding them by traffic bollards to prevent ramming. In many cases, video surveillance is also an integral component of ATMs while additional surveillance cameras are also mounted in close proximity to ATMs to monitor and record users and the immediate area around the ATM. In other cases, financial institutions have relocated ATMs to safer areas and have installed panic alarms that immediately notify police of a problem (Prenzler, 2011).

Other simple physical protection systems include vibration and motion sensors that alert officials that the ATM has been moved or stolen, while monitoring ATMs with

> **ram raiding** Ramming ATMs (automatic teller machines) with vehicles or heavy equipment to demolish and force them open for their cash.

CCTV technologies. ATMs are oftentimes equipped with Global Positioning System (GPS) technologies that can immediately shut down the device if some type of tampering is detected while also tracking them if they are stolen (Lizie & Dhas, 2015). In more extreme cases, banks in Brazil have installed incinerators in their ATMs, which automatically set currency on fire inside the machine if tampering is detected (Gold, 2014). In order to protect users, meanwhile, ATMs are often found in well-lit areas that are monitored by CCTV cameras. In other cases, users must swipe their card to gain entry into an ATM booth, providing an added layer of security from human threats.

Since ATMs are part of an organization's information system, they are also susceptible to several types of cyberattacks that can include hacking and malware. In these cases, ATMs can be targeted or used as the instrument of a cybercrime. As a target, DoS and DDos attacks can disable ATMs, which was the case in 2003, where the Bank of America's 13,000 ATMs were unable to process requests (Hahn, Guillen, & Anderson, 2006). In other cases, ATMs may have factory installed defaults, including sequential key codes that a threat can type in on the ATM keypad, giving the threat administrative privileges, where he or she can then withdraw money or reprogram the machine (Saket et al., 2012).

ATM card holders are vulnerable to attack. To deter against personal crimes at ATM locations, banks often use video surveillance systems Bank cards (ATM's, gift cards, credit cards, and other magnetic strip-based cards) are also vulnerable to attack. ATM card holders can be phished and spoofed for their personal PIN-related information. Threats can also engage in skimming activities where adversaries install a card reader device on the ATM that collects information stored on the magnetic strip of the user's bank card. Combined with this covert reader, there may be a hidden camera (or the threat may shoulder surf or eavesdrop on the user when typing in the PIN), subsequently capturing the user's PIN. The account information collected from the ATM card is then transferred to another card (called cloning); combined with the PIN, a personal account can then be compromised (Adepoju & Alhassan, 2010). In an effort to prevent skimming, beginning in 2016, bank and credit card companies will be switching to embedded microchips in their cards that provide a unique number or code that is used by the bank for each transaction. In other cases, PINs can also be skimmed off the ATM's keypad using electronic recording devices. There is also card trapping (or card jamming). Here, a user's ATM card is physically trapped in the machine's card slot while the person's PIN is also collected in some manner. When the person leaves, the criminal retrieves the card, withdrawing money from the owner's account. There is also the Lebanese loop. Here, a threat inserts a thin, clear plastic sleeve fitted with a small wire or thread into the ATM card reader slot. After a legitimate user inserts the ATM card, it slides into the sleeve where the machine cannot read it and the owner cannot retrieve the card. Thinking the machine "ate it," the legitimate user leaves. After stealing the owner's PIN in some manner, the criminal then extracts the sleeve containing the card, using it to withdraw funds (Sharma, 2012). In those cases where threats already have a valid ATM bank card, criminals can also PIN crack the card by simply typing in numbers or using electronic devices to solve the numerical code. In many cases, PIN cracking is easy because users have not created strong PINs. The research on PIN security shows that individuals often do not use random numbers for their PIN passwords. Instead, they may use sequential numbers (e.g., 1234), common PINs (e.g., 1212), numbers related to their birth dates, or reuse other numbers from other accounts (Bonneau, Preibusch, & Anderson, 2012).

User Authentication and Financial Institution Security

User authentication is also a security concern for the financial sector. Three types of user authentication are shown in Box 7-2. Traditionally, authentication was achieved in face-to-face transactions by simply providing photo identification to a teller. With e-banking, however, transactions rely on passwords and tokens. A password is simply a secret word,

skimming A form of ATM/debit card fraud where adversaries install a card reader device on the ATM that collects information stored on the magnetic strip of the user's bank card.

card trapping A form of debit card/ATM fraud. Where a user's ATM card is physically trapped in the machine's card slot while the person's PIN is also collected in some manner. Also called card jamming.

Lebanese loop A type of debit card/ATM fraud where the user's card is trapped in the card slot of the machine and is later retrieved by the criminal(s).

PIN cracking A form of ATM/debit card fraud where the criminal simply types in numbers or uses electronic devices to solve the numerical PIN code.

AUTHENTICATOR TYPES

1. **Knowledge**—"what the user knows." These are based on secrecy or obscurity. They include memorized PINS and passwords, and other "quasi-secret" information, such as favorite colors, mother's maiden name, etc. (Gorman, 2003; Jones, Anton, & Earp, 2007).

2. **Objects**—are based on what a person has. These are items that a person physically possesses.

They include RFID cards, smart cards, and one-time password generating cards or cryptographic keys, and other tokens (Gorman, 2003; Jones et al., 2007).

3. **Identification**—based on "who you are." These include biometrics (retina, fingerprints, and voice) and other identifiers including passports, driver's licenses, diplomas, etc. that are unique to a person (Gorman, 2003; Jones et al., 2007).

phrase, or number (such as a PIN). A token, meanwhile, is a physical device that aids or performs in the authentication process (Gorman, 2003). For example, an ATM card can be considered a token because it aids in the authentication process—a user needs an ATM card and a PIN to access an account. In the case of online financial transactions, a user ID and a PIN password are required to gain access. Generally, the more the layers of authentication that exist, the better the account is protected against unauthorized use and access. For example, a PIN accompanied with a biometric is much stronger than just requiring a PIN. However, authentication must also be balanced with the demands of consumers (and employees) who want security measures tempered with their ability to readily access information and accounts.

SECURITY SPOTLIGHT

Do you conduct some or all of your banking activities online? If so, what steps are you taking personally to ensure security of your financial data and resources? What steps do the banking institutions you use take to keep customers' financial data and resources safe? If possible, arrange a telephone call with a security professional at an online banking institution you use. Ask the person about which security practices have been established by the bank to protect customers, and how (if at all) these practices have evolved over time to meet changing needs and challenges.

► Courthouse and Courtroom Security

Expanding space requirements at the local, state, and federal levels has pressured jurisdictions to construct new courtroom buildings, expanding the courts and increasing the number of judicial personnel, litigants, jurors, and ancillary activities associated with legal proceedings. In addition to litigation activities, courthouses may contain other government agencies, receive deliveries, and have adjacent or underground parking areas. They are also transfer points for defendants and convicted criminals, and function as venues for public ceremonial events.

In recent years, incidents of assault, bombings, and homicide have increased in American courthouses. Consider, for example, the following incident. On March 11, 2005, Brian Nichols, 33, on trial for rape, was being transported through a courthouse in Atlanta, Georgia. Nichols overpowered his sheriff's deputy escort, took her firearm, and proceeded to the courtroom, where he fatally shot the presiding judge and a court reporter. Later, Nichols killed a sheriff's deputy outside the courthouse. In the course of his 24-hour escape ordeal,

Nichols also hijacked three cars and a tow truck, and shot an off-duty Immigration and Customs Enforcement agent to death, stealing the agent's car as well. Early the next morning, Nichols forced his way into a woman's apartment. He subsequently surrendered to the police without incident (Burnett, 2006). While this is an extreme case, other common court security issues include unruly spectators, protestors, escape attempts by defendants, threatened witnesses, and the intimidation and harassment of jurors, judges, prosecutors, and courthouse staff. The most vulnerable areas include courtrooms, judges' chambers, probation and parole offices, clerk of court offices, and areas where witnesses may encounter one another.

Now, courthouse building exteriors and perimeters must be protected against a possible bombing attack. After the bombing of the Alfred P. Murrah federal building in Oklahoma City in 1995, virtually all government buildings were identified as potential targets for terrorists (Thomas, 2001). To assist in target hardening courthouses, the Conference of State Court Administrators (2012) has published 10 essential guidelines for a comprehensive courthouse security program that are shown in Box 7-3.

To further increase the level of security in courthouses, access control devices (card access, controlled entry and exit points), CCTV surveillance systems, and metal detectors are now commonplace. Surveillance systems, duress alarms, and security glass also provide additional protection (Champion, Hartley, & Rabe, 2008).

Another component of an effective courthouse security program includes security personnel. At the local and county level, **bailiffs** are court officials whose primary duty is courtroom security and maintaining order during trials. Oftentimes, these bailiffs are deputy sheriffs who are assigned to the court. Some states also require that courts have full-time security administrators who are responsible for overseeing courthouse security. Besides the courtroom itself, an effective security program will also include sworn law enforcement personnel or civilian contract or proprietary security personnel who are responsible for the perimeter, screening, and patrolling the noncourtroom areas of the facility, during and after normal business hours (Cade, 1989; Hardenbergh, 2005).

At the federal level, the security of courthouses and courtrooms is the responsibility of the U.S. Marshals Service (USMS). The USMS is responsible for conducting threat assessments and developing security plans for federal courthouses, and protecting and investigating threats against federal judges. The USMS is also responsible for physical security activities throughout the 94 federal districts in the United States, comprising approximately 400 courts. USMS personnel are responsible for the personal protection of judges, prisoner transport and holding, and security in other areas of the courthouse, including interview rooms and office spaces. In many cases, the USMS also contracts with private security companies. These Court Security Officers (CSOs) perform a variety of security-related activities, including patrol, access control, and package screening (Reese, 2010).

bailiff Court security officer.

BOX 7-3

ESSENTIAL GUIDELINES FOR COURTHOUSE SECURITY

1. Operational security: or standard operating procedures
2. Facility security planning: self-audit of security practices
3. Emergency preparedness and response/continuity of operations
4. Disaster recovery
5. Threat assessment
6. Incident reporting procedures
7. Adequate (and increased) funding for security-related measures
8. Updated security equipment
9. Strong partnership for security between the courts, police, and county officials
10. New courthouse designs

Courthouse security also relies upon proper building design. Modern courthouses segment human activities into four zones based on function: (1) public; (2) private; (3) prisoner; and (4) interface. Using the defense in depth approach, access into each sphere should be through a controlled area. The public sphere includes a secure perimeter and parking areas separated from court staff, and separate entrances and screening of all individuals with the use of magnetometers (metal detectors) that use electronic fields to detect metal objects. Waiting areas should be easy to surveil and protected from vandalism, and there should be separate elevators for the public. A well-designed system will also ensure that the courthouse is closed after normal business hours. The private circulation zone is the area reserved for court staff, judges, jurors, and authorized visitors. These areas should also have separate elevators, and policies and procedures related to escorting visitors. The prisoner zone, meanwhile, should include a dedicated vehicular entrance for prisoners (a sally port), and secure holding areas that are separated "sight and sound" from the public and private zones. This secure area should also have separate corridors for transporting defendants to courtrooms. Finally, the interface zone can be considered that area where all of the three other zones intersect. These common interface areas include the courtroom, where effective physical security measures related to transport, policies and procedures, design (bulletproof barriers), panic/duress alarms, and nonmovable furniture should be incorporated (Griebel & Phillips, 2001).

> **magnetometers**
> Metal detectors that use electronic fields to detect metal objects.

▶ Educational Institution Security

Statistically, educational institutions are safer than homes. Yet, private and public schools, colleges, and universities are not immune from the hazards and risks that threaten other types of institutions. The FBI estimates that 3.3 percent of all crime in the United States occurs at the 90,000 schools, colleges, and universities that serve over 50 million students (Noonan & Vavra, 2007). As a result, security programs have been created and oftentimes enhanced to protect property, students, faculty, and staff from a myriad of man-made threats. Some of the key issues for K–12 schools and institutions of Higher Education (IHEs) are reviewed in this section.

Elementary and Secondary Schools

School violence is defined as "youth violence that occurs on school property, on the way to or from school or school-sponsored events, or during a school-sponsored event (Centers for Disease Control, 2015a, np). In one of the worst and most publicized incidents of school violence to date, two students, Eric Harris, 18, and Dylan Klebold, 17, went on a lethal rampage at Columbine High School in Littleton, Colorado, on April 20, 1999. Harris and Klebold killed 12 fellow students and a teacher before taking their own lives. This event has led to the "Columbine effect" where school systems throughout the United States have now upgraded and changed their school security practices and policies, due in part to the fear that their particular school could be vulnerable to an active shooter attack (Muschert & Peguero, 2010).

School shootings are actually uncommon. The Center for Disease Control (CDC) reported that during the 2010–2011 school year, there were 11 homicides throughout the United States (Centers for Disease Control, 2015a). Other research from the Department of Education and the Department of Justice shows that there were a total of 116 homicides from July 1992 to June 2006, suggesting that they are rare (a rate of about 0.03 homicides per 100,000 students) (Centers for Disease Control and Prevention, 2008).

Nonlethal violent crimes in schools are far more common than homicides. In the 2010–2011 school year, there were 749,000 reported nonfatal violent victimizations among students 12–18 years of age. These acts included bullying, fighting, weapon use,

> **Columbine effect**
> Schools systems throughout the United States have now upgraded and changed their school security practices and policies due in part to the fear that their particular school could be vulnerable to an active shooter attack.

electronic aggressions (e.g., cyberbullying), and gang violence (Centers for Disease Control, 2015a). Property crimes are also an issue. The data shows that approximately 29 percent of students have their books, clothing, or vehicles damaged on school property one or more times in a school year (Centers for Disease Control and Prevention, 2006), while verbal harassment, bullying, and other forms of intimidation serve to create a hostile learning environment. In 2008, there were about 1.2 million victims of nonfatal crimes at school, including 619,000 thefts and 629,800 violent crimes (simple assault and serious violent crime) among students between ages of 12 and 18. In 2009, 8 percent of students reported being threatened or injured on school property with a weapon, such as a gun, knife, or club (U.S. Department of Education, Institute of Education Sciences, 2011).

Violence against faculty and staff is also an issue. School staff are the target of harassment and intimidation, and other property and violent crimes from students and even parents on and off school grounds. The research shows that approximately 30 percent of school staff had experienced some form of nonphysical violent event, while 7 percent were threatened and 4 percent were physically assaulted by a student within the current or past school year (McMahon et al., 2014). Even witnessing these events can have short and long-term implications for school staff that could lead to disengagement from their duties. Staff could also experience job burnout, resign, and be less engaged with students, negatively impacting the quality of instruction and student success in the classroom. These and other actions constitute workplace violence where progressive schools have developed comprehensive training programs directed at prevention (Barton-Bellessa, Johnson, Shon, & Austin, 2014; Johnson & Barton-Bellessa, 2014). To address these issues, many schools have created comprehensive antiviolence prevention programs that focus on creating a positive school culture, student success, and prosocial conduct in the classroom. These programs are directed toward changing student behaviors, and having teachers improve their classroom management and communication with students. Improved school policies and practices directed toward violence reduction, threat analysis and intervention, and training staff in de-escalation and violence-reduction strategies are effective. Additionally, including parents and the community (after school programs, mental health, and social services) to ensure that youth are engaged in prosocial behaviors outside the school environment are also effective in reducing youth violence (Espelage et al., 2014).

In response to these threats, some schools (and school systems) have enhanced their physical protection systems, installing metal detectors (magnetometers) and biometric fingerprint scanning to identify authorized students and personnel. Some school districts, especially in tough inner-city neighborhoods, have their own police or security departments to ensure that threats do not enter school grounds or the facility itself (Michel, 2000). Some of these countermeasures have been criticized. Some screening procedures may also be slow, making students late or tardy for their courses. Besides delays, other individuals have raised concerns that schools have become more custodial and institutional in nature instead of a nurturing environment because of visible CCTV surveillance systems, metal detectors, and security personnel, generating a culture of fear among students that may inhibit the learning process. Therefore, school security measures must be balanced with the need for security and the need for an effective, nurturing, and positive learning environment. Some research on this issue that analyzed national-level data concluded that visible security measures did not have any impact on student academic performance or success, postsecondary aspirations, or attendance (Tanner-Smith & Fisher, 2016).

Crime prevention through environmental design (CPTED) has also been applied successfully in schools to reduce crime and noncrime incidents, and to improve the quality of life in schools. These CPTED strategies increase the surveillance of students, manage the access and flow of students and faculty, and create a sense of ownership. These CPTED-based strategies can also lead to a more caring and positive learning environment. Some of these strategies are shown in Box 7-4.

CPTED STRATEGIES IN SCHOOLS

1. *Natural surveillance* involves the placement of physical features that maximize visibility. Example: The strategic use of windows that look out on the school entrance so that students can see into the school and know that others can see them.

2. *Access management* involves guiding people by using signs, well-marked entrances and exits, and landscaping. It may also include limiting access to certain areas by using real or symbolic barriers. Example: Landscaping that reduces access to unsupervised locations on the school grounds.

3. *Territoriality* is defined by a clear delineation of space, expressions of pride or ownership, and the creation of a welcoming environment. Example: Motivational signs, displays of student art, and the use of school colors to create warmth and express pride.

4. *Physical maintenance* includes repair and general upkeep of space. Example: Removing graffiti in restrooms in a timely manner and making the necessary repairs to restrooms, light fixtures, and stairways to maintain safety and comfort.

5. *Order maintenance* involves attending to minor unacceptable acts and providing measures that clearly state acceptable behaviors. Example: Maintaining an obvious adult presence during all times as students move from one location to another.

Source: Centers for Disease Control (2015b).

Legislation and several types of collaborative programs have also been developed by national, state, and local governments to improve safety and security in schools. Because a large number of school violence situations do not occur on school property or in schools, legislation has been directed toward the area around schools. For example, most states have, through legislation, created safe-school zones. These zones include school transportation systems and off-campus school activities. The safe-school zones give rise to zero-tolerance policies focusing on weapons and drug-related offenses occurring in these zones. Other efforts include the following:

> **safe-school zone**
> School campus areas, transportation systems, and off-campus activity venues that give rise to zero-tolerance policies focusing on weapons and drugs.

- Federal regulations enacted in 1994 require drug- and alcohol-use testing for all school bus drivers.

- School districts are collaborating with the courts, probation agencies, and youth-service professionals to share information and monitor students who have criminal records.

- School districts are developing crisis prevention and intervention policies and procedures.

- Many schools now conduct criminal background checks on prospective employees, and have enlisted parents and volunteers (who must also submit to a criminal history check) to monitor facilities and school activities.

Other efforts include a more holistic approach to school violence and crime. Since 1999, the U.S. Secret Service and the U.S. Department of Education have collaborated to identify potential threats and prevent violence in schools. These federal agencies established the Safe-School Initiative. Their efforts resulted in the development of a guide to managing threatening situations and creating safe school environments. The guide, *Threat Assessments in Schools,* provides school administrators with facts regarding school violence (Fein, 2002). The book lists 10 key findings based on their analysis of school violence events in the United States:

> **Safe-School Initiative**
> Created in 1999, a partnership between the U.S. Department of Education and the Secret Service to identify and address threats in schools and prevent school violence.

1. Incidents of targeted violence at school rarely are sudden, impulsive acts.

2. Prior to most incidents, other people knew about the attacker's idea and/or plan to attack.

3. Most attackers did not threaten their targets directly prior to advancing the attack.

4. There is no accurate or "useful" profile of students who engage in targeted school violence.

5. Most attackers engaged in some behavior, prior to the incident that caused others concern, or indicated a need for help.

6. Most attackers had difficulty coping with significant losses or personal failures. Many had considered or attempted suicide.

7. Many attackers felt bullied, persecuted, or injured by others prior to the attack.

8. Most attackers had access to and had used weapons prior to the attack.

9. In many cases, other students were involved in the attack in some capacity.

10. Despite prompt law enforcement responses, most attacks were stopped by means other than law enforcement intervention; most were brief in duration (Fein, 2002, pp. 17–25).

The research also suggests that an effective school violence security program should be based on proactive efforts to identify and address potentially violent behaviors prior to an event, coupled with an effective physical protection system. Some of the recommendations to reduce school violence and to create a climate and culture of safety include: fostering a culture of respect among students and adults, making connections with students and faculty to increase trust, encouraging responsible bystander behaviors where students break the "code of silence," reporting suspicious behaviors to school personnel, and preventing bullying in schools. An effective safety and security program also includes a threat assessment investigation that is similar to the Secret Service's model of investigating specific threats and potentially threatening actions (Fein, 2002).

> More information on school safety can be found at www.secretservice.gov/ntac or the U.S. Department of Education at www.ed.gov/offices/OESE/SDFS

Institutions of Higher Education

> **Institutions of Higher Education (IHEs)** Post-secondary schools including colleges and universities.

Institutions of Higher Education or IHEs have longer instructional days and unique problems in comparison to K–12 institutions. Some are residential campuses with dormitories, apartments, and single-family residences. In most cases, these institutions are very permeable, and encourage public discourse and host events for the public. In some cases, these postsecondary institutions may experience crime. The research shows that 97 percent of all reported campus criminal activities include robberies, sexual assaults, illegal drug use, domestic violence, and property-related offenses ("School and crime," 2015).

In effect, IHEs, like other institutions, are a microcosm of society. In some cases, homicides occur. One particular incident that will be used as a case study at the end of this chapter, was the Virginia Tech shooting that occurred on April 16, 2007, where Cho Seung Hui killed 32 fellow students and then committed suicide. Although multiple homicide incidents on America's college campuses occur and receive widespread attention, they remain quite rare. The United States has approximately 4,200 college and university campuses—home to nearly 16 million students—where an average 15 homicides occur per year. Yet, the publicity associated with campus killings can cause fear and anxiety among student populations (Noonan & Vavra, 2007).

Types of IHE Security Programs

Higher education institution security is relatively new. Most colleges and universities did not have formalized security or police departments prior to World War II. However, as student populations became more politicized in the late 1950s and throughout the 1960s, the threat of civil disorder became more evident. Anti-Vietnam War sentiment and the radical behaviors of some during the civil rights movement led to violent demonstrations and riots on several college campuses. During the 1970s and 1980s, enrollment in institutions at all educational levels increased dramatically. Violent crime, sexual assaults, homicide, and theft increased along with the increase in student populations (Dunn, 1999; Simonsen, 1998; U.S. Department of Justice, Bureau of Justice Statistics, 2006).

IHE security operations can be categorized into four types: (1) watchmen-guards whose primary responsibility is to protect property; (2) contracting services with a security company or local police agency; (3) proprietary (in-house) security; and (4) police agencies (Powell, 1981). Research by the U.S. Department of Justice shows that 92 percent of all public colleges and universities that have enrollments of 2,500 students or more use sworn police officers, who in most cases are armed, and are on duty 90 percent of all days and times. In comparison, 38 percent of private IHEs use sworn police who are on-duty during 80 percent of all days and times (Reaves, 2015).

The research also shows that these officers perform a variety of security-related tasks that include access control, CCTV surveillance, central alarm monitoring, event security, emergency management, key control, parking administration, vehicle registration, and responding to medical emergencies. In some cases, private security personnel are also used to supplement patrol coverage or for special events. The research also shows that many IHEs that have police departments also offer a range of security-related services performed by students. These activities can include safety escorts for other students, special event security, auxiliary patrols, building lock-ups, and residence hall security (Reaves, 2015).

Like K–12 institutions, IHEs have a legal standard of care that must be met that includes effective physical, personnel, and information security. This standard of care also requires conducting threat assessments and having comprehensive anticrime and violence programs. Some elements include zero tolerance policies related to violence, sexual assault, and alcohol- and drug offenses, and firearms restrictions on campuses. Colleges and universities have also created comprehensive training programs related to dating violence, sexual assault, and drug and alcohol abuse. Specific security activities have included modifying the physical environment of campuses, "building out" crime, installing more lighting and emergency phones, and ensuring that students and faculty have ready access to panic alarms that are now oftentimes located directly on computer desktops where a person simply has to "click" for help.

Another common element of IHE security operations are the use of emergency notification systems and social networking tools to alert students and staff of security-related issues. Emergency notification systems alert students and college personnel about emergencies and other hazardous situations, such as poor weather and closures. These notification systems can include the use of digital signs in common areas, sirens or alarm systems, and text and email messaging (Young, 2008). In many cases, colleges contract with vendors for these messaging services. With some systems, designated college officials notify the vendor of the emergency notification system who subsequently sends text messages, voice mails, and emails to enrolled individuals. Depending upon design, colleges can automatically enroll all students, faculty, and staff, who can then "opt out" or unsubscribe from the emergency messaging system. Other notification systems require an "opt in" where users are required to register for notifications. Generally, these "opt in" communication systems have lower participation rates (Gow, McGee, Townsend, Anderson, & Varnhagen, 2009;

> **emergency notification system**
> A method of alerting individuals about emergencies and other hazardous situations.

Sullivan, Hakkinen, & DeBlois, 2010). Other universities also use social networking tools, such as Facebook or their homepages, to share security and crime-related information (Shelton, 2009). These systems are commonplace. Popular notification methods used included email (100 percent), text messages (99 percent), and websites (98 percent). Nearly two-thirds (63 percent) of the campuses had opt in systems that allowed first-year students to enroll voluntarily (Reaves, 2015).

IHE Legislation

The federal government has also passed legislation related to IHE security. The Jeanne Clery Disclosure of Campus Security Policy and Campus Crime Statistics Act of 1990 (or Clery Act's) primary goal is to increase transparency on crime and crime reporting on college campuses. The Clery Act requires postsecondary institutions to collect and disseminate campus crime statistics to students, parents, faculty, and staff. The Act was passed through the efforts of many, including the parents of Jeanne Clery, a 19-year-old woman who was raped and killed in her residence hall room at Lehigh University, on April 5, 1986. The law applies to all colleges and universities that participate in federal financial aid programs. The Clery Act was amended in 1992 and 1998, expanding reporting requirements. The 1998 amendments also formally named the law in memory of Jeanne Clery. By October 17, 2000, colleges and universities throughout the United States were required to post their crime statistics on the U.S. Department of Education's website.

> **Clery Act** Named for Jeanne Clery. This 1990 federal law requires all colleges and universities that participate in federal financial-aid programs to collect, maintain, and disclose information about crime on or near their campuses.

Learn more about college campus crime and security at www.ope.ed.gov/security.

According to federal officials, postsecondary institutions traditionally underreported crime in spite of the 1990 federal law, requiring submission of crime data. The Clery Act amendments closed a number of loopholes through which colleges could exclude some reported crimes. The amendments expand the definition of a campus to include city streets and other properties that meander through college campuses. Colleges and universities are also required to survey local police, dormitory leaders, and rape crisis centers for criminal allegations that may not have been reported to college officials. All criminal complaints, proven or not, must be documented and reported under the 1998 Clery Act amendments ("An education in crime stats," 2000; U.S. Department of Education, 2007).

To control the issue of drug and alcohol use and abuse on college campuses, on August 16, 1990, the U.S. Department of Education made some amendments to the Drug-Free Schools and Communities Act enacted by Congress on December 12, 1989. The amendments require each institution of higher learning, as a condition to participation in a federal financial aid to students program, to certify that it had adopted and implemented a program to prevent the unlawful possession, use, or distribution of illicit drugs and alcohol by students and employees (U.S. Department of Education, 2007).

> **Drug-Free Schools and Communities Act** Enacted by Congress on December 12, 1989. Require institutions of higher learning to certify that they have adopted and implemented a program to prevent the unlawful possession, use, or distribution of illicit drugs and alcohol by students and employees.

SECURITY SPOTLIGHT

Go to the U.S. Department of Education's Campus Safety and Security website (http// www.ope.ed.gov/security) and look up campus crime statistics for the IHE you attend. How does your institution compare to similar IHEs in your area and state? Arrange a meeting with someone from the security office at the educational institution where you are enrolled. Ask what security challenges the college or university has encountered during its history and what processes, systems, and practices the school has adopted to improve security of faculty, students, administrative personnel, facilities, and data.

▶ Health Care Security

Health care is the fifth largest industry in the United States. More than 30,000 health care facilities administer care to millions of people. Health care facilities include about 6,000 hospitals in the United States, ranging from 25 to 2,500 beds that served over 35 million people in 2013 ("Fast facts," 2015). Other types of health care facilities include clinics, medical offices, extended care, and outpatient facilities that must provide a safe and secure environment for patients, staff, and visitors. As security-related problems in hospitals increase, the Joint Commission has increased minimum standards for hospital security. To assist in the design and administration of security programs in health care facilities, in 1968 the International Association for Healthcare Security and Safety (IAHSS) was established to provide a professional forum for health care security managers. The IAHSS provides security administrators with industry guidelines and professional certifications for guards and supervisors.

> **health care facility**
> Hospital, medical center, health clinic, nursing home, or similar facility.

As a profession, health care security developed gradually over the last 100 years. During the first half of the twentieth century, health care security was limited to the minor role hospital maintenance staff played in providing security. In the 1950s, off-duty police officers were used to provide security in emergency rooms and other sensitive areas. Today, virtually every major urban hospital, as well as many rural and other health care facilities, has safety and security programs. Security in a health care environment is an absolute necessity for the following reasons:

> **International Association for Healthcare Security and Safety (IAHSS)**
> Professional organization for health care security managers.

- Hospitals and other health care facilities have a moral responsibility to serve the public. This obligation requires the provision of a safe and secure environment.

- Health care enterprises have a legal responsibility to protect persons and property. The legal duty to protect is even greater when patients are unable to care for themselves. Negligence on the part of hospitals has led to compensatory damage awards by juries. A safe environment reduces and limits liability.

- Accreditation and regulatory requirements of the Joint Commission (formerly the Joint Commission for Accreditation of Healthcare Organizations [JCAHO]) and the Occupational Safety and Health Administration (OSHA), coupled with numerous other federal, state, and local statutes, require security in health care facilities.

> **The Joint Commission**
> Formerly the Joint Commission for Accreditation of Healthcare Organizations (JCAHO). Requires minimum security standards for hospitals and health care facilities.

- Health care organizations have a fiduciary responsibility to maintain a sound financial position. Thus, cost containment through the prevention of loss due to crime, waste, and natural phenomena is necessary.

- Good public and employee relations are maintained, in part, through the provision of a safe and secure environment.

Health care facilities, including hospitals and medical centers, tend to be a reflection of the environments in which they are located. The types and levels of security also vary in hospitals based on vulnerability and threats. For example, if facilities are located in high-crime areas, the threat of crime on or near facility property is also high. Major urban medical centers function much like small cities. They never close. Each has retail outlets, pharmacies, restaurants, and offices, and many have multiple buildings. Many patients are unable to care for themselves, much less protect themselves from dangerous situations. Theft, fire, natural disasters, accidents, personal attacks, and sexual assaults are constant threats. Shoplifting may occur in the gift shops, patients or visitors may become violent, and power failures may threaten life-support systems. Drugs are stolen from pharmacies, cars from parking lots, and babies from maternity wards ("University Health Care provides," 2000). Rival gang members may even pursue an injured gang member into an emergency room for revenge.

Policies, procedures, equipment, and strategies for preventing loss in health care facilities are as numerous as the facilities are diverse. Electronic surveillance systems monitor patients, staff, and visitors. Security personnel patrol the buildings and high-risk areas, including emergency rooms, and other areas that may be prone to violence and crime, including parking ramps. Health care security personnel conduct internal investigations, inspections, audits, and surveys. They also provide other interdepartmental support, such as escort and mail services. They also develop safety and security plans, test emergency protection systems, and control access.

Access control is difficult in many health care facilities. Numerous entrances and exits coupled with busy medical staff and a constant flow of newcomers help create an environment where control and surveillance of pedestrian traffic is difficult. Photo identification badges for staff and card access controls using RFID technologies assist with access control. Hospitals may also use biometrics in some high-security locations including research areas, patient records, and information-technology centers. Loss prevention and self-protection training is being provided to more staff, especially those who work alone in a community health environment.

Information security is also an issue. The research shows that one of the primary challenges to health care data is security, followed by management of that data ("2015 healthcare outlook," 2015). Special security practices are needed to protect electronic databases and computer-based information storage and transmission systems in health care settings. These practices are important, considering the increased use of computers and the sharing of patient and personnel data between departments and among health care organizations through electronic medical records (EMR), and electronic health records (EHR) technology. Data transmission interceptions and access to email and Internet connections threaten the privacy of countless individuals. The Health Insurance Portability and Accountability Act of 1996 (HIPAA) mandated national standards for the electronic storage and transmission of health insurance transactions, including information on claims, enrollment eligibility, payments, and benefits. The law also mandates strict standards to protect the privacy of a patient's identity and personal health information among medical personnel and the public (Dolan, 1999; U.S. Department of Health and Human Services, Office of Civil Rights, 2007).

Another area in a hospital where there is a need for increased security is in birthing wards or nurseries. To prevent infant abductions from these areas, hospitals have increased security measures and have modified their policies and procedures to meet the Joint Commission accreditation. Generally, they include lock down procedures related to abductions, limiting access to infants by hospital staff, educating staff and parents on abduction risk, placing identically numbered matching wrist bands on the parents and infants, verifying the identity of parents and visitors, foot printing babies immediately after birth, and having the staff wear color-coded identification badges specific to the nursery/birth wards. These areas also have enhanced access control for parents and visitors and increased security for infants. For example, infants are equipped with RFID ankle bracelets/security tags upon birth that continually track them while alerting security personnel and staff if the tag has been tampered with, or the infant has been moved outside the controlled area (Vincent, 2009).

To address workplace violence issues, many health care facilities require that staff be trained in aggression management techniques. One specific aggression management program (AMP) is Professional Assault Response Training (PART). PART involves a comprehensive and systematic approach to security that is designed to minimize risks associated with assaultive behavior of patients, visitors, and others in a health care environment. PART emphasizes the roles of supervision, policy enforcement, and de-escalation of conflict. The training focuses on identification of the symptoms and motives of violent behavior, the development of alternative courses of action, the determination of

> Health Insurance Portability and Accountability Act of 1996 (HIPAA) A federal law mandating national standards for electronic health insurance transactions, including claims, enrollment, eligibility, payments, and benefits.

levels of dangerousness, response techniques, and use of force. PART helps health care employees develop the skills necessary to manage risk associated with assaultive behavior, mitigate liability, maintain a safe environment, and conform to legislatively mandated training requirements (Professional Growth Facilitators, 2000).

Extended Care/Nursing Home Security

Extended or assisted care facilities, the largest segment of which consists of nursing homes, serves a population that often have physical or cognitive impairments. What is unique about this population of individuals is that oftentimes, the facility becomes their home. As a result, residents oftentimes require or demand the presence and a feeling of physical security in their "home" than other health care facilities (Lewin, 2001; Parmelee & Lawton, 1990). Although typically smaller in size and scope than hospitals, these facilities can be vulnerable to natural and environmental disasters, fire, theft of resident property, patient abuse, and slip and fall-related accidents. Of greater concern are residents who may have cognitive impairments who may inadvertently wander (also called elopement) away from the facility. To address this issue, many facilities have alarmed doors and/or have their patients wear RFID bracelets that activate an alarm if they should leave the facility (Aud, 2004). In some situations, nursing homes will also use bed-exit alarms that are used to prevent falls and wandering (Capezuti, Brush, Lane, Rabinowitz, & Secic, 2009).

Since most nursing homes and assisted care facilities are small, the protective function is usually assigned to a nonsecurity professional, often the business manager for a facility who must be trained in security. In addition, budgetary realities dictate the need for personnel multitasking in small health care facilities. Thus, the safety and security function is often given a low priority. However, through the use of alarms, closed-circuit television (CCTV), controlled access systems, and policies and procedures, an increased protection of people, property, and information can be realized. Liaison with local agencies as well as a thorough investigation of all injuries, losses, and security violations can help minimize protection problems (Colling, 2001; International Association for Healthcare Security and Safety, 2007; Simonsen, 1998).

▶ Entertainment Security

Theme parks, mega events, and casinos provide recreational outlets for individuals. These venues also pose unique threats and opportunities for criminal activities and from natural threats.

Theme Parks

Theme parks are often considered packaged experiences that include unique forms of entertainment (i.e., water parks, amusement rides), dining, and oftentimes lodging facilities. They are often characterized as geographically large, having sizeable numbers of guests whose populations fluctuate by weather, season, and events. Theme parks, such as Disneyland and Disney World, Busch Gardens, Sea World, and Universal Studios draw millions of people each year where visitors trust that they will be secure and safe from human and mechanical threats. Surveys of theme park managers show that quality and safety security are the two top elements of visitor satisfaction (Tsang, Lee, Wong, & Chong, 2012).

Because of the size and clientele, unique safety and security-related issues need to be considered. For example, it can be anticipated that there will be more medical-related events due to slip and falls, exhaustion, and pre-existing medical issues. The nature of theme parks may also require that security personnel have specialized skills. Many theme parks, such as Disney World in Orlando, Florida, attract people from around the world. This will require that security personnel (and other staff) possess language and cultural competency skills in order to make guests feel comfortable and secure. To ensure that the security function is not "institutional" or coercive in nature, security measures, including physical barriers and surveillance systems, should blend with the environment and go unnoticed by the average visitor.

crowd management Security activities directed toward effective crowd control or management techniques.

One relatively unique security issue in theme parks is crowd management. Large crowds require that security activities be directed toward effective crowd control or management techniques. In most parks, long lines develop at attractions, where waiting periods and levels of frustration can increase. Crowd situations can sometimes lead to increased stress among patrons, resulting in verbal and even physical assaults; individuals who witness the actions of frustrated guests may also feel unsafe. To address this issue, the security function in theme parks should emphasize public relations activities that ensure maintaining positive attitudes among guests (and staff), while also creating a sense of order and control by enforcing parks rules, such as "line jumping," mediating disputes between guests, and preventing assaultive behaviors. In some cases, long lines (or the impression of long lines) can be managed by creating "subzones" or smaller "parks within parks," having well designed queues that provide an impression that the line is shorter than it is, and using diversionary activities for long waits that could include staff dressed as cartoon characters entertaining individuals standing in line (Mowen, Vogelsong, & Graefe, 2003). Another way to reduce or eliminate long lines is by using technologies. For example, one method involves patrons being issued devices that are similar to existing restaurant pagers. These pagers alert them that they are ready to board their attraction (Chu, Hung, & Lu, 2014).

Another security issue involves the emergency evacuation of guests and staff. Unlike other settings, such as the workplace, guests are more vulnerable to injury or death when an emergency event/disaster occurs because they are unfamiliar with the park layout and they are not trained in evacuations. Emergency evacuations can be based on man-made events ranging from terrorist attacks, fires, violent crimes, and natural events, such as storms. The safe and timely evacuation of guests relies on park design followed by well-designed emergency evacuation plans and properly trained staff. Some of the factors that need to be considered include the design and placement of roads, which are known as movement points, obstacles (i.e., buildings and water), land features (that do not include buildings or other obstacles), and the characteristics of the event/disaster itself that can slow an evacuation. To ensure that evacuation plans are effective, security personnel and park planners can use computer generated models to identify evacuation routes, barriers, and estimate the time it takes to evacuate (Solmaz & Turgut, 2013).

Mega Events

mega events Large events that are often international in nature and attract large numbers of spectators and tourists.

Another issue is security at mega events that occur within private and public institutions. Mega events are large events that are often international in nature and attract a large numbers of spectators and tourists. Generally, a mega event is based on scale: the number of athletes, the number of spectators, and the geographic size of the event. Some examples of a mega event can include the Olympics, the Super Bowl, the World Cup and other large sporting events and festivals. Since 9-11, security at these mega events has expanded and has become much more sophisticated.

Like other locations, accidents, theft, assault, robbery, vandalism (during and after hours), bomb threats, and terrorism (such as Boston Marathon bombing in 2013) are some

Yankee Stadium Mega Event.
(Photo courtesy of James Tourtellotte/U.S. Customs and Border Protection.)

vulnerabilities that exist. However, each event may have unique or specific vulnerabilities. For example, during the Islamic pilgrimage from Hajj to Mecca in Saudi Arabia in 2015, over 700 people were killed in a stampede. An estimated 2 million people were present (Hubbard, 2015). In other cases, sporting events tend to draw fans who may become quite unruly, which is commonplace among football fans in Britain and Europe where their disorderly activities are a social phenomenon defined as "hooliganism" (Dunning, Murphy, & Williams, 2014). Additionally, the presence of alcohol and an emotional and competitive spirit between persons can lead to security issues. The size of the crowd itself contributes to security issues too: perceptions of anonymity in large crowds may make some persons act differently because they perceive that they cannot be readily identified. Because these events draw large numbers of people, they can also be an effective location to protest, which was the case in the 2012 London Olympic games where security personnel also had to address individuals protesting against some of the large corporate sponsors of the games, the displacement of populations to build facilities for the events, and concerns that the Olympics were too corporate in nature (Boykoff & Fussey, 2014).

Mega events have some relatively unique security traits. First, these events oftentimes involve international or national organizations, such as the International Olympic Committee or the National Football League (NFL) that may place certain security-related conditions on the host nation, city, and location. For example, the NFL requires pat down searches of individuals entering arenas whose costs are borne by the team owners (Schimmel, 2006) and ultimately ticket holders. Next, these events also involve the coordination of security activities between public and private organizations. The Winter Olympics in Canada was organized through a special body, the Integrated Security Unit, where the Royal Canadian Mounted Police (RCMP) was the lead agency; other government agencies such as the Vancouver Police Department, Canada Border Services Agency (CBSA), Canadian Forces, police agencies across Canada, and the Canadian Security Intelligence Service (CSIS) also played a role ("Olympic security estimated to cost $900M," 2009). The 2012 Olympics in London also relied heavily upon private security personnel who worked with governmental services including police and emergency services that were coordinated through a central command structure (Jennings & Lodge, 2011). Last, these mega events are expensive. The cost of security at the 2002 Winter Olympic Games in Salt Lake City, Utah, approached $350 million, twice the cost of the entire 1980 Winter Olympics in Lake Placid, New York (Zeigler, 2002). The cost for the 2012 Olympics in London was estimated at $2 billion Euros.

Gaming and Casino Security

A casino is a business or organization that provides gambling opportunities through games of chance. The majority of gaming casinos are open 24 hours per day, 365 days a year. Customers can arrive at one of these casinos at any time, searching for a pleasurable experience at the game tables and slots, restaurants, and concert venues. The primary objectives of casino security include protecting legitimate patrons who usually carry large sums of cash and have credit cards, jewelry, and luggage in their possession who are vulnerable to various property-related crimes. Security is also responsible for access control and crowd management, the surveillance of patrons and employees, physical security, investigating employees, and responding to and investigating reports of theft. Security personnel also need to address vice-related crimes including prostitution and drug dealing that can occur on and near casino properties. They also need to ensure that the casino is in compliance with gaming laws, while working with state-level gaming commission investigators when incidents occur (Major, 1998; National Indian Gaming Commission, 2007).

One primary security issue is access control. Because casinos are private property, security can ban individuals who violated gaming laws or committed some other security-related infraction. In some cases, persons may voluntarily self-exclude themselves for a variety of reasons including a gambling addiction. Under self-exclusion, a gambler can complete a self-exclusion agreement that states that she/he would like to be prohibited from access to the casino for a set period of time. This information is then entered into the casino's database along with a photograph of the person. If the person does enter the casino during this time period (where oftentimes the person is readily detected because of facial recognition software), security personnel then have the authority to remove him or her (Ladouceur, Sylvain, & Gosselin, 2007). Besides voluntary bans, casino security can also ban individuals for cheating, various criminal activities, card counting, and arrest them for trespass if they should return. Oftentimes, this information is shared with other casinos throughout the world by the means of interconnected "cheater" databases. Law enforcement agencies may also have access to this information (Gabel, 2012; Jonas, 2006).

Gaming-related theft and fraud is also a primary security issue. Casinos use a five-part strategy to prevent or detect theft through the casino's games:

- Through the *command* component, casinos organize security and surveillance.

- Through the *control* component, casinos utilize security and surveillance to influence circumstances for a favorable outcome.

- Good *communication* is the component used to link elements and personnel.

- *Compliance* is the most vital component of the antifraud strategies. Compliance with house rules and agency regulations is a necessity. A significant portion of the losses to casinos results from irregular or minimal compliance with rules and regulatory agency policy.

- The introduction of *antitheft technology* to the gaming industry helps as well. In addition to surveillance equipment, many casinos have installed automatic card-shuffling machines to prevent collaboration between criminals and bribed card game dealers (McDonald & Barfield, 2007; Nichter, 2000).

Casinos have perhaps the most sophisticated surveillance systems. Continuous surveillance and the recording of suspicious people and security personnel are used to monitor

Casinos often use state-of-the-art security and surveillance systems using digital CCTV and multiplexers to protect assets and detect unauthorized guest activities, including cheating.
(Photo courtesy of Shutterstock.)

patrons and employees. Some common elements include digital color cameras, facial recognition software, and the analysis of license plates to compare this information to known casino violators and return customers. Other forms of surveillance include RFID technologies that track cards and chips, and "smart tables" that can track the flow of money to specific players. Casinos also use other software programs that will track where guests register, monitoring loyalty card (or "players card") holders to see what other casinos they are playing in and how much, and in what casinos they spend their money (Gabel, 2012).

Internal threats are also a concern for casinos. In order to prevent internal theft, fraud and collusion with patrons at gaming tables, and engaging in vice-related and property crimes within the facility, casinos need to conduct comprehensive criminal background investigations on potential employees. Once hired, meanwhile, effective policies and procedures must exist that include the surveillance of casino staff. These policies can include video surveillance of cashier, counting and vault areas, instituting a two-person rule that requires a minimum of two people to transport cash and other valuables, strict inventory and signature policies related to money handling to deter theft, rewarding employees for reporting security-related issues, and strict accounting procedures. Technological changes to the gaming environment have also led to increased security. For example, many casinos now dispense paper receipts instead of tokens or coins from slot machines. These paper receipts reduce some cash handling procedures for the casino and increase the security of patrons who no longer have to carry large quantities of winnings to cashier stations.

Museum Security

Due to the rare and sometimes irreplaceable nature of museum inventories, special attention must be given to criminal and noncriminal events. The two most common threats against museums are theft and vandalism. In the case of museums, theft can be divided into three groups: (1) opportunistic, where an outsider takes the opportunity to steal an object; (2) pre-determined, where the criminal, after consulting with dealers and other individuals who can sell the item for him, steals the object(s); and (3) fakes and forgeries, where an insider threat substitutes a fake for the real item (Agrawal & Naqvi, 2013). In many cases, major thefts are the product of a contractual arrangement between the thief and the illegitimate consumer or client. However, the most frequently stolen works in museums and art galleries tend to be small items that can be concealed and easily sold. In many cases, insider threats steal and sell items to unscrupulous rare book or art dealers, or sell the items themselves to collectors, using modern auction sites, such as eBay (Cremers, 2015). Museums are also vulnerable to vandalism. For example, in 2007, four individuals broke into the Musee d'Orsay in Paris where one of the intruders punched a hole in Claude Monet's Le Pont d'Argenteuil (The Argenteuil Bridge) masterpiece painting. In another case, a patron kissed a painting valued at $2.8 million leaving lipstick residue on it. It cost $45,000 to restore the paining (Brisman, 2011).

Museums must also be prepared for natural threats. Fire, floods, leaking roofs, and the environment are common threats to collections. Museums are also vulnerable to acts of civil unrest and warfare where a nation's cultural heritage and history can be vandalized or destroyed. To address these and other issues, in 2002, the International Council on Museums (ICOM) created the Museum Emergency Programme (MEP) which trains museum personnel in risk assessment, disaster management, and emergency response (Menegazzi, 2006). Museums and art galleries must also be vigilant regarding purchases of additional pieces for the collection that could impact their reputation and expose them to legal issues. Reproductions and fakes, as well as stolen goods require museums to conduct investigations on the providence of the item to ensure its authenticity, and to verify that the current owner has legal ownership of the item.

To protect museum assets, comprehensive physical security and access control programs, continuous inventory control procedures, and the authentication and appraisal of new works can greatly reduce losses to museums and galleries. Irreplaceable and rare items and materials should be maintained in restricted areas where access can be monitored and controlled. Acquisitions should be authenticated to deter and detect criminals who specialize in the creation of fraudulent pieces or the disposition of stolen works. Objects in museum collections should also be properly cataloged and secured. Maintaining and monitoring appropriate air quality and temperature standards also preserves rare items. In addition, emergency management planning and procedures, video surveillance, security personnel, and vigilant curatorial staff help to protect the contents of museums (Hough, 1999; Longmore-Etheridge, 2007).

Zoo and Aquarium Security

A zoological park or aquarium is defined as any permanent cultural institution that owns and maintains wildlife that represent more than a token collection and, under the direction of a professional staff, provides its collection with appropriate care and exhibits them in an aesthetic manner to the public on a regularly scheduled, predictable basis (American Zoo and Aquarium Society, 2007). Zoos and aquariums also exhibit, conserve, and preserve the earth's fauna and flora in an educational and scientific manner. Currently, there are over 170 zoos and aquariums in North America. Facilities that house rare and exotic plants, animals, fish, and other wildlife have special security needs. Many plant and animal species are near extinction. Precautions must be taken to ensure their safety and good health. They must be protected from environmental disasters, mistreatment by human beings, and assaults from predators. Some zoological parks are small, while others cover hundreds of acres. The Zoological Society of San Diego, in addition to its world famous zoo, maintains a 1,800-acre wildlife preserve, The Wild Animal Park, which contains more than 2,500 animals.

One of the most valuable assets that zoos need to protect are animals. In some cases, animals can be stolen. For example, on December 27, 2000, two female koalas were reported stolen from the San Francisco Zoo. Although the zoo has a 24-hour security operation, the koalas were discovered missing by an animal keeper. Apparently, the thieves stole the marsupials during the previous evening. The suspect(s) climbed onto the koala exhibit roof, penetrated a skylight, and entered the koala facility through a furnace door. Zoo officials were extremely concerned for the rare creatures' safety because the stress associated with improper care could be deadly (Mason, 2000). On December 28, 2000, two teenage boys were arrested and charged with burglary, possession of stolen property, and felony theft in connection with the koalas' disappearance. Apparently, the two boys took the koalas to give to their girlfriends ("Two teens arrested in theft of koalas," 2000).

Zoo and aquarium assets are also subject to vandalism, accidents, health-related issues, theft, shoplifting and after hours trespass. Ticket and credit card fraud, auto theft, and violence against persons are potential threats in zoological parks. Bus and tram rides require safety considerations. People undertaking close encounters with dangerous wildlife, users of ATMs, and endangered species necessitate special protection, security, and safety precautions. Moreover, food service areas' compliance with health regulations must be monitored (Bagott, 2003). Zoos also need to comply with security standards. In 1999, zoo officials from Atlanta, Georgia, faced several security challenges in their 10-year quest to house giant pandas at the facility. Pandas in the wild are found only in the central region of China, and their fate is controlled by the Chinese government. Since 1972, Chinese officials have lent pairs of pandas to zoos to conduct research. In addition to stringent health, safety, and habitat requirements, Chinese officials wanted the Atlanta zoo to provide continuous audio–video monitoring of the pandas and allow open access to the monitoring by Chinese researchers. Through integration of CCTV and Internet technology, continuous monitoring of the pandas is provided and the Chinese can observe the pandas at any time (White, 2001).

Facilities that house rare and exotic animals have special security needs.
(Photo courtesy of Patrick Ortmeier.)

As zoos and aquariums seek to place visitors closer to wildlife in a natural habitat, traditional physical barriers, such as glass enclosures and cages, are being eliminated. As a result, the risk of improper interactions with wildlife as well as the possibility of wildlife theft increases. Birds and snakes are most vulnerable, especially as objects of theft, because they are easy to conceal and sell. Critical to the success of any zoo or aquarium security program is planning and personnel training. Contingency plans that can be activated quickly provide guidance for personnel in an emergency, especially in the event of an animal's escape. A comprehensive training program, for facility staff as well as security personnel, creates security awareness and helps promote rapid and appropriate responses to crime and emergency situations (American Zoo and Aquarium Society, 2007; Bagott, 2003).

Many zoos and aquariums are accredited by the American Zoo and Aquarium Association (AZA). To be accredited, all aspects of wildlife care must be highly professional. In addition, the zoo or aquarium must demonstrate significant support through donations, volunteerism, and membership. Other factors that are heavily considered in the accreditation process include fiscal viability, educational activities, operations, strategic plans, physical facilities, visitor services, management of the collection, participation in conservation and research programs, safety and emergency procedures, and security measures (Hosey, Melfi, & Pankhurst, 2013).

A QUICK SURVEY

Consider all the institutional settings with which you have interacted. In any of the settings with which you have interacted, have you become aware that a security breach occurred? If so, check any and all of the following settings in which this has occurred.

- Bank or other financial institution
- Courthouse or courtroom
- Elementary school
- Secondary school
- College or university
- Health care facility
- Religious institutions

In your view, what led to the security breaches in the settings you checked? What could security personnel have done differently to prevent the breaches?

▶ Religious Institutions and Security

Unfortunately, religious institutions can be the targets of crime. In August 2012, Wade Page, a white supremacist, entered the 17,000-square foot Sikh temple in Oak Creek, Wisconsin, with a handgun, killing six worshipers. During the spree, Page was shot and killed by the police who responded to the call ("Police identify," 2012). While church shootings are rare, religious institutions face many other personal and property-related issues that can impact the reputation of the institution, and even the religion itself to some degree. In many cases, religious institutions can contain expensive religious icons, artifacts, and artworks that could be stolen. Because of intolerance, some institutions can be the targets for vandalism and arson. Members can also be targeted. What also makes the security function challenging in these settings is that oftentimes, they vary in size and function. Some are large multiuse facilities that serve as a place of worship and education where they could be located in high-crime urban areas. These institutions often have an "open door" policy welcoming all individuals. They can also serve as community centers where the institution is involved in a variety of community outreach and charitable activities. In many cases, these institutions are open on a 24-hour basis and are unsupervised after normal business hours.

To address these issues, unobtrusive and "invisible" administrative (policies and procedures) and procedural controls need to be established. Some key considerations include the following:

- Child abuse—to address this threat all personnel should undergo background investigations; institutions may also want to develop a "two-person" policy, requiring two individuals to be present at all times when an at-risk person is present (based on age, gender, or disability). A risk analysis of the surrounding area around the facility should also be conducted.

- Child abductions—to deter and prevent abductions, policies and procedures must exist. Parents/guardians should be required to register their child(ren) at all events, while positive matching policies should exist where, for example, the parent and child are given matching wristbands. Emergency procedures for suspected abductions should also exist and children should be kept in secure areas. All staff should be trained in child abduction procedures, and children should not be left unattended in any area of the institution, including restrooms.

- Emergency response—all church personnel (including volunteers) need to be trained in emergency response procedures related to fire, medical emergencies, lock downs (in the case of violent crimes) and evacuations for man-made and natural events. Emergency response also includes training and liaison with law enforcement and fire personnel.

- Physical protection systems—CPTED-related modifications to the perimeter and interior, fencing, locks, lighting, and CCTV should be part of the comprehensive security plan. The physical security component also includes securing certain assets and areas, based on use and time-related variables. Particular areas and assets should be target hardened against theft and vandalism. If open after hours, the use of volunteer staff may be an effective deterrent for some criminal activities. Greeters and ushers during normal business hours may also serve as a deterrent.

- Cash handling—a common element in many religious institutions is presence of cash from donations. As such, cash handling procedures need to be in place. Common cash handling procedures can include cash bags that have seals to prevent reopening them, "two-person" carry and counting procedures, emptying all donation boxes/locations periodically, and signage that notifies would-be criminals that there is no cash on hand. Members can also be encouraged to donate using electronic fund transfers and checks instead of cash.

Another issue is mismanagement and embezzlement of church funds. Religious institutions often rely upon volunteers who are placed in positions of trust. In many cases these individuals may have very little oversight of their activities. These financial crimes have fiscal ramifications. For example, in 1990 the comptroller of the Diocese in Buffalo, New York was convicted of embezzling $8 million (Fleckenstein & Bowes, 2000). If not the dollar losses themselves, financial crimes by staff can erode trust in the institution, leading to a loss in its reputation, declining donations, and members leaving for a trustworthy religious institution.

Summary

Common safety and security principles and practices apply across the broad spectrum of public and private institutions that serve diverse populations. The nature of banking and financial transactions has changed dramatically, increasing targets of opportunity for the would-be criminal, particularly among ATM and card users. Courthouses and courtrooms are no longer safe havens where adversaries can settle disputes without fear of disruption, injury, or death. Now, courthouses need to have effective security programs and be properly designed to separate individuals based on their function. Staff and users of services provided at medical facilities, K–12 schools, and institutions of Higher Education (IHE) also face relatively unique security issues. Oftentimes, these are associated with quality of life issues and property-related crimes. However, violent threats are also an issue that must be addressed. Entertainment-related venues including theme parks, mega events, casinos, and museums that attract large numbers of individuals must also have effective security programs to address various criminal activities. Some of these locations also require well-developed crowd management and evacuation plans. Even religious institutions are vulnerable to security issues that can impact their reputation, members, and financial health. While each of these institutions has unique security concerns, one common denominator is that the security function is critical in protecting patrons through the design and administration of a comprehensive security program. By protecting patrons, increased levels of trust are built between the users and the organization, ensuring that the potential for return business exists. These programs will also ensure that loss to the organization is minimized or eliminated.

Career Opportunities

Banking/Financial services security: Security positions within the financial services industry (retail banking, credit companies, mortgage lending, insurance companies) typically require a bachelor's degree in business, financial, or security management. Entry-level salaries range from $40,000–$65,000.

Contract services: Almost any security service provided through a proprietary (in-house) security organization or unit can be provided by a contract security company. Security vendors offer a wide range of personnel, equipment, and services including security officers, patrol, armored car (aka "cash in transit"), alarm systems, surveillance, investigations, and consulting. Due to competition, entry-level wages for most unarmed security officers is $10–$15 per hour.

However, contract security supervisors and managers earn higher salaries.

Casino/Gaming security: Casino and gaming security personnel provide traditional security services related to physical and personnel security. They also engage in sophisticated surveillance activities within casino and gaming establishments. Depending upon company and location, entry-level salaries range from $23,000–$34,000 annually.

Educational institution security: A wide range of employment opportunities exist in elementary, secondary, and postsecondary educational institutions. Most schools and college campus security operations provide traditional security services. Salaries are similar to police officers, ranging from $30,000–$60,000 annually.

Key Terms and Concepts

ATM *143*
Bailiffs *146*
Bank Protection Act of
   1968 *141*
Card trapping *144*
Casino security *158*
Clery Act *152*
Columbine effect *147*
Crowd management *156*
Drug-Free Schools and
   Communities Act *152*

Emergency notification systems *151*
Financial institution *140*
Health care facilities *153*
Health Insurance Portability and
   Accountability Act of 1996
   (HIPAA) *154*
Institutions of Higher Education
   (IHEs) *150*
International Association for
   Healthcare Security and Safety
   (IAHSS) *153*

Joint Commission *153*
Lebanese loop *144*
Magnetometers *147*
Man trap *143*
Mega event *156*
PIN crack *144*
Ram raiding *143*
Safe-School Initiative *149*
Safe-school zones *149*
Skimming *144*

Discussion Questions and Exercises

1. Although commonalities exist, numerous unique hazards threaten specific types of industries and organizations. Identify one unique security-related issue in each of the major sectors reviewed in this chapter.
2. Choose one specific security application from this chapter. List the types of crime and other hazards that threaten the operation, and design measures to prevent the threats from materializing.
3. What are some key security issues for financial institutions?
4. Courthouse and courtroom security is a major concern. When designing a courthouse, how should it be designed, based on zones of operations?
5. What are some of the major issues for K–12 schools? How can they be addressed?
6. Review security in your Institution of Higher Education. What type of security program exists? What types of security practices and hardware exist?
7. What are some specific security issues or concerns for nursing homes?
8. Cheating and defrauding in casinos are major security threats. What strategies can be used to detect theft in casinos?
9. What types of security practices should a museum have to prevent theft and vandalism?
10. Identify an upcoming mega event. What security issues do you foresee? How can these issues be addressed?

Your Turn

Analyzing the Virginia Tech Incident

One of the deadliest single-perpetrator shooting rampages in the history of the United States occurred at Virginia Polytechnic Institute and State University (Virginia Tech) in Blacksburg, Virginia, on April 16, 2007. The shooter, Cho Seung Hui, killed 32 students and faculty and wounded 30 others before taking his own life.

The killing spree began shortly after 7:00 a.m. at West Ambler Johnson Hall, a dormitory on the Virginia Tech campus. The following is a brief summary of early morning events:

7:15 A.M.

Police receive a 911 phone call, reporting shots fired at Johnson Hall. Police find a female student and male resident advisor fatally wounded. Based on witness interviews, police believe the shootings are an isolated domestic incident. Police do not initiate campus-wide security measures. Police focus on the female victim's boyfriend, a student at nearby Radford University. Police later stop and interrogate the boyfriend on a highway in Blacksburg.

9:26 A.M.

Virginia Tech authorities issue first mass email, reporting the 7:15 A.M. shooting and warning students and staff.

9:45 A.M.

Police receive a phone call about a shooting at Norris Hall, a science and engineering classroom building, about 15 minutes walking distance from West Ambler Johnson Hall. After the perpetrator, Cho Seung Hui, chained the Norris Hall exterior doors shut, he killed 30 students and faculty in their classrooms before killing himself.

9:50 A.M.

A second mass email by Virginia Tech officials reports a gunman is loose on campus.

9:55 A.M.

A third mass email reports the shootings at Norris Hall and that the gunman is in custody.

Subsequent to the mass killing, it was learned that the killer, Cho Seung Hui, had been treated for mental illness.

1. In your view, were any or all of the killings at Virginia Tech preventable? If so, what could have been done to prevent them, and by whom?
2. Do you think that police and security measures and responses were appropriate? Why or why not? If not, what would have constituted more appropriate responses from police and university security personnel?

3. Are sufficient safety and security measures in place on school and college campuses in general?

4. Conduct research online or in your library to discover what actions the Virginia Tech massacre prompted key stakeholders to take. Consider actions taken by emergency services organizations, university administrators, Virginia's state government, families of the victims and the shooter, and mental health professionals.

5. Research the news media's coverage of the Virginia Tech shootings and the shooters' mental state. Consider the benefits and risks of the press coverage. For example, a benefit might be that details about how events unfolded during the shootings could help other universities strengthen their security measures. A risk might be that the extensive attention given to the shooter could cause other mentally ill individuals to plan a similar massacre in hope of getting media attention and a permanent place in history.

6. What impact did the Virginia Tech shootings have on the debate over gun control in the United States and on gun laws?

8 Commercial, Office, and Residential Security

LEARNING OBJECTIVES

After completing this chapter, the reader should be able to:

1 *identify security threats unique to specific industries*

2 *describe asset protection priorities as well as loss prevention policies, procedures, and systems associated with the following:*
- *industrial security*
- *shipping/cargo security*
- *utilities security*
- *hospitality security*
- *retail security and loss prevention*
- *office complex security*
- *residential security*

▶ Introduction

Although a comprehensive exploration of every security environment and service is beyond the scope of a single book, this chapter is designed to introduce the reader to numerous security practices and applications in organizations that operate in the commercial, industrial, and retail sectors. The commercial sector is involved in the buying and selling of goods and services. Commercial businesses include industrial manufacturing facilities, the shipping/cargo industry, utilities, hotels, and retail establishments. Other businesses that operate out of office complexes also require security. Finally, this chapter will explore residential and retail security issues.

▶ Industrial Security

Industrial security is the practice of ensuring safety and security in manufacturing environments and managing loss through the risk management process. Industrial security can also be defined as identifying and managing natural and man-made threats that are imposed on the organization that could cause loss (Russell & Arlow, 2015). The purpose of an industrial security program is the protection of company assets. According to the Siemens Electric (2013), the purpose and goal of industrial security is to "protect industrial machines and plants against unauthorized access, sabotage, espionage and malicious manipulation" (p. 3). To achieve these goals, organizations must have a clear plan of action and specific security objectives—a program that

industrial security The practice of ensuring safety and security in manufacturing environments and managing loss through the risk management process.

progressively and continually identifies and assesses risks, followed by the creation and administration of sound, appropriate, and cost-effective security measures to mitigate and prevent loss.

Already, this textbook has identified some common industrial security threats. Accidents, fire, natural disasters, internal theft, and sabotage constitute some of the major threats to industrial complexes. Accidents may result in lost productivity, property damage, personal injury, death, and damage to a company's reputation. Internal theft is a major contributing factor to loss in and around industrial manufacturing facilities. Theft of tools, raw materials, component parts, finished products, equipment, time, and technology are the primary means through which dishonest employees contribute to loss. Vulnerable areas include loading docks, shipping and receiving areas, warehouses, tool storage areas, trash containers, distribution points, and data systems (Fennelly, 1992). Sabotage occurs when the manufacturing process is intentionally disrupted or when machinery or products are intentionally destroyed. External human-based threats also abound. Natural disasters can destroy an entire industrial facility or disable it for long periods of time. Criminal activities can threaten employees and the organization itself, while espionage is a real threat to manufacturing organizations.

State and federal regulations and laws often require industries to have minimum levels of security. Many private organizations and numerous colleges and universities also conduct classified research and produce classified material for government use. To ensure compliance with federally mandated security requirements, these private industries and academic institutions participate in the National Industrial Security Program (NISP). NISP security-compliance regulations apply to contractors performing for numerous government agencies, including the U.S. Department of Defense, U.S. Department of Energy, CIA, and Nuclear Regulatory Commission (Federation of American Scientists, 2007; Kovacich & Halibozek, 2003). Furthermore, insurance companies often impose security measures as a condition for coverage. And, in other cases, companies can impose security requirements on other companies that they are doing business with to ensure security throughout the supply chain.

▶ Shipping/Cargo Security

cargo security Security efforts directed toward the movement of goods.

Container Security Initiative (CSI) Established in 2002 by the CBP to protect global trade and border security by deploying CBP personnel around the world to ensure cargo container security.

Depending upon the product, cost, and company needs, cargo (freight) can be shipped by different modes that include rail, road, sea, inland water, and air. In most cases, companies rely upon intermodal transport (and supply) chains that include sea, rail, and truck before a product reaches the consumer market (Tong, Wang, Wen, & Kummer, 2010). The cargo industry is a complex network of inter-related companies that are involved in the shipping transaction. To ship by sea, for example, it involves the company or manufacturer, shipping companies, inland carriers, sea terminal operators at ports, a shipping line, another sea port, inland carriers, warehouses, more inland carriers, and finally the recipient of the cargo. At any point in the transportation chain, cargo can be stolen, vandalized, and hijacked. Legitimate forms of cargo transport can also be used for smuggling drugs and even human beings. Unsecure transportation chains can be used by terrorist organizations to transport or deploy chemical, biological, radiological, and nuclear (CRBN) weapons.

Following the events of 9-11, the United States and many other nations strengthened their cargo security standards. One area that received a great deal of attention was sea cargo. It is estimated that 90 percent of world trade is by sea, where approximately 140 million containers are shipped annually throughout the world (Fransoo & Lee, 2013; United Nations, 2015). To address the security threats that exist with the shipping industry, in 2002, U.S. Customs and Border Protection created the Container Security Initiative (CSI). The primary goal of the CSI is

CORE ELEMENTS OF THE CSI

- Identify high-risk containers. CBP uses automated targeting tools to identify containers that pose a potential risk for terrorism, based on advance information and strategic intelligence.
- Prescreen and evaluate containers before they are shipped. Containers are screened as early in the supply chain as possible, generally at the port of departure.

- Use technology to prescreen high-risk containers to ensure that screening can be done rapidly without slowing down the movement of trade. This technology includes large-scale X-ray and gamma ray machines and radiation detection devices.

Source: From CSI: Container Security Initiative. Published by U.S. Customs and Border Protection.

to protect the United States against a terrorist attack where the container is used to deliver the weapon (US Customs and Border Protection, 2011). In a much broader perspective, the CSI also protects global trade and the economic security of the United States. To meet these goals, CBP staff is assigned to foreign ports where they prescreen cargo containers bound for the United States. The three core elements of the CSI can be found in Box 8-1.

In 2006, U.S. Congress enacted the Security and Accountability for Every Port Act of 2006 (Public Law 109–347) to enhance the CSI. Also known as the *SAFE Port Act*, this Act requires that 100 percent of all containers originating from foreign ports be X-rayed or scanned for radiation at a foreign or U.S. port before being allowed to leave for their final destination. The SAFE Port Reauthorization Act of 2011 amended the SAFE Port Act to allow more time to develop and evaluate nonobtrusive imaging and radiation detection equipment (Nolan, 2013).

A complement to the CSI is the Customs-Trade Partnership against Terrorism (C-TPAT) which is a partnership between the private sector and the U.S. Customs and Border Protection (CBP) agency. Unlike the CSI, C-TPAT is a voluntary program where U.S. importers and Mexican and Canadian manufacturers (and other companies in select foreign countries) have their cargo security-related practices and procedures validated by the CBP to ensure that they are "trusted traders," and meet minimum cargo security standards related to the handling, conveyance, tracking, and recordkeeping of cargo. Member companies must also ensure that they meet physical security measures (fencing, lighting, CCTV, locks) and physical access controls at their sites. They must also have information security protocols, hiring standards including background checks for employees, and effective security training programs. Participating companies must also ensure that their partners in the supply chain also meet minimum CBP security standards. CBP personnel also audit these companies in order to maintain their status. Based on compliance, companies are classified by tiers. Tier 1 certified importers have fewer cargo examinations, have front of line inspections if an inspection is needed, and can use FAST (fast and secure transport) lanes at land borders. Tier 2 importers, meanwhile, have even fewer inspections while Tier 3 status companies have zero inspections and have a "Green Lane," where the vehicles and cargo do not have to stop for inspection (US Customs and Border Protection, 2006). The advantage of belonging to C-TPAT is that the cargo of C-TPAT members is "fast-tracked" through the screening and inspection processes in various countries, where cargo is searched less often than nonmembers. C-TPAT membership also ensures that cargo is shipped and received in a timely manner, reducing wait time for goods (Voss & Williams, 2013).

Approximately 90 percent of the world's goods are shipped in containers (Yang & Wei, 2013), which are large steel boxes that have fixed dimensions (made for stacking)

> **Security and Accountability for Every Port Act of 2006** Also known as the SAFE Port Act. This federal law requires that 100% of all containers originating from foreign ports be X-rayed or scanned for radiation at a foreign or U.S. port.

> **Customs-Trade Partnership against Terrorism (C-TPAT)** Partnership between the private sector and the U.S. Customs and Border Protection (CBP) agency.

that can be loaded onto aircraft, ships, trains, and semi-trucks. These containers are screened upon entry into a port or terminal, where trucks hauling the containers will drive through a radiation portal monitor (RPM), which is a passive scanning tool that detects radiation. The contents of the containers will also be scanned using X-rays, while another sensor using pulsed-neutron elemental analysis (called PELAN, which stands for pulsed elemental analysis with neutrons) is used to detect the presence of chemicals and explosives. This technology bombards all materials in the container with pulsed neutrons. The elements of each item in the container are then identified and quantified to determine if a potential threat exists. These systems also use optical character recognition (OCR) software that records license plates and container identification numbers to verify the legitimacy of the container and the truck hauling it (Orphan, Muenchau, Gormley, & Richardson, 2005).

Because these containers are inter-model and "end-to-end," security measures for the full lifecycle of the containers now exist where containers can be tracked throughout the entire transit process. Some of the new physical security measures include "smart containers" that use Global Positioning Systems (GPS) and satellites, RFID, and e-seals to track shipping containers from their point of origin to their final destinations (Erera, Kwek, Goswami, White, & Zhang, 2003). The purpose of these devices is to detect unauthorized breaches, to monitor the internal environment for the safety of the product (e.g., temperature), and to detect illegal cargo, including weapons, humans, and drugs (Giermanski, 2008). In addition to sensors attached or placed in containers, other security technologies are being used to detect shifts or changes in the alignment of stacked containers on ships and at terminals (Kim, Deng, Gupta, & Murphy-Hoye, 2008). While these technologies are very effective in scanning items, human beings are still responsible for interpreting and assessing any security-related issues. For example, if suspicious regions of interest (ROIs) are identified in a container's contents, a physical search of the container by security personnel is conducted (Kolkoori, Wrobel, Hohendorf, & Ewert, 2015). Therefore, organizations need to properly select and train qualified security personnel who have the aptitude and skills to identify suspicious or prohibited items (Michel, Mended, Deruiter, Koomen, & Schwaninger, 2014).

Vehicle & Cargo Inspection System (VACIS). The Mobile VACIS system is a truck-mounted gamma-ray imaging system for inspecting vehicles and cargo in multiple, temporary or remote locations.
(Photo courtesy U.S. Custom and Border Protection.)

Air cargo is another transportation security issue. Air cargo can be defined as any type of property that is transported by freight aircraft or in the belly holds of passenger aircraft. Approximately 7.6 billion pounds of cargo are transported daily by U.S. carriers alone; 20 percent of this cargo is transported by passenger aircraft, where about 15 percent of commercial passenger airline profit ($60 billion annually) is attributed to cargo transport (Abeyratne, 2013; McNeill, 2010). Air cargo security has been identified as the weakest link in aviation security, making it an attractive means to commit a variety of crimes (Sury, Ritzmann, & Schwaninger, 2012). Some risks associated with air cargo security include explosive and incendiary devices concealed in cargo, the shipment of undeclared or undetected hazardous materials, including chemical, radiological, biological, and nuclear (CRBN) items that can be used as weapons of mass destruction, the theft and smuggling of goods, sabotage, and even aircraft hijackings (Elias, 2007). To address air cargo security concerns, Congress passed the Aviation and Transportation Security Act (Public law 107–71) in 2001, which required that by 2010, 100 percent of all cargo carried aboard passenger aircraft be screened by the Transportation Security Administration (TSA).

> **Aviation and Transportation Security Act of 2001** Federal law that created the Transportation Security Administration.

▶ Utilities Security

Utilities are public or private companies that provide services to the public. They are often called "public works." Some common utilities include electric, water (and wastewater), gas, oil, and telecommunications companies. These utilities are some of the sectors that comprise the nation's Critical Infrastructure and Key Resources (CIKR), which is defined as "The framework of interdependent networks and systems comprising identifiable industries, institutions (including people and procedures), and distribution capabilities that provide a reliable flow of products and services essential to the defense and economic security of the United States, the smooth functioning of government at all levels, and society as a whole" (Moteff & Parfomak, 2004, p. 4). The need for security in the utility industry existed prior to the 9-11 attacks. However, after the 9-11 attacks, the need for utility security gained renewed attention from companies, state regulatory agencies, and the federal government.

> **Critical Infrastructure and Key Resources (CIKR)** Public and privately controlled resources and assets that are deemed most critical to national public health and safety, governance, economic and national security, and maintaining public confidence.

The utility industry has some unique characteristics that impact the need for and the provision of security-related activities. First, what is somewhat unique about utility industries is that, in most cases, they are privately owned companies that provide a monopolized service to the public (i.e., the provision of water and electricity). Since only one company may be providing the service, there is a greater duty to the public that the utility is safe and secure and the provision of services will not be interrupted. Next, a great deal of the utility infrastructure is centralized. Most utilities are large scale, where, for instance, there is a single natural gas- or coal- powered electrical plant that is responsible for providing power to a large population of users in a specific geographical region. Because of the centralization, supplies are "brittle," meaning they can easily break or become disrupted (Lovins & Lovins, 1981). As a result of this vulnerability, utility companies need to have effective security measures and contingency plans to mitigate service outages. Last, many components of the utility industry are difficult to secure. For example, there are over 130,000 miles of electric transmission lines in the United States (Smith, 2014). There are also thousands of miles of natural gas and water pipelines in the United States that are vulnerable to natural and man-made events.

> **utility security** Security practices directed toward the utilities sector that include private and/or public companies (gas, electric, water, and wastewater) that provide services to the public.

Already this textbook has identified common man-made and natural threats to organizations that also apply to the utility industry. In some cases, man-made threats can be unique. For example, in February 2014, individuals attacked an electrical transmission substation owned by Pacific Gas and Electric company near San Jose, California. The suspects first entered a utility tunnel, cutting telephone cables. Then, they carried out a sniper attack on

The protection of industrial facilities against man-made and natural threats is a primary security concern.
(Photo courtesy of U.S. Dept of Energy.)

an adjacent substation, shooting 17 transformers, shutting down the substation. It took 27 days to repair the damage (Smith, 2014). Furthermore, pipelines in the United States that are used to transport natural gas and other products have been targeted by extremist groups (Parfomak, 2012). Some of the measures used against these man-made threats include lighting, fences, access control, and long-range cameras. Advanced remote sensing technologies such as Light Detection and Ranging (LiDAR) use remote sensing technologies to monitor and compare images of a certain area, subsequently reporting any image changes in the area (Talarico, Sorensen, Reniers, & Springael, 2016). Even though utilities may be privately owned, they are often regulated by state utility commissions and federal agencies that may require minimum security levels. These utility companies also provide security-related activities out of their own self-interest (Beecher & Kalmbach, 2013; Phelan, 2014).

▶ Hospitality Security

The hospitality industry includes those organizations and institutions that provide lodging, food and beverage, recreation, and entertainment services to guests. This industry consists of resorts, motels and hotels, clubs, bars, spas, restaurants, and similar facilities. The U.S. Department of Labor estimates that it is the third largest industry in the United States, employing approximately 14 million people (Henderson, 2013). Unfortunately, the hospitality industry is vulnerable to man-made and natural threats that must be managed. This section will primarily focus on hotel security.

According to the research, safety and security is considered the most important factor for travelers and hotel guests (Pizam, 2010). Unlike some of the other institutions that were analyzed in this chapter, hotel security can be more challenging based on the notion that the guests are paying for an experience. As such, their hotel stay must be positive. However, the presence of security measures (i.e., guards and access control) could actually worry guests, creating a false impression that the hotel is unsafe or it has had prior incidents. This could lead to perceptions that the guest's stay was "bad," resulting in early departures and the lack of return business. These concerns require that hotel security programs operate "invisibly" to guests, finding a balance between the psychological (a "safe" and secure environment) and physical security needs of guests and the need for effective security and safety practices.

The nature and extent of security in this industry sector varies. It depends upon the threat environment, the type of guests staying at the hotel, and the types of meetings or conventions that may exist. In many cases, hotels may rely upon contract security for large events and during evening hours when hotel and guest property may be more vulnerable to crimes. In other instances, hotels may have full-time proprietary security personnel due to the threat environment, and the philosophy of the hotel that recognizes that safety and security is a primary need and a marketing tool. Regardless of the structure, the security functions in hotels are related to safety, health, information security, insurance, emergency response, and loss prevention for guests, employees, and the organization.

Externally, thieves, burglars, prostitutes, and drug dealers find that lodging establishments make very attractive targets. Guests can steal ashtrays, towels, and linen for souvenirs and vandalize hotel and motel property. Credit card and check fraud, shoplifting, and non-payment of room charges are also commonplace. In other instances, "mega events" which include large-scale conferences and sporting events, such as the World Cup, Super Bowl, and Olympics, that draw large crowds of individuals into the area and lodging facility may result in new or expanded vulnerabilities in the context of crime. To ensure that the quality of life in the hotel is maintained, increased numbers of security personnel will most likely be needed to address crime, disorder and guest-related emergencies. Hotels also need to be concerned about terrorism. In 2011, many U.S. hotels participated in a joint venture between the U.S. Department of Homeland Security and the American Hotel and Lodging Association titled "If You See Something, Say Something," a 15-second public service announcement that was televised through welcome channels in hotels throughout the United States that encouraged guests and hotel staff to report suspicious activities (Ritchie, 2015).

Emergency management is also a key element of hotel security. Perhaps one of the most common emergency situations in the lodging industry is fire. A well-planned and executed fire prevention strategy coupled with appropriate fire detection and extinguishing equipment will reduce heavy losses, injuries, or deaths due to fire. All staff should also be trained in evacuation procedures; guests could be slowed by the sheer numbers of persons trying to leave, some guests may have mobility-related disabilities; and because it is an unfamiliar setting, guests may require more time to find exits, slowing their evacuation (AlBattat & Som, 2013). In some cases, emergencies are remote "one in a million" occurrences. Consider, for example, an electrical blackout in 2003 that wiped out a large portion of the Eastern and Midwest U.S. for two days, disrupting electrical services to an upscale 180-room hotel that was at 100 percent occupancy. Because the backup generator only provided limited emergency lighting in select areas of the hotel, flashlights were distributed to all guests. The security director also organized "meet and greet" picnic receptions on the hotel patios in the evening, where guests were provided free nonalcoholic beverages and picnic food. Later, it was determined that only a few guests checked out of the hotel. The completed comments cards showed that guests were impressed with the speed of response and assurance by security that everyone was fine, regardless of the lighting limitations. Because of the actions of a progressive security department, the hotel saved thousands of dollars and preserved its reputation.

Hotel security programs also need to deal with internal issues. Staff, for example, must be protected from guests and coworkers. Bullying, sexual harassment, and other forms of violence are unfortunate occurrences. These actions can result in psychological trauma, poor performance, and high staff turnover (Ram, 2015). Lack of internal controls can result in the theft of hotel property, including cash, linen, supplies, dishes, and silverware. Guests and guest rooms are targets of theft as well. Employee theft and misconduct issues can be prevented through a comprehensive pre-employment screening program on all prospective employees that may uncover poor employment and criminal conviction histories, credit problems, and propensity toward drug and alcohol abuse.

Organizations also have a duty of care to provide invitees (guests) and employees, requiring them to provide adequate levels of security. Guests themselves are vulnerable to foreseeable accidents including slip and falls that could result in civil liability claims against the hotel. The resulting litigation costs and adverse judgments from lawsuits also affect the profitability and reputation of lodging facilities. Courts have held motels and hotels liable for theft of guest property and injuries and assaults on guests by employees as well as outsiders (Ivancevich & Ivancevich, 2012).

All employees also need to be trained in security. Housekeeping staff could leave a guest room door open and unattended, resulting in a theft of a guest's personal property. Poorly or undertrained front desk staff may provide a guest's room number verbally, allowing a threat within earshot to later target the guest for theft or a violent crime. All staff should be trained in respecting the confidentiality of guests in and outside of the workplace. Because hotel staff may possess keys and card access devices, they should be trained in the key and card control and protection. In many cases, these and other issues can be addressed through the existence of well-developed policies and procedures and effective leadership and supervision.

Common safety and security measures include adequate lighting on the hotel perimeter and parking areas, secured entrances to the hotel, smoke alarms, fire sprinklers, and card access to rooms to protect guests and their assets against common property crimes, and in some cases, serious violent crimes, including robbery and assault. Another common security measure is the use of CCTV surveillance in common areas of the hotel, including lobbies and hallways. Hotels (and casinos) also use biometrics, including facial recognition software, to verify guests. Also, fingerprint readers for in-room safes and access to elevators, floors, and guest rooms are now common security features (Meyersa & Millsb, 2007).

Another specialized type of resort hotel includes cruise ships and gated resorts. In a simplistic sense, cruise ships are basically floating hotel resorts. These cruise ships experience unique safety and security problems. Ships and boats are usually in motion when operating, and steep, narrow passageways and stairwells are hazards. Probably the greatest threat to cruise lines is the potential for accidents, medical emergencies (such as an outbreak of a food-borne illness), slip and fall claims, and the resulting liability and lawsuits. In addition, although thieves cannot escape unless a ship or boat is in port, theft remains a major threat in a maritime environment.

Gated resorts are often found in under-developed or high-crime countries, such as Mexico. Gated resorts, as the name implies, physically separate travelers from the local setting to increase their security and impression of the area, providing all of the amenities needed for a pleasurable trip. In many cases, these resorts also offer off-site excursions. These events are often highly structured where the resort will contract with trusted contractors or use their own staff and transportation to ensure guest safety (Manuel-Navarrete & Redclift, 2012).

▶ Retail Security and Loss Prevention

shrinkage Reduction in inventories not accounted for through sales or other legitimate activities.

One particular issue that the retail sector must address is the serious problem of inventory shrinkage. Shrinkage is defined as the reduction in inventories not accounted for through sales or other legitimate activities. It is the difference between the inventory that is on hand for sale and what the retail establishment indicates should be available for sale (Chan, 2003). According to the 2015 National Retail Security Survey, retailers lost $44 billion to "shrink" in 2014. The majority of this shrink can be attributed to shoplifting (38 percent) and employee/internal theft (34.5 percent). Other causes of loss include administrative/paperwork error (16.5 percent) and vender fraud/error (6.8 percent). Losses of this nature can force a retail operation into bankruptcy. To compensate for actual losses, a retail outlet is required to generate, through additional sales, many times the amount of the loss. For example, if a retail store operates on a 5 percent net profit margin and experiences an actual loss of $50, it must generate additional sales of $1,000 to offset the loss. Similarly, if the same store experiences a $500 loss, it must generate additional sales of $10,000 before profitability returns.

Internal Employee Theft and Retail Crime

Internal employee theft is one major issue for retailers. Employees oftentimes have direct access to cash and merchandise, work alone, and are familiar with how to defeat or circumvent existing retail loss prevention measures. Some crimes employees can commit include:

> **internal employee theft** Theft by individuals employed by the organization.

- Theft of cash.
- Price alterations or switching.
- Abuse of the refund system.
- Undercharging of, or not charging for, merchandise to a friend or relative.
- Theft of merchandise.
- Kickbacks from vendors.
- Damaging merchandise with the intention of purchasing it later at a discounted price.
- Failing to record sales on the cash register and pocketing the cash from a customer.

Point-of-sale (POS) theft schemes are a particular problem for retailers. These occur when store employees defraud their employer through sales and return-related activities. In one common scheme, an employee "under-rings" a sale on a cash register, but charges the customer the full value, stealing or "pocketing" the difference. Other POS-related schemes can include return-related activities where an employee conducts a false return transaction, pocketing the money. One common way to control POS fraud or theft is to use transaction exception reporting systems. These computerized systems analyze typical transactions and identify "out of the ordinary" transaction patterns and sales that are then reviewed by loss prevention personnel (Wesley & Wanat, 2013).

> **Point-Of-Sale (POS)** Cash registers or other locations where customers can pay for goods and services.

> **transaction exception reporting systems** Used in loss prevention. These systems analyze typical transactions and analyze and identify "out of the ordinary" transaction patterns (sales and returns).

One example of POS fraud can be found with Dunkin' Brands (which owns Dunkin' Donuts and Baskin-Robbins) where POS theft was totaling millions in loss each year. To reduce loss from POS theft, the company's security team integrated video and POS data, and used exception-reporting software to zero in on suspicious transactions. The team also used a third-party data investigation service that queried Dunkin' Brands POS transaction database and then confirmed any fraud-related issues with CCTV footage from the particular location. The security team would then inform the franchisee of the suspected issue. The franchisee could then review the transaction and surveillance video to confirm the security team's suspicions and take appropriate actions. At one store, after several offending employees were discovered and fired, revenues increased by 30 percent (Goodchild, 2010).

More information about loss prevention careers, certification programs and careers can be found at: http://www.losspreventionfoundation.org and at the National Retail Federation: https://nrf.com

Internal theft can be prevented, or at least reduced, through the establishment of sound pre-employment screening procedures, strict cash-handling procedures, refund policies, cash register software that identifies suspicious transactions, random audits, a code of conduct for employees, and management's attention to employee behavior. Independent honesty shopping services may be used to test employee cash-handling procedures and customer service. The honesty shopper, posing as a customer, observes employee behavior and reports to management on sales personnel's efficiency, courtesy, and violations of store policies and procedures (Davies, 2007). Other internal controls include the separation of duties, authorizations, and inspections. It has also been determined that assigning employees full responsibility for loss in a specific location, such as storerooms, will serve as an incentive to prevent theft by other employees (Mishra & Prasad, 2006).

Technologies can also be used to monitor the flow of merchandise and improve inventory control while reducing internal loss. For example, radio frequency identification (RFID) tags can be tracked by computer systems. Companies can trace the flow of products, determining if loss occurs because of damage and spoilage, transaction errors, misplacement of merchandise, theft by internal and external sources, or fraud committed by suppliers. These RFID tags can also provide real-time or continuous monitoring of goods where managers can monitor inventory levels, while the loss prevention function can monitor and track where loss occurs (Chen, Jan, Tsai, Ku, & Huang, 2012).

External Threats and Retail Crime

External threats in the retail sector abound. In addition to vandalism, burglary, robbery, and other common crimes, merchants are also vulnerable to some unique forms of fraud. Payment fraud includes bad checks, credit cards, and bankcards. The three elements of any payment fraud include failures in (1) payment initiation, where a third party service initiates payment through the person's Internet-enabled account; (2) authentication (confirming the payer's identity); and (3) approval, which involves failing to screen the payment for any suspicious elements (Sullivan, 2014). For example, credit card fraud resulting from the use of a stolen or fictitious credit card may be reduced through a careful examination of the credit card and the signature of the cardholder, accompanied by verification of the signature and positive identification of the purchaser. Coupon fraud occurs when customers (or employees) redeem coupons for cash in lieu of the purchase of the item for which the coupon was issued (Nocella, 2000). Retail losses may also occur because of refund fraud that are fraudulent or attempted claims for a refund on merchandise. These can be prevented through an effective refund policy. Ideally, refunds should be tightly controlled and issued from a centralized service desk. To prevent refund fraud by customers, retail merchants can develop a database of individuals who request refunds. Suspicious refunds are checked against the database to determine how often the person seeking a refund attempts to return merchandise. Additionally, when a refund is requested, a review of the company's inventory list may verify if the item returned was actually sold. Transaction reports, which include sales records, voided sales receipts, and other activities performed by the cash registers each day, may also be used. Loss prevention personnel should audit these reports to identify suspicious activity (Hayes, 2014).

Shoplifting is perhaps the most recognized criminal activity in the retail sector. Shoplifting is defined as the theft of goods from the selling floor when a store is open for business, the theft of goods displayed for sale, or theft from a retail establishment. It occurs whenever persons lawfully or unlawfully present on a retail premises misappropriate merchandise for their own use. Shoplifting is basically as old as the retail sector. It can be traced to the 1500s in London, England, where bands of thieves called "lifters" would steal items from shop owners (Shteir, 2011). In many states, the crime of shoplifting is defined and

radio frequency identification (RFID) Tags or similar devices attached to products or goods. Provide real-time or continuous monitoring of assets.

payment fraud Types of retail crimes that include bad checks, credit cards, and bankcards.

coupon fraud Occurs when customers or employees redeem coupons for cash in lieu of the purchase of the item for which the coupon was issued.

refund fraud Defrauding a retailer by returning stolen or ineligible items for a cash or credit refund.

shoplifting Misappropriation (theft) of retail merchandise.

expanded to include acts of retail fraud, which involves defrauding a retailer through return fraud, switching price tags, and not properly scanning items for purchase. The methods of theft vary and can include: hiding items under or in clothing, purses, and bags; switching price tags; placing items in another product's packaging; using a booster box (a box with a spring-loaded trap door) or shopping bag; or simply wearing items out of a store.

One relatively new issue for retailers is *self-scan checkout kiosk fraud.* Many retailers now provide customers the option of using a self-scan checkout (SSC) kiosk where customers scan merchandise themselves at a self-serve POS terminal instead of having a store employee do it for them. Because an employee is not physically present at the terminal, the potential for fraud and theft exists. For example, customers may switch UPC codes on items to defraud merchants, or they simply may not scan items. In order to prevent fraud, these terminals often have smart shelves, which are basically scales that compare the weight of the item placed on the scale to the registered weight of the merchandise, based on the UPC. In order to deter and prevent theft at these kiosks, retailers need to enhance their zones of control that focus on surveillance and design to increase perceptions of being detected and apprehended. Changes in surveillance could include expanding the number of staff at these locations, increasing surveillance technologies such as CCTV, and have different types of sensors on the terminals themselves to alert customers and staff that an issue exists. Changes are done in the design to increase or recreate perceptions of control by moving SSC's away from exits, narrowing the checkout lanes, and having barriers that allow for a single entrance and exit are effective. Positioning the main SSC control podium near the store exit to remind shoppers that they are being electronically monitored is another way to decrease theft (Beck, 2011).

There are different types of shoplifters. Opportunistic or amateur shoplifters known as snitches are the most common type of shoplifters, accounting for up to 90 percent of all thefts. These are individuals that steal when the opportunity presents itself. There are also professional shoplifters, known as boosters. These individuals cause the most dollar losses for retailers. Professional shoplifters can include persons who work alone and whose major or only source of income is shoplifting. Oftentimes, professional shoplifters work in teams, where the roles of some members are to divert the attention of the store personnel from the person(s) committing the actual theft (Hayes, 2014; Klemke, 1992). Professional shoplifters are often involved in organized retail crime activities as shown in Box 8-2.

> **snitches** Amateur shoplifters.

> **boosters** Professional shoplifters.

> **organized retail crime (ORC)** Criminal organizations that focus on retail theft and defrauding of merchants.

BOX 8-2

ORGANIZED RETAIL CRIME

One of the most daunting problems facing retailers today is organized retail crime (ORC). ORC involves professional boosters and fences who steal and then resell the merchandise through legitimate and illegitimate channels (Finklea, 2011). Besides shoplifting, ORC-related activities also include cargo theft, gift card fraud, ticket switching, credit card fraud, the sale of counterfeit goods to merchants, and return fraud. The total loss attributed to ORC in the United States exceeds annual losses due to automobile theft. According to the National Retail Federation's (NRF) Organized Retail Crime Survey (2014), 90 percent of the participating merchants in the study reported being a victim of ORC. These ORC criminals work in teams, oftentimes selling their stolen goods online, or physically at flea markets and even stores. In response to the rise in ORC, many states have passed specific laws related to ORC. Furthermore, the Retail Industry Leaders Association, the National Retail Federation, and the FBI collaborated to develop the Law Enforcement Retail Partnership Network (LERPnet). Traditionally, individual retailers reported thefts to their local police agencies, but retail crimes were not tracked across jurisdictions. However, with LERPnet, retail crime incidents are entered into a secure national database. The information can be shared among retail loss prevention personnel and public law enforcement agencies, allowing participants to track and apprehend ORC offenders (National Retail Federation, 2007; 2014).

One broad way to understand theft choices by shoplifters is the use of the CRAVED model. Under the CRAVED model, items that are concealable, removable, available, valuable, enjoyable, and disposable are the most common items stolen from retailers (Clarke, 1999). Determining where stolen items are sold is also important in gaining a comprehensive understanding of where items are going and who is buying them. The research shows that up to 18 percent of all stolen goods are sold on the Internet. In some cases, goods are presold on Internet sites. The majority of stolen goods, meanwhile, are sold through "traditional" means such as fences (Clarke & Petrossian, 2012). With modern technologies, such as RFID tagged merchandise, loss prevention (LP) staff can actually trace stolen items from where they are sold and to the homes of the buyer's of the stolen goods.

Shoplifting Prevention Strategies

An effective shoplifting prevention strategy also includes deterrence and detection through the use of appropriate display of merchandise, surveillance equipment and people, package and fitting room inspections, properly enforced refund procedures, locking devices, and alarms. One of the key considerations is that the retailers must determine how much and what type of security is needed, based on the actual or the probability of loss, balanced with the costs involved in protecting assets from theft. Shoplifting prevention programs should also be comprehensive in nature. Research involving the use of eye-tracking devices that were placed on active shoplifters who were placed in simulated store environments found that a combination of item packaging, electronic article surveillance, item placement, and diligent staff were the most effective shoplifting countermeasures (Lasky, Fisher, & Jacques, 2015). Other research has also validated that a comprehensive approach to controlling shoplifting is effective. Interviews of known and admitted shoplifters have found that target hardening, natural surveillance, effective guardianship, and formal surveillance techniques are effective deterrents" (Cardone & Hayes, 2012).

Several types of security countermeasures are used to deter and detect shoplifters. Some countermeasures are based on the concept of benefit denial where the stolen product will be damaged in some manner during or after the commission of the theft, denying the person any benefit related to the stolen item(s). For example, ink tags placed on items are designed to break open and stain the item if they not properly removed by store staff with a special tool (DiLonardo & Clarke, 1996). There are also many deterrence and detection-based antishoplifting measures. Some of the more common countermeasures that are used include mirrors, and advanced CCTV systems such as article surveillance that monitors specific items and alerts staff when the item is moved. Public viewing monitors (PVMs) where the public can also view CCTV surveillance cameras, is another "layer" of surveillance to detect shoplifters. Modifying the shopping environment using CPTED strategies (territoriality, natural surveillance) to prevent the opportunity to commit theft are commonplace. Some recommendations include: placing CRAVED items in visible areas to improve natural surveillance by staff and customers, and target hardening some items by placing them in cases, or securing them with locks and cords. Some store design strategies include: decentralizing cashier stations to improve natural surveillance, minimizing blind spots; keeping isles wide and open to improve surveillance, ensuring that there is adequate and uniform lighting; using visible signage (i.e., "customers are under CCTV surveillance" or "Shoplifters will be Prosecuted"); creating territories (sub areas) in the stores where staff can guard their specific department/area; and using low store fixtures to enhance natural surveillance (Carmel-Gilfilen, 2011). Other design issues that need to be considered include limiting the amount of exits and paying special attention to high-risk areas, such as changing rooms and restrooms.

Many retailers also use **electronic article surveillance (EAS)** that detect and alert store personnel that an article is leaving the store or the zone of control. While technologies do vary, EAS tags are placed on items by store personnel, or in many cases, they are built into the item (called source tagging). The components of an EAS system include gates, the actual tag, and the deactivator. Gates are pedestal or tower-looking readers where one serves as a transmitter and the other a receiver. They are located near exits, restrooms, and changing rooms. When an active EAS tag enters the area between the two towers, the tag/antenna is detected by the receiver, which then activates an alarm. To deactivate an EAS tag, store staff can remove the tag or deactivate it by sliding the tag over a deactivator, which is built into the cashier checkout countertop. These tags are often considered compliments to an RFID system. EAS systems are designed solely for security, while RFID is primarily designed and used for visibility, tracking, and inventory control and uses more expensive and sophisticated technologies (Liard, 2004). To defeat EAS systems, shoplifters may try to shield the items they are trying to steal. One common means is through the use of a "booster bag" or a Faraday cage where a person places the stolen object(s) in a tin foil lined bag that shields the EAS tag from the reader devices (Panigrahy, Jena, & Turuk, 2011). There are also **"bottom" of basket (BoB) detectors**. These are mirrors, sensors, and cameras that monitor and alert store personnel that there are items located in the lower tray of the shopping cart. BoB loss is estimated at $2 billion annually for U.S. retailers (Dulyakorn, Pavaganun, Mangalabruks, Fujii, & Yupapin, 2011).

While **loss prevention** is the primary goal, retailers also have the option of arresting offenders. All states have **Merchant's privilege laws** that allow retailers (and their designees) to arrest offenders for misdemeanor, felony theft, and fraud-related crimes. If a retail establishment's policy is to apprehend shoplifters, staff needs to be fully trained on the laws of arrest and detention. In order to avoid civil claims related to false arrest, false imprisonment, excessive force, and defamation, retailers have strict policies for an arrest. At a minimum, these policies require loss prevention personnel to observe the suspect (1) approach; (2) select; (3) conceal; and (4) carry away (and perhaps convert it by eating it or removing it from its original packaging) the merchandise before an arrest can occur. Staff must also maintain continuous surveillance of the suspect to ensure that the suspect did not dispose of the item. The suspect should also be apprehended past the last possible POS and outside the store in order to validate that the person did not intend to pay for the item(s). The actual arrest, meanwhile, must be reasonable, conducted in a professional manner, be as discreet as possible, and not cause any undue stress on the suspect. All information regarding the arrest must also be confidential (LaBruno, 2011).

Merchants can also seek recovery for the loss or damage of their items that were stolen. Under **civil demand**, merchants can "demand" payment for the loss or damage in addition to the costs associated with the theft under the threat of civil action if the person refuses to pay. They are basically penalty fees that include the value of the item, in addition to a fee that is calculated based on the value of the item. Depending upon the state, for example, if the item stolen was worth $10, the merchant can legally multiply the loss by 10 times its actual value, demanding $110 from the accused. If the person fails to comply with the civil demand letter, then merchants can seek **civil recovery** for their losses in a civil court (Johnson & Carter, 2009).

Retailers are also vulnerable to **cargo theft**. In most cases, retailers have distribution warehouses that serve as a supply hub for stores in a region where contracted (also known as third party logistics providers—3PLs) or company semi-trucks transport the merchandise. This merchandise (or cargo) is vulnerable to theft during transit. Theft could also occur in the warehouse parking lot, waysides or rest areas, or at truck stops. This is also a serious problem in other nations. In order to prevent insider collusion, many companies do not inform drivers of the contents of the trailer and keep cargo

Electronic Article Surveillance (EAS) Technologies that monitor, detect, and alert store personnel that an article is leaving the store or the zone of control.

bottom of basket (BoB) detectors Mirrors, sensors, and cameras that monitor and alert store personnel that there are items located in the lower tray of the shopping cart.

loss prevention Security measures used to reduce loss or shrinkage in the retail sector.

Merchant's privilege laws Specific laws that allow retailers (and their designees) to arrest offenders for misdemeanor and felony theft and fraud-related crimes.

civil demand Civil law process where merchants can contractually "demand" payment for the loss or damage in addition to the costs associated with the theft under the threat of civil action if the person refuses to pay.

civil recovery Civil law process that allows merchants to seek financial compensation for their losses in civil court if a person fails to comply with the civil demand.

cargo theft The criminal theft of cargo.

▼

manifests sealed from their (and others) review. Trailers are also "e-sealed" with RFID and GPS tracking systems (Zhang, 2013). Research of cargo theft in the Middle East and Europe found that most cargo theft occurs at nonsecure locations. The items stolen are oftentimes based on volume of goods (and entire trailer) and not on value, suggesting that the thieves did not know the contents of the trailer (Ekwall & Lantz, 2015).

A QUICK SURVEY

Which of the following settings are places where you have personally spent a significant amount of time and where security breaches have occurred? Check any and all that apply.

- An office building where an organization you work for is located
- Your own residence, or that of a friend or a relative
- A retail store where you have shopped

For each setting you checked, what was the nature of the security breach or breaches? What steps were taken to reduce the risk of additional breaches? Who took these steps? In your view, were these steps effective? Why or why not?

► Office Building Security

Most office buildings are open to the public and provide convenient entry and exit points. In those settings where there are multiple tenants, access control can be difficult to manage; few office buildings restrict access to lobbies, different floors, individual business offices, or restrooms. Major office building security threats include fire, poor or inadequate emergency evacuation routes, terrorist activities, bombs or bomb threats, theft, burglary, trespass, vandalism, robbery, and violent crimes. Office equipment, supplies, payroll checks, cash, proprietary information, copper from phone lines and cables, and even recyclable materials within office buildings are often the targets for thieves and burglars.

The risk of loss or injury in office buildings can be minimized in several ways:

- Security personnel, contract or proprietary, should be employed.
- Assets such as cash and valuables, and sensitive proprietary information can be stored in vaults.
- Restrooms should be locked with passkeys or card access and restricted to tenants and their guests.
- Maintenance and custodial personnel should be properly screened prior to employment.
- Common areas and parking facilities should be patrolled regularly.
- Access control and surveillance systems should be utilized.
- Fire drills and inspections of fire prevention and protection equipment should take place on a regular basis.

After the World Trade Center terrorist bombing in New York City in 1993, several high-rise office building management teams increased security. Measures implemented included improved access control, security patrols, staff awareness training, new policies and procedures, contingency planning, improved blast-resistant window glazing, and forms of perimeter fortification. During the 7 years prior to the 1993 incident, $60 million was spent at the World Trade Center to improve security and counter the threat of terrorism. However, it appears that only the high-profile facilities made measurable security improvements. In spite of the bombings at the World Trade Center in 1993 and the Murrah federal building in Oklahoma City in 1995, many office building security managers still believed their facilities were relatively safe from terrorism (Gips, 2000). This false sense of security was shattered on September 11, 2001. Since the loss of New York's World Trade Center(s) on 9-11, many high-rise facilities throughout the United States have improved security and safety measures dramatically (Craighead, 2009).

Ultimately, the type, amount, and cost of security measures employed in and around an office building will depend on the size, location, and the nature and extent of threats identified in the risk management process. The number of tenants, the type of businesses involved, and crime rate within the area must also be considered when planning and administering a safety and security program for an office building. In some cases, office buildings have united to provide and improve their own security. For example, in 2009, more than a dozen businesses in Oakland, California formed community-benefit associations in two sections of the city after Oakland reduced city services to close a $30 million budget deficit. The two associations eventually comprised about 100 member businesses. The associations have hired unarmed security guards who patrol the streets (White, 2010).

SECURITY SPOTLIGHT

Select an office building or complex in your area. Identify security measures that have been taken to protect the building as well as the people and assets within the building. In your view, could additional measures be taken? If so, which?

▶ Residential Security

Individuals spend a great deal of their time in a residential environment. People eat, sleep, socialize, and sometimes work in single-family homes, apartments, and condominiums. The home may be located in the inner city, a suburb, or a rural area. It may also be part of a planned or gated community, or it may be part of a public housing complex. While each of these types of homes vary to some degree, they all nevertheless have some common safety and security issues.

Homes are vulnerable to a variety of safety-related issues. One major safety issue in the home is fire. According to the U.S. Fire Administration (2014), in 2013, there were over 380,000 residential fires in the United States that caused over 2,755 deaths and 12,450 injuries, resulting in about $7 billion in losses. The primary cause of home fires is related to cooking, followed by heating, and then electrical malfunctions. To reduce the risk of fire injury and death, detectors, suppression devices, and preplanned evacuation and escape routes must exist. Other safety-related issues include accidents and loss due to human actions. "Designing out" hazards and avoiding or modifying various personal behaviors and practices in the home can help prevent these.

Homes are also vulnerable to a variety of natural threats related to wind, water, and fire. Oftentimes, loss from natural threats can be managed through risk transfer activities, such as taking out insurance to recover any financial loss related to the natural event.

COMMON BURGLARY SAFEGUARDS

- Ensure that the residence does not appear unoccupied.
- Maintain key control and keep doors and windows locked.
- Leave lights and a radio on while residents are away. Use timing devices to control lights.
- Do not admit strangers to the residence.
- Know neighbors. Trusted neighbors may check on the home and retrieve mail and newspapers during an absence.
- Keep an inventory of valuables, and provide it to the police if a burglary occurs.
- Do not leave notes visible that indicate an absence.
- Do not broadcast travel plans.
- Consider installing an alarm system: the least expensive alarm is a dog that barks at strangers.

In ther cases, homeowners can manage risk by modifying the environment. For example, in earthquake-prone areas, structures can be reinforced in order to absorb tremors. In fire-prone areas, homeowners can also modify the construction of their homes, where they can use asphalt shingles instead of wood and eliminate brush and other combustible materials to create firebreaks (which are gaps in combustible materials) around the perimeter of the home ("Homeowner's guide," 2005; Ponkshe, 2015).

Homes are also vulnerable to burglary, theft, and vandalism. Occupants can be exposed to violent crimes in some cases. One of the most common vulnerabilities is burglary. The residence is an ideal target for burglars because the possibility of being caught is minimal. Nationally, only about 15 percent of all residential burglaries are solved, resulting in an arrest. Most burglaries are committed when the home is unoccupied and the possibility of detection and apprehension is minimized. In most cases, less than $1,000 in goods is stolen where electronics and small personal effects (i.e., jewelry) are the most common targets. In addition, many homicides are committed in the home, often as a result of a long history of domestic conflict (Barlow, 2000; Berzofsky, Langton, Moore, & Walters, 2013).

Physical security in the form of lighting, good locks on doors and windows, access control features, and the secure storage of valuables can deter or minimize the impact of an unauthorized intrusion. Increased security awareness using common residential crime prevention measures are found in Box 8-3.

Other target hardening strategies include the use of steel shutters that cover and secure windows (Cozens & Davies, 2013). Individuals may contract with a security company or have their own proprietary security personnel.

In many cases, homes are equipped with home security systems that are installed and monitored by alarm companies to detect intrusion and fire. Some homes are now "smart homes." Smart homes allow the owner(s) to have the ability to electronically monitor specific home functions remotely. Some common examples of smart home technologies include the ability to operate lighting or adjust a thermostat online or through a smart phone application. Many of these smart devices also allow for real-time surveillance. Depending upon the sensors that are installed in the home, they can also alert the homeowner of any intrusion, motion, or smoke and fire-related issue (De Silva, Morikawa, & Petra, 2012).

Besides the home itself, the external environment can also be modified to deter and perhaps prevent burglaries and other crimes. Neighborhoods can be modified using CPTED principles (some of the key elements are found in Box 8-4). Urban planners and developers can limit the number of exits through streets and design cul-de-sacs (dead-end streets with a turnaround area) to prevent travel and increase the surveillance of vehicles. Other CPTED strategies include increasing lighting and ensuring that landscaping does not offer areas of concealment and increases natural surveillance of homes in the specific area (Poyner, 2013). Some neighborhoods may also employ security patrols to supplement existing public police services. In an effort to create a more secure environment, many residential areas have neighborhood watch programs or are gated to restrict access. Through local community policing efforts, resources are often available to assist residential property managers in their efforts to secure property and deter illegal activities.

SECURITY SPOTLIGHT

Assess the risks to your residence, whether you live in an apartment, condominium, stand-alone house, or dormitory. What measures do you and others (e.g., campus security, a condo association, your family members, or an apartment building owner) currently take to ensure that your residence is secure? What additional measures (if any) would you recommend? Why?

BOX 8-4

KEY ELEMENTS OF CRIME PREVENTION THROUGH ENVIRONMENTAL DESIGN

Crime prevention through environmental design is based on certain assumptions relating to how space is to be designed and used. First, all human space has a designated purpose that lays the foundation for the social, legal, cultural, or physical definitions that prescribe desired and acceptable behaviors. Second, facilities and communities are designed to support and control the desired behaviors. The basic concepts of territorial reinforcement, access control, and surveillance are inherent in the approach. These basic concepts are accomplished through any combination of the following:

- A clear border definition of the controlled space. Public and private spaces must be clearly delineated.
- Clearly marked transitional zones. The user must be forced to acknowledge movement into the controlled space.
- Relocation of gathering areas. The design must formally designate gathering areas in locations with good access control and natural surveillance capabilities.

- Safe activities in unsafe locations. Safe activities serve as magnets for normal users and communicate to abnormal users that they are at a greater risk of detection.
- Unsafe activities in safe locations. Vulnerable activities should be placed within tightly controlled areas to help overcome risk and make normal users feel safer.
- Use of space to provide natural barriers. Conflicting activities may be separated by distance and natural terrain to avoid fear-producing conflict.
- Improved scheduling of space. The effective use of space reduces actual risk as well as the perception of risk for normal users.
- Appropriate space allocation and design. This increases the perception of surveillance.
- Reduction in isolation and distance. Design efficiencies and improved communication systems increase the perception of surveillance and control (Crowe, 2000).

Summary

Commercial businesses and homes are vulnerable to man-made and natural threats. To mitigate and prevent risk, industries need to have security and risk management programs in place. For those companies that rely upon the shipment of goods, cargo security is an important security concern. At any point in the transportation or supply chain, cargo can be stolen, vandalized, or hijacked. Shipping modes can also be used by terrorist groups. Following the events of 9-11, the United States and other nations throughout the world strengthened cargo security measures. Some security measures include the CSI, the SAFE Port Act, and the C-PTAT partnership. Ports and terminals also use a variety of advanced security screening tools to check the contents of containers, while the containers themselves are monitored and equipped with tracking devices that include RFID and GPS tracking. Since cargo is transported by air, air freight companies and passenger airlines must also be screened and inspected. Security is particularly important for those industries in the utility sector that include water/wastewater, electricity, and gas. Since they provide monopolized (but publically regulated) services that cannot be readily replaced or replicated, they have a greater duty to the public to ensure that their services are not interrupted.

Security in the hospitality, retail, office, and residential sectors was also reviewed. Safety and security in hotels has also been identified as an important issue for travelers and hotel guests. Hotels have a duty of care to protect guests from man-made internal (or employee) crimes related to theft. They also have a duty to protect guests from crimes and natural and man-made hazards. Additionally, the retail sector is vulnerable to shrinkage. This shrinkage can be the result of internal and external factors. Some internal issues are based on Point of Sale (POS) theft schemes and other types of internal theft that can be controlled through administrative controls and the tracking of merchandise. One of the primary external threats is the shoplifter. Shoplifters can be amateurs or professionals who account for the most dollar losses in retail theft. These professional shoplifters are often involved in organized retail crime (ORC) activities, reselling stolen merchandise through legitimate and illegitimate channels. To combat the shoplifters, merchants have a variety of shoplifting prevention strategies they can use that include CPTED, EAS, and employee training. Under the Merchant's Privilege statute, merchants can also arrest for retail crimes and seek damages through the civil demand and recovery process. In many cases, industries have their operations and administrative functions in large office campuses or complexes that are shared with other organizations, making access control difficult where employees and guests are vulnerable to property and personal crimes. Finally, residential home security is important. Fire and property and personal-related crimes can be mitigated through properly designed safety and security systems. In other cases, entire neighborhoods can be designed with crime prevention in mind, where CPTED principles, including security services, citizen patrols, and partnering with the police are proven and effective countermeasures to crime.

Career Opportunities

Industrial Security: Industrial security professionals protect a wide range of manufacturing and government contractor facilities. Government contractors must protect classified information in accordance with the NISP. Entry-level industrial security managers typically possess a college degree and earn between $55,000 and $75,000. The average annual salary for executive-level security managers is over $100,000.

Loss Prevention Officers and Managers: The field of loss prevention is large and diverse. LP staff conduct apprehensions, investigations, and perform a variety of surveillance and physical security activities. Depending upon the actual company LP staff and managers may also be responsible for occupational safety, supply chain security, organized retail crime, and information security. LP managerial positions, meanwhile, range from $40,000–$65,000 annually; district managers are higher, often exceeding $65,000.

Key Terms and Concepts

Aviation and Transportation Security Act of 2001 *171*

Benefit denial *178*

Boosters *177*

Bottom of basket (BoB) detectors *179*

Cargo security *168*

Cargo theft *179*

Civil demand *179*

Civil recovery *179*

Container Security Initiative (CSI) *168*

Coupon fraud *176*

CRAVED *178*

Critical Infrastructure and Key Resources (CIKR) *171*

Customs-Trade Partnership against Terrorism (C-TPAT) *169*

Electronic article surveillance (EAS) *179*

Industrial security *167*

Internal employee theft *175*

Loss prevention *179*

Merchant's privilege laws *179*

Optical character recognition (OCR) *170*

Organized retail crime (ORC) *177*

Payment fraud *176*

PELAN *170*

Point-of-sale (POS) *175*

Radiation portal monitor (RPM) *170*

Radio frequency identification (RFID) *176*

Refund fraud *176*

Security and Accountability for Every Port Act of 2006/ SAFE Port Act *169*

Shoplifting *176*

Shoplifting prevention strategy *178*

Shrinkage *174*

Smart containers *170*

Snitches *177*

Transaction exception reporting systems *175*

Utility security *171*

Discussion Questions and Exercises

1. Security organizations within retail operations often differ in their approaches to loss prevention. Some focus most protection resources toward externally motivated crime prevention while others emphasize internal theft prevention. Is one approach better than the other? How should protection resources be allocated in any organization?

2. What are some common threats to residential security? How can they be managed?

3. What are some unique characteristics of the utility industry? How do these impact the level and type of security they need to provide?

4. What are some common security issues in the hospitality industry?

5. What are some of the common laws that govern shipping/cargo security?

6. What is C-PTAT. As a company, why should it be C-PTAT certified?

7. What are some common security measures found in ports/terminals throughout the world?

8. What is shrinkage? What are some ways to prevent shrinkage?

9. What is civil demand? What is civil recovery?

10. What are some common shoplifting prevention strategies?

Your Turn

Managing Retail Crime

Fawn's hardware is currently experiencing a great deal of shrink. This small chain store currently does not have a loss prevention function per se. Generally, each of the four store's managers is responsible for loss prevention activities. A discussion with the owner and the managers regarding shrink was held after the chain's annual audit showed that both large and small items were missing from the inventory list. In fact, one of the "lost" items included a large snow blower. As a security consultant what would be some new practices that you would encourage to reduce the amount of shrink that the company is experiencing?

9   Homeland Security

LEARNING OBJECTIVES

After completing this chapter, the reader should be able to:

1. explain the concept and philosophy of homeland security
2. identify security threats unique to homeland security
3. understand the role and findings of the 9-11 Commission
4. explain the main components of the USA PATRIOT Act
5. describe the structure, mission, and agendas of the Department of Homeland Security (DHS)
6. explain the functions of homeland security
7. describe government and private sector responsibilities, especially as they relate to the DHS and the philosophy of homeland security
8. explain the role of the private sector in homeland security
9. explain the NIPP and NIMS programs
10. articulate some of the key elements of securing airlines, airports, and ground transportation systems (critical infrastructure)

▶ Introduction

Prior to September 11, 2001, few Americans were familiar with the concept of homeland security. Since 9-11, homeland security efforts against terrorism have become a priority. While there is no one definition of homeland security, the Government Accountability Office (GAO) defines it as "a combination of law enforcement, disaster, immigration, and terrorism issues. It is primarily the responsibility of civilian agencies at all levels. It is a coordination of efforts at all levels of government" (Reese, 2012, p. 5). Homeland security, however, involves more than the prevention of terrorist acts. Broadly speaking, homeland security encompasses a wide range of activities designed to address natural and man-made threats in the United States. The Homeland Security Council and United States of America (2007) lists three missions of homeland security: (1) prevent and disrupt terrorist acts; (2) protect the American people, critical infrastructure, and key resources; and (3) respond to and recover from incidents that do occur. To achieve these missions, federal, state, and local agencies, along with the private sectors, use a variety of strategies and practices to achieve the philosophical and practical goals of making America safer.

Major organizational changes have occurred within the federal government to address homeland security. Additionally, states, private businesses, and individuals are keenly aware of the need to prevent and respond effectively to catastrophic events. This chapter reviews some major homeland security legislation and programs. It also reviews the role of the private sector in fulfilling the homeland security mission. Specific homeland security challenges, including natural, technological, and accidental hazards, and transportation security are also reviewed in this chapter.

► Homeland Security: A Historical Perspective

The concept and philosophy of homeland security did not emerge in the aftermath of 9-11. Rather, the notion of homeland security in the United States has evolved throughout the nation's history. The U.S. Constitution (Article 4, Section 4) established a republic in which the primary responsibility for homeland security (maintenance of law and order) rests with state and local governments. The federal government's role is secondary, prompted to intervene when state and local governments are unable to cope with disorder or disaster. In fact, the Constitution severely limits the federal government's ability to intervene in criminal matters within the United States. As time has passed, the national government has become more actively involved with homeland security issues by asserting federal authority when incidents (1) threaten the unity principle of the federal system of government; (2) threaten national security and involve foreign nations; or (3) violate laws enacted by Congress.

Violence, terror, and natural or man-made disasters—as well as national government responses to these events—are not new to America. For example, the federal government responded in the aftermath of devastating fires in Portsmouth, New Hampshire, in 1803 and in Chicago, Illinois, in 1871; flooding in Johnstown, Pennsylvania, in 1889; and the San Francisco earthquake in 1906. The federal government aided cities and states during the Whiskey Rebellion of 1794; the Pullman Strike of 1894; and the riots of the 1960s. The federal government also intervened during the Great Depression of the 1930s.

Beginning with World War I, the federal role in homeland security expanded. The United States was no longer isolated from other countries. The emergence of globalism, the rise of corporate culture, and reduced emphasis on states' rights altered Americans' lives and the way they viewed the federal government's role. There were 10 presidential cabinet positions in 1945, suggesting a relatively limited federal government. By 2006, there were 20. Further, the Vietnam War placed increased emphasis on international intelligence (information) gathering. In 1986, Congress authorized the FBI to investigate attacks occurring against U.S. citizens outside the United States. However, except for a few individuals in the FBI, Central Intelligence Agency (CIA), military, and other government agencies, international terrorism and its prevention did not appear in the public's consciousness until September 11, 2001 (Rosenbach, Peritz, & LeBeau, 2009).

Contemporary definitions of homeland security certainly include terrorism as a feature. Yet terrorism is not new. The assassination of Roman Emperor Julius Caesar in 44 B.C. was an act of terrorism. Religious and political groups that took shape during the Middle Ages spread terror among their enemies in the form of mass murder. The origin of WWI was based on the assassination of Archduke Franz Ferdinand and his wife Sophie by Serb nationalist Gavrilo Princip in Sarajevo on June 28, 1914 (Weissman, Busch, & Schouten, 2014). Currently, high-tech communications, rapid modes of transportation, and the availability of weapons of mass destruction (WMDs) create new challenges that differ markedly from their early historical counterparts (Oliver, 2007; Simonsen & Spindlove, 2007; Ward, Kiernam, & Mabrey, 2006).

► The 9-11 Commission and Homeland Security

Following the September 11, 2001, terrorist attacks against the United States by Al Qaeda, the independent, bipartisan *National Commission on Terrorist Attacks Upon the United States*, also known as the 9-11 Commission, was established in 2002. The task of the Commission was to prepare a full and complete account of the circumstances surrounding the 9-11 terrorist attacks, including events leading up to the attacks as well as the government's response. The Commission was also tasked with the responsibility

> **9-11 Commission**
> Commission tasked with investigating the 9-11 attacks and the state of readiness that existed in the United States at the time to fight terrorism.

to provide recommendations against future terrorist attacks. Created by an act of Congress and signed into law by President George W. Bush, the Commission was composed of five Republicans and five Democrats. The Commission was co-chaired by former New Jersey governor, Thomas Kean (Republican), and Lee Hamilton (Democrat), former U.S. Representative from Indiana's Ninth District. The Commission conducted hearings and interviewed numerous individuals regarding the 9-11 attacks and the state of readiness that existed in the United States at that time to fight terrorism (9-11 Commission, 2004).

On July 22, 2004, the 9-11 Commission issued a final report, culminating an exhaustive 20-month investigation of the 9-11 terrorist attacks. The Commission cited systemic failures and charged that elected and appointed government officials in the Congress, the administrations of Presidents Bill Clinton and George W. Bush, the CIA, and the FBI failed to grasp the seriousness of terrorism as an imminent threat. Although the Commission stopped short of stating that the 9-11 attacks could have been prevented, it noted many government missteps. The 9-11 Commission's (2004) recommendations included the following:

- Create a single, high-level intelligence director to supervise and oversee the 15 intelligence agencies of the United States.

- Create a National Counterterrorism Center to coordinate data collection and analysis among intelligence-gathering agencies, including the CIA and FBI.

- Develop a global diplomatic and public relations strategy to dismantle the terrorist network that Osama bin Laden created and to defeat the radical fundamentalist Islamic ideology that encourages and supports terrorist groups.

- Improve homeland security measures, including national standards for issuing driver licenses and other forms of identification, create terrorist watch lists, and increase the use of biometric identifiers to screen travelers at seaports, borders, and airports.

- Improve oversight of intelligence gathering and counterterrorism activities by the U.S. Congress, especially during transitions between presidential administrations. This recommendation supports radical changes, including a proposal for either a single, joint House–Senate intelligence oversight committee or separate House and Senate committees, with direct budget authority over the U.S. intelligence function (National Commission on Terrorist Attacks Upon the United States, 2004).

Intelligence Reform and Terrorism Prevention Act of 2004 Fashioned after the recommendations of the 9-11 Commission; provided for the creation of a national intelligence center and a director to oversee 15 U.S. intelligence agencies.

Implementing Recommendations of the 9-11 Commission Act of 2007 Federal law that elevated the importance of risk factors in determining federal homeland security funding for states and cities.

In response to the Commission's recommendations, President George W. Bush signed executive orders on August 27, 2004, that are designed to strengthen the CIA director's power over intelligence agencies and create a national counterterrorism center.

Furthermore, a CIA inspector general's executive summary released in August 2007 reinforced the 9-11 Commission's findings. Although the CIA report did not identify a single point of failure, it concluded that CIA resources devoted to counterterrorism were mismanaged prior to 9-11. The report faulted nearly 60 senior CIA administrators, including the director, for systemic failure to follow through with counterterrorism operations and properly share and analyze critical data (U.S. Central Intelligence Agency, 2007).

Based on the 9-11 Commission findings, homeland-security related legislation followed. In response to the Commission's report, President George W. Bush signed the Intelligence Reform and Terrorism Prevention Act of 2004 into law on December 17, 2004. Fashioned after recommendations of the 9-11 Commission, the law provided for the creation of a national intelligence center and a Director of National Intelligence (DNI) to oversee the nation's intelligence agencies. The law was also written to increase border and immigration security while also requiring that visa applicants be interviewed by security officials. Other components of the legislation included enhanced immigration policies, increasing the penalty for transporting undocumented immigrants to 10 years, and the deportation and detention of any immigrant found to have ties to terrorist organizations. It also contains "lone wolf" provisions that redefine that any non-U.S. citizen who engages in a terrorism-related action against the United States as an agent of a foreign power under the existing Foreign Intelligence Surveillance Act (FISA). By defining individual "lone wolfs" as state agents, governmental officials seeking electronic surveillance and physical searches from the FISA court do not have to prove a connection between that person and a terrorist group. The FISA court, meanwhile, does not need probable cause to approve the order (Bazan, 2004).

Later, in July 2007, Congress enacted the "Implementing Recommendations of the 9-11 Commission Act of 2007." The law elevated the importance of risk factors in determining federal homeland security funding for states and cities. The law also funded a program to improve emergency communications systems. Some of the key elements of this legislation included communications interoperability grants for first responders to improve communications among the federal, state, local, and tribal agencies during disasters and terrorism-related events, and changes to strengthen the existing incident command system. The Act also called for improving intelligence sharing through the creation of a state, local, and regional fusion center initiative. The goal of these fusion centers is information and intelligence sharing where all levels of government and the private sector would share security-related information. This Act also requires that the DHS develop private sector preparedness best practices guidelines for infrastructure security while maintaining a National Asset Database to improve critical infrastructure security in the United States (PL 110-53 (8/3/07)).

> fusion centers Information sharing centers or hubs that collect, analyze, and disseminate data to assist law enforcement and homeland security partners in preventing, protecting against, and responding to crime and terrorism.

> USA PATRIOT Act of 2001 Officially titled the Uniting and Strengthening America by Providing Appropriate Tools Required to Intercept and Obstruct Terrorism, this federal law broadens law enforcement criminal investigative authority.

▶ The USA PATRIOT Act

The events of 9-11 also provided the catalyst to create more proactive terrorism prevention strategies. In response to the 9-11 attacks, Congress enacted the USA PATRIOT Act (Uniting and Strengthening America by Providing Appropriate Tools Required to Intercept and Obstruct Terrorism Act) of 2001. Key points of the original law are found in Box 9-1.

The law dramatically increased the criminal investigative authority of local, county, state, and federal law enforcement agencies. The law also strengthens law enforcement's ability to jail suspects, broadens search and seizure authority, enhances prosecutors' power, promotes the sharing of intelligence, and provides for more restrictive border security (U.S. Congress, 2001). The USA PATRIOT Act has been amended since its creation. In 2003, the U.S. Senate voted to retain the USA PATRIOT Act's 2005 sunset provision and passed a limited version of the Act. On March 9, 2006, President George W. Bush signed the USA PATRIOT Improvement and Reauthorization Act of 2005 into law. The 2005 legislation

> USA PATRIOT Improvement and Reauthorization Act of 2005 A 2005 legislation that reauthorized expiring provisions of the USA PATRIOT Act of 2001, added dozens of additional safeguards to protect Americans' privacy and civil liberties, and strengthened port security.

BOX 9-1

KEY SECTIONS OF THE USA PATRIOT ACT

- Enhanced domestic security against terrorism
- Enhanced surveillance activities by law enforcement personnel
- Anti-money laundering/terrorist financing
- Border protection enhancements
- Removing obstacles related to terrorism investigations

- Providing for victims of terrorism, public safety officers and their families
- Increased information sharing for critical infrastructure protection
- Strengthening criminal laws against terrorism
- Improved intelligence

Source: From USA Patriot Act, 2001.

reauthorized expiring provisions of the USA PATRIOT Act of 2001, added dozens of additional safeguards to protect Americans' privacy and civil liberties, strengthened port security, and expanded mechanisms to combat the spread of methamphetamine. The reauthorizing legislation made permanent 14 of the 16 sunsetted USA PATRIOT Act provisions and placed 4-year sunsets on the other 2 (USA PATRIOT Act, Sections 206 and 215, respectively) that authorized roving surveillance and the authority to request production of business records under the Foreign Intelligence Surveillance Act (FISA) of 1978, as amended. The Foreign Intelligence Surveillance Act established a Foreign Intelligence Surveillance Court (FISC) that is responsible for judicial oversight of the intelligence community's activities. FISA also established and regulates legal procedures for the physical and electronic surveillance and collection of foreign intelligence information between or among foreign powers to protect the United States against an actual or potentially grave attack, sabotage, or international terrorism. Among the 14 USA PATRIOT Act provisions made permanent are the ability to:

- facilitate enhanced information-sharing and coordination between national security and law enforcement personnel.
- add certain chemical weapons offenses, international terrorism, nuclear and WMD threats, and computer espionage offenses to the list of wiretap predicates.
- allow Internet service providers to disclose customer records voluntarily to the government in emergencies involving an immediate risk of death or serious physical injury.
- permit victims of computer trespass (hacking) crimes to request law enforcement assistance in monitoring trespassers on their computers (U.S. Department of Justice, 2007b).

Other changes to the original act have occurred. In 2015, Congress passed the USA Freedom Act also known as the "Uniting and Strengthening America by Fulfilling Rights and Ensuring Effective Discipline Over Monitoring Act of 2015." This Act restored some of the provisions of the original USA PATRIOT Act that were to expire, extending these provisions until 2019. This Act also ends the bulk collection of American phone records and places some restrictions on FISA courts. The Act also strengthened some national security provisions, including the monitoring of foreign nationals entering the United States for up to 72 hours. It also increases prison sentences for those convicted of supporting terrorist organizations, enhances the investigation of WMDs, and preserves some of the intelligence gathering activities used by federal agencies including the FBI.

The threat of the use of weapons of mass destruction (WMD) is particularly frightening. Many nation-states as well as nonstate organizations possess or have access to nuclear, biological, or chemical (NBC) devices that have the potential to cause loss of life and property destruction on a scale never before experienced. In recent years, WMD classifications expanded to include chemical, biological, radiological, nuclear, and explosive (CBRNE) agents. As the threat of terrorism increases, organizations will find it necessary to implement terrorism prevention procedures and install CBRNE detection devices at or near facility perimeters (Asal, Ackerman, & Rethemeyer, 2012).

▶ The U.S. Department of Homeland Security

The 9-11 attacks led to massive structural changes in homeland security-related activities at the federal level. In response to the threat of terrorism, the U.S. Department of Homeland Security (DHS) was created by the Homeland Security Act of 2002 (U.S. Congress, 2002). Representing the largest transformation of the U.S. government

DHS SIX POINTS AGENDA

A six-point agenda for the Department of Homeland Security was developed and announced in July 2005, by Secretary Michael Chertoff, to ensure that the DHS's policies, operations, and structures are aligned in the best way to address the potential threats—both present and future—that face the United States. The six-point agenda includes the following:

1. Increase overall preparedness, particularly for catastrophic events.

2. Create better transportation security systems to move people and cargo more securely and efficiently.
3. Strengthen border security and interior enforcement and reform immigration processes.
4. Enhance information sharing with our partners.
5. Improve DHS financial management, human resource development, procurement, and information technology.
6. Realign the DHS organization to maximize mission performance.

Source: From Department Six-point Agenda. © 2015. Published by U.S. Department of Homeland Security.

since the 1947 creation of the U.S. Department of Defense, the Homeland Security Act consolidated 22 domestic agencies with nearly 180,000 employees. Currently, there are over 230,000 DHS employees who are found in five different directorates which are basically departments that oversee multiple divisions. The DHS is currently a cabinet level department in the U.S. government. Its primary responsibility is ". . . protecting the United States and its territories from and responding to terrorist attacks, man-made accidents, and natural disasters." Its six-point agenda to meet its responsibilities can be found in Box 9-2.

The organization of the DHS can be found in Figure 9-1 ■.

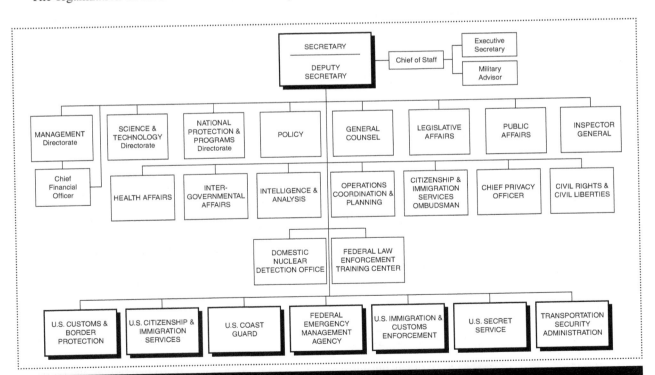

FIGURE 9-1 Homeland Security Organizational Chart
Source: Patrick J. Ortmeier, Johnson, Introduction to Security: Operations and Management, 5e. © 2018, Pearson Education, Inc., New York, NY.

DHS Main Components

The major components of the DHS include the following:

- The Directorate for Management is responsible for Department budgets and appropriations, expenditure of funds, accounting and finance, procurement, human resources, information technology systems, facilities and equipment, and the identification and tracking of performance measurements.

- The Directorate for Science and Technology is the primary research and development arm of the Department. It provides federal, state, and local officials with the technology and capabilities to protect the homeland.

- The Directorate for National Protection and Programs works to advance the Department's risk-reduction mission. Reducing risk requires an integrated approach that encompasses both physical and virtual threats and their associated human elements.

- The Office of Policy is the primary policy formulation and coordination component for the DHS. It provides a centralized and coordinated focus to the development of Department-wide, long-range planning to protect the United States.

- The Office of General Counsel is responsible for all legal determinations and oversees all DHS attorneys. The General Counsel is also the Department's regulatory policy officer, managing the rulemaking program and ensuring that all DHS regulatory actions comply with relevant statutes and executive orders.

- The Office of Legislative Affairs serves as the primary liaison to members of Congress and their staffs, the White House and executive branch, and other federal agencies and governmental entities that have roles in assuring national security.

- The Office of Public Affairs coordinates the public affairs activities of all of the Department's components and offices, and serves as the federal government's lead public information office during a national emergency or disaster.

- The Office of Inspector General is responsible for conducting and supervising audits, investigations, and inspections relating to the programs and operations of the DHS, recommending ways the DHS may carry out its responsibilities in the most effective and efficient manner possible.

- The Office of Health Affairs coordinates all medical activities of the DHS to ensure appropriate preparation for and response to incidents having medical significance.

- The Office of Intergovernmental Affairs coordinates and advances federal interaction with state, local, tribal, and territorial (SLTT) governments. It is also responsible for opening the homeland security dialogue with executive-level partners at the SLTT levels, along with the national associations that represent them.

- The Office of Intelligence and Analysis is responsible for using information and intelligence from multiple sources to identify and assess current and future threats to the United States.

- The Office of Operations Coordination and Planning is responsible for monitoring the security of the United States on a daily basis and coordinating activities within the Department and with state governors, homeland security advisors, law enforcement partners, and critical infrastructure operators in all 50 states and more than 50 major urban areas nationwide.

- The Office of Citizenship and Immigration Ombudsman helps individuals and employers who need to resolve a problem with U.S. Citizenship and Immigration Services (USCIS) and to make recommendations to fix systemic problems and improve the quality of services provided by USCIS.

- The Privacy Office works to minimize the impact on the individual's privacy, particularly the individual's personal information and dignity, while achieving the mission of the DHS.
- The Office for Civil Rights and Civil Liberties provides legal and policy advice to DHS leadership on civil rights and civil liberties issues, investigates and resolves complaints, and provides leadership to Equal Employment Opportunity Programs.
- The Domestic Nuclear Detection Office works to enhance the nuclear detection efforts of federal, state, territorial, tribal, local governments, and the private sector to ensure a coordinated response to such threats.
- The Federal Law Enforcement Training Center provides career-long training to law enforcement professionals to help them fulfill their responsibilities safely and proficiently.

There are several agencies housed under the DHS. As shown in Figure 9-1, they include the following:

- U.S. Customs and Border Protection (CBP) is responsible for protecting the nation's borders to prevent terrorists and terrorist weapons from entering the United States, while facilitating the flow of legitimate trade and travel.
- U.S. Citizenship and Immigration Services is responsible for the administration of immigration and naturalization adjudication functions and establishing immigration services policies and priorities.
- U.S. Coast Guard protects the public, the environment, and U.S. economic interests in the nation's ports and waterways, along the coast, on international waters, and in any maritime region as required to support national security.
- Federal Emergency Management Agency (FEMA) prepares the nation for disasters, manages federal response and recovery efforts following any major national incident, and administers the National Flood Insurance Program.
- U.S. Immigration and Customs Enforcement (ICE), the largest investigative arm of the DHS, is responsible for identifying and confronting vulnerabilities at the nation's border as well as entities associated with the nation's economy, transportation, and infrastructure.
- U.S. Secret Service protects the president and other high-level officials and investigates counterfeiting and other financial crimes, including financial institution fraud, identity theft, computer fraud, and computer-based attacks on the nation's financial, banking, and telecommunications infrastructure.
- The Transportation Security Administration (TSA) protects the nation's transportation systems to ensure freedom of movement for people and commerce.

Federal Emergency Management Agency (FEMA) Federal agency that manages federal response and recovery efforts following a major national incident.

U.S. Immigration and Customs Enforcement (ICE) Largest investigative arm of the DHS, which is responsible for identifying and confronting vulnerabilities at the nation's border.

Transportation Security Administration (TSA) Federal agency with primary responsibility for commercial aviation and transportation security.

Advisory Panels and Committees

The DHS advisory panels and committees include the following:

- The Homeland Security Advisory Council provides advice and recommendations to the secretary on matters related to homeland security. It is comprised of leaders from state and local government, first responder communities, the private sector, and academia.
- The National Infrastructure Advisory Council provides advice to the secretary of Homeland Security and the president on the security of information systems for the public and private institutions that constitute the critical infrastructure of the nation's economy.

- The Homeland Security Science and Technology Advisory Committee serves as a source of independent, scientific and technical planning advice for the undersecretary for Science and Technology.

- The Critical Infrastructure Partnership Advisory Council was established to facilitate effective coordination between federal infrastructure protection programs with the infrastructure protection activities of the private sector and of state, local, territorial, and tribal governments.

- The Interagency Coordinating Council on Emergency Preparedness and Individuals with Disabilities was established to ensure that the federal government appropriately supports safety and security for individuals with disabilities in disaster situations (U.S. Department of Homeland Security, Office of the Press Secretary, 2007).

In addition to creating the DHS, a provision of the Homeland Security Act of 2002 created civil liability protections for those engaged in the development and sales of antiterrorism technology. The subsection is entitled the Support Anti-Terrorism by Fostering Effective Technologies Act (SAFETY Act) of 2002. The SAFETY Act created certain liability limitations for claims arising from an act of terrorism when antiterrorism technologies have been deployed. Those who sell antiterrorism technologies can apply to the DHS for SAFETY Act designation and certification. Once certified by the DHS that the technology is a "qualified anti-terrorist technology" in the event of a terrorist attack and civil liability claim, damage awards are capped and sellers/manufacturers are exempt from paying punitive damages.

Homeland Security: Function and Mission

While the term homeland security is often associated with terrorism, its task is actually much broader. According to the DHS, the vision of homeland security is based on the key concepts of (1) security; (2) resilience or the capacity to withstand a disruptive event; and (3) customs and exchange, which is concerned with ensuring the efficient enforcement of lawful trade, travel, and immigration ("Our Mission," n.d.). While oftentimes associated with just the federal government, under the vision of homeland security, federal, state, local, tribal and private sector organizations (especially those in the nation's critical infrastructure) are responsible for carrying out the DHS's five core missions that can be found in Box 9-3.

▶ The Role of the Private Sector in Homeland Security

The DHS's 2014–2018 Strategic Plan shows that homeland security depends upon stakeholder engagement and partnerships to achieve its five core missions. The private sector is one of these partners. While there are many homeland security partnerships and programs, two of the more common ones include NIPP and NIMS.

The National Infrastructure Protection Plan

The original Homeland Security Act of 2002 tasked the DHS with the responsibility of protecting the nation's critical infrastructure and key resources. In 2006 the DHS issued its National Infrastructure Protection Plan (NIPP) to protect the nation's critical infrastructure and key resources (CIKR) which are public and privately controlled resources and assets that are deemed most critical to national public health and safety, governance, economic and national security, and maintaining public confidence. The DHS has identified

BOX 9-3

HOMELAND SECURITY MISSIONS

1. *Preventing terrorism and enhancing security*—preventing the current and revolving threat of international and domestic-based terrorism is the cornerstone of homeland security. The goals of this mission include preventing terrorist attacks and the acquisition of chemical, biological, radiological, and nuclear (CRBN) weapons. Another goal is related to protecting and securing the nation's critical infrastructure, making these systems more resilient to attacks.

2. *Securing and managing borders*—this mission is directed toward securing the nation's borders and working internationally with other nations and private sectors organizations. The goals related to this mission are threefold: (1) effectively control U.S. air, land, and sea borders; (2) safeguard lawful trade and travel; and (3) disrupt and dismantle transnational criminal organizations.

3. *Enforcing and administering immigration laws*—the goals of this mission include: (1) strengthening and administering the U.S. immigration system; and (2) preventing unlawful immigration.

4. *Safeguarding and securing cyberspace*—cybercriminals and nation-states are a threat to the economy and national security. Some of the goals to prevent cybercrime include (1) creating safe, secure, and resilient cyber environments by identifying, prioritizing, and managing threats to governmental and private sector networks; and (2) promoting cybersecurity, knowledge, and innovation.

5. *Ensuring resilience to disasters*—resilience to major accidents, deliberate attacks, and disasters is accomplished through hazard mitigation, preparedness, and emergency response and recovery efforts. The goals of this mission include (1) mitigating hazards by strengthening the capacity of governments and organizations to withstand threats and hazards; (2) enhancing preparedness through capacity building and enhancing disaster preparedness capabilities.

Source: From Quadrennial Homeland Security Review Report, by Janet Napolitano, 2010.

16 critical infrastructure sectors that require protective actions to prepare for, or mitigate against, a terrorist attack or other hazards. These sectors are shown in Box 9-4.

The purpose of NIPP is to ensure that the nation's critical infrastructure and key resources (CIKR) are resilient. The DHS defines *resilience* as "the ability to prepare for and adapt to changing conditions and withstand and recover rapidly from disruptions . . . [it] includes the ability to withstand and recover from deliberate attacks, accidents, or naturally occurring threats or incidents." ("What is security," 2015) Basically, NIPP provides

BOX 9-4

CRITICAL INFRASTRUCTURE AND KEY RESOURCES SECTORS

- Chemicals
- Commercial facilities
- Communications
- Critical manufacturing
- Dams
- Defense industrial base
- Emergency services
- Energy sector
- Food and agriculture
- Financial services
- Governmental facilities
- Health care and public health
- Information technology
- Nuclear reactors, materials, and waste
- Transportation systems
- Water and wastewater systems

Source: U.S. Department of Homeland Security.

The critical infrastructure also includes the protection of monuments to maintain public confidence.
(Photo courtesy of U.S. Custom and Border Protection.)

a structure and framework for governments and the private sector to collaborate on security-related issues by developing a comprehensive public–private risk management program for the nation's CIKRs (see Figure 9-2 ■). Its core missions are to prevent, protect, mitigate, respond to, and recover from any events that can compromise the nation's critical infrastructure. These risk management activities are directed toward the physical, cyber, and human elements that exist in the nation's critical infrastructure.

The DHS is the lead federal entity that provides expertise, funding, administration, coordination of activities, and outreach to CIKR-related organizations. There are also federal Sector-Specific Agencies (SSAs) assigned to their specific CIKR sector. For example, the Department of Agriculture is assigned to assist industries in the Food and Agricultural Sector in their homeland security-related activities. Meanwhile, the Environmental Protection Agency (EPA) is tasked with water security. An example of the water sector's vision and mission statement is found in Box 9-5.

Additionally, state, local, and tribal and territorial (SLTT) governments are responsible for sharing information and coordinating homeland security efforts with the DHS and

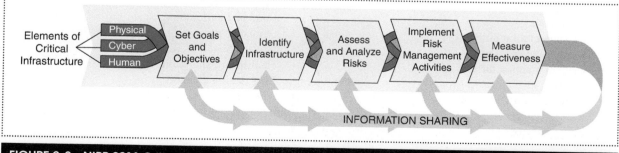

FIGURE 9-2 NIPP 2013 Critical Infrastructure Risk Management Framework

EPA'S SECTOR-SPECIFIC PLAN FOR THE WATER SECTOR: VISION AND MISSION STATEMENT

Water sector vision statement: A secure and resilient drinking water and wastewater infrastructure that provides clean and safe water as an integral part of daily life, ensuring the economic vitality of and public confidence in the Nation's drinking water and wastewater service through a layered defense of effective preparedness and security practices in the sector.

EPA's water security mission statement: To provide national leadership in developing and pro-moting programs that enhance the sector's ability to prevent, detect, respond to, and recover from all hazards.

Source: From Private Security Report of the Task Force on Private Security Published by ANON, published by National Criminal Justice Reference Service, 1976.

many other regulatory organizations. NIPP also relies upon advisory councils composed of experts from the private sector, academia, and state and local governments to provide advice. Companies also voluntarily participate in and carry out NIPP objectives in support of the philosophy of homeland security and to ensure and improve their levels of safety and security.

In support of NIPP, sector-specific plans (SSPs) were developed through a collaborative process involving federal sector-specific agencies; private sector owners and operators; state, local, and tribal entities; and other security partners. These SSPs define roles and responsibilities, catalog existing security authorities, institutionalize already existing security partnerships, and establish the strategic objectives required to achieve a level of risk-reduction appropriate to each individual sector. Each SSP also establishes a sector-specific risk-reduction consultative network to exchange best practices and facilitate rapid threat-based information sharing among the federal, state, local, tribal, and private sectors. Strategic objectives include the following:

> **sector-specific plans (SSPs)** Part of the NIPP. SSPs define roles and responsibilities, catalog existing security authorities, institutionalize already existing security partnerships, and establish the strategic objectives required to achieve a level of risk-reduction appropriate to each individual sector.

- Protecting critical sector assets, systems, networks, and functions prior to a terrorist attack or natural disaster.
- Rapidly reconstituting critical assets, systems, and networks after an incident.
- Planning for emergencies and updating response plans.
- Ensuring timely, relevant, and accurate threat information sharing among the law enforcement and intelligence communities and key decision makers in the sector.
- Educating stakeholders on infrastructure resiliency and risk management practices (U.S. Department of Homeland Security, Office of the Press Secretary, 2007).

Current revisions to NIPP by the Obama Administration in 2013 through Policy Directive 21 (PPD-21), Critical Infrastructure Security and Resilience, places greater emphasis on cybersecurity where the DHS has established the C3 program. This voluntary program emphasizes:

- converging critical infrastructure community resources to support cybersecurity risk management and resilience through use of the framework;
- connecting critical infrastructure stakeholders to the national resilience effort through cybersecurity resilience advocacy, engagement, and awareness; and
- coordinating critical infrastructure cross-sector efforts to maximize national cyber-security resilience (NIPP, 2013).

National Incident Management System

On February 28, 2003, President George W. Bush issued Homeland Security Presidential Directive/HSPD-5, Management of Domestic Incidents in response to some of the recognized emergency response failures tied to the 9-11 attacks. This Directive tasked the DHS to create and administer a National Incident Management System (NIMS). The Federal Emergency Management Agency (FEMA) is the lead agency under the DHS that is responsible for administering NIMS. FEMA provides credentialing (validating personnel requirements and providing authorization to perform certain functions during incidents) and technical assistance to emergency response providers. More specifically, the National Integration Center (NIC), which is part of FEMA's National Preparedness Directorate, provides the support and credentialing of emergency responders through its NIMS Support Center (Walsh et al., 2012).

At the crux of NIMS is that emergency service providers need to have a common incident management framework. Through a common framework, emergency response personnel at the federal, state, and local levels and the private and nongovernmental sectors will have a standardized and coordinated system for emergency management and subsequent incident response activities. Therefore, NIMS is not an operational plan for incidents. The purpose of NIMS is to unite or coordinate incident response and management activities throughout the United States. According to the DHS, "NIMS provides a consistent nationwide framework and approach to enable government at all levels (Federal, State, tribal, and local), the private sector, and nongovernmental organizations (NGOs) to work together to prepare for, prevent, respond to, recover from, and mitigate the effects of incidents regardless of the incident's cause, size, location, or complexity" (p. 1). Its goal is to establish a "common standard where all emergency responders will follow the same principles, use the same terms, concepts and organizational processes so they operate in unison during an emergency event, regardless of its size or scope" (Walsh et al., 2012, p. 12). For example, under NIMS, there is a specific Incident Command Structure (ICS) that is made up of functional areas that include command, operations, planning, logistics, and finance/administration (Walsh et al., 2012). The primary goal of a common standard is that during an emergency, organizations will be better prepared and properly organized to address incidents.

NIMS is premised on the concept that all incidents begin and end locally. As such, emergency response is the responsibility of local entities. However, when local emergency response resources are overwhelmed (or anticipated to be overwhelmed), the federal government can intervene where its role in these situations is to support and not command the situation. This support, meanwhile, is best achieved when all of the parties involved operate under a unified system of emergency management and incident response.

NIMS has five main components: (1) preparedness, (2) communications and information management, (3) resource management, (4) command and management, and (5) ongoing management and maintenance. The preparedness component ensures that emergency response parties are prepared for all incidents. Preparedness requires planning, effective procedures and protocols, training programs, qualified personnel, proper equipment, and evaluation of the degree of preparedness. The communications and information management component is premised on the fact that any incident relies on information systems and communication where interoperability, resiliency, and

> **National Incident Management System (NIMS)** A disaster and emergency plan that provides unified federal, state, county, and local approach to disasters with an emphasis on preparedness, standardization, mutual aid, and resource management.

communications redundancy and reliability are some key features of an effective emergency management communications system. Resource management, meanwhile, is premised on the fact that any incident needs proper equipment and personnel based on the incident requirements. Command and management is also a key consideration where a properly designed incident command system, public information, and multiagency coordination are important. Last, ongoing management and maintenance is directed toward the oversight and coordination of the NIMS program by NIC/FEMA (Walsh et al., 2012). To meet the five main components, DHS and FEMA provide training and funding for emergency service providers.

NIMS is simply not an incident management program for governmental agencies. NIMS also includes the private and NGO sectors. Transportation systems, hospitals, and many other private sector organizations that are considered to be part of the critical infrastructure can be directly impacted by an event. If not directly impacted, they will have indirect impacts on their operations. Some events, for example, will lead to more civilians demanding medical care while hotels may be needed to temporarily house evacuees. In the case of a large wildfire, public sector fire services may be overwhelmed where local industries could provide fire-trained personnel and equipment to assist. The NIMS Integration Center provides 12 recommendations on how the private sector can assist (NIMS, 2015). These are shown in Box 9-6.

BOX 9-6

PRIVATE SECTOR NIMS IMPLEMENTATION ACTIVITIES

1. *Adopt NIMS for your company.*

2. *Identify points of contact* for emergencies in your company and share them with local emergency management officials.

3. *Use the Incident Command System (ICS)*—manage all emergency incidents and preplanned (recurring/special) events using ICS organizational structures, doctrine, and procedures, as defined in NIMS.

4. *Support integrated multiagency coordination systems (MACs)*—ensure your organization has connectivity capability between local incident command posts (ICPs), local 911 centers, local emergency operations centers (EOCs), the state EOC, and regional/federal EOCs.

5. *Establish a public information system*—gather, verify, coordinate, and disseminate information both within your organization and with others (i.e., media, local emergency management, and other private sector partners) during an incident.

6. *Revise plans*—organizational plans and standard operating procedures (SOPs) should incorporate NIMS components, principles, and policies, to include planning, training, response, exercises, equipment, evaluation, and corrective actions.

7. *Promote mutual aid*—establish a memorandum of understanding/memorandum of agreement with the government agencies and other private sector organizations to share resources and personnel.

8. *Maintain NIMS training*—emergency preparedness personnel in your organization as well as any emergency responders or teams (fire brigade/EMS) can adopt training programs in conformance with the NIMS National Standard Curriculum.

9. *Exercise NIMS*—participate in state, regional, tribal, and/or local NIMS-based exercises.

10. *Inventory response assets*—inventory your response assets. Share this inventory with your local emergency response authority.

11. *Coordinate mutual aid requests*—exercise your response asset inventory during exercises and training opportunities.

12. *Use plain language*—apply standardized and consistent terminology, including the establishment of plain language communication standards across your organization and when you are communicating with other private sector partners and local emergency management organizations.

Source: U.S. Department of Homeland Security.

▶ Terrorism and Homeland Security

Terrorism prevention is one of the primary missions of homeland security. There is considerable disagreement on the definition of *terrorism*, largely because a definition depends on an interpretation of the motivation of the participants. What is terrorism to one person may be a selfless act to another. Thus, defining terrorism is not a simple process. Broadly speaking, terrorism involves the use of violence or threats to intimidate or coerce others. Terrorism may be used by an individual or a group. Within a narrow context, terrorism is defined as an act of violence committed against an innocent person, or noncombatant, for the purpose of achieving a political end through fear and intimidation (Barlow, 2000; Deutch, 1997). The definition of terrorism continues to evolve as terrorists and their motives, targets, and methods change. Domestic and foreign terrorists include individuals, street gangs, political and religious zealots, and highly organized national and international organizations (Maniscalco & Christen, 2002; Martin, 2009; Siegel, 2010; Simonsen & Spindlove, 2007; White, 2012). In addition, drug cartels are involved in what has come to be known as narcoterrorism. Drug cartels terrorize politicians, kidnap and execute government officials and corporate executives, and extort services and economic resources from international business concerns.

International terrorism is also a homeland security concern. International terrorists do not confine themselves to a nation-state. Numerous international terrorism have occurred over the past several years. Of course, the most devastating terrorist attacks to occur on U.S. soil took place on September 11, 2001. Terrorists connected with Osama bin Laden hijacked four commercial aircraft. Two of the aircraft were flown into the twin, 110-story towers of the World Trade Center in New York City. One was flown into the Pentagon. The fourth crashed into the ground in rural Pennsylvania after passengers overpowered the terrorists; the plane's target is not known, although it was suspected to be Washington, DC. Subsequently, the World Trade Center towers collapsed. Approximately 3,000 deaths resulted from the 9-11 terrorist attacks ("America under attack," 2001). Besides 9-11, the first decade of the twenty-first century had other large terrorist attacks. On March 11, 2004, terrorists linked to Al Qaeda bombed four commuter trains during the morning rush hour in Madrid, Spain, killing 191 people and injuring hundreds more. In August 2004, two Russian passenger airliners crashed, killing a total of 89 people. Extremists in Chechnya claimed responsibility. On July 7, 2005, three subway trains in London were bombed, killing 56 and wounding 700 people. Islamic extremists were blamed for the London attacks. On July 11, 2006, explosive devices were detonated in seven trains in Mumbai (formerly Bombay), India, killing nearly 200 people (Rabasa, 2009). More recently, on November 13, 2015 terrorists affiliated with ISIS killed 130 citizens and injured many others in their organized attacks throughout the city of Paris.

Acts of domestic terrorism also stem from domestic causes. The FBI defines domestic terrorism as "acts of violence that are a violation of the criminal laws of the United States or any state, committed by individuals or groups without any foreign direction, and appear to be intended to intimidate or coerce a civilian population, or influence the policy of a government by intimidation or coercion, and occur primarily within the territorial jurisdiction of the United States." According to some authors, domestic terrorism in the United States is "alive and well" and is more common than international terrorism (Napps & Enders, 2015; Stewart, 2012). Consider for example the 2016 Orlando night club massacre where 29-year-old Omar Mateen killed 49 and injured more than 50 others, making it the worst mass shooting in U.S. history. President Obama described the shooting as "an act of terror and an act of hate," while the director of the FBI stated that Mateen was radicalized to some degree by the Internet ("Orlando gunman," 2016). In another incident, in 1995, Timothy McVeigh bombed the Alfred P. Murrah federal office building in Oklahoma City; 168 men, women, and children died.

> **terrorism** Use of violence or threats to intimidate or coerce.

An aerial view of the World Trade Center and surrounding area after the 9-11 attacks.
(Photo courtesy of Reuters/Alamy Stock Photo.)

McVeigh was subsequently convicted in U.S. district court in Denver and executed for the killing of several federal law enforcement agents who were present in the building at the time of the bombing (Deutch, 1997). Other examples of domestic terrorism threats can include right and left wing extremist groups. Right wing groups can include neo-Nazis, militias, and sovereign citizen groups, which have been reported by law enforcement as the most serious terrorism threats in their jurisdictions (Kurzman & Schanzer, 2015). Other threats include left wing groups (revolutionaries and Marxist organizations) and special interest extremist groups such as the Animal Liberation Front (ALF) and the Earth Liberation Front (ELF) that have committed more than 1,000 criminal acts in the United States since 1976 (Testimony, 2015).

This homegrown terrorism is attracting increased attention. Homeland Security Secretary Janet Napolitano acknowledged in 2010 that the terrorists who want to attack the United States are increasingly legal U.S. residents rather than individuals traveling to the United States from abroad. These individuals may have little or no formal connection to terrorist groups such as Al Qaeda, and can be radicalized by watching jihadist videos, listening to sermons, and reading training manuals on the Internet. This trend could present challenges for the nation's intelligence system, Napolitano said, because the system has traditionally been tailored to uncovering identities of foreign terrorists and disrupting specific plots. Combating this new trend will require the DHS to continue building relationships with police, and it will require local law enforcement agencies to strengthen their skills in identifying indications of possible terrorist activities ("Napolitano warns police," 2010).

Some domestic terrorists do acquire terrorism skills abroad and return home to initiate attacks, further complicating the issue. A study by the Homeland Security Policy Institute of the George Washington University and the Swedish National Defense College's Center for Asymmetric Threat Studies described a growing threat from Westerners who leave home to train or fight jihad (holy war), and are then sent back to their home countries armed with terror expertise and tasked with launching domestic attacks. Because these terrorists have different reasons for turning to terrorism and come from different backgrounds and ethnicities, they are difficult to identify and track. The study's authors advise Western countries to share passenger data to improve travel security, highlight the harsh realities of foreign training camps in public communications, and give greater visibility to fighters who have turned away from jihad (Baldor, 2010).

To combat domestic terrorism, the Justice Department launched the Nationwide SAR (Suspicious Activity Reporting) Initiative (NSI). This joint initiative between the DHS and the FBI sets up *fusion centers*, where reports of suspicious activities and crimes made by citizens and local police are collected and analyzed. NSI uses a standardized process for gathering and sharing information among federal, state, local, and tribal agencies, with the aim of detecting and reporting underlying patterns of "precursor conduct"—activities that may signal a potential terrorist attack. Precursor conduct includes the following:

- Surveillance. Individuals are recording or monitoring activities, taking notes, or using observation equipment near a site.

- Asset deployment. Abandoned vehicles, stockpiled suspicious materials, and suspicious persons are deployed near vulnerable locations.

- Suspicious persons. A person who does not appear to belong is present in the workplace, neighborhood, business establishment, or near a vulnerable location.

- Suspicious questioning. Someone is trying to gain information in person or by phone, mail, email, or other communication method regarding a key facility or its personnel.

- Supplies acquisition. Someone is attempting to improperly acquire explosives, weapons, ammunition, dangerous chemicals, uniforms, badges, flight manuals, access cards, or identification for a key facility or to legally obtain items under suspicious circumstances that could be used in a terrorist act.

- Practice runs. Behaviors that may be related to preparing for a terrorist activity. They can include mapping out routes, playing out scenarios with other people, monitoring key facilities, and timing traffic lights or traffic flow ("Calling all eyes," 2010).

In addition to collecting data about possible domestic terrorism plots, fusion centers also collect and distribute criminal intelligence. The intent of these centers is to develop a system that fosters efficient receipt, sorting, and sharing of vital information needed to uncover terrorist plots before they can be carried out. Though the use of fusion centers has led to the discovery of dangerous individuals who would not otherwise have been found, some observers are concerned that the centers could violate citizens' privacy and civil rights. The centers take steps to protect these rights, including not running names through databases unless there is reasonable suspicion to do so and preventing the misuse of government and commercial databases that contain large amounts of personal information (Dilanian, 2010).

Specific forms of legislation have also been passed to address various types of terrorism. The Bioterrorism Act of 2002, otherwise known as the Public Health Security and Bioterrorism Preparedness and Response Act of 2002, seeks to improve the ability of the United States to prevent, prepare for, and respond to bioterrorism and other public health emergencies. As of 2007, the DHS requires owners of chemical facilities containing certain quantities of specified chemicals to complete a preliminary screening assessment that determines the level of risk associated with the facility. If a chemical facility preliminarily qualifies as high risk, its owners are required to prepare and submit a security vulnerability assessment and site security plan. Submissions are validated through audits and site inspections. DHS provides technical assistance to facility owners and operators as needed. Security standards are required to achieve specific outcomes, such as securing the perimeter, controlling access, deterring theft of potentially dangerous chemicals, and preventing internal sabotage.

▶ Homeland Security: Natural, Technological, and Accidental Hazards

Besides terrorism, homeland security efforts are directed at natural, technological, and accidental hazards. Natural disasters include drought, earthquakes, extreme heat, floods, hurricanes, landslides, severe weather, thunderstorms and lightning, tornadoes, volcanoes, wildfires, and winter weather. Technological and accidental hazards include any accident or emergency that can cause short- and long-term harm to individuals, organizations, and the environment. Examples include accidents associated with nuclear power, chemical, and petrochemical companies. They can also include hazardous materials such as explosives, flammable and combustible substances, poisons, and radioactive materials. These substances are most often released into the air and water as a result of small and large scale industrial and transportation-related accidents. They are caused by the impact of human action on the natural environment. They can take numerous forms that include oil spills and toxic waste spills.

Hurricane Katrina that struck the Gulf Coast on August 29, 2005, was one of the worst natural disasters in the history of the United States. In its wake, Katrina left nearly 1,300 people dead, hundreds of thousands homeless, and billions of dollars in property damage. Most of the destruction occurred in Alabama, Mississippi, and Louisiana. In New Orleans, two major levees broke a full day after Katrina struck, allowing water to pour into the city's streets. An estimated 80 percent of the city was flooded. New Orleans plunged into chaos as people drowned, looters ravaged businesses, health-related problems multiplied, public safety and security services disintegrated, and billions of dollars' worth of property was damaged or destroyed. Several reports cited flaws in planning for and response by the local, state, and federal government (particularly DHS and FEMA) as responsible the increased death, injury, and destruction (Jordan, 2006).

Because of some failures and gaps in emergency response, on October 4, 2006, President George W. Bush signed the Post-Katrina Emergency Reform Act of 2006 into law. This Act established new leadership positions within the DHS, brought additional functions into FEMA, created and reallocated disaster-related duties to other components within the DHS, and amended the Homeland Security Act of 2002 in ways that directly and indirectly affected the organization and functions of various entities within the DHS. The changes to the DHS became effective on March 31, 2007. The primary goal of this Act was to create a "New FEMA" that was tasked with increased responsibilities in the area of homeland security preparedness for disasters. To ensure that FEMA would be better prepared to assist in disasters, it was given more autonomy to act in emergencies, elevating its status within the DHS (see Figure 9-1). The Act also created 10 regional offices throughout the United States to better assist local entities and respond to disasters (Bea, 2006).

Some of the primary goals in disaster management set forth by FEMA and the NIMS program include mitigation, preparedness, response, and recovery.

Mitigation activities prevent an emergency, reduce the chance of an emergency happening, or reduce the damaging effects of unavoidable emergencies. They occur before and after emergencies. They are designed to mitigate the impact or shock of a disaster. Floodplain mitigation activities, for example, are designed to reduce the loss associated with a water-related emergency. Here, communities could build floodwalls, construct strong levees, prevent the building of structures in low-lying areas and even return some residential areas to "green" or undeveloped areas allowing floodwaters to flow into those undeveloped areas (Kousky & Walls, 2014; Wenger, 2015).

Preparedness activities include plans or preparations made to save lives and to help response and rescue operations. These occur before and after emergencies (Anderson, 2012). Examples of a preparedness activity include storing food and water in anticipation of a tropical storm or hurricane that could lead to supermarkets not being able to supply citizens, and public water sources becoming contaminated from storm water.

Post-Katrina Emergency Reform Act of 2006 Federal law that added functions to FEMA and amended the Homeland Security Act of 2002

mitigation activities A component of disaster management: prevent an emergency, reduce the chance of an emergency happening, or reduce the damaging effects of unavoidable emergencies.

preparedness activities Include plans or preparations made to save lives and assets and to assist in response and recovery-related operations.

An aerial view from a Missouri National Guard UH-60 Black Hawk helicopter shows the effects of flooding in Valley Park, Mo., Dec. 30, 2015. (Photo courtesy of Missouri National Guard photo/U. S. Department of Defense.)

response The actions or activities taken during an incident.

recovery efforts Actions taken after an event occurs in an effort to return to a pre-event or normal state.

pandemic Large-scale epidemic. Occurs when a disease emerges for which there is little or no immunity in the human population.

Food Safety Modernization Act (FSMA) Signed by President Barack Obama in January 2011. Designed to build a new system of food-safety oversight, with an emphasis on prevention of outbreaks of food-borne illnesses.

Response, meanwhile, involves actions or activities taken during an incident. These response activities are conducted by local agencies and private sector organizations in addition to the federal government, particularly the DHS and FEMA. For example, in 2012, a large tornado struck Moore, Oklahoma. In response to this disaster, FEMA sent preliminary damage assessment, search and rescue crews, disaster survivor teams, and management assistance teams to assist in the recovery efforts (Anderson, 2012).

Last, recovery efforts are those actions taken after an event occurs in an effort to return to a normal state. They occur after an emergency. Recovery can take a long period of time. For example, communities and organizations that were damaged by Hurricane Sandy that struck the Eastern United States on October 29, 2012, were still rebuilding in 2015. To assist in the recovery effort, FEMA and the U.S. Small Business Administration disbursed over $16.9 billion for recovery efforts in New York alone ("*FEMA aid*," 2015).

Public health-related issues are also a homeland security issue. A pandemic (large-scale epidemic) occurs when a disease emerges for which there is little or no immunity in the human population. A pandemic strains health care systems and supplies and may cause widespread economic and social disruption. An example of a pandemic can include strains of avian influenza. When a pandemic influenza virus emerges, its global spread is considered inevitable. Government agencies as well as businesses are advised to develop contingency plans for coping with a pandemic, especially if the organization's personnel travel to foreign countries. The federal government develops and disseminates pandemic preparedness guidelines. The guidelines include planning checklists that address health and safety, continuity of operations, resources required, and emergency communications (U.S. Department of Health and Human Services, 2007).

Even food safety-related issues are a part of homeland security. To address food safety issues the FDA Food Safety Modernization Act (FSMA), signed by President Barack Obama in January 2011. The FSMA is designed to build a new system of food-safety oversight, with an emphasis on prevention of outbreaks of food-borne illnesses. Such outbreaks have become more common with the globalization of food supply chains and consolidation of farms and food manufacturing plants. With globalization and consolidation, a food-safety failure at a single farm or in a single plant could threaten immense numbers of people and the food supply chain. The FSMA has key provisions including increased FDA inspection frequency, expanded access to food companies' records, import certification authority, and mandatory recall authority.

▶ Transportation Security

The September 11, 2001, terrorist attacks changed the course of transportation security in the United States. In response to the obvious need to improve aircraft and airport security, the federal government began to assume responsibility for the security function in November 2001. One of the first legislative responses to the 9-11 attacks was Congressional passage of the Aviation and Transportation Security Act of 2001 on November 19, 2001. The law created the *TSA* that was originally placed in the Department of Transportation. The TSA officially assumed its duties on February 17, 2002. The TSA was later transferred to the newly created DHS when the Homeland Security Act of 2002 was passed. The role of the TSA is broad. While perhaps best known for its role in aviation security, the TSA also oversees security-related activities for highways, rail, maritime, transit systems, and pipelines. Currently, the TSA has approximately 56,000 employees who are primarily located in the aviation sector.

> **Aviation and Transportation Security Act of 2001** Federal law that created the Transportation Security Administration.

Aviation Security

Airports accommodate millions of people annually, and aircraft typically cross numerous jurisdictional boundaries Many airports are quite large where daily, thousands of travelers use the airport for travel and dining. Air cargo theft, airline ticket fraud, theft of passenger luggage and items from vehicles in parking lots, traffic control problems, and the potential for fire and major disasters are some threats for airports. Not all criminal activity in airports originates with external sources. Theft, sabotage, and personal injury also result from employee actions. In addition, bomb threats, actual bombings, the taking of hostages, terrorist activities, even disruptive behavior from passengers created a need for increased security in the air travel and transport industry. All of the approximately 450 commercial airports in the United States are considered high-security risks, with the highest risk airports located in large urban areas. Large airports in other countries face similar risks—a fact made all too clear in January 2011, when a suicide bomber blew himself up in Moscow's busiest airport, killing 35 people (Stewart & Mueller, 2014; Ward et al., 2006).

Airport security measures are relatively old and they have evolved with the changing threat environment. Historically, airline and airport security developed primarily as a result of the skyjackings that occurred during the 1960s. The U.S. government's initial response was to place sky marshals on commercial airline flights. In 1972, the Federal Aviation Administration (FAA), the federal agency that was responsible for regulating air transportation in the United States pre-9-11, began to require specific minimum security measures at major airports. These measures included:

> **Federal Aviation Administration (FAA)** Federal agency responsible for regulating air transportation in the United States.

- screening of all persons and baggage entering aircraft departure areas.
- the availability of law enforcement support with the ability to respond to screening points within 5 minutes.
- the development of security plans by airlines and airport management.
- the development of airport disaster plans.

In 1987, the FAA assumed the responsibility for enforcing comprehensive safety and security standards and programs for airports and the airline industry. In 1988, with the enactment of Federal Aviation Regulation (FAR) 107.14, the U.S. government required heightened access controls at commercial airports and restricted access to commercial aircraft. Later in October 1996, Congress passed additional legislation that mandated additional security features and screening. The screening was designed to ensure that dangerous articles and explosive devices were not introduced into controlled areas. However, the wage rate and training provided to screening personnel was often minimal because many airlines responsible for screening did not wish to pay more than necessary. The airlines maintained they were in the transportation business, not the security business (Vincent, 2000). On February 7, 1997, the White House Commission on Aviation Safety and Security issued its report. The report included 57 recommendations, 31 of which dealt with improvements in security for the traveling public. The Commission recommended that the federal government consider aviation security a national security concern. This resulted in $100 million increase in the fiscal year 1999 budget request for upgrades in civil aviation security. The FAA used the money to continue with the installation of explosive detection systems and devices as well as hardened cargo containers to control explosions that could occur in the baggage compartments of commercial aircraft (Thomason, 2000).

A pre-9-11 major problem at U.S. airports was the fragmentation of the responsibility for security. Apparently, no single entity, whether it be the airlines, the FAA, or the jurisdiction associated with the location of the airport facility, was able to assume overall responsibility for the security function. Although all domestic aviation activities were licensed, certified, or supervised by the FAA, the airport security duties were performed by local police agencies or by private security companies in cases where the airport was privately owned. In addition, domestic commercial airports are not federal facilities, despite the federal authority overriding their operations. Thus, lack of standard operating procedures at many airports added to the confusion. Recommendations for improvement included placement of the security function within the federal government, with uniform passenger, luggage, and cargo screening standards under the auspices of the FAA (Slepian, 2000). The events of 9-11 and the passage of the Aviation Security Act of 2001 basically led to the federalization of security personnel and the standardization of security practices in the nation's airports. Federalization of commercial aviation security resulted in the removal of contract private security personnel (in most cases) from passenger- and baggage-screening points in the majority of U.S. airports.

The TSA is perhaps best known for its role in aviation security. The TSA provides trained federal employees for passenger and baggage screening within airports. The TSA also supplies sky marshals (air marshals) that are covertly assigned to commercial flights. Funding for TSA operations comes from a tax that all flyers pay as part of their airline ticket that is collected by the airlines and then paid to the TSA. The TSA, however, does not provide security for the entire airport complex. Basically, the TSA is concerned about security on an aircraft. As such, the TSA is responsible for "gate side" activities, meaning that it screens flyers and baggage entering the secure area of airport. The TSA is also responsible for ensuring that airport staff (who could be an insider threat) are cleared for employment and are screened when entering airport terminals. However, in other areas of the airport, police and private security are responsible for security (Salant, 2002; U.S. Department of Homeland Security, Transportation Security Administration, 2003). Consider, for example, O'Hare International Airport that is located in Chicago, Illinois. O'Hare has millions of passengers pass through its terminals annually. Here, TSA screens passengers and flyers and verifies staff working at the airport, while the City of Chicago Police Department patrols the airport grounds and the common areas of the airport (Johnson, Yalda, & Kierkus, 2010). The TSA is also responsible for partnering with airports and companies in the development of effective passenger and screening technologies. It also certifies security companies and screeners that perform security operations in some airports in the United States. Called the Screening Partnership Program, these companies must comply with all TSA requirements and procedures. To date, there are approximately 21 airports in the United States that are classified as SPP airports (Screening Partnership Program, 2015).

Strategies for Passenger Screening and Explosives Detection

Like other organizations, airports take a defense in depth and layered approach to security. These security measures include the use of surveillance systems and patrol at the perimeter, followed by more extensive screening inside the airport. For example, airline security personnel and U.S. Customs agents are trained to identify suspicious passengers, luggage, and cargo. Additionally, some airlines have initiated extensive security training programs for their employees. Positive identification of passengers, baggage/passenger matching, and random baggage searches became part of the preboarding passenger-screening procedure by TSA personnel post 9-11. Additionally, before a traveler can enter the gate side of the airport, he or she must have a valid boarding pass and a valid government-issued photo identification—usually a driver's license. However, driver licenses issued in many states are easy to counterfeit. In response, Congress passed the REAL ID Act of 2005. The Act is contained in Division B of the Emergency Supplemental Appropriations Act for Defense, the Global War on Terror, and Tsunami Relief, 2005. The Act imposes prescriptive federal standards for driver licenses and identification cards. Specifically, the law requires that counterfeit-resistant security features be incorporated into each driver's license or ID card, and physical security measures be specified for locations where licenses and cards are issued (U.S. Congress, 2005). Tighter controls over international air travel have been implemented as well. Since January 2007, all commercial air travelers, including citizens of the United States, Canada, Mexico, and Bermuda are required to present a passport to enter the United States from another country, even when arriving from another part of the Western Hemisphere (U.S. Department of Homeland Security, 2007).

> **REAL ID Act of 2005**
> Federal law that imposes minimum standards for driver licenses, including verification of personal information provided by license applicants and counterfeit-resistant security features incorporated into each license.

The TSA also uses other security measures and practices to identify potential threats at airports. The TSA uses risk-based security (RBS) practices that differentiate the level of screening persons receive based on their potential threat level. As part of this RBS, the TSA also has staff trained in behavioral detection and analysis. These behavior detection officers identify potentially high-risk individuals through observations and verbal interactions, diverting them for more physical screening. In other cases, the TSA uses the practice of managed inclusion, where the screening of some travelers is expedited ("Testimony on the TSA," 2013). Flyers can also participate in the TSA Secure Flight program that is reviewed in Box 9-7.

Various technologies are also used to screen travelers and baggage. First, there are the traditional X-ray scanners that examine items that are fed through the detection machines; liquids and laptops are separated so they can be better analyzed. These devices provide the staff with a 2D image of the items under analysis. More advanced systems provide color 3D images. People, meanwhile, are first screened by walking through metal detection gates where they are screened for any metal objects (Almazroui, Wang, & Zhang, 2015). There are also trace-detection portal machines. With these machines, a person enters a chamber where an air sample is then taken of the person and his possessions. This air sample is then scanned using mass spectrometry which checks for trace elements that are related to explosives (or even drugs). Airports can also use explosive trace detection devices where TSA staff will swab a person's hands or luggage. The cotton swab is then inserted into the ETD unit and analyzed for explosive residue ("TSA expands," 2010).

A TSA officer monitors a baggage screening X-ray system.
(Photo courtesy of U.S. Department of Homeland Security.)

Another relatively new technology is backscatter analysis that uses advanced imaging technology (AIT) to detect metallic and nonmetallic objects on a person. Here, a person enters a scanner unit and is bombarded with X-rays that are backscattered toward detectors, providing a detailed image of the person and items the person possesses. (Mowery et al., 2014). While these are considered nonintrusive in comparison to a "pat-down" search that requires physical contact, they have been controversial because the backscatter image provides TSA with a "nude" image of the traveler, raising some privacy concerns. While passengers can opt out of backscattering screening, those who choose to do so must submit to an "enhanced pat-down" by a TSA agent, which some passengers have decried as too invasive ("TSA chief," 2010).

SECURITY SPOTLIGHT

Research airline security procedures used in the United States and compare them with those used in the United Kingdom. What similarities and differences do you find? Which procedures do you consider most effective? Why? What, if any, trade-offs do the procedures entail?

Trucking Industry Security

The development of semi-trucks in the early 1900s precipitated the decentralization of the manufacturing industry that relied on horse, rail, and sometimes watercraft to transport cargo. Trucks permitted goods to be moved farther, faster, and less expensively than ever before. Economic development was no longer limited to regions serviced by railroads and commercial waterways. The trucking industry experienced tremendous growth after World War II. Low-fixed-cost trucks captured a large portion of the cargo transportation business. Today, trucks transport nearly 75 percent of freight shipped within the United States (Sweet, 2006).

THE SECURE FLIGHT PROGRAM

Secure Flight is a behind-the-scenes program that streamlines the travelers' watch-list matching process. It aims to improve the travel experience for all passengers, including those who have been misidentified in the past. Under the Secure Flight Final Rule, TSA requires airlines to collect and transmit to TSA the Secure Flight Passenger Data (SFPD) including the following:

- name as it appears on government-issued ID when traveling
- date of birth
- gender
- redress number (for inquiries or attempts to seek resolution regarding difficulties the traveler experienced during screening at transportation hubs while crossing U.S. borders) if available.

The TSA determined that mandating the provision of date of birth and gender would reduce the number of passengers misidentified as a match to the watch list, particularly for individuals who have similar names to those on the watch lists. The program's key goals are to identify known and suspected terrorists, prevent individuals on the No Fly List from boarding an aircraft, subject individuals on the Selectee List to enhanced screening to determine if they are permitted to board an aircraft, facilitate passenger air travel, and protect individuals' privacy.

By assuming watch-list matching responsibilities from the airlines, the TSA maintains that it is decreasing the risk of compromised watch-list data by limiting its distribution; providing earlier identification of potential matches, allowing for speedier notification of law enforcement and threat management; providing a fair, equitable, and consistent matching process across all airlines; reducing instances of misidentified individuals; and offering consistent application of an integrated redress process for misidentified individuals via the DHS's Travel Redress Inquiry Program.

Source: Transportation Security Administration (2011).

The increased use of trucks necessitated improved safety and security measures. The Federal Motor Carrier Safety Administration (FMCSA) was established as a separate administration within the U.S. Department of Transportation (DOT) on January 1, 2000. The primary mission of the FMCSA is to reduce collisions, injuries, and fatalities involving large trucks and buses. It develops, monitors, and ensures compliance with commercial licensing standards for drivers, carriers, and states. Secondarily, the FMCSA is involved with security, especially with regard to the safe and secure transportation of hazardous materials. Through enforcement of the federal hazardous materials regulations (HMRs), the FMCSA addresses hazardous materials classification and packaging, employee training, communications, and hazardous materials transportation operational requirements (Federal Motor Carrier Safety Administration, 2007). In May 2003, as part of an effort to prevent terrorist incidents, the U.S. TSA began checking the backgrounds of 3.5 million truckers who haul hazardous materials. Trucks carry over 90 percent of the almost 1 million daily shipments of hazardous materials in the United States. Over 60,000 materials are listed as hazardous. The list includes a wide range of substances, from nail polish, gasoline, and corrosives to nuclear waste. Those who are illegal immigrants, deemed mentally incompetent, or have recent convictions for possession of controlled substances cannot transport hazardous materials (Brandman, 2007; Miller, 2003).

> **Secure Flight** A behind-the-scenes program that streamlines the passenger screening process at airports.

> **Federal Motor Carrier Safety Administration (FMCSA)** Federal agency tasked with improving security and reducing injuries and fatalities involving large trucks and buses.

Railroad Security

Railroads help to integrate cities, countries, and continents. They also contribute greatly to economic development and they function as an important strategic resource. A tremendous amount of cargo is transported by railroads. Responsibility for the enforcement of

A TSA VIPR Team patrols Washington DC's Union Station.
(Photo courtesy of U.S. Department of Homeland Security.)

Federal Railroad Administration (FRA) Federal agency responsible for the promulgation and enforcement of federal rail safety regulations.

Visible Intermodal Protection Response (VIPR) Teams TSA officers assigned to some commuter railway lines and stations.

Maritime Transportation Security Act (MTSA) of 2002. Fully implemented on July 1, 2004, the MTSA requires vessels and ports to conduct vulnerability assessments, develop security plans, and engage in activities designed to protect the nation's ports, vessels, and waterways.

railway safety regulations rests with the Federal Railroad Administration (FRA), which is part of the U.S. Department of Transportation. The FRA also administers railroad assistance programs, conducts research in support of improved railroad safety, and consolidates federal governmental support of rail transportation activities (Federal Railroad Administration, 2007). Human cargo is also transported by railroad. In response to the threat of terrorism, TSA officers are assigned to some commuter railway lines and stations. For example, one particular program is called RAILSAFE, where TSA personnel called Visible Intermodal Protection Response (VIPR) Teams along with Amtrak Police and local law enforcement authorities patrol and randomly inspect baggage and conduct explosives checks on trains and train stations on high-volume travel days ("TSA supports passenger," 2015).

The TSA also has jurisdiction over some rail-security issues. For example, the TSA has inspection authority over all rail carriers. The TSA (1) also has a chain of custody procedures that require freight handlers to have secure handoff procedures and physically inspect rail cars prior to shipment; (2) requires freight and rail carriers to have a designated rail security coordinator who serves as liaison to the DHS; (3) reports procedures for threats and significant security concerns to TSA; and (4) tracks procedures that can readily identify the location of cars containing security-sensitive materials ("DHS announces," 2008). The railroad industry also employs proprietary security officers and police. In some states, railroad security personnel are commissioned as peace officers with full police powers while on duty and on railroad property. Local, county, and state law enforcement agencies as well as the FBI and ICE provide assistance as well.

Maritime Security

The maritime component of the transportation industry includes the use of a vast network of canals, rivers, lakes, oceans, and ports to transport people and cargo. The primary agency under the DHS that is responsible for maritime security is the U.S. Coast Guard. In response to the terrorist attacks of 9-11, Congress passed the Maritime Transportation Security Act (MTSA) of 2002. This law is the United States equivalent of the International Ship and Port Facility Code (ISPS). The MTSA was fully implemented on July 1, 2004. The MTSA requires vessels and ports to conduct vulnerability assessments, develop security plans, and engage in activities designed to protect the nation's ports, vessels, and waterways. Specifically, the MTSA-required security plans must include provisions for passenger-, vehicle-, and baggage screening procedures, security patrols, restricted areas, personnel identification procedures, access control measures, and the installation of surveillance equipment. Developed with risk-based methodology, the MTSA regulations focus on the elements of the maritime industry that are at a high risk for involvement in a transportation security incident. Thus, the MTSA regulations apply to large passenger ships, tankers, barges, cargo, and towing vessels, offshore oil and gas platforms, and ports that handle hazardous cargo and service the types of vessels identified in the MTSA. The MTSA also requires Area Maritime Security Committees be located in all of the nation's ports to coordinate activities of relevant federal, state, and local agencies; the maritime industry; and the boating public (U.S. Coast Guard, 2007).

The TSA is also involved in maritime security. Under the MTSA, the TSA is responsible for administering the Transportation Worker Identification Credential (TWIC) which allows access to secure areas of ports and vessels. The TWIC application and background investigation is conducted by the TSA. If cleared under TWIC, the employee is issued a biometric security smart card, which grants him access to secure areas in ports and vessels. The TSA also has responsibilities for screening passengers using commercial watercraft. For example, vehicles boarding the Cherry Branch-Minnesott Beach Ferry near Havelock, North Carolina are screened for explosives using backscatter technology before they are cleared for boarding ("Maritime security pilot," 2008). TSA personnel, in collaboration with the vessel operators' security staff also screen for contraband prohibited under U.S. law and cruise line policies and procedures.

Summary

The philosophy and practice of homeland security encompasses a wide range of public and private organizational activities designed to prevent and respond to events including terrorism, accidents, and disasters that threaten the security of communities and the United States. The goal of homeland security is to prevent and disrupt terrorist attacks, protect the American people and the nation's CIKR, and respond to and recover from incidents that do occur. While an old concept, homeland security regained renewed interest and priority following the terrorist attacks in the United States on September 11, 2001, where various weaknesses were found in the response and recovery efforts of emergency personnel from all levels of government.

Following the September 11 attacks, there were major changes in homeland security at all levels of government. The USA PATRIOT Act, one of the first pieces of legislation passed after the 9-11 attacks, included new initiatives to fight terrorism, increase border protection, and provide law enforcement agencies with new alternatives to investigate and fight terrorism. Later in 2002, the Department of Homeland Security was created through the Homeland Security Act of 2002. This legislation led to the creation of a new cabinet level position within the U.S. government, the reassignment of existing federal agencies to the DHS, and the creation of the TSA. Today, the philosophy and practice of homeland security is better refined. It is based on the key concepts of security, resilience, and customs and exchange. Its missions include: preventing terrorism, securing and managing the borders, enforcing immigration laws, safeguarding cyberspace, and ensuring resilience to disasters. To achieve these diverse missions, the DHS has created the NIPP. This program is designed to protect the nation's CIKR where DHS personnel in concert with other forms of government and the private sector engage in risk management activities to prepare for and mitigate against terrorist attacks and other hazards. Additionally, FEMA is responsible for the administration of the NIMS program. The primary goal of NIMS is to ensure that a uniform and unified incident management framework exists at all levels of government and in the private sector. By having a uniform incident management system, it is anticipated that if any incident does occur, local agencies that are primarily responsible for the incident can properly respond to and address the issue.

This chapter also identifies that there are some specific threats to homeland security. These can include international and domestic-based terrorists, where it has been determined that domestic terrorist organizations and individuals associated with those groups are often a greater concern than international groups. Other threats include natural, technological, and accidental hazards. Natural disasters, for example, can cause a great deal of damage and disruption where governments and the private security need to have effective mitigation, preparedness, response, and recovery programs in place. The transportation sector which is part of the nation's critical infrastructure, is also a homeland security issue. Since 9-11, there have also been major changes to airport security. Now, the TSA is responsible for the screening of passengers and baggage instead of security personnel employed by the airlines. Besides aviation, the TSA is also responsible for security-related activities in the railroad and maritime sectors that are also vulnerable to terrorism and other issues.

Career Opportunities in Homeland Security

Career opportunities in homeland security exist in both the private and public sectors. In the private sector, all organizations located in the CIKR-related field will require security officers and specialists who can conduct security audits and engage in risk-management activities to meet NIPP-related goals and standards. These private sector organizations will also require NIMS credentialed security staff to ensure that their organization is prepared for man-made and natural disasters.

The public sector, especially the DHS provides a variety of entry level and advanced security positions. One common entry-level position is Transportation Security Officer (TSOs). According to information from usajobs.gov, TSOs provide for security and the protection of air travelers, airports, and aircraft. Some specific duties include:

- Operating various screening equipment and technology to identify dangerous objects in baggage, cargo, and on passengers, and preventing those objects from being transported onto aircraft.
- Performing searches and screening, which may include physical interaction with passengers (e.g., pat-downs, search of property, etc.), conducting bag searches and lifting/carrying bags, bins, and property weighing up to 70 lbs.

- Controlling terminal entry and exit points.
- Interacting with the public, giving directions, and responding to inquiries.
- Maintaining focus and awareness while working in a stressful environment which includes noise from alarms, machinery and people, crowd distractions, time pressure, and disruptive and angry passengers, in order to preserve the professional ability to identify and locate potentially life threatening or mass destruction devices, and to make effective decisions in both crisis and routine situations.
- Engaging in continuous development of critical thinking skills, necessary to mitigate actual and potential security threats, by identifying, evaluating, and applying appropriate situational options and approaches. This may include application of risk-based security screening protocols that vary based on program requirements.
- Retaining and implementing knowledge of all applicable standard operating procedures, demonstrating responsible and dependable behavior, and being open to change and adapting to new information or unexpected obstacles.

Other DHS-related positions can also be found on usajobs.gov.

Key Terms and Concepts

Discussion Questions and Exercises

1. What agencies comprise the Department of Homeland Security?
2. Identify threats to homeland security and develop a protection strategy for each threat identified.
3. Are organizations and individuals other than public law enforcement responsible for the prevention of terrorist acts?
4. Analyze the findings of the 9-11 Commission.
5. What are the key missions of the Homeland Security?
6. Explain the National Infrastructure Protection Plan (NIPP). What is the role of the private security sector in NIPP?
7. Explain the National Incident Management System (NIMS). What is the role of the private sector in NIMS?
8. Define terrorism. What are some of the terrorist-based threats that can jeopardize homeland security?
9. What is the role of the TSA?
10. How can the philosophy of homeland security protect against accidents and natural and technological issues?

Your Turn

Spotting Potential Terrorist Activities

The NSI established fusion centers where reports of suspicious activities made by citizens and local police can be collected and analyzed to generate meaningful intelligence for local, state, and federal law enforcement officials. Authorities depend on ordinary citizens to provide reports. With fusion centers in mind, consider the following scenario and questions.

Miguel works in an agricultural supply store in the Midwest United States. One day, he notices a young man purchasing a ton of ammonium nitrate fertilizer from the store. He has never seen this individual in the store. Later that week, Miguel is socializing at a bar with friends. Carla, a friend who works at a nearby gas station, mentions seeing someone purchasing large quantities of racing fuel in 5 gallon containers, placing them in the back of his pickup truck. Carla's story reminds Miguel of the man he saw in the store, and he says, "I guess some people have big gardens, and some are really into racing." Carla says, "It's funny that we both saw someone doing something unusual." Another friend remarks, "Well, it ain't illegal to buy fertilizer or fuel."

The following week, while running errands in the city, Miguel walks by a large cargo van sitting vacant near a large civic center. The building has a banner advertising an upcoming performance by a famous rock band. A few days later, Miguel is in the city again. He sees the same used van, still sitting in the same place.

1. Does any of the three activities Miguel has noticed and heard about strike you as indicating potential terrorist plans in the works? Why or why not?

2. If you learned that all three activities were carried out by the same individual, would you be more or less likely to conclude that Miguel and his friends have observed a potential terrorist plot? Explain your response.

3. Is there anything in Miguel's conversation with his friends at the bar that suggests an opportunity for them to share knowledge and thus build more

collective insight into the behaviors they have observed? (Hint: What information do Miguel and Carla possess in common that, if shared, could shed additional light on the situation?)

4. If you believe that one or more of the activities observed by Miguel and his friends suggest possible terrorist plans, how would you advise these individuals to report the activities in question? To whom should they report the activities?

Postscript: In 1995, a young man bought a ton of ammonium nitrate fertilizer from a farm supply store. Later, he went to a raceway and purchased large quantities of racing fuel. Still later, he bought a used car and left it parked for several days near a nondescript federal building. None of these activities was illegal, and each went unreported. The young man who carried out each of these activities was Timothy McVeigh—the domestic terrorist responsible for the April 1995 attack in Oklahoma City that killed 168 people and wounded hundreds more. McVeigh constructed an "ANFO" (Ammonium Nitrate/Fuel Oil) bomb in a rental truck to carry out the attack ("Calling all eyes," 2010).

PART 4

Security Management

The chapters in this section examine specific security management-related activities. Chapter 10 examines the concepts and practices of management and leadership and ethics in organizations. Chapter 11 focuses on specific managerial activities in the context of personnel management and planning and budgeting. Chapter 12 is devoted to the risk management process.

10 Management, Leadership, and Ethics in Security Organizations

LEARNING OBJECTIVES

After completing this chapter, the reader should be able to:

1 *explain some of the key differences between private and public administration*

2 *describe some of the key characteristics of a bureaucracy*

3 *explain what management means*

4 *explain some of the key responsibilities of managers*

5 *explain how the concept and practice of management has evolved in organizations*

6 *understand what effective supervision is and why it is important*

7 *know the difference between management and supervision*

8 *explain and apply the concept of leadership in organizations*

9 *understand some of the behavioral assumptions of leadership style*

10 *know how to ensure ethics and integrity in organizations through ethical leadership*

► Introduction

The management of people and organizations is old. Its origins can be traced to over 3,000 years ago to ancient Iraq where Sumerian Priests kept records of business transactions and the Roman Catholic Church that used traditional bureaucratic principles, including a chain of command, the delegation of responsibilities, and specialized job descriptions in its organization (Pindur, Rogers, & Suk Kim, 1995). Since these early origins, the management of contemporary organizations has become much more advanced. Nevertheless, there still remain some common elements. These common elements are based on the fact that any organization must be properly managed, employees need effective supervision, and effective leadership must exist at all positions and levels. Moreover, employees and the organization itself must be ethical.

This chapter will introduce the reader to the principles of management, supervision, leadership, ethics, and the need for effective administration in organizations. To properly administer requires effective managers who know how to manage and an understanding of the various roles they perform, based on their position in the company. Organizations also need competent line level supervisors. Regardless of the position held in an organization, leadership and ethics are also key attributes of the modern security organization.

The Need for Effective Administration

All organizations must be properly administered. In a broad sense, administration is a process that involves two or more people working collaboratively to accomplish a predetermined vision or goal. To administer means to carry out or execute organizational policies, procedures, and processes to meet defined objectives. The process emerges from the need to cooperate with others on complex, difficult, or multiple tasks to achieve common objectives of an organization, community, or society.

Administrative activities are carried out in public and private sector organizations. Public administration is defined as the business of administering public policy and law as delegated by the government (Graben & Fitz-Gerald, 2013) while private administrative activities are carried out by companies to meet company goals and objectives. Some of the major differences between the two are related to the goals they need to meet and their scope. For example, two primary goals of the private sector are profit maximization and serving the needs of the organization. In the public sector, meanwhile, efficiency—not profit—and accountability to the public are primary concerns where administrators are responsible for making and carrying out governmental policy that ensures that the social welfare needs of the public are being met. Tables 10-1 ■ and 10-2 ■ show some characteristics and differences between the private and public sectors.

The proper administration of organizations requires that they be properly structured. Administrative and work-related functions oftentimes have unique attributes, where logically, communications, coordination, and productivity would improve if similar functions were consolidated to some degree. As organizations become large and oftentimes specialized, they need to have better coordinated activities to meet their goals (Downs, 1967).

The traditional administrative structure is based on Max Weber's Theory of Bureaucracy. Weber (1864–1920) was critical of the effectiveness of existing administrative structures that were based on family-like or feudalistic structures. He proposed new or more effective structures based on rational-legal principles and authority. Weber believed that the ideal form of organization and administrative activities for bureaucracies (large organizations in the governmental sector) are based on six points:

> **administration**
> Process through which two or more people collaborate to accomplish a predetermined goal.

> **public administration**
> Refers to administration of public sector organizations.

> **Max Weber's Theory of Bureaucracy**
> Theory of management based on a hierarchy of authority, formalization, and clearly defined organizational rules.

> **bureaucracy** A type of administrative structure; large organizations that have formal rules and are hierarchically structured.

TABLE 10-1 Defining Characteristics of Public Administration

Characteristic	Explanation
Public affairs oriented	Public administration focuses on the management of public agencies and organizations.
Impartial and fair	All citizens are entitled to a particular government service and must be treated in a uniform manner.
Apolitical	The policies of government may be political, but the detailed execution of these policies is administrative.
Public service oriented	Public administration exists to serve the public, and profit is not a motive for its operations.
Publicly funded	Funds for public administration are appropriated by law and derived primarily from tax revenues.
Publicly documented	Administrative records and financial documents are public information that must be made available for review by all citizens.
Accountable to the public	Public administration is subject to legislative and judicial review at all times.
Selectively staffed (civil service)	Qualified personnel are selected on the basis of demonstrated merit through civil service examinations.
Hierarchical	Public agencies are official and formal and consist of levels of positions.

Source: Patrick J. Ortmeier, Johnson, Introduction to Security: Operations and Management, 5e. © 2018, Pearson Education, Inc., New York, NY.

TABLE 10-2 Defining Characteristics of Private Administration

Characteristic	Explanation
Private enterprise	Private administration exists to fulfill a private rather than public obligation or interest.
Private or corporate ownership	Private individuals, groups, or stockholders own private organizations.
Competitiveness	The organization may be in competition with other enterprises engaged in producing the same product or service.
Profit incentive	Except for certain nonprofit private organizations, the incentive is to generate profit.
Financing regulated by market price	Revenue is based on the ability to sell the product or service.
Privacy of information and records (within limits)	Information is proprietary and the property of the owner(s).
Accountability to owners and stockholders	The organization and its employees are held accountable to the organization's owners rather than the public.
Some freedom in selection and termination of employees	The organization is not bound by civil service rules related to hiring or termination of employees.
Freedom to regulate work methods and organization	The organization is not bound by civil service regulations.

Source: Patrick J. Ortmeier, Johnson, Introduction to Security: Operations and Management, 5e. © 2018, Pearson Education, Inc., New York, NY.

(1) A well-defined formal hierarchy and chain of command distinguishes the level of authority within an organization. Individuals who hold higher positions will supervise and direct lower positions within the hierarchy.

(2) Management by rules and regulations provides a set of standard operating procedures that facilitate consistency in both organizational and management practices.

(3) Division of labor and work specializations are used to align employees with their organizational tasks. This way, an employee will work on things with which he or she has experience and knows how to do well.

(4) Managers should maintain an impersonal relationship with employees to promote fair and equal treatment of all employees so that unbiased decisions can be made.

(5) Competence, not personality, is the basis for job appointment. An employee should be chosen, placed and promoted within an organization based on his or her level of experience and competency to perform the job.

(6) Formal written records are used to document all rules, regulations, procedures, decisions, and actions taken by the organization and its members to preserve consistency and accountability.

Based on Weber's writings, these large governmental organizations became known as bureaucracies. Those individuals working in these organizations were referred to as bureaucrats (Jaffee, 2008).

Weber's theory of bureaucracy resulted in many organizations using his points to restructure to improve the control and regulation of their activities and to ensure technical competence among workers (Stoner & Freeman, 1989). While it was originally designed and applied to public organizations, these bureaucratic principles and elements were also integrated into many private sector organizations. Therefore, elements of Weber's bureaucratic principles can be found in many organizations today. For example, many private sector organizations have some type of merit system for promotion and they have formal written policies and procedures to ensure consistency and accountability.

With the rise of the human relations movement in the 1930s and beyond, many organizations have changed their organizational and administrative structures, using post-bureaucratic principles. Characteristics of post-bureaucratic organizations include re-organizing the structure and role of managers and employees in organizations. For example, post-bureaucratic structures are less hierarchical and more networked and more nurturing toward employees (Maravelias, 2003). They are structured around "fluid/flexible decision making processes; network[s] of specialized functional relationships; open and visible peer review processes; open and permeable boundaries; broad public standards of performance; expectation of change" (Hodgson, 2004, p. 84).

> **post-bureaucratic organizations** Structures that are less hierarchical, more networked, and more nurturing toward employees.

► What is Management?

The administration of an organization also requires effective management. Management is defined as "the process of planning, organizing, leading, and controlling the efforts of organizational members, and using all other organizational resources to achieve stated organizational goals" (Stoner & Freeman, 1989, p. 4). All organizations must have effective management to survive and compete.

> **management** The process of planning, organizing, leading, and controlling the efforts of organizational members, and using all other organizational resources to achieve stated organizational goals.

Core Functions of Management

Even though organizations may differ in their scope or function, the literature has identified some core managerial activities. One of the traditional ways to understand the role of management is through Gulick and Urwick's (1937) POSDCORB model that posits that managers are responsible for *planning, organizing, staffing, directing, coordinating, reporting, and budgeting*. These functions are shown in Box 10-1.

> **POSDCORB** Acronym that describes administrative activities: Planning, Organizing, Staffing, Directing, Coordinating, Reporting, and Budgeting.

BOX 10-1

MANAGERIAL FUNCTIONS

Planning	Planning—choosing a course of action and outlining what needs to be done. Planning requires establishing standards and creating evaluation measures to ensure that organizational goals and objectives are achieved. It is a basic managerial activity that requires an understanding of where the organization is and where it wants to be.
Organizing	Establishing formal structures of authority and coordinating and defining work subdivisions necessary to get the job done.
Staffing	Involves human resource-related functions, including recruitment, selection, and the training of employees.
Directing	Is related to leadership. Directing is making correct decisions and ensuring that all resources, including personnel, are used properly to achieve organizational goals.
Coordinating	Ensuring that personnel and resources work together toward specific goals and objectives.
Reporting	Keeping superiors and subordinates informed as to what is going on by making sure that information keeps flowing through the organization. Reporting includes both verbal and written forms of communication.
Budgeting	Includes all aspects of the budgeting process, including fiscal planning, accounting, and expense controls.

Source: Patrick J. Ortmeier, Johnson, Introduction to Security: Operations and Management, 5e. © 2018, Pearson Education, Inc., New York, NY.

TABLE 10-3 Managerial Roles and Behaviors

Interpersonal	Managing through people
Figurehead	Engaging in social-related activities; serving as a symbolic leader of the organization.
Leader	Leading, motivating, and inspiring employees.
Liaison	Networking skills and techniques to establish and maintain relationships in and outside the organization.
Informational	**Managing through information**
Monitor	Finding and acquiring work-related information.
Disseminator	Sharing information effectively with others in the organization.
Spokesperson	Transmitting information to outsiders.
Decisional	**Managing through action**
Entrepreneur	Solving problems creatively and coming up with and implementing novel solutions to problems/issues.
Disturbance handler	Resolving and managing conflicts and addressing crisis or conflict situations.
Resource allocator	Planning and scheduling activities; managing a budget.
Negotiator	Participating in negotiations with one's team, department and/or organization and individuals and groups that come into contact with the organization.

Source: Patrick J. Ortmeier, Johnson, Introduction to Security: Operations and Management, 5e. © 2018, Pearson Education, Inc., New York, NY.

---

interpersonal role
Managerial roles directed toward establishing and maintaining relationships by serving as a liaison, figurehead, and leader.

informational role
Managerial roles directed toward serving as a spokesperson and monitoring and disseminating information.

decisional roles
Managing through actions and following through on decisions by serving as an entrepreneur, disturbance handler, resource allocator, and negotiator.

management levels
Different layers of management in a company based on managerial roles and responsibilities.

The original POSDCORB model has been modified over the years by other authors. Table 10-3 ■ shows Mintzberg's 10 managerial roles. Mintzberg (1989), proposed that these 10 managerial roles require three interdependent behaviors: (1) interpersonal, (2) informational, and (3) decisional. In their interpersonal role, managers as leaders guide and motivate employees; their primary purpose is to integrate the needs of the organization with the needs of the employee. In this interpersonal role, they perform a variety of ceremonial functions including providing tours, taking customers to lunch (figureheads), and serving to link the organization with the external environment. In their informational role, managers as monitors collect information from internal and external sources (clients, reports, conferences) that keep them informed of issues and trends. As a disseminator, managers filter and pass on factual, value-based information to superiors and employees where they then serve the role of spokesperson. In their decisional roles, managers serve as: (1) entrepreneurs, making changes freely to improve the organization while adapting to changing conditions; (2) disturbance handlers, addressing employee conflict and disputes between units in the company; (3) resource allocators, scheduling and prioritizing how time will be spent at work; and, as (4) negotiators, intervening on behalf of the organization in nonroutine situations with individuals and groups that come into contact with the organization (Johnson, 2005).

Managerial Levels

There are also different management levels in organizations. These levels are based on a hierarchical organizational structure where management levels are below or subordinate to another management level, with the exception of the top level. These hierarchical structures oftentimes resemble a pyramid where there are top, mid, and line level managers (Sirmon, Hitt, Ireland, & Gilbert, 2011). At each level, managers have different responsibilities and levels of authority. For example, top level managers may operate in an abstract and conceptual world and may not know operational and daily work-related employee activities because this is not their role in the organization. Positions at this level include president, vice president, chief executive officer (CEO), chief financial officer, chief operations officer, and chief technological officer. Middle managers, meanwhile, make broader organizational goals and issues visible to lower level managers. These managers are often responsible for a specific unit in the organization and fall between senior management and line level managers. Some examples of middle management positions include human resource, senior project, operations, training, and accounting managers. Line or entry level managers are more concerned with and involved in the technical aspects of company operations, concentrating on the daily quantity and quality-related activities. Some position names at this level include team and project leaders, section heads, sales, and account managers (Sveningsson & Alvesson, 2003).

Based on these levels, some authors propose that managerial activities exist on a continuum from strategic to operational management. At the strategic level, managerial activities focus on the entire organization. Here, top level executives are involved in long-term planning activities that shape the organization's objectives and direction. On the other end is operational management. Operational management is concerned about the day-to-day operations, where for example, managers at this level will be concentrating on the performance of the line level workers, making sure that they have the correct tools and resources to perform their jobs. These managers ensure that the tactical strategies are carried out and translated into action. In the middle, meanwhile, are those mangers who are concerned with tactical management. These individuals are responsible for carrying out the specific organizational functions using the best approaches or tactics to meet or achieve the strategic plan created by top management, making sure that the strategic goals are implemented at the operational level. For example, from a strategic level, key organizational managers may be under pressure from stakeholders and governmental regulations to develop policies, practices, and strategies that are aligned with the organization's security goals. At the tactical level, these managers have to develop appropriate plans to meet and carry out the specific goals created by top level managers. Furthermore, at the operational level, security managers are responsible for the delivery of security services the organization provides, ensuring that there is enough staffing while staff is properly trained to perform security-related activities (Stoner & Freeman, 1989).

The Evolution of Managerial Thought

Two of the early schools of managerial thought include scientific management (1890s–1930s) or the classical management movement, and the Human Relations Movement (1930s and beyond).

Classical management is based on scientific and administrative management. Scientific management is focused on productivity, while administrative management focuses on the complete organization, looking at ways to increase organizational effectiveness and efficiency (Pindur et al., 1995). One of the early contributions to classical managerial thought in the United States was based on the works of Frederick Taylor (1856–1915) and the practice of Scientific Management, which is also considered the classical school of managerial thought. Scientific management is premised on the principle that organizations carefully investigate the work activities needed in a company and then set appropriate performance standards that employees should meet. To accomplish this, Taylor recommended the use of scientific fact finding to determine what workers ought to be able to perform, based on their equipment, materials, and the correct way to perform tasks. This fact finding required a systematic analysis of the production processes, examining the true nature of the work, finding the right employees for the job, and making sure that employees had the right tools, machinery, and resources from the company. The goal was to increase the productivity and skill levels of workers. Because appropriate production rates could now be estimated, scientific management could also lead to increased pay for workers if they exceeded normed standards, since they would receive incentive pay for their hard work. As such, the company would benefit through increased productivity, and, employees would perceive the process as fair, especially if they could make more money (Flynn, Schroeder, & Sakakibara, 1994; Johnson, 2005).

hierarchical organizational structure Where management levels are below or subordinate to another management level, with the exception of the top level.

operational management Managerial activities directed at day-to day operations.

tactical management Managers responsible for carrying out the specific organizational functions using the best approaches or tactics to meet or achieve the strategic plan created by top management, making sure that the strategic goals are implemented at the operational level.

scientific management Classical management concept that focused on worker productivity.

One of the more common ways to scientifically study work was through time studies. These time studies first required that jobs be broken down into their most simplest or rudimentary tasks where an investigator then calculated the time it took to complete each task. Following this analytical stage, the constructive stage then re-designed and standardized each position or job, determining what precise movements were needed by the workers and what tools and other resources were required to maximize production. For example, Taylor applied these principles of scientific management to workers at the Bethlehem Steel Company of South Bethlehem, Pennsylvania. These workers were responsible for loading "pig iron," which were 92 pound slabs of iron that they had to load onto rail cars. Through time-and-motion studies, Taylor calculated that an average worker could load 45 tons a day. Based on this calculation, the company then set a norm, expecting that each worker load a minimum of 45 tons; more than 45 tons would result in a bonus for the employee's hard work (Johnson, 2005).

There are some drawbacks to this managerial approach. First, the principles of scientific management did not apply well in assembly line factors. In assembly line positions, workers were tied to a rigid production rate. They were dependent on other workers for productivity norms and there were no benefits to getting jobs done earlier or faster because they were paid solely by the hour with no opportunity for bonuses (Johnson, 2005). Furthermore, Scientific Management was found to be dehumanizing. With its concern for production, it did not consider the personal needs of the worker. The focus under scientific management was production rather than the human side of management, where oftentimes the worker was simply considered to be an extension of the machine (McKinlay & Zeitlin, 1989). These classical management concepts still exist in the actual practice and mindset of some managers. The need to cut costs, increase productivity, and increase organizational effectiveness are all elements of classical management theory.

Human Relations Movement New management approach that emerged in the 1930s that concentrated on the needs of workers and not just production.

Beginning in 1930s, another approach to management emerged: the Human Relations Movement. The human relations movement is best associated with psychologist Eton Mayo from Harvard University and his research of how worker productivity could be improved at the Western Electric Hawthorne Plant in Chicago, Illinois (1924–1927). Originally, the primary goal of Mayo's work was to determine if increased lighting (which Mayo called illumination studies) would improve productivity. In order to determine if lighting was important, Mayo and his team of researchers divided workers into two groups: one group of workers had increased lighting and other group had the same level of lighting. Then, they carefully recorded worker productivity and actions with management. Mayo found increased productivity with both groups. Mayo concluded that the productivity increased markedly over time because of the changed interpersonal relationships between supervisors and workers, where management became more relaxed and better communicated with employees. Upon further investigation on why productivity increased, Mayo determined that people worked harder because they believed that management was concerned about them. This phenomenon was later coined the Hawthorne effect (Bramel & Friend, 1981; Johnson, 2005).

Hawthorne effect Phenomenon that people worked harder because they believed that management was concerned about them.

From this and other research, the management of organizations shifted from solely production needs to a concern for the worker and participative management. The basic premise of the human relations movement is that the workplace is not simply a production system. Instead, it is a social system that is involved in the production of goods and services where workers have psychosocial needs that need to be met by management and the workplace. This concern for workers and the subsequent theories and practices have been collectively named the human relations movement in management (Bruce, 2006). Since the early Hawthorne Electric studies, many more researchers have used the social and behavioral sciences, sociology, and psychology—to study human behavior in relationship to management and organizations, resulting in a multitude of organizational theories to assist in the development of the re-design of the workplace and managerial activities. Now, motivations, workers' needs, leadership, worker empowerment, team building, and decision-making are just some of the issues that organizations are addressing to improve effectiveness and efficiency and the quality of work life for employees. This change from solely production to human relations also required new forms of management, requiring that managers in contemporary organizations be educated and acutely aware that the management of people is a complex but nevertheless rewarding challenge.

The Role of Supervision in the Workplace

Supervision is defined as directing people in the workplace. Supervision can be considered efforts to support workers to enable them to get their work done. Supervision is different from management. Supervisors have an internal focus having direct and daily contact with line level employees, addressing daily operations, individuals, and groups of employees. In this capacity, one of the primary roles of a supervisor is to ensure that employees are supported for their work-related efforts. Managers, meanwhile, often have an external or outward focus and limited contact with line level employees. They are more concerned with the external environment, oftentimes working with other businesses and clients on larger, more strategic issues that can affect the organization.

> **supervision**
> Directing people in the workplace toward organizational goals.

Supervision also differs from management based on span of control (the number of subordinates under one's control), problem solving, and even knowledge. Management often oversees entire departments, units, or special programs or projects. Security managers, meanwhile, may be responsible for the entire function in the organization. A security supervisor, meanwhile, may be responsible for a particular location and shift. Supervisors may deal with repetitious or similar problems related to personnel (managing employee conflict, absenteeism) and productivity (e.g., equipment failures) that are relatively short term in nature. Managers often address larger problems that could be more critical to the success of the organization, requiring long-term solutions and impacts. In the context of knowledge, meanwhile, supervisors will have an in-depth understanding of line level operations. They have most likely performed the same work performed by line level employees. Managers, however, may have never performed specific tasks related to line level activities and operations (Cohen, 2011; Howard & Wech, 2012; Varnali, 2015).

Because of their direct contact, supervisors need to cultivate and maintain positive relationships with employees. Building positive relationships involves social exchange. Supervisors need to care about employees' well-being or welfare at work, value their contributions to the organization, and treat them fairly. In "exchange" employees will have a higher degree of attachment to the supervisor and organization, and be more creative and committed to the organization, leading to better quality work and productivity (Paillé, Grima, & Bernardeau, 2013). Trust must also exist. Trust is oftentimes earned slowly, but it goes away fast. Trust can be considered a "social lubricant" that leads to better working relationships between employees and supervisors (Bennis & Nanus, 1985). Some of the behaviors that build trust between supervisors and employees include: competence, equity, integrity, discretion, loyalty, and transparency, keeping promises, receptivity, and availability (Butler & Ehrlich, 1991).

▶ Leadership

The management of organizations and supervision of staff also requires leadership. The universal phenomenon called leadership has been the subject of a great deal of research from both the theoretical and the practical points of view. Leadership has been described as a trait, the art of inducing compliance, an exercise of influence, a kind of behavior or act, a form of persuasion, a power relationship, an instrument in goal attainment, an effective interaction, a differentiated role, and an initiation of structure (Bass, 1990). Leadership has also been defined as acts or behaviors that result in a shared direction, alignment to goals

> **leadership** Occurs anytime one motivates, influences, or mobilizes an individual or group.

and values and commitment for change, and developing teams (Drath et al., 2008). It has also been defined as directing and coordinating work relationships while showing consideration for others (Fiedler, 1967), an activity that mobilizes people to do something (Heifetz, 1994), and a social meaning-making process that takes place as a result of an activity or work in a group (Drath & Palus, 1994).

Leadership should not be confused with supervision or management. Leadership, as a concept and practice, attempts to motivate, influence, or mobilize an individual or group. Supervision and management, on the other hand, involves directing people toward organizational goals (Hersey & Blanchard, 1982). Although supervision and leadership may be exercised or exhibited by the same individual, both represent distinct concepts. Leadership produces change by establishing direction, aligning people, motivating, and inspiring. Supervision and management bring a measure of order and consistency to organizations by planning and budgeting, organizing and staffing, and controlling (Kotter, 1990). In other words, supervision and management follow leadership (Covey, 1998). Bennis (2009) distinguished leadership from management along numerous dimensions (see Table 10-4 ■). As one author stated, the leader is the one who climbs the tallest tree, surveys the situation, and cries out, "Wrong jungle!" The manager responds with "Shut up! We are making progress" (Covey, 1998).

Leadership is a trait and attribute. Not all managers or supervisors make good leaders. And, not all leaders make good supervisors or managers. Ideally, good supervisors are also good leaders. The concept of leadership is often misunderstood because definitions of leadership vary and the process for leadership development is vague. However, substantial evidence exists that leads progressive thinkers to believe that leadership skills are essential for all workers in contemporary society (Drucker, 1994). These leadership skills must also entail global leadership competencies. These global leadership competencies are developed by: (1) eliminating cultural ignorance through enhancing knowledge, awareness, and an understanding, appreciation and acceptance of other cultures, which in turn (2) changes attitudes and values of other cultures, leading to (3) transformations in oneself where globalized behaviors and attitudes become internalized, effortless, and a way of life (Chin, Gu, & Tubbs, 2001). For example, a new survey by the American Management Association and the Institute for Corporate Productivity (2015) found that approximately 50 percent of organizations have made the development of global leadership skills a priority in their organizations. These skills include emphasizing a global mindset among employees, requiring critical thinking, inclusiveness, cultural agility and awareness, creativity and innovation, emotional intelligence, cultural competency, and political savvy to work with individuals and organizations throughout the world in the competitive global economy.

TABLE 10-4 Management versus Leadership

A manager	A leader
Administers	Innovates
Is a copy	Is an original
Maintains	Develops
Focuses on systems and structure	Focuses on people
Relies on control	Inspires trust
Has a short-range view	Has a long-range perspective
Asks how and when	Asks what and why
Keeps an eye on the bottom line	Keeps an eye on the horizon
Accepts the status quo	Challenges the status quo
Is the classic good soldier	Is not dependent on others
Does things right	Does the right thing

Source: Patrick J. Ortmeier, Johnson, Introduction to Security: Operations and Management, 5e. © 2018, Pearson Education, Inc., New York, NY.

Leadership is not a position within a company. In some cases, individuals will assume that managers are leaders. However, this is not always the case. Leadership is every person's responsibility, and each employee can assume a leadership role. The CEO of an organization is probably the most important strategic initiator. The CEO plays a significant role in defining the organization's philosophy, values, mission, and priorities. The CEO is instrumental in creating the climate conducive to successful change and positive outcomes. The CEO is also in the best position to assist with the creation of a vision for the future. Ideally, middle and upper level managers should lead as well as manage. Rather than insulate themselves from line supervisors and operations personnel, upper and middle managers should interact with subordinates, assisting the latter through mentoring, coaching, and team building. Upper and middle managers are in an excellent position to act as conduits, monitoring for and adjusting the pace of change.

Line supervisors are in a pivotal leadership position to facilitate the achievement of goals. These supervisors help line personnel achieve accountability and performance objectives. It has been stated that the quantity and quality of performance can be linked directly to the quality of supervision. Line supervisors are in the best position to assume a leadership role in reviewing individual productivity, making recommendations for improvement, and taking corrective action when appropriate. Finally, regardless of the size of an organization or the number of levels of authority or supervision, it is the line person who has the most direct role in serving the mission of the organization. The line person is in the best position to directly impact the lives of the people who are served. Thus, considerable training and education resources should be expended to develop ethical leadership competencies in line as well as senior personnel. Furthermore, ethical leadership development should be viewed as a lifelong process, not an event (Baker, 2011; Johnson, 2009; Meese & Ortmeier, 2004; Ortmeier, 1997, 2003; Ortmeier & Davis, 2012).

Leadership Theories

Throughout the twentieth century, numerous theorists attempted to define leadership. An important breakthrough in understanding the concept of leadership occurred with the publication of *Leadership* by James MacGregor Burns in 1978. Burns characterized leadership as either transactional leadership (when one person takes the initiative, making contact with others for the purpose of the exchange of valued things) or transformational leadership (when one or more persons engage with others in a way that the leader and nonleader raise one another to higher levels of motivation and morality). The function of transactional leadership is to ensure compliance of subordinates through contingent rewards (such as praise) and punishment in order to maintain the organization's operations and goals, rather than to change it (Blanchard & Johnson, 1992; Burns & Becker, 1988). Transformational leadership, on the other hand, focuses on the three behavior patterns of charisma, intellectual stimulation, and individualized consideration to inspire employees to be the best they can be (Bass, 1985). Tichy and Ulrich (1984) presented the transformational leader as the model for future leadership excellence. They cited three identifiable activities associated with transformational leadership: creation of vision (view of a future state, mobilization of commitment), acceptance of a new mission, and institutionalization of change (new patterns of behavior must be adopted).

Although leadership originally focused on traits or inbred qualities that a person possessed since birth, today it is believed that leadership skills can be acquired or modified extensively through learning. These skills include keeping communication channels open and functioning effectively, solving problems, planning, initiating action, and accepting responsibility. Such skills are not inherited; they are learned (McGregor, 1960). Also critical to the success of the leader are skills in facilitation of team interaction, effective team problem solving, and training (Miskin & Gmelch, 1985).

> **transactional leadership** Leadership style where the leader seeks employee compliance through rewards and/or punishment.

> **transformational leadership** When one engages another in a way that the leader and nonleader raise one another to higher levels of motivation and morality.

An effective leader is likely to demonstrate excellent communication and interpersonal skills. A leader is likely to be both relations-oriented and task-oriented, manage conflict successfully, and mobilize and direct individuals toward higher objectives (Bass, 1981). Orton (1984) cited the importance of quality decision-making, commitment, and the ability to employ situational strategies. Motivational, or person-oriented behaviors, tend to promote follower satisfaction, although they may not contribute to group productivity (Bass, 1981). McGregor (1966) suggested that people already possess motivation and desire full responsibility.

Leadership competence has also been expressed in terms of the ability to plan, organize, and set goals. Leaders must create clear-cut and measurable goals based on advice from all elements of an organization. Likert (1961, 1967) discovered that high-producing leaders make clear what the objectives are and give people freedom to complete the task. Argyris (1964) suggested that it is in an individual's nature to be self-directed and to seek fulfillment through the exercise of initiative and responsibility. Hersey and Blanchard (1982) suggested that leadership involves goal setting, organizing, setting time lines, and directing. Contemporary experts often focus on leadership competencies. Bennis (1984, 1993a) identified four competencies of leadership:

- Management of attention—the ability to attract followers.
- Management of meaning—the ability to communicate one's viewpoint or vision.
- Management of trust—reliability.
- Management of self—the ability to know one's skills and use them effectively.

Daniel (1992) identified 13 leadership competencies. They include a goal orientation, a bottom-line focus, the ability to communicate and enforce standards, initiative, strategic influence, communication of confidence, and interpersonal sensitivity. Good leaders also develop and coach others, give performance feedback, collaborate and build teams, solve problem, project a good image and reputation, and possess self-confidence. Kotter (1993) pointed out that good leaders articulate a vision, involve people in decision-making, and recognize and reward success. Drath and Palus (1994) stated that leaders must be trained to participate in, rather than exercise, leadership by learning community-oriented, meaning-making capacities, such as the capacity to understand oneself as both an individual and a socially embedded being; the capacity to understand systems in general as mutually related, interacting, and continually changing; the capacity to take the perspective of another; and the capacity to engage in dialogue. Leaders must be flexible and demonstrate initiative, integrity, and the ability to empower others (Davids, 1995).

Essential leadership competencies can be grouped into five major categories. The communications and related interpersonal competencies category addresses one's ability to communicate with diverse populations. Through motivational competencies, a person demonstrates the ability to encourage others and build proactive relationships. Problem-solving competencies focus on problem identification, critical and analytical thinking, and situation analysis. Planning and organizing competencies are used to create a vision, prioritize, delegate, and define goals and objectives. Actuation-implementation competencies address the ability to implement a vision and evaluate results (Ortmeier, 1997, 2006).

The real test of leadership lies in the performance of the individuals and groups being led (Bass, 1981). The competencies applied in a particular circumstance depend on the situation, the people involved, the action to be taken, and the desired results (Byrnbauer & Tyson, 1984). Leadership skills are especially important in an asset protection environment. As the primary protection officers for most organizations, security personnel must respond to threats against people and property and assume control in high stress and dangerous situations. The ability to communicate well, maintain integrity, exercise effective judgment, reduce hostility, promote safety, and restore normal operations requires ethical leadership competence (More, Vito, & Walsh, 2012; Ortmeier, 1997, 2006; Ortmeier & Meese, 2010).

Think of someone you know whom you consider an effective leader. In your view, what makes this individual an effective leader? Consider the individual's personal characteristics, skills, behaviors, and impact on others.

Behavioral Assumptions and Leadership Style

Numerous factors and conditions operate to create behavioral assumptions that influence a person's perception of another individual, circumstances, and leadership style (Adler & Towne, 2007). Behavioral assumptions about people and how to motivate them influence leader behavior. If a leader harbors false assumptions about people, the beliefs can cause a leader to use inappropriate motivational techniques with followers. Correct behavioral assumptions can result in positive outcomes (Fournies, 2000). Although many of the assumptions and the accompanying models for direction and control of human beings were developed for managerial personnel, the concepts apply to leaders as well. Four specific theories, perspectives, or models that explain the interrelationship of effective leadership and human motivation and behavior include Theory X and Y, the Managerial Grip, the Situational Leadership Model, and Path-Goal Leadership.

One of the most widely quoted models for recognizing and distinguishing assumptions about motivation was developed by Douglas McGregor in the 1950s. In his classic work, *The Human Side of Enterprise*, McGregor (1960) explored theoretical assumptions about human nature and human behavior as it relates to ethics, management, leadership, and motivation. McGregor proposed that two sets of leadership or managerial assumptions regarding human behavior appear to exist. He referred to the traditional view of leadership and managerial direction and control as Theory X and the view that leadership and management should be based on the integration of individual and organizational goals as Theory Y. Theory X includes the following leadership and managerial assumptions:

> **Theory X** Leadership and managerial assumption that employees dislike work and will avoid work if possible.

- The average human being has an inherent dislike of work and will avoid work if possible.
- Because of the dislike for work, most people must be coerced, controlled, directed, or threatened with punishment to get them to put forth adequate effort toward the achievement of objectives.
- The average human being is self-centered, prefers to be directed, wishes to avoid responsibility, has relatively little ambition, and wants security above all.

> **Theory Y** Leadership and managerial assumption that assumes that employees are ready to work for individual and group goals.

McGregor suggested that Theory X leaders and managers did not account for critical factors associated with motivation. These factors include a few simple generalizations about human beings. First, human beings are "wanting" animals. As soon as one need is satisfied, it is replaced with another. Second, human needs are organized in a hierarchy of importance. Third, a satisfied need is not a motivator of behavior. According to McGregor, Theory X leaders and managers ignore these generalizations. They direct and control through the exercise of authority.

Theory Y leaders and managers, on the other hand, operate with a different set of assumptions regarding human behavior. Theory Y assumptions include the following:

- The expenditure of physical and mental effort in work is as natural as play or rest.
- External control and the threat of punishment are not the only means for bringing about effort toward objectives. People will exercise self-direction and self-control in the service of objectives to which they are committed.

- Commitment to objectives is a function of the rewards associated with their achievement.

- The average human being learns, under proper conditions, to accept as well as seek responsibility.

- The capacity to exercise a relatively high degree of imagination, ingenuity, and creativity in the solution to problems is widely, not narrowly, distributed in the population.

- Under the conditions of modern industrial life, the intellectual potentialities of the average human being are only partially realized (McGregor, 1960).

Theory Y assumptions are dynamic rather than static, and they represent significantly different implications for leadership and management than do Theory X assumptions. Theory Y assumptions focus on human growth. Theory X leaders and managers blame followers and workers for failure to achieve goals. Theory Y implies that poor productivity is more often the result of poor leadership and management. Theory Y focuses on the integration of goals: the creation of conditions through which members of a group or organization may achieve their own goals as well as the goals of the enterprise. Thus, motivation, the potential for growth, the ability to assume responsibility, and the readiness to work toward individual as well as group goals are present in all people. The leader's responsibility is to recognize, harness, and channel these characteristics toward common goals by creating a climate and methodology conducive to success (Gomez-Mejia & Balkin, 2012; Hellriegel, Jackson, & Slocum, 2005; McGregor, 1960).

An adaptation of Theory Y, called Theory Z, was created by William Ouchi in the early 1980s. Theory Z is a leadership and management style that advocates trusting followers and employees and creating an environment in which followers and employees feel as though they are an integral part of the group or organization. According to Theory Z, a relationship of trust promotes increased productivity and goal achievement (Ouchi, 1981).

> **managerial grid** Five leadership styles that integrate varying degrees of concern for people and production.

The managerial grid developed by Robert Blake and Jane Mouton (1985) identifies five leadership styles that integrate varying degrees of concern for people with concern for production and goal achievement (Figure 10-1 ■). Blake and Mouton's five leadership styles are arranged on a grid. The impoverished leadership style (1,1) demonstrates low concern for people, production, and goal achievement. Leaders utilizing this style exert minimal effort and wish to maintain the status quo. Through the country club style (1,9), leaders demonstrate high concern for people but low concern for production and goal achievement. Leaders create a secure and comfortable environment in the hope that followers will produce. Low concern for people and high concern for production and goal achievement characterize the produce or perish leadership style (9,1). Leaders use coercive powers to achieve results and show little concern for the personal needs of followers. Through the middle-of-the-road style (5,5), leaders strive to balance follower personal needs with a concern for productivity and goal achievement. Through the team style (9,9), leaders demonstrate high concern for people as well as productivity and goal achievement. Blake and Mouton believed that 9,9 was the optimal style. The 9,9 approach is consistent with McGregor's Theory Y. Leaders at 9,9 strive for teamwork and commitment to goal achievement among team members.

> **Situational Leadership Model** Leadership and managerial model that suggests that supportive (people-centered) and directive (production- and goal-centered) leadership behaviors should be contingent on the readiness level of followers and workers.

Paul Hersey and Ken Blanchard (1982) created a Situational Leadership Model that suggests that supportive (people-centered) and directive (production- and goal-centered) leadership behaviors should be contingent on the readiness level of followers and workers. Supportive leadership behavior is consistent with open communication links between a leader and followers. Leaders listen, encourage, and involve followers in decision-making. Directive leadership behaviors are consistent with situations requiring structure, control, direct supervision, and a reliance on one-way (leader-to-follower) communication.

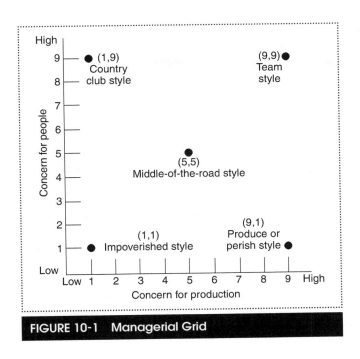

FIGURE 10-1   Managerial Grid

Follower readiness (maturity, experience, expertise) determines the follower's ability to set high and attainable task-related goals and willingness to assume responsibility for achieving the goals. The level of supportive or directive leadership behaviors is dependent on different levels of follower readiness. According to the Situational Leadership Model, leaders use a delegating, participating, selling, or telling style, depending on follower readiness.

The leadership style with the highest probability of successfully and effectively inducing the desired behaviors of a follower who is skilled, competent, and motivated is that of delegating. This involves monitoring and observing on the part of the leader. This kind of empowering behavior should only be entered into with a follower who is in fact demonstrating at a sustained and acceptable level, otherwise the leader risks making followers feel abandoned. The participating leadership style is used to encourage, assist, and maintain communication between the leader and follower when the follower is performing at a sustained and acceptable level, but may be feeling a little insecure about the leader completely backing off or fully empowering the employee. These individuals do not need to be told how to do the task anymore because the follower is performing, but they do need some help from their leader to build their confidence in their own ability. The selling style requires the most actions from a leader. It is used appropriately when a follower is starting to perform or is new to a task and is also willing, committed, or motivated to perform. The follower needs not only the task direction from the leader like how and when to do the job, but also the support and encouragement to achieve the specific tasks. The telling style is used appropriately for those followers who not only are not performing but are either insecure about their ability to do so or downright unwilling to do the task. In this instance, followers need clear and specific instructions and possibly even consequences for nonperformance. Relationship or supportive behavior at this juncture could be misconstrued by followers as confirming their level of performance as acceptable if the leader is not careful to tie it incrementally and specifically with improvements in performance (Hersey & Blanchard, 1982; Hersey, Blanchard, & Johnson, 2008).

Path-Goal Leadership A leadership theory that assumes that followers will be motivated if they believe that that they are capable of performing tasks assigned, that their efforts will result in a certain result, and that the rewards for completing the tasks are worthwhile.

Although many leadership theories include motivation of others as an objective, the stated purpose of Path-Goal Leadership is to enhance performance and satisfaction by focusing on motivation as a primary ingredient of leadership. The underlying assumption of Path-Goal Leadership theory is that followers will be motivated if they believe that they are capable of performing tasks assigned, that their efforts will result in a certain result, and that the rewards for completing the tasks are worthwhile. Through the application of path-goal theory, the leader's challenge is to select the correct "path" and implement a leadership style that best meets a follower's motivational needs to achieve the end goal.

Although complex, the application of the path-goal theory of leadership considers leadership behaviors, follower characteristics, and task and environmental characteristics. The theory suggests that there are four types of leadership behaviors that can be used: (1) directive, where a leader tells subordinates what needs to be done, guiding them in the process; (2) supportive, which considers the needs of the workers and their welfare, supporting them through the task; (3) participative, which involves consulting with workers for their advice on how the task should be done; and (4) achievement oriented, where the leader has faith in the workers and sets challenging tasks for them, enhancing their passion and drive to excel. Which leadership behavior is used also is contingent on what followers need, want, or prefer in the context of leadership. This theory also proposes that the specific task and environment also determines leadership behaviors. For example, common tasks will require minimal intervention by leaders. Meanwhile, more complex and unique tasks may require leaders to "step in," find alternatives, and remove any "roadblocks" that exist (House, 1996; Meese & Ortmeier, 2004; Northouse, 2010).

▶ Ensuring Ethics and Integrity

ethics A branch of philosophy that studies morality. Involves moral principles and focuses on the concepts of right and wrong and standards of behavior.

morality The standards, beliefs, or intangible principles of what is good or bad, or right or wrong.

unethical Lacking moral principles; not willing to follow rules and codes of conduct.

integrity A person who has sound moral principles and the quality of being honest.

values Beliefs of a person, group, organization, and society that are considered worthwhile upon which personal decisions and conduct are based.

The role of any manager, supervisor, and employee, as well as organizations themselves is to be ethical. Ethics is a branch of philosophy that studies morality. Morality, meanwhile, can be understood as the standards, beliefs, or intangible principles of what is good or bad, or right or wrong. Morally correct values are at the core of ethical behavior. Doing the right thing at the right time, delivering what is promised, taking responsibility for one's own actions, and treating others with courtesy and respect lie at the heart of ethical conduct. These standards are based on ethical principles that have been developed through a person's education and life experiences and through the actions of organizations (also referred to as business ethics) that create ethical codes of conduct that they expect individuals to follow. In some cases, however, the examination of a person's (or an organization's) actions or beliefs could lead another to conclude that the individual was unethical; this individual did not conform to the acceptable or approved standards of personal, social, or business standards—the person lacked moral principles when acting. If a person has sound moral principles, then he or she is said to have integrity. The lack of integrity, meanwhile, can result in the person or organization being perceived as unethical.

Another term often used in the study of ethics is values. Values are the beliefs of a person, group, organization, and society that are considered worthwhile upon which personal decisions and conduct are based. These values are general beliefs that are important to the individual, group, or organization (Dean, 1994). Values provide behavioral rules and actions that are not based on "right or wrong," which is the case with morals. These can include societal values that are based on the norms of the community, organizational values that represent the beliefs of an organization, and professional values that are reflected by an occupation or discipline. These values may be ethical or unethical. For example, criminals have values, but their behaviors may be unethical. In the field of policing, a common subcultural value is secrecy and not "ratting on" or reporting fellow officers who engaged in unethical and criminal activities (Crank & Crank, 2014).

According to Raiborn and Payne (1990), there are four fundamental ethical principles that are used to make decisions. They include integrity, justice, competence, and utility: "integrity means to be of sound moral principle, to have the characteristics of honesty, sincerity, and candor [being open and telling the truth, even though a person may not want to hear the truth]. Justice reflects impartiality, conscientiousness and good faith. Competence is defined as capable, reliable, and duly qualified. Utility indicates a quality if being useful and philosophical, providing the greatest good for the greatest number (or the least harm to the greatest number)" (pp. 884–885).

Ethical principles can be applied using four different standards. From the lowest to the highest levels, they include: (1) basic, which can be considered minimally accepted behaviors, such as the letter of the law; (2) currently attainable, which is behavior that is deemed basically moral by society; (3) practical, which is achievable but nevertheless difficult, requiring extreme diligence to achieve; and (4) theoretical, where the decision is made in the spirit of morality and would have the highest potential for good (Raiborn & Payne, 1990).

Two examples show the differences among these standards. First, OSHA regulations establish minimum workplace health and safety standards—a basic standard. While "ethical" because a company is meeting the law, an employee's health and safety might be enhanced significantly if the employer sets standards for employee safety that are higher than the OSHA-established minimums. In many cases, these standards are attainable ethical standards that can be achieved through increased training and the installation of increased safety measures that exceed OSHA standards that will result in greater levels of worker safety. Additionally, the employer can also strive for the higher practical and theoretical standards to further ensure that employees are safe and protected from workplace hazards. Second, consider the example of a homeless person trespassing on company property. Per company policy unauthorized individuals must be removed by security personnel. Removing this person has achieved the basic ethical standard of "doing one's job." However, the security officer who removed the individual now calls a homeless shelter (or a social service agency) to ensure that the person has a secure and warm shelter for the evening. At the basic ethical standard, all the officer had to do was remove the person from company property—that was the minimal or basic ethical requirement—doing one's job. At a higher ethical standard, meanwhile, the officer recognized that he/she could help the person too, demonstrating a higher attainable ethical standard that required just a little more work on his/her part to achieve a "higher" ethical end goal.

These two examples also show that personal choice is a factor in ethical conduct. Meese and Ortmeier (2004) write about choices in decisions and ethics. They state that the importance of choice in ethics is often confused with the notion that values are subjective and people merely choose their own set of values. This assumption is misleading because most ethical decisions involve a choice between already established possibilities. Personal moral values are rarely one's own values alone. By their very nature, values are shared and exist outside those who embrace the values. A person does not choose the alternative. Rather, the person chooses among alternatives. Most people live in a pluralist society, an environment with no single code of ethics but several sets of moral values emanating from a variety of cultures and subcultures. For example, members of a street gang may subscribe to a particular set of values where they may not believe it unethical to kill a rival gang member. A security person may be reluctant to intervene to stop another's inappropriate behavior. Although it may be incorrect, this is the security person's choice. The individual challenge oftentimes is to choose and follow an appropriate set of values.

Ethical Dilemmas

ethical dilemma
Occurs when a person
has the choice
between two or more
different ethical
options.

In some cases, individuals encounter ethical dilemmas in their personal and professional lives. An ethical dilemma occurs when a person has a choice between two or more different ethical options. However, none of the options will fully resolve the issue and it brings about a negative consequence based on personal and societal morals. A genuine moral dilemma occurs in a situation from which the decision-maker cannot emerge "clean," no matter what the decision. Some common unresolvable moral dilemmas are often related to conflicts between the law, religion, and morality. Depending upon the issue, resolving these moral dilemmas can be stressful and difficult. A proper resolution of a moral dilemma involves using logic and philosophy to generate the "best" action by carefully inspecting the elements of the situation, identifying principles involved, and then deciding upon what principle takes precedence in the particular situation (Langlois, Lapointe, Valois, & de Leeuw, 2014).

Some contemporary ethical dilemmas facing the security industry include the use of Private Military Companies (PMCs) as force multipliers in state-sponsored wars throughout the world. In these situations, private security personnel may be involved in force situations that could result in the death of civilian populations, leading to a moral dilemma related to profit over human rights (Lucas, 2015). At the individual level, meanwhile, security personnel face moral dilemmas continually. For example, can falsifying information in a report to achieve a good end (convicting a known internal thief) be justification for using unethical and possibly illegal means, to achieve this end? Could inaction lead to a lawsuit by the victim of the dangerous person who was not apprehended because ethical means to arrest were not available? Other common dilemmas include seeing unethical activities (theft, misuse of property, time fraud) in the workplace where a person's loyalty to the organization or loyalty to a coworker may create a moral dilemma on what to do. In many cases, these ethical dilemmas are easy to resolve. In other cases, meanwhile, they may call for intense thought and deliberation requiring time and consultation with others.

Unethical Activities

Unfortunately, unethical activities occur among employees, within organizations and even by organizations. Certain cognitive processes and socialization with others reinforce unethical conduct and influence the onset and proliferation of undesirable behaviors. Thus, psychological and social forces help produce misconduct and unethical actions. However, one should not lose sight of the role of choice when engaged in unethical and unprofessional conduct. Given a security person's position of trust, unethical (even illegal) behavior results when the person makes a conscious decision to act in a way that is not appropriate to the situation. While circumstantial reasons, peer pressure, loyalties, social factors, or psychological problems may exist, or there is a corporate culture that promotes unethical activities, the fundamental ingredient for unethical conduct is a conscious decision by the actor.

Potential ethical problem areas in security management include corruption, discrimination, violation of rights to privacy, violation of rights under the U.S. Constitution, negligence, use of excessive force, violations of organizational policies or procedures, and violations of any existing professional code of ethics. Although real or imagined unethical behavior may involve a very small number of individuals, the negative impact of this behavior can be devastating. People engage in unethical conduct when they accept gratuities, practice racism and discrimination, misuse privileged communications and confidential information, misappropriate property, obstruct justice, engage in inappropriate behaviors, and invoke a code of silence with respect to another person's unethical behavior (Byers, 2000; Foss, 2003; Ortmeier, 2006; Ortmeier & Meese, 2010; Solomon, 1996).

Ethical Standards

To control and prevent unethical actions, organizations must have ethical standards. Ethical standards dictate behavior(s) when law or precedent, which may prescribe appropriate behavior(s), does not exist. Whenever one possesses the power of discretional decision-making, the decision should conform to what one ought to do. The ends do not always justify the means. Conducting oneself according to an acceptable ethical standard means doing the right thing at the right time. Maintenance of personnel and personal integrity in organizations is paramount. It involves more than effective pre-employment screening procedures, periodic performance appraisals, and internal security controls. Personnel integrity also involves promotion of and adherence to a code of ethics and appropriate standards of professional conduct. Most institutions, agencies, and professions have a code of ethics that prescribes ethical conduct. As exemplified by the ASIS International Code of Ethics, standards of ethical behavior must emanate from the organization as well as the individual. This ASIS Code of Ethics can be found in Box 10-2.

> **ethical standards**
> Standards that dictate behavior when law or precedent, which may prescribe behavior, does not exist.

> **code of ethics**
> Standards of professional conduct.

Ethical Leadership

Today organizations require ethical leadership. Ethical leadership is defined as "the demonstration of normatively appropriate conduct through personal actions and interpersonal relationships, and the promotion of such conduct to followers through two-way communication, reinforcement, and decision-making" (Brown, Treviño, & Harrison, 2005, p. 120). Ethical leadership is every person's responsibility. As already indicated in this chapter, leadership is a trait and an attitude. It is not a position. Every person in an organization can and should assume an ethical leadership role. To be an ethical leader, some researchers propose that a person first needs to have a high moral identity, which then guides and regulates his or her moral actions. These moral actions then translate into actions that are consistent with what is means to be a moral person, resulting in that person being perceived as an ethical leader (Mayer, Aquino, Greenbaum, & Kuenzi, 2012). Ethical leadership can also be considered to be altruistic in nature. It is not egoistic in nature where the person is interested in his or her own personal gain. Instead, actions and decisions are made in the context of "what is best in the context of the greatest good for the greatest number."

> **ethical leadership**
> Demonstration of normatively appropriate conduct through personal actions and interpersonal relationships, the promotion of such conduct to followers through two-way communication, reinforcement, and decision-making.

Any ethical leadership program rests on the two pillars of the manager as a moral person and as a moral manager. As a moral person, managers must project to employees that they possess certain traits, behaviors, and decisions that are ethical. Some of these traits include integrity, honesty, and trustworthiness. Next, ethical leaders demonstrate ethical behaviors through their actions. Some of these actions include: (1) "doing the right thing" or engaging in activities that are morally correct; (2) showing concern for people by treating them with respect, dignity, and trust; (3) being open (having candor), which involves being a good listener and approachable where employees can share their concerns and issues without fear of reprisal; and (4) personal morality, which requires making sure that a manager's personal morality is not in question. Last, in their role as a decision-maker, ethical leaders also have and hold onto a core set of ethical values and principles; they are fair and objective; they have a concern and ethical sensitivity for the community and society; and, they follow ethical decision rules (Trevino, Hartman, & Brown, 2000). One common decision rule is based on the "Golden Rule" (e.g., "do unto others as you would have them do unto you"). Another way to see if one's actions are ethical is to consider if the decision was televised in the local nightly news where the public could see and judge the person's actions to determine if they were ethical. These components of a moral person will also serve to establish what the manager will most likely do in situations.

The second pillar of ethical leadership involves taking the ethical moral message to the rest of the organization—moral managing. As a moral manager, individuals must make ethics an obvious and recognized component of their leadership style. By placing ethics at the forefront of all activities, employees will know what is expected and how to act. These ethical values will then serve as a "glue" that holds organizations together. Some of the key elements of moral managing include engaging in visible actions "modeling the way," while also recognizing that both actions and words can have a profound impact on how other employees perceive what is right or wrong, impacting how they will act. Next, moral managers also communicate their ethics to others on what the organization expects and values; this will serve to educate and guide other employees when making ethical decisions. Last, managers should reward employees for following organizational values and making ethical decisions; they also discipline employees for unethical conduct (Trevino et al., 2000).

Ethical leadership is critical to the success of an organization. It has been found to be associated with transformational leadership, employee willingness to put more effort into his or her work (organizational commitment), and higher levels of job satisfaction (Kim & Brymer, 2011). Ethical leadership also promotes ethical conduct, resulting in increased levels of organizational citizenship behaviors, less misconduct and absenteeism, while making the organization more credible in the business community and attractive for future employees (Dinc & Aydemir, 2014). Conversely, unethical "bad leaders" who engage in deceptive activities can create dysfunctional environments leading to increased absenteeism, low morale, increased employee turnover, decreased levels of job satisfaction, and reduced productivity (Erickson, Shaw, & Agabe, 2007).

In the context of public and private administration alike, some observers have begun advocating a new model of leadership focused on managerial judgment and practice grounded in ethics. According to Haque (2011), the primary force behind the recent worldwide global recession—marked by trillions of dollars of financial assets destroyed, trillions of dollars in shareholder value vanished, and stalling worldwide gross domestic product (GDP)—is overreliance on outdated Industrial Age leadership ideals. These ideals include rampant exploitation of resources and top-down command of resource allocations, as well as withholding of information from stakeholders to control them and a single-minded pursuit of profit for its own sake. All of these actions could be considered unethical.

Haque maintains that adherence to these ideals has produced "thin value"—short-term economic gains that accrue to some people far more than others, and that have not made people happier or healthier (e.g., a greater good). It has left resources depleted and has spawned conflict, organizational rigidity, economic stagnation, and nihilism. To reverse the situation, public and private organizations must adopt a new set of ideals:

- *Renewal*—Use resources sustainably to maximize efficiencies.
- *Democracy*—Allocate resources democratically to foster organizational agility.
- *Peace*—Practice economic nonviolence in business.
- *Equity*—Create industries that make the least well off better off.
- *Meaning*—Generate payoffs that tangibly improve quality of life.

While adopting these ideals requires ambitious and sustained changes in administration and management practices, some organizations (Haque cites Google, Wal-Mart, and Nike as examples) have begun making those changes and generating attention-getting results. The willingness and ability to change demonstrated by such renowned organizations suggest that more ethical models of leadership—models that create more value for more people than value created through Industrial Age ideals—are possible.

The ASIS Code of Ethics

Many security organizations have a code of conduct or ethical statements. In most cases, these ethical statements exist in policy and procedure manuals and are "brought to life" through ethical conduct and leadership in the organization. Besides internally generated statements and beliefs, the American Society for Industrial Security International (ASIS) has created its own code of conduct for its members and the security industry. This Code of Ethics is shown in Box 10-2.

BOX 10-2

ASIS CODE OF ETHICS

PREAMBLE

Aware that the quality of professional security ultimately depends upon the willingness of practitioners to observe special standards of conduct and to manifest good faith in professional relationships, the American Society for Industrial Security adopted the following code of ethics and mandates its conscientious observance as a binding condition of membership in or affiliation with the Society:

ARTICLE I

A member shall perform professional duties in accordance with the law and the highest moral principles.

Ethical Considerations

I-1   A member shall abide by the law of the land in which the services are rendered and perform all duties in an honorable manner.

I-2   A member shall not knowingly become associated in responsibility for work with colleagues who do not conform to the law and these ethical standards.

I-3   A member shall be just and respect the rights of others in performing professional responsibilities.

ARTICLE II

A member shall observe the precepts of truthfulness, honesty, and integrity.

Ethical Considerations

II-1   A member shall disclose all relevant information to those having a right to know.

II-2   A right to know is a legally enforceable claim or demand by a person for disclosure of information by a member. Such a right does not depend upon prior knowledge by the person of the existence of the information to be disclosed.

II-3   A member shall not knowingly release misleading information nor encourage or otherwise participate in the release of such information.

ARTICLE III

A member shall be faithful and diligent in discharging professional responsibilities.

Ethical Considerations

III-1   A member is faithful when fair and steadfast in adherence to promises and commitments.

III-2   A member is diligent when employing best efforts in an assignment.

III-3   A member shall not act in matters involving conflicts of interest without appropriate disclosure and approval.

III-4   A member shall represent services or products fairly and truthfully.

ARTICLE IV

A member shall be competent in discharging professional responsibilities.

Ethical Considerations

IV-1   A member is competent who possesses and applies the skills and knowledge required for the task.

IV-2   A member shall not accept a task beyond the member's competence nor shall competence be claimed when not possessed.

(Continued)

BOX 10-2 (*Continued*)

ARTICLE V

A member shall safeguard confidential information and exercise due care to prevent its improper disclosure.

Ethical Considerations

V-1   Confidential information is nonpublic information, the disclosure of which is restricted.

V-2   Due care requires that the professional must not knowingly reveal confidential information or use a confidence to the disadvantage of the principal or to the advantage of the member or a third person unless the principal consents after full disclosure of all the facts. This confidentiality continues after the business relationship between the member and the principal has terminated.

V-3   A member who receives information and has not agreed to be bound by confidentiality is not bound from disclosing it. A member is not bound by confidential disclosures made of acts or omissions which constitute a violation of law.

V-4   Confidential disclosures made by a principal to a member are not recognized by law as privileged in a legal proceeding. The member may be required to testify in a legal proceeding to information received in confidence from the principal over the objection of the principal's counsel.

V-5   A member shall not disclose confidential information for personal gain without appropriate authorization.

ARTICLE VI

A member shall not maliciously injure the professional reputation or practice of colleagues, clients, or employers.

Ethical Considerations

VI-1   A member shall not comment falsely and with malice concerning a colleague's competence, performance, or professional capabilities.

VI-2   A member who knows, or has reasonable grounds to believe, that another member has failed to conform to the Society's Code of Ethics shall present such information to the Ethical Standards Committee in accordance with Article XIV of the Society's Bylaws (ASIS International, 2007).

Source: From Code of Ethics © 2016. Used by permission of American Society for Industrial Security International (ASIS).

Summary

This chapter examines security administration in the context of management, supervision, and leadership. In order to be successful, security organizations must be properly supervised, managed, and led. Regardless of the fact if the security organization operates or is part of the public or private sector, individuals have a variety of administrative activities to carry out to achieve organizational goals and objectives. These activities may differ according to if they exist in the public or private sectors. However, a common denominator is that organizations need effective managers. Managers perform a variety of functions that include planning, organizing, staffing, directing, coordinating, reporting, and budgeting (POSDCORB). Their functions can also be examined in the context of their interpersonal, informational, and decisional roles

they perform, and can also be analyzed on strategic, tactical, and operational management.

Managerial roles are contingent upon how jobs are designed and performed. One of the early models to design jobs and manage was based on Scientific Management that required a systematic analysis of the job and the correct ways for employees to perform the work. Later, with the emergence of human relations movement, the management of organizations shifted from solely production needs to the concern for the worker and participative management. All organizations also need effective supervisors who have an internal focus, working directly with the line level employees, overseeing their work-related activities, and dealing with the repetitious issues related to employees and production.

Regardless of the actual position held, this chapter has also shown the need for effective leadership. Leadership is an attribute and attitude that should be held and used by all the members of the organization. Leadership is not a position. Individuals should strive to be transformational and possess some key competencies where they develop and coach others, articulating a vision and modeling the way. Of paramount importance is that leaders (and all employees) be ethical where morally correct values are at the core of ethical behavior. In the case of managers, meanwhile, their actions need to rest on the pillars of the manager being a moral person and a moral manager. By ensuring ethics at the forefront of all activities, employees will know what is expected and how to act in the workplace. External stakeholders, meanwhile, will have an increased respect for employees and the company itself.

Key Terms and Concepts

Administration *217*

Bureaucracy *217*

Code of ethics *233*

Decisional roles *220*

Ethical dilemmas *232*

Ethical leadership *233*

Ethical standards *233*

Ethics *230*

Hawthorne effect *222*

Hierarchical organizational structure *220*

Human Relations Movement *222*

Informational role *220*

Integrity *230*

Interpersonal role *220*

Leadership *223*

Operational management *221*

Management *219*

Management levels *220*

Managerial grid *228*

Max Weber's Theory of Bureaucracy *217*

Morality *230*

Path-Goal Leadership *230*

POSDCORB *219*

Post-bureaucratic organizations *219*

Public administration *217*

Scientific management *221*

Situational Leadership Model *228*

Supervision *223*

Tactical management *221*

Theory X *227*

Theory Y *227*

Transactional leadership *225*

Transformational leadership *225*

Unethical *230*

Values *230*

Discussion Questions and Exercises

1. What is the difference between a manager and supervisor? What are their main responsibilities in organizations?
2. Define leadership. What are some attributes of a good leader?
3. What are some of the core functions of management? What are the three managerial behaviors according to Mintzberg?
4. What are the key elements of Scientific Management and the Human Relations Movement?
5. What are the six points or elements of a bureaucracy, according to Weber?
6. Explain Theory X and Theory Y. How does this theory tie into the management and supervision practices?
7. Explain the Managerial Grid. What is the worst style of leadership? Why? Which is considered the "best" type of leadership? Why?
8. Explain the Situational Leadership Model. What are the main elements of this model?
9. Define ethics? What are morals? What are values? What is an ethical dilemma?
10. What is ethical leadership? What are the two pillars of any ethical leadership program?

Careers in Security Management

The review of career-related sites on the Internet shows the many opportunities in security management. Oftentimes, these positions are direct hire. In other cases, individuals will need to start at an entry level position to learn about the organization and then be promoted to a managerial position. Regardless of the entry point, careers exist in both the contract and proprietary sectors. Depending upon the sector, experience, and degrees held by the applicant, entry-level salaries range from $40 to $60,000. Advanced managerial positions can easily reach $80–$100,000 (or higher) annually.

Your Turn

Demonstrating Ethical Leadership in the Face of Workplace Theft

Surveys indicate that many workers are reluctant to report unethical practices, including stealing, in the workplace. Although a federal law (Sarbanes-Oxley) was passed to counter unethical corporate behavior and protect workers who report unethical activities, many employees still face loss of their jobs or ridicule if they "whistleblow" on corporate misconduct (Spherion, 2006).

Furthermore, it has been reported that nearly 25 percent of young workers aged 18–24 do not believe that stealing office supplies for personal use is wrong. Many steal employer property, including pens, pencils, paper, self-adhesive notepads, and paper clips without regard to the activity's illegality. Employee theft costs American businesses over $40 billion each year (Wulfhorst, 2006).

Unethical behavior, dishonesty, and theft in the workplace often occur in a gradual incremental process. Theft, in particular, stems from a complex set of causes. Foremost among them is simply that an opportunity to steal arises, because the chances of getting caught are low. Additional causes include low workforce morale, employees' sense that they are being underpaid, and minimal consequences for getting caught stealing (Walsh, 2000).

As seemingly insignificant misconduct and theft go undetected, perpetrators often rationalize larger transgressions. Even high level executives can become tempted to steal. Consider Dale Frantz, the former chief information officer of Auto Warehousing Company. Frantz embezzled more than $500,000 from his company during 2007–2009 and was sentenced to nearly 6 years in prison. He used a number of strategies to steal the funds, including writing up fraudulent invoices for expense reports and changing legitimate reports to maximize his reimbursements. In addition, he used company funds to buy computer equipment that he resold on the Internet (McMillan, 2010).

1. Do you believe that ethical behavior can be learned? If yes, who do you believe should take responsibility for teaching ethics?

2. If you observed a theft in your workplace, would you assume a leadership role and take action against the misconduct? If yes, what action(s) would you take?

3. Given your knowledge of the causes behind workplace theft, what steps would you advise organizations to take in order to discourage and minimize stealing by employees and thereby protect the organization's assets?

4. How would you go about strengthening your ethical leadership skills?

Simulation exercises may be used to rehearse responses to various security scenarios such as armed security personnel conducting a simulation at a nuclear power facility.

11   Managing People and Organizations

LEARNING OBJECTIVES

After completing this chapter, the reader should be able to:

1. explain the purpose of recruitment and selection
2. describe some of the techniques used in the recruitment and selection process
3. define and explain negligent hiring and retention
4. identify the purpose and methods used in employee development and training programs
5. explain the purpose of employee performance appraisals
6. explain the difference between a policy and a procedure
7. identify some of the key elements and issues related to scheduling
8. explain and describe plans, goals, and objectives
9. distinguish between and explain the different types of plans used in organizations
10. discuss and explain budgeting and different types of budgets

▶ Introduction

Regardless of the position held in an organization, it is important to understand what managers do and the logic or purpose of these diverse activities. This chapter reviews some core managerial responsibilities found in the proprietary and contract sectors of the security industry. Some specific human resource functions that are examined in this chapter include personnel recruitment and selection, employee training and development, and performance appraisals. Legal issues related to negligent hiring and retention and the use of off-duty officers are also analyzed. Additionally, the key elements of policies and procedures, scheduling, planning, and budgeting are reviewed.

▶ Personnel Recruitment and Selection

Recruitment and selection activities are important in ensuring that organizations have the correct human resources to successfully perform all job functions while maintaining a competitive advantage in the marketplace. Without an effective recruitment and selection process, organizations can experience high turnover rates and churn. Turnover is the voluntary quit of an employee from the organization who moves on to a new position; it is the rotation of workers out of the organization in a given time period (Price, 1977). In the field of private security, historically, the turnover rate in some sectors was (and still is) high, ranging between 100 and 300 percent in some cases (Cunningham & Taylor, 1985). Churn, meanwhile, is when the agency has no appreciable gain in the quality and skill levels of new employees that are hired (Johnson, 2005). A properly designed and administered recruitment and selection process can ensure higher rates of retention, reducing employee turnover and churn.

Recruitment is the process of attracting and finding suitable candidates for job vacancies in the organization. It is a process that "encompasses all organizational practices and decisions that affect either the number or type of individuals who are willing to apply for, or to accept a given vacancy" (Rynes, 1990, p. 5). The goal of any recruitment process is to create a qualified pool of candidates. From this pool of applicants, an organization can then select the best qualified person, based on the identified predetermined knowledge, skills, and abilities (KSAs) that are needed for that particular position (Jain, 2014). Personnel selection, meanwhile, is the process of evaluating and choosing the most appropriate and qualified candidate for the job from the pool of applicants based on the existing selection criteria used (Gatewood, Feild, & Barrick, 2010).

Recruiting candidates for a vacancy is conducted in a variety of ways. In some cases, organizations already possess the necessary talent and can use the internal labor market (ILM) to find candidates inside the company, filling the position through promotion or transfer instead of looking outward (Bidwell & Keller, 2014). Externally, the recruitment process may involve newspaper and trade journal advertising, college and university career fairs, the Internet, former employees, friends and relatives of employees, applications on file, labor organizations, employment agencies, and community job fairs. Recruiting acceptable candidates is critical and it can be difficult. During good economic times, organizations may find it even more challenging to recruit new hires due to the lack of interested or available candidates. Numerous laws also regulate the employment process, making the recruitment (and selection process) complex and time consuming.

Following the recruitment stage, various selection tools are used to find the most qualified applicant. The selection process begins with a preliminary pre-employment screening to determine the applicant's suitability for employment. These pre-employment screening tools "affords an employer multiple "touch points" where it can assess an individual's qualifications, personality, and potentially eliminate applicants with a violent past or a disposition that places them at risk to commit an act of violence in the workplace" (Sugahara & Sugahara, 2014, p. 187). The primary goal of these selection tools is to find the most qualified applicant for the position. Depending upon the position and organizational preferences, common selection tools include the job application, resume, aptitude tests, psychological and integrity (honesty) tests; appropriate physical agility or fitness tests; a medical examination; criminal history, driving record, and credit checks; and, an interview (Johnson, 2005; Moran, 2011).

Hiring Off-duty Police Officers

Some interesting situations may develop when private organizations employ off-duty public law enforcement officers (called moonlighting) to work in a private security setting. Although the reasons (more training and the ability to exercise public police powers) for employment of off-duty public law enforcement officers are legitimate and understandable, private employers should be aware of the potential legal implications that may arise when private security personnel have public police powers. One particular legal issue is related to operating under the color of law where police officers and their employer(s) can be sued under federal statute U.S.C. 42 §1983 if this "color of law" standard is proven.

Generally, private organizations cannot be sued under Section 1983 because they are not a governmental entity and employees are not considered under law to be performing public functions as "state agents." However, when a private entity hires off-duty police officers, it can expose itself to liability under Section 1983 if these individuals use specific powers granted to them through their public employer. While this standard is sometimes vague and inconsistent among the federal courts, two main elements that are often considered to establish "acting under color of law" is if the off-duty officer used official powers of his or her public office to accomplish the harm and if the victim reasonably believed that a government employee was causing the harm and the person committing the harm used this belief to achieve or complete the damage, injury, or harm (Miller, 2015). Although the respondent to a lawsuit may prevail, the cost of defending one's actions could be quite expensive. To avoid these claims, adequate training is one way to reduce liability. Off-duty police officers should be trained in the law as it relates to private security operations, restricting their official police powers in the course of activities as a private security officer. Most important, private employers who employ off-duty police officers in a security capacity should be aware that unique legal issues arise in a public police officer–private employer relationship (Nemeth, 2005; Ortmeier & Meese, 2010; Peck, 1999).

> **color of law** A legal standard. A person who is operating under *authority of* any *law*, statute, ordinance, regulation, or custom.

Negligent Hiring and Retention

The hiring of an employee must be more than an intuitive guess. Although state and federal privacy statutes make pre-employment screening challenging, failure to complete a diligent inquiry into the suitability of persons employed may constitute negligent hiring and can have devastating consequences for the organization. Poor hiring decisions result in losses due to theft, high attrition rates, increased insurance claims and premiums, vicarious liability, and negligent hiring lawsuits. A thorough background investigation on a prospective employee is not a luxury, it is a necessity. As numerous court judgments show, employers are held liable for the actions of employees when the employer failed to investigate properly and the investigation would have uncovered the risk.

> **negligent hiring** Possible civil liability associated with failure to complete a diligent inquiry into the suitability of a person for employment.

The elements of negligent hiring include the following:

- The person in question was an employee of the organization.
- The employee was unfit for employment in the position.
- The employer knew or should have known the employee was unfit.
- The plaintiff was injured by the employee in the course of an employment-related activity.
- The employer owed a duty of care to the plaintiff.
- The hiring of the employee was the proximate (legal) cause of the injury to the plaintiff (Cheeseman, 2010).

An employer may also be held liable for negligent supervision or retention of an employee. Negligent retention involves a situation in which the employer does not take disciplinary or remedial action after becoming aware of a risk factor. The elements of negligent retention include the following:

> **negligent retention** Possible civil liability associated with employer's failure to take disciplinary or remedial action after becoming aware that an employee is a risk factor.

- The employee was hired by the employer.
- After hiring, the employer became aware that the employee is a potential threat or risk.
- The employer retains the employee in the position, knowing the risk.
- The plaintiff's injurious contact with the employee was connected to or within the scope of his or her employment.
- The plaintiff was injured during the contact.

To avoid negligent retention lawsuits, the employer must thoroughly investigate claims of misconduct, such as sexual harassment and violent behavior(s) on the part of any employee. If an investigation uncovers a credible issue, the employer is legally obligated to take appropriate action to remove the threat through reassignment or termination. If not, and the employee continues with the issue in question, the company may be civilly liable for the damage, injury, or harm the person(s) caused against the complainant(s). Employer liability for the actions of an employee may extend beyond the employment relationship. A former employer may be held liable if a generally positive reference is provided for a former employee, despite knowledge that the person is a potential threat (American Society for Industrial Security, 1998; Cheeseman, 2010; Hess & Wrobleski, 2009).

Two common actions that can lead to a negligent retention lawsuit include sexual harassment and a hostile work environment. Sexual harassment refers to a pattern of behaviors that involves unwelcomed lewd remarks, offensive touching, intimidation, and other conduct or communication of a sexual nature that is offensive to a reasonable person. Violent behavior may involve threats as well as acts resulting in physical contact (Bland, 2000; Cheeseman, 2010; Kovacich & Halibozek, 2003). Sexual harassment is a form of employment discrimination under Title VII of the Civil Act of 1964, as amended. A hostile work environment, meanwhile, is harassment by employees, supervisors, or the employer that is sufficiently "severe or pervasive" to create an intimidating or abusive workplace which alters the employee's work conditions (Plump & Ketchen, 2013). In these and other work-related incidents employers can be held liable if they are negligent in failing to address or prevent the actions from occurring (Davis, 2013).

► Employee Development and Training

Employee development is an ongoing process of encouraging employees to seek new forms of knowledge, skills, and abilities to ensure organizational success in the highly competitive marketplace. They are also strategic human resource efforts taken by companies to improve personal, professional, and organizational growth. It is considered to be one of the most essential functions of human resource management (Jawahar, 2012). Consider, for example, a security company that provides health and wellness programs, a workout center, and personal finance courses to employees. While these employer-initiated actions are not directly tied to work-related tasks, they nevertheless can serve to improve employee satisfaction levels and self-esteem. In turn, employees may have increased levels of motivation and performance in their work-related responsibilities.

There are basically two ways to improve the skill levels of an organization's workforce: hiring qualified individuals who already possess certain skills, and improving skill levels of employees through training. Training is the process by which employees obtain work-related skills through structured or guided ways (Westhead & Storey, 1996). Some of the benefits of training include improved productivity, better quality products or services provided, enhanced morale, and increased customer satisfaction. Training may serve as a liability reduction tool. However, employee training programs can also be expensive due in part to workers being paid to go to training sessions and the costs directly related to training (Johnson, 2005). Regardless of cost, the economic benefits of training have been reported to be more than the costs related to turnover and hiring new employees (Becker, 2011).

In order to determine what type of training is needed, organizations often conduct a training needs analysis. A training needs analysis (TNA) is the process of identifying what types of training are needed, based on the skills or knowledge required by workers

---

sexual harassment Pattern of behavior that involves unwelcome lewd remarks, offensive touching, intimidation, and other conduct or communication of a sexual nature that is offensive to a reasonable person.

hostile work environment Workplace behaviors and actions that a reasonable person would consider intimidating, *hostile,* or abusive.

employee development The ongoing process of encouraging employees to seek new forms of knowledge.

training Process by which employees obtain work-related skills through structured or guided ways.

training needs analysis (TNA) Process of identifying what types of training are needed, based on the skills or knowledge required by workers to effectively complete the task.

▼

to effectively complete the task. This TNA process is continual in nature where the human resource function is constantly evaluating the skill levels of employees and the changing demands and tasks in the workplace (Johnson, 2005; Rothwell, Hohne, & King, 2012).

There are different forms of training. In-service training is training provided to existing employees that is paid for and provided by the organization. The goal of in-service training is to improve and update competency in specific skill areas by providing employees structured training opportunities. They are usually directed at the needs of the agency more than the personal needs of the employee (Johnson, 2005; Young & Lambie, 2007). These types of training are often conducted in-house, and can be done "on the job" while the person is working. In cases where specialized training is needed, employees can be sent to specific locations for the training. They can also be conducted by other employees or contracted trainers. In-service training can also be general and specific. General training activities provide skills that are used by many employers. These skills are often directly transferable to other organizations. There is also specific training which creates skills that are useful to a single employer that are not readily transferable (Stevens, 1996). Consider, for example, a security company that provides "basics of patrol" training. An employee receiving this type of training can easily transfer these skills to another security company if he or she decides to leave the organization.

> **in-service training**
> Continuous professional training for current or existing employees.

Employee development programs also include education opportunities. Education encompasses general knowledge development that is useful in all aspects of life. It is "learning undertaken in educational institutions in pursuit of qualifications" (Gibb, 2002, p. 6). Unlike skills-based training, education is oftentimes nontechnical, experiential, and general in nature. For example, in higher educational institutions (colleges and universities), learners are exposed to various disciplines (psychology, sociology, political science, and economics) and educated in interpersonal communications, human relations, written and oral communications, critical thinking, and problem solving (Hansen & Brooks, 1994).

> **education** General knowledge development that is useful in all aspects of life. Learning undertaken in educational institutions in pursuit of qualifications.

▶ Performance Appraisal

A performance appraisal is a systematic and objective assessment of how well an employee is performing. It is used to establish standards, appraise employee performance, make human resource decisions, and provide documentation to support those decisions. An objective, well-documented performance appraisal, that is conducted according to legally permissible human resource policies and procedures, may be the best defense against litigation arising from claims of inappropriate discipline or wrongful termination. The appraisal focuses on objective performance, not on the person, and on strengths as well as weaknesses. The appraisal process should be designed to enhance performance. The ideal appraisal process includes the supervisor's evaluation of the employee and a self-evaluation made by the employee. In addition, some formal appraisal processes include peer evaluations and assessments conducted by the employee's clients or consumers (George & Jones, 2012; Ortmeier & Davis, 2012).

> **performance appraisal** Systematic assessment of employee performance.

Performance appraisals should be a daily activity where supervisors continuously work with and coach employees. In fact, it makes no sense to see performance productivity-related issues occur and not address them immediately. As such, performance appraisal is an ongoing activity by supervisors and managers where employees are coached and counseled on a continual basis (Johnson, 2005). In most cases, organizations also have a more formal meeting to review and officially document and employee's performance. This appraisal meeting is one of the most important parts of the appraisal process. It is constructive, emphasizing strengths, and pointing out areas for improvement. This meeting is also used as a catalyst for achieving future goals. An appraisal meeting should be held in a trusting, private environment with adequate, uninterrupted time allotted for open, honest, and frank discussion. The content of the appraisal meeting is kept confidential and shared with others on a need-to-know basis only, since the discussion may often include information that could adversely impact the reputation of the worker with his or her peers (Hartel & Fujimoto, 2015).

The outcomes of performance appraisal meetings are also used for employment-based decisions. One common performance-based action is promotion. A promotion is advancement into a higher position in the organization. It serves as a means to fill job vacancies, as a reward and morale booster, and as an incentive for employees to perform better. Employees with the best records in production, quality of work, and cooperation should be the ones promoted. The promotion process should be fair, objective, and based on the candidate's ability to perform in the new position. A competitive process involves the use of standardized objective assessments of the candidate's qualifications and current performance as well as an evaluation of the candidate's strengths and weaknesses as predictions of future performance (Lewis, Goodman, & Fandt, 2008; Mosley, Megginson, & Pietri, 2005).

Another common type of performance appraisal is discipline-related. Discipline is a corrective action designed to bring about change in an individual's behavior (Bielous, 1993, p. 17). The primary purpose of a disciplinary action is to improve performance and behavior rather than punish or seek revenge. The disciplinary process serves to educate the employee on appropriate performance and behaviors in the organization. Except in rare instances, when policy or law may warrant immediate termination, a uniformly applied system of progressive discipline should be used. Under this system, corrective action progresses through the following steps: verbal warning, verbal warning noted in employee's record, written reprimand, suspension, demotion, and termination. The agency or business must also have a written policy that addresses uniform standards of behavior and these policies must be enforced in a fair and uniform manner against all employees to ensure perceptions of fairness and to avoid any discrimination-related legal claims (Johnson, 2005).

If disciplinary action is warranted, employer-related actions should be immediate, consistent, and fair. Disciplinary action is more likely to be viewed as fair if reasonable, if employees are provided notice of acceptable standards of performance and conduct and are informed of the consequences for violating them. The employer's representative should present the behavioral problem in specific terms by providing the date, time, and place of the incident as well as the organizational rule or policy violated. Discussions should remain impersonal and agreement on the direction of behavioral change should be obtained (Certo & Certo, 2012; Slater, 2000).

Failure to discipline appropriately can have far-reaching negative consequences, especially when illegal activities are involved. Obviously, theft of an organization's assets, liability associated with negligence, and settlements resulting from lawsuits exact a heavy toll from businesses and government operations. In some cases, losses result from extremely subtle activities. For example, the pilferage of employees' personal property, including lunch items from communal refrigerators in the workplace, impact negatively on employee morale. Low morale tends to reduce productivity, resulting in incalculable losses to an organization.

▶ Policies and Procedures

Security managers will also be responsible for knowing, following, enforcing and oftentimes, writing policy. A policy is a general statement of intent describing how situations should be handled. Policy statements also show preferences and provide guiding principles for employees and the organization (Alpert & Smith, 1994; Rudd, Mills, & Litzinger, 2008). Policy statements describe general goals and focus on a wide range of

promotion Advancement into a higher position in the organization; a means to fill job vacancies, a reward or morale booster, and an incentive for employees to perform better.

discipline Corrective action designed to bring about change in an individual's behavior.

progressive discipline Corrective actions progressing through several steps including verbal warnings, written reprimands, suspensions demotions, and/ or terminations.

policy General statement that describes goals or states an organization's position on issues or topics.

personnel issues, such as selection, discipline, promotion, and termination. They often address behavioral problems associated with substance abuse, sexual harassment, discrimination, as well as workplace violence and safety, and the use of force. Policies also show values: affirmative action, equal opportunity employment, conflict of interest, and ethics are some examples. Furthermore, policies can be used to help create accountability for managerial and employee-based activities. In fact, in some cases, policies are considered the constitution of the workforce, clearly describing acceptable levels of conduct and explaining what the company expects and values. Existing policies will require periodic revision, and additional policies may be created as new situations or issues arise.

A procedure outlines a series of steps to be followed when carrying out a policy. Procedures outline specific operational protocols and describe detailed responses to incidents or events. Procedures often cover a wider range of activities and they are more specific than policies. Some examples of procedures include: blood-borne pathogens/universal precautions, evidence handling, emergency procedures (bomb threat, active shooter, and fire), patrol procedures, and handling sensitive and classified information. In some situations, case law will require new procedures. For example, in its *Graham v. Conner* (1989) decision, the U.S. Supreme Court determined the legal standards and guidelines regarding the use of force. Now, for force to be considered reasonable and not excessive in nature, the level of force used must be objectively reasonable and based on the totality of circumstances related to the particular incident. Because of this decision, security companies must ensure that they have a correct use of force policy and detailed procedures related to when force can be legally and ethically used.

> **procedure** Outline a series of steps to be followed when carrying out policy.

Policies and procedures serve many functions. First, they provide guidance for security staff on what to do in certain situations. In doing so, policies serve to restrict activities by staff. They serve to frame discretionary decisions by staff, ensuring that they act in a professional, legal, and ethical manner. Next, well-designed policies and procedures also serve as a liability reduction tool. For example, in most cases, employers have many policies and procedures for high-risk/liability situations such as use of force and arrest where the policy and procedures clearly dictate what actions are appropriate. These comprehensive and up to date policies ensure that the organization is in compliance with existing laws and regulations, serving to reduce legal risk/liability against staff and the organization. Policies and procedures are also a training tool. Their existence serves to notify and educate staff on what is appropriate. And, if an issue should occur, the policy and procedure manual can be used for disciplinary purposes to correct behaviors and actions. However, precise guidance may not be appropriate in all situations. Security personnel often work alone in settings that require the exercise of independent judgment and discretion. Thus, overreliance on standardized procedures can discourage critical thinking, problem solving, initiative, and imagination (Cordner & Scarborough, 2010; Dalton, 2003; Fay, 1999; Greer & Plunkett, 2007; Robbins & Coulter, 2009).

▶ Scheduling

Scheduling is the process of assigning individuals to work various days, times, and locations. Scheduling can be a complex task for managers, requiring careful planning to make sure that an adequate number of personnel are assigned, while also ensuring that the scheduling of personnel is fiscally responsible. In fact, scheduling is sometimes considered an art, where supervisors or managers must balance the needs of the organization with those of the employee. For example, failing to meet the personal needs of employees (an adequate number of hours, adequate notification of when and where they are working and a "fair" schedule) can lead to increased discontent and turnover in the organization.

> **scheduling** The process of assigning individuals to work various days, times, and locations.

scheduling cycle
The number of days, weeks, and months in the scheduling horizon.

scheduling periods
Single or multiple days a person is scheduled to work.

Some of the common elements of scheduling include the scheduling cycle, scheduling periods, shifts, and touring schedule. The scheduling cycle is the time period for which the schedule operates (called the horizon). For example, an employer may create a six-month schedule that is then disseminated to employees. Within this cycle, an employee will know exactly when he or she is scheduled. The date and times may differ (e.g., by week or biweekly), but the employee nevertheless knows in advance the work schedule. There are also scheduling periods. These periods can be considered "time subsets" within the cycle over which the scheduling takes place. In the case of the above example, the manager must schedule employees for two-week periods that delineate the specific days and times the employee is scheduled to work. These two-week periods are then compiled into the six-month schedule (the cycle) that is published and disseminated to employees. Generally, employees prefer longer schedule cycles (e.g., months) so they can plan their personal activities far into the future. However, long scheduling cycles (and periods) for employers can be difficult to determine, especially if they are operating in unpredictable or rapidly changing work environments. Within each scheduling period, staffing levels also need to be determined. These staffing levels may fluctuate based on changes in the activities in the organization. For example, during normal business hours there are more employees and visitors present, requiring more staff, in comparison to other time periods. There are also shifts. A shift is a period of time that has a start and end time. Common shift lengths include 8-, 10-, and 12-hour days. Within each shift and planning period there are different tasks or responsibilities for each person working. Scheduling also requires considering touring scheduling, which is a combination of the number of the days worked and not worked. For example, a 5-7 tour involves 5 days on and 2 days off, while a 4-3 is 4 days on and 3 days off (Alfares, 2003; Morris & Showalter, 1983).

Scheduling also involves a comprehensive labor needs assessment, the calculation of the total number of work hours required, and a determination of the workforce's impact on the budget. The goal of workforce scheduling is to maximize coverage with minimum resources without sacrificing quality. Visually, a schedule might be presented as follows:

Position	Days	Hours	Total Hours/Week
Security director	Vary	Vary	40
Supervisor 1	Mon–Fri	2300–0700	40
Supervisor 2	Tue–Sat	0700–1500	40
Supervisor 3	Wed–Sun	1500–2300	40
Supervisor 4	Vary	Vary	40
Assignment 1	24/72	400–2400	168
Assignment 2	Mon–Fri	0800–1600	40
Assignment 3	Mon–Fri	1600–2400	40
Assignment 4	Mon–Fri	1200–2000	40
TOTAL			488

Scheduling must also be cost-effective. Since salaries and wage rates vary among positions and individuals, the total hours indicated on the previous schedule example cannot simply be multiplied by a flat hourly rate. Rather, the dollar amount budgeted for each position must be calculated separately. For example, if the wage rate for Assignment 2 is $15 per hour, the total direct labor cost for that position is $600 per week, or $31,200 per year. Statutorily mandated and related payroll costs (such as social security and unemployment taxes), training, and discretionary benefit packages could easily account for an additional 40 percent in indirect labor costs for each position. Thus, a $31,200 position may actually cost $43,680 per year (Moran, 2010; Ortmeier, 1999; Payton & Amaral, 2004).

Careful attention should also be paid to make sure that employees do not work more than 40 hours per pay period (usually a week). The Fair Labor Standards Act (FLSA) mandates that employees who work more than 40 hours in a pay period be paid 1.5 times their base wage. The scheduling process should also consider the elements of a collective bargaining agreement (if one exists) that may specify additional terms and conditions related to shift bidding, seniority provisions for assigning individuals and shifts, and assignment of overtime, if available (Decenzo & Robbins, 2015).

Another part of the scheduling process is determining the number of coverage hours and employees needed for each tour. After personnel assignments (posts) are determined, the number of coverage hours is calculated. For example, if an employee is to be assigned to a workstation or post, 24 hours per day, 7 days a week, the result is the equivalent of 168 hours (24 × 7 = 168 hours). When calculated that an individual works 40 hours per week, 4.5 **full-time equivalent (FTE)** persons will be needed to cover this particular post. This accounts for vacations and sick leave without unnecessary overtime. The position could be filled with any combination of full-time or part-time employees.

> **full-time equivalent (FTE)** Equivalent to a person, or combination of persons, assigned to work full time (40 hours per week).

There are 2,080 (52 weeks × 40 hours per week) working hours available per year for each FTE. However, this calculation is based on the assumption that the position is filled by a full-time person and no vacation, holidays, or sick leave time is taken. Therefore, adjustments must be made to reduce the number of hours a full-time person is available for work if vacation, holiday, and sick leave benefits are provided. To account for 2,080 working hours, two part-time workers could fill the assignment at 1,040 hours each. If a contract service provides security personnel, the client organization need only provide the number of workforce hours exclusive of any calculation for time off (Johnson, 2005).

When a post must be staffed 24 hours per day, 7 days per week (continuous staffing), most organizations maintain at least three 8-hour shifts to ensure 24-hour service. Some organizations add a fourth shift for peak activity periods, as in the following example:

A Shift	2300 hours–0700 hours	(11:00 p.m.–7:00 a.m.)
B Shift	0700 hours–1500 hours	(7:00 a.m.–3:00 p.m.)
C Shift	1500 hours–2300 hours	(3:00 p.m.–11:00 p.m.)
D Shift (optional)	1900 hours–0300 hours	(7:00 p.m.–3:00 a.m.)

Organizations may also utilize what is commonly referred to as the 4–10 plan: three 10-hour shifts that overlap during peak periods. Fewer people are scheduled for each shift, but a greater number are available during peak periods. Ten plans also tend to improve the morale of employees. Employees work four 10-hour shifts and have 3 days off, as in the following example:

A Shift	2400 hours–1000 hours	(midnight–10:00 a.m.)
B Shift	0800 hours–1800 hours	(8:00 a.m.–6:00 p.m.)
C Shift	1600 hours–0200 hours	(4:00 p.m.–2:00 a.m.)
D Shift (optional)	1700 hours–0300 hours	(5:00 p.m.–3:00 a.m.)

Organizations also use 12-hour shifts. Under this plan, employees work 3 or 4 days a week, alternating every 7-day period. The plan requires only two shift changes every 24 hours, instead of three, reducing the number of shift changes and resulting in more time for the actual work assignment. Some of the benefits of the 12-hour shift include more days off from working. Drawbacks, meanwhile, can include more worker-related fatigue issues because of longer shifts (Johnson, 2005).

Planning

A **plan** is a sequence of actions. Plans define an organization's goals, establish strategies for achieving those goals, and integrate and coordinate organizational efforts (Robbins & Coulter, 2009). Plans must have clear goals and objectives in order to be successful.

> **plan** A sequence of actions that define an organization's goals, establish strategies for achieving those goals, and integrate and coordinate organizational efforts.

organizational goals
Desired states of affairs or preferred results that organizations attempt to realize and achieve.

organizational objectives Define or explain how to achieve organizational goals.

vision statement Future-oriented statements that describe what the organization is committed to and will look like in the future.

mission statement A statement that that describes what the organization is and its core purpose(s). These statements guide the actions of the organization.

Organizational goals are "desired states of affairs or preferred results that organizations attempt to realize and achieve" (Etzioni, 1961, p. 366). These goals are aligned with the vision and mission statements, and outline what the company wants to achieve in a set time period. These goals are clear, precise and measurable, realistic to achieve, and are an end state (Ayers, 2015). To achieve these goals, organizational objectives are created which define or explain how to achieve the goals. These objectives can be considered the steps or activities needed to reach the end goal. Clear goals and objectives serve to facilitate planning, they are a motivational tool for employees, serve as an evaluation tool for employers, and allow employees and managers the ability to monitor their progress toward these end goals (Johnson, 2005).

Effective plans are based on organizational vision and mission statements. Organizational values are used to create a vision statement, which are living documents that are future oriented and describe what the organization is committed to and will look like in the future. These statements are also used as a guide for planners and to inform the public of the organization's future state (Lipton, 1996). These vision statements are short in length and are specific. A mission statement, meanwhile, defines the organizations "unique and enduring practice" (Bart, 1996, p. 212). The purpose of these (oftentimes lengthy) statements is to identify its products, to set it apart from other organizations, and to increase and improve performance. These mission statements are considered to be the most visible component of the organization's strategic plan. These statements do not set objectives or goals; instead, they clarify beliefs and expectations and help establish the direction of the company (Galpin, 2013). For example, the vision statement of Starbucks Coffee is to *"to establish Starbucks as the premier purveyor of the finest coffee in the world while maintaining our uncompromising principles while we grow."* Its mission statement is much broader and shows Starbucks' beliefs: *"To inspire and nurture the human spirit – one person, one cup and one neighborhood at a time"* (Gregory, 2015). The vision and mission statements for the U.S. Department of Homeland Security can be found in Box 11-1.

SECURITY SPOTLIGHT

Go to the Internet and locate a security company. What is its vision statement? What is its mission statement?

decision-making The process of making choices and determining the best course of action from a series of possible alternatives, based on the plan.

Effective planning also requires sound decisions. Decision-making is the process of making choices and determining the best course of action from a series of possible alternatives, based on the plan (Johnson, 2005). A decision is simply a way or a series of steps or stages to reach the end goal. Consider the following example: the general plan for the trip

BOX 11-1

DHS VISION AND MISSION STATEMENT

VISION

A homeland that is safe, secure, and resilient against terrorism and other hazards.

DEPARTMENT MISSION

We will lead efforts to achieve a safe, secure, and resilient homeland. We will counter terrorism and enhance our security; secure and manage our borders; enforce and administer our immigration laws; protect cyber networks and critical infrastructure; and ensure resilience from disasters. We will accomplish these missions while providing essential support to national and economic security and maturing and strengthening both the Department of Homeland Security and the homeland security enterprise.

Source: From Department Vision and Mission. © 2012. Published by Department of Homeland Security Strategic Plan.

is to travel by vehicle from point A to B. The decision, meanwhile, is what roads will be driven to reach the final destination. In some cases, the decision-making process and the decisions made are not always popular among manager and employees. The impact a decision has on the organization, its people, its clients, and the community requires careful consideration. Change causes stress and anxiety. However, if well-defined and communicated, each decision may be viewed as an opportunity for development, progress, and advancement of individual and organizational goals and objectives.

Types of Plans

There are several different types of plans used to pursue company goals. A strategic plan is designed with the entire company in mind, defining the direction and mission of a company, leading it from where it is now to where it would like to be in the future (Knight, 2013). Strategic plans are long term in nature and can be considered guides that managers can use to set priorities in implementing programs and ensuring that resources (such as personnel and funding) are directed toward the organizational objectives and goals (Johnson, 2005; Myrna, 2012). Next, tactical plans need to be developed to reach the objectives and goals that are found in the strategic plan. These plans are more specific and detailed in nature; they are designed to be achieved in a short time frame and meet a specific goal outlined in the strategic plan. These plans turn strategic plans into reality where, for example, specific departments are responsible for carrying them out in the short term (Lombardi, Schermerhorn, & Kramer, 2007).

> **strategic plan**
> Long-range plans designed with the entire company in mind, defining the direction and mission of a company, leading it from where it is now to where it would like to be in the future.

These tactical plans, meanwhile, are implemented through operational plans. Operational plans are low-level in nature; they provide specific details and action steps that need to be carried out. Compared to tactical and strategic plans, these are more detailed and define specific activities, processes, and tasks and procedures that will be accomplished by various departments and individuals to review and show how they are moving toward accomplishing the strategic goals (Barry, 1998). These operational plans can include both single use and repeat plans. Single-use plans are only used once and are no longer needed when the objectives of the plan are accomplished. Budgets and special projects are examples of single-use plans. A repeat-use (standing) plan, on the other hand, may be used several times. Repeat-use plans are implemented each time a given situation or incident occurs. Unless modified, repeat-use plans change little over time. Examples of repeat-use plans include policies and procedures (Collins, 2008; Ortmeier & Meese, 2010; Perry, 1996).

> **tactical plan**
> Short-range plans that are specific and detailed in nature; they are designed to be achieved in a short time frame and meet a specific goal outlined in the strategic plan.

> **operational plans**
> Provide specific details and action steps needed to be carried out by an individual or group.

Consider, for example, these three types of plans in the context of the fictitious ACME security company. Here, the company's strategic plans are related to improving profitability, growth, and market share in the next 5 years, where top level managers develop long term plans to ensure that the goals are met. Next, middle managers create tactical plans that are aligned with and support the strategic plan. For example, one tactical plan includes testing some new digital surveillance cameras that use state of the art video analytics software to identify and track individuals. Through the creation of this new product, profitability and growth can be achieved. In the context of operational plans, meanwhile, lower-level managers in the company could re-examine scheduling and create new procedures to save the company money.

> **single-use plan**
> A plan that is used once and no longer needed when the objectives of the plan are accomplished.

Performance Measures

Achieving excellence in any organization involves special attention to evaluating the effectiveness of plans through the use of *performance measures*. Even carefully developed plans can fail without an evaluation of progress and outcomes. After a plan is implemented, the evaluation process begins. The process is exercised continuously throughout the life of the operation. Evaluation involves measuring performance, comparing performance with stated objectives, reporting results, and taking corrective actions, if necessary.

> **repeat-use (standing) plan**
> A plan implemented each time a given situation or incident occurs. Unless modified, repeat-use plans change little over time.

Evaluation has both predictive and after-the-fact aspects. Through predictions, the evaluator attempts to anticipate the possibility of undesirable outcomes and prevent deviation from established standards. Crime prevention is an example of predictive evaluation. After-the-fact evaluation analyzes an event or deviation from established standards to determine what corrective action is required. A determination of the cause of a theft is an example of after-the-fact evaluation.

The first step in the evaluation process is to measure performance based on the standards (objectives) established during the planning process. The standards are units of measurement that serve as reference points for evaluating results. There are several types of standards—tangible, numerical, and intangible:

tangible standards
Standards that are quite clear, specific, identifiable, and generally measurable; typically expressed in terms of dollars, numbers, physical properties, and time.

- Tangible standards are quite clear, specific, identifiable, and generally measurable. They measure quantity and quality. They may be used to assess incident reduction efforts, and appraise individual employee performance. Tangible standards are expressed in terms of numbers, dollars, physical properties, and time.

numerical standard
Quantifiable standards that can be measured and expressed numerically.

- Numerical standards are quantifiable, such as the amount of crime reduction or number of personnel who successfully complete a training program. Examples of monetary standards include the impact of a budget or payroll and maintenance costs. Physical standards refer to quality, durability, and other factors related to physical composition. Vehicle durability can be determined with physical standards. Time standards refer to the speed with which a task might be completed.

intangible standards
Characteristics that are difficult to measure. Examples include attitude, morale, and reputation.

- Intangible standards relate to human characteristics that are difficult to measure. They take no physical form, yet they are as important as tangible standards. Examples of intangible standards are a desirable attitude, high morale, ethics, cooperation, and the organization's reputation. In some cases, crime prevention cannot be measured utilizing a tangible standard. It is difficult, if not impossible, to measure the amount of crime that has been prevented unless a number of criminal incidents occurred before a prevention program was initiated. Thus, measuring a monetary return on investment (ROI) for security-related expenditures is often a challenge. Security's value-added contribution (VAC) to the organization is often incalculable. In many situations, security's VAC may be more qualitative than quantitative. Employees and clients may feel safer and experience less fear of crime. Thus, morale, productivity, and the quality of organizational life improve.

Methods for measuring performance include qualitative and quantitative data that include personal observation, written and oral reports of subordinates, automatic recording systems, inspections, tests, and surveys. Whatever type of data is used, performance standards should be based on realistic targets. Failure to meet a performance standard can result from a variety of causes. The identification of causes rather than the symptoms is extremely important if appropriate corrective action is to be taken. Those closest to the situation should be consulted to determine why the performance standards are not being met. Participation of all affected by the measurements is an essential ingredient in this process. The sooner a deviation from a standard is identified, the sooner the situation can be corrected. Evaluation and assessment, therefore, is a continuous process.

After a careful analysis of any deviation from the plan, changes may be necessary. Modifications to the original plan should not be viewed negatively. Objectives and standards stated in the original plan are often based on forecasts. If the deviation is extreme, it may be necessary to evaluate the planning process itself. There may be several reasons why a deviation from an established standard has occurred. It is possible that the standards could not be achieved because they were based on faulty forecasts or assumptions or because an unforeseen problem arose that distorted the anticipated outcome. Failure might have occurred in some other activity that supported the activity being evaluated. It is also possible that the employee who performed the task was unqualified, was not given adequate directions, was negligent, or did not follow required directions or procedures.

In recent years, the use of metrics has become popular as a means to evaluate performance. Metrics, as relates to performance, involves procedures designed to quantify and periodically assess processes that can be measured. The metrics (measurements) are compared to previous or similar assessments. Metrics are often used in management to track productivity, identify trends, and calculate resource consumption. The metrics tracked may be key performance indicators (benchmarks) against which similar activities are compared. In a security setting, metrics can be used to calculate ROI and VAC.

> **metrics** As it relates to performance, involves procedures designed to quantify and periodically assess processes that can be measured.

Well-managed security operations collect an enormous amount of information (e.g., traffic patterns, crime and accident incident reports, and safety hazards). Utilizing a metrics-based performance measurement system, security information is quantified and aligned with organizational priorities (e.g., expense reductions, risk management, mitigation of liability, ROI, VAC, life safety, and legal requirements).

Consider this simple example:

1. A review of incident reports reveals that nine minor vehicle collisions occurred within a month in the organization's parking lots.

2. The location and time of each incident is identified on a map of each parking lot.

3. An analysis reveals that most collisions occur at the end of the workday (5:00 p.m.) at a parking lot exit near a highway on-ramp.

4. A security officer is assigned to direct traffic at the relevant parking lot exit at the end of each workday.

5. Incident reports are reviewed periodically to assess the collision reduction strategy.

Thus, metrics can be used to identify vulnerabilities and map risks, determine allocation of resources, and assess results. Sound metrics procedures and protocols are specific, measurable, attainable, relevant, and timely.

Quality performance standards are probably the most difficult to measure. Quality can be an elusive concept and it means different things to different people. Basically, quality means that the product or service meets or exceeds predetermined expectations. Quality assurance, continuous quality improvement, and total quality management (TQM) initiatives involve administrative activities that attempt to maximize effectiveness of an organization through the continual improvement of the quality of its people, processes, products, and environment. To ensure quality performance, initiatives must be based on decisions and founded on facts rather than on intuition. Participants must also take personal responsibility for quality, improve teamwork and commitment, and focus on the end user and service. As such, quality assurance is a way of life or an underlying philosophy within many organizations and simply not a program (Campbell, 2006; Dalton, 1995; Goetsch & Davis, 2010; Haberer & Webb, 1994; Lewis et al., 2008; "Measuring up," 2011; Peters, 1987).

> **quality assurance** Initiatives carried out to maintain, improve, and promote quality levels in services and/or products.

Quality assurance initiatives involve goal setting, trust, cohesiveness, increasing information flow, and resolving conflict. To succeed, quality assurance initiatives must incorporate an internal and external customer focus, be obsessed with quality, long-term commitment, teamwork, employee involvement, and empowerment. Managers must incorporate education and training, freedom from control, and unity of purpose. The initiatives must also use the scientific approach (i.e., objectivity) to decision-making and problem solving.

Some managers make errors when implementing quality assurance initiatives. They may attempt a quality initiative by delegating responsibility to an outside expert rather than applying the leadership necessary to get everyone within the organization involved (Clemmer, 1992; Gomez-Mejia & Balkin, 2012). Additionally, employees must learn how to be team players. An organization must often undergo a cultural change before teamwork can succeed. Creating teams before learning about teamwork and quality assurance methods will be counterproductive and will create more problems than the teams will solve.

Organizations must develop quality initiatives concurrent with plans for integrating them into all elements of the organization. None of the approaches to quality management is truly a one-size-fits-all proposition. Quality programs must be tailored to fit organizational needs. According to Goetsch and Davis (2010), quality initiatives should include commitment, team building, training, vision and guiding principles, broad objectives, communication, a plan for implementation, project identification, feedback, and modification of the organizational infrastructure as necessary.

▶ Budgeting

> **budget** A plan expressed in financial terms; list of possible expenditures.

The financial impact of each action plan must also be determined. A budget is defined as "plan quantified in monetary terms, prepared and approved prior to a defined period of time, usually showing planned income . . . and or expenditure to be incurred during that period and the capital to be employed to attain a given objective" (Burkhead, 1996, p. 119). Budgets serve multiple purposes. They are used to forecast expenditures and revenues, and as quantitative standards against which one can measure and compare resource consumption. Budgets also assist in the planning process; they show the priorities of a company, and they inform stakeholders of the company's priorities. For example, if a security company has budgeted a large amount of money toward training employees, this shows that the company is forward thinking and concerned about its quality of services (Johnson, 2005).

Some of the different types of budgeting formats that can be used by organizations are shown in Box 11-2. The type of budget used depends on the circumstances, information needs, organizational policy, and the past budgeting practices of companies.

BOX 11-2

TYPES OF BUDGETS

- *Line item budgets* are considered traditional budgets. These budgets work from a base (the prior year's budget) where monies are added or subtracted from the yearly baseline. Line item budgets include a description of items and the cost of each item/activity. These budgets provide a lot of detail on how money will be spent and they allow planners to compare the prior year's budget to the current year's budget. They focus on what is to be spent: not the goal or outcome of the activities.

- *Performance-based Budgets (PBB)* are designed to show that monies are used wisely. They focus on outputs. The goal of these types of budgets is to ensure and prove that expenditures have had an impact. These types of budget formats enhance efficiency by examining the costs of certain activities relative to the outputs. While being

more cost-effective in nature and containing more detail on unit costs, one of the main drawbacks is that the outcomes of services provided by security (crime prevention, reduced property loss, improved quality of worklife), cannot be easily or accurately measured in a monetary cost-benefit format.

- *Zero-based budget (ZBB)* is considered to be "what if" budgeting. Unlike line item budgets, this budget has no annual base. Instead, managers must prioritize activities and needs and justify why they need the money they do. This type of budgeting focuses on what needs to be done and then finds the best methods of doing them through a cost-benefit analysis. In this type of format, managers are required to think in terms of budget consequences and what their main priorities are.

Source: Based on Johnson, B.R. (2005). Principles of Security Management, Upper Saddle River, NJ: Prentice Hall.

Budget preparation is an integral part of the planning process. It is an essential planning tool tied to the established goals and objectives developed as alternative courses of action. Areas to consider in budget preparation include past operations, present conditions, and future expectations. Revenue forecasts and projected expenditures are also useful elements to budget preparation. The budget process should be continuous, flexible, and responsive to the changing needs of the organization (Johnson, 2005).

In the budgeting process, an analysis must also be made of the cost and benefit of each item listed in the budget. A cost-benefit analysis is an estimate of a potential value of an activity or action compared to its cost (Walsh, Levin, Jaye, & Gazzard, 2013). The analysis is a systematic process through which one attempts to determine the value of the benefits derived from an expenditure and compare the value with the cost. The cost-benefit analysis usually involves three steps.

> **cost-benefit analysis** A systematic process through which one attempts to determine the value of the benefits derived from an expenditure, comparing the value with the cost.

- The identification of all possible consequences of an expenditure.

- The assignment of a monetary value to each consequence (cost and benefit) associated with the expenditure.

- The discounting of anticipated future costs and revenues accruing from the expenditure to express those costs and revenues in current monetary terms (ASIS International Guidelines Commission, 2007).

Industry standards indicate that security-related costs should be less than 2 percent of the value of the asset to be protected. Higher protection cost percentages are justifiable only if special circumstances exist. Security expenditures exceeding 5 percent of the value of the protected item are rarely justifiable (American Society for Industrial Security, 1998; Bassett, 2006).

The cost-benefit analysis can assist with the calculation of the return on investment (ROI) of security-related expenditures and the value-added contribution (VAC) of the security program. ROI refers to the net savings that result when security measures are in place. The VAC refers to those anticipated threats that do not materialize because of the security program. The ROI and VAC can be difficult to quantify unless one has a baseline for comparison. For example, a reduction in the number of thefts after protective measures are enacted is quantifiable. Savings can also be estimated in such diverse areas as illicit drug use and employee attrition. However, without a basis for comparison (i.e., how much overall crime is prevented), security's productivity can be questioned because its VAC is not quantifiable in specific terms. Thus, selling the security program and its budget can be challenging. To overcome the challenge, the security manager must be creative. The manager must also be assertive and pursue collaborative asset protection activities with personnel in other organizational units, such as operations, sales, marketing, human resources, information technology, and community relations (Bragdon, 2006; Dalton, 1995; Harowitz, 2003; Johnson, 2005; Jones & Arnold, 2003; Sommer, 2003).

> **return on investment (ROI)** Net cost savings that result from security measures employed.

> **value-added contribution (VAC)** The nature of extent of value that the security functions contributes to the organization.

To justify security-related expenditures, asset protection and loss prevention must be viewed by budget decision-makers as something more than an expense item. In addition, everyone in the organization must view the security function as vital and integral to the agency and corporate strategy. In business, chief executive officers (CEOs) actions are often driven by earnings before taxes, interest, depreciation, and amortization. The CEO is interested in profitability. Therefore, the security professional must present budget requests that are supported with quantifiable evidence that security expenditures will increase profitability. The sophisticated security manager speaks the language of business, and highlights how security improves earnings through efficiency and loss prevention.

Summary

The management of organizations is a complex and rewarding activity and process. Managers perform a variety of functions in the modern organization. Human resource management activities related to the recruitment and selection of employees are important to ensure that the correct employee is chosen, to reduce turnover, and prevent any legal issues that should arise. Once an employee is hired, companies also need to engage in employment development activities that are directed toward educational opportunities and in-service training to ensure that employees possess those skill levels to perform to acceptable levels. Employees must also be properly assessed through well-designed performance appraisal methods that provide objective and constructive feedback.

This chapter has also reviewed the importance of policies and procedures, scheduling, planning, and budgeting. Security managers are responsible for knowing, following, enforcing, and oftentimes, writing policies and procedures that provide guidance for security staff on what to do in situations. Another common managerial activity is scheduling which requires balancing the needs of the organization and employees. Managers are also responsible for planning; plans define an organization's goals, establish strategies for achieving these goals, and integrate and coordinate organizational efforts to meet its vision and mission. Finally, managers engage in budget-related activities. These budgets serve many functions, one of which is ensuring that financial resources are used prudently in the delivery of security-related activities and services. All of these and other managerial functions are will contribute to and are critical for organizational success.

Career Opportunities

Several managerial career opportunities exist in the field of security management. Two are shown below:

Industrial Security Managers

Industrial security professionals protect a wide range of manufacturing and government contractor facilities. Government contractors must protect classified information in accordance with the National Industrial Security Program (NISP). Entry-level industrial security managers typically possess a college degree and earn between $55,000 and $75,000. The average annual salary for executive-level industrial security managers is over $100,000.

Chief Security Officers

Many large corporations employ Chief Security Officers (CSOs). The CSO's position (rank) within the organization is similar to the corporation's chief financial officer (CFO). CSOs often hold the title of vice president for security, loss prevention, or asset protection. CSOs are responsible and accountable for a wide range of activities. They:

- develop and implement loss prevention strategy.
- gather information and assess risk.
- engage in organizational preparedness.
- prevent and respond to major incidents.
- manage disaster recovery efforts.
- coordinate with those responsible for investor and government relations, public affairs, and core business activities.
- protect people, physical and information assets, and organizational reputation.

Chief security officer positions typically require a bachelor's degree or higher in security management or business. In addition, CSOs must possess broad-based knowledge, skills, and abilities. They must be able to:

- develop and maintain professional relationships.
- demonstrate exceptional leadership and management abilities.
- provide security-related subject-matter expertise.
- function as a team member.
- anticipate, recognize, and appraise security-related risks.
- think creatively and solve problems, using high-quality analytical skills.
- effectively communicate recommended courses of action.
- demonstrate integrity.
- adjust and respond rapidly to changing conditions.

Compensation potential is high. CSOs may earn up to $400,000 annually.

Key Terms and Concepts

Budget *252*

Churn *240*

Color of law *241*

Cost-benefit analysis *253*

Decision-making *248*

Discipline *244*

Education *243*

Employee development *242*

Full-time equivalent (FTE) *247*

Hostile work environment *242*

In-service training *243*

Intangible standards *250*

Internal labor market (ILM) *240*

Metrics *251*

Mission statement *248*

Moonlighting *240*

Negligent hiring *241*

Negligent retention *241*

Numerical standards *250*

Operational plans *249*

Organizational goals *248*

Organizational objectives *248*

Performance appraisal *243*

Personnel selection *240*

Plan *247*

Policy *244*

Pre-employment screening *240*

Procedure *245*

Progressive discipline *244*

Promotion *244*

Quality assurance *251*

Recruitment *240*

Repeat-use (standing) plan *249*

Return on investment *253*

Scheduling *245*

Scheduling cycle *246*

Scheduling periods *246*

Sexual harassment *242*

Single-use plans *249*

Strategic plan *249*

Tactical plans *249*

Tangible standards *250*

Training *242*

Training needs analysis (TNA) *242*

Turnover *239*

Value-added contribution *253*

Vision statement *248*

Discussion Questions and Exercises

*1. What is recruitment? What is selection? What are some common recruitment and selection tools?

2. What are some issues related to hiring off-duty police officers? How can this issue be managed?

3. Explain negligent hiring.

4. What is sexual harassment? What is a hostile work environment? How can management prevent these activities?

5. What is the difference between training and education?

6. What is the difference between a policy and a procedure? Why are policies and procedures important in the management of organizations?

7. What are some of the common elements of a schedule? What are some key considerations when scheduling employees?

8. What is a plan? What are some elements of a plan?

9. What is a goal? What is an objective?

10. What is a budget? What are the purposes of budgets? What are some different types of budgets?

Your Turn

The ACME security company is currently expanding in size due to the acquisition of a new long-term contract with a large, multinational firm that will require immediate hiring and training at least 60 new full-time security staff to provide security services to the company. Already, ACME is experiencing a large turnover among its line level staff: almost 120 percent annually. Exit interviews from employees leaving the organization have shown that they are bored with the job, dissatisfied with the existing scheduling process that provides them only two weeks advanced notice of their shift and tours, and they are frustrated due to the lack of direction on "what to do" when working. Combined with ACME's existing high turnover, concerns exist among management that this new contract will lead to increased turnover, added costs related to training, and dissatisfaction from clients related to the "revolving door" of new security employees in their organizations.

1. In your view, could ineffective pre-employment processes by ACME have led to high turnover?

2. As a security manager, what are some ways to ensure that the "right" people are recruited? What would be some good recruitment sources and why? How could these reduce turnover?

3. What would be some good selection tools to use to ensure that right people are hired and turnover is reduced?

4. What are some employee development techniques to reduce turnover?

5. In your opinion, how could the organization make work schedules more attractive for new hires?

6. Because of the need to immediately hire 60 new staff, how will you ensure that the ACME company is not at risk for a negligent hire and retention claim?

12   Risk Assessment, Security Surveys, and Continuity Planning

LEARNING OBJECTIVES

After completing this chapter, the reader should be able to:

1   *define risk*

2   *describe and explain the risk management process*

3   *list and describe the types of risk that threaten individuals and organizations*

4   *explain the risk assessment process*

5   *explain the purpose of security surveys*

6   *identify attributes of risk*

7   *discuss management techniques associated with risk elimination, reduction, and mitigation*

8   *explain the purpose of business continuity plans*

9   *understand the main components of disaster contingency plans*

10   *evaluate risks to determine vulnerability, probability, and criticality of loss*

▶ Introduction

A major focus for security managers is identifying and managing risk. Public and private sector organizations are vulnerable to many different types of risk in the course of normal and abnormal operations. This chapter will examine the concept and practice of risk management, which includes the process of identifying and assessing risk. It also reviews the key points and concepts related to the creation of a comprehensive risk management program, which relies upon a variety of strategies and practices to eliminate or mitigate the impact of loss. This chapter also examines business continuity and contingency planning activities that are integral to any risk management program in organizations.

▶ The Concept of Risk

Risk is defined as the possibility of suffering harm or loss, exposure to the significance or probability of loss or damage, an element of uncertainty, or the possibility that the results of an action may not be consistent with the planned or expected outcomes. Risk can also be thought of as any activity (or inactivity) in a particular setting that produces consequences or outcomes that are uncertain where humans and/or something of human value is at stake (Aven & Renn, 2009). According to Broder (2000), three key elements need to be considered in determining risk: (1) the assets that an organization has; (2) the degree of exposure the company has; and (3) the types of losses a company could experience.

From a security perspective, **risk management** is defined as the process involved in the anticipation, recognition, and appraisal of a risk, and the initiation of action to eliminate the risk entirely or reduce the threat of loss to an acceptable level. A risk is a known or foreseeable threat to an organization's assets: people, property, information, or reputation. It exists in several domains as shown in Figure 12-1 ■.

Risk, in most cases, cannot be totally eliminated. However, an effective risk management program can reduce risk and its impact to the lowest possible level, maximizing asset protection while minimizing protection costs (Fay, 2000; Fischer & Janoski, 2000; Kovacich & Halibozek, 2003; Robbins & Coulter, 2009; Simonsen, 1998; Sweet, 2006). Failure to recognize and take action against a risk is potentially costly for any organization. Materialized risk increases the cost of doing business. It may increase insurance premiums, and expose the organization to criminal as well as civil liability. In addition to direct costs associated with a reduction in organizational assets, indirect costs are incurred when the organization experiences loss of market share, its reputation, or competitive edge. Losses in shareholder equity and reductions in productivity also result. A risk event may adversely impact profitability for private business and affect a public organization's ability to render services (American Society for Industrial Security, 1998; Collins, 2008; Fay, 2000).

All risk management programs use rational decision-making processes. They should involve all key stakeholders in the organization, including management and line level personnel who can provide information regarding risk and existing vulnerabilities. Effective risk management programs also need to examine the external risk environment, where key stakeholders outside the organization should also be included. Consider, for example, the risk management model shown in Figure 12-2 ■. Here, the four fundamental elements of the risk management process include: (1) identification; (2) assessment; (3) management; and (4) measurement. The process begins with the identification of the types of risks an organization may be exposed to. Following the identification of the risk, the risk management team then needs to assess the impact that the risk(s) may

risk Possibility of suffering harm or loss; exposure to probability of loss or damage; an element of uncertainty.

risk management Process involved in the anticipation, recognition, and appraisal of a risk and the initiation of action to eliminate the risk entirely or reduce the threat of harm to an acceptable level.

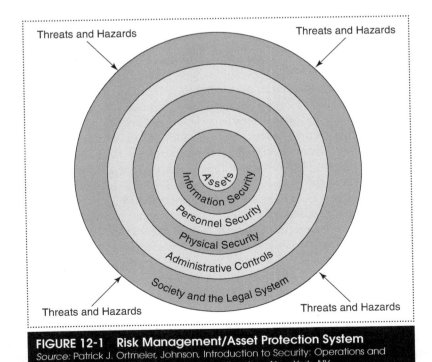

Threats and Hazards

Threats and Hazards

Threats and Hazards

Threats and Hazards

Assets
Information Security
Personnel Security
Physical Security
Administrative Controls
Society and the Legal System

FIGURE 12-1   Risk Management/Asset Protection System
Source: Patrick J. Ortmeier, Johnson, Introduction to Security: Operations and Management, 5e. © 2018, Pearson Education, Inc., New York, NY.

FIGURE 12-2　The Risk Management Cycle
Source: Patrick J. Ortmeier, Johnson, Introduction to Security: Operations and Management, 5e, © 2018, Pearson Education, Inc., New York, NY.

have on the organization. Next, the identified vulnerabilities or weaknesses need to be properly managed, which can involve a variety of proactive efforts that will be reviewed later in this chapter. Finally, the measurement stage usually involves testing the entire risk management plan and specific components, and various countermeasures in order to determine if the plan actually met its objectives. Once tested, the risk management team can then evaluate the effectiveness of the plan, adjusting it accordingly (Broder, 2000; Johnson, 2005; Roper, 1999).

The risk management plan needs to be measured for effectiveness. Consider, for example, disaster planning. Disaster and emergency plans should be tested to identify weaknesses and assess their viability prior to an actual incident. Such plans are typically evaluated through the use of exercises designed to simulate, as closely as possible, a major disaster or emergency event. Discussion-based and operations-based exercises can be used to simulate catastrophic events and evaluate responses. One of the most widely used discussion-based planning tools is tabletop exercises. Here, an event scenario is presented to stakeholders in a roundtable format. Participants discuss how their functional areas would respond to the event. Facilitators provide basic information (place, time, magnitude, resource limitations) concerning the event, conduct the exercise, and guide the discussion. Facilitators also introduce additional information, such as damage reports and changing conditions, as the exercise proceeds (Van Niekerk et al., 2015).

Operations-based exercises are more complex. Participants are required to role-play and act out their responses. Personnel with simulated injuries are treated, participants use emergency equipment, and criminal perpetrators (if any) are apprehended. In addition to the actual participants in the simulation, operations-based exercises typically employ an exercise director, controllers who provide new information, a group of people who represent external organizations and individuals interfacing with the exercise participants, actors who role-play as victims and bystanders, and exercise evaluators. The actions of the participants are the focus of the exercise. Discussion-based as well as operations-based exercises are assessed through after-action evaluations and reports (Gomez-Mejia & Balkin, 2012; Haque, 2011; Nason, 2007).

This risk management process is also continual in nature. Because the risk environment is oftentimes changing, these plans and response strategies must also be updated, modified, and evaluated to ensure that the risks are eliminated or there is minimal impact in an organization (Broder, 2000; Johnson, 2005; Roper, 1999).

▶ Identifying Risk

Risk assessment first requires the identification of risks. Generally, risk can be separated into the major categories of dynamic and static risk. Within these two categories of risk exposure, meanwhile, risk managers will further classify the risk into the categories of pure and speculative. Each of these is reviewed below.

Dynamic risk exists where conditions in the environment may fluctuate or are subject to change (McLeman & Smit, 2006). Examples include areas of the world that are subject to weather extremes, communities that depend on seasonal tourism, or changing political conditions in some nations. To manage these events, dynamic risk management activities occur. For example, risk managers can use dynamic modeling to determine dynamic risk. Dynamic modeling analyzes the behaviors of a specific event over time. For example, in the case of a wildfire, terrain, wind, moisture levels, meteorological events, and fuel loads are all dynamic variables that can influence the growth and spread of the fire (Fiorucci, Gaetani, & Minciardi, 2008). While oftentimes considered only in a negative perspective, improving economic conditions, decreased costs on production materials, and changes in government policy in another nation that improves company revenues are positive outcomes related to dynamic risk. As such, dynamic risk can result in a loss or gain. It can also be pure or speculative in nature.

> **dynamic risk** Exists when threat conditions fluctuate.

Static risk is constant and unchanging risk that is always present. These are risks that an organization can foresee and manage through mitigation and avoidance strategies. It can be either pure or speculative in nature. Here, the risk environment is in a steady state. For example, the probability of a person dying is 100 percent—the risk of death always exists. Static risks may include theft, accidents, and natural events, such as storms that could cause loss. In other cases, an organization could be exposed to static risk if a single supplier provides a critical component needed to manufacture one of its products. The loss of that supplier could mean the product manufacturing process would be slowed or stopped. To mitigate against this risk, an organization could find an alternative supplier to ensure business continuity. These types of risks can be pure or speculative in nature (Vallabhaneni, 2013). And, they may result in some type of loss.

> **static risk** Constant and unchanging risk, as in the possibility of an earthquake or severe storm.

Pure risk exists when there is a potential for injury, damage, or loss with no possible benefit or gain. Potential medical claims resulting from accidents may be classified as pure risks. The threat of criminal attack and natural disasters are also examples of pure risk. These events increase operating costs, a form of loss. These types of risk can be insured where an individual or company (the insured) can transfer that risk to the insurer who has a greater financial ability to pay for the loss (Masci, 2012). Consider, for example, vehicle insurance. Here, a person takes auto insurance because the risk of an auto accident exists that could lead to property and personal injury. A pure risk always leads to loss.

> **pure risk** Potential for harm or loss with no possible benefit.

Speculative risk exists when there is a potential for benefit or loss. This type of risk is based on uncertainty. These are situations where the possibility for either a gain or loss is possible, depending on the consequences of an activity or inactivity (Halek & Eisenhauer, 2001). For example, engaging in the activity of gambling has both positive and negative outcomes. With this activity, therefore, speculative risk exists because a person or organization could win or lose. This type of risk is voluntary in nature where the organization or person makes a decision to place itself in a situation knowing that

> **speculative risk** Potential for benefit or loss, depending on consequences of activity or inactivity.

although the event may be "risky," there is the possibility for some type of gain or loss. New product research and development, and business ventures into new markets and regions of the world are examples of speculative risk (Sherman, Weston, Willey, & Mansfield, 2014).

In addition to the potential of exposure to dynamic or static risk that is pure or speculative in nature, risk can be further classified into the categories of operational, legal, and reputational risk. These types of risk can also be pure or speculative. These are reviewed in detail below.

Operational risk is defined as an organization's potential for loss owing to significant deficiencies in system reliability or integrity (Johnson, 2005). It is "the risk of loss resulting from inadequate or failed internal processes, people and systems or from external events" (Basel Committee on Banking Supervision, 2004, p. 149). For example, the investigation of the British Petroleum Deepwater Horizon oil spill in 2010, which killed 11 people and was the largest oil spill in U.S. history, showed that it was the result of systemic errors at the operational level (Saad & Arakaki, 2014). The BP Report (2010) concluded that ". . . a complex and interlinked series of mechanical failures, human judgments, engineering design, operational implementation and team interfaces came together to allow the initiation and escalation of the accident. Multiple companies, work teams, and circumstances were involved over time" (p. 4). All organizations are basically exposed to operational risks. In order to control loss and reduce line level accidents, many organizations now have comprehensive **operational risk management (ORM)** programs that are concerned with identifying distinct elements of operations, including individuals and the systems in which they work, to reduce or mitigate the possibility of something going wrong (Pinto & Magpili, 2015).

Legal risk arises from violations or nonconformity with laws, rules, regulations, or prescribed practices (Katz & Claypoole, 2001). This concept can include legal compliance risk where a company could fail to follow legally binding rules related to existing rules and regulations. Legal risk also exists when organizations enter into or negotiate agreements or contracts, potentially exposing them to contract-related risk. Legal risk also includes tort liability, where a company could be sued for negligence-related activities, which in turn could lead to litigation risk that is associated to a company losing a legal case (de Frahan, 2015).

Reputational risk is the value of an organization's (or even a person's) reputation. Organizations need to be concerned that their business practices could negatively impact how customers, investors, employees, the media, activists, business partners, and the community perceive the organization (Fombrun, Gardberg, & Barnett, 2000). These negative opinions (whether true or not) could affect revenue levels, lead to increased litigation, and a decline in its customer base and market share. Some authors consider this to be the most serious of all types of risk because it could seriously damage a company. Overcoming the risk can also be a lengthy and expensive process (Suomi & Järvinen, 2013). Consider, for example, an incident involving Wendy's International in 2005. Anna Ayala, a customer, reported that she found a severed human thumb in her chili that she purchased from one of its restaurants in San Jose, California. Ayala went public about the incident with her attorney, threatening to sue Wendy's Corporation, and even sharing information about the incident during an interview on the *Good Morning America* television program. The resulting internal investigation by Wendy's corporate security department and local police found that the restaurant was not responsible for the severed thumb in the chili; the thumb actually came from a coworker and friend of Anna Ayala's husband who sold it to him for $100, which she then "planted" in the chili. Anna Ayala and her husband were subsequently charged for attempted grand theft. Because of the media attention, sales at Wendy's restaurants plummeted nation-wide (Manning, 2008). Additionally, in November and December, 2013, hackers broke into Target Stores and stole payment card information from approximately 40 million customers.

operational risk An organization's potential for loss owing to significant deficiencies in system reliability or integrity.

operational risk management (ORM) Programs that are concerned with identifying distinct elements of operations including individuals and the systems in which they work to reduce or mitigate the possibility of something going wrong.

legal risk Risk that arises from violations or nonconformity with laws, rules, regulations, or proscribed practices.

reputational risk Risk to an organization's or person's reputation.

It was estimated that the direct loss was close to $1 Billion, sales dropped 46 percent, the CEO of Target was forced to resign, and the company was sued by customers and banks. To ensure customer confidence, Target engaged in a massive public relations campaign to build customer confidence while also offering discounts to get shoppers to return (Berg, 2014; Weinstein, 2013).

In some cases, these types of risk are independent of one another. In other cases, they are inter-related (Johnson, 2005). Consider, for example, failure of a company to follow OSHA-related guidelines that results in an industrial accident involving damage to company machines and injuries to employees. First, the company has experienced operational losses due to broken machinery. The company is also exposed to legal risk, where it may be found liable in federal court for failing to follow OSHA-related safety standards, having to pay some fines for its actions. Through civil litigation, meanwhile, the organization will have to pay damage awards to employees who are impacted by the organization's action. At the same time, the media publicity around the incident may give the company a poor reputation related to worker safety, leading to further issues related to recruiting new employees and lost revenues from companies and individuals that boycott the company.

▶ Risk Assessment Techniques

Risk assessment and management involve processes that have been used by insurance companies and organizations for decades. They involve deliberate actions aimed at loss prevention and the mitigation of risk. Through the process of *risk management,* security professionals anticipate, recognize, and analyze potential risks and loss-creating threats, implementing strategies to mitigate loss and damage. The analysis of risk is based on the identification of past, existing, and future organizational risks. Continuous risk assessment also enables the security professional to provide sound data upon which to solicit funding and make informed decisions regarding the allocation of scarce resources.

As a method for identifying and evaluating risks, a risk assessment involves a critical, objective analysis of an organization's entire protective system and its vulnerabilities. Basically, risk assessment is a decision-making process that relies upon a comprehensive analysis of security-related issues. It is a process that requires identifying risk factors, modeling their relationships, and then integrating them to form a risk assessment argument that results in a comprehensive risk management program that uses various countermeasures to improve security in the organization (Lee, 2011). This decision-making process primarily relies upon objective information to make sound security-related decisions that will affect the design and operation of physical, personnel, and information security operations in the organization.

> **risk assessment**
> Critical, objective analysis of an organization's entire protective system and its vulnerabilities.

The ASIS International Guidelines Commission (2007) has developed some recommended practices for conducting general security risk assessments. The following is a brief outline of the Commission's recommended approach.

- Develop an understanding of the organization and identify the human, physical, and information assets at risk.
- Specify loss risk events and vulnerabilities.
- Establish the probability of loss risk and determine the frequency of loss events.
- Determine the impact of loss events, including the financial, psychological, and other costs associated with a loss event.
- Develop options to prevent or mitigate losses.
- Study the feasibility of implementing each option.
- Perform a cost-benefit analysis.

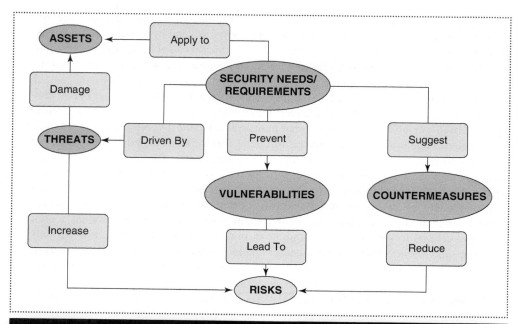

FIGURE 12-3   Common Criteria Security Model
Source: Patrick J. Ortmeier, Johnson, Introduction to Security: Operations and Management, 5e. © 2018, Pearson Education, Inc., New York, NY.

Another way to understand risk and to conduct effective risk assessments is to use the criteria found in the **common criteria security model** (Lee, 2011). This model provides individuals performing risk assessments a cognitive map which serves to identify attributes of risk. As shown in Figure 12-3 ■, this process can be complex. Some of the main points of this model include the following:

- Assets have risk.
- Threats damage assets and increase risk.
- Vulnerabilities (weaknesses) lead to risk.
- Security measures apply to assets, are driven by threats, prevent vulnerabilities, and suggest countermeasures.
- Countermeasures reduce risk.

Security Surveys

A proper risk assessment requires objective and sound data. This information is obtained through a comprehensive **security survey** or audit that identifies vulnerabilities and risks that an organization can or is exposed to. Security surveys can be considered an exhaustive analysis of how various elements can affect the safety and security of the organization (Johnson, 2005). At a minimum, these surveys are designed to collect data regarding organizational vulnerabilities or weaknesses related to legal, personal, and property-related risk (Broder, 2000). They are an objective understanding of the current state of security and safety in an organization, where the subsequent findings will serve as an educational tool for management and function as a basis for safety and security planning activities and programs within the organization. Subsequent actions taken as a result of the findings in the survey will reduce exposure to loss and liability and serve as an instrument for positive change (Johnson, 2005). In-house security personnel can conduct security surveys. Organizations can also contract with companies or individuals who have expertise and specialization in conducting security surveys. Regardless of who conducts the surveys, they must be well planned and have organizational support. The surveys must also be comprehensive and have the appropriate scope and depth to have a meaningful and positive impact on security operations and the organization (Johnson, 2005).

The processes used to collect information during the risk assessment vary and depend on the situation. This data may be collected utilizing subjective and objective techniques. *Subjective (qualitative) measures* include the use of forecasting, employee surveys, expert opinion, and the Delphi technique. The Delphi technique involves a process through which several individuals or experts provide input on a given issue and ultimately arrive at a consensus on a prediction or list of needs and priorities. *Objective (quantitative) measures* include the use of data from audits, marketing, operations research, and incident reports. Information from threat assessments, investigations, risk analyses, inspections, and security (loss prevention) surveys is also used (Bunning, 1979; Jacobson, 1997; Oliver, 2007).

There are various formats that can be used when conducting security surveys. In some cases, an organization can used a structured approach, using pre-existing survey instruments or checklists. These can be purchased from vendors or created by the organization itself. Depending on the needs of the organization, the survey forms can be relatively simple where the user simply checks a box to verify the presence or lack of effective security countermeasures. These checklists can be comprehensive and easy to complete and they may be inexpensive to administer. However, one main drawback that they may have is that the content of the checklist does not provide enough depth or detail; it may not include all of the vulnerabilities that a company may be exposed to, resulting in the organization overlooking some critical vulnerabilities. In other cases, organizations may rely upon more advanced tools that could include in-depth interviews and the use of sophisticated software programs that are designed specifically for conducting security surveys (Johnson, 2005).

> **Delphi technique**
> Process through which several individuals or experts provide input on an issue and arrive at consensus on a prediction or list of needs or priorities.

Conducting the Survey

Depending upon the scope of the security survey, several sources of information can be used. For example, the availability of public services, utilities, and health care, along with political and economic conditions, must be evaluated. Local police crime statistics, Uniform Crime Report (UCR), NIBRS, and National Crime Victimization Survey (NCVS) data and criminal intelligence reports are excellent sources of information. Additionally, general economic conditions, data related to natural disasters, and industry trends are also vital to the risk assessment process (ASIS International Guidelines Commission, 2007). The general area or neighborhood surrounding the facility should also be analyzed. Consideration must also be given to aesthetic qualities and susceptibility to catastrophic events, such as floods. The perimeter near the facility should be evaluated in terms of its parking, fencing, landscaping, and signage. The survey of the building itself should include points of entry, exits, access control, locks and keys, alarm systems and lighting, and vulnerability to intrusion.

Information regarding internal issues must also be examined. These include computer and data storage areas, mechanical and utility rooms, telecommunication rooms, mailrooms, and executive office suites. In addition, alarm and surveillance systems, fire protection, personnel security, and information security must also be reviewed. Also, an organization's internal documents (i.e., incident reports and complaints received) and civil claims can provide critical risk assessment data (ASIS International Guidelines Commission, 2007). A review of organizational policies and procedures used in the management of human resources and in the protection of property and information is important; procedures for investigations and the collection of business and criminal intelligence, as well as reporting systems, operations, and liaison activities, must also be evaluated. Finally, employees should be consulted

$$\text{Vulnerability} \times \text{Probability} \times \text{Criticality} = \text{Risk Level}$$

FIGURE 12-4   Calculating Risk Levels
Source: Patrick J. Ortmeier, Johnson, Introduction to Security: Operations and Management, 5e. © 2018, Pearson Education, Inc., New York, NY.

during the security survey. Employees typically know where vulnerabilities lie. Input from employees also assists with the creation of employee ownership of the security program. Ownership, or buy-in, with employees is critical to program success (Johnson, 2005).

Assigning Risk Levels

Based on the information collected in the survey, the next stage is to identify and prioritize risk levels. As shown in Figure 12-4 ■, risk levels are based on vulnerabilities (weaknesses), the probability of occurrence, and the impact on the organization (criticality) if such an event should occur. Based on these three variables, risk managers can then prioritize each risk, addressing high-risk issues first and then design appropriate countermeasures.

Assigning risk levels begins with identifying vulnerabilities. In the context of security, a vulnerability is a security flaw or weakness that can be exploited by a threat which can subsequently lead to damage, injury, or harm. It is the degree of exposure to an event. If an individual or organization is vulnerable, it is exposed to the possibility that the risk or threat will materialize. A security professional must consider vulnerability as loss. Factors to consider when calculating vulnerability include threat identification and location, accessibility, adequacy of security measures, and the availability of response personnel and emergency equipment.

Next, the probability, which is the likelihood of loss or occurrence, must be considered. Probability is the "odds" of an event occurring, based on the current state of security (or lack thereof). It is expressed in its magnitude of occurrence. For example, an event is certain when the probability of occurrence is 100 percent (or 1.0). Likewise, it can also be totally uncertain if the probability of occurrence is 0. In most cases, the probability of occurrence is not 0 or 1.0. Instead, it falls between the two extreme measures where security managers must use both objective and subjective criteria to generate a correct probability of occurrence value. For example, if a company is located in the Gulf States, it is vulnerable to the impact of tropical storms and perhaps hurricanes. This is based on past natural events as well as forecasting the probability of future events. Likewise, a company that owns a series of convenience stores is at risk for armed robberies. Factors that can increase the probability of an armed robbery are the location of the store, the hours it is open, local crime rates, and existing security practices used. In some cases, estimating the probability of occurrence is based on objective criteria. In other cases, it relies on subjective information, where expertise of those individuals conducting the assessment is relied upon.

Once the probability of occurrence is determined, then the risk management process should determine criticality. Criticality can be thought of as the importance of the asset in achieving mission or organizational success and how damage or loss of the asset could adversely impact the organization (Moteff, 2005; Vellani, 2006). It can also be considered "asset value" (FEMA, 2003). When considering criticality, for example, the organization needs to ask the question: "if the event should occur, what will be the nature and extent of the loss?" In other words, one must foresee the likely impact and consequences associated with the loss. For example, if a product research and development organization stores all of its data at a single location and the IT system is destroyed during a flood, the loss to the organization would be devastating. A criticality assessment involves an evaluation of each human, physical, and information asset to determine its value as well as prioritizing the allocation of security resources to protect the most critical assets.

vulnerability Gaps or weaknesses in the protection of an organization's assets.

probability The likelihood of loss or occurrence.

criticality The importance of the asset in achieving mission or organizational success.

Quantifying Risk: Examples

The actual estimation of the degree of risk can be complex. In some cases, companies can use highly sophisticated software programs. In other instances, quantifying risk can be much easier. For example, FEMA (Federal Emergency Management Agency) uses a 10-point rating scale for calculating criticality (which it refers to as asset value) and the probability of occurrence: 1 is very low; 2–3 is low; 4 is medium low; 5–6 is medium; 7 is medium high; 8–9 is high; and 10 is very high. For vulnerability, a 10-point scale ranging from 1 (no or very low) to 10 (where one or more major weaknesses exist) is used. All three values (criticality x probability x vulnerability) are then multiplied together to generate a numerical risk factor. For example, values of 1–60 denote a low risk, 61–175 is considered medium risk, and values 176 or greater are considered high risk. Once these values are calculated, loss prevention resources are then allocated to protect assets exposed to the highest risk value first. With time and resources permitting, then the organization can address other less serious security issues that have lower values.

A sample template used by FEMA (2003) is shown in Figure 12-5 ■. Here, a fictitious company performed a security assessment, examining specific functions in a company (administration and engineering), and threats that included cyber, armed, vehicle bomb, and chemical, biological, and radiological (CBR) attacks. This assessment shows that the administrative function has a high risk of a cyberattack, while engineering has a high risk of an attack involving a vehicle bomb. In the case of a cyberattack against the administrative functions of the company, the criticality level was 5, the threat rating was 8, and the vulnerability rating was 7 ($5 \times 7 \times 8 = 280$). In the case of engineering, meanwhile, a vehicle bomb attack was identified as the most serious risk factor—not a cyberattack. Here, it was determined that the loss of the engineering function (the asset value) is high (8), the threat of an attack, based on existing threat environment is medium (6), while existing security measures show that the organization is highly vulnerable to an attack (8). Based on these scores, the first security issue that should be addressed by the company are vehicle bomb attacks against engineering (score of 384), followed by enhancing security measures against cyberattacks in the administrative functions in the organization (score of 280).

Function	Cyberattack	Armed Attack (Single Gunman)	Vehicle Bomb	CBR Attack
Administration	280	140	15	90
Asset value (*criticality*)	5	5	5	5
Threat rating (*probability*)	8	4	3	2
Vulnerability rating	7	7	9	9
Engineering	128	160	384	144
Asset value	8	8	8	8
Threat rating	8	5	6	2
Vulnerability rating	2	4	8	9

FIGURE 12-5 Sample FEMA Risk Quantification Table

Source: Patrick J. Ortmeier, Johnson, Introduction to Security: Operations and Management, 5e. © 2018, Pearson Education, Inc., New York, NY.

In some cases, a thorough risk assessment may reveal a low probability that a breach of security or disastrous event will occur. However, the security manager should not disregard low-probability risks; failure to protect against such risks can be a fatal error. The impact of the bombings at the World Trade Center in New York City in 1993, and the federal building in Oklahoma City in 1995, and the terrorist attacks of 9-11 provide ample evidence of the consequences associated with disregarding low-probability risk (Garcia, 2000; Jopeck, 2000; Oliver, 2007; Scalet, 2007).

risk states A method to categorize risk based on subjective ("social world") and objective (physical world") criteria.

Another way to categorize risk is to place it into states instead of numbers. According to Macgill and Siu (2004), any given risk state is based on two core dimensions: (1) the current base of scientific knowledge or facts (the physical world); and (2) social aspects such as happiness and the quality of life of individuals (the social world). As such, risk is a "physical entity coupled with a characteristic social orientation" (p. 321). This perspective also assumes that risk is always in a state of change or flux since risk states can adjust with social views and changes in scientific knowledge. These socially constructed realities and the physical nature of risk can be further divided into four subcategories, based on the damage, injury, or harm (known as detriment) and the level of concern or people's positions related to the particular risk. Figure 12-6 ■ shows these risk states.

As shown is Figure 12-6, risk exists on two axes. The vertical social axis relies on the socially constructed realities of risk (e.g., risk acceptability ranging acceptable to unacceptable). The horizontal axis relies on the factual, scientific perspectives related to the risk (ranging from low to high, based on the degree of expected damage, injury, or harm). To determine the appropriate risk, state analysts should ask "Physical World" questions such as if the risk issue at that particular time is "big" or if there is any factual doubt. Questions related to the "Social World" include the acceptability of, and the level of agreement between individuals regarding the risk.

Depending upon the risk state, the organizations can then develop appropriate risk management responses, based on scientific fact and the constituencies involved. For example, in "State A," a risk manager could use risk acceptance strategies since the risk is socially acceptable and the scientific facts suggest that loss would be low if the event occurred. In the context of "State C," meanwhile, risk avoidance strategies would be used since the risk is socially unacceptable and there is a high degree of objective, scientific proof that the specific risk is simply too high or dangerous.

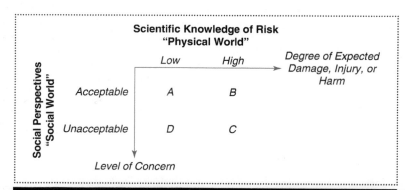

FIGURE 12-6 Risk States

A—high acceptability; low expected detriment; B—high acceptability; high expected detriment; C—low acceptability; high expected detriment; D—low acceptability; low expected detriment.

Source: Patrick J. Ortmeier, Johnson, Introduction to Security: Operations and Management, 5e. © 2018, Pearson Education, Inc., New York, NY.

▶ Risk Management Techniques

Once risks are identified, the next stage of any risk management program is addressing them. Organizations have a variety of risk management options or countermeasures they can choose from. What options are selected oftentimes depend upon the type of risk, the organizational philosophy, the risk environment in which the organization operates, personal choice, and the costs associated with protecting the asset. Several variables are considered when determining which technique is appropriate. For example, if the cost of protecting an asset is more expensive than the asset's value, then the acceptance technique should be used. Some of the more common types of risk management are shown below.

One risk management techniques is risk elimination. The elimination of the risk may be possible, even though total elimination of risk is difficult in most cases (Nakayachi, 1998). For example, many organizations face the risk of loss from fire. Removing all flammable materials from a facility will eliminate the threat of fire fueled by the flammable materials. It will not, however, eliminate the threat of fire fueled by a different source. The total elimination of risk, therefore, is oftentimes unattainable.

> **risk elimination**
> Efforts to reduce risk.

Since elimination of risk is most likely unattainable, organizations have other risk management techniques or options they can choose from to mitigate or reduce the impact of any loss. Mitigation activities can be grouped into five categories: (1) avoidance; (2) reduction; (3) spreading; (4) transfer; and (5) acceptance. All of these are shown in Figure 12-7 ■.

> **mitigation** Efforts to reduce the impact of loss.

Risk avoidance is making decisions and engaging in activities that create less risk. It is simply managing risk by avoiding "risky" things (Johnson, 2005). For example, high fat foods and smoking are risk factors for cardiovascular disease and cancer. To control the risk of heart disease or cancer, individuals may avoid high-fat foods in their diet and not smoke cigarettes. Likewise, some areas of a city may have a higher risk factor for being victimized by criminals. To manage this risk, individuals may simply avoid high-crime areas.

> **risk avoidance**
> Making decisions and engaging in activities that create less risk. Managing risk by avoiding "risky" things.

Avoidance is one way to deal with uncertainty and risk in organizations. Businesses may choose more predictable and safe options over speculative or more risky options. In the context of security, risk avoidance is generally associated with the elimination of various activities that are identified and considered too risky and cannot be managed in any other way. It is the complete elimination of the risk. For example, some regions and countries in the world are too risky for company executives and operations due to unstable governments and the threat of terrorism. Because the risk is so high and security practices cannot effectively mitigate (reduce) the risk, the end solution would be to avoid those areas.

Organizations can also engage in risk reduction activities. They are designed to reduce the consequences and likelihood of any loss associated with the specific risk(s). In a broad sense, risk reduction is reducing risk to its lowest level (Jha, 2010). In the context of natural disasters, for example, risk reduction is defined as the "conceptual framework

> **risk reduction**
> Activities designed to reduce the consequences and likelihood of any loss associated with the specific risk(s).

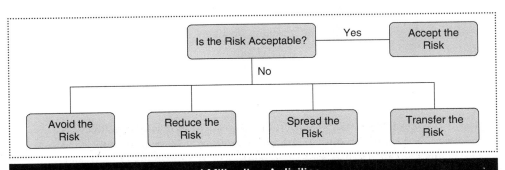

FIGURE 12-7   Risk Management Mitigation Activities
Source: Patrick J. Ortmeier, Johnson, Introduction to Security: Operations and Management, 5e. © 2018, Pearson Education, Inc., New York, NY.

of elements considered with the possibilities to minimize vulnerabilities and disaster risks throughout society, to avoid (prevention) or to limit (mitigation and preparedness) the adverse impacts of hazards, within the broad context of sustainable development" (Ginige, Amaratunga, & Haigh, 2009, p. 557). Some examples of risk reduction activities include modifying environmental safety controls by installing new safety equipment on machines, creating effective policies and procedures, and installing new forms of physical security (Johnson, 2005).

risk spreading Practices designed to spread or separate assets to mitigate or reduce loss.

Risk spreading is a common mitigation tool. It is based on the belief of "not putting all of your eggs in one basket." For example, a company may have off-site data storage based on the logic that if the internal system should fail, the data can still be retrieved from the external storage site. Other examples include compartmentalizing factory buildings to separate the risk of production loss due to fire or some other event. Some companies also have production facilities located throughout the United States and even the world. While often based on logistics, in a security perspective having multiple production facilities, instead of just one, will ensure continued production if one factory was shut down because of a long- or short-term man-made or natural event. Risk spreading is even used by the U.S. Secret Service. In most cases, the President and Vice-President of the United States travel separately to ensure that the "risk" to the effective leadership of the United States is not disrupted if something should happen to the President. Another example of risk spreading is the practice of asset redistribution. Investors, for example, do not invest solely in one company or market. Instead, they spread their financial assets in various companies and stock markets throughout the world to lessen the impact of any financial losses that could occur in one specific market, region, or company.

risk transfer Shifting the risk burden onto someone else.

In other cases, risk management may involve transfer. Risk transfer is defined as shifting the risk burden onto someone else (Ghosh, 2013). It can also be understood as "sharing with another party the burden of loss, or benefit of gain, for a risk" (Sadgrove, 2015, p. 321). One common example of risk transfer is insurance. Through insuring a particular activity, financial ramifications are now the burden of the insurance company. The transfer of risk also occurs through contractual agreements. Consider, for example, a company that uses contract security. Oftentimes, the contract between the parties results in a lot of liability (legal risk) being shifted from the organization itself to the contract security provider.

risk acceptance Accepting that some type or degree of loss will occur.

Finally, there is risk acceptance. In some cases, an organization, even after considering or using risk reduction, spreading, and transfer methods, will simply accept that some loss will occur (Johnson, 2005). Oftentimes the decision to accept risk is based on cost: if it would cost more to protect the asset than what it is worth, an acceptable and rational practice would be to accept the fact that it can be lost. For example, retailers have a variety of security countermeasures to deter, detect, and deny the opportunity for retail theft. Even though these reduce the risk, retail crime still occurs. Retail theft is simply an unfortunate outcome of doing business. Therefore, the retailer "accepts" some level of loss because the protection of all items would be difficult to achieve, and very expensive.

SECURITY SPOTLIGHT

Select two assets at the educational institution you attend or the organization where you are employed. For each asset you selected, calculate the risk level associated with that asset, by assigning numerical values for vulnerability (1 to 3), probability (1 to 3), and criticality (1 to 5). Which of the assets has the highest risk level? What could be done to mitigate that risk level?

▶ Continuity and Contingency Planning

As already reviewed in Chapter 9, the management of risk also requires the creation of continuity and contingency plans. Business continuity plans (BCPs) and the activities derived from these plans are designed to ensure that normal business operations are not disrupted by disasters, emergencies, crises, or other significant events. The primary goals of these plans are to "prevent, mitigate, prepare for, respond to, resume, recover, restore and transition from a disruptive (crisis) event in a manner consistent with its strategic objectives" (Shaw & Harrald, 2006, p. 3). A business continuity plan typically includes information related to: line of succession, notification of stakeholders, plan activation, recovery, and resumption (return to normal operation). The primary goal of any continuity plan is to ensure that business operations continue during an interruption event (Polelle, 2000).

> business continuity plan (BCPs) A plan designed to ensure that significant events do not disrupt normal business operations.

Continuity plans are essential for organizations in both the private and public sectors. In the private sector, loss due to risk can adversely impact the short- and long-term success of a company, leading to serious financial losses and even the firm going out of business. For example, failure to maintain continuous operations can negatively affect a business' revenue stream—a danger that seems to have captured executives' attention. In a survey of Fortune 1,000 companies, respondents cited business continuity as among their top three concerns, behind cyber/communications security and workplace violence (Securitas, 2010). In the public sector, meanwhile, the public is dependent on many critical functions such as police, fire, and 911 that must be maintained under all circumstances. Without an ability to restore public services to normal operations, property can be destroyed and lives may be lost.

Contingency Plans

Contingency planning is the planning and preparation for events that could impact individuals and the organization. These plans are an integral component of the risk management process and they are part of continuity plans. These contingency plans can be thought of as using various (contingent) strategies or alternative courses of action in order to deal with the "what ifs" if an event should occur. It addresses operational elements that are most likely to be adversely affected by change. These plans are considered the first step of emergency preparedness. Consider, for example, a person who has a vehicle that is not dependable and is prone to breaking down. To make sure that the person can still make an important meeting, the contingency plan will involve having back up forms of transportation, including friends or a rental car to ensure that the meeting is attended. Contingency plans can also be thought of as the "Plan B" or worst case scenario plan.

> contingency plan Plan implemented only if a certain event, such as a natural disaster, occurs.

There are several types of contingency plans. Some are simple, while others are complex. For example, the response to an accident requiring basic first aid may be relatively simple, while a response to an environmental disaster can be very detailed and complex. Disasters can impact an entire community or region. Therefore, a contingency plan should address all conceivable variables and requirements. For example, a chain of command designating authority relationships must be created. This includes command staff as well as a designated emergency coordinator. The plan must state its purpose, the types of emergencies covered, and the transition process from normal to emergency operations. Plan execution instructions and supporting information must be included. Maps and information on procedures, local resources, mutual-aid agreements, and liaison personnel are essential. The locations of the emergency control and operations center must be identified and communications channels should be described in the plan. Provisions must be made to secure vital agency and organizational records and databases. This includes data files, incorporation certificates, bylaws, client lists, stock records, board meeting minutes, and financial records. Emergency shutdown procedures, personnel protection systems, the roles of supervisors, emergency evacuation routes, and shelter locations must be specified. All contingency plans should be published in a manual, and employees must be trained regarding their response in the event of a disaster. Finally, the plan should be tested periodically to ensure organizational readiness and to assess the need for changes to the plan (Collins, 2008; Haddow & Bullock, 2010; Meese & Ortmeier, 2004; Papi, 1994).

Contingency Plans and Emergency Management

Disaster and emergency planning is critical to business survival. America's businesses form the mainstay of the nation's economy. Thus, businesses must be prepared to survive and manage the consequences of and recover from natural and environmental disasters. Safe and secure businesses help to secure the economy and the nation. Businesses must identify possible emergencies that might affect the business; develop plans to respond to those emergencies; involve, protect, and communicate with all stakeholders (employees and customers); establish liaison with public safety agencies; and, safeguard the business' physical and information assets.

National Incident Management System (NIMS) A disaster and emergency plan that provides unified federal, state, county, and local approach to disasters with an emphasis on preparedness, standardization, mutual aid, and resource management.

While most emergencies are handled internally and locally, major incidents often require the assistance of several jurisdictions, including the state and federal governments. As reviewed in Chapter 9, the National Incident Management System (NIMS) was developed through the DHS to promote collaboration among first responders from different jurisdictions and public safety disciplines. Through NIMS, which sets forth the process for responding to events, agencies are better able to respond to natural disasters and emergencies, including acts of terrorism. NIMS benefits include an emphasis on preparedness, mutual aid, and resource management as well as standardized command structures, and a unified approach to incident response (Federal Emergency Management Agency, 2007). NIMS also serves as the foundation for the *National Response Framework,* which is a guide that promotes an all-hazards approach and a unified response to incidents. The framework incorporates best practices from law enforcement, firefighting, public works, emergency medical services, public health, emergency management, homeland security, and the private sector for managing serious local and large scale events.

The Framework's Response Doctrine includes the following elements:

1. Engaged Partnerships: Avoid dominoes of sequential failure. Layered, mutually supporting capabilities; plan together; understand strengths/weaknesses, know where gaps are. Develop shared goals; align capabilities so none allows other to be overwhelmed.

2. Tiered Response: Incidents must be managed at the lowest possible jurisdictional level and supported by additional response capabilities when needed.

3. Scalable, Flexible, and Adaptable Operational Capabilities: As incidents change in size, scope, and complexity, the number, type, and source of responses must be able to expand to meet requirements.

4. Unity of Effort through Unified Command: Effective unified command indispensable to all response activities; requires clear understanding of roles and responsibilities; shared objectives. Each agency maintains its own authority, responsibility, and accountability.

5. Readiness to Act: Readiness to act balanced with an understanding of risk. Requires clear, focused communications. Disciplined processes, procedures, and systems. From individuals, families, communities to local, State, and Federal agencies, national response depends on instinct and ability to act (U.S. Department of Homeland Security, 2008, p. 6).

Some of the main components of contingency plans in a disaster include: (1) emergency response; (2) business recovery; and (3) business resumption activities. *Emergency response* is defined "as all the activities for identifying, detecting, planning, training, analyzing vulnerability and responding to unanticipated events that may result in injury and/or loss of human lives and damage and/or destruction of critical infrastructure elements" (Jain & McClean, 2003, p. 1). The goals of emergency response include: (1) increasing the likelihood that people at risk will take precautions, preventing injury, and saving lives; (2) reducing anxiety levels and avoiding unnecessary care-seeking by unthreatened populations; and (3) facilitating relief efforts (James, Hawkins, & Rowel, 2007). These are response and assistance-related activities that occur during and immediately after an event. They are the immediate efforts to save lives, protect property, and maintain and restore continuity of services (Boersma, Comfort, Groenendaal, & Wolbers, 2014).

Response efforts depend upon the event. If large enough, these events could also include the use of local first responders, including police, fire, and emergency medical personnel. For example, a fire in a facility would involve security personnel, other internal staff assigned to emergencies, and the local fire department. Some large scale events, meanwhile, will require state and federal response activities where additional personnel, equipment, and expertise are required. These large scale events are often associated with natural disasters, including tornadoes and hurricanes where FEMA and other federal agencies, state and local agencies, and the private sector respond collectively.

Next, recovery efforts are conducted immediately after emergency response to the event. The primary (but nevertheless complex) goal of recovery is to have the organization recover as fast as possible after an event (McEntire, 2014). Consider the example of a ship hitting an iceberg: here, the primary recovery goal of the captain and crew is to "plug the hole" as fast as possible so the ship will not sink. Once the hole is plugged, then it can continue or resume with its voyage, conducting repairs as it goes. Another analogy of recovery can be found in the game of football where a player gets tackled after running the ball. Here, the player recovers from the tackle and then resumes the game.

> **recovery efforts**
> Part of disaster management. Actions taken after an event occurs in an effort to return to a pre-event or normal state.

Many organizations have highly qualified and trained emergency response personnel.
(Photo courtesy of Randy Montoyo/Sandia National Laboratories.)

Even if organizations have risk management plans, they may be exposed to various events that create a "hole" or crisis for the organizations. Like the previous ship analogy, the organization will need to "plug the hole" first and then continue on with its operations. The goal of business recovery is to get the organization up and running again to an acceptable level or condition as fast as possible so it can perform essential business functions. While not at pre-event functions, it is nevertheless performing essential business functions. It is "limping along" and performing at an "acceptable level" and engaging in various restoration activities (Halibozek, Kovacich, & Jones, 2008). Depending upon the crisis, this could take months or even years to accomplish. In some cases, recovery efforts may never result in a pre-event condition. The events of a crisis or disaster could profoundly affect social and economic conditions of society and organizations (Hiltz, Diaz, & Mark, 2011).

All recovery activities must be properly planned prior to the event and prioritized. Part of the planning process is to establish recovery time objectives (RTOs). These RTOs are specific activities and the estimated duration of time that will be needed to restore and/or replace critical activities and processes to prevent any unacceptable consequences. These RTOs are based on priority and they are often sequential in nature. These plans and subsequent actions are directed at recovering critical and essential operations first that are crucial to organizational survival, followed by important, but less serious functions. Once these critical operations are re-established, then the organization can address other issues that the event has impacted (Elliot, Swartz, & Herbane, 2010). For example, one critical component in most organizations today is the information technology (IT) function. In this context, FEMA (2015) recommends that companies should anticipate and develop recovery plans related to IT system components that include: computer room environment, hardware (networks, servers, and computers), connectivity to service providers, and data recovery. Once data recovery efforts have resulted in the organization re-establishing its IT function, then it can begin establishing its production capabilities.

Last, business resumption activities are directed at restoring the organization to pre-event conditions. Resumption activities occur after recovery actions have brought the organization back to an operational state once systems are available (Payne, 2008). Resumption is tied to recovery. Resumption is impaired if recovery efforts are not achieved (Green & CITP, 2007). As such, organizations need to have effective recovery plans followed by resumption plans. These plans deal with "how, where, when, and who will be responsible and what they will do when a significant event occurs" (Freeman, 2002, p. 3). These plans are actually created pre-event to ensure that the organization can resume its operations as fast as possible. As is the case in recovery-related activities, these processes can be long and complicated. Consider, for example, if the critical infrastructure in an area or region is heavily impacted and is subsequently going through recovery activities. In this case, resumption efforts within the organization will be slowed since these specific activities are oftentimes tied to the state or condition of the external environment (Botten & Riggs, 1998).

> **recovery time objectives (RTOs)** Specific activities and the estimated times it will take to restore and/or replace critical activities and processes.

> **business resumption activities** Activities are directed at restoring the organization to pre-event conditions.

Summary

Risk is defined as the possibility of suffering harm or loss, exposure to the probability of loss or damage, an element of uncertainty, or the possibility that the results of an action may not be consistent with expected outcomes. Risk management, meanwhile, is the process of identifying and managing risk. To identify risk and an organization's vulnerabilities or weaknesses, risk assessment tools are used. These risk assessments often use security surveys, which are an objective and comprehensive analyses of an organization's risks and its vulnerabilities. Based on the information collected in the security survey where risks and vulnerabilities are identified, the next stage of the risk management process is to prioritize the risk based on existing vulnerabilities or weaknesses, the probability that the event could occur, and the criticality of the issue in question. All three of these factors are equally important. Once identified and prioritized, then reduction, spreading, and transfer-related strategies can be used to manage the risk.

This chapter has also reviewed business continuity planning which is part of the risk management process. Continuity plans and subsequent activities are designed to ensure that operations are uninterrupted if an adverse event should occur. To ensure continuity, organizations must also have contingency plans. These contingency plans can be thought of as using various (contingent) strategies to deal with the "what ifs" if an actual event should occur. Serious events such as disasters also require a comprehensive continuity plan. These plans must include response, recovery, and resumption activities.

Key Terms and Concepts

Business continuity plans (BCPs) *269*
Business resumption activities *272*
Common criteria security model *262*
Contingency planning *269*
Criticality *264*
Delphi technique *263*
Dynamic risk *259*
Legal risk *260*
Mitigation *267*
National Incident Management System (NIMS) *270*

Operational risk *260*
Operational risk management (ORM) *260*
Probability *264*
Pure risk *259*
Recovery efforts *271*
Recovery time objectives (RTOs) *272*
Reputational risk *260*
Risk *256*
Risk acceptance *268*
Risk assessment *261*

Risk avoidance *267*
Risk elimination *267*
Risk management *257*
Risk reduction *267*
Risk spreading *268*
Risk states *266*
Risk transfer *268*
Security survey *262*
Speculative risk *259*
Static risk *259*
Vulnerability *264*

Discussion Questions and Exercises

1. Explain why risk management is an important component of an organization's security program.
2. Explain the purpose of a risk management program. What are the four major components of a risk management program? Why is it a cycle? Why should a risk management program be continual in nature?
3. Describe the types of risk. Provide examples of each.
4. What is risk assessment? What is its role in risk management?

5. What is the purpose of a security survey? What are some key elements of these surveys?
6. How is an asset evaluated to determine its vulnerability, probability, and criticality of loss?
7. What are the four ways to mitigate risk? Provide examples of each.
8. What is a continuity plan? Provide an example.
9. What is a contingency plan? Provide an example.
10. Explain the three stages in a disaster-related contingency plan.

Your Turn

Conducting a Safety and Security Survey

Conduct a safety and security survey of your home or a small business:

1. Identify a small business and obtain permission from the owner (or the person in charge) to conduct the survey.

2. Identify five risks the organization or home is vulnerable to.
3. Classify and prioritize each type of risk.
4. Provide some ideas on how to mitigate these risks.

PART 5

Trends and Challenges

This section considers critical developments in the realm of security and challenges facing the security profession. Chapter 13 reviews the nature and extent of security operations in other parts of the world. Chapter 14 looks ahead to the future, anticipating developments in key areas, including the security profession, legislative trends, terrorism, and globalization.

13 Security in an International Perspective

LEARNING OBJECTIVES

After completing this chapter, the reader will be able to:

1. *identify the main social and political factors that led to the growth of private security throughout the world*

2. *explain how the private security industry is regulated and controlled in other regions of world, compared to the United States*

3. *assess the quality of the private security industry throughout the world*

4. *compare and contrast security needs and practices throughout the world*

5. *identify some unique private security activities throughout the world*

6. *explain some of the key deficiencies in the regulation of private security industries in various regions of the world*

7. *explain the role of private security military companies*

8. *Identify major issues related to the use of private military security companies*

9. *explain the nature and extent of maritime piracy and various ways to secure maritime shipping*

10. *explain the various private and public organizations involved in the regulation and control of private security companies throughout the world*

▶ Introduction

This chapter examines the private security industry throughout the world. By examining the evolution and growth of security throughout the world, a greater understanding of some themes, commonalities, and unique practices and issues can be identified. A global analysis will also provide some insight into the potential strengths and weaknesses and areas for improvement in the U.S. private security industry. Some of the specific regions reviewed in this chapter include the former Communist states from the Soviet Union, Yugoslavia, and nations in Southeastern Europe. Security practices in the European Union and the United Kingdom are also reviewed. In addition to the European continent, this chapter also reviews security activities and issues in the continent of Africa and Central and South America, exposing unique security activities and factors that led to its evolution and growth in these regions of the world. This chapter also reviews two contemporary international issues in private security: the use of private military security companies (PMSCs) and international piracy that has a large impact on maritime security operations. A review of existing international regulations and agreements, specifically the Montreux Document, the ICoC, and the role of the UN in regulating the private security industry is also part of this chapter.

► The Private Security Industry in Europe

The former USSR and Warsaw Pact Countries

Since the early 1990s, the private security industry in the former Warsaw Pact countries has experienced a large growth. The collapse of the former Soviet Union and its Warsaw Pact countries, and the resulting transformation from Communism to a democratic and capitalistic system resulted in these counties experiencing a new phenomenon—the shift from a political system that relied upon state control of security of most industries to the emergence of a market-driven private sector that was no longer directly controlled by the state. Because of this change, private security has expanded in number and scope in many (if not all) of these "new" countries (Lehmbruch & Sanikidze, 2014; Sergevnin & Kovalyov, 2013). This growth was due in part to the demand for increased security needs in the new private business sector, the rise in crime, and the resulting need for additional security-related activities that are no longer provided at adequate levels by the state (Van Steden & Sarre, 2007). To meet these new needs, former (and current) intelligence and former military personnel sought out more financially lucrative opportunities in the private sector (Lehmbruch & Sanikidze, 2014; Sergevnin & Kovalyov, 2013). In other cases, the demand for security led to the nation's government contracting its state-security-related services to private firms. This served as a new, nongovernmental revenue stream that specific state ministries used for their operations, resulting in some of these agencies actually becoming "quasi-private security" agencies. For example, in Lithuania, the Police Protection Office was retained by the national police because it was profitable and it provided a revenue stream from the private sector (Lehmbruch, 2012).

In many of these emerging post-Communism democratic and capitalistic nations, there have been some issues with the growth of private security. One particular issue is that in many cases, legislation followed the creation of the industry. In this context, the private security industry emerged to meet security-related issues, but there was no legislation or regulations controlling the industry's actions. Because of the lack of regulation combined with weak and sometimes corrupt governmental structures, corrupt and illegal activities between the private sector and governmental officials arose. For example, in some cases, former police and governmental officials that were part of the old authoritarian oppressive governmental or state security sector (e.g., the KGB) created their own questionable private security companies (Bachmann, Stewart, & Fisher, 2015). Because of their close connections to the government, corrupt and monopolistic agreements between the government and some security companies emerged (Hensell, 2012; Kupatadze, 2015). Consider for example, the Ukraine. From 2005 to 2012, the State Protection Service (DSO), which was a special police unit in the Ministry of the Interior, was actually contracting its security-related services to the private sector, oftentimes forcing banks into contracts with the DSO instead of private sector security companies (Markus, 2015). Issues related to using state resources to generate profits, conflict of interests, and claims of unfair competition between state agencies and the private security industry also existed in other former communist states (Lehmbruch & Sanikidze, 2014).

Yugoslavia and Southern Eastern Europe

In the 1990s, this region of the world also saw a break from socialism and a swing to democracy and capitalism. In the former state of Yugoslavia, for example, the private security industry has grown rapidly since the 1990s, due in part to demands from private sector businesses and the public sector not providing satisfactory security-related services. In Slovenia, former police started their own private security companies, which resulted in a transfer of some negative practices from public policing to the private sector. As was the case under Marshal Tito and former Communism, the state was involved in a great deal of surveillance-related activities against its citizenry. With the new private security sector, meanwhile, some private companies engaged in similar activities that were now prohibited (by law) by the police and public sector. These actions oftentimes widened the "surveillance net" that the police performed when the Communist state existed, which led to an initial distrust and fear of the private sector security industry by the citizenry (Šelih, Završnik, Aas, Gorkič, & Kanduč, 2012). The research also shows that private security sector often partners with the existing public police in crime prevention efforts. This has resulted in decreases in crimes, such as armed robberies in commercial banking institutions (Vukadin, Borovec, & Golub, 2013). Since the worldwide recession in 2008, the private sector has expanded in this region due in part to deceased funding of the police. Based on current research, private security personnel have now gained a degree of trust among the citizenry. In some counties, private security personnel are ranked second, next to the police as a legitimate and trusted means of security (Lobnikar, Sotlar, & Modic, 2015).

Like many other countries, the industry also emerged in the field where little or no laws existed. However, these new countries are now passing laws related to the regulation and control of their activities. One example of early legislation can be seen in Slovenia. It first passed security-related legislation related to licensing and training in 1994. Later, in 2011, Slovenia's Ministry of the Interior took over the licensing and regulation of its private security industry, requiring mandatory training of security personnel. Even though regulations and licensing do exist, issues related to circumventing licensing, labor rights of employees, poor salaries, dangerous working conditions, and the supervision of company operations exist (Šelih et al., 2012). In neighboring Croatia, meanwhile, the private security industry is also large and state regulated. It has been estimated that the ratio of private security to citizens is 1:280 compared to the police whose ratio is 1:236. Here, security personnel are regulated under the Act of Private Protection, which is administered by the Ministry of the Interior. Like Slovenia, private security personnel have limited powers. They can only engage in preventive protection activities and serve as a deterrent to crime ("Private security," 2015).

This region also experienced a civil war from 1992 to 1995, leading to some challenges in the development of the private security industry in a post-conflict society. These challenges included the presence of multinational security forces (e.g., the United Nations) that delayed the creation of the private security industry because these forces provided de-facto security services. Other challenges included the lack of a "rule of law" and resistance to creating a private security sector because some of the people involved in its establishment also took part in the conflict, leading to public trust issues (Sotlar, 2009). Some other issues that existed in these post-conflict nations included: (1) the lack of professionalism in the sector; (2) the lack of expertise, appropriate legislation, political will, and resources to regulate the sector; (3) an underdeveloped private security market or no demand for its services because of a destroyed infrastructure; and (4) the development of the industry not being a priority, since the reconstruction of society was the primary concern of these nations (Soltar, 2009).

> **plural policing**
> The practice of sharing and/or transferring traditional public sector police services to the private sector.

This growth and expansion of private security has also resulted in plural policing. This term is related to the fact that in many regions of the world, policing-related activities are no longer the sole or sovereign domain of the public sector. Instead, other private sources of security and public policing exist, work with, and complement existing levels of state-supplied policing services (Murray, 2006). This pluralism can be seen with the ratio of private to public police (in these and other European countries) that is almost equal to, or in some cases, exceed the number of public police personnel (Lobnikar et al., 2015).

While it has been determined that private security companies do not pose a threat to the stability of some governments in Southeastern Europe (Albania, Bosnia and Herzegovina, Bulgaria, Croatia, the Former Yugoslav Republic of Macedonia, Moldova, and Serbia and Montenegro), some concerns that exist are related to criminal activities and improper relationships with political and paramilitary groups. Acts of predatory entrepreneurialism, where corrupt private security companies extort local businesses for "protection" was also identified (Aidis, Estrin, & Mickiewicz, 2012). Regardless of these issues, the private security sector in many of the former Yugoslav states has been found to have a stabilizing effect; it employs a large number of individuals and it supplements existing state delivered security efforts (Sotlar, 2009).

Other countries in Southeastern Europe (Albania, Bulgaria, Kosovo, and Serbia) have also seen growth in their private security sectors. The Geneva Center for the Democratic Control of Armed Forces (DCAF), an international foundation that studies security sector governance (SSG), conducted a series of studies in Southeastern Europe to determine the sector's current state and issues within it. DCAF found that a relatively large grey market for security personnel exists in Albania, Bulgaria, and Serbia. These grey markets exist when unlicensed security firms and individuals perform security-related activities in the country. For instance, shopping malls, clubs, and supermarkets may have their own security functions that are not licensed through the state. In Albania, meanwhile, the general conclusion was that even though legislation directly related to private security exists, there was still a lack of oversight of private security agencies, corruption, poor self-organization of the private sector, and poor record keeping by the Albanian Government due to the legal vacuum following the elimination of the communist regime in the early 1990s. The field was also determined to be a "reservoir of employment" for the low skilled segment of the workforce (Klopfer & vanAmstel, 2015).

Kosovo and Serbia have similar issues according to DCAF. One unique attribute of the private security industry in Kosovo is that its structure was influenced by the United Nations. Out of concerns that former paramilitary personnel would enter the private security field and use their positions to destabilize the country, in 1999, the United Nations enacted legislation that prohibited domestic private security personnel from being armed, only allowing international security companies to provide armed services. This was done to avoid any issues or concerns related to former military groups gaining power through their presence in the private security industry. With new legislation in 2011, security personnel are now licensed. Other findings from DCAF were that the private security sector in Kosovo was "disorganized and disjointed" where the Division for private security companies (part of the Ministry of Internal Affairs) lacks institutional support, financial resources, and the capacity to perform its regulatory role. Finally, Serbia has one of the largest numbers of individuals (30,000–50,000) employed in private security. Under legislation passed in 2013, security personnel must pass required training requirements and companies have to be licensed. Professional security organizations have also developed and corruption in the industry is less of an issue due in part to the fact that many companies demand quality services. It was also determined that security clients were closely aligned with political parties and the industry was a very competitive market where companies undercut one another with lower contract bids, driving employee wages down (Klopfer & vanAmstel, 2015).

The European Union

The European Union (EU) is an economic and political union of 27 member states. Like other regions of the world, the need for security is strong in the EU. Research shows that the ratio of security per 10,000 residents is 31.11, compared to 36.28 for the public police. The industry itself accounts for approximately 35 billion Euros annually (CoESS, 2011). Compared to the United States, the private security sector is more regulated and controlled at the state level where companies and employees have to meet licensure standards. However, one common gap in legislation that exists among many EU countries is that in-house security personnel are not licensed, resulting in some proprietary companies having lower standards in comparison to their regulated counterparts in the contract security side. A summary of the security legislation and facts related to security personnel in the EU countries, along with Bosnia and Herzegovina, Croatia, Macedonia, Norway, Serbia, Switzerland, and Turkey can be found in Box 13-1.

Geneva Center for the Democratic Control of Armed Forces (DCAF) International foundation that studies security sector governance (SSG).

grey markets A market where the goods sold or used is not necessarily illegal. However, the sale, or use of the goods is illegal because it violates existing laws and legal restrictions.

European Union (EU) Economic and political union of 27 European member nations.

THE PRIVATE SECURITY INDUSTRY IN EUROPE

Economic and Industry Facts:

- Average market growth 2005–2010: 13.3 percent
- Total number of private security companies: 52,300
- Licensing for private security companies is mandatory by law: 94 percent
- Authority in charge of drafting/amending legislation:
  - Police: 41 percent
  - Ministry of Interior: 53 percent
  - Ministry of Justice: 16 percent
  - Other: 25 percent
- Authority in charge of controls/inspections of industry:
  - Police: 41 percent

- Ministry of Interior: 38 percent
- Other: 18 percent
- Ministry of Justice: 3 percent

Private security guard facts:

- Licensing of private security guards is mandatory by law: 88 percent
- Average age: 35 years
- Gender: males (83 percent); females (17 percent)
- Average staff turnover: 33 percent
- Mandatory uniforms: 95 percent
- Mandatory identification cards: 98 percent

Source: Patrick J. Ortmeier, Johnson, Introduction to Security: Operations and Management, 5e. © 2018, Pearson Education, Inc., New York, NY.

Confederation of European Security Services (CoESS) Located primarily in the European Union, an umbrella organization for security-related companies.

To increase professionalism, while representing the needs of the security industry, in 1989, the Confederation of European Security Services (CoESS) was created. The CoESS is a private sector umbrella organization composed of private security employers' associations in the EU, representing approximately 50,000 security companies and 1.7 million employees. Headquartered in Belgium, CoESS' core objective is to "defend the interests of its national member federations and of their member private security services companies, both at European and at international level, and to represent those joint interests, in particular through its involvement in the work aimed at harmonizing national private security legislation and regulations" (CoESS, 2013, p. 1). In doing so, CoESS and its working committees (guard, cash-in-transit, electronic surveillance, airport security, maritime security, social dialogue, and enlargement efforts to expand CoESS and the industry) work with European countries and legislative bodies in the development of security legislation and policy. While engaged in lobbying activities and considering itself to be a privileged partner in the development of policies and legislation with European nations, CoESS is also actively involved in security-related research and providing the sector with documentation (including position papers) on best practices in the field.

While security-related standards are generally higher in comparison to United States, there are no universal security regulations that exist among European counties. This can lead to issues and confusion for those companies (such as cash-in-transit) operating between states, making security-related business within the EU difficult (CoESS, 2011). Authors have also raised concerns that private security companies can become involved in corrupt activities including cigarette smuggling and the control and distribution of illegal drugs in areas where they operate (Gounev & Bezlov, 2012).

For more information on the Confederation of European Security Services (CoESS), go to www.coess.org

One of the primary concerns in Europe is that private security companies can impact the human rights and fundamental freedoms of individuals. To address this concern, many countries have adopted conventions related to human rights and law. For example, the Council of Europe's (an intergovernmental organization that promotes human rights)

Recommendation No. R (87) 19 has been adopted by many nations. This Recommendation recognizes the importance of private security and its role in crime prevention. It also states that its functions should not jeopardize individual freedoms and public order and should not encroach on the functions of the police. Other points in the Recommendation include the creation of minimum standards and training for staff, distinctive uniforms, and the need for a positive relationship between the private security industry and the police. Later, in 2005, this human rights issue was raised again by the Council of Police Matters, Council of Europe, where concerns related to common minimal standards and inadequate oversight and control of private security operations in some member states were raised (Born, Caparini, & Cole, 2007).

The United Kingdom

Compared to the United States, the United Kingdom (England, Northern Ireland, Scotland, and Wales) has national standards and regulations for the private security industry. In 2003, the United Kingdom established the Security Industry Authority (SIA) under the Private Security Industry Act of 2001. The SIA is a governmental entity that is responsible for licensing individuals, managers, and security companies operating in the transit of cash and valuables, door supervision, public space surveillance, guards, and close protection. The SIA also conducts inspections and establishes competency and minimum training standards for trainers in the private sector who deliver SIA certification programs. It also publishes and conducts research and maintains a register of license holders. Under the SIA licensing program, applicants can complete different training modules that include the common core, conflict management, and physical intervention, depending upon the sector they would like to work in. Upon successful completion of required training, individuals can then apply for licensure to work in a specific security sector that they were trained in. These sectors include: manned guarding, cash and valuables in transit, close protection, door supervision, public space surveillance (CCTV), security guarding, immobilization, restriction and removal of vehicles, and key holding. Each sector requires individual licensure, and through the SIA's register of license holders, companies can verify that the individual is properly licensed to perform specific security functions. Security personnel, meanwhile, are required to wear identification badges that are issued by the SIA that clearly shows on the badge what the person is licensed to perform (Security Industry Authority, 2013). This Act, however, does not regulate in-house or proprietary security personnel.

> **Security Industry Authority (SIA)** Established under the Private Security Industry Act of 2001 in the United Kingdom. The SIA is a governmental entity that is responsible for licensing individuals, managers, and security companies operating in the transit of cash and valuables, door supervision, public space surveillance, guards, and close protection.

Public–private partnerships are also present in the United Kingdom. One example of a partnership is Project Griffin where the London Metropolitan Police considers the private sector to be a spoke in its "security wheel." Started in 2004, by the city of London and the London Metropolitan Police, one of the major goals of this program is to have "Griffin-trained" security personnel available if the city of London should have some major incident, such as a terrorist attack (Sarre, 2012). Its focus is to enhance community awareness, surveillance, and reporting in order to "advise and familiarise managers, security officers and employees of large public and private sector organisations across the capital on security, counter-terrorism and crime prevention issues" (Project Griffin, 2015, np). Under this program, private security personnel are trained and "Griffin certified" to assist public sector police personnel. Companies also participate in Awareness Days that are sponsored by local police that train security personnel on how to respond to emergency events and recognize suspicious individuals and behaviors. Other activities include Bridge Calls, which use modern technologies to meet and keep all participants aware of security-related issues and threats; and Emergency Deployments that involve Griffin-certified security personnel to support and assist (as civilians only) the police by patrolling and establishing barricades and performing other tasks in emergency

> **Project Griffin** Public Private partnership in the City of London involving the London Metropolitan Police, private organizations, and private security.

Project Argus
Created by the United Kingdom's National Counter Terrorism Security Office (NaCTSO) where Counter Terrorism Security Advisors (CTSAs) train individuals in the office and retail, night clubs, hotels, education, health, and architectural design and planning sectors on crime prevention and antiterrorism techniques.

Project Kraken
UK-based antiterrorism security program administered by the National Crime Agency; increases vigilance among the UK's 20,000 miles of coastline and waterways.

Project Pegasus
UK-based antiterrorism and security program directed toward increasing vigilance in the aviation community.

Project Servator
Created by the City of London Police in February, 2014. The primary objective of this program is to address terrorism and other crimes by randomly deploying increased numbers of police officers in London and developing stronger relationships with citizens, British Transport Police, the private security sector, and businesses.

Ring of Steel
Nickname for security measures that exist around the City of London.

situations (Project Griffin, 2015). There are also "Griffin Days" where security personnel are trained by police personnel on terrorism and public safety-related issues and practices (White & Gill, 2013).

The United Kingdom has also created other security-related partnerships that are found in specific sectors. These include Project Argus, Kraken, Pegasus, and Servator. Project Argus was created by the National Counter Terrorism Security Office (NaCTSO) where Counter Terrorism Security Advisors (CTSAs) train individuals in the office and retail, night clubs, hotels, education, health, and architectural design and planning sectors on crime prevention and antiterrorism techniques. The goal of this program is to increase resilience against terrorist attacks in locations that attract large crowds by helping companies develop response and business continuity plans (Coaffee, Moore, Fletcher, & Bosher, 2008; Malcolm, 2013). Next, Project Kraken, which is administered by the National Crime Agency, increases vigilance among the United Kingdom's 20,000 miles of coastline and waterways, while Project Pegasus is directed toward increasing vigilance in the aviation community (Project Kraken, 2015; Project Pegasus, 2015). Finally, Project Servator was launched by the city of London police in February, 2014. The primary objectives of this program are to address terrorism and other crimes by randomly deploying increased numbers of police officers in London and developing stronger relationships with citizens, the British transport police, the private security sector, and businesses (Project Servator, 2015; "Survey finds," 2014).

The city of London extensively uses physical security measures, creating a "Ring of Steel" around the City. The origins of the city of London's Ring of Steel program trace back to Belfast, Northern Ireland, in the 1970s and 1980s. To combat Irish Republican Army (IRA) violence that included the use of explosives (1,800 incidents from 1970 to 1975 alone) and car bombs being detonated in Belfast's business district, security forces installed concrete barriers, barbed wire, steel gates, and conducted physical searches of pedestrians entering the zone (Brown, 1985). The city of London's "Ring of Steel" also relies on the principles of defensible space, where street closures, gates, concrete jersey barriers, bollards, extensive CCTV cameras and surveillance (where it is estimated that the average Londoner is recorded 300 times a day), CPTED strategies, and the construction of new blast-resistant buildings are used to enhance perimeter security around the entire city in order to deter threats and to virtually seal the city, if necessary. Various governmental buildings within the city itself have also been fortified to the point where some, such as the U.S. Embassy, are now considered a fortress (Coaffee, 2004; Fussey & Coaffee, 2011).

The United Kingdom also extensively uses CCTV surveillance in many of its cities and towns. Beginning in 1975, the London transport installed CCTVs in some of its underground (subway) stations. By 1994, approximately 79 cities and towns had installed open street CCTV systems as a crime prevention tool, where their use rapidly expanded after 2000. One of the early locations that used CCTV was in King's Lynn that installed over 250 cameras in its business district in 1992, leading to a 98 percent reduction of crime in the city center. Here, private security personnel monitor CCTV cameras in a central command room and alert police personnel of any suspicious or crime-related issues who then respond. This system was financed by the police, local authorities, and by private businesses (McCahill & Norris, 2002; Webster, 2004; Williams & Johnstone, 2000). The reason for the growth in CCTV surveillance was that it reduced crime, it addressed the terrorism threat, and it was consistent with political goals related to privatization of the public services where private security companies would build, equip, staff, and maintain the equipment. Its growth can also be credited to the British government that provided millions of pounds in grants to local authorities, businesses, hospitals, and schools that relied on CCTV as an integral component of its public space crime control and policing strategies (Williams & Johnstone, 2000). To address legal issues related to privacy rights, the U.K. government has also passed various laws such as the CCTV Code of Practice in 2000 that dictates how long data can be retained and limitations on who has access to it.

► The African Continent and Private Security

Private security activities also abound in the continent of Africa. It is estimated that Africans spend about 15 percent of their income on private security services. Most citizens pay for private security activities (Schouten, 2011). There are two perspectives that explain the growth of the private security industry in Africa. One perspective is based on the failed or weak state concept where the industry grew because of a nonexistent or weak governmental infrastructure in some nations that could not provide effective security-related services. Another explanation is based on philosophical changes of the role of the state in the provision of security. This perspective proposes that new or neoliberal state policy decisions do not clearly delineate public–private boundaries and services. Instead, these policies encourage and endorse private security companies to work with existing state services, leading to complex security networks that knit together public and private actors (Abrahamsen, 2013).

Private security activities in Africa are concentrated in capital cities, near international organizations, or around critical infrastructures to "facilitate sustaining, formal, planned operations under adverse conditions" (Schouten, 2011, p. 60). Its role in many cases is to promote a safe and predictable economic environment. This stability then serves to attract foreign investment, which in the long term creates stronger nation-states (Schouten, 2011). In many African nations, private security forces are used to protect mining operations and other "economically valuable enclaves" (Ferguson, 2005, p. 379). An example of security practices in the diamond industry can be found in Box 13-2. In many cases, the security sector is controlled by transnational security firms such as G4S (Group 4 Securicor) that claims it is the largest employer in the continent of Africa. Other security providers and private military companies (PMCs) are also present, where they are responsible for peacekeeping missions (Schouten, 2011).

Private security forces are also used by NGOs and the United Nations (and its partner organizations). These organizations contract with private security companies for personnel security activities, escorting staff and protecting certain residential areas in major cities through armed patrols. Because of their activities, private security companies may also serve to stabilize societies. Unlike state security forces that can be corrupt in nature because they may represent the interests of the government, private security companies are oftentimes tied to international organizations and businesses where they become "legitimate guardians of economic activities" that are approved by the state and corporation (Schouten, 2011).

South Africa has been reported to have the largest private security sectors in the African continent. The industry accounts for 2 percent of the country's Gross Domestic Product, has over 6,000 registered companies, and employs over 1.4 million individuals (Berg & Nouveau, 2014). Since the 1990s, it has also been the fastest growing industry in South Africa (Clarno, 2014). The massive growth of the private security industry in South Africa can be traced to the increase of crime and violence in the late 1980s, the elimination of its Apartheid (a system of racial segregation) policies, and the subsequent decline of the political power and social status of whites in South Africa in the 1990s. Combined with these political changes, many former white police officers formed their own private security companies that were readily accepted by the white minority who were the primary users of these services. In many cases, these private security companies provided (and still do) armed response services that were in high demand and considered indispensable, based in part on the fears that the black majority would be seeking revenge against the minority white citizenry. These new private security forces were readily accepted. In fact, some individuals concluded that all that basically occurred during the transition was simply a change in uniform where the public police now wore private security uniforms (Diphoorn, 2015). Unlike other African nations, because of

BOX 13-2

SECURITY PRACTICES IN THE AFRICAN DIAMOND INDUSTRY

The diamond industry is oftentimes the major source of income for governments and citizens for many African nations. As such, the protection of diamonds is a serious security issue. The Debswana Diamond Company (a partnership between DeBeers and the Republic of Botswana) is the major employer in Botswana and the second largest producer of diamonds in the world. From 1988 to 2011, the company reported that it detected 673 theft incidents from its four mines ("Our operations," 2016). The three most common ways employees stole diamonds was concealing them in the anus (36%), buttocks (30%), and socks and hair (14%). Other methods of concealment included the mouth (5%) under the scrotum (2%), in clothing (2%), in underwear (2%), and other means (10%). In other cases of theft, employees have become much more creative. In one instance in a Namibian open pit diamond mine, employees smuggled homing pigeons into the mine site in their lunchboxes. Diamonds were attached to the pigeons' legs that subsequently flew to their respective homes. This technique was discovered by security staff who found a pigeon struggling to fly because it was overloaded with diamonds (Hart, 1999; Mokgoabone, 2014).

To address the issue of internal employee theft, diamond companies use a variety of security countermeasures. One traditional method has been the use of guards and physical searches that includes strip and cavity searches. CCTV is also used extensively in work areas and toilets. Advanced CCTV surveillance including "spider cameras," which are small tripod mounted cameras that are placed adjacent to workers, and FLIR (Forward Looking Infrared) cameras that monitor mine locations after hours to detect trespassers and thieves are also used ("FLIR imaging cameras," 2014). Court decisions in African nations have determined that these security practices are legal. Laws in some African companies are also designed to deter diamond theft. Botswana's Semi-Precious and Precious Stones (Protection) Act of 1969 allows police to conduct searches anytime and anywhere when they suspect that a person may be in possession of rough or uncut stones. It is also criminal to possess precious stones that are picked up or found by chance at any place or in any land. If this should occur, individuals are required to surrender the stone(s) to the nearest Botswana police station.

Beginning the early 1900s, mine employees have also been x-rayed to detect diamonds that have been swallowed and concealed in the body by other means. Currently, low dose x-ray scanners developed by the DeBeers family of companies (specifically Debtech) are used in South Africa and Namibian mines. These scanners only take seconds to scan the body for foreign objects. Debswana in Botswana is also using DeBeer's Scannex low dose scanner to take full body images of miners to better deter and detect theft. While more effective at locating diamonds than searches alone, Debswana also reports that this technology is also being used as a means of restoring the dignity of mine employees because it replaces invasive and humiliating physical strip and cavity searches (Solomons, 2015; Tebogo, 2014).

Source: Patrick J. Ortmeier, Johnson, Introduction to Security: Operations and Management, 5e. © 2018, Pearson Education, Inc., New York, NY.

the high violent crime rate, security officers are often armed and engage in deadly force events (Schneider, 2013).

There are some concerns with the South African private security industry. Because of its strong presence in performing policing-related functions in public spacing, it is argued that oftentimes there is a "blurring" of the public and private police activities, leading to legal and philosophical issues related to the role of private security in public spaces. Next, in-house security forces and activities are not regulated by law, raising some concerns that this sector is unregulated and outside the control of the state. Last, because the sector is heavily armed and large in size, the potential for criminality and human rights issues exist; this issue may require a shift by the state from regulatory to more accountability types of industrial oversight to prevent any abuses by security companies and employees (Berg & Noveau, 2014).

▶ The Private Security Industry in Central and South America

Since the 1990s, Central and South American nations have also experienced growth in the private security sector due to a large increase in violent crime and the inability (and perhaps corruption) of the public sector police being unable to address crime-related issues. The 1990s also saw changes in many governmental structures and the democratization of the region in addition to an increased demand for private security services—primarily from the middle and upper class citizenry. As early as 2007, it was estimated that there were 611 security personnel per 100,000 residents compared to the police who had a ratio of 187 per 100,000 (Shifter, 2012). In fact, it is estimated that in Central America, private security personnel outnumber the police in every country in the region (Meyer & Seelke, 2011) by a ratio of at least 1.8/1.0 (Muggah & Aguirre, 2013). In some countries including Brazil, Columbia, El Salvador, Honduras, and Mexico, it is estimated that the ratios are even higher. For example, in Brazil and Mexico respectively, there are approximately 470,000 and 450,000 registered private security personnel. In fact, Brazil has the highest reported citizen spending levels on private security in the region (Muggah & Aguirre, 2013). It is estimated that from 2002 to 2012 the industry grew by 64 percent (Brooks, 2014). This is due in part to the fact that the Brazilian police system has been determined to be uncontrollable and corrupt and the nation has a very high violent crime rate. These two factors have led to what some authors refer to as a militarized cityscape that includes gated communities, bullet-proof cars, and armed guards (Larkins, 2015).

One particular nation that has experienced growth in its private security industry is Guatemala, which transitioned to a democratic state in 1996. Here, it is estimated that there are 5 times as many private security personnel than public police where 1.8 percent of the nation's Gross Domestic Product is related to private security operations. While the growth of security can be credited to increases in crime, it can also be attributed to that fact that private security is a cultural artifact of earlier governmental policy that dates back to the 1950s. Prior to 1996, state governmental officials were primarily tasked with fighting insurgents and communists. As such, the government provided minimal local police services, expecting its citizenry to engage in their own self-protection and security activities in the form of civil patrols and the creation self-defense organizations. With the transition to democracy, these early forms of citizen-based security activities readily transitioned into a private security industry (Argueta, 2012).

In some instances in South America, corporate private security personnel partner with governmental entities to provide security-related services. Consider, for example, the Canadian-owned company Petrominerales that has oil operations in the nation of Columbia. Having over 200 employees in Columbia (in addition to other employees that need to visit Columbian operations), the company decided that it needed to have a private security force to protect employees against threats from narcoterrorist organizations and street gangs who were involved in kidnapping for ransom, the sabotage of oil pipelines, the illicit drug trade, and violent crimes. To protect its assets, Petrominerales created a layered security approach that included a security department, security contractors, and military agreements. The security department included Columbian nationals and former Columbian military personnel who were responsible for physical security activities. The company also hired contract security personnel to provide guard and executive protection activities for corporate visitors and for the company's expatriates living in the capital. The company also fostered positive relationships with the Columbian military that provided additional security services in high-threat areas controlled by rebel groups. In this capacity, the military provided security in areas around the company's drilling sites, while the Petrominerales security staff provided security services at the site itself (Finley, 2013).

Select a foreign nation that you are interested in. What is the nature and extent of the private security industry in that country? What regulations exist? What issues, if any exist with the industry?

► International Issues and Private Security

High Seas Piracy

piracy The act of boarding or attempting to board any ship with the apparent intent to commit theft or any other crime and with the intent or capability to use force in furtherance of the act.

Piracy is an old crime and profession. In modern day society, piracy is defined by the United Nations Article 101 as "the act of boarding or attempting to board any ship with the apparent intent to commit theft or any other crime and with the intent or capability to use force in furtherance of the act" (Bernaerts, 1988, p. 57). Figure 13-1 ■ shows the extent of armed robbery (piracy in territorial waters) and piracy attacks (in international waters) against ships throughout the world in 2014.

Acts of piracy threaten international trade, disrupt shipping, increase expenses related to shipping because of longer trade routes taken to avoid the piracy threat, and reduce maritime trade in high-risk areas that subsequently impact the Gross Domestic Product of those affected countries (Bensassi & Martínez-Zarzoso, 2012). According to the International Maritime Organization (IMO) (2013), the peak year for piracy was 2011 with over 500 known incidents. In the Somali area alone, the cost to the global economy (due to an increased military presence, increased security measures by shippers, ransom payments, increased speeds to elude pirates, and piracy-related insurance) was estimated in 2011 at $6 billion U.S. dollars (Zamparini, 2014). This increase in piracy over the last 20 years can be explained in part due to the growing global economy that has resulted in more shipping trade and the inability of some states (such as Somalia which is considered a failed state) to police their territorial waters. Advancements in technologies related to watercraft, the availability of weapons, and communications have also led to better equipped and organized criminal gangs that often carry out these attacks (Liss, 2003).

Maritime piracy is an issue throughout the world. Some of the high-risk areas for piracy include: (1) the Straits of Malacca; (2) Indonesia; (3) Malaysia; (4) the Philippines; (5) Vietnam; (6) Bangladesh; (7) India, (8) the Niger Delta; and (9) the Gulf of Aden/Red

FIGURE 13-1   Piracy Attacks: 2014
Source: Patrick J. Ortmeier, Johnson, Introduction to Security: Operations and Management, 5e, © 2018, Pearson Education, Inc., New York, NY.

Sea, including the coast of Somalia and the Horn of Africa (Menefee & Mejia, 2012). While piracy off the coast of Somalia has a high number of incidents and receives a lot of media attention, piracy in the South China Sea, particularly around Indonesia and Straits of Malacca (the narrow sea lane between Indonesia and Malaysia) has had more reported incidents, due in part to lax law enforcement, increased shipping in the area, and the fact that pirates can hide in the many island chains that exist in the area (Schoenberger, 2014).

In most cases, the motives for pirates are financial in nature where the vessel and/or crew and the ship's contents may be held for ransom. In other cases, pirates may steal cargo or the ship's fuel (Jones, 2014). Three examples of piracy incidents that were reported to the International Maritime Organization (IMO) in 2014 can be found in Box 13-3.

In many cases, pirate gangs may have some level of sophistication and organization. Consider Somali-based pirates. In some incidents of piracy near Somalia and in the Gulf of Aden, pirates rely on a "mothership," which is a larger ship (that is oftentimes stolen) that serves as a floating operational base from where smaller, faster, and more agile speedboats carry out the actual attacks on vessels. The pirates, meanwhile, are oftentimes young males who are equipped with modern weaponry including rocket propelled grenades (RPGs) and machine guns, who board the ships, take the crew captive, and then transport the ship to Somali territorial waters, which was considered a sanctuary for pirates (Percy & Shorthand, 2013). On land, meanwhile, some of these pirate gangs use intermediaries who negotiate a ransom for the release of the ship, its crew, and/or contents with ship owners and insurance companies (Donohue, Pugh, & Sabrie, 2014).

Several security-related activities have been used by vessels to combat Somali-based piracy in the Gulf of Aden. First, countries throughout the world have provided naval

---

BOX 13-3

PIRACY INCIDENTS: 2014

Indonesia: On 04 July, 2014, at approximately 1938 LT, armed pirates attacked and hijacked a Honduras flagged product tanker MT Moresby 9 while underway around 34nm WNW of Anambas Island, Indonesia. The pirates took all crewmembers as hostage and damaged all the communication equipment. They hijacked the tanker and sailed it to an unknown location. Owners reported the incident to the authorities who searched the area. On 05 July, 2014, the owners advised that they had established contact with the hijacked tanker. The pirates had stolen part of the oil cargo and escaped. The Malaysian Maritime Enforcement Agency (MMEA) is investigating the incident.

Nigeria: Eight armed pirates in a high-powered boat attacked a Panamanian chemical tanker MT Cher, while underway around 75nm WSW of Brass, Nigeria at approximately 1055 LT on 06 February, 2014. The tanker raised the alarm, made evasive maneuvers, sent distress messages, and activated the SSAS alert. The pirates maneuvered alongside the tanker and boarded using a long ladder. The crew cut off the power supply to the vessel and retreated into the citadel. After around five hours, the crew emerged and noticed that the pirates had used sledgehammers to break into stores and cabins and loot ship and crew property. The tanker's communication equipment was destroyed. The crew managed to start the emergency generators and other necessary machinery, inform the owners, and sail to Lagos.

Somalia: On 17 January, 2014, a Marshall Islands flagged product tanker MT Nave Atropos was attacked and fired upon by armed pirates while underway at position Latitude 15:06 North and Longitude 054:23 East, around 115nm south of Salalah, Oman, off Somalia at approximately 1804 UTC. Armed pirates in a skiff launched from a mother vessel nearby chased and fired upon the tanker underway. The Master raised the alarm, increased speed, altered course, and activated SSAS Alert, contacted UKMTO (United Kingdom Maritime Trade Operations) and all nonessential crewmembers were mustered in the citadel. The on board armed security team returned fire resulting in the pirates aborting the attack. A coalition helicopter arrived to assist.

Source: From Piracy and Armed Robbery Against Ships. © 2014. Used by permission of ICC International Maritime Bureau.

Suspected Somali pirates in the Gulf of Aden are being held by U.S. Navy personnel. High seas piracy is an international security issue.
(Photo courtesy of Jason R. Zalasky/U.S. Navy.)

Internationally Recommended Transit Corridor (IRTC) A security transit corridor for shipping in the Gulf of Aden that is patrolled by multinational naval vessels.

forces to deter and respond to pirate attacks. In conjunction with these joint naval forces an **Internationally Recommended Transit Corridor (IRTC)** was created that is patrolled by a variety of naval forces. This corridor is 492 miles long and has east and west shipping lanes that are each 5 miles wide. The purpose of this transit corridor is to group ships together to increase their safety against attacks as they travel through the Gulf. The Maritime Security Centre, Horn of Africa (MSCHOA) is responsible for grouping ships together; ships contact the organization through its website, providing detailed information on their size and capable speeds. MSCHOA then organizes the ships into groups based on their capable speeds into "Gulf of Aden Transits." Vessels then enter into the corridor in groups at various intervals and times to ensure that they travel through high-risk areas in the corridor in number and not during the night (Group Transit Explanation, 2010; NATO Shipping Center, 2015; Pristrom, Yang, Wang, Zhang, & Yan, 2015). MSCHOA also publishes a Best Management Practice (BMP) manual to assist companies and ships in how to protect against piracy attacks off the coast of Somali in the Gulf of Aden (BMP4, 2011).

Ships also use various target hardening strategies. They include the use of: warning signs; concertina wire to deter, delay, and prevent boarding; electrified barriers; alarm systems to alert crews; and the use of water (fire hoses, water cannons, and water spray rails) to prevent boarding if an attack should occur. Other practices include evasive maneuvering; the use of CCTV to monitor and detect attacks; and lighting (including search lights) to deter pirate attacks. In the context of personnel security, meanwhile, the BMP manual also recommends that crews have a safe muster (meeting) point in the event of an attack or the ship should construct a citadel. A citadel is basically a secure room that is resistant to attack and penetration, where all crew can go into in the event of an attack and wait for rescue (BMP4, 2011).

citadel A secure room that is resistant to attack and penetration.

Some vessels and shipping companies use private security personnel who are referred to as **private maritime security contractors (PMSCs)**. These PMSCs can be armed or unarmed. It is estimated that approximately one-quarter of all commercial ships now use armed security on board their vessels, not including armed security patrol boats. However, they are operating in a legal vacuum because international law has not kept pace with this new

private maritime security contractors (PMSCs) Armed or unarmed private security personnel on ships.

practice (Brown, 2012). Due to the lack of international laws and regulations, each Flag State (the nation which the ship registers under) has its own regulations regarding the use of PMSCs. However, in most cases, these Flag States have no official stance on the use of armed PMSCs; only a few prohibit the use of armed security ("Oceans Beyond Piracy," 2015).

International agreements exist to fight the world piracy problem. States near the Straits of Malacca and Singapore and the South China Sea have ratified the Regional Cooperation Agreement on Combating Piracy and Armed Robbery against Ships in Asia (ReCAAP). Under ReCAAP, participating countries are responsible for "(1) managing the piracy and armed robbery incidents within its territorial waters, (2) acting as a point of information exchange with the ISC, (3) facilitating its country's law enforcement investigations, and (4) coordinating surveillance and enforcement for piracy and armed robbery with neighbouring focal points" (Ho, 2009, p. 433). The member nations have also created and funded an Information Sharing Center (ISC), which is located in Singapore. This center collects data on piracy-related activities in the region and publishes monthly reports of piracy incidents (Ho, 2006).

In the Middle East, the Djibouti Code of Conduct (DCoC) was adopted by 20 countries in the region (Djibouti, Ethiopia, Kenya, Madagascar, Maldives, Seychelles, Somalia, the United Republic of Tanzania, Yemen, Comoros, Egypt, Eritrea, Jordan, Mauritius, Mozambique, Oman, Saudi Arabia, South Africa, Sudan, and the United Arab Emirates). Like ReCAAP, DCoC was created to improve regional cooperation of maritime piracy in the Red Sea, Western Indian Ocean, and the Gulf of Aden by the signatory countries. Some of the key activities include: (1) information sharing, (2) training, (3) the creation of laws against piracy and other maritime crimes, and (4) enhancing the capacity of member nations by developing and enhancing law enforcement capabilities and strengthening their abilities to fight piracy. Some specific activities of DCoC partner nations include the creation of a regional maritime monitoring plan, which records and tracks all shipping in the area (Djibouti Code of Conduct, 2015). The UN, the International Maritime Organization (IMO), and several other countries, including the United States and Canada (Guilfoyle, 2008), also support activities under the DCoC.

> **Regional Cooperation Agreement on Combating Piracy and Armed Robbery against Ships in Asia (ReCAAP)** Agreement among states located near or around the Straits of Malacca and Singapore and the South China Sea to fight high seas piracy.

> **Djibouti Code of Conduct (DCoC)** Agreement adopted by 20 countries in the Middle East to address high seas piracy.

Private Military Security Companies (PMSCs)

Private military security companies (PMSCs) provide military-related services to nation-state clients for monetary compensation. To be considered a PMSC, the following characteristics exist. They must be: (1) market-oriented; (2) professional (a business headquarters, trained staff, and business structure); (3) organized under private law (not public); and (4) a legally registered company (Branović, 2011). Unlike mercenaries who are individuals hired to overthrow governments, PMSC personnel work for legitimate nations where their main goal is to support and enhance the contracting nation's military capabilities (Johnson, 2005).

> **private military security companies (PMSCs)** Private security companies that provide military-related services to clients.

The origins of PMSCs can be traced to the 1970s and 1980s, when British-based companies began to offer military training, support, and consulting services to various nations. However, with geopolitical changes in the 1990s, former military superpowers such as the former Soviet Union and the United States no longer provided the same political and military support to many underdeveloped and unstable nations in the world, particularly in the continent of Africa that was experiencing many civil wars. As such, a new "opportunity structure" existed for entrepreneurial individuals who started professional military firms to assist struggling nations that had small and ill-trained and ill-equipped military forces. Oftentimes, individuals employed by these companies were former military personnel that had the requisite expertise to provide clients with trained contract military personnel and equipment (Spicer, 1999). PMSCs were heavily used in the continent of Africa. From 1990 to 2008, 33 different countries in Africa used PMSCs in military conflicts (Akcinaroglu & Radziszewski, 2013). One PMSC that existed in the 1990s was the South African company, Executive Outcomes (EO). EO was primarily staffed by former South African military personnel.

In 1995, the nation of Sierra Leone contracted with EO for $35 million to take back and secure oilfields that were captured by rebels. Because the government could not pay the contract, EO later accepted diamond-mining concessions (e.g., "blood diamonds") for its services (Patterson, 2009). PMSCs were also used by the U.S. military in the 1990s in the Balkans region where companies such as Military Professional Resources Inc. (MPRI) and DynCorp performed training-related functions in Croatia and Bosnia (Kinsey, 2006).

There are many benefits associated with PMSCs. PMSCs can support weak nation-states that do not have the capacity to have a strong standing military (Leander, 2005). PMSCs can provide a "surge" effect, serving as force multipliers for some countries that require additional military resources. These companies can also provide a great deal of expertise and specialization for clients (Avant, 2006). PMSCs have also been reported to be able to respond to crises faster (while also being better prepared) in comparison to the abilities of many nations and even NATO forces, making them an attractive alternative for peacekeeping missions. They are also able to get the tasks done faster since they are under contractual guidelines and not tied up by political issues, as could be the case of regular military organizations. In some cases, PMSCs are also cost-effective for nations; states are not burdened with the costs of a large, standing army (Wallwork, 2005).

There are some issues with PMSCs. First, these companies have operated in a "legal limbo" where there is a lack of international law that governs their use. Other issues include the poor quality of services that some companies provide, based in part on the use of unqualified staff (Avant, 2006). There are also issues related to human rights abuses that may occur when these forces are used, due in part to the current lack of international law and conventions to control such abuses from private actors (Cameron, 2006). Furthermore, there are philosophical and ethical issues related to the private sector being involved in warfare-related activities for profit instead of the public good. There may also be a long-term impact of the presence of these companies. Professional soldiers may leave the public military to seek out better financial opportunities in the private sector (Avant, 2006). Last, the use of PMSCs can alter foreign policy; their presence and use can alter geo-political relationships between nations and destabilize certain parts of the world (Kinsey, 2006).

PMSCs were brought to the forefront with the global war on terror, especially their activities in Operation Enduring Freedom in Afghanistan (2001–2014) and Iraq (2003–2011). Because of a downsized U.S. military, combined with a philosophical shift toward privatization and the need for specialized services that governments could not readily provide, the United States (and other coalition nations including the United Kingdom) contracted with several PMSCs to provide security-related services in these combat zones. In fact, it was estimated that private contractors accounted for 54 percent of all U.S. government personnel in Iraq and Afghanistan in 2010 (Whitmore, 2014). Of these private contractors, many were private security companies that provided support and security services. These services included: base security, armed escorts, personnel security, the training of civilian and military and police personnel, and intelligence-related activities (Kinsey, 2006). Those companies that performed armed services raised a great deal of debate. One company that received a lot of attention and criticism was the U.S. firm Blackwater (now defunct) whose employees were involved in many force-related incidents that involved civilian deaths (Singer, 2007). One of the more infamous incidents occurred in September 16, 2007, in Iraq, where Blackwater employees killed 17 unarmed civilians and injured another 34 in Baghdad's Nisour Square. This incident led to the government of Iraq denying Blackwater a license to operate in the country and Congressional investigations (Scahill, 2011).

Because of potential abuses and concerns related to these use of these PMSCs, some legislation does exist to regulate and control them. In 2008, U.S. Congress passed the Duncan Hunter National Defense Authorization Act (2008) that placed restrictions on the use of military contractors. The Act states that their use and function should be determined by local military commanders and not by other individuals outside the military chain of command. It also

Duncan Hunter National Defense Authorization Act (2008) U.S. legislation that placed restrictions on the use of military contractors by the U.S. military.

stated that military contractors "are not authorized to perform inherently governmental functions in an area of combat operations" (p. 4535). In addition, the National Defense Authorization Act for Fiscal Year 2008, (2008) created additional regulations for private military contractors operating under contract with the U.S. Government. Section 862 of the Act requires that the Secretary of Defense and State register and maintain appropriate records of military contractors and their weapons and other equipment (armored vehicles, helicopters, etc.). The Act also mandates that PMSCs report force-related incidents, comply with United States and host country laws, and follow Department of Defense training regulations.

▶ Regulating the International Private Security Industry

In many cases, private security companies that operate internationally have limited control over their activities. Generally, their activities are governed by the laws that exist in those countries where they operate. In many instances, however, these companies may operate in failed nation-states or in countries whose infrastructure is severely weakened by warfare. As a consequence of these factors, these nations may have no laws or regulatory mechanisms to "police" private security companies. In fact, even in those nations that do have strong infrastructures and stable legal systems, the need and demand for the services from government and multinational firms operating in those countries may result in the host nation "turning a blind eye" to the actions of these private security personnel. In addition to weak governmental controls, to date, there is limited international regulation of the private security industry. Some of the regulations that currently exist include the Montreux Document, the International Code of Conduct, and actions by the United Nations.

The Montreux Document

To ensure that security companies, especially PMSCs, adhere to or follow existing international law and follow humanitarian principles and human rights, the Montreux Document was created in 2008. This document was the initiative of the Swiss government, the International Committee of the Red Cross (ICRC), and 17 nations (Afghanistan, Angola, Australia, Austria, Canada, China, France, Germany, Iraq, Poland, Sierra Leone, South Africa, Sweden, Switzerland, the United Kingdom of Great Britain and Northern Ireland, Ukraine, and the United States). This document is not legally binding and it does not take a stance on PMSCs. Instead, it provides 27 recommendations or "best practices" that are based on human rights and humanitarian law that nations can adopt. It is also designed to assist nations in creating policies, regulations, and laws for the use of PMSCs. It also establishes the responsibilities that contracting (those countries that hire PMSCs); territorial (those states in the same region or territory where PMSCs operate); and home states (those nations that the PMSCs are based) have regarding PMSCs. Some of the specific recommendations include:

> **Montreux Document**
> Nonlegal document that provides 27 recommendations or "best practices" that are based on human rights and humanitarian law that nations can adopt regarding the use of Primate Military Companies.

- the creation of laws that criminally prosecute, extradite, or surrender persons for committing crimes and breaches of the Geneva Conventions and international law;
- the obligations of states to respect international humanitarian law;
- taking appropriate measures (in some circumstances) to prevent, and provide effective remedies for relevant misconduct of PMSCs and their personnel;
- not to contract PMSCs to carry out activities (such as direct warfare) that international humanitarian law explicitly assigns to a state agent or authority.

This document is also designed to assist PMSCs in ensuring that their practices conform to the principles of humanitarian goals and human rights law while holding PMSCs accountable for their actions. Some of the recommendations include the following:

- Respect the relevant national law, in particular the national criminal law, of the state in which they operate, and, as far as applicable, the law of the states of their nationality.
- The status of the personnel of PMSCs is determined by international humanitarian law, on a case-by-case basis, in particular according to the nature and circumstances of the functions in which they are involved.
- PMSCs are obliged to comply with international humanitarian law or human rights law imposed upon them by applicable national law, as well as other applicable national law such as criminal law, tax law, immigration law, labor law, and specific regulations on private military or security services.

Superiors of PMSC personnel, including governmental officials, whether they are military commanders or civilian superiors, or directors or managers of PMSCs, may be liable for crimes under international law committed by PMSC personnel under their effective authority and control, as a result of their failure to properly exercise control over them in accordance with the rules of the Geneva Convention (The Montreux Document, 2008).

The International Code of Conduct

International Code of Conduct for Private Security Providers Association (ICoC) Guidelines created by private military companies as a means of self-regulating the industry.

There is also the International Code of Conduct for Private Security Providers Association (ICoC) which was created by private security companies as a means of industrial self-regulation. The Private Security Providers Association is a Swiss nonprofit organization that is composed of private security providers, states, and civil society organizations (nongovernmental organizations and institutions) that equally comprise the organization's board of directors who make ICOC policy. The purpose of the Association is to promote, govern, and oversee the implementation of the ICoC. In November, 2010, the Association created and published the *International Code of Conduct* (ICoC) for its membership that is based in part on the principles of the UN Global Compact and International Human Law. The mandate of the Association includes: (1) certification of member companies to ensure that they meet the Code of Conduct; (2) monitoring company compliance and activities; and (3) handling complaints on alleged violations of the Code of Conduct. Similar to the Montreux Document that was created and endorsed by states, the ICoC can be adopted followed by Civil Societies (institutions and nongovernmental organizations) that provide or are impacted by the operations of private security organizations (ICoCA, 2015). Some of the elements of the Code are shown in Box 13-4.

The United Nations

Working Group on the use of mercenaries A United Nations Working Group tasked with the creation of new standards and guidelines for the use of private security military companies.

The United Nations has also been involved in the regulation of the private security industry. Historically, the United Nations has been concerned with human rights, state sovereignty, and issues related to the self-determination of people. To date, the United Nations has not established any specific international protocols regarding the use of private security or PMSCs. Nevertheless it has recognized and has become involved in addressing issues and controversies regarding private security-related activities. To investigate private security and private military companies, in 2005, the Human Rights Council of the United Nations created the Working Group on the use of mercenaries. The purpose of this Working Group is to create new standards and guidelines for the use of private military security companies (PMSCs) in order to ensure that human rights

BOX 13-4

ELEMENTS OF THE ICOC

- Private security companies and other private security service providers (collectively "PSCs") play an important role in protecting state and nonstate clients engaged in relief, recovery, and reconstruction efforts, commercial business operations, and diplomacy and military activity. In providing these services, the activities of PSCs can have potentially positive and negative consequences for their clients, the local population in the area of operation, the general security environment, the enjoyment of human rights and the rule of law.

- The *Montreux Document On Pertinent International Legal Obligations and Good Practices for States Related to Operations of Private Military and Security Companies During Armed Conflict* recognizes that well-established rules of international law apply to States in their relations with private security service providers and provides for good practices relating to PSCs. The "Respect, Protect, Remedy" framework developed by the special representative of the United Nations (UN) Secretary-General on Business and Human Rights, and welcomed by the UN Human Rights Council, entails acting with due diligence to avoid infringing the rights of others.

- Building on these foundations, the Signatory Companies to this International Code of Conduct for Private Security Service Providers (the "Code") endorse the principles of the Montreux Document and the aforementioned "Respect, Protect, Remedy" framework as they apply to PSCs. In so doing, the Signatory Companies commit to the responsible provision of security services so as to support the rule of law, respect the human rights of all persons, and protect the interests of their clients.

- The Signatory Companies affirm that they have a responsibility to respect the human rights of, and fulfill humanitarian responsibilities toward, all those affected by their business activities, including personnel, clients, suppliers, shareholders, and the population of the area in which services are provided. The Signatory Companies also recognize the importance of respecting the various cultures encountered in their work, as well as the individuals they come into contact with as a result of those activities.

- The purpose of this Code is to set forth a commonly agreed set of principles for PSCs and to establish a foundation to translate those principles into related standards as well as governance and oversight mechanisms.

- Signature of this Code is the first step in a process toward full compliance. Signatory Companies need to: (1) establish and/or demonstrate internal processes to meet the requirements of the Code's principles and the standards derived from the Code; and (2) once the governance and oversight mechanism is established, become certified by and submit to ongoing independent auditing and verification by that mechanism. Signatory Companies undertake to be transparent regarding their progress toward implementing the Code's principles and the standards derived from the Code. Companies will not claim they are certified under this Code until certification has been granted by the governance and oversight mechanism as outlined below.

- This Code complements and does not replace the control exercised by competent authorities, and does not limit or alter applicable international law or relevant national law. The Code itself creates no legal obligations and no legal liabilities on the Signatory Companies, beyond those which already exist under national or international law. Nothing in this Code shall be interpreted as limiting or prejudicing in any way existing or developing rules of international law.

Source: From The International Code Of Conduct For Private Security Service Providers. Published by International Code of Conduct Association.

are followed, and to "monitor and study the effects on the enjoyment of human rights, particularly the right of peoples to self-determination, of the activities of private companies offering military assistance, consultancy and security services on the international market, and to prepare a draft of international basic principles that encourage respect for human rights by those companies in their activities" ("Working group," 2015).

To date, the Working Group has surveyed and collected data from many nations regarding their use and regulation of PMSCs. In the context of Africa, for example, it was found that PMSC legislation exists on a spectrum from highly regulated and controlled to lacking effective security-related legislation. In Asia, meanwhile, the Working Group determined that even though legislation does exist in each country examined, there nevertheless exists the potential for human rights violations. One of its recommendations is that the Human Rights Council of the United Nations establish a technical assistance program to assist countries in developing stronger forms of legislation, in addition to the creation of a convention on the use of private security and private military companies ("Annual report," 2013).

Of interest is that the United Nations has been criticized for its use of private military companies in many of its peacekeeping and humanitarian missions throughout the world. However, because of the lack of military expertise, economics, and low levels of commitment by member nations to deploy their military personnel to peacekeeping and humanitarian missions, the United Nations has resorted to using private military companies. Because of some of the issues related to private military companies, the United Nations, however, is placed in an ethical dilemma if it should partner with PMSCs (Schildknecht, 2015). As indicated in a DCAF report (Ostensen, 2011), "In an ideal world the United Nations would probably not buy PMSC services in the first place" (p. 67). However, because of practical needs, the UN needs the services of PMSCs. As such, it was recommended by DCAF that the UN endorse the ICoC Code into PMSC contracts, and since the use of PMSCs are "well established and unlikely to cease" (p. 68) in its operations, it should work on ensuring that issues with their use does not arise.

Summary

This chapter has shown that regardless of the region of the world, there are some common elements, themes, and controversies associated with the private security industry. In all regions of the world, the private security industry is quite large where oftentimes the number of security personnel is equal to or exceeds existing numbers of public police-related personnel. While specific activities and functions may differ to some degree based on perceived threats that often include high crime rates, another common element is that the security industry emerged to meet the demands of the citizenry and new businesses in a market economy. Another common theme is that the private security industry is relatively young; in some areas of the world, the industry is approximately 30 years old and it has experienced tremendous growth following political and economic changes. Even though the sector is relatively young, many nations have nevertheless enacted legislation related to the licensure of security companies and employees. Like Eastern and Southern Europe, Africa, and Central and South America, the private security industry in the EU and the United Kingdom is also large and regulated by state; in Europe, there is also the Confederation of European Security Services (CoESS), an organization that lobbies for and represents the needs of the security industry through Europe and the EU.

This chapter has also identified two contemporary issues related to international security. One particular issue is piracy, which exists throughout the world. To address this security threat, several strategies have been adopted by ships, companies, and nations that include changes in physical security, changes to shipping practices, and collaborative partnerships and efforts to monitor and respond to the piracy threat. Next, private military security companies, which are private security companies that provide military-related services, have received a great deal of criticism. While providing necessary services in many regions and countries in the world, they have been criticized at a philosophical level and for human rights-related violations. To date, no international laws to regulate the private security industry exist. There is, however, the Montreux Document that was created by governments to assist nations in creating effective legislation to regulate this industry while the private security industry has created its own standards (the ICoC) as a means of industrial self-regulation.

Career Opportunities in International Security

One particular career opportunity that exists in international security is employment with Private Military Security Companies. While these companies have been associated with the recent conflicts in the Middle East, their services are needed throughout the world, where they contract with nongovernmental organizations, governments, and the private sector to provide physical security, personnel security, and other specialized security-related functions. Two particular companies that provide these services are Triple Canopy and Aegis. The review of their websites shows the diverse services they provide and the respective salaries for these positions.

Key Terms and Concepts

Citadel *288*

Confederation of European
   Security Services
   (CoESS) *280*

Djibouti Code of Conduct
   (DCoC) *289*

Duncan Hunter National Defense
   Authorization Act (2008) *290*

European Union (EU) *279*

Geneva Center for the Democratic
   Control of Armed Forces
   (DCAF) *279*

Grey market *279*

International Code of Conduct for
   Private Security Providers
   Association (ICoC) *292*

Internationally Recommended
   Transit Corridor (IRTC) *288*

Montreux Document *291*

Piracy *286*

Plural policing *278*

Private maritime security
   contractors (PMSCs) *288*

Private military security companies
   (PMSCs) *289*

Project Argus *282*

Project Griffin *281*

Project Kraken *282*

Project Pegasus *282*

Project Servator *282*

Regional Cooperation Agreement
   on Combating Piracy and Armed
   Robbery against Ships in Asia
   (ReCAAP) *289*

Ring of Steel *282*

Security Industry Authority
   (SIA) *281*

Working Group on the use of
   mercenaries *292*

Discussion Questions and Exercises

1. What are some common elements and themes found in the evolution and development of the private security industry in the former Communist states?
2. Explain the degree of regulation and control of the private security in Europe.
3. Reflect on the growth and development of security in the United States. What are some similarities and differences of the growth and evolution of security in the United States compared to other nations?
4. Explain the role and function of the Confederation of European Security Services (CoESS).
5. What are some of the different ways foreign nations regulate their private security industries?
6. What are some of the primary issues with private security companies in other regions of the world?
7. What are the two explanations for the growth of the private security industry in Africa?
8. What are some specific challenges post-conflict nations encounter regarding the growth and development of a private security industry?
9. Define piracy. What factors contribute to piracy? What are some common security practices used to address the piracy problem?
10. What are private military security companies? Explain their growth, use, and issues.

Your Turn

Reflect on London's "Ring of Steel." Apply this concept to your home town (or a specific area in your home town). How would you target harden this area against identified threats by using physical security measures and existing private security resources?

14   The Future

LEARNING OBJECTIVES

After completing this chapter, the reader should be able to:

1. identify and discuss future trends and challenges in the field of security

2. evaluate the impact of globalization on the provision of security services

3. explain transnational private policing

4. discuss the concept of human security and the role of corporations in ensuring human security in the future

5. explain and identify some future threats and how security can mitigate them

6. identify some of the new, emerging security-related technologies that will be used in the future

7. discuss some future legislative issues in the field of security

8. explain the changing nature of terrorism and the role of security in counterterrorism efforts

9. explain and identify some of new knowledge, skills, and abilities security personnel will need in the future

10. discuss the importance of value added and evidence-based practices for security organizations

▶ Introduction

This chapter examines changes the security industry will experience in the future due to globalization, legislation, technology, and world events including terrorism. These changes will also result in new challenges for the security industry in the context of the knowledge skills and abilities needed by security professionals. The future will also see the growth of security as an academic discipline. While all of these (and other factors) will prove to be challenges, they are also opportunities for the industry to become more specialized and recognized as a legitimate entity in risk management, loss, and crime prevention.

▶ Globalization

Globalization is term and a process. As a term, it is the growing interconnectedness and expanded flow of information, technology, capital, goods, services, money, and people throughout the world. As a process, globalization has led to greater interdependencies of world markets and economies. Globalization has also changed the nature of business, where competitive pressures have forced many businesses to decentralize, enter global markets, create virtual corporations (electronically linked partnerships), and collaborate in joint ventures with business partners throughout the world (Miller, Miller, & Davidenko, 2015). Globalization has also changed human interactions and the political and social fabric of many nations (Pieterse, 2015). While beneficial, globalization also creates new vulnerabilities and challenges for security managers. The safety and security of almost all aspects of an organization's personnel and property are affected by globalization as companies physically move into new parts of the world and workers are exposed to an increased number of threats.

globalization Internationalization of economic and business activities; commercial, travel, and communications activities spanning the entire globe.

Globalization has resulted in the growth of private security operations and firms that operate around the world. Transnational private policing is the term used that describes multinational firms and corporations engaged in security-related activities in more than one nation. In many cases, these security operations exist in multiple countries and regions of the world. As a consequence, "these multifunctional organizations form complex transnational security networks by virtue of the interaction of their parent companies and branch plants with other commercial and non-commercial security providers" (denBoer, 2005, p. 198). Contract security companies are already involved in transnational private policing. The world's largest security company is the English-based G4S (Group 4 Securicor) that operates in approximately 110 countries. G4S employs over 620,000 individuals and it generated £6.8 billion in revenues in 2014 (G4S, 2015). Another large transnational company is Swedish-based Securitas that employs approximately 320,000 employees in 53 different countries (Securitas, 2015). With increased globalization and the need for more security, transnational firms will undoubtedly increase in the future.

transnational private policing Term used that describes multinational firms and corporations engaged in security-related activities in more than one nation.

In some cases, private security organizations may form a global security assemblage. Global security assemblages are hybrid private/public arrangements where local and state authorities work with private security providers to deliver security-related services. As a result of these assemblages, there may no longer be a clear definition of activities, power, and authority in the future. Instead, "the authority and goals of the state are routinely exercised and negotiated with those of private security providers and their clients" (Abrahamsen & Williams, 2009, p. 8). Another issue that exists with the presence of these large multinational security companies that have created these assemblages is that that by their sheer size and political power, they may have the ability to influence and de-stabilize states and affect their economies.

global security assemblages Hybrid private/public arrangements where local and state authorities and private security providers work together to provide security-related services.

Transnational crimes will also become more of a concern. Transnational organized crimes are criminal acts that are committed in more than one state, where the planning, preparation control, and direction takes place in a different country from where the crime is actually being committed (Finckenauer & Chin, 2006). These crimes are committed by transnational organized crime groups who are involved in drug smuggling, human trafficking, cybercrimes, financial fraud, and kidnapping for ransom activities. The private sector will become more vulnerable to these crimes due to their increased exposure as they expand operations in regions of the world that lack both the laws and effective responses to these types of crimes.

transnational organized crimes Criminal acts that are committed in more than one state, where the planning, preparation control and direction takes place in a different country from where the crime is actually being committed.

Besides increased vulnerability, the contract and proprietary sectors will also become more involved in combatting these criminal activities. The resources and expertise they have to investigate and address them may surpass those found in the public sector. In some cases, the public sector may not have the personnel, resources, and skills to address globalization-related crimes. Or, these crimes and criminal groups will not be a pressing issue to address because they do not impact the country directly or the crime groups themselves are basically a de-facto political and cultural artifact of that nation in question. This is especially the case in underdeveloped countries where transnational crimes are predicted to occur more often in the future (Finckenauer & Chin, 2006). Besides these points, public sector agencies often lack jurisdictional powers to investigate many of these crimes; their powers stop at their respective borders, while the transnational crimes do not. And, even though there are international organizations, they may also lack adequate resources and skills to address all crimes. However, the private sector does not have jurisdictional boundaries *per se*. As such, they will assume a greater role and responsibility in investigating and policing these crimes, partnering with existing public resources, and creating an environment of shared intelligence and trust (Broadhurst, 2003).

Human Security and Globalization

human security
A universal issue that is based on ensuring people freedom from fear and wants.

Because of globalization and the greater role of security in organizations throughout the world, the security industry will also see a demand for and growth of risk management activities in human security. Human security can be understood as a universal issue that is based on protecting people from fear and wants. It is shift from understanding security in the perspective of people and not just states, identifying particular threats and vulnerabilities to individuals, groups, and societies. It is a philosophical approach that takes the position that all people should have the "the right to live in freedom and dignity, free from poverty and despair … with an equal opportunity to enjoy all their rights and fully develop their human potential" (Gómez & Gasper, 2013, p. 2). The increased recognition of human security supports existing corporate social responsibility (CSR) functions, which are activities by companies that provide some type of social benefit to improve the quality of life for communities and society. These CSR-related activities are commonplace among large, multinational organizations, where for example, they have provided material support for nations and cities that have been impacted by natural disasters (Johnson, Connolly, & Carter, 2011).

corporate social responsibility (CSR)
Activities by companies that provide some type of social benefit to improve the quality of life for communities and society.

Human security consists of seven components that are shown in Box 14-1. While the private security function already indirectly or directly addressees some of the elements of human security, in the future it will undoubtedly become more immersed in the human security function.

Meeting human security needs has traditionally been the responsibility of governments (Leaning & Arie, 2000). However, the private security function (both contract and proprietary) can positively impact all of these different types of human security to some degree through the provision of material activities and by ensuring safety and security. In some cases, the security function has already had a role in economic, environmental, personal, community, and political security in many developing nations. As companies move into more underdeveloped

---

BOX 14-1

THE SEVEN COMPONENTS OF HUMAN SECURITY

- *Economic Security*—an assured basic income—usually from productive and remunerative work.
- *Food Security*—where all people at all times have both physical and economic access to basic food.
- *Health Security*—minimum protection from disease and unhealthy lifestyles.
- *Environmental Security*—human beings rely on a healthy physical environment; protection from long and short-term man-made and natural threats.
- *Personal Security*—protection from sudden unpredictable violence committed by the state, individuals, and groups.
- *Community Security*—protecting people, communities, and ethnic groups from oppressive practices and the loss of their traditional values.
- *Political Security*—people should be able to live in a society that honors their basic human rights.

Source: Patrick J. Ortmeier, Johnson, Introduction to Security: Operations and Management, 5e. © 2018, Pearson Education, Inc., New York, NY.

and unstable nations throughout the world that could be experiencing war, genocide, famine, and climate change, the provision of human security needs will become more of a private endeavor. This may lead to a philosophical shift for the security function, from the physical, personnel, and informational to a more human-centered approach. In many situations, this will not be an option for companies. It will be a necessity to ensure a secure and stable workforce where companies (and the security function) will become more heavily involved in the provision of food, medical services, housing, and personal security-related activities. Of these, food, water, and energy security issues will be some primary concerns for the security function.

Food security is already an issue in many regions of the world. Food security is concerned with the availability, access to, utilization of, and the stability of food supplies to individuals (Ericksen, 2008). Already, the agricultural sector in the United States has been identified as part of the nation's critical infrastructure. The agricultural industry from "farm to table" is vulnerable to contamination with biological agents (such as *E. coli* and Salmonella) and man-made poisons. The agricultural sector is also vulnerable to supply disruptions due to natural and man-made disasters and disease. It is also vulnerable to "Barnyard terrorism," which is an attack on the agriculture sector by terrorist groups. For example, an attack on America's beef industry would lead to an immediate stoppage of the industry leading to large economic losses, food shortages, and panic (Spellman, 2008). Already, the U.S. government and private sector companies have sought to ensure food security through legislation and the introduction of various security practices throughout the entire supply chain. However, this same level of diligence may not exist in many emerging nations and regions of the world that are involved in the world food trade, making them more vulnerable to food security-related issues (Souza-Monteiro & Hooker, 2013).

Food security will be an increasing issue in the future, due in part to global warming, limited fresh water, a growing global population, warfare, and even energy shortages (Kneafsey, Dowler, Lambie-Mumford, Inman, & Collier, 2013). The resulting outcome of food insecurity could lead to famine, hunger, and destabilized governments and regions. In fact, some authors propose that food security is more of a threat than traditional forms of terrorism (Brown, 2012). These issues related to food security will impact organizations operating in high risk regions. Therefore, issues related to food security will become an important variable for security managers to consider in the risk management process and the design of security programs.

Water security will also become a bigger issue throughout the world, including the United States. Water security can be defined as "the availability of an acceptable quantity and quality of water for health, livelihoods, ecosystems and production, coupled with an acceptable level of water-related risks to people, environments and economies" (Grey & Sadoff, 2007, p. 547). It is estimated that only 2.5% of the water's world supply is fresh water (ODNI, 2012). This supply of fresh water is not evenly distributed around the world and it is diminishing in volume and quality; it is already estimated that 780 million people throughout the world do not have access to clean water (Gleick & Ajami, 2014). It is expected to get worse. The Office of the Director of National Intelligence (ODNI) (2012) published a report on water security, concluding that: "Between now and 2040, fresh water availability will not keep up with demand absent more effective management of water resources. Water problems will hinder the ability of key countries to produce food and generate energy, posing a risk to global food markets and hobbling economic growth. As a result of demographic and economic development pressures, North Africa, the Middle East, and South Asia will face major challenges coping with water problems" (p. 1).

As with food insecurity, the predicted declining supplies of fresh and clean water can lead to social disruption, political instability, state failures, warfare, and disease. All of these issues will have a "trickle down" effect on organizations operating in those

food security
Activities directed toward the availability, access to, utilization of, and the stability of food supplies to individuals.

Barnyard terrorism
Attacks on the agriculture sector by terrorist groups.

water security
The availability of an acceptable quantity and quality of water for health, livelihoods, ecosystems and production.

Water security is an issue in the United States. Nevada's Lake Mead (pictured) has experienced a large drop in its water level. The Colorado River Basin lost nearly 53 million acre feet (the volume of one acre of surface area to a depth of one foot) of freshwater from 2006 to 2014, according to a study from NASA. The Colorado River is the only major river in the southwestern United States. Its basin supplies water to about 40 million people in seven states, as well as irrigating roughly four million acres of farmland.
(Photo courtesy of U.S. Bureau of Reclamation.)

nations and regions of the world that are experiencing water security-related issues. Already, some large international companies in the agricultural sector that are responsible for over 90% of global water consumption (e.g., irrigation) are addressing this issue. Companies including Bunge, Archer Daniels Midland (ADM), Cargill, and Nestle, which are the biggest traders of virtual water (the hidden flow of water in various commodities), are involved in water risk management-related activities and water sustainability, based on concerns raised by shareholders and advocacy groups (Sojamo & Larson, 2012). Water-related issues will also become an issue for the critical infrastructures of many nations creating energy insecurity because the two resources are inextricably linked. The World Bank estimates that by 2035 many nations will have serious energy and water issues. Due to the depleted water sources, hydroelectric sources of energy will be affected, leading to energy shortages, brownouts, and blackouts (Zerrenner, 2014).

It can be safely assumed that water security will become more of an issue in the future for companies. In some cases, water usage can be a direct threat to companies. Consider for example, the 2003 incident involving the Ice Mountain Water Company (a division of Nestle' Water) where four incendiary devices were found in the Big Rapids, Michigan, pumping facility. The Earth Liberation Front (ELF), an "eco-terrorist" group, took credit for the action, claiming that the company was stealing water for profit (Gleick, 2006). Indirectly, water shortages will also require companies to consider water insecurity in the risk management process. As part of this water risk management process, companies will need to identify and address direct human threats including radicalized groups and individuals targeting the company and its assets because of its water use practices and policies. Natural water issues and uncertainties including drought and famine will also result in challenges for security.

An expanding global economy will increase the demand for many natural resources, including oil. This increased demand will lead to issues related to energy security, which is a global security issue. In a broad sense, energy security is "the assured continuity of energy supply, or a situation in which energy products are readily available through the usual commercial outlets and processes" (Noël, 2014, p. 205). Threats against the world's energy sources can lead to serious social, economic, and political issues. For instance, it is currently estimated that there are over 3 million miles of unprotected oil and gas pipelines throughout the world. Often located in remote and politically unstable regions of the world, these pipelines are "soft" or easy targets for criminals and "oil terrorists." Already, there have been attacks by terrorist organizations including Al-Qaeda against oil facilities in Saudi Arabia. Other lesser known rebel and terrorist groups operating in Columbia, Algeria, and other oil-rich nations throughout the world have also attacked oil-related industries and their assets. This has led to increases in governmental and private security efforts to secure pipelines and facilities, and protect employees (Luft, 2009).

energy security
The assured continuity of energy supply, or a situation in which energy products are readily available through the usual commercial outlets and processes.

As multinational companies move into new regions including the Caspian Sea, South America, and Africa for new sources of oil, the use of private security forces to secure these areas will undoubtedly increase. This will lead to a philosophical shift among Exploration and Production (E&P) and pipeline companies. Security will no longer be an option. It will be an inherent need. These security-related activities can lead to human rights issues. Already security forces employed by multinational companies in the Niger Delta have been accused of using deadly force against criminals and vandals near oil pipelines in the region (Stokes, 2007). In Myanmar, meanwhile, private security personnel have been accused of violence including rape and even genocide against groups opposed to the oil industry (Sovacool & Cooper, 2013).

The quest for new, renewable, and noncarbon energy sources, including wind and solar, will also result in new security challenges. Like other computer-driven businesses, these industries will be vulnerable to cybercrimes including data breaches and Supervisory Control and Data Acquisition (SCADA) based attacks. SCADA-based attacks could interrupt power supplies and result in long-term damage to wind turbines (Trantham & Garcia, 2015). These large farms will also need to be protected against human threats. Already, there have been an increased number of reported thefts of copper from wind turbines that have about one ton of copper in each turbine (Greensolver, 2015). Because of their location in rural environments, companies will need to increase their site security using innovative physical security controls to prevent wind turbine looting. To address these issues, in 2014, the Federal Energy Regulatory Commission (FERC), which is a governmental agency that regulates the interstate transmission of energy (gas and electricity), instructed the North American Reliability Corporation to develop physical security reliability standards. These standards require energy companies to take three steps to improve physical security. They include: (1) performing risk assessments on their facilities, (2) evaluating threats and vulnerabilities at their facilities, and (3) developing and implementing security plans to address the threats and vulnerabilities (FERC, 2014). Already insurance companies including Lloyds of London and security experts are conducting risk analyses of wind farms where the general conclusion is that threats do exist. The best way to address these issues is to improve the security culture (and awareness) that this industry is vulnerable to a myriad of security-related issues (Dvorak, 2015). With the increased shift to these energy sources, the need to protect them will be a high priority.

Federal Energy Regulatory Commission (FERC)
An independent government agency that regulates the interstate transmission of natural gas, oil, and electricity. FERC also regulates natural gas and hydropower projects.

Large wind farms that are often located in isolated areas have specific security needs.
(Photo courtesy of U.S. Department of Energy.)

SECURITY SPOTLIGHT

To gain a firsthand sense of the impact of globalization, consider all the ways globalization has affected you personally, in the context of security. For example, have you worried about your personal safety while vacationing or working in a country characterized by political instability? Have you purchased a food product that was recalled because it contained unsafe ingredients or toxins originating from an overseas supplier? Has your computer become vulnerable to cyberattacks from distant sources around the world?

▶ Technology

New technologies will result in increased vulnerabilities for companies. The growing two-way flow of technology between the developing world and the West, the increasing size of the computer-literate workforce in developing countries, and efforts by global corporations to diversify their high-technology operations will foster the spread of new technologies. These technologies will invariably lead to increased security threats. The theft of intellectual property, the increased threat of cyberattacks from individuals, companies, nation-states, and terrorist groups to disrupt critical information networks and, even more likely, to cause physical damage to information systems will increase. As a crime facilitation device, computer-based technologies will allow for greater instant connectivity, communication, and learning. It will enable transnational crime groups and terrorist threats to become increasingly decentralized, evolving into an eclectic array of networks, cells, and individuals that do not need a stationary headquarters to plan and carry out operations. Instead, training materials, weapons know-how, and fundraising will become virtual (online) in nature, where social media tools can be one method to share information, mobilize individuals, and be used to commit crimes. In fact, it has already been determined that street gangs and terrorist groups

Drones are already used for surveillance-related activities along the Mexican and Canadian borders.
(Photo courtesy of U.S. Custom and Border Protection.)

are using social media sites as crime facilitation devices (Pyrooz, Decker, & Moule, 2015). With the increased use of computers and the growth of social media sites, this threat will continue to expand in scope and intensity. In addition to being the "tool" to facilitate nefarious activities, computer-based technologies will also increasingly be the target of crime.

New technologies will significantly change security industry practices. Already, **drones** (also referred to as Unmanned Ariel Vehicles (UAVs)) are used by the military and private military security companies throughout the world. In the United States, they are being used by private security contractors working under contract with the U.S. Government who operate drone aircraft in support of border patrol surveillance activities (Peña, 2014). The FBI, Secret Service, and other federal and state-level agencies are also using them for law enforcement and surveillance-related functions. The Federal Aviation Administration (FAA) has estimated that there will be over 30,000 unmanned aircrafts in the United States in the next 20 years (Saranya, Pavithira, Premsai, Lavanya, & Govindarajan, 2015). To control drone surveillance-related activities, some states have already passed legislation requiring police to have valid warrants before deploying drones, while the FAA requires private sector owners to register their drones through its Unmanned Aircraft System (UAS) registry. The International Association of Chiefs of Police (IACP) has also created model policies on the use of drones, prohibiting weapons from being mounted on them while also requiring that agencies secure search warrants before using them for surveillance-related activities (Rae, 2014). These drones may revolutionize the private security industry. As these technologies become more advanced and less cost-prohibitive, it is likely that the security industry will also use drone surveillance as a supplement to or a replacement to existing human forms of patrol. Specific applications may include their use in mega sporting events and patrolling gated communities. Drones will also be used in the rail industry to inspect and monitor track, while the guard industry will also use UAVs as a supplement to or replacement of traditional guard staff.

drones Unmanned Ariel Vehicles (UAVs).

UAVs will not be the only technological revolution. The Defense Advanced Research Projects Agency (DARPA), an agency of the U.S. Department of Defense, has created unmanned ground vehicles that patrol military bases. Called Mobile Detection Assessment Response System (MDARS), a Patrol Unit Vehicle (PUV) equipped with a variety of sensors and weapons randomly patrols assigned areas. In addition to being able to be directly controlled by an operator in a command center, MDARS can perform semi-autonomous activities that include randomized patrols to detect and respond to various threats. These vehicles may be more reliable and more "random" in their patrol habits than humans and have the capacity to operate in all climates. With the downsizing of the military and the need for increased market share, the private sector may be a new market for these high-tech unmanned vehicles (Carroll, Nguyen, Everett, & Frederick, 2005).

For more information on current security-related technologies, go to http://www.darpa.mil/

Last, CCTV-related surveillance technologies and communications will continue to advance. One future area in video surveillance that will see great growth is video analytics. Video analytics is the interpretation of events that are recorded or monitored by CCTV cameras (Lee, Park, & Yoo, 2013). They are computer-based technologies and programs that are designed to track and identify individuals in large groups, record the number of people entering an organization, monitor the movement and motion of objects, and even perform gaze analysis that tracks where individuals are looking (Connell et al., 2013). Other video analytics include license plate recognition, facial detection, strange object recognition, secured access points surveillance, and auto-tracking suspects (Srilaya, Kumar, Boggavarapu, & Vaddi, 2013). These video-analytical tools will become increasingly important as a means to sift through large amounts of digital data to identify security-related issues.

> ## Legislative Trends in Security

The twenty-first century also presents new legal challenges. The elimination of, and alterations to nation-states and societies, the changing nature of the workplace, homeland security, increased use of high technology, and the expansion of global competition help to create an environment where the legal aspects of security management constantly evolve (Kovacich & Halibozek, 2003; Simonsen & Spindlove, 2007). Specific crime-related issues including school violence, mass shootings, and terrorism will also result in legislative changes that will have an impact on security operations and related laws. The progressive, informed, and visionary security manager takes advantage of any opportunity to learn about new laws and their implications.

Currently, there is no federal legislation that regulates the hiring and training of security personnel throughout the United States. This is not a surprising issue. The U.S. government structure was founded on the concept of states' rights. The system of government, established by the U.S. Constitution's Tenth Amendment, recognizes the sovereignty of states where powers not delegated to the federal government by the Constitution are reserved to the states or the people. As such, states can enact laws that serve the needs of their constituents as long as they do not violate the U.S. Constitution—it is their right— while the federal government is limited on what laws it can pass that interferes with those rights the state and its people retain. Because of states' rights, there is limited federal legislation related to the control and regulation of the private security industry at the state and local level. This point parallels the control the federal government has on the local police. In the case of regulating and controlling the police, instead of federal law, each state has specific laws and has legislatively created Police Officers Standards and Training (POST)

video analytics The interpretation of events that are recorded or monitored by CCTV cameras.

states' rights System of government established by the U.S. Constitution's Tenth Amendment that recognizes the sovereignty of states where powers not delegated to the federal government by the Constitution are reserved to the states or the people.

organizations that are responsible for establishing minimum training requirements and licensure for police officers. The only oversight the federal government basically has is when the police violate the civil rights of a citizen, which can lead to an investigation by federal agencies and subsequent civil and criminal actions in the federal courts (Southerland, Merlo, Robinson, Benekos, & Albanese, 2007).

However, this is not to say that federal government will not have the ability to influence the nature and quality of the private security industry. The federal government has the ability to legislatively create additional laws and regulations regarding minimum qualifications and training for private security personnel operating in the federal sector. These standards, in effect, could lead to states re-evaluating their standards to be more consistent with federal standards. Furthermore, as the sector begins to perform more quasi-public functions, engaging in activities traditionally reserved only for state actors, the potential for Fourth (use of force and search and seizure) and Fifth Amendment issues (e.g., confessions and interrogations) will arise. In this context, the federal courts, through their decisions, will indirectly effect security-related operations by modifying existing case law. Because of these federal court decisions, state governments may also need to pass legislation to govern the industry and individuals employed in it.

Currently, 41 states have some type of state regulation regarding licensure for private security firms. In most cases, these existing laws regulate the contract industry only; the proprietary sector is regulated by standards established by organizations themselves (Strom et al., 2010). However, the review of state legislation shows that even with the increased threat of terrorism and recognition for the need for more security since 9-11, there have only been moderate increases in security-related licensing and training requirements. Additionally, private security companies themselves often have minimum training standards that surpass existing state legislation (Nalla & Crichlow, 2014). What may become the driving forces for legislative change, however, are misconduct and use of force-related incidents in the private security industry. The theory of punctuated equilibrium posits that public policy is often characterized by long periods of stability, which is the case of private security law that has not received a great deal of attention or changed over the years. However, this stability can be punctuated by a serious event that shifts public opinion, which then leads to governmental policy changes. For example, some police agencies in the United States were confronted with some high-profile force-related incidents in 2014 and 2015 that led to policy changes and calls for more oversight. Similar high-profile and serious incidents in the private sector can also result in demands from the public for increased controls and legislation. Since several sectors of the security industry (contract, guard, and armored car) have a great deal of contact with the public, it can be safely assumed that similar force-related incidents will occur in the private security sector in the future. The resulting public sentiment will be the driving force behind increased security licensing, regulation, and training—especially when the public discovers deficiencies in existing legislation in some states.

> **punctuated equilibrium** A theory that posits that public policy is often characterized by long periods of stability that is then "punctuated" and changed by a serious event.

► Terrorism

The international community's conflict with transnational and domestic terrorists will continue well into the twenty-first century. Some success with dismantling terrorist organizations and disrupting their leadership has been achieved—most notably with the killing of Al-Qaeda chief Osama bin Laden in May, 2011 (Hoffman, 2013). However, new structures for terrorist organizations have emerged, based on leaderless groups and illicit networks (not organized under traditional hierarchical structures led by a chain of command) and driven by a philosophy instead of a core group of leaders. These new fluid structures may be more adaptable and harder to detect and assess than traditional terrorist organizations (Jones, 2008). In the future, it will be more difficult to determine if they are truly a terrorist organization, a criminal enterprise, or a gang. Perhaps, the only common denominator is that all are threats to individuals and organizations.

To date, some counterterrorism initiatives have experienced relative success. Cooperative international efforts have improved border and transportation security, enhanced information security, disrupted terrorist financing, and restricted terrorist activities. For example, in March 2011, the European Commission released a U.S. counterterrorism program that aims to track the finances of terrorism suspects. Under the program, U.S. agencies can obtain access to European banking data held by the Society for Worldwide Interbank Financial Telecommunication (SWIFT), which is a cooperative that routes trillions of dollars in transactions between financial institutions, brokerage houses, and stock exchanges. The Commission asked the United States to:

- Make the benefits of the program more transparent, so the public would support it.

- Make other relevant aspects of the program known, such as how much data the United States will access through SWIFT.

- Provide more information about its justifications for requesting information from SWIFT and to make those requests in writing so that European officials can evaluate them.

- Post more information on the U.S. Treasury Department's website about what types of information in SWIFT's database can be corrected, erased, or blocked (Kanter, 2011).

Despite progress in combatting terrorism, major challenges remain. Several nation-states continue to sponsor terrorism, providing weapons, training, advice, and funding. The appeal and spread of Al-Qaeda and ISIS (also known as the Islamic State) and radical ideologies continues. As security improves in one area, terrorists target other venues or adapt their tactics to meet changing conditions. In addition, organizational and structural issues related to information sharing and limited or noncooperation between law enforcement organizations may also impair the world's war on terror (O'Connell, 2008).

In a simplistic sense, terrorists seek and exploit vulnerabilities in the physical, personnel, and information protection systems in the private and public sector. To ensure that many of these vulnerabilities no longer exist or are exploited, counterterrorism efforts in the future will rely more upon horizontal (among intelligence agencies) and vertical (among local police agencies) relationships that include the private security sector (O'Connell, 2008). An effective "War on Terror" will also require a paradigm shift by many public sector organizations and antiterrorism experts that the private sector has a lot to offer in this war. According to Howard and Riebling (2006), "In counterterrorism, the community includes private-sector infrastructure and multinational corporations. Security policymakers must encourage partnerships not only with private citizens, but with business leaders and corporate-security chiefs" (p. 3).

In this context, public private partnerships at all levels (international, federal, state, and local) will become more important (Gill & Phythian, 2006; Howard & Riebling, 2006). At the international level, in 2007, the United Nations formed the United Nations Counter Terrorism Implementation Task Force (CTITF), a partnership between the private and public sectors. The rationale for including the private sector in antiterrorism efforts was based on the fact that terrorists perform indiscriminate attacks on soft targets in the private sector and the protection of these targets relies on active participation by all parties who are affected (Lucas, 2012). In addition, many private sector organizations possess resources and expertise that can supplement and enhance antiterrorism efforts. In many cases, these companies already have locations in high-risk settings and may have extensive contacts with the local population, collecting essential information that can lead to the generation of intelligence for the global community.

public private partnerships Partnerships between public and private sector organizations.

United Nations Counter Terrorism Implementation Task Force (CTITF) Partnership between the private and public sectors directed against world terrorism.

One of the most infamous threats in the 1990s and early twenty-first century was Al-Qaeda ("The Base") that often engaged in expeditionary terrorist activities, which involves violence from perpetrators outside the targeted country (Tankel, 2014). In the past, Al-Qaeda selected and trained terrorists in one country, and then clandestinely inserted a team into another country to attack a preplanned objective. The Al-Qaeda attacks on the USS *Cole*, in 2000 in Yemen that killed 17 U.S. sailors, the events of 9-11 by Al-Qaeda (Phares, 2014), and the November 2015 ISIS attacks in Paris France that killed 129 are examples of expeditionary terrorist activities (Pierot, 2015). Terrorist groups have adapted, and are now radicalizing citizens of the target nation (aka "homegrown terrorists") and training them in terrorist tactics. Through intermediaries, web-based propaganda, and subversion of immigrant expatriate populations, terrorist organizations can now finance, inspire, and radicalize local citizens to carry out attacks. The Madrid bombing in 2004 that killed 191, the London terrorist attacks of 2005 that killed 52 and injured another 700 are just two examples of the homegrown approach adopted by terrorist organizations (Argomaniz, 2015; Hafez & Mullins, 2015). This homegrown terrorism also includes citizens who are radicalized and then travel to a foreign country or provide financial or material support to terrorist organizations (Brooks, 2011).

New tactics and strategies must be developed to combat new forms of terrorism. In addition to targeting violent extremist networks and individual terrorists, the new threats demand the application of counterinsurgency techniques that focus on protecting, securing, and winning the support of populations at risk of radicalization. Trusted networks of private and government organizations and individuals, along with integrated civil–military measures, are keys to the success of this new approach (U.S. Department of State, 2007).

The National Intelligence Council (NIC) affirms the opinions of other experts regarding the threat of terrorism. The NIC is a center for strategic thinking within the U.S. government that reports to the Director of National Intelligence (DNI) and provides analyses on foreign policy issues to the president and senior policymakers. Periodically, the NIC produces a National Intelligence Estimate (NIE), a forward-looking assessment on national security issues. NIEs are classified intelligence estimates (rather than predictions) that express the composite views of 16 U.S. intelligence agencies. They present intelligence analysts' judgments regarding the capabilities, vulnerabilities, and probable courses of action of foreign groups and nations (National Intelligence Council, 2007b).

In April, 2006, the DNI released an unclassified NIE that assessed the threat of terrorism in the near future. While published in 2006, these issues are contemporary and are still a future concern for security managers and the intelligence community. Some of the underlying elements of the spread of jihad (holy war) throughout the world are shown in Box 14-2.

expeditionary terrorist activities Terrorist-based violence from perpetrators outside the targeted country.

homegrown terrorists Domestic, not foreign, terrorists committed by citizens of the affected nation.

counterinsurgency techniques Tactics and strategies designed to protect, secure, and win the support of at-risk populations prone to insurgency.

National Intelligence Estimate (NIE) A forward-looking assessment on national security issues. NIEs are classified intelligence estimates (rather than predictions) that express the composite views of 16 U.S. intelligence agencies.

jihad Holy war.

BOX 14-2

THE UNDERLYING ELEMENTS OF THE SPREAD OF JIHAD

1. Entrenched grievances, such as corruption, injustice, and fear of Western domination, leading to anger, humiliation, and a sense of powerlessness;
2. The Iraq jihad;
3. The slow pace of real and sustained economic, social, and political reforms in many Muslim majority nations; and,
4. Pervasive anti-U.S. sentiment among most Muslims—all of which jihadists exploit (National Intelligence Council, 2006, p. 2).

Besides Al-Qaeda, the NIE described other potential threats to the U.S. homeland. The NIE assessed that the Lebanese Hizballah, a Shiite Muslim extremist group, will consider attacks against the U.S. homeland if Hizballah perceives the United States to be a direct threat to the group or Iran. Furthermore, the number of radical, self-generating Muslim extremist groups within the United States and other Western countries is increasing, fueled by anti-American rhetoric presented in the media and on Internet sites. Finally, non-Muslim single-issue groups such as right-wing white supremacists, anarchists, antiabortion activists, and animal rights groups will probably launch small terrorist attacks within the United States (National Intelligence Council, 2007b).

Shifts in International Terrorism

The key factors that spawned international terrorism show no signs of abating over the years. The revival of Muslim identity will create a framework for the spread of radical Islamic ideology inside and outside the Middle East, including Southeast Asia, Central Asia, and Western Europe. This revival has been accompanied by a deepening solidarity among Muslims caught up in national or regional separatist struggles. Uprisings in Syria, Palestine, Chechnya, Iraq, Kashmir, Mindanao, and southern Thailand have emerged in response to government repression, corruption, and ineffectiveness. Informal networks of charitable foundations, *madrassas* (Islamic seminaries), *hawalas* (informal banking systems), and other mechanisms will continue to proliferate and be exploited by radical elements; and alienation among unemployed youth will swell the ranks of those vulnerable to terrorist recruitment (Hasan, 2015; Kis-Katos, Liebert, & Schulze, 2014).

It is also expected that Al-Qaeda will be superseded by similarly inspired Islamic extremist groups. Al-Qaeda is no longer the nucleus of any worldwide terrorist conspiracy and has not been for some time. In fact, public opinion polls in the Middle East show that most Muslims in many Middle Eastern nations do not support and actually revile the actions of Al-Qaeda. However, there is a substantial risk that broad Islamic movements akin to Al-Qaeda will merge with local separatist movements. One of these is the Islamic State or ISIS whose origins can be traced to Sunni extremist forces fighting coalition forces in Iraq in 2003. Then called Al-Qaeda in Iraq (AQI) and led by Abu Musab al-Zarqawi (who was later killed by a U.S. air strike in 2006), it then re-emerged in 2011 and seized territory in Northeast Syria, which it uses as its base of operations, while also seizing large amounts of land and major cities in Iraq in 2014. Unlike Al-Qaeda whose main goal is global terrorism, ISIS seeks to eliminate the geographic borders and nations that were created in the Middle East by the Western powers after World War I. In place of these nation-states, ISIS wants to re-establish a *caliphate* (an ancient Muslim ideal of a pure Islamic state governed by Sharia law), and restore the original borders of the Ottoman Empire (Cronin, 2015).

Other militant terrorist groups are emerging in countries other than Afghanistan, such as Yemen and many nation-states throughout Africa. Experts agree that the shifting nature of terrorism overall presents a major challenge. Individuals and organizations that use terror are mobile and constantly mutating. Thus, these enemies have no fixed and definitive identity. Moreover, their methods are blending with those of other organizations: criminal organizations use terror, and terrorists use the means of criminal organizations. Under these conditions, it is difficult, if not impossible, to combat terrorism by simply compiling lists of individuals or organizations that must be captured, prevented from boarding aircraft, or eliminated. Data that is collected becomes out of date quickly, making it irrelevant even if it is processed by the best available computer. To move out of the current culture of reaction, retrospection, and data compilation, the intelligence community will need to master the art of early detection of the threats and dangers presented by the modern world. This transition will require expert observation—but in the context of what threats may emerge and how their nature may change. Such expert knowledge will hinge on day-to-day connections with the real world—by the entire law enforcement community, ranging from small towns to large cities (Bauer, 2011). It will also rely upon the collection of information and the generation and dissemination of intelligence by the private security industry.

Terrorist attacks will continue to primarily employ conventional weapons involving small arms and light weapons (SALW) that are readily available for purchase from many unstable countries in the world (Strazzari & Tholens, 2014). However, a strong interest in terrorist groups acquiring chemical, biological, radiological, and nuclear (CBRN) weapons increases the risk of a major terrorist attack. Already, it is reported that most terrorist organizations have considered their use. Because of the diffusion of knowledge (e.g., the Internet) and the increased availability of some of these weapons, this risk of CBRN weapons has increased. In addition, some of the older, larger, and organized groups may also have the financial abilities to purchase CBRN weapons (Asal, Ackerman, & Rethemeyer, 2012). To manage this risk, initiatives including the G8 Global Partnership Against the Spread of Weapons and Materials of Mass Destruction have been created. The goal of the partnership is to limit the availability of CBRN-related weapons, destroying stockpiles of chemical weapons around the world, and increasing the safety and security of the storage of spent nuclear fuel (Akbulut, 2013). One primary concern is terrorists acquiring biological agents, which could cause mass casualties. Of these, existing diseases such as smallpox, hemorrhagic fever, anthrax, and plague, which are easily obtainable in the "public domain" in comparison to other biological agents, are a primary concern. These agents are easily transmitted between persons, can cause mass panic, and have the highest mortality rates; they are considered to be the greatest threat (Cannons, Amuso, & Anderson, 2006).

> **CBRN weapons**
> Chemical, biological, radiological, and nuclear weapons.

▶ Growth and Challenges

Security personnel at all levels must acquire new, more sophisticated skills to compete in and demonstrate the competencies needed in the future. Specialized training, education, and experience in security will be a necessity rather than a luxury. As the security profession becomes even more complex and sophisticated, security managers will be chosen from the ranks of those with specialized training, education, and experience in security rather than simply relying on retired law enforcement officers. Security managers are also likely to assume a broader range of responsibilities, as evidenced by position titles that reflect facilities management, continuity of operations, and risk management functions. Security managers must also possess the multidimensional competencies of loss prevention expert, intelligence gatherer, investigator, administrator, visionary planner, financier, resourceful inventor, and effective communicator.

In the future, line level security personnel and managers will need to have greater cultural competency skills to successfully operate in and meet the needs of their clients in an increasingly diverse population. Culture is defined as "patterns of thinking, feeling, and acting that are rooted in common values and societal conventions" (Mazaheri, Richard, Laroche, & Ueltschy, 2014, p. 255). It can also be thought of as inherited and collective assumptions, core values, customs, rituals beliefs and behavioral norms, and societal expectations (Gallivan & Srite, 2005; Sil, 2000). Cultural or intercultural competency, in a broad sense, is having the knowledge, skills, and abilities to work and live in a culturally diverse world (Moran, Abramson, & Moran, 2014). Intercultural competency is developmental in nature. It is a personal process that involves having the right attitude (respecting and valuing other cultures, openness or withholding judgment, curiosity and discovery, and tolerating ambiguity); and, possessing knowledge and comprehension skills (cultural self-awareness, deep cultural knowledge, and language skills) regarding other cultures. If a person has acquired these skills, then he or she should be able to properly internalize cultural issues (empathy, adaptability, and taking an ethno-relative view of situations) and

> **culture** Patterns of thinking, feeling, and acting that are rooted in common values and societal conventions.

> **intercultural competency** Having the knowledge, skills, and abilities to work and live in a culturally diverse world.

then engage in external actions (i.e., appropriate forms of communication and behaviors). Developing intercultural competency skills is continuous and lifelong; culturally competent individuals repeatedly seek out the opportunity to learn, understand, and appreciate other cultures (Deardorff, 2015). Intercultural competency is also an organizational responsibility. Organizations must value and promote diversity and inclusion, creating a core set of values and principles, while modeling pro-cultural behaviors and attitudes on both a philosophical end goal and as a means to improve profitability.

In some security disciplines, organizations may encounter challenges in recruiting sufficient numbers of security personnel who have specialized skills. Cybersecurity professionals will be one of the greatest needs. In fact, the lack of adequately trained cybersecurity professionals has already been identified as a human capital crisis. This crisis is due in part to individuals not entering the field and educational institutions not providing the correct training and education (CSIS, 2013; Hettema et al., 2014). The Department of Homeland Security has recognized the need for highly trained cybersecurity staff. To increase the interest in this field, DHS partnered with the National Initiative for Cybersecurity Education (NICE), which is led by the National Institute of Standards and Training (NIST). The purpose of NICE is to promote cybersecurity education, awareness, and to establish standards for professional development and training in the field of cybersecurity. Another goal of the program is to increase the skill sets of individuals working in cybersecurity. In 2013, NICE established some common KSAs (Knowledge, Skills, and Abilities) for cybersecurity workers. The primary goal of this National Cybersecurity Workforce Framework (the Workforce Framework) "is the foundation for increasing the size and capability of the US cybersecurity workforce. It provides us with a shared language and frame of reference to organize the way we think and talk about cybersecurity work. It also helps us understand what is required of the cybersecurity workforce across government, industry, and academia" (National Initiative for Cybersecurity Careers and Studies, 2015, np). Additional strategies by the DHS to increase the number of cybersecurity professionals in its ranks include increasing university recruitment efforts and attending hacker conventions to find skilled employees (Rashid, 2011).

Partnerships

Despite the differences between the private and public policing sectors in their primary duties and responsibilities (generally, private v. public interests), the relationship between the sectors has evolved positively since the 1980s and especially after 9-11. One early example of partnerships was when ASIS International and the IACP joined forces through Operation Cooperation (1999), which studied and provided guidelines for police and private security professionals to work together. The impetus for the creation of the partnership was due in part to the growth in security services, coupled with the success of community policing practices in the public sector that forged alliances with citizen groups. Activities associated with Operation Cooperation include networking, information and resource sharing, crime prevention, training, joint operations, and the development and promotion of state and federal legislation of mutual interest (Connors, Cunningham, & Ohlhausen, 1999).

Since the terrorist attacks of 9-11, public law enforcement–private security partnerships have been viewed as critical to preventing terrorism-related activities. For example, in 2005, the Law Enforcement–Private Security Consortium and the U.S. Department of Justice, Office of Community Oriented Policing created Operation Partnership. Operation Partnership established guidelines on how to develop and improve law enforcement and private security partnerships in the United States. These cooperative relationships between and among private security organizations, government operations, and public law enforcement demonstrate a growing trend toward *private/public interdependence* (Law Enforcement-Private Consortium, 2009). Joint public and private ventures, investigations,

National Initiative for Cybersecurity Education (NICE) Organization led by the National Institute of Standards and Training (NIST) to promote cybersecurity education, awareness; establishes standards for professional development and training in the field of cybersecurity.

Operation Cooperation Partnership between ASIS International and the International Association of Chiefs of Police (IACP) in 1999 that studied and provided guidelines for police private security professionals to work together.

Operation Partnership A project created by the U.S. Department of Justice, Office of Community Oriented Policing in 2005 that provides guidelines on how to develop and improve law enforcement and private security partnerships in the United States.

emergency planning efforts, crime prevention programs, and the privatization of some public police services that are mutually advantageous will undoubtedly continue into the future. This can be attributed to resource limitations in the public sector combined with the increased recognition of the resources the private sector possesses that can be used to address new security challenges.

Changes in Security-Related Services

There will also be changes related to the services companies provide. To date, many contract and proprietary security organizations are "one-dimensional," providing security-related services only. However, the field itself and of what security encompasses has dramatically increased in the first part of the twenty-first century. Now, security is inter-related with a variety of issues associated with human resource management, occupational safety, labor relations, and management. In the future, contract security firms will provide "one stop shopping" for clients where all of their physical, personnel, and IT-related security needs can be provided by one source. The security function, in many cases, will therefore shift from a "craft" to a "knowledge-based" entity. Already, CoESS posits that the "modern" security organization will be the following:

> What should the new security company then look like? Managing a guard service process is not the same as running an installation department that is getter more and more IT-driven. If the aim is to provide total concept offerings, the company should be capable of bringing a number of skills together and of transforming an organisation from a silo culture into a collaborative mode. Indeed, a multitude of operationally stand-alone installation and service flow management processes need to culminate seamlessly into a security solution (Cools & Pashley, 2015, p. 28).

When considered in this context, security will also become more involved in the strategic decision-making in organizations. In many cases, this will result in a paradigm shift for employees and clients where the broad services of the security function will be recognized for its **value-added** contribution to organizational success. The services and benefits it provides results in increased financial savings or profits for the organization.

This value-added approach will become increasingly important for organizations. Intensified global competition will result in greater demands for fiscal accountability for all organizations where the security function will be required to prove its worth. To prove its effectiveness or worth, value-added models will be increasingly used to measure security outcomes. In a basic sense, these models (that often rely on statistical procedures) isolate and measure the impact that a policy, practice, or program has on various outcomes and measures. For example, in teaching, the outcome is learning that is often measured by standardized tests. In the security profession, meanwhile, cost-savings, loss reduction, and more abstract but nevertheless important outcomes related to safety and security will be used to justify security-related expenditures.

This increased need and demand for a value-added approach also will result in the use of more **evidence-based practices (EBPs)** in the profession. Already used in many public sector agencies, EBPs are specific actions and policies that consistently show (with scientific reliability) that they "work," based on defined outcomes. These outcomes can include cost-effectiveness, reduced crime, increased satisfaction levels, and reduced injury rates. EBPs will also serve to identify ineffective practices and gaps in performance. In the future, it can be anticipated that both the contract and proprietary sectors will need to provide sound objective evidence that their existing security programs and practices are effective in the context of cost and other pre-determined measures. EBPs will also be important in contract renewals. They also serve as a marketing tool by the contract sector that they are providing effective services. The proprietary sector will also use EBPs.

value-added
Services and benefits of the activity provide increased financial savings or profits for the organization.

evidence-based practices (EBPs)
Specific actions and policies that consistently show (with scientific reliability) that "they work," based on defined outcomes, such as cost effectiveness, reduced crime, increased satisfaction levels, and reduced injury rates.

Research into "what works" will also result in better practices throughout the sector and it will lead to security having its own body of knowledge, enhancing the reputation of the entire profession (Aarons, Cafri, Lugo, & Sawitzky, 2012).

Changes in Higher Education

In the case of security, the field is still young and evolving where there will be an increase in the number of higher educational institutions that will offer security-related degrees. Many higher educational institutions have already created security programs to provide an education in "security." However, one issue that the field of security has wrestled with over the years is defining the intellectual boundaries that comprise the discipline of "security." In the future, this discussion will continue where it will be important for the profession to identify and define a common educational core. To further frame and define security as a profession and an academic discipline, there will also be increased demands for security programs to be accredited. Through accreditation, security programs will have a common core curriculum ensuring the graduates are competent, since they have successfully completed a given set of coursework and obtained that requisite knowledge skills and abilities related to the security profession. Accreditation will also ensure academic rigor, integrity, and program legitimacy in the field (Ramsay, 2013).

> **surveillance studies** The study of surveillance practices in the world, using a variety of scholarly disciplines including economics, psychology, political science, and sociology.

The demand for better educated and trained security personnel will also increase due to the changing and increased threat environment. Already, many higher education institutions offer programs in Homeland Security, Private Security, Security Management, Loss Prevention, and Information Security. With new and emerging threats, security programs in higher education institutions will continue to provide specialized courses and degree programs. One relative new area is Surveillance studies. **Surveillance studies** is the study of surveillance practices in the world, exploring the issue from a variety of disciplines including economics, psychology, political science, and sociology (Gilliom & Monahan, 2013). With the increased demand for security professionals, combined with an heightened awareness of the field, it can be anticipated that there will be continued interest in the field as a career path and a deliberate career choice. To further address this need, certification and training programs offered by private organizations including the American Society for Industrial Security (ASIS) are predicted to "erase the distinction between the public and private worlds" (Lippert, Walby, & Steckle, 2013, p.219).

Summary

The future holds great promise for those who wish to pursue a career in security. Technological advances, legislative changes, and terrorism create new challenges for the security professional. The field of security will experience the growth of transnational private policing activities. Security companies will be part of a global assemblage of actors that will address complex issues related to transnational organized crime. Security practices will also expand to meet the personal needs of clients and citizens in emerging and underdeveloped nations as companies expand and direct their CSR activities toward the elements of human security. In fact, human security will become a strategic and practical concern for organizations in the near future, leading to the security function expanding its role in the organization to provide these services and needs. Globalization will also create new threats and challenges related to water, food, and energy security. Another area where there will

Clery Act Named for Jeanne Clery. This 1990 federal law requires all colleges and universities that participate in federal financial-aid programs to collect, maintain, and disclose information about crime on or near their campuses.

Color of law A legal standard. A person who is operating under *authority of* any *law*, statute, ordinance, regulation, or custom.

Closed-circuit television (CCTV) Video surveillance system closed to external transmission.

Cloud A metaphor for internet-based computing where organizations (and individuals) use external computer services.

Cloud computing Assessing computer resources and data owned and operated by a third-party data center.

Code of ethics Standards of professional conduct.

Columbine effect School systems throughout the United States have now upgraded and changed their school security practices and policies due in part to the fear that their particular school could be vulnerable to an active shooter attack.

Combination lock Dial or push-button lock commonly used with safes, vaults, padlocks, and vehicle doors.

Combustible hazards Products of fire that can be grouped into toxic gasses, heat, and smoke.

Common criteria security model A model or cognitive map that identifies the attributes of risk.

Common law Unwritten law based on custom or tradition.

Communications security (COMSEC) All efforts to protect information transmission from unauthorized interception.

Comparative negligence Legal doctrine that takes the position that the plaintiff did something that contributed to the damage, injury, or harm.

Compensatory damages Designed to compensate a plaintiff in a lawsuit for actual losses incurred.

Competitive intelligence The legal act of defining, gathering, and analyzing intelligence about competitor's products, promotions, sales etc. from external sources.

Computer crime Generally, any crime committed utilizing computer technology.

Confederation of European Security Services (CoESS) Located primarily in the European Union, an umbrella organization for security-related companies.

Confidentiality Keeping data private, allowing its access to authorized persons only. In the context of information security, it means that unauthorized disclosure of information would be prejudicial to the interests of the organization.

Confidential communication Any communication carried out under circumstances reasonably indicating that any party to the communication desires it to be confined to the parties involved in the communication.

Consideration A component of a contract. Consideration for the promise or benefit given to the other party. Is the point that the contract must have some type of value.

Conspiracy Criminal plan involving at least two people. In some states, it requires an act toward the completion of the intended (planned) crime.

Constitutional law That branch of law that is concerned with the examination, interpretation, and application of the U.S. Constitution.

Container Security Initiative (CSI) Established in 2002 by the CBP to protect global trade and border security by deploying CBP personnel around the world to ensure cargo container security.

Contingency plan Plan implemented only if a certain event, such as a natural disaster, occurs.

Continued reliability Employee background investigations conducted continuously or periodically to ensure that employees have ongoing suitability to hold their positions.

Continuous evaluation process (CEP) See continued reliability.

Contract Legally binding voluntary agreement between or among parties.

Contract security service Security organization that provides security services to individuals or other organizations for a fee.

Copyright Protects against unauthorized use of virtually any creative writing or expression that can be physically observed.

Corporate kidnapping The abduction of employees for ransom, where the company is solicited for the ransom payment. Also called executive kidnapping.

Corporate social responsibility (CSR) Activities by companies that provide some type of social benefit to improve the quality of life for communities and society.

Cost-benefit analysis A systematic process through which one attempts to determine the value of the benefits derived from an expenditure, comparing the value with the cost.

Counterinsurgency techniques Tactics and strategies designed to protect, secure, and win the support of at-risk populations prone to insurgency.

Countermeasures Actions directed against the actions of man-made and natural threats.

Coupon fraud Occurs when customers or employees redeem coupons for cash in lieu of the purchase of the item for which the coupon was issued.

Court of last resort A state's highest court; U.S. Supreme Court.

Courts of general jurisdiction A level in state courts that can try any case brought before it.

Courts of limited jurisdiction Courts that are limited in the types of cases they are authorized to try.

Covenants not to compete (CNCs) Contracts (also known as restrictive covenants because they restrict behaviors) that are designed to prohibit direct competition and knowledge transfer by former employees to other organizations competing with the company.

Covert operations   Undercover, secret, or surreptitious operations.

CRAVED   A shoplifting model. Items that are Concealable, Removable, Valuable, Enjoyable, and Disposable are the most common items stolen from retailers.

Credit card fraud   Economic crime utilizing a credit card or credit card accounts.

Credit history   An applicant or employee's financial history.

Crime   Offense against a society; an intentional act, or omission to act, in violation of the criminal law, committed without defense or justification and punished by society as a felony, misdemeanor, or infraction.

Crime Awareness and Campus Security Act   1990 federal law requiring postsecondary educational institutions to collect and disseminate campus crime statistics. See Clery Act.

Crime prevention strategies   Education, treatment, diversion, rehabilitation, and deterrence through law enforcement and security. Proactive efforts and policies that reduce the occurrence of criminal activities.

Crime prevention through environmental design (CPTED)   Theory and practice associated with protecting people and the environment through the proper design of facilities and communities.

Crimes against persons   Offenses committed by physical contact with the victim, in the presence of the victim with the victim's knowledge, or by placing the victim in fear of immediate harm; violent crime.

Crimes against property   Offenses committed against property—not persons.

Criminal history checks   Criminal background investigations conducted by human resource or security personnel on new and current employees.

Criminal investigation   An investigation that focuses on actual or suspected criminal activity.

Criminal law   The body of law that relates to crime. It regulates social conduct and/or prescribes whatever is threatening, harmful, or otherwise endangering to the property, health, safety, and moral welfare of people.

Criminal negligence   A form of criminal intent; the actor can foresee the result and fails to exercise the degree of care that a reasonable and prudent person would exercise in similar circumstances.

Criminology   The scholarly and scientific examination of the causes of crime and deviance.

Critical information   Information vital to a mission. All forms and types of information as defined in the U.S. Economic Security Act of 1996.

Critical Infrastructure and Key Resources (CIKR)   Public and privately controlled resources and assets that are deemed most critical to national public health and safety, governance, economic and national security, and maintaining public confidence.

Critical Infrastructure Partnership Advisory Council   Established to facilitate effective coordination between federal infrastructure protection programs with the infrastructure protection activities of the private sector and of state, local, territorial, and tribal governments.

Criticality   The importance of the asset in achieving mission or organizational success; how damage or loss of the asset could adversely impact the organization.

Crowd management   Security activities directed toward effective crowd control or management techniques.

Cryptographic security   The transformation (secret writing) of the data being transmitted in order to make it unintelligible to an unauthorized interceptor.

Cryptography   Science of secret writing; transformation of data to render it unintelligible to an unauthorized interceptor.

Culture   Patterns of thinking, feeling, and acting that are rooted in common values and societal conventions.

Customs-Trade Partnership against Terrorism (C-TPAT)   Partnership between the private sector and the U.S. Customs and Border Protection (CBP) agency.

Cybercrimes   Criminal activities where computers and computer networks are the target, tool, instrument, or place of criminal activity.

Cybersecurity   Computer security efforts directed at the protection of information systems computers, networks, software, and computer-related information from theft or damage.

Debit card   An electronic bank card that withdraws money from a bank account.

Decisional roles   Managing through actions and following through on decisions by serving as an entrepreneur, disturbance handler, resource allocator, and negotiator.

Decision-making   The process of making choices and determining the best course of action from a series of possible alternatives, based on the plan.

Decryption   Conversion of crypto text to plain text.

Defamation   Damaging a person's reputation by making public statements that are both false and malicious. Defamation can take the form of libel or slander.

Defend Trade Secrets Act   A 2016 legislation directed toward the enhancement of penalties for trade secret theft and economic espionage.

Defense in depth   Strategies use a layered approach to security where mutually supporting security countermeasures are used to protect assets.

Defense Security Services (DSS)   An agency of the Department of Defense that is responsible for administering the NISP.

Degrees of proof   Standards by which guilt or liability must be established in criminal and civil cases.

Delay functions   Slow an adversary's progress.

Delphi technique   Process through which several individuals or experts provide input on an issue and arrive at consensus on a prediction or list of needs or priorities.

Denial of service (DoS) Attack occurs when a perpetrator uses a computer network to flood another computer server with large fictitious packets of data, overloading the system and causing the server to "crash" or to slow down considerably.

Detection elements Detect adversaries, weapons, contraband, and other threats.

Deterrence-based strategies Security strategies to deter an adversary from committing the act.

Digitization The conversion and electronic storage of an image or information to a computer's digital language.

Digitized information Information that is created, stored, manipulated, and transmitted electronically.

Disasters Extreme large-scale man-made or natural events that result in casualties, destruction, damage, and disruptions that affect large groups of people. The degree of damage often overwhelms the response capabilities of local emergency response systems, communities, and individuals.

Disaster recovery The ability to recover from a disaster in a manner that does not adversely impact continuity of operations.

Discipline Corrective action designed to bring about change in an individual's behavior.

Discretionary access control (DAC) Under these models, the owner of the information or the system administrator decides or delegates who is going to have access to the information.

Distributed denial of service (DDoS) attack Where a large network of computers have been compromised (often thousands that have been infected with malware), flooding the organization's server(s) with data to slow or crash it.

Djibouti Code of Conduct (DCoC) Agreement adopted by 20 countries in the Middle East to address high seas piracy.

Documentation Any medium used to create a record of an event or communication.

Drones Unmanned Ariel Vehicles (UAVs).

Drug-Free Schools and Communities Act Enacted by Congress on December 12, 1989. Require institutions of higher learning, as a condition to participation in a federal financial aid to students program, to certify that it had adopted and implemented a program to prevent the unlawful possession, use, or distribution of illicit drugs and alcohol by students and employees.

Duncan Hunter National Defense Authorization Act (2008) U.S. legislation that placed restrictions on the use of military contractors by the U.S. military.

Dynamic risk Exists when threat conditions fluctuate.

E-contract An electronic contract.

Early warning systems (EWS) Preventative management where the organization uses a variety of baseline data to monitor employee actions with the goal of preventing a counterproductive action, such as workplace violence, before it occurs.

Earth Liberation Front (ELF) An "eco-terrorist" group.

Economic espionage Foreign power sponsored or coordinated intelligence activity directed at the U.S. government or U.S. corporations, establishments, or persons for the purpose of unlawfully obtaining proprietary economic information.

Economic Espionage Act of 1996 Federal law created to deter and prosecute domestic and foreign efforts toward the theft of trade secrets and economic espionage activities.

Education General knowledge development that is useful in all aspects of life. Learning undertaken in educational institutions in pursuit of qualifications.

Electronic article surveillance (EAS) Technologies that monitor, detect, and alert store personnel that an article is leaving the store or the zone of control.

Electronic locks Access control devices that do not rely upon traditional keys and instead use some type of proximity or card access device.

Emanations security Prevent the compromise of information through the capture of acoustical emanations. Also called TEMPEST.

Embezzlement Fraudulent appropriation of property by a person to whom the property has been entrusted.

Emergency notification system A method of alerting individuals about emergencies and other hazardous situations.

Emergency response Activities for identifying, detecting, planning, training, analyzing vulnerabilities and responding to unanticipated events that may result in injury and/or loss of human lives and damage and/or destruction of critical infrastructure elements.

Employee development The ongoing process of encouraging employees to seek new forms of knowledge.

Employee Polygraph Protection Act of 1988 1988 federal law that severely restricts the use of the polygraph or similar instruments by private-sector organizations.

Employee retention Strategies to retain productive employees to avoid expenses associated with recruitment and training of new employees.

Employment law Refers to common law and statutory provisions that regulate the employment relationship.

Encryption Conversion of plain text to crypto text.

Energy security The assured continuity of energy supplies, or a situation in which energy products are readily available through the usual commercial outlets and processes.

Engineering controls Physical changes to the workplace, which are used to separate workers from threats.

Environmental crime Human activities that violate or harm the environment in some manner.

Environmental disaster Term associated with exposure to hazardous materials, conventional and nuclear power failures, and gas line or water main breaks.

Environmental Protection Agency (EPA) Federal agency responsible for enforcement of federal environmental laws and regulations.

Ethical dilemma   Occurs when a person has the choice between two or more ethical options.

Ethical leadership   Demonstration of normatively appropriate conduct through personal actions and interpersonal relationships, the promotion of such conduct to followers through two-way communication, reinforcement, and decision-making.

Ethical standards   Standards that dictate behavior when law or precedent, which may prescribe behavior, does not exist.

Ethics   A branch of philosophy that studies morality. Involves moral principles and focuses on the concepts of right and wrong and standards of behavior.

European Union (EU)   Economic and political union of 27 European member nations.

Evaluation   Process used to measure performance, compare performance with stated objectives, report results, and take corrective action.

Evidence   Information used to make a decision. In a judicial proceeding, includes testimony, writings, material objects, and other items presented to prove or disprove the existence or nonexistence of a disputed fact.

Evidence-based practices (EBPs)   Specific actions and policies that consistently show (with scientific reliability) that "they work," based on defined outcomes, such as cost effectiveness, reduced crime, increased satisfaction levels, and reduced injury rates.

Executive protection   Activities designed to maintain the safety, security, and health of a human asset.

Expeditionary terrorist activities   Terrorist-based violence from perpetrators outside the targeted country.

Express kidnappings   Short-term types of executive/corporate kidnapping.

Expressed contract   Written or verbal contract in which all terms are explicitly stated.

FAA   See Federal Aviation Administration.

Fair Labor Standards Act (FLSA)   Passed by Congress in 1938. The Act forbids the use of oppressive child labor; established minimum wage and overtime pay for workers.

False alarm   An alarm that is activated as a result of a defect in the sensor itself or its application.

Federal Aviation Administration (FAA)   Federal agency responsible for regulating air transportation in the United States.

Federal Emergency Management Agency (FEMA)   Federal agency that manages federal response and recovery efforts following a major national incident.

Federal Energy Regulatory Commission (FERC)   An independent government agency that regulates the interstate transmission of natural gas, oil, and electricity. FERC also regulates natural gas and hydropower projects.

Federal Motor Carrier Safety Administration (FMCSA)   Federal agency with a mission to improve security and reduce injuries and fatalities involving large trucks and buses.

Federal Railroad Administration (FRA)   Federal agency responsible for promulgation and enforcement of federal rail safety regulations.

Felony   A crime for which the potential penalty may be a fine and/or imprisonment of more than 1 year, or death.

Financial audit   Evaluation of an accounting system; transactions are sampled to confirm records are free of significant errors.

Financial institution   Bank, credit union, brokerage house, insurance company, or any other institution where financial transactions are the primary function.

Fire   A state, process, or instance of combustion in which fuel or other material is ignited and combined with oxygen, giving off heat, light, and flame.

Fire annunciator   Devices that control and monitor the various parts and components of a fire alarm system.

Fire brigade   Private firefighting units and personnel.

Fire extinguisher   Portable and fixed fire suppression systems.

Fire hazard abatement   Involves the use of fire abatement codes typically established at the municipal government level.

Fire inspection   Determines if reasonable life safety conditions exist within a facility.

Fire inspection programs   Fire safety surveys, testing of fire systems.

Fire investigation   Involves fire cause determination and investigation of criminal actions.

Fire load   The total energy content of combustible materials in a given area.

Fire prevention   Policies and practices designed to prevent a fire from occurring.

Fire prevention enforcement   Adoption and administration of fire prevention codes, enforcement procedures, and notices.

Fire protection systems   Procedures and fire suppression systems and activities designed to minimize harm to persons and property after a fire has started.

Fire safety education   Fire prevention and fire reaction training.

Fire tetrahedron model   A fourth element of the fire triangle that consists of a chemical chain reaction.

Fire triangle   Heat, fuel, and oxygen necessary for a fire to occur.

Firewall   In computer security, the electronic tool used to restrict access to computer databases. A filter that is placed on a gateway between an organization's system and the internet where traffic can be blocked based on protocols (or rules) that are created by system administrators.

Flashover   The sudden increase in flame in the fire setting.

Food Safety Modernization Act (FSMA) Signed by President Barack Obama in January 2011. Designed to build a new system of food-safety oversight, with an emphasis on prevention of outbreaks of food-borne illnesses.

Food security Activities directed toward the availability, access to, utilization of, and the stability of food supplies to individuals.

Foreign Intelligence Surveillance Act (FISA) Federal law passed in 1978; created procedures for the physical and electronic surveillance and collection of foreign intelligence information between or among foreign powers.

Frankpledge system Ancient policing/watch practice in England where all able bodied men were required to serve the crown by participating in security-related activities (called the Watch) patrolling the tything unit and responding to criminal activities when citizens raised the hue and cry.

Fraud Involves practically any scheme or device used by a person to deceive another.

Free-burning phase Where the fire has become more intense and there is an ample supply of oxygen where open or visible flaming is present.

Free Will A philosophical perspective that proposes individuals rationally and freely choose their actions, always choosing to engage in pleasurable activities while avoiding or minimizing any pain related to their action(s).

FSMA See Food Safety Modernization Act.

Fuel load The mass of combustibles, including furnishings and building components in a given area that determines if a fire will occur and the nature and extent of the fire if fuel is present.

Full-time equivalent (FTE) Equivalent to a person, or combination of persons, assigned to work full time (40 hours per week).

Fusion centers Location where reports of suspicious activities made by citizens and police are collected and analyzed. Aim is to detect activities that may signal a potential terrorist attack.

General deterrence The concept that individuals will be deterred from engaging in a criminal or deviant act out of the fear of getting caught and punished.

Geneva Center for the Democratic Control of Armed Forces (DCAF) International foundation that studies security sector governance (SSG).

Globalization Internationalization of economic and business activities; decentralization; commercial, travel, and communications activities spanning the entire globe.

Global security assemblages Hybrid private/public arrangements where local and state authorities and private security providers work together to provide security-related services.

Grey market A market where the goods sold or used is not necessarily illegal. However, the sale, or use of the goods is illegal because it violates existing laws and legal restrictions.

Guard forces Proprietary, contract, or hybrid security personnel.

Hacker An expert at programming and solving problems with a computer; can refer to a person who illegally accesses restricted computer databases.

Hallcrest Report I 1985 study of private security in America.

Hallcrest Report II A study of the private security in America that was published in 1990; reaffirmed the need for training and regulation of the security industry.

Hawthorne effect Phenomenon that people worked harder because they believed that management was concerned about them.

Hazards Underlying conditions or situations that increase the potential that harm will occur.

Health care facility Hospital, medical center, health clinic, nursing home, or similar facility.

Health Insurance Portability and Accountability Act of 1996 (HIPAA) A federal law mandating national standards for electronic health insurance transactions, including claims, enrollment, eligibility, payments, and benefits. The law also mandates standards to protect privacy of personal health information.

Hierarchical organizational structure Where management levels are below or subordinate to another management level, with the exception of the top level.

Homegrown terrorists Domestic, not foreign, terrorist activities committed by citizens of the affected nation.

Homeland Security A combination of law enforcement, disaster, immigration, and terrorism issues, at all levels of government.

Homeland Security Act of 2002 Federal law that created the U.S. Department of Homeland Security and consolidated 22 separate federal agencies from several departments into one; effective March 1, 2003.

Homeland Security Advisory Council Provides advice and recommendations to the Secretary of Homeland Security on matters related to homeland security. Comprised of leaders from state and local government, first responder communities, the private sector, and academia.

Homeland Security Science and Technology Advisory Committee Serves as a source of independent, scientific, and technical planning advice for the undersecretary for Science and Technology.

Hospitality industry Organizations and institutions that provide lodging, food and beverage, recreation, and entertainment services to guests.

Hostile work environment Workplace behaviors and actions that a reasonable person would consider intimidating, hostile, or abusive.

Human error Unintentional, human mistake.

Human Factors Analysis and Classification System Model that examines the causal factors of accidents in a systems perspective.

Human Relations Movement New management approach that emerged in the 1930s that concentrated on the needs of workers and not just production.

Human security A universal issue that is based on ensuring people freedom from fear and wants.

Hurricane Katrina The devastating hurricane that hit the Gulf Coast of the United States in August 2005.

Hybrid disasters A type of man-made disaster. Are the result of human activities and decisions compounded with natural forces, such as wind, tornadoes, earthquakes, and lightning.

Hybrid security organization A security operation that employs proprietary security staff and uses contract security personnel to supplement existing proprietary security staff.

ICE See U.S. Immigration and Customs Enforcement.

Identity theft A crime committed when an imposter fraudulently uses another's personal identification information to obtain credit, merchandise, or services in the name of the victim.

Impeachment In a judicial proceeding, refers to an attack on the credibility of a witness; possible result of cross-examination of a witness.

Implementing Recommendations of the 9-11 Commission Act of 2007 Federal law that elevated the importance of risk factors in determining federal homeland security funding for states and cities.

Implied contract Contract resulting from the actions of the parties.

Implied contract A contract that is "unspoken" and results from the actions of the parties where they believe that an agreement exists.

Incident report Used to document an event or reported criminal activity.

Incipient stage A fire is in its beginning stage where some heat and small amounts of fire gases are being produced.

Indemnity/hold harmless clause Clause in a contract through which the indemnified person or organization is held harmless for the action/inaction of another.

Index crimes Contained in Part I of the Uniform Crime Report (UCR): murder, forcible rape, robbery, aggravated assault, burglary, larceny (theft), auto theft, arson.

Indictment Formal criminal charge issued by a grand jury.

Industrial Defense Program Created in 1952 by the U.S. government where those military branches affiliated with the Key Facility were responsible for working with that particular company that had primary responsibility for physical security and emergency management.

Industrial espionage The theft of trade secrets by individuals and companies.

Industrial security The practice of ensuring safety and security in manufacturing environments and managing loss through the risk management process.

Industrial self-regulation Organizations voluntarily adhering to industry standards and self-created codes or principles of conduct in addition to mandated laws and regulations (if they exist).

Inergen systems Fire suppression systems that provide a gaseous alternative to other types of fire extinguishing agents.

INFOSEC The protection of information and information systems.

Information In a criminal proceeding, the formal criminal charge issued by a prosecutor in a state felony case.

Information gathering Part of a hacker attack. Where a hacker tries to gain as much information about the target and existing computer security.

Informational role Managerial roles directed toward serving as a spokesperson and monitoring and disseminating information.

Information security (INFOSEC) One of the three pillars of an effective security program. Security of information creation, processing, storage, retrieval, transmission, dissemination, and disposition. The protection of information assets and systems against any threat.

Information system A discrete (and integrated) set of information resources organized for the collection, processing, maintenance, use, sharing, dissemination, or disposition of information.

Infraction Minor civil or criminal offense not amounting to a misdemeanor or felony.

Infrared (IR) camera Detects changes in infrared light radiation from area covered by cameras.

Infrared sensors Sensors that detect changes in heat or thermal energy.

Inherent risk Unavoidable risk due to the nature of activity.

Initial appearance The defendant's first appearance before a court. A nonadversarial proceeding before a magistrate (or judge) to set bail.

Injunction A judicial decree by the court that the tortfeasor engages in or ceases a particular activity or course of conduct.

In-service training Continuous professional training for current or existing employees.

Institutional Anomie Theory Posits that crime and deviance is the result of the commitment to the goal of material success, no matter how it is achieved, to be pursued by everyone in society, under conditions of open, individual competition.

Institutions of Higher Education (IHEs) Post-secondary schools including colleges and universities.

Intangible standards Employee characteristics that are difficult to measure. Examples include attitude, morale, and reputation.

Integrity An organization has processes to ensure that information and/or data is not modified, destroyed, or altered in some manner from storage and transfer. A person who has sound moral principles.

Integrity tests Tests used to detect a person's propensity toward dishonesty and unethical acts.

Intellectual property Information created through research and development, such as chemical formulas and software designs.

Intelligence Reform and Terrorism Prevention Act of 2004 Fashioned after the recommendations of the 9-11 Commission; provided for the creation of a national intelligence center and a director to oversee 15 U.S. intelligence agencies.

Intentional torts Willful tort activity. Examples include assault, false imprisonment, and defamation of character.

Interagency Security Committee (ISC) Chaired by the Department of Homeland Security is composed of representatives from approximately 53 federal agencies. The goal of this committee is to develop model physical security standards for federal buildings, based on the threats and vulnerabilities present and industry best practices.

Intercultural competency Having the knowledge, skills, and abilities to work and live in a culturally diverse world.

Intermediate appellate courts Appellate courts between trial courts and courts of last resort.

Internal employee theft Theft by individuals employed by the organization.

Internal labor market (ILM) Finding candidates inside the company, filling the position through promotion or transfer instead of looking outward.

International Association for Healthcare Security and Safety (IAHSS) Professional organization for health care security managers.

International Code of Conduct (ICoC) Document created by the ICoC that provides guidelines for the use of Private Military Security Companies.

International Code of Conduct for Private Security Providers Association (ICoC) Guidelines created by private military companies as a means of self-regulating the industry.

Internationally Recommended Transit Corridor (IRTC) A security transit corridor for shipping in the Gulf of Aden that is patrolled by multinational naval vessels.

Internet An interconnected system of computer networks.

Interpersonal role Managerial roles directed toward establishing and maintaining relationships by serving as a liaison, figurehead, and leader.

Interview Face-to-face encounter between the candidate and the employer's representative.

Investigation A systematic process through which information is gathered, analyzed, and reported.

Ionization sensor Sensor that detects products of combustion, including heat, flame, smoke, and invisible toxic gases.

IR sensors Sensors that respond to infrared emissions in heat.

Irritant gases Products of combustion that can be lethal, but at a minimum they impair one's vision and ability to breathe.

ISIS Also known as the Islamic State.

Islamic State Middle East Terrorist Group.

Jersey barrier Modular concrete barriers that can be used to prevent, control traffic flow and speed, and/or deter vehicular traffic.

Jihad Holy war.

Job description Position description; identifies the principal elements, scope of authority, and responsibilities involved in a job.

Job specifications Outline specific skills, competencies, and personal qualities necessary to perform a job adequately.

Job task (occupational) analysis Identifies the job functions (duties) a worker is expected to perform. Breaking the job down to its essential tasks.

Key-operated lock A common lock in residential and commercial settings; utilizes notched key inserted into the lock's keyway.

Keypad lock Generally, an electronic lock that utilizes microcomputer technologies and touch pads.

Law Enforcement Assistance Administration (LEAA) Now defunct federal program, established through the Omnibus Crime Control and Safe Streets Act of 1968 that provided federal monies to fight crime and improve the criminal justice system.

Leadership Occurs anytime one motivates, influences, or mobilizes an individual or group.

Lebanese loop A type of debit card/ATM fraud where the user's card is trapped in the card slot of the machine and is later retrieved by the criminal(s).

Legal risk Risk that arises from violations or nonconformity with laws, rules, regulations, or proscribed practices.

Library Collection of books and other media.

Limitations of liability clauses Are sections in the contract that limit, define, and articulate the maximum liabilities of the party if there is some type of legal challenge or action.

Line item budget Detailed budget that includes a description and the cost of each item. These budgets work from a base (the prior year's budget) where monies are added or subtracted from the yearly baseline.

Line of sight sensor (LOS) Senor that requires a clear "line of sight" between the sensor's sending and receiving unit.

Line security Involves protection of telephone cables, modems, local area networks (LANs), and similar communications systems.

Local alarm system When activated, produces an alarm signal in the immediate vicinity of the protected premises.

Locks Delay devices used to deter adversaries.

Logic bombs Software programs that remain "silent" until a certain computer activity (keystrokes, opening a program) or date and time is met.

Logical controls   Products and processes used to protect access to and the flow of data in an information system. Also known as technical controls.

Loss prevention   Security measures used to reduce loss or shrinkage in the retail sector.

Magnetometers   Metal detectors that use electronic fields to detect metal objects.

Malicious code attack   Occur when individuals (usually hackers) gain access to user and/or computer administrator accounts in order to shut down or raise havoc in a computer server or network.

Malware   Malicious software used to inflict damage to, or insert a virus into, a computer database.

Management   The process of planning, organizing, leading, and controlling the efforts of organizational members, and using all other organizational resources to achieve stated organizational goals.

Management levels   Different layers of management in a company based on managerial roles and responsibilities.

Managerial grid   Five leadership styles that integrate varying degrees of concern for people and production.

Mandatory access control (MAC)   Have fixed rules or attributes that allow access to information or information systems.

Man-made disasters   Disasters that are result of hazards that are created by humans, not the natural environment, which expose humans to some type of threat.

Man trap   Used in physical security and access control applications. Are small rooms or vestibules that have two interlocking doors, "trapping" a person in the room, if necessary.

Maritime Transportation Security Act (MTSA) of 2002   Fully implemented on July 1, 2004, the MTSA requires vessels and ports to conduct vulnerability assessments, develop security plans, and engage in activities designed to protect the nation's ports, vessels, and waterways.

Maslow's hierarchy of needs   A theory that explains human motivation and development. Created in 1958, Maslow hypothesized that in order for humans to excel, they have prepotent or *a priori* needs that must be met before progressing on to more advanced, complex needs.

Mass private property hypothesis   Areas of public life that were once the domain or control of the public police are now under the control of private companies.

Max Weber's Theory of Bureaucracy   Theory of management based on a hierarchy of authority, formalization, and clearly defined organizational rules.

Mega events   Large events that are often international in nature and attract large numbers of spectators and tourists.

Mens rea   The element of a crime that focuses on the offender's guilty mind or criminal intent (a design, resolve, or purpose of the mind) to commit a criminal act.

Mental disorder   A psychological disorder generally associated with a defect or disease of the mind.

Merchant's privilege laws   Specific laws that allow retailers (and their designees) to arrest offenders for misdemeanor and felony theft and fraud-related crimes.

Metrics   As it relates to performance, involves procedures designed to quantify and periodically assess processes that can be measured.

Metropolitan Police Act of 1829   1829 British law, promoted by Sir Robert Peel, that established first public, full-time police department in the world.

Microwave motion sensor   Sensor that utilizes high-end radio frequencies rather than sound. Similar in operation to ultrasonic motion sensor.

Misdemeanor   Crime for which the potential penalty may be a fine and/or confinement for up to 1 year.

Mission statement   Language designed to help operationalize an organization's action plan.

Mitigation   Efforts to reduce loss of life and property by lessening the impact of disasters.

Mitigation activities   A component of disaster management: prevent an emergency, reduce the chance of an emergency happening, or reduce the damaging effects of unavoidable emergencies.

Mobile Detection Assessment Response System (MDARS)   Patrol Unit Vehicle (PUV) equipped with a variety of sensors and weapons that randomly patrols assigned areas.

Montreux Document   Nonlegal document that provides 27 recommendations or "best practices" that are based on human rights and humanitarian law that nations can adopt regarding the use of Private Military Companies.

Moonlighting   When private organizations employ off-duty public law enforcement officers to work in a private security setting.

Morality   The standards, beliefs, or intangible principles of what is good or bad, or right or wrong.

MTSA   See Maritime Transportation Security Act.

Municipal ordinances   Laws created by cities, towns, or villages.

Museum   Facility used to preserve and display artistic and historic objects.

Mutuality of obligation   An element of a contract. The parties "have a meeting of the minds" and have agreed to the basic terms and conditions of the contract and agree to be bound by the contract.

Narrative report   Used to narrate what happened, record statements, and document additional information acquired subsequent to an original report.

Natech disasters   Another term for hybrid disasters. Disasters where natural forces "trigger" technological disasters.

National Cargo Security Council (NCSC)   Functions as a clearinghouse for cargo theft information.

National Commission on Terrorist Attacks Upon the United States (The 9-11 Commission) An independent bipartisan commission established in 2002 to investigate the events leading to the terrorist attacks of September 11, 2001. Recommended improvements to security and intelligence gathering capabilities.

National Crime Victimization Survey (NCVS) Random-sample survey conducted by the U.S. Census that determines the victimization crime rate per 1,000 persons.

National Incident-Based Reporting System (NIBRS) Enhanced UCR; requires and provides more detailed information than the UCR.

National Incident Management System (NIMS) A disaster and emergency plan that provides unified federal, state, county, and local approach to disasters with an emphasis on preparedness, standardization, mutual aid, and resource management.

National Infrastructure Advisory Council Provides advice to the secretary of Homeland Security and the president on the security of information systems for the public and private institutions that constitute the critical infrastructure of the nation's economy.

National Infrastructure Protection Plan (NIPP) Issued by the DHS in 2006. Outlines 16 critical infrastructure sectors that require protective actions to prepare for, and mitigate against a terrorist attack or other hazards.

National Industrial Security Program (NISP) Program that regulates the private industry's access to and use of classified government information.

National Initiative for Cybersecurity Education (NICE) Organization led by the National Institute of Standards and Training (NIST) to promote cybersecurity education, awareness; establishes standards for professional development and training in the field of cybersecurity.

National Intelligence Estimate (NIE) A forward-looking assessment on national security issues. NIEs are classified intelligence estimates (rather than predictions) that express the composite views of 16 U.S. intelligence agencies.

National Law Enforcement Agencies Federal agencies; have broad territorial and narrow subject matter jurisdiction. Also known as federal law enforcement agencies.

National Labor Relations Act (NLRA) Also known as the Wagner Act. Federal law that grants employees the right to belong to labor unions (and strike) in the private sector.

Nationwide SAR (Suspicious Activity Reporting) Initiative (NSI) Joint initiative between the DHS and the FBI where reports of suspicious activities made by citizens and local police are collected and analyzed in fusion centers.

Natural disaster Sudden, extraordinary misfortune caused by a force of nature.

Negligence Generally, a lack of due care or diligence that an ordinary, reasonable, and prudent person would have exercised in similar circumstances.

Negligence torts Emerge from those situations in which a tortfeasor fails to exercise ordinary and prudent care when carrying out specific tasks and activities, causing some type of damage, injury, or harm to another.

Negligent hiring Possible civil liability associated with failure to complete a diligent inquiry into the suitability of a person for employment.

Negligent retention Possible civil liability associated with employer's failure to take disciplinary or remedial action after becoming aware that an employee is a risk factor.

Network segmentation Securing, isolating, and separating vital network components into subnetworks to better protect the entire system by compartmentalizing an attack and any damage if it should occur.

NSI See Nationwide SAR (Suspicious Activity Reporting) Initiative (NSI).

Nuisance alarm An alarm caused by an event that is not a true intrusion or security issue.

Numerical standards Quantifiable performance standards that can be measured and expressed numerically.

Nursing home Extended care facility for the elderly and infirm.

Objective (quantitative) measures Used in risk assessment, planning, and evaluation. Include audits, inspections, surveys, marketing, and reports.

Occupational safety The protection of a company and human assets against accidents, injuries, and harm as the result of noncriminal actions by humans and mechanical/industrial failures.

Occupational Safety and Health Act (OSHA) Federal law created to protect worker health and safety.

Offer Part of a contract. A promise made by one of the parties to do or not do something, provided that the terms of the offer are accepted.

Operating expense Expense incurred as a result of organizational operations. Examples include rent, utilities, contract services, training, insurance, and licensing fees paid.

Operation Cooperation Partnership between ASIS International and the International Association of Chiefs of Police (IACP) in 1999 that studied and provided guidelines for police private security professionals to work together.

Operational management Managerial activities directed at day-to day operations.

Operation Partnership A project created by the U.S. Department of Justice, Office of Community Oriented Policing in 2005 that provides guidelines on how to develop and improve law enforcement and private security partnerships in the United States.

Operational plans Provide specific details and action steps needed to be carried out by an individual or group.

Operational risk An organization's potential for loss owing to significant deficiencies in system reliability or integrity.

Operational risk management (ORM) Programs that are concerned with identifying distinct elements of operations including individuals and the systems in which they work to reduce or mitigate the possibility of something going wrong.

Operations Security (OPSEC) Risk assessment activities designed to identify potential vulnerabilities that an adversary may exploit to obtain critical information.

Optical character recognition (OCR) Used in cargo security and other applications. Software that records license plates and container identification numbers to verify the legitimacy of the container and vehicle hauling it.

Organizational goals Desired states of affairs or preferred results that organizations attempt to realize and achieve.

Organizational objectives Define or explain how to achieve organizational goals.

Organize To create an orderly structure or arrangement.

Organized crime Refers to a relatively permanent group of individuals who systematically engage in illegal activities and provide illegal services.

Organized retail crime (ORC) Criminal organizations that focus on retail theft and defrauding of merchants.

OSHA See Occupational Safety and Health Act. Passed in 1970, the Act established the Occupational Safety and Health Administration (OSHA) and established specific safety requirements for employers.

Overseas Security Advisory Council (OSAC) Created in 1985, a partnership between 34 private and public sector organizations and the U.S. Department of State, Diplomatic Security Service to address and identify security-related issues in foreign countries.

Oxidation An exothermic reaction or process where oxygen combined with other substances, releases heat energy.

Pandemic Large-scale epidemic. Occurs when a disease emerges for which there is little or no immunity in the human population.

Part I crimes FBI UCR crime data comprising eight index crimes. See Index Crimes

Part II crimes FBI UCR crime data consisting of crimes against property

Passenger profiling techniques Used to identify smugglers and possible terrorists attempting to board commercial forms of transportation.

Passive infrared sensor Detects changes in heat or thermal energy (infrared light radiation) in protected area.

Password Unique identifier necessary to gain access, as in a code inputted to access a computer file or program.

Password stewardship Protecting and maintaining effective computer passwords and effectively securing passwords.

Patent A novel, useful, and nonobvious invention protected by federal law from unauthorized replication or use.

Path-Goal Leadership A leadership theory that assumes that followers will be motivated if they believe that that they are capable of performing tasks assigned, that their efforts will result in a certain result, and that the rewards for completing the tasks are worthwhile.

Payment fraud Types of retail crimes that include bad checks, credit cards, and bankcards.

PELAN Pulsed Elemental Analysis with Neutrons. Device used to detect the presence of chemicals and explosives in or on containers, vehicles, etc.

Peremptory challenge A challenge to a potential trial juror's qualifications for which no reason need be given; limited in number.

Performance appraisal Systematic assessment of employee performance.

Performance-based budget Budget designed to show that monies are used wisely, focusing on outputs. The goal of these types of budgets is to ensure and prove that expenditures have had an impact.

Perils Situations or events that can cause loss, injury, or damage. Threats are a synonym of perils.

Perimeter lighting Use of street lights, floodlights, search lights, and Fresnel lights to illuminate facility perimeter and/or protection zone.

Perimeter security A continuous line of security (barriers, illumination systems, personnel) used to monitor or control a facility's perimeter and prevent unauthorized access.

Personal identification number (PIN) Numerical password used to authenticate a user.

Personal property Anything, tangible or intangible, other than land and anything in it or permanently attached to it (real property, real estate).

Personnel integrity Individual honesty and appropriate behavior.

Personnel security One of the three pillars of any security program. Protection of persons associated with an organization as well as protection from individuals who seek to harm the organization.

Personnel selection Process of evaluating and choosing the most appropriate and qualified candidate for the job from the pool of applicants based on the existing selection criteria used.

Phishing A form of computer-based identity theft where the perpetrator uses email and malicious websites to obtain personal information.

Photoelectric sensor A fire-related sensor; detects airborne particles, including smoke, in an environment.

Physical security One of the pillars of an effective security program. Devices, lighting, surveillance and alarm systems, and security personnel devoted to access control.

Physical security measures Physical measures (i.e., locks, walls, gates) used to protect assets.

PIN cracking A form of ATM/debit card fraud where the criminal simply types in numbers or uses electronic devices to solve the numerical PIN code.

Piracy The act of boarding or attempting to board any ship with the apparent intent to commit theft or any other crime and with the intent or capability to use force in furtherance of the act.

Plan A sequence of actions that define an organization's goals, establish strategies for achieving those goals, and integrate and coordinate organizational efforts.

Plan review A process or requirements used by local governments to ensure that businesses are in compliance with building codes and other laws and ordinances.

Planned redundancy In the context of computer security, is the use of multiple firewalls to prevent cyberattacks while ensuring that there are no system failures or connectivity issues by being able to route traffic through different devices.

Plural policing Related to the fact that in many regions of the world, policing-related activities are no longer the sole or sovereign domain of the public sector.

Point-of-sale (POS) Cash registers or other locations where customers can pay for goods and services.

Policy General statement that describes goals or states an organization's position on issues or topics.

Portals Secure access points or openings.

POSDCORB Acronym that describes administrative activities: Planning, Organizing, Staffing, Directing, Coordinating, Reporting, and Budgeting.

Post-bureaucratic organizations Structures that are less hierarchical, more networked, and more nurturing toward employees.

Post-incident procedures Procedures and activities by the organization immediately after an event.

Post-Katrina Emergency Reform Act of 2006 Federal law that added functions to FEMA and amended the Homeland Security Act of 2002.

Postsecondary institutions Colleges, universities, and other post–high school education and training institutions.

Precursor conduct As defined by the NSI, activities that may signal a potential terrorist attack.

Pre-employment screening Selection tools used to determine the applicant's suitability for employment.

Preliminary hearing In the pretrial stages of a criminal proceeding, hearing at which the judge determines if probable cause exists that a crime was committed and that the person charged committed the offense.

Preparedness activities Part of disaster management. Include plans or preparations made to save lives and assets and to assist in response and recovery-related operations.

Preponderance of evidence The standard or degree of proof needed to prevail in a civil case. This degree of proof is met if the evidence demonstrates a probability—at least a 51% likelihood—that the facts in the issue are true.

Prevention and control strategies The use of engineering and administrative controls to create a solid, comprehensive physical security program.

Principal The person being protected in the executive protection process.

Private citizen powers to arrest Private person's powers of arrest, as compared with those of a public police officer.

Private justice system Rules, regulations, standards of conduct, and punishments established by private enterprises.

Private maritime security contractors (PMSCs) Armed or unarmed private security personnel on ships.

Private military security companies (PMSCs) Private security companies that provide military-related services to clients.

Private police Private security; protective services typically financed through private funding sources.

Private/public partnerships Joint private and public ventures.

Private Security Advisory Council (PSAC) Was tasked to advise the LEAA on security-related issues and how the private sector could assist in preventing crime.

Private Security Officer Employment Authorization Act of 2004 Allows employers to conduct criminal history checks of applicants for, and holders of, positions in which the primary duty is to perform security services, including positions held by contract and proprietary security personnel.

Privatization of public security services Public services provided by private organizations (contractors).

Probability The likelihood of loss or occurrence.

Procedural elements Policies and standard operating procedures for security operations and personnel.

Procedural security measures Policies and procedures that are in place to address a security issue/concern.

Procedure Outline a series of steps to be followed when carrying out policy.

Products of combustion Flame, heat, smoke, and toxic gases.

Professional development Training, education, and experiences designed to assist a person to perform well.

Progressive discipline Corrective actions progressing through several steps including verbal warnings, written reprimands, suspensions demotions, and/or terminations.

Project Argus Created by the United Kingdom's National Counter Terrorism Security Office (NaCTSO) where Counter Terrorism Security Advisors (CTSAs) train individuals in the office and retail, night clubs, hotels, education, health, and architectural design and planning sectors on crime prevention and antiterrorism techniques.

Project Griffin Public Private partnership in the City of London involving the London Metropolitan Police, private organizations, and private security.

Project Kraken UK-based antiterrorism security program administered by the National Crime Agency; increases vigilance among the UK's 20,000 miles of coastline and waterways.

Project Pegasus UK-based antiterrorism and security program directed toward increasing vigilance in the aviation community.

Project Servator Created by the City of London Police in February, 2014. The primary objective of this program is to address terrorism and other crimes by randomly deploying increased numbers of police officers in London and developing stronger relationships with citizens, the British Transport Police, the private security sector, and businesses.

Promotion Advancement into a higher position in the organization; a means to fill job vacancies, a reward or morale booster, and an incentive for employees to perform better.

Property laws The body of law that deals with the lawful possession and ownership of tangible and intangible property.

Proprietary alarm system Alarm system owned and operated onsite by the protected user.

Proprietary information Virtually any information belonging to an individual or organization.

Proprietary security Security program controlled and financed directly by the protected organization.

Protection zone Specific area protected through security measures.

Protective operations The final stage in the executive protection process. Complex and coordinated efforts between mobile and fixed protection staff and a command center to monitor and protect the movements of the principal(s).

Proximate cause Legal cause; the actor can foresee (anticipate) the consequences of an act or omission to act.

Psychological perspectives Theories that propose that offenders have some underlying psychological abnormality that was a causal factor of their commission of a crime.

Psychological tests Used to determine an individual's emotional stability and mental health.

Psychopaths Individuals who have underdeveloped regions of the brain that regulate and control impulse and emotion. They are highly aggressive, impulsive, and show little remorse or empathy for their actions.

Psychosis A break from reality, where a person suffers from hallucinations and delusions and is not aware of his or her break with reality.

Public administration Refers to administration of public sector organizations.

Public alarm system Typically, an alarm system connected directly to a public 911 emergency dispatch center or police department.

Public law enforcement Generally refers to police officers working for a city, county, state, federal, or other type of public police or law enforcement agency.

Public private partnerships Partnerships between public and private sector organizations.

Punctuated equilibrium Theory that posits public policy is often characterized by long periods of stability that is then "punctuated" and changed by a serious event.

Punitive damages Civil awards above and beyond the actual losses experienced by the action. Designed to punish a respondent in a lawsuit.

Pure risk Potential for harm or loss with no possible benefit.

Pyrolysis A chemical or thermal decomposition of combustible organic materials that are broken down by heat, and oxidation.

Quality assurance Continuous quality improvement; initiative designed to promote and assure quality.

Quality assurance initiative Collaborative effort that involves goal setting, trust, cohesiveness, increasing information flow, and conflict resolution; actions designed to improve the quality of products and services provided.

Radiation portal monitor (RPM) Passive scanning tool that detects radiation in vehicles, containers, and other objects.

Radio frequency identification (RFID) Tags or similar devices attached to products or goods. Provide real-time or continuous monitoring of assets.

Railway Police Act Granted police powers to railway security personnel in 1865 in Pennsylvania, leading to the creation of the Reading Railroad Rail and Coal Police.

Ram raiding Ramming ATMs (automatic teller machines) with vehicles or heavy equipment to demolish and force them open for their cash.

REAL ID Act of 2005 Federal law that imposes minimum standards for driver licenses, including verification of personal information provided by license applicants and counterfeit-resistant security features incorporated into each license.

Realistic job preview Where an employer provides realistic expectations on the part of new and existing employees.

Real property Land and anything permanently (or semipermanently) attached to land; real estate.

Reasonable doubt A term that means the evidence presented by the prosecution leaves "no reasonable doubt" in the belief of a juror or judge that the defendant is guilty of the crime in question.

Recovery efforts Part of disaster management. Actions taken after an event occurs in an effort to return to a pre-event or normal state.

Recovery time objectives (RTOs) Specific activities and the estimated times it will take to restore and replace critical activities and processes.

Recruitment Process of locating and attracting suitable candidates to fill job vacancies.

Refund fraud Defrauding a retailer by returning stolen or ineligible items for a cash or credit refund.

Refund policy Refunds tightly controlled from central location; sales receipt required; audit refund procedure.

Regional Cooperation Agreement on Combating Piracy and Armed Robbery Against Ships in Asia (ReCAAP) Agreement among states located near or around the Straits of Malacca and Singapore and the South China Sea to fight high seas piracy.

Relative value The subjective value of a component piece of information, based on its contribution to the entire system.

Repeat-use (standing) plan A plan implemented each time a given situation or incident occurs. Unless modified, repeat-use plans change little over time.

Reputational risk The value of an organization's or person's reputation.

Resilience The ability to prepare for and adapt to changing conditions and withstand and recover rapidly from disruptions. Includes the ability to withstand and recover from deliberate attacks, accidents, or naturally occurring threats or incidents.

Respondeat superior A legal doctrine where employers are responsible (or vicariously liable) for the negligent actions of their employees when their actions are within the scope of their employment.

Response strategies Security-related activities that interrupt the actions of an adversary.

Response A part of disaster management. The actions or activities taken during an incident.

Resume Subjective account of a person's background. Used as a pre-employment screening device.

Resumption Activities directed at restoring the organization to pre-event conditions.

Return on investment (ROI) Net cost savings that result from security measures employed.

RFID See Radio Frequency Identification.

Ring of Steel Nickname for security measures that exist around the City of London.

Riot Relatively spontaneous group violence.

Risk Possibility of suffering harm or loss; exposure to probability of loss or damage; an element of uncertainty.

Risk acceptance Accepting that some type or degree of loss will occur.

Risk assessment Critical, objective analysis of an organization's entire protective system.

Risk avoidance Making decisions and engaging in activities that create less risk. Managing risk by avoiding "risky" things.

Risk elimination Efforts to reduce risk.

Risk management Process involved in the anticipation, recognition, and appraisal of a risk and the initiation of action to eliminate the risk entirely or reduce the threat of harm to an acceptable level.

Risk management techniques Strategies and tactics designed to eliminate risk, reduce the probability loss will occur, or mitigate damage, if a threat materializes.

Risk reduction Activities designed to reduce the consequences and likelihood of any loss associated with the specific risk(s).

Risk spreading Practices designed to spread or separate assets to mitigate or reduce loss.

Risk states A method to categorize risk based on subjective ("social world") and objective (physical world") criteria.

Risk transfer Shifting the risk burden onto someone else.

Role-based access control (RBAC) An access control policy for computer-based information that grants access based on the job and tasks that individual users have in the organization.

Routine activities theory A criminological theory that posits that the opportunity to commit a deviant or criminal act consists of three elements: (1) suitable target; (2) a motivated and likely offender; and the (3) lack of capable guardianship.

SAFE Port Act See Security and Accountability for Every Port Act of 2006.

Safe-School Initiative Created in 1999, a partnership between the U.S. Department of Education and the Secret Service to identify and address threats in schools and prevent school violence.

Safe-school zones School campus areas, transportation systems, and off-campus activity venues that give rise to zero-tolerance policies focusing on weapons and drugs.

Safety The absence of accidents.

Safety analysis Identifying and assessing workplace hazards.

Scheduling The process of assigning individuals to work various days, times, and locations.

Scheduling cycle The number of days, weeks, and months in the scheduling horizon.

Scheduling periods Single or multiple days a person is scheduled to work.

Scientific management Classical management concept that focused on worker productivity.

Secret Unauthorized disclosure of information could damage the organization.

Sector-specific plans (SSPs) Part of the NIPP. SSPs define roles and responsibilities, catalog existing security authorities, institutionalize already existing security partnerships, and establish the strategic objectives required to achieve a level of risk-reduction appropriate to each individual sector.

Secure Flight A behind-the-scenes program that streamlines the travelers' watch-list matching process. It aims to improve the travel experience for all passengers, including those who have been misidentified in the past. Under the Secure Flight Final Rule, TSA requires airlines to collect and transmit to TSA the Secure Flight Passenger Data (SFPD).

Security Freedom from risk or harm; safety.

Security and Accountability for Every Port Act of 2006 Also known as the SAFE Port Act. This federal law requires that 100% of all containers originating from foreign ports be X-rayed or scanned for radiation at a foreign or U.S. port before being allowed to leave a US port.

Security awareness   The depth and degree of security-related knowledge that organizational members possess, apply, and use in the workplace.

Security Industry Authority (SIA)   Established under the Private Security Industry Act of 2001 in the United Kingdom. The SIA is a governmental entity that is responsible for licensing individuals, managers, and security companies operating in the transit of cash and valuables, door supervision, public space surveillance, guards, and close protection.

Security management   Multifaceted and interdisciplinary management tactics and strategies designed to secure persons, property, and information and prevent losses from any source.

Security services   Public and private security services designed to protect people, property, and information.

Security survey   Risk assessment tool used to evaluate and identify risks and security hazards/deficiencies.

Security Systems Integration   Unification of all security systems into one system.

Selection   In pre-employment screening, the process of evaluating and choosing the most appropriate and qualified person from a pool of applicants.

Self-Scan Checkout Kiosk Fraud   Retail fraud committed at self-scan checkouts.

Sensitive compartmented information (SCI)   Security systems, policies, and procedures designed to restrict access to information on a need-to-know basis.

Sensor   Device that senses a specific condition, including motion, sound, temperature, or vibration.

Session locks   Prevent unauthorized users from accessing information from "open" computers.

Sexual harassment   Pattern of behavior that involves unwelcome lewd remarks, offensive touching, intimidation, and other conduct or communication of a sexual nature that is offensive to a reasonable person.

Sheriff   Historically, the chief law enforcement officer of a county.

Shire reeve   Individuals who were elected by the hundredmen who supervised the tything systems within shires.

Shoplifting   Misappropriation (theft) of retail merchandise.

Shoplifting methods   Hiding items, defeating sensors, switching price tags, use of a booster box, wearing stolen item, grab and run.

Shoplifting prevention strategy   Deterrence, detection, surveillance, inspections, enforced refund procedures, locks, alarms, observant personnel.

Shrinkage   Reduction in inventories not accounted for through sales or other legitimate activities. It is the difference between the inventory that is on hand for sale and what the retail establishment indicates should be available for sale.

Single-issue groups   Radical groups; right-wing white supremacists, anarchists, antiabortion activists, and animal rights groups whose purpose and goals are directed toward a single issue/idea.

Single-use plan   A plan that is used once and no longer needed when the objectives of the plan are accomplished.

Sir Robert Peel   The British Home Secretary credited with creating the first full-time police department in 1829 in metropolitan London.

Site work elements   Anything beyond 5 feet from the building include landforms (such as hills or depressions) standoff distances, and perimeter barriers such as fences that could assist or impede security efforts.

Situational awareness   Being aware of one's surroundings and having the ability to identify dangerous situations and threats.

Situational Leadership Model   Leadership and managerial model that suggests that supportive (people-centered) and directive (production- and goal-centered) leadership behaviors should be contingent on the readiness level of followers and workers.

Skimming   A form of ATM/debit card fraud where adversaries install a card reader device on the ATM that collects information stored on the magnetic strip of the user's bank card.

Smart card   An access control card that has an embedded circuit that connects to or has RFID capabilities.

Smart containers   Shipping containers that use Global Positioning Systems (GPS) and satellites, RFID and e-seals to track shipping containers from their point of origin to their final destination(s).

Smoldering stage of fire   The last stage of the fire where oxygen levels are not high enough to sustain the fire, even though there is the presence of heat and fire gases.

Snitches   Amateur shoplifters.

Social engineering   Nontechnical and nonphysical means to steal information. Psychologically manipulating people to divulge confidential information.

Social learning theories   Propose that people learn how to be deviant. Because these theories posit that crime can be learned, obviously such actions can be "unlearned."

Social structure theories   Use social and environmental characteristics of the place or location to explain crime.

Specific deterrence   The concept that actual infliction of a punishment on a person caught committing an offense would serve to prevent that person from committing future offenses.

Speculative risk   Potential for benefit or loss, depending on consequences of activity or inactivity.

Spoofing   Trickery to gain access to a computer/information system.

Sprinkler systems Fire suppression systems that use pipes containing suppression fluids that are distributed through sprinkler heads.

Spyware A form of software that collects personal information without the victim's consent. The victim's personal data is secretly obtained using a variety of methods, including logging the victim's keystrokes or Internet browsing history, or by accessing documents on the victim's computer hard drive.

SSP See Sector Specific Plans.

Stages of combustion Are the stages of a fire involving the incipient, free-burning, and smoldering phases.

Standoff zone The distance of the asset from the threat.

State action An intrusion into a person's rights either by a governmental entity or by a private party that can only be enforced by governmental action.

States' rights System of government established by the U.S. Constitution's Tenth Amendment that recognizes the sovereignty of states where powers not delegated to the federal government by the Constitution are reserved to the states or the people.

State, county, and local law enforcement agencies Public police agencies with narrow territorial jurisdiction and broad subject matter jurisdiction (general police powers).

Static risk Constant and unchanging risk, as in the possibility of an earthquake or severe storm.

Statute Written law that is the product of legislative activity.

Statute of Westminster of 1285 Established local responsibility for police and security-related activities in walled cities and towns.

Strain/anomie theories Use the "place" or location to explain crime, proposing that the entire value system and socioeconomic structure of the modern U.S. economy promotes deviance and crime.

Strategic business intelligence Seeks to forecast the long-range implications of business activities.

Strategic plan Long-range plans designed with the entire company in mind, defining the direction and mission of a company, leading it from where it is now to where it would like to be in the future.

Street crime Generally, refers to crimes such as murder, rape, robbery, assault, burglary, larceny (theft), auto theft, and arson.

Strict liability Liability attached even though the person liable was not at fault or did not intend any harm.

Subjective (qualitative) measures Used in risk assessment, planning, and evaluation. Includes expert opinion, forecasting, and the Delphi technique.

Substance abuse Refers to the inappropriate use of controlled substances.

Supervision Directing people in the workplace toward organizational goals.

Supervisory Control and Data Acquisition (SCADA) A category or specific type of application-based software that is used in various control systems to monitor processes and the physical function of equipment.

Support Anti-Terrorism by Fostering Effective Technologies Act (SAFETY Act) of 2002 A subsection (subtitle) of the Homeland Security Act of 2002. It created liability protections for sellers of qualified antiterrorism technologies and others in the supply and distribution chain of those products.

Surreptitious investigative methods Secret (undercover) investigative methods.

Surveillance Covert or overt observation of persons or property.

Surveillance studies The study of surveillance practices in the world, using a variety of scholarly disciplines including economics, psychology, political science, and sociology.

Systems design and engineering Tools used by professionals, such as architects and engineers, to design security features into a facility.

Tactical management Managers responsible for carrying out the specific organizational functions using the best approaches or tactics to meet or achieve the strategic plan created by top management, making sure that the strategic goals are implemented at the operational level.

Tactical plans Short-range plans that are specific and detailed in nature; they are designed to be achieved in a short time frame and meet a specific goal outlined in the strategic plan.

Tangible standards Standards that are quite clear, specific, identifiable, and generally measurable; typically expressed in terms of dollars, numbers, physical properties, and time.

Target hardening Crime prevention strategies that make items more difficult to steal items or reduce victimization.

Task Force Report on Private Security Published by the National Commission on Criminal Justice Standards and Goals in 1976; recommended minimum training and licensing requirements for private security.

Technical controls See logical controls.

Technical security The prevention of adverse technical surveillance through the use of intrusion devices. Term used to describe the development and implementation of countermeasures identified in risk assessments; prevention of adverse technical surveillance caused by the use of intrusion devices.

TEMPEST See Emanations Security.

Terrain Following Sensor Sensor that follows the contours of the terrain, allowing for full coverage of an area with no blind spots.

Terrorism Use of violence or threats to intimidate or coerce.

The Joint Commission Formerly the Joint Commission for Accreditation of Healthcare Organizations (JCAHO). Requires minimum security standards for hospitals and health care facilities.

Theory A thought or an idea that is supported by a hypothesis (a proposed explanation) and supported by scientific evidence.

Theory X Leadership and managerial assumption that employees dislike work and will avoid work if possible.

Theory Y Leadership and managerial assumption that assumes that employees are ready to work for individual and group goals.

Theory of collective security Posits that individuals will engage in self-protection activities when they perceive instability or insecurity with existing forms of protection provided by the government.

Thermal sensor Senses heat in a protected area.

Thief takers Forerunners of modern day detectives that recovered stolen goods for a fee; provided for in British Highwayman Act of 1692.

Threats Where a hazard has materialized into a tangible or definite threat that can cause some type of damage, injury, or loss.

Title VII of the Civil Rights Act of 1964 Prohibits discrimination in employment on the basis of gender, race, religious preference, national origin, and age throughout the employment relationship including hiring, promotions, pay, and retirement.

Top secret Unauthorized disclosure of information that could cause grave danger to the organization.

Tort Private wrong committed against a person or property. It is a civil, rather than criminal, wrong for which the law provides a remedy.

Trademark Protects against unauthorized use of a distinctive mark, name, word, symbol, or device that identifies the goods of a particular commercial enterprise.

Trade secrets Ideas, software code, organizational knowledge that has some type of commercial value.

Traditional budget A budget that includes a simple percentage increase over the previous budget.

Traffic control Use of physical security and facility design to control vehicular and pedestrian traffic patterns.

Traffic treadles Shred and deflate vehicle tires. Rigid barriers withstand large kinetic energy forces and prevent a vehicle from running over or pushing the barrier out of the way.

Training Process by which employees obtain work-related skills through structured or guided ways.

Training needs analysis (TNA) Process of identifying what types of training are needed, based on the skills or knowledge required by workers to effectively complete the task.

Transactional leadership Leadership style where the leader seeks employee compliance through rewards and/or punishment.

Transaction exception reporting systems Used in loss prevention. These systems analyze typical transactions and analyze and identify "out of the ordinary" transaction patterns (sales and returns).

Transaction report Sales records, voided sales receipts, and other activities performed by cash registers each day.

Transborder Crosses borders; generally refers to event in one country that impacts another country.

Transnational organized crimes (TOCs) Criminal acts that are committed in more than one state, where the planning, preparation control and direction takes place in a different country from where the crime is actually being committed.

Transnational private policing Term that describes multinational firms and corporations engaged in security-related activities in more than one nation.

Transcript A written record; typically refers to a written record of a judicial proceeding.

Transformational leadership When one engages another in a way that the leader and nonleader raise one another to higher levels of motivation and morality.

Transportation Security Administration (TSA) Federal agency with primary responsibility for commercial aviation and transportation security.

Trial court Court where a criminal or civil trial takes place.

Trojan horse A computer program that appears to be legitimate and useful, but it is actually malware.

TSA See Transportation Security Administration.

Turnover The voluntary quit of an employee from the organization who moves on to a new position; the rotation of workers out of the organization in a given time period.

Type I attacks Cyberattacks where the computer/computer system is the target.

Type II attacks Where the computer is used as an instrument of the crime.

Tything An early form of policing in pre-modern England where family groups of 10 belonged to a territorial-based tithing unit. These tything (or tithings) units were supervised by a tythingman (a forerunner of the constable) who was responsible for dealing with crime and disorder in the tythings and sometimes beyond.

Ultrasonic motion sensor Transmits extremely high frequency (beyond a human being's audible range) sound energy.

Undercover investigation A surveillance through which the surveillant, using an assumed identity or cover, personally encounters a subject under investigation.

Unethical Lacking moral principles; not willing to follow rules and codes of conduct.

Uniform Crime Report (UCR) Annual report published by the FBI; includes crime statistics reported voluntarily to the FBI by law enforcement agencies throughout the United States. Generates the crime rate.

Unintentional tort Emerges from a situation in which the person(s) liable did not intend harm but the person failed to exercise the care of an ordinary, reasonable, and prudent person.

United Nations Counter Terrorism Implementation Task Force (CTITF) Partnership between the private and public sectors directed against world terrorism.

U.S. court of appeals Intermediate appellate court in the federal court system.

U.S. Department of Homeland Security (DHS) A department of the federal government responsible for protecting the United States from and responding to terrorism, disasters, and other major national incidents.

U.S. district court Trial court in the federal court system.

U.S. Immigration and Customs Enforcement (ICE) Largest investigative arm of the DHS, which is responsible for identifying and confronting vulnerabilities at the nation's border.

U.S. Secret Service Protects the President and other high-level officials and investigates counterfeiting and other financial crimes, including financial institution fraud, identity theft, computer fraud, and computer-based attacks on the nation's financial, banking, and telecommunications infrastructure.

U.S. Supreme Court Court of last resort in the United States. The only court created by the U.S. Constitution.

USA Freedom Act Also titled the Uniting and Strengthening America by Fulfilling Rights and Ensuring Effective Discipline Over Monitoring Act of 2015. This Act restored some of the provisions of the original USA PATRIOT ACT that were to expire, extending these provisions until 2019.

USA PATRIOT Act of 2001 Officially titled the Uniting and Strengthening America by Providing Appropriate Tools Required to Intercept and Obstruct Terrorism, this federal law broadens law enforcement criminal investigative authority.

USA PATRIOT Improvement and Reauthorization Act of 2005 A 2005 legislation that reauthorized expiring provisions of the USA PATRIOT Act of 2001, added dozens of additional safeguards to protect Americans' privacy and civil liberties, and strengthened port security.

Utility security Security practices directed toward the utilities sector that include private and/or public companies (gas, electric, water, and wastewater) that provide services to the public.

Value-added Where the services and benefits of the activity provide results in increased financial savings or profits for the organization.

Value-added contribution (VAC) The nature of extent of value that the security function contributes to the organization.

Values Beliefs of a person, group, organization, and society that are considered worthwhile upon which personal decisions and conduct are based.

Vehicle barrier systems Physical security barriers designed to deter or prevent vehicles from accessing a facility or specific area.

Vicarious liability Liability incurred as a result of situations in which organizations or third parties may be held liable for the intentional or unintentional actions of others with whom they have a relationship.

Victimless crime Participants enter into the activity voluntarily. Examples include illegal gambling and drugs, prostitution, and pornography.

Video analytics The interpretation of events that are recorded or monitored by CCTV cameras.

Violence prevention program Specific security programs designed to mitigate and prevent workplace violence incidents.

Violent Crime Control and Law Enforcement Act of 1994 (HR 3355) provided municipalities funding for improvements in lighting, emergency phones, and other security-related activities and functions; another $10 million in funding was allocated to increasing public transportation security, including the use of private security personnel.

VIPERS See Visible Intermodal Protection Response Teams.

Virginia Tech Virginia Polytechnic Institute and State University; site of deadliest single-perpetrator shooting rampage in U.S. history; where Cho Seung Hui killed 32, wounded 30, and killed himself.

Virtual private networks (VPNs) Computer networks that encrypt information between two points to protect information through untrusted internet connections.

Virtual security organization When the organization does not have a specific security department, the security function is integrated with the entire operation or merged with another department.

Viruses Malicious pieces of code that are secretly installed or implanted into a computer system, "infecting" or contaminating the system and devices that use or are connected to the system.

Vishing Similar to the traditional phishing scam. Instead of being directed by an email to an Internet site, the victim is asked to provide personal information by means of a telephone, using Voice over Internet Protocol (VOIP).

Visible Intermodal Protection Response (VIPR) Teams TSA officers assigned to some commuter railway lines and stations.

Vision statement Future-oriented documents that describe what the organization is committed to and will look like in the future.

***Voir dire* examination** "Speak the truth" examination of a prospective trial juror to determine juror's suitability for jury service. The prospective juror's qualifications may be challenged for cause or a party may exercise a peremptory challenge.

Volumetric sensor Sensor that is designed to fill a certain area, such as a room.

Vulnerability Gaps or weaknesses in the protection of an organization's assets.

Wagner Act See the National Labor Relations Act (NLRA).

Warfare A man-made event that includes civil and insurgency-related events.

Watch Pre-modern/ancient form of policing in England and America where citizens were responsible for security-related activities.

Water security The availability of an acceptable quantity and quality of water for health, livelihoods, ecosystems and production, coupled with an acceptable level of water-related risks to people, environments, and economies.

Weapons of mass destruction (WMD) Chemical, biological, radiological, nuclear, and explosive (CBRNE) agents.

White-collar crime Offense committed by a person or group in the course of an otherwise respected and legitimate occupation or financial activity. Generally, refers to crimes such as corruption, bribery, tax evasion, embezzlement, industrial espionage, and other economic crimes.

Working Group on the use of mercenaries A United Nations Working Group tasked with the creation of new standards and guidelines for the use of private security military companies in order to ensure that human rights are followed.

Workplace aggression Behaviors by a person or persons in or outside of organizations that are intended to psychologically or physically harm workers.

Workplace deviance Voluntary behavior that violates significant organizational norms and, in doing so, threatens the well-being of the organization or its members, or both.

Workplace prevention programs Programs that mitigate and address violent episodes in the workplace.

Workplace violence (WPV) Violent acts including both physical assaults and threats of assaults directed toward workers and those in the workplace.

Workplace violence prevention plan Policies, procedures, training of employees, liaison with community services, security, enforcement of codes of conduct, assistance programs.

Worms Carry viruses and allow Trojans to be replicated in the entire computer system.

Zero-based budget (ZBB) A budget that has no annual base. Under this type of budgeting, managers must prioritize their needs, based on available funding.

Zoological park Permanent cultural institution that owns and maintains wildlife that represents more than a token collection and exhibits the collection to the public. Also include aquariums.

References

12 CFR 208.61—Bank security procedures. Retrieved from https://www.law.cornell.edu/cfr/text/12/208.61

17799. *The Information Management Journal, 39*(4), 60–66.

2015 healthcare outlook. (2015). Retrieved from http://www.cit.com/wcmprod/groups/content/@wcm/@cit/documents/images/2015-healthcare-outlook-report.pdf

9/11 Commission. (2004). *Final report of the National Commission on Terrorist Attacks Upon the United States.* Washington, DC: U.S. Government.

A comparative analysis of complex organizations: on power, involvement, and their correlates. Published by Free Press © 1961.

A Cross Section of the Issues and Research Activities Related to Both Information Security and Cloud Computing. Published by Medknow Publications & Media Pvt. Ltd, © 2011.

Aarons, G. A., Cafri, G., Lugo, L., & Sawitzky, A. (2012). Expanding the domains of attitudes towards evidence-based practice: The evidence based practice attitude scale-50. *Administration and Policy in Mental Health and Mental Health Services Research, 39*(5), 331–340.

Abadinsky, H. (2013). *Organized crime* (10th ed.). Belmont, CA: Cengage.

Abeyratne, R. (2013). Air cargo security: The need for sustainability and innovation. *Air and Space Law, 38*(1), 21–32.

About OSAC. (2015). Retrieved from www.osac.gov

Abrahams, R. (2003). What's in a name? Some thoughts on the vocabulary of vigilantism and related forms of informal criminal justice. In D. Feenan (Ed.), *Informal criminal justice* (pp. 25–40). London: Ashgate.

Abrahamsen, R. (2013). Privatization of force and violence. In D. M. Anderson, N. Cheeseman, & A. Scheibler (Eds.), *Routledge handbook of African politics* (pp. 49–59). New York: Routledge.

Access Control & Security Systems Integration. (1999). *1999 salary survey.* Atlanta, GA: Security Lock Distributors.

Accident identification in nuclear power plants using hidden Markov models. Engineering Applications of Artificial Intelligence by Kee-Choon C Kwon, Jin-Hyung Kim. Published by Elsevier, © 1999.

Acker, J. R., & Brody, D. C. (2004). *Criminal procedure: A contemporary perspective* (2nd ed.). Boston, MA: Jones and Bartlett Publishers.

Ad hoc terms of reference for the Council for Police Matters. (2005, 21–21 April). (PC–PM) relating to the regulation of private security services' CM 924th Meeting of Deputies, Council of Europe, Strasbourg.

Adams, D. (1995). Internal military intervention in the United States. *Journal of Peace Research, 32*(2), 197–211.

Adepoju, A. S., & Alhassan, M. E. (2010). Challenges of automated teller machine (ATM) usage and fraud occurrences in Nigeria—A case study of selected banks in Minna Metropolis. *Journal of Internet Banking and Commerce, 15*(2), 1–10.

Adler, R. B., & Towne, N. (2007). *Looking out/looking in* (12th ed.). Fort Worth, TX: Harcourt College Publishing.

Aerts, J., & Botzen, W. (2014). Adaptation: Cities' response to climate risks. *Nature Climate Change, 4*(9), 759–760.

Agbiboa, D. E. (2014). Terrorism without borders: Somalia's Al-Shabaab and the global jihad network. *Journal of Terrorism Research, 5*(1). doi: http://doi.org/10.15664/jtr.826

Agrawal, R. C., & Naqvi, S. A. A. (2013). Dimensions of theft in museums. In *Museum Security* (pp. 123–127, 84–89). New Delhi: Indira Gandhi National Centre for the Arts.

Ahrens, M. (2008, January). *Lightning fires and lightning strikes.* Quincy, MA: National Fire Protection Association.

Aidis, R., Estrin, S., & Mickiewicz, T. M. (2012). Size matters: Entrepreneurial entry and government. *Small Business Economics, 39*(1), 119–139.

Akbulut, H. (2013). *The G8 Global Partnership: From Kananaskis to Deauville and beyond.* Austrian Institute for International Affairs (ed) Working Paper, 67.

Akcinaroglu, S., & Radziszewski, E. (2013). Private military companies, opportunities, and termination of civil wars in Africa. *Journal of Conflict Resolution, 57*(5), 795–821.

AlBattat, A. R., & Som, A. P. M. (2013, July–September). Emergency preparedness for disasters and crises in the hotel industry. *SAGE Open, 3*(3), 1–10.

Alekseeva, N., Geller, F., Patterson, J., Fitz-Gerald, M., Horton, R., & Minagar, A. (2012). Urgent and emergent psychiatric disorders. *Neurologic Clinics, 30*(1), 321–344.

Alexander, B., & Green, J. (2015, April 2). What's the airline's legal liability for Germanwings crash? CMM. Retrieved from Germanwings Flight 9525 "mental health" civil liability leave. Available from http://www.cnn.com/2015/04/02/opinions/green-alexander-legal-liability-germanwings/

Alexander, D. (2005). Towards the development of a standard in emergency planning. *Disaster Prevention and Management: An International Journal, 14*(2), 158–175.

Alfares, H. K. (2003). Flexible 4-day workweek scheduling with weekend work frequency constraints. *Computers & Industrial Engineering, 44*(3), 325–338.

Alhaqbani, B., & Fidge, C. (2008, January). Access control requirements for processing electronic health records. In *Business process management workshops* (pp. 371–382). Berlin, Heidelberg: Springer.

Almazroui, S., Wang, W., & Zhang, G. (2015). Imaging technologies in aviation security. *Advances in Image and Video Processing, 3*(4), 12–24.

Almirall, J. R., & Furton, K. G. (2004). *Analysis and interpretation of fire scene evidence*. Baca Raton, FL: CRC Press.

Alpert, G. P., & Smith, W. C. (1994). Developing police policy: An evaluation of the control principle. *American Journal of Police, 13*(2), 1–20.

America under attack. (2001, September 11). *Newsweek Extra Edition, 88*(12-A), 1–64.

American Public Transportation Association. (2010). Ornamental fencing systems to control access at transit facilities. Retrieved from http://staging.apta.com/resources/standards/Documents/APTA-SS-SIS-RP-006-10.pdf

American Society for Industrial Security. (1998). *ASIS International presents introduction to security for business students*. Alexandria, VA: American Society for Industrial Security.

American Society for Industrial Security. (2012). Security professionals' salaries up 2 percent in 2012. Retrieved from https://www.asisonline.org/News/Press-Room/Press-Releases/2012/Pages/SecurityProfessionals-SalariesUp.aspx?PF=1

American Society for Industrial Security. (2013). The United States security industry: Size and scope, insights, trends, and data. Retrieved from ASIS.org

American Zoo and Aquarium Society. (2007). *Accreditation\ fact sheet 2007*. (Online). Available from : http://www.aza.org/dept/accred/accredfacts.htm

An education in crime stats. (2000, November 15). *Law Enforcement News, 26*(543), 1, 10.

Anderson, D. R. (2011). Restricting social graces: The implications of social media for restrictive covenants in employment contracts. *Ohio State Law Journal, 72*(4), 881–908.

Anderson, L. (2012, June 16). *Oklahoma tornado response & how to help*. Retrieved from http://www.fema.gov/blog/2013-05-21/oklahoma-tornado-response-how-help

Anderson, T. (2002, December). On the money. *Security Management, 46*(12), 49–50, 68–69.

Andress, J. (2011). The basics of information security: Understanding the fundamentals of INFOSEC in theory and practice (1st ed.). Amsterdam: Elsevier.

Annual report of the Working Group on the use of mercenaries as a means of violating human rights and impeding the exercise of the rights of peoples to self-determination. (2013, July). United Nations Human Rights Council.

Annual report to Congress on foreign economic collection and industrial espionage—2003. (2003, February). Washington, DC: Office of the National Counterintelligence Executive.

Annual Report and Form 20-F, 2010, Copyright © 2010. Published by British Petroleum.

Anti-Pinkerton Act, 5 U.S. Code § 3108.

Arce, I., & Levy, E. (2003). An analysis of the slapper worm. *Security & Privacy, IEEE, 1*(1), 82–87.

Argomaniz, J. (2015). The European Union policies on the protection of infrastructure from terrorist attacks: A critical assessment. *Intelligence and National Security, 30*(2–3), 259–280.

Argueta, O. (2012). Private Security in Guatemala: Pathway to its proliferation. *Bulletin of Latin American Research, 31*(3), 320–335.

Argyris, C. (1964). *Integrating the individual and the organization*. New York: Wiley.

Armour, S. (2003, February 10). Wal-Mart takes hit on worker treatment: Lawsuits, unions slam megaretailer. *USA Today*, p. B01.

Asal, V. H., Ackerman, G. A., & Rethemeyer, R. K. (2012). Connections can be toxic: Terrorist organizational factors and the pursuit of CBRN weapons. *Studies in Conflict & Terrorism, 35*(3), 229–254.

Asia's Energy Energy Supply and Maritime Security, Copyright © 2014. Published by Routledge

ASIS International. (2007). *Code of ethics*. Alexandria, VA: ASIS International.

ASIS International Guidelines Commission. (2007). *General security risk assessment guidelines*. Alexandria, VA: ASIS International.

Aud, M. A. (2004). Dangerous wandering: Elopements of older adults with dementia from long-term care facilities. *American Journal of Alzheimer's Disease and Other Dementias, 19*(6), 361–368.

Auerbach, J. S. (1964). The La Follette Committee and the CIO. *The Wisconsin Magazine of History, 48*(1), 3–20.

Avant, D. (2006). Private military companies and the future of war. Foreign Policy Research Institute.

Aven, T., & Renn, O. (2009). On risk defined as an event where the outcome is uncertain. *Journal of Risk Research, 12*(1), 1–11.

Aviation and Transportation Security Act. (2001). (Public law 107–71).

Ayers, R. S. (2015). Aligning individual and organizational performance goal alignment in federal government agency performance appraisal programs. *Public Personnel Management, 44*(2), 169–191.

Babu, G. R., Kumar, G. A., & Tiwari, V. (2015). Security risks associated with the cloud computing. *International Journal of Research, 2*(6), 101–103.

Bachmann, K., Stewart, R., & Fisher, K. J. (2015). Risks and rewards: Lessons from Central and Eastern Europe's transitional justice experiences. In R. Stewart & K. Fisher (Eds.), *Transitional justice and the Arab spring* (pp. 112–128). New York: Routledge.

Bagott, J. (2003, May). It's all happening at the zoo. *Security Management, 47*(5), 46–50, 52, 54, 56.

Baker, T. E. (2011). *Effective police leadership: Moving beyond management* (3rd ed.). Flushing, NY: Looseleaf Publications, Inc.

Baker, W. H., & Wallace, L. (2007). Is information security under control? Investigating quality in information security management. *Security & Privacy, IEEE, 5*(1), 36–44.

Baldor, L. C. (2010, October 1). *Report: US, EU must join to stop homegrown terror.* Associated Press.

Ballantyne, B. (2006). Medical management of the traumatic consequences of civil unrest incidents. *Toxicological Reviews, 25*(3), 155–197.

Banday, M. T., & Mir, F. A. (2012, December). A study of Indian approach towards cyber security. In *Emerging technology trends in electronics, communication and networking (ET2ECN), 2012 1st International Conference on* (pp. 1–6). IEEE.

Barling, J., Dupré, K. E., & Kelloway, E. K. (2009). Predicting workplace aggression and violence. *Annual Review of Psychology, 60*, 671–692.

Barlow, H. D. (2000). *Criminal justice in America.* Upper Saddle River, NJ: Prentice Hall.

Barnhorn, D., & Pegram, J. E. (2011). Speak the truth and tell no lies: An update for the Employee Polygraph Protection Act. *Hofstra Labor & Employment Law Journal, 29*(1), 141–189.

Barry, B.W. (1998, April). A beginner's guide to strategic planning. *The Futurist, 32*(3), 33–36.

Bart, C. K. (1996). High tech firms: Does mission matter? *Journal of High Technology Management Research, 7*(2), 209–225.

Barton-Bellessa, S. M., Johnson, B. R., Shon, P. C., & Austin, C. W. (2014). Exploratory study of school crime and rural teacher and staff victimization: A research note. *JIJIS, 14*, 9.

Based on "Preventing Violence at Work, by Bonnie S. Michelman, 2011. https://sm.asisonline.org/Pages/Preventing-Violence-at-Work.aspx.

Bass, B. M. (1981). *Stogdill's handbook of leadership: A survey of theory and research.* New York: The Free Press.

Bass, B. M. (1985). *Leadership and performance beyond expectations.* New York: The Free Press.

Bass, B. M. (1990). *Handbook of leadership.* New York: The Free Press.

Bassett, J. (2006, September). When your CEO says "show me the money." *Security Technology & Design, 16*(9), 84–86.

Bauer, A. (2011, January). War on terror or policing terrorism? Radicalization and expansion of the threats. *The Police Chief*, pp. 46–52.

Bauer, S., Bernroider, E. W., & Chudzikowski, K. (2013, December). End user information security awareness programs for improving information security in banking organizations: Preliminary results from an exploratory study. In *Proceedings of the eighth pre-ICIS workshop on information security and privacy* (Vol. 1).

Bazan, E. B. (2004, December). *Intelligence Reform and Terrorism Prevention Act of 2004:" Lone Wolf" Amendment to the Foreign Intelligence Surveillance Act.* Library of Congress. Washington, DC: Congressional Research Service.

Bea, K. (2006). *Federal emergency management policy changes after Hurricane Katrina: A summary of statutory provisions.* Washington, DC: Congressional Research Service.

Beck, A. (2011). Self-scan checkouts and retail loss: Understanding the risk and minimising the threat. *Security Journal, 24*(3), 199–215.

Becken, S. (2012). *Future tourism: Political, social and economic challenges.* New York: Routledge.

Becker, T. M. (1974). The place of private police in society: An area of research for the social sciences. *Social Problems, 21*(3), 438–453.

Becker, W. S. (2011). Are you leading a socially responsible and sustainable human resource function? *People & Strategy, 34*(1), 18–24.

Beecher, J. A., & Kalmbach, J. A. (2013). Structure, regulation, and pricing of water in the United States: A study of the Great Lakes region. *Utilities Policy, 24*, 32–47.

Bell, M. P., Quick, J. C., & Cycyota, C. S. (2002). Assessment and prevention of sexual harassment of employees: An applied guide to creating healthy organizations. *International Journal of Selection and Assessment, 10*, 160–167.

Bennis, W. (2009). *On becoming a leader.* Basic Books.

Bennis, W. G. (1984, September). The four competencies of leadership. *Training and Development Journal, 38*(9), 14–19.

Bennis, W. G. (1993). *An invented life: Reflections on leadership and change.* Reading, MA: Addison-Wesley.

Bennis, W. G., & Nanus, B. (1985). *Leaders: The strategy for taking charge.* New York: Harper & Row.

Benny, D. J. (2014). *Industrial espionage: Developing a counterespionage program.* Boca Raton, FL: CRC Press.

Bensassi, S., & Martínez-Zarzoso, I. (2012). How costly is modern maritime piracy to the international community? *Review of International Economics, 20*(5), 869–883.

Bento, A., & Bento, R. (2004). Empirical test of a hacking model: An exploratory study. *Communications of the Association for Information Systems, 14*(1), 678–691.

Berg, J. (2014, February 3). *Target as target.* Retrieved from http://www.riskandinsurance.com/target-as-target/

Berg, J., & Nouveau, J. P. (2014). Towards a third phase of regulation: Re-imagining private security in South Africa. *South African Crime Quarterly, 38,* 23–32.

Bernaerts' Guide To The 1982 United Nations Convention On The Law Of The Sea Copyright © 1988. Published by Fairplay Publications Ltd.

Bernard, T. J., Snipes, J. B., & Gerould, A. L. (2010). *Vold's theoretical criminology* (6th ed.). New York: Oxford University Press.

Berzofsky, M., Langton, L., Moore, A., and Walters, J. H. (2013, June 20). Financial loss due to household burglary increased from 1994 to 2011. Washington, DC: Bureau of Justice Statistics. NCJ 241754.

Bessho, M., & Shimizu, K. (2012). Latest trends in LED lighting. *Electronics and Communications in Japan, 95*(1), 1–7.

Bhandari, A., Sangal, A. L., & Kumar, K. (2015). Destination address entropy based detection and traceback approach against Distributed Denial of Service attacks. *International Journal of Computer Network and Information Security (IJCNIS), 7*(8), 9–20.

Bhattacharya, S., & Guriev, S. (2006). Patents vs. trade secrets: Knowledge licensing and spillover. *Journal of the European Economic Association, 4*(6), 1112–1147.

Bidwell, M., & Keller, J. R. (2014). Within or without? How firms combine internal and external labor markets to fill jobs. *Academy of Management Journal, 57*(4), 1035–1055.

Bielous, G. (1993, April). How to discipline effectively. *Super-Vision, 54*(4), 17–19.

Biskup, J., & Lochner, J. H. (2007). Enforcing confidentiality in relational databases by reducing inference control to access control. In *Information security* (pp. 407–422). Berlin, Heidelberg: Springer.

Bix, B. H. (2012). *Contract law: Rules, theory, and context.* New York: Cambridge University Press.

Black, H. C. (1990). *Black's Law Dictionary.* St. Paul, MN: West Publishing.

Blake, R. R., & Mouton, J. S. (1985). *The managerial grid.* Houston, TX: Gulf.

Blanchard, K., & Johnson, S. (1992). *The one minute manager.* New York: Morrow.

Bland, T. S. (2000, January). Get a handle on harassment. *Security Management, 44*(1), 62, 64–67.

Bland, T. S., & Stalcup, S. S. (1999, June). Accurate applications. *Security Management, 43*(6), 38–39.

BMP4. (2011, August). The maritime security centre—Horn of Africa (MSCHOA). Retrieved from http://www.imo.org/en/MediaCentre/HotTopics/piracy/Documents/1339.pdf

Bobbio, N. (1993). *Thomas Hobbes and the natural law tradition.* University of Chicago Press.

Boersma, K., Comfort, L., Groenendaal, J., & Wolbers, J. (2014). Editorial: Incident command systems: A dynamic tension among goals, rules and practice. *Journal of Contingencies and Crisis Management, 22*(1), 1–4.

Bonneau, J., Preibusch, S., & Anderson, R. (2012). A birthday present every eleven wallets? The security of customer-chosen banking PINs. In *Financial Cryptography and Data Security* (pp. 25–40). Berlin, Heidelberg: Springer.

Born, H., Caparini, M., & Cole, E. (2007). *Regulating private security in Europe: Status and prospects.* Geneva Centre for the Democratic Control of Armed Forces.

Bose, I., & Leung, A. C. M. (2014). Do phishing alerts impact global corporations? A firm value analysis. *Decision Support Systems, 64,* 67–78.

Botha, R. A., & Eloff, J. H. (2001). A framework for access control in workflow systems. *Information Management & Computer Security, 9*(3), 126–133.

Botten, L. H., & Riggs, D. A. (1998, July). 2.1.2 Contingency and disaster recovery engineering: A discipline within a discipline. In *INCOSE International Symposium, 8*(1), 75–81.

Bottom, N. R. (1983). An informational theory of security. *Computers & Security, 2*(3), 275–280.

Bouncing back from the one-two punch. (2005, Fall). Shell Oil Corporation. Retrieved from http://www.torma.com/pdf/Shell-EPW.pdf

Bowers, D. M. (2013). *Access control and personal identification systems.* Boston, MA: Butterworth-Heinemann.

Boyce, J. G., & Jennings, D. W. (2002). *Information assurance: Managing organizational IT security risks.* Boston, MA: Butterworth-Heinemann.

Boykoff, J., & Fussey, P. (2014). London's shadow legacies: Security and activism at the 2012 Olympics. *Contemporary Social Science, 9*(2), 253–270.

Bragdon, B. (2006, July). What security's worth. *CSO, 5*(7), 10.

Bramel, D., & Friend, R. (1981). Hawthorne, the myth of the docile worker, and class bias in psychology. *American Psychologist, 36*(8), 867–878.

Brandman, B. (2007, January–February). Cargo theft: A costly epidemic. *Loss Prevention, 6*(1), 46–50, 52.

Branović, ž. (2011). *The privatisation of security in failing states: A quantitative assessment.* Geneva Centre for Democratic Control of Armed Forces (DCAF).

Bratton, W. J. (2011, February). Reducing crime through prevention not incarceration. *Criminology & Public Policy, 10*(1), 63–68.

Brenner, B. (2010, October). Sea change. *CSO, 10,* 26.

Briggs, R. (2001). *The kidnapping business.* London: Foreign Policy Centre.

Brisman, A. (2011). Vandalizing meaning, stealing memory: Artistic, cultural, and theoretical implications of crime in galleries and museums. *Critical Criminology, 19*(1), 15–28.

Broadhurst, R. G. (Ed.). (2003). *Bridging the GAP—A Global Alliance Perspective on Transnational Organised Crime.* Proceedings, March 21–24, 2002, Hong Kong Police Force: Hong Kong Government Printer (pp 299, xxix: foreword, HK Chief Justice Andrew K. N. Li).

Broder, J. F. (2000). *Risk analysis and the security survey* (2nd ed.). Boston: Butterworth-Heinemann.

Brody, D. C., Acker, J. R., & Logan, W. A. (2010). *Criminal law* (2nd ed.). Gaithersburg, MD: Jones and Bartlett Publishing.

Bromet, E. J., Havenaar, J. M., & Guey, L. T. (2011). A 25 year retrospective review of the psychological consequences of the Chernobyl accident. *Clinical Oncology, 23*(4), 297–305.

Brooks, R. A. (2011). Muslim "homegrown" terrorism in the United States: How serious is the threat? *International Security, 36*(2), 7–47.

Brooks, S. G. (2005). *Producing security.* Princeton, NJ: Princeton University Press.

Brooks, S. M. (2014). Insecure democracy: Risk and political participation in Brazil. *The Journal of Politics, 76*(04), 972–985.

Brown, J. (2012). *Pirates and privateers: Managing the Indian Ocean's private security boom.* Sydney: Lowy Institute for International Policy.

Brown, L. R. (2012). *Outgrowing the Earth: The food security challenge in an age of falling water tables and rising temperatures.* Taylor & Francis.

Brown, M. E., Treviño, L. K., & Harrison, D. A. (2005). Ethical leadership: A social learning perspective for construct development and testing. *Organizational Behavior and Human Decision Processes, 97,* 117–134.

Brown, S. (1985). Central Belfast's security segment: An urban phenomenon. *Area, 17*(1), 1–9.

Bruce, K. (2006). Henry S. Dennison, Elton Mayo, and human relations historiography. *Management & Organizational History, 1*(2), 177–199.

Bukowski, R. W., Peacock, R. D., Averill, J. D., Cleary, T. G., Bryner, N. P., Walton, W. D., ... Kuligowski, E. D. (2007). *Performance of home smoke alarms: Analysis of the response of several available technologies in residential fire settings.* National Institute of Standards and Technology. Fire Research Division. Building and Fire Research Laboratory.

Bunning, R. L. (1979). The Delphi technique: A projection tool for serious inquiry. In *The 1979 annual handbook for group facilitators* (pp. 174–181). San Diego, CA: University Associates.

Bureau of Labor Statistics. (2015a). Occupational employment and wages, May 2014. Retrieved from http://www.bls.gov/oes/current/oes339021.htm

Bureau of Labor Statistics. (2015b, January 23). *Union Members Summary.* Retrieved from http://www.bls.gov/news.release/union2.nr0.htm

Burkhead, J. (1996). *Government budgeting.* John Willey and Sons.

Burnett, L. A. (2006). Security in administrative hearings. *Journal of the National Association of Administrative Law Judiciary, 26*(2), 361–385.

Burns, J. M. (1978). *Leadership.* New York: Harper & Row.

Burns, L. R., & Becker, S. W. (1988). Leadership and decision making. In S. M. Shortell & A. D. Kaluzny (Eds.), *Health care management: A text in organization theory and behavior* (2nd ed.) (pp. 142–186). New York: Wiley.

Burrough, B. (2009). *Public enemies: America's greatest crime wave and the birth of the FBI, 1933–34.* Penguin.

Burstein, H. (1996). *Security: A management perspective.* Englewood Cliffs, NJ: Prentice Hall.

Business Resumption Planning: A Progressive Approach, Copyright © 2002. Published by SANS Institute

Butler, M. C., & Ehrlich, S. B. (1991). Positional influences on job satisfaction and job performance: A multivariate, predictive approach. *Psychological Reports, 69*(3), 855–865.

Byers, B. (2000, September/October). Ethics and criminal justice: Some observations on police misconduct. *ACJS (Academy of Criminal Justice Sciences) Today, 21*(3), 1, 4–7.

Byrnbauer, H., & Tyson, L. A. (1984, September). Flexing the muscles of technical leadership. *Training and Development Journal, 38*(9), 48–52.

Cabera, C. (2014, January 26). Actress' murder spotlights dangers in South American nations. *The Tampa Tribune.* Retrieved from tbo.com

Cade Jr, W. A. (1989). Security challenge: Order in the court. *Security Management, 33*(6), 38–42.

Calder, A., & Bland, S. (2015). Chemical, biological, radiological and nuclear considerations in a major incident. *Surgery (Oxford), 33*(9), 442–448.

Calder, J. D. (2010). Law, politics, and occupational consciousness: Industrial guard unions in the United States, 1933–1945. *Journal of Applied Security Research, 5,* 64–106.

Cameron, L. (2006). Private military companies: Their status under international humanitarian law and its impact on their regulation. *International Review of the Red Cross, 88*(863), 573–598.

Campbell, G. K. (2006, August). How to use metrics. *CSO, 5*(8), 40–44.

Cane, A. B. (2015). Finding external review of the merits of suitability determinations for national security employees after Kaplan v. Conyers. *Federal Circuit Bar Journal, 24,* 625–699.

Cannons, A., Amuso, P., & Anderson, B. (2006). Biotechnology and the public health response to bioterrorism. In *Microorganisms and bioterrorism* (pp. 1–13). Springer US.

Canton, L. G. (2003). *Guard force management* (updated edition). Boston, MA: Butterworth-Heinemann.

Capezuti, E., Brush, B. L., Lane, S., Rabinowitz, H. U., & Secic, M. (2009). Bed-exit alarm effectiveness. *Archives of Gerontology and Geriatrics, 49*(1), 27–31.

Cardone, C., & Hayes, R. (2012). Shoplifter perceptions of store environments: An analysis of how physical cues in the retail interior shape shoplifter behavior. *Journal of Applied Security Research, 7*(1), 22–58.

Carlson, T. (2001). Information security management: Understanding ISO 17799. *Lucent Technologies Worldwide Services.*

Carmel-Gilfilen, C. (2011). Advancing retail security design: Uncovering shoplifter perceptions of the physical environment. *Journal of Interior Design, 36*(2), 21–38.

Carr, C., Morton, J., & Furniss, J. (Winter, 2000). The Economic Espionage Act: Bear trap or mousetrap? *Texas Intellectual Property Law Journal, 8*(2), 159–209.

Carroll, D. M., Nguyen, C., Everett, H. R., & Frederick, B. (2005, May). Development and testing for physical security robots. In *Defense and security* (pp. 550–559). International Society for Optics and Photonics.

Carroll, J. M. (2014). *Computer security.* Boston: Butterworth-Heinemann.

Çelik, S. S. (2015). Lost treasures: Locks. *International Journal of Science Culture and Sport, 3*(1), 96–112.

Center for Strategic & International Studies (CSIS). (2013). *A human capital crisis in cybersecurity: Technical proficiency matters.* Washington, DC: Center for Strategic and International Studies.

Centers for Disease Control and Prevention. (2002). Violence: Occupational hazards in hospitals. National Institute for Occupational Safety and Health. Available at http://www.cdc.gov/niosh/injury/traumaviolence.html (Accessed 27 August 2005)

Centers for Disease Control and Prevention. (2006, June 9). *Morbidity and Mortality Weekly Report.* Atlanta, GA: U.S. Department of Health and Human Services.

Centers for Disease Control and Prevention. (2008). School-associated student homicides—United States, 1992–2006. *MMWR* 2008, *57*(02), 33–36.

Centers for Disease Control and Prevention. (2015a). *CDC Health Information for International Travel 2016.* Oxford University Press.

Centers for Disease Control and Prevention. (2015c). Youth violence: Using environmental design to prevent school violence. Retrieved from http://www.cdc.gov/violenceprevention/youthviolence/cpted.html

Certo, C. C., & Certo, T. (2012). *Modern management* (12th ed.). Upper Saddle River, NJ: Pearson Prentice Hall.

12 CFR 208.61—Bank security procedures. Published by United States Government Publishing Office.

Champion, D. J., Hartley, R. D., & Rabe, G. A. (2008). *Criminal courts: Structure, process, and issues* (2nd ed.). Upper Saddle River, NJ: Pearson Prentice Hall.

Chan, A. (2003, January). Web-based loss prevention: The fast track to controlling shrink. *Loss Prevention & Security Journal, 3*(1), 12–14.

Cheeseman, H. R. (2010). *Business law* (7th ed.). Upper Saddle River, NJ: Pearson Prentice Hall.

Chen, Y. Y., Jan, J. K., Tsai, M. L., Ku, C. C., & Huang, D. C. (2012). On the security of RFID-based monitoring mechanism for retail inventory management. *KSII Transactions on Internet and Information Systems (TIIS), 6*(2), 515–528.

Cheung, S. N. S. (1982, January). Property rights in trade secrets. *Economic Inquiry, 20,* 40–53. doi:10.1111/j.1465-7295.1982.tb01141.x

Chin, C. O., Gu, J., & Tubbs, S. L. (2001). Developing global leadership competencies. *Journal of Leadership & Organizational Studies, 7*(4), 20–31.

Choi, M., & Lee, C. (2015). Information security management as a bridge in cloud systems from private to public organizations. *Sustainability, 7*(9), 12032–12051.

Chu, L., Hung, F. Y., & Lu, Y. C. (2014, August). Analysis and simulation of theme park queuing system. In *Intelligent information hiding and multimedia signal processing (IIH-MSP), 2014 Tenth International Conference on* (pp. 9–12). IEEE.

CISCO 2014 Annual security report. (2014). San Jose, CA.

Clark, H. L., & Jayaram, S. (2005). Intensified international trade and security policies can present challenges for corporate transactions. *Cornell International Law Journal, 38,* 391.

Clarke, R. V. (1999). "Hot products: Understanding, anticipating and reducing demand for stolen goods." *Police Research Series,* Paper 112, Policing and Reducing

Crime Unit, Research Development and Statistics Directorate, Home Office, London, UK.

Clarke, R. V., & Petrossian, G. (2012). The problem of shoplifting. Retrieved from http://www.popcenter.org/problems/shoplifting/print/

Clarno, A. (2014). Beyond the state: Policing precariousness in South Africa and Palestine/Israel. *Ethnic and Racial Studies, 37*(10), 1725–1731.

Clayton, M. (2010). Stuxnet malware is "weapon" out to destroy... Iran's Bushehr nuclear power plant. *Christian Science Monitor,* p. 21.

Clemmer, J. (1992, April). 5 common errors companies make starting quality initiatives. *Total Quality, 3,* 7.

Coaffee, J. (2004). Rings of steel, rings of concrete and rings of confidence: Designing out terrorism in Central London pre and post September 11th. *International Journal of Urban and Regional Research, 28*(1), 201–211.

Coaffee, J., Moore, C., Fletcher, D., & Bosher, L. S. (2008). Resilient design for community safety and terror-resistant cities. *Proceedings of the ICE: Municipal Engineer, 161* (2), 103–110.

Codebook: Inclusion Criteria and Variables. Published Study of Terrorism and Responses To Terrorism, © 2015.

Code of Ethics Copyright © 2016. Used by permission of American Society for Industrial Security International (ASIS).

CoESS. (2013, November). CoESS contribution to the Advisory Group on land transport security (LANDSEC 3). Retrieved from http://www.coess.eu/_Uploads/dbsAttachedFiles/141114_CoESS_Contribution_to_LANDSEC_Best_Practices_Rail_Security.pdf

Cohen, B. J. (2011). Design-based practice: A new perspective for social work. *Social Work, 56*(4), 337–346.

Cohen, C. F., & Cohen, M. E. (2007, December). On-duty and off-duty: Employee right to privacy and employer's right to control in the private sector. *Employee Responsibility Rights Journal, 19*(4), 235–246.

Cohen, L. E., & Felson, M. (1979). Social change and crime rate trends: A routine activity approach. *American Sociological Review, 44*(4), 588–608.

Cohen, M. (2004, July). Elements of an effective workplace violence program. *The Colorado Lawyer, 33*(7), 57–62.

Cole, G. F., & Smith, C. E. (2011). *The American system of criminal justice* (12th ed.). Belmont, CA: Wadsworth/Thomson Learning.

Coleman, J. (2000, August). Trends in security systems integration. *Security Technology & Design, 10*(8), 38–40, 42–44.

Coleman, J. W. (1994). *The criminal elite: The sociology of white-collar crime.* New York: St. Martin's Press.

Coleman, L. (2006). Frequency of man-made disasters in the 20th century. *Journal of Contingencies and Crisis Management, 14*(1), 3–11.

Colling, R. L. (2001). *Hospital and healthcare security* (5th ed.). Burlington, MA: Elsevier.

Collins, K. (2008). *Exploring business.* Upper Saddle River, NJ: Pearson Prentice Hall.

Collins, L. R. (2000). *Disaster management and preparedness.* CRC Press.

Combating piracy and armed robbery in Asia: The ReCAAP InformationSharing Centre (ISC). Copyright © 2009. Published by Elsevier Ltd.

Comparisons of variables between fatal and nonfatal accidents in manufacturing industry, International Journal of Industrial Ergonomics by Yong Jeong. Published by Elsevier, © 1999.

Conference of State Court Administrators. (2012). CCJ/COSCA *Court security handbook.*

Connell, J., Fan, Q., Gabbur, P., Haas, N., Pankanti, S., & Trinh, H. (2013, March). Retail video analytics: An overview and survey. In *IS&T/SPIE electronic imaging* (pp. 86630X–86630X-6). International Society for Optics and Photonics.

Connors, E. F., Cunningham, W. C., & Ohlhausen, P. E. (1999). *Operation Cooperation: A literature review of cooperation and partnerships between law enforcement and private security organizations.* Washington DC: US Department of Justice.

Conti, R. (2014). Do non-competition agreements lead firms to pursue risky R&D projects? *Strategic Management Journal, 35*(8), 1230–1248.

Coon, D., & Mitterer, J. O. (2012). *Introduction to psychology: Gateways to mind and behavior* (13th ed.). Belmont, CA: Wadsworth.

Cooter, M. (n.d.). Don't be in denial about DDos attacks. Retrieved from http://www.contextpr.co.uk/technology-insights/dont-denial-ddos-attacks/

Cordin, E., Rowan, L., Odgers, P., Barnes, A., & Redgate, R. (2008). $37 billion: Counting the cost of employee misunderstanding. *A White Paper commissioned by Cognisco.*

Cordner, G. W., & Scarborough, K. E. (2010). *Police administration* (7th ed.). Newark, NJ: Matthew Bender & Company.

Corporate codes of conduct: A collective conscience and continuum, Copyright © 1990. Published by Springer International Publishing.

Corritore, C. L., Kracher, B., & Wiedenbeck, S. (2003). On-line trust: concepts, evolving themes, a model. *International Journal of Human-Computer Studies, 58*(6), 737–758.

Cote, A. E., Grant, C. C., Hall, J. R., Powell, P. A., & Solomon, R. E. (2008). *Fire protection handbook* (Vol. 2). National Fire Protection Association.

Council of Europe, Committee of Ministers. (1987). *Recommendation No. R (87) 19 of the Committee of Ministers to Member States on the Organization of Crime Prevention*. Retrieved from http://www.coe.int/t/dg1/legalcooperation/economiccrime/organisedcrime/Rec_1987_19.pdf

Covey, S. R. (1998). *The seven habits of highly effective people*. New York: Simon & Schuster.

Cozens, P., & Davies, T. (2013). Crime and residential security shutters in an Australian suburb: Exploring perceptions of 'Eyes on the Street', social interaction and personal safety. *Crime Prevention & Community Safety, 15*(3), 175–191.

Craighead, G. (2009). *High-rise security and fire life safety* (3rd ed.). Boston, MA: Butterworth-Heinemann.

Crank, J., & Crank, J. P. (2014). *Understanding police culture*. New York: Routledge.

Cremers, T. (2015). Rogues gallery: An investigation into art theft … and the curator did it. Retrieved from www.museum-security.org/insider-theft.pdf

Criminal Resource Manual, U.S. Department of Justice. (2015). Sections 1124–1128. Retrieved from http://www.justice.gov/usam/criminal-resource-manual

Critical Foundations. Published by The White House.

Cronin, A. K. (2015, March/April). ISIS is not a terrorist group. Why counterterrorism won't stop the latest Jihadist threat. *Foreign Affairs, 94*(2), 87–98.

Crowe, T. D. (2000). *Crime prevention through environmental design: Applications of architectural design and space management concepts* (2nd ed.). Oxford: Butterworth-Heinemann.

CryWolf. (2015). Retrieved from https://falsealarm.louisvilleky.gov/

Cunningham, W. C., & Taylor, T. H. (1985). *The Hallcrest report: Private security and police in America*. Portland, OR: Chancellor Press.

Cunningham, W. C., Strauchs, J. J., & Van Meter, C. W. (1990). *The Hallcrest report II: Private security trends 1970–2000*. Boston, MA: Butterworth-Heinemann.

Dabling, J. G., McLaughlin, J. O., & Andersen, J. J. (2012, October). Design and performance testing of an integrated detection and assessment perimeter system. In *Security Technology (ICCST), 2012 IEEE International Carnahan Conference on* (pp. 34–42). IEEE.

Dalton, D. R. (1995). *Security management: Business strategies for success*. Boston, MA: Butterworth-Heinemann.

Dalton, D. R. (2003). *Rethinking corporate security in the post-9/11 era: Issues and strategies for today's global business community*. Boston, MA: Butterworth-Heinemann.

Daniel, T. (1992, March). Identifying critical leadership competencies of manufacturing supervisors in a major electronics corporation. *Group and Organizational Management: An International Journal, 17*(1), 57–71.

Darbra, R. M., Palacios, A., & Casal, J. (2010). Domino effect in chemical accidents: Main features and accident sequences. *Journal of Hazardous Materials, 183*(1), 565–573.

Davids, M. (1995, January/February). Where style meets substance. *Journal of Business Strategy, 16*(1), 48–55, 57–60.

Davies, J. (2007, June 13). Smoking out shoplifters. *San Diego Union Tribune*, pp. C1, C4.

Davies, S. J., & Hertig, C. A. (2007). *Security supervision and management: The theory and practice of asset protection*. Boston: Butterworth-Heinemann.

Davis, L. A. (2013). Who's the boss—A distinction without a difference. *Barry Law Review, 19*(1), 155–173.

de Frahan. (2015). What does "Legal Risk" mean? Retrieved from http://www.frahanblonde.com/sites/default/files/articles/1503_What%20does%20legal%20risk%20mean.pdf

De Maeyer, D. (2007). Setting up an effective information security awareness programme. In *ISSE/SECURE 2007 Securing electronic business processes* (pp. 49–58). Vieweg.

De Silva, L. C., Morikawa, C., & Petra, I. M. (2012). State of the art of smart homes. *Engineering Applications of Artificial Intelligence, 25*(7), 1313–1321.

Dean, P. J. (1994). Some basics about ethics. *Performance + Instruction, 33*(10), 42–45.

Deardorff, D. K. (2015). How to assess intercultural competence. In Z. Hua (Series Ed.), *Research Methods in Intercultural Communications Series. Research methods in intercultural communication: A practical guide* (pp. 120–134). West Sussex, UK: Wiley-Blackwell.

Dębowska-Ludwin, J. (2011). Early Egyptian tomb security—middle class burials from Tell el-Farkha. *Studies in Ancient Art and Civilization*, (15), 31–36.

Decenzo, D. A., & Robbins, S. P. (2015). *Fundamentals of human resource management*. John Wiley & Sons.

Defend Trade Secrets Act of 2016, S.1890, 114th Cong. (2015–2016).

Defining Homeland Security: Analysis and Congressional Considerations. Published by Congressional Research Service, © 2012.

Defense Security Services. (2015). About us. Retrieved from http://www.dss.mil/

Definitions of "Inherently Governmental Function" in Federal Procurement Law and Guidance. Copyright © 2014. Published by Congressional Research Service.

DeLeire, T. (2000). The wage and employment effects of the Americans with Disabilities Act. *Journal of Human Resources, 35*(4), 693–715.

Dempsey, J. S. (2010). *Introduction to private security* (2nd ed.). Belmont, CA: Wadsworth.

Department of the Army. (1966). AR 580-20 National Security Armed Forces Industrial Defense Program. Washington, DC: Department of the Army.

Derudder, B., Faulconbridge, J. R., Witlox, F., & Beaverstock, J. V. (Eds.). (2012). International business travel in the global economy. UK: Ashgate Publishing Ltd.

Deutch, J. (1997, September 22). Terrorism. Foreign Policy, p. 10.

DHS announces security standards for freight and passenger rail systems. (2008, November 13). Retrieved from https://www.tsa.gov/news/releases/2008/11/13/dhs-announces-security-standards-freight-and-passenger-rail-systems

DHS Launches the C³ Voluntary Program, A Public-Private Partnership to Strengthen Critical Infrastructure Cybersecurity. Copyright © 2013. Published by The Department of Homeland Security.

Dickens, R. L. (2007). Finding common ground in the world of electronic contracts: The consistency of legal reasoning in clickwrap cases. Marquette Intellectual Property Law Review, 11(2), 379–412.

Dilanian, K. (2010, November 15). "Fusion centers" gather terrorism intelligence—and much more. Los Angeles Times.

DiLonardo, R. L., & Clarke, R. V. (1996). Reducing the rewards of shoplifting: An evaluation of ink tags. Security Journal, 1(7), 11–14.

Dinc, M. S., & Aydemir, M. (2014). Ethical leadership and employee behaviours: an empirical study of mediating factors. International Journal of Business Governance and Ethics, 9(3), 293–312.

Dinev, T. (2006). Why spoofing is serious internet fraud. Communications of the ACM, 49(10), 76–82.

Diphoorn, T. G. (2015). Twilight policing: Private security and violence in urban South Africa. University of California Press.

Djibouti Code of Conduct. (2015). Retrieved from http://www.imo.org/en/OurWork/Security/PIU/Pages/DCoC.aspx

Doboli, A., Curiac, D., Pescaru, D., Doboli, S., Tang, W., Volosencu, C., ... Istin, C. (2008). Cities of the future: Employing wireless sensor networks for efficient decision making in complex environments. State University of New York, Tech. Rep.

Dodd, V. (2011). Cost of English riots much higher than first thought, Met police report suggests. The Guardian. Retrieved from http://www.theguardian.com/uk/2011/oct/24/england-riots-cost-police-report

Dolan, M. (2004). Psychopathic personality in young people. Advances in Psychiatric Treatment, 10(6), 466–473.

Dolan, T. G. (1999, August). Healthcare security: A very insecure profession. Security Technology & Design, 9(8), 10–12, 14.

Donohue, W. A., Pugh, F., & Sabrie, S. (2014). Somali piracy negotiations: Resolving the paradoxes of extortionate transactions. Negotiation and Conflict Management Research, 7(3), 173–187.

Dowart, J. M. (1979). ONI: The Office of Naval Intelligence. Annapolis, MD: Naval Institute Press.

Downs, A. (1967). Inside bureaucracy. Boston: Little, Brown.

Doyle, C. (2006, March). Administrative subpoenas in criminal investigations. A brief legal analysis. Washington, DC: Congressional Research Service.

Doyon-Martin, J. (2015). "Cybercrime in West Africa as a result of transboundary e-waste." Journal of Applied Security Research, 10(2), 207–220.

Drath, W. H., & Palus, C. J. (1994). Making common sense: Leadership as meaning-making in a community of practice. Greensboro, NC: Center for Creative Leadership.

Drath, W. H., McCauley, C. D., Palus, C. J., van Velsor, E., O'Connor, P. M. G., & McGuire, J. B. (2008). Direction, alignment, commitment: Towards a more integrative ontology of leadership. Leadership Quarterly, 19, 635–653.

Drucker, P. F. (1994, November). The age of social transformation. The Atlantic Monthly, pp. 53–80.

Drysdale, D. (2011). An introduction to fire dynamics. West Sussex, United Kingdom: John Wiley & Sons.

Dubber, M. D. (2015). An introduction to the Model Penal Code. New York: Oxford University Press.

Duhart, D.T. (2001, December). Violence in the workplace, 1993-99. Washington, DC: Bureau of Justice Statistics.

Dulyakorn, N., Pavaganun, C., Mangalabruks, B., Fujii, Y., & Yupapin, P. (2011). BOB loss-preventing for modern trade retail product safety. Procedia Engineering, 8, 353–359.

Duncan Hunter National Defense Authorization Act for Fiscal Year 2009, Public Law 122 Stat. 4356. (2008, October 14).

Dunn, M. (1999). Critical elements in school security. In J. Agron & L. Anderson (Eds.), Under siege: Schools as the new battleground (pp. 13–14, 16). Atlanta, GA: Access Control & Security Systems Integration.

Dunning, E., Murphy, P. J., & Williams, J. (2014). The roots of football hooliganism (RLE sports studies): An historical and sociological study (Vol. 2). Routledge.

Durston, G. J. (2012). Whores and highwaymen: Crime and justice in the Eighteenth-Century Metropolis. Waterside Press.

Dvorak, P. (2015, October 1). Cyber security and wind-farm penetrations. Retrieved from http://www.windpowerengineering.com/uncategorized/cyber-security-and-wind-farm-penetrations/

Ekwall, D., & Lantz, B. (2015). Cargo theft at non-secure parking locations. *International Journal of Retail & Distribution Management, 43*(3), 204–220.

Elias, B. (2007, July). *Air cargo security*. Washington, DC: Library of Congress, Congressional Research Service.

Elliott, D., Swartz, E., & Herbane, B. (2010). *Business continuity management: A crisis management approach* (2nd ed.). New York: Routledge.

Ellison, C. C., & Brokaw, J. T. (2014, April). What are your real barrier requirements? In *Structures Congress 2014* (pp. 611–622). American Society of Civil Engineers.

Erera, A. L., Kwek, K. H., Goswami, N., White, C. C, & Zhang, H. (2003). Cost of security for sea cargo transport. *White Paper, The Logistics Institute—Asia Pacific,* National University of Singapore, Singapore.

Ericksen, P. J. (2008). Conceptualizing food systems for global environmental change research. *Global Environmental Change, 18*(1), 234–245.

Erickson, A., Shaw, J. B., & Agabe, Z. (2007). An empirical investigation of the antecedents, behaviors, and outcomes of bad leadership. *Journal of Leadership Studies, 1,* 26–43.

Espelage, D., Anderman, E. M., Brown, V. E., Jones, A., Lane, K. L., McMahon, S. D., ... Reynolds, C. R. (2014, November). Preventing violence against teachers. *American Psychologist, 44*(10), 58–67.

Estlund, C. L. (2006). Between rights and contract: Arbitration agreements and non-compete covenants as a hybrid form of employment law. *University of Pennsylvania Law Review, 155*(2), 379–445.

Eytan, R. (2005). Cost effective retrofit of structures against the effects of terrorist attacks: The Israeli experience. In *Proceedings of the Structures Congress and Exposition* (pp. 2161–2172).

Fact Sheet: National Infrastructure Protection Program Sector-Specific Plans. Copyright © 2007. Published by U.S Department of Homeland Security.

Fagin, J. A. (2007). *Criminal justice* (2nd ed.). Boston, MA: Pearson Allyn & Bacon.

Farmer, L. (2005). *Criminal law, tradition and legal order: Crime and the genius of Scots law, 1747 to the present.* Cambridge University Press.

Fast facts on U.S. hospitals. (2015). Retrieved from http://www.aha.org/research/rc/stat-studies/fast-facts.shtml

Fay, J. J. (1999). *Model security policies, plans and procedures.* Woburn, MA: Butterworth-Heinemann.

Fay, J. J. (2000, August). SICM: A risk management tool. *Security Technology & Design, 10*(8), 22–24, 26.

Fay, J. J. (2007). *Encyclopaedia of security management.* Boston: Butterworth-Heinemann.

FBI, Frequently Asked Questions, Foreign Counterintelligence. Published by Federal Bureau of Investigation, © 2016.

Federal Bureau of Investigation. (2014a). *Internet crime report.* Washington, DC: U.S. Department of Justice.

Federal Bureau of Investigation. (2014b). Violations of the federal bank robbery and incidental crimes Statute, Title 18 United States Code, Section 2113. Washington, DC: U.S. Department of Justice.

Federal Bureau of Investigation. (2015). Economic Espionage. Retrieved from http://www.fbi.gov/about-us/investigate/counterintelligence/economic-espionage

Federal Emergency Management Administration. Published by Federal Emergency Management Administration, © 2015.

Federal Emergency Management Administration. (2015). *FEMA Glossary.* Retrieved from https://www.trainingfema.gov/programs/emischool/el361toolkit/glossary.htm

Federal Emergency Management Agency. (2003). *Risk Management Series: Reference manual-to mitigate potential terrorist attacks against buildings.* Government Printing Office.

Federal Emergency Management Agency. (2007). *Welcome to the National Incident Management System Integration Center.* (Online). Available from http://www.fema.gov/emergency/nims/index/shtm

Federal Emergency Management Agency. (2011). Putting out fires. Retrieved from https://www.fema.gov/media-library-data/1445532597685-7b1af8a601e33d9994baeca9826baeae/Section_5_BT_IG_Unit_2_508.pdf

Federal Emergency Management Agency. (2015). *IT disaster recovery plan.* Retrieved from http://www.ready.gov/business/implementation/IT

Federal Energy Regulatory Commission. (2014, March 7). FERC directs development of physical security standards. Retrieved from http://www.ferc.gov/media/news-releases/2014/2014-1/03-07-14.asp#.Vo8qk85N3II

Federal Motor Carrier Safety Administration. (2007). *About FMCSA.* (Online). Available from http://www.fmcsa.dot.gov/about/aboutus.html

Federal Railroad Administration. (2007). *About the FRA.* (Online). Available from http://www.fra.dot.gov/us/content/2

Federation of American Scientists. (2007). *Project on government secrecy.* (Online). Available from http://www.fas.org/sgp/library/nispom.html

Fein, R. A. (2002). *Threat assessment in schools: A guide to managing threatening situations and to creating safe school climates.* DIANE Publishing.

Feinman, J. M. (2000). *Law 101: Everything you need to know about the American legal system.* New York: Oxford University Press.

Felson, M. (2002). Crime in everyday life. Thousand Oaks, CA: Pine Forge Press.

FEMA aid reaches $16.9 billion for New York's Hurricane Sandy Recovery. (2015). Retrieved from https://www.fema.gov/news-release/2015/10/21/fema-aid-reaches-169-billion-new-yorks-hurricane-sandy-recovery

Fennelly, L. J. (1992). Security applications in industry and institutions. Woburn, MA: Butterworth-Heinemann.

Fennelly, L. J. (2012). Effective physical security. Boston: Butterworth Heinemann.

Ferguson, J. (2005). Seeing like an oil company: Space, security, and global capital in neoliberal Africa. American Anthropologist, 107(3), 377–382.

Fest, G. (2001, January 22). Desk rage. San Diego Union Tribune, pp. C1, C2.

Fiedler, F. E. (1967). A theory of leadership effectiveness. New York: McGraw-Hill.

Final report of the Defense Science Board Task Force on globalization and security. (1999). Washington, DC: Office of the Under Secretary for Defense for Acquisition and Technology.

Finklea, K. M. (2011). Organized retail crime. DIANE Publishing.

Finley, G. (2013). Petrominerales: Security management programs in Columbia. In M. G. Santos & S. J. Randall (Eds.), Calgary papers in military and strategic studies (pp. 35–42). Calgary, AB: Centre for Military and Strategic Studies.

Fiorucci, P., Gaetani, F., & Minciardi, R. (2008). Development and application of a system for dynamic wildfire risk assessment in Italy. Environmental Modelling & Software, 23(6), 690–702.

Fischer, L. F., & Morgan, R. W. (2002). Sources of information and issues leading to clearance revocations (No. PERSEREC-TR-02-1). Monterey, CA: Defense Personnel Security Research Center.

Fischer, R. J., & Green, G. (2008). Introduction to security (8th ed.). Burlington, MA: Elsevier.

Fischer, R. J., & Janoski, R. (2000). Loss prevention and security procedures: Practical applications for contemporary problems. Woburn, MA: Butterworth-Heinemann.

Fischer, R. J., Halibozek, E. P., & Walters, D. (2012). Introduction to security. Butterworth-Heinemann.

Fisher, L. E. (1995). The Great Wall of China. New York: Simon and Schuster.

Fisher, R. (2010). Introduction to security (8th ed.). Boston: Elsevier.

Fishman, T. C. (2002, August). The myth of capital's good intentions. Harper's Magazine.

Fitzhenry, B. (2007, February). An eye on it all. Security Products, 11(2), 26D–26E.

Fleckenstein, M. P., & Bowes, J. C. (2000). When trust is betrayed: Religious institutions and white collar crime. Journal of Business Ethics, 23(1), 111–115.

FLIR imaging cameras secure diamond mines in Namibia day and night. (2014, October 27). Retrieved from http://www.asmag.com/print_article.aspx?id=17702

Flynn, B. B., Schroeder, R. G., & Sakakibara, S. (1994). A framework for quality management research and an associated measurement instrument. Journal of Operations Management, 11(4), 339–366.

Fombrun, C. J., Gardberg, N. A., & Barnett, M. L. (2000). Opportunity platforms and safety nets: Corporate citizenship and reputational risk. Business and Society Review, 105(1), 85–106.

Foss, B. (2003, January 1). Pain of scandals may yield benefits. San Diego Union Tribune, pp. C1, C8.

Fournies, F. (2000). Coaching for improved work performance. New York: McGraw-Hill.

Fradkin, P. L. (2002). Stagecoach: Wells Fargo and the American West. New York: Simon & Schuster.

Frandsen, A. C., Hiller, T. B., Traflet, J., & McGoun, E. G. (2013). From money storage to money store: Openness and transparency in bank architecture. Business History, 55(5), 695–720.

Franke, U., Johnson, P., & König, J. (2014). An architecture framework for enterprise IT service availability analysis. Software & Systems Modeling, 13(4), 1417–1445.

Fransoo, J. C., & Lee, C. Y. (2013). The critical role of ocean container transport in global supply chain performance. Production and Operations Management, 22(2), 253–268.

From protecting the United States and its.....and natural disasters. Published by San Roberto Instituto, © 2015.

Fussey, P., & Coaffee, J. (2011). Olympic rings of steel: Constructing security for 2012 and beyond. In C. J. Bennett & K. D. Haggerty (Eds.), Security Games (pp. 36–54). New York: Routledge.

G4S. (2015). G4S Annual Report. Retrieved from http://www.g4s.com/en/Investors/2014%20Annual%20Report/

Gabel, J. D. (2012). CSI Las Vegas: Privacy, policing, and profiteering in casino structured intelligence. UNLV Gaming LJ, 3, 39.

Gallagher, F. J., & Grassie, R. P. (2000, September). Alarm management: The key ingredient in effective security management operations. Security Technology & Design, 10(9), 12–14, 16, 18.

Gallivan, M., & Srite, M. (2005). Information technology and culture: Identifying fragmentary and holistic perspectives of culture. Information and Organization, 15(4), 295–338.

Galpin, T. (2013). Creating a culture of global citizenship. *Journal of Corporate Citizenship, 49*, 34–47.

Garcia, M. L. (2000, June). Truth and consequences. *Security Management, 44*(6), 44–48.

Garcia, M. L. (2001). *The design and evaluation of physical protection systems.* Boston: Butterworth-Heinemann.

Garcia, M. L. (2006). *Vulnerability assessment of physical protection systems.* Boston: Butterworth-Heinemann.

Gatewood, R., Feild, H., & Barrick, M. (2010). *Human resource selection.* Independence, KY: Cengage Learning.

Genge, B., Graur, F., & Haller, P. (2015). Experimental assessment of network design approaches for protecting industrial control systems. *International Journal of Critical Infrastructure Protection*, 1–15.

George, B., & Watson, T. (1992). Regulation of the private security industry. *Public Money & Management, 12*(1), 55–57.

George, J. M., & Jones, G. R. (2012). *Understanding and managing organizational behavior* (6th ed.). Upper Saddle River, NJ: Pearson Prentice Hall.

Gest, T. (2001). *Crime and politics.* New York: Oxford University Press.

Ghosh, M. (2013). Mainstreaming disaster risk reduction in development: From risk to resilience—a report on first session of NPDRR at Vigyan Bhavan, New Delhi, India. *Library Hi Tech News, 30*(8), 1–5.

Gibb, S. (2002). *Learning and Development: Processes, Practices and Perspectives at work.* Palgrave Macmillan.

Giermanski, J. (2008). Tapping the potential of smart containers. *Supply Chain Management Review, 12*(1), 38–44.

Gigliotti, R., & Jason, R. (1999). Approaches to physical security. In L. J. Fennelly (Ed.), *Handbook of loss prevention and crime prevention* (3rd ed.). Boston, MA: Butterworth-Heinemann.

Gill, P., & Phythian, M. (2006). *Intelligence in an insecure world.* Malden, MA: Polity Press.

Gilliom, J., & Monahan, T. (2013). *SuperVision: An introduction to the surveillance society.* Chicago, IL: University of Chicago Press.

Gips, M. A. (2000, May). Building in terrorism's shadow. *Security Management, 44*(5), 42–44, 46–50.

Gips, M. A. (2007, March). My short life as an EP specialist. *Security Management, 51*(3), 52–56, 58–60.

Givens, A. D., & Busch, N. E. (2013). Information sharing and public-private partnerships: The impact on homeland security. *Homeland Security Review, 7*(2), 1–28.

Gleick, P. H. (2006). Water and terrorism. *The world's water 2006-2007.* Washington: Island Press.

Gleick, P. H., & Ajami, N. (2014). *The world's water volume 8: The biennial report on freshwater resources* (Vol. 8). Washington: Island Press.

Global Water Security, Copyright © 2012. Published by Office of the Director of National Intelligence.

Goetsch, D. L., & Davis, S. (2010). *Quality management* (6th ed.). Upper Saddle River, NJ: Pearson Prentice Hall.

Gold, S. (2014). Financial services sector puts voice biometrics at heart of fraud battle. *Biometric Technology Today, 2014*(4), 5–9.

Goldstein, P. (2007). *Intellectual property.* New York, NY: Portfolio.

Goluch, G., Ekelhart, A., Fenz, S., Jakoubi, S., Tjoa, S., & Mück, T. (2008, January). Integration of an ontological information security concept in risk aware business process management. In *Hawaii International Conference on system sciences, Proceedings of the 41st annual* (p. 377). IEEE.

Gomez-Mejia, L. R., & Balkin, D. (2012). *Management.* Upper Saddle River, NJ: Pearson Prentice Hall.

Goodchild, J. (2010, November). Donuts to dollars. *CSO, 9*(11), 28.

Goode, E. (1992). *Collective behavior.* Fort Worth, TX: Harcourt Brace Jovanovich.

Gorman, L. O. (2003). Comparing passwords, tokens, and biometrics for user authentication. *Proceedings of the IEEE, 91*(12), 2021–2040.

Gounev, P., & Bezlov, T. (2012). Corruption and criminal markets. In P. Gounev & V. Ruggiero (Eds.), *Corruption and Organized Crime in Europe: Illegal Partnerships.* London: Routledge.

Gow, G. A., McGee, T., Townsend, D., Anderson, P., & Varnhagen, S. (2009). Communication technology, emergency alerts, and campus safety. *Technology and Society Magazine, IEEE, 28*(2), 34–41.

Graben, S., & Fitz-Gerald, A. (2013). Mind the gap: The importance of local institutional development in peace-building-funded security interventions. *Conflict, Security & Development, 13*(3), 285–316.

Graham v. Conner, 490 U. S. 386 (1989).

Green, R. P., & CITP, C. (2007). How CFOs should tackle information management. *Financial Executive, 23*(10), 44–48.

Greene, J. D., & Tappen, A. R. (2000, July). Designing retrofit fire alarm systems: Part 2. *Security Technology & Design, 10*(7), 60–63.

Greensolver. (2015). Site Security Solutions: How to protect your wind energy assets. Retrieved from http://greensolver.net/site-security-solutions-protect-wind-energy-assets/

Greer, C. R., & Plunkett, W. R. (2007). *Supervisory management* (11th ed.). Upper Saddle River, NJ: Pearson Prentice Hall.

Greer, W. (1979). *History of alarm security.* Washington, DC: National Burglar and Fire Alarm Association.

Grey, D., & Sadoff, C. (2007). Sink or swim? Water security for growth and development. *Water Policy, 9,* 545–571.

Griebel, M., & Phillips, T. S. (2001). Architectural design for security in courthouse facilities. *The ANNALS of the American Academy of Political and Social Science, 576*(1), 118–131.

Griffin, A. (2015). Shy Godiva: Digital likeness and the Personal Data Protection and Breach Accountability Act. *Wake Forest Journal of Business & Intellectual Property Law, 15*(2), 314–364.

Group Transit Explanation. (2010, August). Retrieved from www:shipping.nato.int

Guha-Sapir, D., Hoyois, P., & Below, R. (2014, September). Annual Disaster Statistical Review 2013: The numbers and trends. Available from http://www.cred.be/sites/default/files/ADSR_2013.pdf

Guilfoyle, D. (2008). II. Piracy off Somalia: UN Security Council resolution 1816 and IMO Regional counter-piracy efforts. *International and Comparative Law Quarterly, 57*(03), 690–699.

Gulick, L., & Urwick, L. (1937). *POSDCORB.* New York: Institute of Professional Administration.

Guo, X., Tiller, D. K., Henze, G. P., & Waters, C. E. (2010). The performance of occupancy-based lighting control systems: A review. *Lighting Research and Technology, 42*(4), 415–431.

H.R. 3355. (1994, August 21). Violent Crime Control and Law Enforcement Act of 1994.

Haberer, J. B., & Webb, M. L. W. (1994). *TQM: 50 ways to make it work for you.* Menlo Park, CA: Crisp Publications.

Haddow, G. D., & Bullock, J. A. (2010). *Introduction to emergency management* (4th ed.). Boston, MA: Butterworth-Heinemann.

Hafez, M., & Mullins, C. (2015). The radicalization puzzle: A theoretical synthesis of empirical approaches to Homegrown Extremism. *Studies in Conflict & Terrorism, 38*(11), 958–975.

Hahn, J., Guillen, D. P., & Anderson, T. (2006). Process control systems in the chemical industry: Safety vs. security. *Process Safety Progress, 25*(1), 40–43.

Hails, J. (2012). *Criminal evidence* (7th ed.). Florence, KY: Cengage Learning.

Halek, M., & Eisenhauer, J. G. (2001). Demography of risk aversion. *Journal of Risk and Insurance, 68*(1), 1–24.

Halibozek, E., Kovacich, G. L., & Jones, A. (2008). *The corporate security professional's handbook on terrorism.* Burlington, MA: Butterworth-Heinemann.

Hall Jr, J. R. (2006). An analysis of automatic sprinkler system reliability using current data (p-19). Quincy, MA: National Fire Protection Association.

Hamm, M. S. (2007). *Terrorism as crime: From Oklahoma City to Al-Qaeda and beyond.* NYU Press.

Hamper, B. (1991). *Rivethead: Tales from the Assembly Line.* New York, NY: Warner Books.

Handbook of Forensic Sociology and Psychology by Stephen J. Morewitz, Mark L. Goldstein, copyright year 2013. Published by Springer Science & Business Media.

Hannah, D. R. (2005, Jan–Feb). Should I keep a secret? The effects of trade secret protection procedures on employees' obligations protect trade secrets. *Organizational Science, 16*(1), 71–84.

Hannan, T. H. (1982). Bank robberies and bank security precautions. *The Journal of Legal Studies, 11*(1), 83–92.

Hansen, C. D., & Brooks, A. K. (1994). A review of cross-cultural research on human resource development. *Human Resource Development Quarterly, 5*(1), 55–74.

Haque, U. (2011). *The new capitalist manifesto: Building a disruptively better business.* Watertown, MA: Harvard Business Press.

Hardenbergh, D. (2005). Protecting America's courthouses. *Judges Journal, 44,* 14.

Hard Won Lessons: The New Paradigm—Merging Law Enforcement and Counterterrorism Strategies, Copyright © 2006. Published by Manhattan Institute for Policy Research..

Hargroves, T. R. (2007). *Long march to freedom: The true story of a Colombian kidnapping.* Texas A&M University Press.

Harman, K., & Messner, W. K. (2012, October). Outdoor perimeter security sensors a forty year perspective. In *Security Technology (ICCST), 2012 IEEE International Carnahan Conference* (pp. 1–9). IEEE.

Harowitz, S. L. (2003, January). The new centurions. *Security Management, 47*(1), 50–52, 54, 56–58.

Harr, J. S., & Hess, K. M. (2006). *Careers in criminal justice and related fields: From internship to promotion* (5th ed.). Belmont, CA: Wadsworth/Thomson Learning.

Harrell, E. (2011, March). *Workplace violence 1993–2009.* Washington, DC: U.S. Department of Justice, Office of Justice Programs. Available from http://www.bjs.gov/content/pub/pdf/wv09.pdf

Harrell, E. (2013). Workplace violence against government employees, 1994–2011. Washington, DC: Bureau of Justice Statistics.

Hart, M. (1999, March). How to steal a diamond. *The Atlantic.* Retrieved from http://www.theatlantic.com/magazine/archive/1999/03/how-to-steal-a-diamond/305488/

Hartel, C. E. J., & Fujimoto, Y. (2015). *Human resource management.* Upper Saddle River, NJ: Prentice Hall.

Hartley, D. (2004). Job analysis at the speed of reality. *Training and Development, 58*(9), 20–22.

Hartley, D., Doman, B., Hendricks, S. A., & Jenkins, E. L. (2012). Non-fatal workplace violence injuries in the United States 2003–2004: A follow back study. *Work (Reading, Mass.), 42*(1), 125–135.

Hasan, R. (2015). Rising extremism in Bangladesh: A voyage towards uncertainty. *Journal of South Asian Studies, 3*(2), 143–153.

Hawaii cites Xerox in worker shooting. (2000, November 8). *San Diego Union Tribune*, p. A10.

Hayes, R. (2014). *Retail security and loss prevention*. Boston: Butterworth-Heinemann.

Hays, C. L. (2001, September 30). Business; A company faces a calamity's personal side. *New York Times*.

Hayton, J. C. (2005). Competing in the new economy: the effect of intellectual capital on corporate entrepreneurship in high-technology new ventures. *R&D Management, 35*(2), 137–155.

Heifetz, R. A. (1994). *Leadership without easy answers*. Cambridge, MA: The Belknap Press of Harvard University Press.

Hellriegel, D., Jackson, S. E., & Slocum, J. W., Jr. (2005). *Management: A competency-based approach* (10th ed.). Cincinnati, OH: South-Western/Thomson Learning.

Henderson, R. (2013). Industry employment and output projections to 2022. *Monthly Labor Review, 136*, 65–83.

Hensell, S. (2012). The patrimonial logic of the police in Eastern Europe. *Europe-Asia Studies, 64*(5), 811–833.

Henson, B. (2010). Preventing interpersonal violence in emergency departments: Practical applications of criminology theory. *Violence and Victims, 25*(4), 553–565.

Herbig, K. L. (2011). *The evolution of adjudicative guidelines in the Department of Defense* (No. PERSEREC-TR-11-04). Monterey, CA: Defense Personnel Security Research Center.

Herrmann, A. (2013). The quantitative estimation of IT-related risk probabilities. *Risk Analysis, 33*(8), 1510–1531.

Hersey, P., & Blanchard, K. H. (1982). *Management of organizational behavior: Utilizing human resources*. Englewood Cliffs, NJ: Prentice Hall.

Hersey, P., Blanchard, K. H., & Johnson, D. E. (2008). *Management of organizational behavior: Leading human resources* (9th ed.). Upper Saddle River, NJ: Pearson Prentice Hall.

Hess, K. M., & Wrobleski, H. M. (2009). *Introduction to private security* (5th ed.). Belmont, CA: Thomson Higher Education.

Hettema, H., Watters, P., Sarrafzadeh, H., Fourie, L., Kingston, T., & Pang, S. (2014). The global cyber security workforce: An ongoing human capital crisis. Retrieved from http://130.217.226.8/bitstream/handle/10652/2457/Cyber2.pdf?sequence=1&isAllowed=y

Hicks, M. J., Snell, M. S., Sandoval, J. S., & Potter, C. S. (1999). Physical protection systems cost and performance analysis: A case study. *Aerospace and Electronic Systems Magazine, IEEE, 14*(4), 9–13.

Hiltz, S. R., Diaz, P., & Mark, G. (2011). Introduction: Social media and collaborative systems for crisis management. *ACM Transactions on Computer-Human Interaction (TOCHI), 18*(4), 18–23.

Ho, J. H. (2006). The security of sea lanes in Southeast Asia. *Asian Survey, 46*(4), 558–574.

Hodgson, D. E. (2004). *The Legacy of Bureaucratic Control in the Post-Bureaucratic Organization*. Sage Publications.

Hoffman, B. (2013). Al Qaeda's uncertain future. *Studies in Conflict & Terrorism, 36*(8), 635–653.

Holder, P., & Hawley, D. L. (1998). *The executive protection professional's manual*. Butterworth-Heinemann.

Homeland Security Council and United States of America. (2007). National Strategy for Homeland Security, 2007. Washington, DC: Department of Homeland Security.

Homeowner's guide to earthquake safety. (2005). Sacramento, CA: California Seismic Safety Commission.

Homer-Dixon, T. F. (1999). *Environment, scarcity and violence*. Princeton, NJ: Princeton University Press.

Horowitz, R. (1998). The Economic Espionage Act: The rules have not changed. *Competitive Intelligence Review, 9*(3), 30–38.

Hosey, G., Melfi, V., & Pankhurst, S. (2013). *Zoo animals: Behaviour, management, and welfare*. Oxford University Press.

Hough, W. O. (1999). Proactive security is called for. In R. R. Robinson (Ed.), *Issues in security management: Thinking critically about security* (pp. 158–162). Woburn, MA: Butterworth-Heinemann.

House, R. J. (1996). Path-goal theory of leadership: Lessons, legacy, and a reformulated theory. *Leadership Quarterly, 7*(3), 323–352.

Howard, J. L., & Wech, B. A. (2012). A model of organizational and job environment influences on workplace violence. *Employee Responsibilities and Rights Journal, 24*(2), 111–127.

Hubbard, B. (2015, September 24). Hajj stampede near Mecca leaves over 700 dead. *New York Times*. Retrieved from http://www.nytimes.com/2015/09/25/world/middleeast/mecca-stampede.html?_r=0

Human Security, A Thematic Guidance Note for Regional and National Human Development Report Teams, Copyright © 2013. Published by United Nations Development Programme

Hunt, W. R. (1990). *Front-page detective: William J. Burns and the Detective Profession, 1880–1930*. Cleveland, OH: Popular Press.

Hussain, S. A., Malik, M. Z., & Menezes, R. G. (2015). The airplane crash in the French Alps: A preventable tragedy. *Asian Journal of Psychiatry, 17,* 109–110.

ICC International Maritime Bureau. (2015). *Piracy and Armed Robbery, Report for the period 1 January–31 December, 2014.* Retrieved from http://www.hellenicshippingnews.com/wp-content/uploads/2015/01/2014-Annual-IMB-Piracy-Report-ABRIDGED.pdf

Information Security Management Best Practice Based on ISO/IEC 17799. Published by ARMA International, © 2005.

Information security policy decision making: An analytic hierarchy process approach, by Hwang, J., & Syamsuddin, I. Published by IEEE, © 2009.

Implementing Recommendations of the 9/11 Commission Act of 2007. PL 110-53 (8/3/07).

Institute for Corporate Productivity. (2015). Developing global-minded leaders to drive high performance. Retrieved from www.i4cp.com

Institute for Economics and Peace. (2014). *Global Terrorism Index, 2014.* Available from www.economicsandpeace.org

Intelligence Reform and Terrorism Prevention Act. (2004) a.k.a. National Intelligence Reform Act *(An act to reform the intelligence community and the intelligence and intelligence-related activities of the United States government, and for other purposes)* S. 2845; Pub.L. 108-458; 118 Stat. 3638. 108th Congress; December 17, 2004.

Interagency Security Committee. (2013). *The risk management process for federal facilities: An interagency security committee standard.* Washington, DC: Department of Homeland Security.

International Association for Healthcare Security and Safety. (2007). *Mission and goals.* (Online). Available from http://www.iahss.org/about_mission.asp

International Code of Conduct Association. (2015). Retrieved from http://icoca.ch/en/the_icoc

International Convergence of Capital Measurement and Capital Standards -a Revised Framework, Copyright © 2004. Published by Bank for International Settlements

International Maritime Organization. (2013, March). *Reports on acts of piracy and armed robbery against ships, Annual report—2013.* Retrieved from http://www.imo.org/en/OurWork/Security/SecDocs/Documents/PiracyReports/208_Annual_2013.pdf

Internet Security Threat Report. (2015). Symantec Corporation. Retrieved from http://www.symantec.com/security_response/publications/threatreport.jsp

IOMA/IOFM. (2011). *2011 report on workplace violence: Complete guide to managing today's and tomorrow's threats.* Greenwich, CT: Institute of Management and Administration.

Islam, S. S., Edla, S. R., Mujuru, P., Doyle, E. J., & Ducatman, A. M. (2003). Risk factors for physical assault: State-managed workers' compensation experience. *American Journal of Preventive Medicine, 25*(1), 31–37.

Ivancevich, S. H., & Ivancevich, D. M. (2012). Mitigating inadequate security claims through effective security measures. *UNLV Gaming Research & Review Journal, 2*(1), 6.

Jacobson, R. V. (1997, September). Look through the risk management window to add up security costs. *Access Control & Security Systems Integration, 40*(9), 59–62.

Jaffee, D. (2008). *Organization theory: Tension and change.* Boston: McGraw-Hill.

James, P., & Goldstaub, J. (1988). Terrorism and the breakdown of international order: The corporate dimension. *Conflict Quarterly, 8*(3), 69–98.

Jawahar, I. M. (2012). Mediating role of satisfaction with growth opportunities on the relationship between employee development opportunities and citizenship behaviors and burnout. *Journal of Applied Social Psychology, 42*(9), 2257–2284.

Jaworowski, Z. (2010, April–June). Observations on the Chernobyl disaster and LNT. *Dose-Response, 8*(2), 148–171.

Jeffery, C. R. (1971). *Crime prevention through environmental design.* Beverly Hills, CA: Sage.

Jelen, G. E. (1994, October). OPSEC for the private sector. *Security Management, 38*(10), 67–68.

Jennings, W., & Lodge, M. (2011). Governing mega-events: Tools of security risk management for the FIFA 2006 World Cup in Germany and London 2012 Olympic Games. *Government and Opposition, 46*(2), 192–222.

Jeong, Y. (1999). Comparisons of variables between fatal and nonfatal accidents in manufacturing industry. *International Journal of Industrial Ergonomic.* Published by Elsevier.

Jha, M. K. (2010). Natural and anthropogenic disasters: An overview. In *Natural and anthropogenic disasters* (pp. 1–16). Netherlands: Springer.

Jidiga, G. R., & Sammulal, P. (2013, July). The need of awareness in cyber security with a case study. In *Computing, communications and networking technologies (ICCCNT), 2013 Fourth International Conference on* (pp. 1–7). IEEE.

Johnson, B. R. (2005). *Principles of security management.* Upper Saddle River, NJ: Pearson Prentice Hall.

Johnson, B. R. (2015, October). Watch the workplace legally. *Security Management, 59*(10), 50–57.

Johnson, B. R., & Barton-Bellessa, S. M. (2014). Consequences of school violence: Personal coping and protection measures by school personnel in their personal lives. *Deviant Behavior, 35*(7), 513–533. doi: 10.1080/01639625.2013.859047.

Johnson, B. R., & Carter, T. (2009). Combating the shoplifter: An examination of civil recovery laws. *Journal of Applied Security Research, 4*(4), 445–461.

Johnson, B. R., Connolly, E., & Carter, T. S. (2011). Corporate social responsibility: The role of fortune 100 companies in domestic and international natural disasters. *Corporate Social Responsibility and Environmental Management, 18*(6), 352–369.

Johnson, B. R., Kierkus, C., & Gerkin, P. (2016, August). Trade secret crimes and offenders: A typology. *Security Management* (forthcoming).

Johnson, B. R., & Kingshott, B. F. (2009). *Safe overseas travel.* New York: Looseleaf.

Johnson, B. R., McKenzie, D. G., & Warchol, G. L. (2003). Corporate kidnapping: An exploratory study. *Journal of Security Administration, 26*(2), 13–30.

Johnson, B. R., Yalda, C. A., & Kierkus, C. (2010). Property crime at O'Hare International Airport: An examination of the routine activities approach. *Journal of Applied Security Research, 5*(1), 42–63.

Johnson, C. E. (2009). *Meeting the ethical challenges of leadership: Casting light or shadow* (3rd ed.). Thousand Oaks, CA: Sage Publications.

Jonas, J. (2006). Threat and fraud intelligence, Las Vegas style. *IEEE Security & Privacy, 4*(6), 28–34.

Jones, C. (2008). Assessing the dangers of illicit networks. *International Security, 33*(2), 7–44.

Jones, D. (2000, August 2). Businesses battle over intellectual property. *USA Today,* pp. 1B–2B.

Jones, J. W., & Arnold, D. W. (2003, February). Trends in personnel testing: A loss prevention perspective. *Loss Prevention & Security Journal, 3*(2), 14–16.

Jones, L. A., Antón, A. I., & Earp, J. B. (2007, October). Towards understanding user perceptions of authentication technologies. In *Proceedings of the 2007 ACM workshop on Privacy in electronic society* (pp. 91–98). ACM.

Jones, S. (2014). Maritime piracy and the cost of world trade. *Competitiveness Review, 24*(3), 158–170.

Jopeck, E. J. (2000, August). Five steps to risk reduction. *Security Management, 44*(8), 97–98, 100–102.

Jordan, L. J. (2006, February 24). White House's Katrina Report calls for fixes. *San Diego Union Tribune,* p. A3.

Journal of Homeland Security and Emergency Management, Copyright © 2006. Published by The George Washington University.

Journal of Homeland Security and Emergency Management, Copyright © 2007. Published by Walter de Gruyter GmbH.

Joyce, P. (2011). *Policing: Development and contemporary practice.* Thousand Oaks, CA: Sage.

Kajalo, S., & Lindblom, A. (2011). An empirical analysis of retail entrepreneurs' approaches to prevent shoplifting. *Security Journal, 24*(4), 269–282.

Kakalik, J. S., & Wildhorn, S. (1971). *The private police industry: Its nature and extent.* Santa Monica, CA: RAND.

Kakalik, J. S., & Wildhorn, S. (1972). *Private Police in the United States: Findings and recommendations.* Washington, DC: U.S. Government Printing Office.

Kanter, J. (2011, March 18). Europe seeks transparency from U.S. on anti-terrorism program. *New York Times.*

Katz, E. M., & Claypoole, T. E. (2001). Willie Sutton is on the Internet. Bank security strategy in a shared risk environment. *North Carolina Banking Institute, 5,* 168–227.

Kearney, R. C., & Mareschal, P. M. (2014). *Labor relations in the public sector.* CRC Press.

Keller, H. J. (1993, October). Advanced passive infrared presence detectors as key elements in integrated security and building automation systems. In *Security Technology, 1993. Security Technology, Proceedings. Institute of Electrical and Electronics Engineers 1993 International Carnahan Conference on* (pp. 75–77). IEEE.

Kempa, M., Stenning, P., & Wood, J. (2004). Policing communal spaces: A reconfiguration of the 'Mass Private Property' hypothesis. *British Journal of Criminology, 44*(4), 562–581.

Kenny, K. (1998). *Making sense of the Molly Maguires.* New York: Oxford University Press.

Khan, F., Amatya, B., Gosney, J., Rathore, F. A., & Burkle, F. M. (2015). *Medical Rehabilitation in Natural Disasters in the Asia-Pacific Region: The Way Forward.* Published by Elsevier B.V.

Kim, S. J., Deng, G., Gupta, S. K. S, & Murphy-Hoye, M. (2008, May). Enhancing cargo container security during transportation: A mesh networking based approach. In *Technologies for Homeland Security, 2008 IEEE Conference on* (pp. 90–95). IEEE.

Kim, W. G., & Brymer, R. A. (2011). The effects of ethical leadership on manager job satisfaction, commitment, behavioral outcomes, and firm performance. *International Journal of Hospitality Management, 30*(4), 1020–1026.

Kinsey, C. (2006). *Corporate soldiers and international security: The rise of private military companies.* London: Routledge.

Kis-Katos, K., Liebert, H., & Schulze, G. G. (2014). On the heterogeneity of terror. *European Economic Review, 68,* 116–136.

Kleiman, L. S., & Kass, D. (2014). Employer liability for hiring and retaining unfit workers: How employers can minimize their risks. *Employment Relations Today, 41*(2), 33–41.

Klemke, L. W. (1992). *The sociology of shoplifting: Boosters and snitches today.* New York: Praeger.

Klopfer, F. & vanAmstel, N. (2015). A force for good. *Mapping the private security landscape in Southern Europe.* Switzerland: DCAF.

Kneafsey, M., Dowler, E., Lambie-Mumford, H., Inman, A., & Collier, R. (2013). Consumers and food security: uncertain or empowered? *Journal of Rural Studies, 29,* 101–112.

Knight, E. J. M. (2013). Strategic human resources management practice, "are we there yet"? A study of the incorporation of a strategic plan. *International Journal of Human Resource Management, 71,* 2104–2111.

Kolkoori, S., Wrobel, N., Hohendorf, S., & Ewert, U. (2015, April). High energy X-ray imaging technology for the detection of dangerous materials in air freight containers. In *Technologies for Homeland Security (HST), 2015 IEEE International Symposium on* (pp. 1–6). IEEE.

Kotter, J. P. (1990). *A force for change.* New York: The Free Press.

Kotter, J. P. (1993). What leaders really do. In W. E. Rosenbach & R. L. Taylor (Eds.), *Contemporary issues in leadership* (3rd ed.) (pp. 26–35). Boulder, CO: Westview Press.

Kousky, C., & Walls, M. (2014). Floodplain conservation as a flood mitigation strategy: Examining costs and benefits. *Ecological Economics, 104,* 119–128.

Kovacich, G. L., & Halibozek, E. P. (2003). *The manager's handbook for corporate security: Establishing and managing a successful assets protection program.* Boston, MA: Butterworth-Heinemann.

Krasnowski, M. (2000, November 10). Fraud charges against Keating dropped. *San Diego Union Tribune,* p. A3.

Krausmann, E., Renni, E., Campedel, M., & Cozzani, V. (2011). Industrial accidents triggered by earthquakes, floods and lightning: Lessons learned from a database analysis. *Natural Hazards, 59*(1), 285–300.

Kravitz, D., & O'Molloy, C. (2014, August 25). The murky world of hostage negotiations: Is the price ever right? *The Guardian.* Retrieved from theguardian.com

Krotoski, M. L. (2009, November). Common issues and challenges in prosecuting trade secrets and economic espionage act cases. *United States Attorneys' Bulletin, 57*(5), 2–23.

Kupatadze, A. (2015). Political corruption in Eurasia: Understanding collusion between states, organized crime and business. *Theoretical Criminology, 19*(2), 198–215.

Kurzman, C., & Schanzer, D. (2015, June 16). The growing right wing terror threat. *New York Times.*

Kwon, K. C., & Kim, J. H. (1999). Accident identification in nuclear power plants using hidden Markov models. *Engineering Applications of Artificial Intelligence.* Published by Elsevier.

LaBruno, L. (2011, January–February). Risks from shoplifter apprehensions: Part II. *Loss Prevention,* pp. 72–73.

Ladouceur, R., Sylvain, C., & Gosselin, P. (2007). Self-exclusion program: A longitudinal evaluation study. *Journal of Gambling Studies, 23*(1), 85–94.

Laforte, C. (2010, October). Bridging the gap. *Security Technology Executive,* p. 52.

Lane, R. (1971). *Policing the city: Boston, 1822–1855.* New York: Atheneum.

Langlois, L., Lapointe, C., Valois, P., & de Leeuw, A. (2014). Development and validity of the Ethical Leadership Questionnaire. *Journal of Educational Administration, 52*(3), 310–331.

Larkins, E. M. R. (2015). *The spectacular favela: Violence in modern Brazil* (Vol. 32). Irvine, CA: University of California Press.

Law Enforcement-Private Consortium & United States of America. (2009). *Operation Partnership: Trends and Practices in Law Enforcement and Private Security Collaborations.*

Lawrence, T. B., & Robinson, S. L. (2007). Ain't misbehavin: Workplace deviance as organizational resistance. *Journal of Management, 33*(3), 378–394.

Leander, A. (2005). The market for force and public security: The destabilizing consequences of private military companies. *Journal of Peace Research, 42*(5), 605–622.

Leaning, J., & Arie, S. (2000). *Human security: A framework for assessment in conflict and transition.* Washington: CERTI/USAID.

Lee, C., & Spisto, M. (2004). International travel, illnesses and the global employee. *Employment Relations Record, 4*(2), 1–11.

Lee, H., Park, S., & Yoo, J. H. (2013, July). A data cube model for surveillance video indexing and retrieval. In *Signal Processing and Multimedia Applications (SIGMAP), 2013 International Conference on* (pp. 163–168). IEEE.

Lee, S. W. (2011, June). Probabilistic risk assessment for security requirements: A preliminary study. In *Secure software integration and reliability improvement (SSIRI), 2011 Fifth International Conference on* (pp. 11–20). IEEE.

Lehmbruch, B. (2012). It takes two to quango: post-Soviet fiscal relations, political entrepreneurship and agencification from below. *ISS Working Paper Series/General Series, 538,* 1–26.

Lehmbruch, B., & Sanikidze, L. (2014). Soviet legacies, new public management and bureaucratic entrepreneurship in the Georgian protection police. Agencifying the police? *Europe-Asia Studies, 66*(1), 88–107.

Leitch, S., & Warren, M. (2009, December). Security issues challenging Facebook. In *Australian Information Security Management Conference* (pp. 136–142).

Lens, J. W. (2011). Punishing for the injury: Tort law's influence on the Constitutional limitations of punitive damage awards. *Hofstra Law Review, 39*, 595–644.

Leon, J. D., Jaffe, D. A., Kaspar, J., Knecht, A., Miller, M. L., Robertson, R. G. H., & Schubert, A. G. (2011). Arrival time and magnitude of airborne fission products from the Fukushima, Japan, reactor incident as measured in Seattle, WA, USA. *Journal of Environmental Radioactivity, 102*(11), 1032–1038.

Leveson, N. (2011). *Engineering a Safer World: Systems Thinking Applied to Safety.* Published by MIT Pres.

Lewin, D. (2002). IR and HR perspectives on workplace conflict: What can each learn from the other? *Human Resource Management Review, 11*(4), 453–485.

Lewin, F. A. (2001). The meaning of home among elderly immigrants: Directions for future research and theoretical development. *Housing Studies, 16*(3), 353–370.

Lewis, L. (1948). Lincoln and Pinkerton. *Journal of the Illinois State Historical Society (1908–1984)*, 367–382.

Lewis, P., Newburn, T., Taylor, M., Mcgillivray, C., Greenhill, A., Frayman, H., & Proctor, R. (2011). Reading the riots: Investigating England's summer of disorder. London: *The Guardian*, London School of Economics.

Lewis, P. S., Goodman, S. H., & Fandt, P. M. (2008). *Management: Challenges for tomorrow's leaders* (5th ed.). Belmont, CA: South-Western/Thomson Learning.

Lewis, R. L. (1993). Appalachian restructuring in historical perspective: Coal, culture and social change in West Virginia. *Urban Studies, 30*(2), 299–308.

Liard, M. J. (2004, June). *The co-existence of EAS and RFID technologies in retail environments.* Natick, MA: Venture Development Corporation.

Lichtenstein, N. (1980). Autoworker militancy and the structure of factory life, 1937–1955. *The Journal of American History, 67*(2) 335–353.

Liebeskind, J. P. (1997). Keeping organizational secrets: Protective institutional mechanisms and their costs. *Industrial and Corporate Change, 6*(3), 623–663. doi: 10.1093/icc/6.3.623.

Likert, R. (1961). *New patterns of management.* New York: McGraw-Hill.

Likert, R. (1967). *The human organization.* New York: McGraw-Hill.

Lipson, M. (1988, July). Private security: A retrospective. *Annuals of the American Academy of Political and Social Science, 498*, 11–22.

Lipton, M. (1996). Demystifying the development of an organizational vision. *Sloan Management Review, 37*, 83–92.

Lippert, R. K., Walby, K., & Steckle, R. (2013). Multiplicities of corporate security: Identifying emerging types, trends and issues. Published by Security Journal.

Liss, C. (2003). Maritime policy in Southeast Asia. *Southeast Asian Affairs*, 52–68.

Liu, C., Li, G., Phang, S. K., & Sun, J. (2008). Effects of boundary conditions on the design of anti-ram bollards. *Transactions of Tianjin University, 14*(5), 384–386.

Lizard Squad Member 'Ryan' explains why it's OK to ruin Christmas. (2014, December 29). Retrieved from https://nakedsecurity.sophos.com/2014/12/29/lizard-squad-member-ryan-explains-why-its-ok-to-ruin-christmas/

Lizie, R. A., & Dhas, Y. S. A. (2015, March). Handheld secured electronic doorstep banking system. In *Circuit, power and computing technologies (ICCPCT), 2015 International Conference on* (pp. 1–5). IEEE.

Lobnikar, B., Sotlar, A., & Modic, M. (2015). Do we trust them? Public opinion on police work in plural policing environments in Central and Eastern Europe. In *Trust and legitimacy in criminal justice* (pp. 189–202). Springer International Publishing.

Lobo-Guerrero, L. (2007). Biopolitics of specialized risk: An analysis of kidnap and ransom insurance. *Security Dialogue, 38*(3), 315–334.

Lohr, S. (2002, May 27). In new era, corporate security looks beyond guns and badges. *New York Times*, pp. C1, C3.

Lombardi, D. J., Schermerhorn, J. R., & Kramer, B. (2007). *Health care management.* John Wiley.

Longmore-Etheridge, A. (2007, April). All along the watchtower. *Security Management, 51*(4), 74–76, 78–80, 82, 84.

Lovins, A., & Lovins, L. H. (1981). Energy policies for resilience and national security. San Francisco: Friends of the Earth. For contract: DCPA01-79-C-0317, Fed. Emerg. Manag. Agency Work Unit #4351-C, Washington, DC.

Lucas, G. (2015). *Military ethics: What everyone needs to know.* Oxford University Press.

Lucas, J. (2012). CTITF Panel Discussion: Public private partnerships in counter-terrorism. Retrieved from http://www.un.org/en/terrorism/ctitf/pdfs/statement_at_public-private_partnerships.pdf

Luft, G. (2009). *Energy security challenges for the 21st century: A reference handbook.* Denver, CO: ABC-CLIO.

Lushbaugh, C. A., & Weston, P. B. (2012). *Criminal investigation: Basic perspectives* (12th ed.). Upper Saddle River, NJ: Pearson Prentice Hall.

Ma, Q., & Pearson, J. M. (2005). ISO 17799: Best practices in information security management? *Communications of the Association for Information Systems, 15*(1), 577–591.

Macgill, S. M., & Siu, Y. L. (2004). The nature of risk. *Journal of Risk Research, 7*(3), 315–352.

McCrory, B., LaGrange, C. A., & Hallbeck, M. S. (2014). Quality and Safety of Minimally Invasive Surgery: Past, Present, and Future. Published by Libertas Academica Ltd.

Major, M. J. (1998, March). A casino's three-pronged approach to security. *Security Technology & Design, 8*(3), 27, 29–33.

Malcolm, J. A. (2013). Project Argus and the resilient citizen. *Politics, 33*(4), 311–321.

Man accused of murder of Long Island gas station clerk at Jericho but pleads not guilty. (2015, August 12). Retrieved from abc7ny.com/news/man-charged-in-nassau-county-armed-robbery-spree-murder-pleads-not-guilty/792213/

Maniscalco, P. M., & Christen, H. T. (2002). *Understanding terrorism and managing the consequences.* Upper Saddle River, NJ: Prentice Hall.

Mann, R. A., & Roberts, B. S. (2009). *Smith and Robertson's business law* (14th ed.). Belmont, CA: Thomson Higher Education.

Mann, T. (1999, October). Seven steps to successful contracting. *Security Management, 43*(10), 46–48, 50–51.

Manning, C. (2008, January–February). The 99 cents chili crisis. *Risk Management, 7*(1), 22–29.

Manuel-Navarrete, D., & Redclift, M. (2012). Spaces of consumerism and the consumption of space: Tourism and social exclusion in the "Mayan Riviera". In *Consumer Culture in Latin America* (pp. 177–193). Palgrave Macmillan.

Maras, M. H. (2012). *Computer forensics: Cybercriminals, laws, and evidence.* Sudbury, MA: Jones and Bartlett Learning.

Maravelias, C. (2003). Post-bureaucracy—control through professional freedom. *Journal of Organizational Change Management, 16*(5), 547–566.

Marcy, L. H. (1916). The Iron Heel on the Mesabi Range. *The International Socialist Review, 17*(2), 72–79.

Maritime security pilot underway in North Carolina. (2008, August 26). Retrieved from https://www.tsa.gov/news/releases/2008/08/26/maritime-security-pilot-underway-north-carolina

Markus, S. (2015). Sovereign commitment and property rights: The case of Ukraine's Orange Revolution. *Studies in Comparative International Development,* 1–23.

Martin, C. G. (2009). *Understanding terrorism: Challenges, perspectives, and issues* (3rd ed.). Thousand Oaks, CA: Sage Publications.

Marx, G. T. (1972). Issueless riots. In J. Short & M. Wolfgang (Eds.). *Collective violence* (pp. 47–59). New York: Aldine-Atherton.

Masci, P. (2012). Insurance and entrepreneurship: A conceptual framework. *Journal of the Washington Institute of China Studies, 6*(1), 23–40.

Mason, M. (2000, December 28). Koalas' lives at risk after theft. *San Diego Union Tribune,* pp. A3, A6.

Mason, M. E. (1998, August). The hands here are disposed to be turbulent: Unrest among Irish trackmen of the Baltimore and Ohio railroad, 1829–1851. *Labor History, 39*(3), 253–272.

Matchett, A. R. (2003). *CCTV for security professionals.* Boston, MA: Butterworth-Heinemann.

Maurer, R. D. (2000a, January). The evolving role of the security director. *Security Technology & Design, 10*(1), 12–14, 16.

Maurer, R. D. (2000b, August). Outsourcing: An option or a threat? *Security Technology & Design, 10*(8), 12–14, 18, 20.

Mawby, R. I. (2013). *Policing across the world: Issues for the twenty-first century.* New York: Routledge.

Mayer, A., Wool, A., & Ziskind, E. (2000). Fang: A firewall analysis engine. In *Security and Privacy, 2000. Proceedings 2000 IEEE Symposium on* (pp. 177–187). IEEE.

Mayer, D. M., Aquino, K., Greenbaum, R. L., & Kuenzi, M. (2012). Who displays ethical leadership, and why does it matter? An examination of antecedents and consequences of ethical leadership. *Academy of Management Journal, 55*(1), 151–171.

McAdams, A. C. (2004). Security and risk management: A fundamental business issue. *Information Management, 38*(4), 36–44.

McCahill, M., & Norris, C. (2002). CCTV in Britain. *Center for criminology and criminal justice* (pp. 1–70). United Kingdom: University of Hull.

McCrie, R. D. (1988). The development of the U.S. security industry. *The Annals of the American Academy of Political and Social Science, 498,* 23–33.

McDonald, J., & Barfield, C. (2007, May 26). Against all odds, cheaters persist. *San Diego Union Tribune,* pp. A1, A15.

McDonald, M. S. (2003). Noncompete contracts: Understanding the cost of unpredictability. *Texas. Wesleyan Law Review, 10,* 137–151.

McDowall, D., & Loftin, C. (1983). Collective security and the demand for legal handguns. *American Journal of Sociology, 88*(6), 1146–1161.

McEntire, D. A. (2014). *Disaster response and recovery: Strategies and tactics for resilience.* John Wiley & Sons.

McEvoy, A. F. (1995). The Triangle Shirtwaist Factory Fire of 1911: Social change, industrial accidents, and the evolution of common sense causality. *Law & Social Inquiry, 20*(2), 621–651.

McGregor, D. (1960). *The human side of enterprise.* New York: McGraw-Hill.

McGregor, D. (1966). *Leadership and motivation.* Cambridge: Massachusetts Institute of Technology Press.

McKinlay, A., & Zeitlin, J. (1989). The meanings of managerial prerogative: industrial relations and the organisation of work in British engineering, 1880–1939. *Business History, 31*(2), 32–47.

McLeman, R., & Smit, B. (2006). Vulnerability to climate change hazards and risks: Crop and flood insurance. *The Canadian Geographer/Le Géographe canadien, 50*(2), 217–226.

McLynn, F. (2013). *Crime and punishment in eighteenth century England.* New York: Routledge.

McMahon, S. D., Martinez, A., Espelage, D., Rose, C., Reddy, L. A., Lane, K., & Brown, V. (2014). Violence directed against teachers: Results from a national survey. *Psychology in the Schools, 51*(7), 753–766.

McMillan, R. (2010a, December). CIO gets six years for embezzlement scheme. *IDG News Service.*

McMillan, R. (2010b, September 21). Was Stuxnet built to attack Iran's nuclear program? PC World. Retrieved from http://www.pcworld.com/article/205827/was_stuxnet_built_to_attack_irans_nuclear_program.html

McNeill, J. B. (2010). Air Cargo Security: How to keep Americans secure without harming the economy. *Heritage Foundation Backgrounder* (2422).

Measuring up. (2011, March). *CSO: Business Risk Leadership, 10*(2), 26–33.

Meese, E., & Ortmeier, P. J. (2004). *Leadership, ethics, and policing: Challenges for the 21st century.* Upper Saddle River, NJ: Prentice Hall.

Mellado, D., Fernández-Medina, E., & Piattini, M. (2007). A common criteria based security requirements engineering process for the development of secure information systems. *Computer Standards & Interfaces, 29*(2), 244–253.

Mendlow, G. (2011). Is tort law a form of institutionalized revenge? *Florida State University Law Review, 39*(1), 129–134.

Menefee, S. P., & Mejia, M. Q. (2012). A "rutter for piracy" in 2012. *WMU Journal of Maritime Affairs, 11*(1), 1–13.

Menegazzi, C. (2006). ICOM activities for the protection of museums in emergency situations. In *Collection Management Seminar on Museums and Private Collections* (pp. 45–65).

Merkow, M. S., & Breithaupt, J. (2014). *Information security: Principles and practices.* Pearson Education.

Merriam-Webster Dictionary. (2015). Available from http://www.merriam-webster.com

Merton, R. K. (1938). Social structure and anomie. *American Sociological Review, 3,* 672–682.

Merton, R. K. (1968). Social Theory and Social Structure. Published by Simon and Schuster.

Messner, S. F., & Rosenfeld, R. (2012). *Crime and the American Dream.* Published by Cengage Learning.

Mexico security memo. (2011, January 10). Retrieved from https://www.stratfor.com/analysis/mexico-security-memo-jan-10-2011

Meyer, P. J., & Seelke, C. R. (2011, March). *Central America regional security initiative: Background and policy issues for congress.* Washington, DC: Congressional Research Service, Library of Congress.

Meyer, S. (2002). Rough manhood: The aggressive and confrontational shop culture of U.S. auto workers during World War II. *Journal of Social History, 36*(1), 125–147.

Meyersa, M., & Millsb, J. E. (2007). *Are biometric technologies the wave of the future in tourism and hospitality?* (Vol. 7, pp. 47907–52086). CERIAS Tech Report 2005.

Michel, R. (2000, September). Learning curve: Access control ensures a safe educational facility. *Security Products, 4*(9), 30–32, 34.

Michel, S., Mendes, M., de Ruiter, J. C., Koomen, G. C., & Schwaninger, A. (2014). Increasing X-ray image interpretation competency of cargo security screeners. *International Journal of Industrial Ergonomics, 44*(4), 551–560.

Middleton, J. F. (1983). Developments in flame detectors. *Fire Safety Journal, 6*(3), 175–182.

Miller, A. Y., Miller, N. V., & Davidenko, L. M. (2015). Formation of integrated industrial companies under current conditions. *Asian Social Science, 11*(19), 70–81.

Miller, D. S. (2007). Returning home and uncertainty in the local newspaper: Risk narratives and policy decisions in the immediate aftermath of Hurricane Katrina. *Journal of Public Management & Social Policy, 13*(2), 79–96.

Miller, D. S. (2015). Off Duty, off the wall, but not off the hook: Section 1983 liability for the private misconduct of public officials. *Akron Law Review, 30*(3), 1–69.

Miller, L. (2003, May 3). U.S. to check background of truckers who haul hazardous goods. *San Diego Union Tribune,* p. A7.

Millwee, S. (2000, February). You have not because you ask not: Cost effective screening that works. *Security Technology & Design, 10*(2), 12–14, 16.

Mintzberg, H. (1973). *The nature of managerial work.* New York: Harper & Row.

Mintzberg, H. (1989). *Mintzberg on management.* New York: Free Press.

Mishra, B. K., & Prasad, A. (2006). Minimizing retail shrinkage due to employee theft. *International Journal of Retail & Distribution Management, 34*(11), 817–832.

Miskin, V., & Gmelch, W. (1985, May). Quality leadership for quality teams. *Training and Development Journal, 39*(5), 122–129.

Modeling and Simulation for Emergency Response: Workshop Report, Standards, and Tools, Copyright © 2003. Published by NTIS - National Technical Information Service.

Mohamed Shaluf, I. (2007). An overview on the technological disasters. *Disaster Prevention and Management: An International Journal, 16*(3), 380–390.

Mokgoabone, K. (2014, August 8). Debswana, BMWU brace for Scannex war. *Sunday Standard*. Retrieved from http://www.sundaystandard.info/debswana-bmwu-brace-scannex-war

Moore, R. (2011). *Cybercrime*. Cincinnati, OH: Anderson Publishing.

Moran, C. (2011, February 6). Agency behind in checking for corrupt border agents. *San Diego Union Tribune*, pp. A1, A2.

Moran, M. (2007, August). What are you worth? *Security Management, 51*(8), 66–68, 70–73.

Moran, M. (2010, August). Pay for performance. *Security Management, 54*(8), 86, 88, 90, 92.

Moran, R. T., Abramson, N. R., & Moran, S. V. (2014). *Managing cultural differences*. Routledge.

More, H. W., Vito, G. F., & Walsh, W. F. (2012). *Organizational behavior and management in law enforcement* (3rd ed.). Upper Saddle River, NJ: Pearson Prentice Hall.

Morris, J. G., & Showalter, M. J. (1983). Simple approaches to shift, days-off and tour scheduling problems. *Management Science, 29*(8), 942–950.

Morris, W. A. (1968). *The Medieval English Sheriff to 1300*, (Vol. 131). New York: Manchester University Press.

Morrison, A. D. (2014, Summer). Misconstruing notice in EEOC administrative processing & conciliation. *Nevada Law Journal, 14*, 785–805.

Mosley, D. C., Megginson, L. C., & Pietri, P. H. (2005). *Supervisory management: The art of inspiring, empowering and developing people*. Belmont, CA: South-Western/Thomson Learning.

Moteff, J. (2005, February). *Risk management and critical infrastructure protection: Assessing, integrating, and managing threats, vulnerabilities and consequences*. Library of Congress. Washington DC: Congressional Research Service.

Mowen, A. J., Vogelsong, H. G., & Graefe, A. R. (2003). Perceived crowding and its relationship to crowd management practices at park and recreation events. *Event Management, 8*(2), 63–72.

Mowery, K., Wustrow, E., Wypych, T., Singleton, C., Comfort, C., Rescorla, E., & Shacham, H. (2014, August). Security analysis of a full-body scanner. In *23rd USENIX Security Symposium (USENIX Security 14)*.

Muggah, R., & Aguirre, K. (2013, October). Mapping citizen security interventions in Latin America: Reviewing the evidence. *NOREF Report*. Available at http://igarape.org.br/wp-content/uploads/2013/10/265_91204_NOREF_Report_Muggah-Aguirre_web1.pdf

Mukherjee, A. S. (2008). *The spider's strategy: Creating networks to avert crisis, create change and really get ahead*. Upper Saddle River, NJ: Pearson.

Mullins, K. (2012, Fall). The Bank Protection Act—What management should know. *The Carolina Banker*, 37–38.

Murray, T. (2006). Comments on the challenges for policing in the 21st century: A global assessment. *Police Practice and Research, 7*(5), 375–377.

Murray-Tuite, P. (2007). Optimizing protective measures with respect to multiple hazards. *Transportation Research Record: Journal of the Transportation Research Board, 2022*, 29–38.

Muschert, G. W., & Peguero, A. A. (2010). The Columbine effect and school anti-violence policy. *Research in Social Problems and Public Policy, 17*, 117–148.

Myrna, J. W. (2012). A rolling stone gathers no moss: prevent your strategic plan from stagnating. *Business Strategy Series, 13*(3), 136–142.

Myyry, L., Siponen, M., Pahnila, S., Vartiainen, T., & Vance, A. (2009). What levels of moral reasoning and values explain adherence to information security rules & quest; an empirical study. *European Journal of Information Systems, 18*(2), 126–139.

Nakayachi, K. (1998). How do people evaluate risk reduction when they are told zero risk is impossible? *Risk Analysis, 18*(3), 235–242.

Nalla, M. K., & Crichlow, V. J, (2014). Have the standards for private security guards become more stringent in the post 9/11 era? An assessment of security guard regulations in the US from 1982 to 2010? *Security Journal*, 1–15.

Napolitano warns police chiefs of homegrown terror threat. (2010, October 26). SecurityInfoWatch.com

Napolitano, J. (2010). *Quadrennial homeland security review report: A strategic framework for a secure homeland*. Washington, DC: Department of Homeland Security.

Napps, C., & Enders, W. (2015). A regional investigation of the interrelationships between domestic and transnational terrorism: A time series analysis. *Defence and Peace Economics, 26*(2), 133–151.

Nason, R. R. (2007, April). Ready for anything? *Security Technology & Design, 17*(4), 46–49.

National Advisory Commission on Criminal Justice Standards and Goals. (1976). *Task force report: Private security*. Washington, DC: U.S. Government Printing Office.

National Commission on Terrorist Attacks Upon the United States. (2004). *The 9/11 Commission report*. (Online). Available from http://www.9-11commission.gov

National Defense Authorization Act for Fiscal Year 2008, Pub. L. No 110–181. (2008, January 28).

National Fire Protection Agency. (2015b). *Ionization vs. photoelectric*. Retrieved from http://www.nfpa.org/safety-information/for-consumers/fire-and-safety-equipment/smoke-alarms/ionization-vs-photoelectric

National Fire Protection Association. (2007). *NFPA 72 national fire alarm code*. Quincy, MA: National Fire Protection Association.

National incident management system. Published by U.S Department of Homeland Security, © 2008.

National Fire Protection Association. (2008). *NFPA fire protection handbook*. Quincy, MA: National Fire Protection Association.

National Indian Gaming Commission. (2007). *Minimum internal control standards*. (Online). Available from http://www.indiangaming.org/cgi-bin/store4/commerce.cgi

National Institute of Standards and Technology.

National Intelligence Council. (2006, April). Declassified key judgements of the National Intelligence estimate trends in global terrorism: Implications for the United States. Retrieved from http://www.dni.gov/files/documents/Special%20Report_Global%20Terrorism%20NIE%20Key%20Judgments.pdf

National Intelligence Council. (2007, July). National intelligence estimate: The terrorist threat to the U.S. Homeland. (Online). Available from http://www.dni.gov/press_releases/20070717_release.pdf

National Retail Federation. (2007). *LERPnet*. (Online). Available from http://www.nrf.com/lerpnet/press.htm

National Retail Federation. (2014). NRF 2014—Organized retail crime survey. Retrieved from https://nrf.com/advocacy/policy-agenda/organized-retail-crime

National Retail Security Survey. (2015). Retrieved from https://nrf.com/resources/retail-library/national-retail-security-survey-2015

NATO Shipping Center. (2015). *Group transits through the IRTC*. Retrieved from www.shipping.natio.int/operations/OS/Pages/GroupTransit.aspx

Nemeth, C. (2011). *Private security and the law* (4th ed.). Boston: Elsevier.

Nemeth, C. P. (2004). *Criminal law*. Upper Saddle River, NJ: Prentice Hall.

Nemeth, C. P. (2005). *Private security and the law* (3rd ed.). Boston, MA: Elsevier.

Nichter, D. A. (2000, September). The house rules. *Security Management, 44*(9), 74–82, 84–86, 88.

NIMS. Frequently asked questions. (2015). Retrieved from https://www.fema.gov/pdf/emergency/nims/nimsfaqs.pdf

Nixon, W. B. (2007, January). Check mate. *Security Products, 11*(1), 56–59.

Nixon, W. B., & Kerr, K. (2011). *Background screening and investigations: Managing hiring risk from the HR and security perspectives*. Boston: Elsevier.

Nocella, H. N. (2000, December). Clipping coupon fraud. *Security Management, 44*(12), 40–42, 44, 46, 48.

Nolan, C. (2013). The Rubik's Cube of cargo security. *The Brief, 42*(3), 58–62.

Noonan, J. H., & Vavra, M. C. (2007). *Crime in schools and colleges*. Washington, DC: Federal Bureau of Investigation.

Norman, J. (2012). *Fire Officer's handbook of tactics*. PennWell Corporation.

Northouse, P. G. (2010). *Leadership: Theory and practice* (5th ed.). Thousand Oaks, CA: Sage Publications.

Northwood, J. (2011). Assaults and violent acts in the private retail trade sector, 2003–2008. *Monthly Labor Review*. Washington, DC: Bureau of Labor Statistics.

Nsouli, S. M., & Schaechter, A. (2002). Challenges of the "e-banking revolution." *Finance and Development, 39*(3), 48–51.

Nunes-Vaz, R., & Lord, S. (2014). Designing physical security for complex infrastructures. *International Journal of Critical Infrastructure Protection, 7*(3), 178–192.

Nye, D. E. (1997, Fall). Shaping communication networks: Telegraph, telephone, computer. *Social Research, 64*(3), 1067–1091.

Nystedt, F. (2003). Deaths in residential fires: An analysis of appropriate fire safety measures. Lund, Sweden: Department of Fire Safety Engineering. Retrieved from http://lup.lub.lu.se/luur/download?func=downloadFile&recordOld=642092&fileOld=642100

Nysten-Haarala, S., Klyuchnikova, E., & Helenius, H. (2015). Law and self-regulation: Substitutes or complements in gaining social acceptance? *Resources Policy, 45*, 52–64.

O'Connor, A. (2011, February 10). Holding flowers and gun, Queens man kills his ex-wife and, later, himself. *New York Times*.

Occupational Safety and Health Administration. (2015). *Guidelines for preventing workplace violence for healthcare and social service workers*. Washington, DC: Author.

Occupational Safety and Health Administration. (2016). Portable fire extinguishers. Retrieved from https://www.osha.gov/SLTC/etools/evacuation/portable_about.html

Occupational violence. (2015). Retrieved from http://www.cdc.gov/niosh/topics/violence/

Oceans Beyond Piracy. (2015). *Introduction to private maritime security companies (PMSCs)*. Retrieved from http://oceansbeyondpiracy.org/

O'Connell, P. E. (2008). The chess master's game: A model for incorporating local police agencies in the fight against global terrorism. *Policing: An International Journal of Police Strategies & Management, 31*(3), 456–465.

Oliver, W. M. (2007). *Homeland security for policing*. Upper Saddle River, NJ: Pearson Prentice Hall.

Olympic security estimated to cost $900M. (2009, February 19). CBC News. (Online). Available from http://www.cbc.ca/news/canada/british-columbia/story/2009/02/19/bc-olympics-cost-colin-hansen.html

Online access with a fingerprint. (2010, December 15). *Security Management Weekly*.

Operational Guidelines for Industrial Security. Published by Siemens AG, © 2013.

Opler, D. (2002). Monkey business in union square: A cultural analysis of the Klein's-Ohrbach's strikes of 1934–1935. *Journal of Social History, 36*(1), 149–164.

OPSEC Professionals Society. (2007). *About OPSEC*. (Online). Available from http://www.opsecsociety.org/about.htm

Organized retail crime. (2015). Available from https://nrf.com/advocacy/policy-agenda/organized-retail-crime

Orlando gunman appears to have been "homegrown extremist." (2016, June 14). Chicago Tribute. Retrieved from http://www.chicagotribune.com/news/nation-world/ct-orlando-nightclub-shooting-20160613-story.html

Orphan, V. J., Muenchau, E., Gormley, J., & Richardson, R. (2005). Advanced γ ray technology for scanning cargo containers. *Applied Radiation and Isotopes, 63*(5), 723–732.

Ortmeier, P. J. (1996, July). Adding class to security. *Security Management, 40*(7), 99–101.

Ortmeier, P. J. (1997, October). Leadership for community policing: Identifying essential officer competencies. *The Police Chief, 64*(10), 88–91, 93.

Ortmeier, P. J. (1999). *Public safety and security administration*. Woburn, MA: Butterworth-Heinemann.

Ortmeier, P. J. (2002). *Policing the community: A guide for patrol operations*. Upper Saddle River, NJ: Prentice Hall.

Ortmeier, P. J. (2003, February). Ethical leadership: Every officer's responsibility. *Law Enforcement Executive Forum, 3*(1), 1–9.

Ortmeier, P. J. (2006). *Introduction to law enforcement and criminal justice* (2nd ed.). Upper Saddle River, NJ: Pearson Prentice Hall.

Ortmeier, P. J., & Davis, J. (2012). *Police administration: A leadership approach*. New York: McGraw-Hill.

Ortmeier, P. J., & Meese, E., III. (2010). *Leadership, ethics, and policing: Challenges for the 21st century* (2nd ed.). Upper Saddle River, NJ: Pearson Prentice Hall.

Orton, A. (1984). Leadership: New thoughts on an old problem. *Training, 21*(28), 31–33.

Ouchi, W. (1981). *Theory Z: How American business can meet the Japanese challenge*. Reading, MA: Addison-Wesley.

Our Mission. (n.d.). Retrieved from dhs.gov

Our operations. (2016). Retrieved from http://www.debswana.com/Pages/default.aspx

Paillé, P., Grima, F., & Bernardeau, D. (2013). When subordinates feel supported by managers: investigating the relationships between support, trust, commitment and outcomes. *International Review of Administrative Sciences, 79*(4), 681–700.

Paine, L. S. (1991, Summer). Trade secrets and the justification of intellectual property. A comment on Hettinger. *Philosophy & Public Affairs, 20*(3), 247–263.

Panigrahy, S. K., Jena, S. K., & Turuk, A. K. (2011, February). Security in Bluetooth, RFID and wireless sensor networks. In *proceedings of the 2011 International Conference on communication, computing & security* (pp. 628–633). ACM.

Papi, V. (1994, February). Planning before disaster strikes. *Security Concepts*, pp. 6, 19.

Paraskevas, A. (2013). Aligning strategy to threat: A baseline anti-terrorism strategy for hotels. *International Journal of Contemporary Hospitality Management, 25*(1), 140–162.

Parfomak, P. W. (2012). Energy storage for power grids and electric transportation: A technology assessment. *Congressional Research Service, 42455*.

Parmelee, P. A., & Lawton, M. P. (1990). The design of special environments for the aged. *Handbook of the psychology of aging* (3rd ed.) (pp. 464–488).

Pastor, J. F. (2007). *Security law and methods*. Boston: Elsevier.

Patey, L. A. (2006, April). *Understanding multinational corporations in war-torn societies: Sudan in focus*. Copenhagen: Danish Institute for International Studies.

Patrick J. Ortmeier, Johnson, Introduction to Security: Operations and Management, 5e, © 2018, Pearson Education, Inc., New York, NY.

Patterson, H. M. (2009). *Privatizing peace: A corporate adjunct to United Nations peacekeeping and humanitarian operations*. New York: Palgrave Macmillan.

Payne, T. (2008). *Practical guide to clinical computer systems: Design, operations, and infrastructure*. San Diego, CA: Elsevier.

Payton, G. T., & Amaral, M. (2004). *Patrol operations and enforcement tactics* (11th ed.). San Jose, CA: Criminal Justice Services.

Peak, K. J., & Glensor, R. W. (2008). *Community policing and problem solving: Strategies and practices* (5th ed.). Upper Saddle River, NJ: Pearson Prentice Hall.

Peck, D. H. (1999, October). When police walk the security beat. *Security Management, 43*(10), 38–40, 42, 45.

Peña, K. (2014). Accountability for private security contractor drone operators on the US-Mexico Border: Applying lessons learned from the Middle East. *Public Contract Law Journal, 44*(1), 137–156.

Percy, S., & Shortland, A. (2013). The business of piracy in Somalia. *Journal of Strategic Studies, 36*(4), 541–578.

Perdikaris, J. (2014). *Physical security and environmental protection.* Boca Raton: CRC Press.

Perrow, C. (1984). *Normal accidents: Living with high-risk technologies.* New York: Basic Books Inc.

Perry, J. L. (Ed.). (1996). *Handbook of public administration* (2nd ed.). San Francisco, CA: Jossey-Bass.

Perry, R. W., & Quarantelli, E. L. (2004). *What is a disaster? New answers to old questions.* Philadelphia, PA: Xlibris Press.

Personnel security clearances: full development and implementation of metrics needed to measure quality of process. (2013, October). Washington, DC: Governmental Accounting Office.

Peters, T. (1987). *Thriving on chaos.* New York: Knopf.

Petersen, W. H., & Petersen, T. R. (1993). Countering the threat of kidnapping. *Risk Management, 40*(5), 57.

Phares, W. (2014). *Future jihad: Terrorist strategies against America.* Macmillan.

Phelan, D. (2014). A summary of State Regulators' responsibilities regarding cybersecurity issues. Washington, DC: National Regulatory Research Institute.

Physical Security. Published by Department of the Army, © 2001.

Pierot, J. P. (2015, November 25). Win the war? No, put an end to it. *Guardian (Sydney),* (1712), 8.

Pieterse, J. N. (2015). *Globalization and culture: Global mélange.* Lahnam: Rowman & Littlefield.

Pindur, W., Rogers, S. E., & Suk Kim, P. (1995). The history of management: A global perspective. *Journal of Management History, 1*(1), 59–77.

Pinheiro, A., & Anderson, D. O. (2012). Improving your workplace violence prevention program. *Occupational Health & Safety, 81*(3), 40–41.

Pinto, A. C., & Magpili, L. (2015). *Operational risk management.* Momentum Press.

Pinto, J. (2014). Expanding the content domain of workplace aggression: A three-level aggressor-target taxonomy. *International Journal of Management Reviews, 16*(3), 290–313.

Pires, S. F., Guerette, R. T., & Stubbert, C. H. (2014). The crime triangle of kidnapping for ransom incidents in Colombia, South America: A 'litmus' test for situational crime prevention. *British Journal of Criminology, 54*(5), 784–808.

Pivateau, G. T. (2014). Enforcement of noncompetition agreements: Protecting public interests through an entrepreneurial approach. *St. Mary's Law Journal, 46,* 483–520.

Pizam, A. (2010). Hotels as tempting targets for terrorism attacks. *International Journal of Hospitality Management, 29*(1), 1–8.

Plump, C. M., & Ketchen, D. J. (2013). Paving a road to well? How the legal pitfalls of wellness programs can harm organizational performance. *Business Horizons, 56*(3), 261–269.

Polelle, M. (2000, January–February). Business resumption planning. *General Practice, Solo & Small Firm Division Magazine, 17*(1), 52–56.

Police identify army veteran as Wisconsin temple shooting gunman. Retrieved from http://www.cnn.com/2012/08/06/us/wisconsin-temple-shooting/

Political topographies of private security in Sub-Saharan Africa Copyright © 1975. Published by Academia.edu.

Ponkshe, S. (2015). Municipal wildfire management in California: A local response to global climate change. *Pace Environmental Law Review, 32,* 600.

Popper, A. F. (2011). In defense of deterrence. *Albany Law Review, 75,* 181–203.

Powell, J. W. (1981). *Campus security and law enforcement.* Boston: Butterworth-Heinemann.

Poyner, B. (2013). *Crime-free housing in the 21st century.* Routledge.

Prahlow, J. (2010). Burns and fire-related deaths. In *Forensic pathology for police, death investigators, attorneys, and forensic scientists* (pp. 481–500). Humana Press.

Prendergast, J. (1995). Oklahoma City aftermath. *Civil Engineering, 65*(10), 42–45.

Prenzler, T. (2011). Strike force Piccadilly and ATM security: A follow-up study. *Policing, 5*(3), 236–247.

President's Commission on Law Enforcement and Administration of Justice. (1967). *Task force report: Police.* Washington, DC: U.S. Government Printing Office.

Price, J. L. (1977). *The study of turnover.* Ames, IA: Iowa State University Press.

Pristrom, S., Yang, Z., Wang, J., Zhang, D., & Yan, X. (2015, June). Major issues associated with maritime security and piracy study. In *Transportation information and safety (ICTIS), 2015 International Conference* (pp. 588–594). IEEE.

Privacy/Data Protection Project. (2015). Retrieved from http://privacy.med.miami.edu/glossary/xd_iso_comm_ops_mgmt.htm

Private Security Services Industry viewsto the European Commission public consultation on the Future of DG HOME Policies. Copyright © 2013. Published by Confederation of European Security Services (COESS).

Private security: Facts & figures. (2015). Retrieved from http://www.tjoeten.be/pdf/CoESS/Croatia.pdf

Private Security Report of the Task Force on Private Security Published by ANON, published by National Criminal Justice Reference Service. © 1976.

Proceedings of The BUHU 9th International Postgraduate Research Conference 2009, Copyright © 2009. Published by University of Salford.

Professional Growth Facilitators. (2000). *Preparation for a violent emergency ... It's not a choice.* San Clemente, CA: Professional Growth Facilitators.

Project Griffin Counter-Terrorism Workshops. Copyright © 2015. Published by FGH Securities Ltd.

Project Kraken. (2015). Retrieved from http://www.nationalcrimeagency.gov.uk/campaigns/project-kraken

Project Pegasus. (2015). Retrieved from http://www.northyorkshire.police.uk/pegasus

Project Servator. (2015). Retrieved from https://www.cityoflondon.police.uk/community-policing/project-servator/Pages/Project-Servator.aspx

Purpura, P. P. (2003). *The security handbook* (2nd ed.). Boston, MA: Butterworth-Heinemann.

Pyrooz, D. C., Decker, S. H., & Moule, R. K. (2015). Criminal and routine activities in online settings: Gangs, offenders, and the Internet. *Justice Quarterly, 32*(3), 471–499.

Rabasa, A. (2009). *The lessons of Mumbai* (Vol. 249). Rand Corporation.

Radvanovsky, R., & Brodsky, J. (Eds.). (2013). *Handbook of SCADA/control systems security.* CRC Press.

Rae, J. D. (2014). Public policy, privacy, and drone technology. In *Analyzing the drone debates: Targeted killing, remote warfare, and military technology* (pp. 98–119). Palgrave Macmillan.

Rajalingam, M., Alomari, S. A., & Sumari, P. (2012). Prevention of phishing attacks based on discriminative key point features of webpages. *International Journal of Computer Science and Security (IJCSS), 6*(1), 1.

Rajendran, L., & Rathinasabapathy, G. (2007, July). Role of electronic surveillance and security systems in academic libraries. In *Information to Knowledge: Technology and Professionals. Proceedings of the conference on recent advances in information science and technology (READIT 2007), MALA & IGCAR, Kalpakkam* (pp. 111–117).

Ram, Y. (2015). Hostility or hospitality? A review on violence, bullying and sexual harassment in the tourism and hospitality industry. *Current Issues in Tourism* (ahead-of-print), 1–15.

Ramdeyal, A., & Eloff, M. M. (2004). A general methodology for the development of an effective information security policy. In *ISSA* (pp. 1–10).

Ramsay, J. D. (2013). The case to accredit Homeland Security Programs: Why outcomes-based accreditation makes sense. *Journal of Homeland Security Education, 2*(13), 19–31.

Rankl, W., & Effing, W. (2010). Smart card security. *Smart card handbook* (4th ed.) (pp. 667–734).

Rashid, F. Y. (2011, March 3). DHS needs to change rules to recruit hackers into U.S. security agencies. *eWeek.*

Rawlings, P. (2002). *Policing: A short history.* Devon: Willan Publishing.

Reamer, F. G. (1995). Malpractice claims against social workers: First facts. *Social Work, 40*(5), 595–601.

Reason, J. (1990). *Human error.* New York: Cambridge University Press.

Reaves, B. A. (2015, January). Campus Law Enforcement, 2011–12. Washington, DC: Bureau of Justice Statistics.

Recommendations for workplace violence prevention programs in late night retail establishments. (2009). Washington, DC: U.S. Department of Labor, Occupational Safety and Health Administration.

Recruitment, Job Choice, and Post-Hire Consequences: A Call For New Research Directions Copyright © 1990. Published by Cornell University.

Reese, S. (2010). *Federal building and facility security.* DIANE Publishing.

Reese, S. (2014, June 17). *Federal building and facility security: Frequently asked questions* (pp. 7–5700). Washington, DC: Congressional Research Service.

Reid, R. N. (2005). *Facility manager's guide to security: Protecting your assets.* New York: The Fairmont Press, Inc.

Remennikov, A., & Carolan, D. (2005). Blast effects and vulnerability of building structures from terrorist attack. *Australian Journal of Structural Engineering, 7*(1), 1–12.

Reneke, P. A. (2013). *Towards smart fire panels.* U.S. Department of Commerce, National Institute of Standards and Technology.

Reprinted with permission from the NFPA web site http://www.nfpa.org/press-room/reporters-guide-to-fire-and-nfpa/all-about-fire, copyright © 2016 NFPA.

Ricks, T. A., Tillet, B. G., & Van Meter, C. W. (1988). *Principles of security.* Cincinnati: Anderson.

Ritchie, M. (2015). Feeling for the State: Affective labor and anti-terrorism training in U.S. Hotels. *Communication and Critical/Cultural Studies, 12*(2), 179–197.

Robbins, S. P., & Coulter, M. (2009). *Management* (2nd ed.). Upper Saddle River, NJ: Prentice Hall.

Robertson, J. C. (2010). *Introduction to fire prevention.* Upper Saddle River, NJ: Prentice Hall.

Robinson, S. L., & Bennett, R. J. (1995). A typology of deviant workplace behaviors: A multi-dimensional scaling study. *Academy of Management Journal, 38*(2), 555–572.

Rogers, C. (2008). A security risk management approach to the measurement of crime in a private security context. In *Acta Criminologica: CRIMSA Conference: Special Edition 3* (pp. 150–166). Sabinet Online.

Rogers, M. K. (2011). The psyche of cybercriminals: A psycho-social perspective. In *Cybercrimes: A multidisciplinary analysis* (pp. 217–235). Berlin, Heidelberg: Springer.

Romanski v. Detroit Entertainment, LLC, 265 F. Supp. 2d 835 (E.D. Mich. 2003).

Roper, C. A. (1997). *Physical security and the inspection process.* Boson: Butterworth Heinemann.

Roper, C.A. (1999). *Risk management for security professionals.* Boston: Butterworth-Heinemann.

Rosenbach, E. B., Peritz, A., & LeBeau, H. (2009). *Confrontation or collaboration? Congress and the intelligence community.* Harvard Kennedy School, Belfer Center for Science and International Affairs.

Rothwell, W. J., Hohne, C. K., & King, S. B. (2012). *Human performance improvement.* Routledge.

Rudd, D., Mills, R., & Litzinger, P. (2008). The functions of implementation. *Economics and Organization of Enterprise, 2*(2), 21–28.

Rugala, E. A., & Isaacs, A. R. (Eds.). (2003). *Workplace violence: Issues in response.* Critical Incident Response Group, National Center for the Analysis of Violent Crime, FBI Academy.

Russell, D. L., & Arlow, P. (2015). *Industrial security: Managing security in the 21st Century.* New Jersey: John Wiley & Sons.

Russell, E. (2008). Writing on the wall: The form, function and meaning of tagging. *Journal of Occupational Science, 15*(2), 87–97.

Rutledge, D. (2000). *California criminal procedure* (4th ed.). Incline Village, NV: Copperhouse Publishing.

Saad, S., & Arakaki, R. (2014, May). An event processing architecture for operational risk management in an industrial environment. In *Proceedings of the 8th ACM International Conference on Distributed Event-Based Systems* (pp. 213–224). ACM.

Sadgrove, K. (2015). *The complete guide to business risk management* (3rd ed.). Burlington, VT: Gower.

Saeed, I. A., Selamat, A., Abuagoub, A. M. A., & Abdulaziz, S. B. (2013). A survey on malware and malware detection systems. *Analysis, 3*(10), 13–17.

Safety and Health Topics. Published by U.S. Department of Labor, © 2015.

Saket, R. K., Sagar, B. B., & Singh, G. (2012). ATM reliability and risk assessment issues based on fraud, security and safety. *International Journal of Computer Aided Engineering and Technology, 4*(3), 279–293.

Salant, J. D. (2002, February 18). Federal government takes over airport security. *San Diego Union Tribune*, pp. A1, A14.

Samaha, J. (2013). *Criminal law* (11th ed.). Boston, MA: Cengage.

San Luis, E., Tyska, L. A., & Fennelly, L. J. (1994). *Office and office building security.* Gulf Professional Publishing.

Sandhu, R. S., & Samarati, P. (1994). Access control: Principle and practice. *Communications Magazine, IEEE, 32*(9), 40–48.

Saranya, C., Pavithira, L., Premsai, N., Lavanya, H., & Govindarajan, R. (2015, February). Recent trends of drones in the field of defense. *International Journal of Electrical and Appliances, 1*(1), 47–55.

Sarre, R. (2012). Public-private cooperation in policing crime and terrorism in Australia. In S. C. Taylor, D. J. Torpy & D. Das (Eds.). *Policing global movement: Tourism, migration, human trafficking, and terrorism.* New York: CRC Press/Taylor and Francis.

Scahill, J. (2011). *Blackwater: The rise of the world's most powerful mercenary army.* Profile Books.

Scalet, S. D. (2006, June). The salary reality. *CSO, 5*(6), 42–43, 45.

Scalet, S. D. (2007, June). Vulnerability assessment's big picture. *CSO, 6*(6), 32–36.

Schat, A. C. H., & Kelloway, E. K. (2005). Workplace violence. In J. Barling, E. K. Kelloway, & M. Frone (Eds.), *Handbook of work stress* (pp. 189–218). Thousand Oaks, CA: Sage.

Schettler, C. (1943). Relation of city-size to economic services. *American Sociological Review, 8*(1), 60–62.

Schildknecht, D. (2015, May 4). Robust UN peacekeeping and private military and security companies. Retrieved from http://www.hscentre.org/security-and-defence/robust-un-peacekeeping-private-military-security-companies/

Schimmel, K. S. (2006). Deep play: Sports mega-events and urban social conditions in the USA. *The Sociological Review, 54*(s2), 160–174.

Schmalleger, F. (2010). *Criminal justice: A brief introduction* (8th ed.). Upper Saddle River, NJ: Pearson, Prentice Hall.

Schneider, G. (2013). The private security industry: A comparison of recent Australian and South African priorities. *Acta Criminologica, 26*(2), 103–123.

Schneider, S. (2014). *Crime prevention: Theory and practice.* Boca Raton, FL: CRC Press.

Schoenberg, R. (2005). Security of healthcare information systems. In *Consumer health informatics* (pp. 162–187). New York: Springer.

Schoenberger, S. (2014, September 6). *Piracy in the South China Sea: Petty theft in Indonesia, kidnapped ships in Malaysia.* Retrieved from http://cimsec.org/piracy-south-china-sea-petty-theft-indonesia-kidnapped-ships-malaysia/12899

Schoepfer, A., & Piquero, N. L. (2006). Exploring white-collar crime and the American dream: A partial test of institutional anomie theory. *Journal of Criminal Justice, 34*(3), 227–235.

School and crime. (2015). 2015 NCVRW Resource guide. Retrieved from http://ovc.ncjrs.gov/ncvrw2015/

Schroll, R. C. (2002). *Industrial fire protection handbook.* Hoboken: CRC Press.

Schumacher, J. (2000, October). How to resolve conflict with proper systems integration. *Security Technology & Design, 10*(10), 36–40, 42–43.

Schweitzer, A. (1980). Countervailing power revisited. *Journal of Economic Issues, 14*(4), 999–1018.

Schweizer, P. (1993). *Friendly spies.* New York: Atlantic.

Screening Partnership Program. (2015). Retrieved from http://www.tsa.gov/for-industry/screening-partnerships

Securitas. (2010). *Top security threats and management issues facing corporate America,* 2010. Retrieved from http://www.pinkerton.com/filebin/images/Interiorpage/2012_Top_Security_Threats.pdf

Securitas. (2015). "About Us." Retrieved from http://www.securitas.com/en/about-us/brief-facts/

Security Beyond the State: Private Security in International Politics, Copyright © 2009. Published by Cambridge University Press.

Security Industry Authority. (2013). *Get licensed. Liverpool. Security Industry Authority.* Retrieved from http://www.sia.homeoffice.gov.uk/Pages/home.aspx

Seigel, M. (2015). Objects of police history. *Journal of American History, 102*(1), 152–161.

Šelih, A., Završnik, A., Aas, K. F., Gorkič, P., & Kanduč, Z. (2012). *Crime and transition in Central and Eastern Europe.* New York: Springer.

Sennewald, C. A. (2003). *Effective security management* (4th ed.). Boston, MA: Butterworth-Heinemann.

Sennewald, C. A., & Christman, J. H. (2011). *Retail crime, security, and loss prevention: An encyclopedic reference.* Butterworth-Heinemann.

Sergevnin, V., & Kovalyov, O. (2013). Policing in Russia. In *Handbook on policing in Central and Eastern Europe* (pp. 191–215). New York: Springer.

Shalloo, J. P. (1929). The private police of Pennsylvania. *The ANNALS of the American Academy of Political and Social Science, 146,* 55–62.

Sharifi, E., Mohammadiasl, K., Havasi, M., & Yazdani, A. (2015). Performance analysis of hardware Trojan detection methods. *International Journal of Open Information Technologies, 3*(5), 39–44.

Sharma, N. (2012). Analysis of different vulnerabilities in auto teller machine transactions. *Journal of Global Research in Computer Science, 3*(3), 38–40.

Shearing, C., & Stenning, P. (1981). Modern private security: Its growth and implications. In M. Tonry & N. Mossis (Eds.). *Crime and justice: An annual review of research* (pp. 193–246). Chicago: University of Chicago Press.

Shelton, K. (2009). Using Facebook following tragedies: A lesson for community colleges. *Community & Junior College Libraries, 15*(4), 195–203.

Sherman, M. B., Weston, H. A., Willey, S. L., & Mansfield, N. R. (2014). Risky business: Managing risk in a complex and connected world. *Management & Avenir,* (8), 159–173.

Shifter, M. (2012). *Countering criminal violence in Central America* (No. 64). New York, NY: Council on Foreign Relations.

Shteir, R. (2011). *The steal: A cultural history of shoplifting.* New York: Penguin.

Siegel, L. J. (2010a). *Criminology: The core* (4th ed.). Belmont, CA: Wadsworth.

Siegel, L. J. (2010b). *Criminology: Theories, patterns, and typologies* (10th ed.). Belmont, CA: Wadsworth/Thomson Learning.

Siegel, L. J., & Senna, J. J. (2008). *Essentials of criminal justice* (6th ed.). Belmont, CA: Wadsworth/Thomson Learning.

Sil, R. (2000). The foundations of eclecticism: The epistemological status of agency, culture, and structure in social theory. *Journal of Theoretical Politics, 12*(3), 353–387.

Sime, J. D. (1985). Movement toward the familiar person and place affiliation in a fire entrapment setting. *Environment and Behavior, 17*(6), 697–724.

Simonsen, C. E. (1998). *Private security in America: An introduction.* Upper Saddle River, NJ: Prentice Hall.

Simonsen, C. E., & Spindlove, J. R. (2007). *Terrorism today: The past, the players, the future* (3rd ed.). Upper Saddle River, NJ: Pearson Prentice Hall.

Singer, P. W. (2007). *Can't win with'em, can't go to war without'em: Private military contractors and counterinsurgency.* Washington, DC: Brookings Institution.

Sirmon, D. G., Hitt, M. A., Ireland, R. D., & Gilbert, B. A. (2011). Resource orchestration to create competitive advantage breadth, depth, and life cycle effects. *Journal of Management, 37*(5), 1390–1412.

Slater, P. (2000, April 3). Thefts eat away at office morale. *San Diego Union Tribune,* p. C1.

Slaveski, S., & Bakreski, O. (2014). Security of classified information as part. *Comprehensive approach as" Sine Qua Non" for Critical Infrastructure Protection* (Vol. 39, p. 107).

Slepian, C. G. (2000, November). Security up in the air. *Security Management, 44*(11), 54–56, 58–59.

Smith, C., & Brooks, D. J. (2013). *Security science.* New York: Butterworth-Heinemann.

Smith, K. (2013). *Environmental hazards: Assessing risk and reducing disaster.* New York: Routledge.

Smith, R. (2014, February 5). Assault on California power station raises alarm. *The Wall Street Journal.* Retrieved from www.wsj.com

Smith, S. (2010, August 4). 911 calls reveal horror as US gunman ran down victims. *AFP.* (Online). Available from http://www.google.com/hostednews/afp/article/ALeqM5gsJKTGz2jPBoFjkLllrnUc41NylA

Social media competitive analysis and text mining: A case study in the pizza industry. Published by Elsevier Ltd, © 2013.

Sofield, L., & Salmond, S. W. (2003). Workplace violence: A focus on verbal abuse and intent to leave the organization. *Orthopedic Nursing, 22*(4), 274–283.

Sojamo, S., & Larson, E. A. (2012). Investigating food and agribusiness corporations as global water security, management and governance agents: The case of Nestlé, Bunge and Cargill. *Water Alternatives, 5*(3), 619–635.

Solmaz, G., & Turgut, D. (2013, December). Theme park mobility in disaster scenarios. In *Global Communications Conference (GLOBECOM), 2013 IEEE* (pp. 377–382). IEEE.

Solomon, R. C. (1996). *A handbook for ethics*. Fort Worth, TX: Harcourt Brace College Publishers.

Solomons, I. (2015, January 23). Scanners to detect diamond theft at Debswana mines. *Mining Weekly*. Retrieved from http://www.miningweekly.com/article/hi-tech-scanners-to-expose-diamond-theft-2015-01-23/rep_id:3650

Sommer, C. J. (2003, March). Survival of the fittest: Corporate success is dependent on strategic synergy. *Loss Prevention & Security Journal, 3*(3), 16–17.

Sotlar, A. (2009). Post-conflict private policing: Experiences from several former Yugoslav countries. *Policing: An International Journal of Police Strategies & Management, 32*(3), 489–507.

Southerland, M. D., Merlo, A. V., Robinson, L., Benekos, P. J., & Albanese, J. S. (2007). Ensuring quality in criminal justice education: Academic standards and the reemergence of accreditation. *Journal of Criminal Justice Education, 18*(1), 87–105.

Southerland, R. (2000, June). Protected against the enemy within. *Access Control & Security Systems Integration, 43*(7), 29–30.

Souza-Monteiro, D. M., & Hooker, N. H. (2013). Food safety and traceability. In *US programs affecting food and agricultural marketing* (pp. 249–271). New York: Springer.

Sovacool, B. K., & Cooper, C. J. (2013). *The governance of energy megaprojects: Politics, hubris and energy security*. Cheltenham: Edward Elgar.

Spellman, F. R. (2008). *Food supply protection and homeland security*. Lanham, ND: Government Institutes.

Spherion. (2006). Spherion snapshot survey finds some workers hesitant to "Blow the Whistle" on unethical workplace activities. (Online). Available from http://www.spherion.com/press/releases/2006/blow_the_whistle_snapshot.jsp

Spicer, T. (1999). *An unorthodox soldier*. London: Mainstream Publishing.

Spivey, J. (2001, January). Banks vault into online risk. *Security Management, 45*(1), 132–134, 136, 138.

Srilaya, B., Kumar, L. V., Boggavarapu, L. N. P., & Vaddi, R. S. (2013). *Surveillance using video analytics*. Retrieved from http://searchdl.org/public/book_series/LSCS/6/537.pdf

Srivastava, H., Dwivedi, K., Pankaj, P. K., & Tewari, V. (2013). A formal attack centric framework highlighting expected losses of an information security breach. *International Journal of Computer Applications, 68*(17), 26–31.

Stanford, D. (2007, January). Global partnering related to nuclear materials safeguards and security: A pragmatic approach to international safeguards work. In *The 11th International Conference on environmental remediation and radioactive waste management* (pp. 1347–1356). American Society of Mechanical Engineers.

Starbucks Coffee's Vision Statement & Mission Statement. Copyright © 2015. Published by Panmore Institute.

START. (2015). *Global Terrorism Database*. Retrieved from http://www.start.umd.edu

Stec, A. A., & Hull, T. R. (2010). *Fire toxicity*. Boca Raton, FL: CRC Press.

Steffey, D. L. (2008). Homeland security and transportation risk. *Encyclopaedia of quantitative risk analysis and assessment*.

Stevens, M. (1996). Transferable training and poaching externalities. In A. L. Booth, & D. J. Snower, (Eds.), *Acquiring skills: Market failures, their symptoms and policy responses* (pp. 21–40). Cambridge: Cambridge University Press.

Stewart, J. K. (1985). Public safety and private police. *Public Administration Review, 45*, 758–765.

Stewart, M. (2014, December 12). Ferguson businesses try to rebuild after protests. *The Huffington Post*. Available from http://www.huffingtonpost.com/2014/12/12/ferguson-businesses-protests_n_6309616.html

Stewart, M. G., & Mueller, J. (2014). Cost-benefit analysis of airport security: Are airports too safe? *Journal of Air Transport Management, 35*, 19–28.

Stewart, S. (2012a). Domestic terrorism: A persistent threat in the United States. *Stratford Global Intelligence*.

Stewart, S. (2012b, March 15). A practical guide to situational awareness. *Security Weekly, Stratfor*.

Stokes, D. (2007). Blood for oil? Global capital, counter-insurgency and the dual logic of American energy security. *Review of International Studies, 33*(2), 245–264.

Stone, J., & Merrion, S. (2004). Instant messaging or instant headache? *Queue, 2*(2), 72–80.

Stoner, J. A. F., & Freeman, R. A. (1989). Management 4th editon. Published by Prentice Hall

Strazzari, F., & Tholens, S. (2014). "Tesco for Terrorists" reconsidered: Arms and conflict dynamics in Libya and in the

Sahara-Sahel Region. *European Journal on Criminal Policy and Research, 20*(3), 343–360.

Strizzi, N., & Meis, S. (2001). Challenges facing tourism markets in Latin America and the Caribbean region in the new millennium. *Journal of Travel Research, 40*(2), 183–192.

Strom, K., Berzofsky, M., Shook-Sa, B., Barrick, K., Daye, C., Horstmann, N., & Kinsey, S. (2010). *The private security industry: A review of the definitions, available data sources, and paths moving forward.* Washington DC: US Department of Justice.

Su, J. Z., Kim, A. K., Crampton, G. P., & Liu, Z. (2001). Fire suppression with inert gas agents. *Journal of Fire Protection Engineering, 11*(2), 72–87.

Subramaniam, C. (2004). Human factors influencing fire safety measures. *Disaster Prevention and Management: An International Journal, 13*(2), 110–116.

Sufian, F., & Majid, M. Z. A. (2014). Banks' efficiency and share prices in an emerging market: A DEA window analysis approach. *Oxford Journal: An International Journal of Business & Economics, 1*(1).

Sullivan, H. T., Hakkinen, M. T., & DeBlois, K. (2010). Communicating critical information using mobile phones to populations with special needs. *International Journal of Emergency Management, 7*(1), 6–16.

Sullivan, R. J. (2014). Controlling security risk and fraud in payment systems. *Federal Reserve Bank of Kansas City, Economic Review, 99*(3), 47–78.

Sullivant, J. (2007). *Strategies for protecting national critical infrastructure assets: A focus on problem solving.* Hoboken, NJ: John Wiley & Sons Inc.

Sun Microsystems integrates access control worldwide. (2000, October). *Access Control & Security Systems Integration, 43*(11), 1, 30, 32, 34.

Suomi, K., & Järvinen, R. (2013). Tracing reputation risks in retailing and higher-education services. *Journal of Retailing and Consumer Services, 20*(2), 207–217.

Support Anti-terrorism by Fostering Effective Technologies (SAFETY) Act, 2002 (Public Law 107-296).

Survey finds Londoners ready to tackle the terrorist threat. (2014, November 10). *The security lion.* Retrieved from https://thesecuritylion.wordpress.com/tag/project-servator/

Sury, P., Ritzmann, S., & Schwaninger, A. (2012, October). Initial results of web based blended learning in the field of air cargo security. In *Security Technology (ICCST), 2012 IEEE International Carnahan Conference on* (pp. 274–279). IEEE.

Sutherland, E. (1949). *White-collar crime.* New York: Dryden.

Sveningsson, S., & Alvesson, M. (2003). Managing managerial identities: Organizational fragmentation, discourse and identity struggle. *Human Relations, 56*(10), 1163–1193.

Sweet, K. M. (2006). *Transportation and cargo security: Threats and solutions.* Upper Saddle River, NJ: Pearson Prentice Hall.

Syamsuddin, I., & Hwang, J. (2010). The use of AHP in security policy decision making: An open office calc application. *Journal of Software, 5*(10), 1162–1169.

Sygnatur, E., & Toscano, G. (2000, Spring). Work-related homicides: The facts. *Compensation and Working Conditions, 2,* 3–8.

Talarico, L., Sorensen, K., Reniers, G., & Springael, J. (2016). Pipeline security. In S. Hakim, G. Albert, & Y. Shiftan (Eds.). *Securing transportation systems* (pp. 281–321).

Taneja, S. (2014). Violence in the workplace: A strategic crisis management issue. *Journal of Applied Business and Economics, 16*(1), 32–42.

Tankel, S. (2014). Indian jihadism: The evolving threat. *Studies in Conflict & Terrorism, 37*(7), 567–585.

Tanner-Smith, E. E., & Fisher, B. W. (2016). Visible school security measures and student academic performance, attendance, and postsecondary aspirations. *Journal of Youth and Adolescence,* 1–16.

Tarlow, P. E. (2011). Tourism risk management in an age of terrorism. *Economía Autónoma, 4*(7), 18–30.

Taveau, J. (2012, March). Secondary dust explosions: How to prevent them or mitigate their effects? *Process Safety Progress, 31*(1), 36–50.

Tebogo, T. (2014, July 28). Scannex to secure diamonds. *Botswana Daily News.* Retrieved from http://www.dailynews.gov.bw/news-details.php?nid=13245

Terry, P., & Tholen, M. (2006). Security barrier design. *Practice Periodical on Structural Design and Construction, 11*(2), 105–111.

Testimony. Published by Federal Bureau of Investigation, © 2004.

Testimony on the TSA Behavior Detection and Analysis Program. (2013). Retrieved from https://www.tsa.gov/news/testimony/2013/11/14/testimony-tsa-behavior-detection-and-analysis-program

Testimony. (2015). Retrieved from https://www.fbi.gov/news/testimony/animal-rights-extremism-and-ecoterrorism

The influence of culture, emotions, intangibility, and atmospheric cues on online behavior, Copyright © 2014. Published by Elsevier Inc.

The Loss Prevention Foundation. (2007). Retrieved from http://www.losspreventionfoundation.org/

The Montreux Document. (2008, September). Geneva, Switzerland: ICRC.

The new security company:integration of services and technology responding to changes in customer demand, demography and technology, Copyright

© 2015. Used by permission of Confederation of European Security Services

The Protective Forces at the Department of Energy. (2010). Hearing Before the subcommittee on Strategic Forces of the Committee on Armed Services. Senate, 111, Cong 1.

The USDA handbook on workplace violence prevention and response. (2001, October). Washington, DC: United States Department of Agriculture.

The Working Group on the use of mercenaries as a means of violating human rights and impeding the exercise of the right of peoples to self-determination. Copyright © 2015. Published by Office of the High Commissioner for Human Rights.

Thomas, L. (2001, January). Security measures for the Miami federal courthouse. Security Products, 5(1), 54.

Thomas, R. S., Bishara, N., & Martin, K. J. (2014). An empirical analysis of non-competition clauses and other restrictive post-employment covenants. Vanderbilt Law and Economics Research Paper, (14–11).

Thomason, R. (2000, September). Airport security for the new millennium. Security Technology & Design, 10(9), 52, 54, 56, 60.

Tichy, N., & Ulrich, D. (1984). The leadership challenge—a call for the transformational leader. SMR Forum. Sloan Management Review, 26(1), 59–68.

Tong, J., Wang, X., Wen, H., & Kummer, S. (2010, November). Analysis and comparison of transport chain between China and Austria. In Logistics Engineering and Intelligent Transportation Systems (LEITS), 2010 International Conference on (pp. 1–5). IEEE.

Transnational European Union: Towards a Common Political Space, Copyright © 2005. Published by Routledge.

Transportation Security Administration. (2011). Frequently asked questions. (Online). Available from http://www.tsa.gov/what_we_do/layers/secureflight/faqs.shtm

Trantham, N., & Garcia, A. (2015, July). Reputation dynamics in networks: Application to cyber security of wind farms. Systems Engineering, 18(4), 339–348.

Trevino, L. K., Hartman, L. P., & Brown, M. (2000). Moral person and moral manager: How executives develop a reputation for ethical leadership. California Management Review, 42(4), 128–142.

Trimmer, H. W. (1999). Understanding and servicing alarm systems (3rd ed.). Woburn, MA: Butterworth-Heinemann.

Trotta, R. Prevention: The key to executive protection. Management Review, 77(8), 35–42.

True III, J. M. (2005). Blue eagle at work: Reclaiming democratic rights in the American workplace. Berkeley Journal of Employment & Labor Law, 26(1), 181–204.

TSA chief likely to face lawmakers' questions on pat-downs, body scans. (2010, November 17). CNN.com

TSA expands the use of Explosives Trace Detection technology at airports nationwide. (2010, February 17). Retrieved from https://www.tsa.gov/news/releases/2010/02/17/tsa-expands-use-explosives-trace-detection-technology-airports-nationwide

TSA supports passenger rail systems security. (2015, September 3). Retrieved from https://www.tsa.gov/news/top-stories/2015/09/03/tsa-supports-passenger-rail-systems-security

Tsang, N. K., Lee, L. Y., Wong, A., & Chong, R. (2012). THEMEQUAL—Adapting the SERVQUAL scale to theme park services: A case of Hong Kong Disneyland. Journal of Travel & Tourism Marketing, 29(5), 416–429.

Tseng, H. R., Jan, R. H., & Yang, W. (2007, November). An improved dynamic user authentication scheme for wireless sensor networks. In Global Telecommunications Conference, 2007. GLOBECOM'07. IEEE (pp. 986–990). IEEE.

Tuttle, H. (2015). Kidnap and ransom in the wake of ISIS. Risk Management, 62(1), 8.

Two teens arrested in theft of koalas. (2000, December 29). San Diego Union Tribune, p. A3.

Tyska, L. A., & Fennelly, L. J. (2000). Physical security: 150 things you should know. Boston: Butterworth-Heinemann.

Understanding School Violence. Published by U.S. Department of Health & Human Services, © 2015.

UNDP. (1994). Human Development Report 1994: New Dimensions of Human Security. New York: Oxford University Press.

United Nations. (2015). IMO profile. Retrieved from https://business.un.org/en/entities/13

United Nations Convention Against Transnational Organized Crime. Copyright © 2004. Published by United Nations Publications.

United Nations Office on Drugs and Crime. (2010). Crime and instability: Case studies of transnational threats. Austria: Vienna.

University Health Care provides health, safety and security for patients. (2000, October). Access Control & Security Systems Integration, 43(11), 44.

UN Use of PMSC? It's a Reality, Not a Hypothetical. Copyright © 2012. Published by The Huffington post.

United States Code, 2012 Edition, Title 18—Crimes and Criminal Procedure. Published by United States Government Publishing Office, © 2015.

U.S. Central Intelligence Agency. (2007). OIG report on CIA accountability with respect to the 9/11 attacks. (Online). Available from http://www.cia.gov/library/reports/ExecutiveSummary_OIG Report.pdf

U.S. Coast Guard. (2007). Maritime Transportation Security Act of 2002. (Online). Available from http://www.uscg.mil/hq/g-cp/comrel/factfile/factcards/MTSA2002.htm

U.S. Chemical Safety and Hazard Investigation Board. (2007, March). *Investigation report: Refinery explosion and fire, BP Texas City, Texas, March 23, 2005.* Available from http://www.csb.gov/assets/1/19/CSBFinalReportBP.pdf

31 U.S. Code § 5312—Definitions and application. Published by United States Government Publishing Office.

U.S. Congress. (2001). *USA PATRIOT Act of 2001 (Public Law 107–56).* Washington, DC: U.S. Government Printing Office.

U.S. Congress. (2002, November 25). *Homeland Security Act of 2002.* Washington, DC: U.S. Government Printing Office.

U.S. Congress. (2005, May 11). Pub. L. No. 109–113.

US Customs and Border Protection. (2006). *Supply chain security best practices catalog.* Washington, DC: U.S. Customs and Border Protection.

US Customs and Border Protection. (2011). *Container Security Initiative in summary.* Washington, DC: US Customs and Border Protection.

U.S. Department of Education. (2007). *Campus security.* (Online). Available from http://www.ed.gov/admins/lead/safety/campus.html

U.S. Department of Education, Institute of Education Sciences. (2011). *Indicators of school crime and safety: 2010.* (Online). Available from http://nces.ed.gov/programs/crimeindicators/crimeindicators2010/index.asp

U.S. Department of Health and Human Services. (2007). *Factsheets.* (Online). Available from http://www.pandemicflu.gov

U.S. Department of Health and Human Services, Office of Civil Rights. (2007). *Fact sheet: Privacy and your health information.* (Online). Available from http://www.hhs.gov/ocr/hipaa/consumer_rights

U.S. Department of Homeland Security. (2008, January 22). National Response Framework. Retrieved from https://www.fema.gov/pdf/emergency/nrf/NRFRolloutBriefingNotes.pdf

U.S. Department of Homeland Security. (2012, February). *Department of Homeland Security Strategic Plan Fiscal Years 2012-2016.* Washington, DC: U.S. Department of Homeland Security.

U.S. Department of Homeland Security. (2015). About DHS. Retrieved from dhs.gov

U.S. Department of Homeland Security, Office of the Press Secretary. (2007). *DHS completes key framework for critical infrastructure protection.* (Online). Available from http://www.dhs.gov/xnews/releases/pr_1179773665704.shtm

U.S. Department of Homeland Security, Transportation Security Administration. (2003). *Aviation and Transportation Security Act (ATSA) Public Law 107-7.* (Online). Available from http://www.tsa.gov

U.S. Department of Justice. (2007). *Fact sheet: USA PATRIOT Act Improvement and Reauthorization Act of 2005.* (Online). Available from http://www.usdoj.gov

U.S. Department of Justice, Bureau of Justice Statistics. (2006). *2006 indicators of school crime and safety.* Washington, DC: U.S. Department of Justice.

U.S. Department of Justice, Federal Bureau of Investigation. (2011). *National Incident Based Reporting System.* Retrieved from https://www.fbi.gov/about-us/cjis/ucr/nibrs/2011

U.S. Department of Justice, Federal Bureau of Investigation. (2013). *National Incident Based Reporting System.* Retrieved from https://www.fbi.gov/about-us/cjis/ucr/nibrs/nibrs-user-manual

U.S. Department of Justice, Federal Bureau of Investigation, Economic Espionage Unit. (2007). *Focus on economic espionage.* (Online). Available from http://www.fbi.gov/hq/ci/economic.htm

U.S. Department of Justice, Private Security Advisory Council to the Law Enforcement Assistance Administration. (1977). *Reports to the LEAA.* Washington, DC: U.S. Government Printing Office.

U.S. Department of Labor, Bureau of Labor Statistics. (2010). *Census of fatal occupational injury summary, 2009.* (Online). Available from http://www.bls.gov/news.release/cfoi.nr0.htm

U.S. Department of State. (2007). *County reports on terrorism.* (Online). Available from http://www.state.gov/s/ct/rls/crt/2006/82727.htm

U.S. Department of State. (2015). Retrieved from www.state.gov

U.S. Department of State Foreign Affairs Handbook. (2014). 5(12) Section 113 p. 35. Retrieved from http://www.state.gov/documents/organization/88382.pdf

U.S. Fire Administration. (2010, April). Nonresidential building fires. Available from http://tkolb.net/FireReports/NonresidentialBuildingFires.pdf

U.S. Fire Administration. (2013, June). Nonresidential building fires (2009–2011). Available from https://www.usfa.fema.gov/downloads/pdf/statistics/v14i5.pdf

US Fire Administration. (2014). *Residential building fire trends, 2004–2103.* Retrieved from https://www.usfa.fema.gov/downloads/pdf/statistics/res_bldg_fire_estimates.pdf

U.S. General Services Administration. (2011). *Alarm and signal systems: Security system management.* (Online). Available from http://www.gsa.gov/portal/content/104644#AlarmSignal. Retrieved from January 23, 2011

U.S. Private Security Advisory Council, (1976). A Report on the Regulation of Private Security Guard Services Including a Model Private Security Licensing and Regulatory Statute. Department of Justice, LEAA : Washington D.C.

USA PATRIOT Act. (2001) H.R. 3162, 107th Cong.

Vallabhaneni, S. R. (2013). *Wiley CIS exam review 2013 focus notes: Part 1, Internal audit basics.* New Jersey: John Wiley & Sons.

Van Niekerk, D., Coetzee, C., Botha, D., Murphree, M. J., Fourie, K., Le Roux, T., & Meyer, S. (2015). Planning and executing scenario based simulation exercises: Methodological lessons. *Journal of Homeland Security and Emergency Management, 12*(1), 193–210.

Van Niekerk, J., & Von Solms, R. (2004, June). Organisational learning models for information security. In *The ISSA 2004 Enabling Tomorrow Conference* (Vol. 30).

van Steden, R., & de Waard, J. (2013). "Acting like chameleons": On the McDonaldization of private security. *Security Journal, 26*(3), 294–309.

van Steden, R., & Sarre, R. (2007). The growth of private security: Trends in the European Union. *Security Journal, 20*(4), 222–235.

Varnali, R. (2015). An exploratory study of the cultural context of organizational climate and human resource practices. *Asia Pacific Journal of Human Resources, 53*(4), 432–447.

Vellani, K. (2006). *Strategic security management: A risk assessment guide for decision makers.* Boston: Butterworth-Heinemann.

Vellani, K. (2007). *Strategic security management: A risk assessment guide for decision makers.* Boston: Elsevier.

Vincent, B. (2000, May). Protection at $5.75 an hour. *Access Control & Security Systems Integration, 43*(6), 1, 47–48.

Vincent, J. L. (2009). Infant hospital abduction: Security measures to aid in prevention. *MCN: The American Journal of Maternal/Child Nursing, 34*(3), 179–183.

Vindevogel, F. (2005). Private security and urban crime mitigation. A bid for BIDs. *Criminal Justice, 5*(3), 233–255.

Violence Occupational Hazards in Hospitals. Published by National Institute for Occupational Safety and Health, © 2002.

Vitale, P. (2011). Wages of war: Manufacturing nationalism during World War II. *Antipode, 43*(3), 783–819.

Voss, M. D., & Williams, Z. (2013). Public–private partnerships and supply chain security: C-TPAT as an indicator of relational security. *Journal of Business Logistics, 34*(4), 320–334.

Vukadin, I. K., Borovec, K., & Golub, T. L. (2013). Policing in Croatia: The main challenges on the path to democratic policing. In *Handbook on policing in Central and Eastern Europe* (pp. 31–55). New York: Springer.

Wagley, J. (2010, November). Be smart about IDs. *Security Management*, pp. 91–92.

Wagner, T. E., & Obermiller, P. J. (2011). A double-edged sword: Social control in Appalachian company towns. In *Engineering earth* (pp. 1917–1935). Springer Netherlands.

Waheed, Y. (2014). Ebola in West Africa: An international medical emergency. *Asian Pacific Journal of Tropical Biomedicine, 4*(9), 673–674.

Wakefield, J. C. (2010). *A toxicological review of the products of combustion.* Health Protection Agency, Centre for Radiation, Chemical and Environmental Hazards, Chemical Hazards and Poisons Division.

Walby, K., & Lippert, R. K. (2014). *Corporate security in the 21st Century.* Published by Palgrave Macmillan.

Walby, K., & Lippert, R. K. (2015). Ford first? Corporate security and the U.S. Department of War's Plant Protection Service's interior organization, 1917–1918. *Labor History, 56*(2), 117–135.

Wallwork, R. D. (2005). Operational implications of private military companies in the global war on terror. Fort Leavenworth, Kansas: United States Army Command and General Staff College School of Advanced Military Studies. Retrieved from http://handle.dtic.mil/100.2/ADA436294

Wal-Mart loses overtime pay lawsuit. (2002, December 20). *The Olympian.* (Online). Available from http://www.theolympian.com/home/news/20021220/business/314505html

Walsh, D. W., Christen, H. T., Callsen, C. E., Miller, G. T., Maniscalco, P. M., & Dolan, N. J. (2012). *National Incident Management System: Principles and practice.* Sudbury, MA: Jones & Bartlet.

Walsh, J. (2000, August). Employee theft. *International Foundation for Protection Officers.*

Walsh, K., Levin, H., Jaye, P., & Gazzard, J. (2013). Cost analyses approaches in medical education: There are no simple solutions. *Medical Education, 47*(10), 962–968.

Walsh, T. J., & Healy, R. J. (1987). *Protection of assets manual.* Santa Monica, CA: The Merrit Company.

Wang, P., Lin, H. T., & Wang, T. S. (2016). An improved ant colony system algorithm for solving the IP traceback problem. *Information Sciences, 326,* 172–187.

War Department. (1943, May 1). *Plant protection for manufacturers. Pamphlet No. 32-1.* Washington, DC: Office of Civilian Defense.

Ward, R. H., Kiernam, K. L., & Mabrey, D. (2006). *Homeland security: An introduction.* New York: LexisNexis/Anderson Publishing.

Wardle, K. A., & Wardle, D. (2004). Glimpses of private life: Roman rock cut tombs of the first and second centuries AD at Knossos. *British School at Athens Studies,* 473–480.

Warner, B. D., Beck, E., & Ohmer, M. L. (2010). Linking informal social control and restorative justice: Moving social disorganization theory beyond community policing. *Contemporary Justice Review, 13*(4), 355–369.

Wasserman, G. A., Miller, L. S., & Cothern, L. (2000, April). *Prevention of serious and violent juvenile offending.* Washington, DC: U.S. Department of Justice, Office of Justice Programs, Office of Juvenile Justice and Delinquency Prevention.

Water Sector-Specific Plan. (2010). Washington, DC: Department of Homeland Security.

Webster, C. W. R. (2004). Evolving standards and regulation: Exploring the development and provision of closed circuit television in the United Kingdom. *Knowledge, Technology & Policy, 17*(2), 82–103.

Weinstein, S. (2013). How target became a target: Massive cyber security breach creates legal and reputational risk for leading U.S. retailer. *Coventry Law Journal, 18*(22), 11–18.

Weisel, D. L. (2007). The problem of bank robbery. *Problem-oriented guides for police. Problem-specific guides series,* (no. 48). U.S. Department of Justice, Office of Community Oriented Policing Services.

Weiss, R. P. (1986). Private detective agencies and labour discipline in the United States, 1855–1946. *The Historical Journal, 29*(01), 87–107.

Weiss, R. P. (2007). From cowboy detectives to soldiers of fortune: Private security contracting and its contradictions on the new frontiers of capitalist expansion. *Social Justice, 34*(3/4), 1–19.

Weissman, S. H., Busch, K. G., & Schouten, R. (2014). Introduction to this issue: The evolution of terrorism from 1914 to 2014. *Behavioral Sciences & the Law, 32*(3), 259–262.

Weiten, W. (2004). *Psychology: Themes and variations* (6th ed.). Belmont, CA: Wadsworth.

Weldes, J. (Ed.). (1999). *Cultures of insecurity: States, communities, and the production of danger* (Vol. 14). University of Minnesota Press.

Wenger, C. (2015). Building walls around flood problems: The place of levees in Australian flood management. *Australian Journal of Water Resources, 19*(1), 3–21.

Wernick, D. A., & Von Glinow, M. A. (2012). Reflections on the evolving terrorist threat to luxury hotels: A case study on Marriott International. *Thunderbird International Business Review, 54*(5), 729–746.

Wesley, R. L., & Wanat, J. A. (2013). *A guide to internal loss prevention.* Elsevier.

Westhead, P., & Storey, D. (1996). Management training and small firm performance: Why is the link so weak? *International Small Business Journal, 14*(4), 13–24.

What Is Security and Resilience. Published by The Department of Homeland Security, © 2015

What is workplace violence? (2002). Washington, DC: U.S. Department of Labor, Occupational Safety & Health Administration. Retrieved from https://www.osha.gov/OshDoc/data_General_Facts/factsheet-workplace-violence.pdf

White, A., & Gill, M. (2013). The transformation of policing from ratios to rationalities. *British Journal of Criminology, 53*(1), 74–93.

White, B. (2010, September 30). The new presence on Oakland's streets. *Wall Street Journal.* Retrieved from http://www.wsj.com/articles/SB10001424052748704654004575518012723731400

White, J. R. (2012). *Terrorism and homeland security* (7th ed.). Belmont, CA: Cengage/Wadsworth.

White, S. (2001, January). Nature watch. *Security Products, 5*(1), 50.

Whitmore, A. (2014). Using open government data to predict war: A case study of data and systems challenges. *Government Information Quarterly, 31*(4), 622–630.

Wiegman, D. A., & Shappell, S. A. (2003). *A human error approach to aviation accident analysis: The human factors analysis and classification system.* Burlington, VT: Ashgate.

Wilberg Fitzsimons, E. (2000, September 28). False alarms trigger fines. *San Diego Union Tribune,* p. B1.

Williams, K. S., & Johnstone, C. (2000). The politics of the selective gaze: Closed circuit television and the policing of public space. *Crime, Law and Social Change, 34*(2), 183–210.

Wimmer, R. (2000, January). Assessing CCTV's roles in public venues. *Security Technology & Design, 10*(1), 32–34.

Winkler, I. (1997). *Corporate espionage.* Rocklin, CA: Prima Publishing.

Witey, F. (1947). Plant protection employees under current federal labor legislation. *University of Illinois Bulletin, 44*(72), 3–19.

Wolensky, K. C. (2008). Freedom to assemble and the Lattimer massacre of 1897. *Pennsylvania Legacies, 8*(1), 24–31.

Workforce Framework Customized User Guides. Copyright © 2015. Published by National Initiative for Cybersecurity Careers and Studies.

Workplace violence in the health sector. Published by World health organisation, © 2002.

Workplace violence prevention strategies and research needs. (2004). Washington, DC: Center for Disease Control and Prevention, National Institute for Occupational Safety and Health.

Workplace violence: Awareness and prevention for employers and employees. (2012). Seattle, Washington: Washington State Department of Labor and Industries. Retrieved from http://www.lni.wa.gov/IPUB/417-140-000.pdf

Wright, S. (2015). *Competitive intelligence, analysis and strategy.* New York: Routledge.

Wulfhorst, E. (2006, June 23). Younger workers more likely to think theft is OK. *San Diego Union Tribune,* p. A2.

Yang, C. C., & Wei, H. H. (2013). The effect of supply chain security management on security performance in container shipping operations. *Supply Chain Management: An International Journal, 18*(1), 74–85.

Young, J. E. (2002). Indemnification clauses in multiple contract transactions. *International Business Law, 30,* 115–118.

Young, J. R. (2008). For emergency alerts, some colleges try sirens. *Chronicle of Higher Education, 54*(31), a22.

Young, M. E., & Lambie, G. W. (2007). Wellness in school and mental health systems: Organizational influences. *The Journal of Humanistic Counseling, Education and Development, 46*(1), 98–113.

Young, S., Balluz, L., & Malilay, J. (2004). Natural and technologic hazardous material releases during and after natural disasters: A review. *Science of the Total Environment, 322*(1), 3–20.

Zalok, E., & Eduful, J. (2013). Assessment of fuel load survey methodologies and its impact on fire load data. *Fire Safety Journal, 62,* 299–310.

Zamparini, L. (2014). Economic issues in maritime transport security. In K. Bichou, J. S. Szyliowicz, & L. Zamparini (Eds.), *Maritime transport security: Issues, challenges and national policies* (pp. 40–51). Northampton, MA: Edward Elgar.

Zeigler, M. (2002, February 16). Olympic security sky-high. *San Diego Union Tribune,* pp. A1, A12.

Zerrenner, K. (2014, February 6). *Can the World Bank's "Thirsty Energy" Effort Create a Culture Shift?* Retrieved from http://www.greenbiz.com/blog/2014/02/06/can-world-banks-thirsty-energy-effort-create-culture-shift

Zhang, R. (2013). A transportation security system applying RFID and GPS. *Journal of Industrial Engineering and Management, 6*(1), 163–174.

Zhou, C., Yu, Q., & Wang, L. (2012). Investigation of the risk of electromagnetic security on computer systems. *International Journal of Computer and Electrical Engineering, 4*(1), 92–98.

Zhu, S., & Levinson, D. M. (2012). Disruptions to transportation networks: A review. In *Network reliability in practice* (pp. 5–20). New York: Springer.

Zuckerman, E. (2003, February 22). Nobody had a chance. *San Diego Union Tribune,* pp. A1, A16.

Doctrine of assumption of risk, 54–55
Domestic terrorism, defined, 200
Drones, 303
Drug-Free Schools and Communities
    Act, 152
Duggan, Mark, 41
Duncan Hunter National Defense
    Authorization Act (2008), 290–291
Dunkin' Brands, 175
Duty, concept of, 53
Dynamic risk, 259

E
Early warning systems (EWS), 110
Economic espionage, 134
Economic Espionage Act (EEA) of
    1996, 135
Economic security, 298
E-contracts, 57
Education, 243
Educational institution security, 147–152
    elementary and secondary schools,
        147–150
    Institutions of Higher Education. See
        Institutions of Higher Education
        (IHEs)
Ego, 37
Egyptians, 5
Electronic article surveillance (EAS),
    179
Electronic locks, 87
Electronic Signature in Global and
    National Commerce Act
    (E-Sign Act), 57
Emanations security (TEMPEST), 132
Emergency management, 173
    contingency plans and, 270–272
Emergency notification systems, 151
Emergency response, 271
Employee development
    training and, 242–243
Employee Polygraph Protection Act of
    1988 (EPPA), 60
Employment law, 59–61
    collective bargaining laws, 60–61
Encryption, 126
Energy security, 301
Entertainment security, 155–162
    mega events, 156–158
    museum security, 159–160
    theme parks, 155–156
    zoo and aquarium security, 160–162
Environmental accidents/disasters, 42–43
Environmental Protection Agency
    (EPA), 196
    water sector vision statement, 197

Environmental security, 298
Equal Employment Opportunity
    Commission (EEOC), 55, 60
Ethical dilemma, 232
Ethical leadership, 233–234
Ethical standards, 233
Ethics, 230–236
    defined, 230
    principles, 231
    and security environment, 19
Europe, private security industry in,
    277–282
European Union (EU), 279–281
Evidence-based practices (EBps),
    311–312
Executive/corporate kidnapping, 113–114
Executive Outcomes (EO), 289–290
Executive protection (EP), 104–105
Expeditionary terrorist activities, 307
Explosives detection strategy, 207–208
Expressed contract, 56
Express kidnappings, 113
Extended care facilities, security of, 155

F
Fair Labor Standards Act (FLSA),
    59–60, 246–247
False alarms, 82
Fargo, William, 8
Federal Aviation Administration (FAA),
    205–206
Federal Aviation Regulation (FAR), 206
Federal Emergency Management
    Agency (FEMA), 31, 193, 203
    risk quantification table, 265f
Federal Energy Regulatory Commission
    (FERC), 301
Federal Motor Carrier Safety
    Administration (FMCSA), 209
Federal personnel security background
    investigation process, 101, 102f
Federal Railroad Administration (FRA),
    210
Felonies, 50
Fencing, 78–80, 78f
Fifth Amendment, 63
Financial institution, defined, 140, 141
Financial institution security, 140–145
    ATM security, 143–144
    user authentication and, 144–145
Fire, 28–33
    causes of, 31
    classification of, 29–30
Fire alarm, 9, 89–90
Fire annunciators, 91
Fire brigade, 90

Fire extinguishers, 30, 91–92
Fire hazard abatement, 89
Fire inspection program, 90
Fire investigation, 89
Fire load, 31
Fire prevention, 89–90
Fire prevention enforcement, 89
Fire protection systems, 91–92
Fire safety education, 90
Fire sensors, 89–90, 91
Fire tetrahedron model, 29
Fire triangle, 29, 29f
Firewall, 132
Five Modes of Adaptation (Merton), 39
Flashover, 30
Food and Drug Administration, 55
Food Safety Modernization Act
    (FSMA), 204–205
Food security, 298, 299
Ford Motor Company's Security
    Services, 11
Foreign Intelligence Surveillance Act
    (FISA), 189, 190
Foreign Intelligence Surveillance Court
    (FISC), 190
Foreseeability, 53
Fourth Amendment, 55
Frankpledge system, 6
Free-burning phase, combustion, 30
Free will, 36
Freud, Sigmund, 37
Fuel load, 31
Fukushima Daiichi Nuclear Power Plant
    disaster, 45
Full-time equivalent (FTE), 247
Fusion centers, 189, 202

G
Gaming industry, security of, 158–159
Gang violence, 39
Gases
    asphyxiant, 30
    irritant, 30–31
Gated resorts, 174
General deterrence, 36
General Motors, 11
Geneva Center for the Democratic
    Control of Armed Forces
    (DCAF), 279
Globalization, 296–301
    defined, 297
    human security and, 298–301
Global security assemblage, 297
Global Terrorism Database (University
    of Maryland), 40
Great Depression, 10